Women & Music

A HISTORY

SECOND EDITION

EDITED BY

KARIN PENDLE

Indiana University Press Bloomington & Indianapolis

Women in the World of Music: Three Approaches

The Special Roles of Women

Preface

Women and Music: A History is a survey of women's activities in music performance, composition, teaching, and patronage from the time of the ancient Greeks to the present, with an emphasis on art music in Europe and North America. This focus is not meant to suggest that women's musical activities, or even their most significant ones, are in any way limited to these areas of the world, but rather to enable students and teachers in standard music history courses to coordinate the material in this book with the topics normally covered in undergraduate surveys. As such surveys have broadened in accordance with today's educational goals, so this edition of *Women and Music* also moves beyond Western art music to include chapters on women in popular music and jazz, as well as approaches to researching and evaluating women's practices and contributions in cultures not part of the Western tradition. The first chapter, dealing with feminist aesthetics as they relate to music, suggests some ways in which music and music making by women could be approached differently from music and music making by men.

The feminist movement of the 1960s and 1970s was the driving force behind the emergence of a wide range of studies and theories focusing on the lives, positions, and contributions of women in society through the ages. As in other fields, scholars in music began to show an interest in the work of the half of the world's population that had been ignored in earlier studies of music history and development. Women's studies came to the fore even more slowly in music than in many other fields, however, perhaps because musicology was (and to some extent still is) dominated by men schooled in traditional methodologies. Even as late as the 1970s, *Women and Music* could not have been written: serious, reliable information on women's musical activities still was too limited and the subjects too widely spread across music's history to support a continuous chronological narrative.

But here, about a decade after *Women and Music* first appeared, we are launching a second edition. This has proved necessary because research and resources have increased beyond expectations, perhaps even beyond dreams. Feminist aesthetics and the application to music of interpretive strategies developed in psychology, literature, and other arts have yielded revelations and controversy. Questions abound: How far can we go in thinking about music in ways that perhaps its composers did not intend? To what extent do nonmusical factors determine a work's style or content? Why is a feminine quality in music only laudable if the composer is a man? Is music by women excluded from study because it is deemed to be of inferior quality in comparison with music by men? What counts as quality anyway? Do evaluative standards differ according to the gender of the composer? Has society shaped the criteria for greatness in ways that keep women out? What, in the end, does it mean to be a woman in music?

For a moment, let us concentrate on selected areas of recent research that have enlightened concepts of society and women's place in it, research that makes this second edition necessary. Materials, programs, and conferences in celebration of the nine-hundredth birthday of Hildegard von Bingen were not entirely about music, but they brought into clearer perspective not only the figure of Hildegard but also the position of nuns and women mystics in the medieval world. Suddenly, it seemed, the doors to the medieval church opened to the varied interior, with Hildegard and her music inside, not outside, society as a whole.

In the mid-1990s, studies of nuns and their music in the years ca. 1600–1725 brought to our attention some brilliant and heretofore neglected published music of North Italian nuns. In so doing, scholars Robert Kendrick and Craig Monson led the way to important revisions of traditional views about the place of nuns, convents, and their music in early modern Europe.[1] No longer could these women (most often patricians) be set aside on the margins of their society. The discovery of their music influenced in turn a reinterpretation of the edicts of the Council of Trent dealing with nuns and their music. These decrees, not unlike pronouncements on nuns' behavior from earlier centuries, had largely been ignored by everyone save the male clerics who continued to debate the issues they raised. But our knowing of women who had actively participated in their society through its convents and music put to question, among other things, handed-down, male-defined views of history and its traditional periodization. For it became obvious that the work of these holy women represented continuity, not a reawakening after a medieval sleep. Surely research that opened to question the accepted

Abbreviations Used in This Book

CAMW	James Briscoe, ed., *Contemporary Anthology of Music by Women*
HAMW	James Briscoe, ed., *Historical Anthology of Music by Women*
IAWM	International Alliance of Women in Music
ILWC	International League of Women Composers
MTA	Sylvia Glickman and Martha Furman Schleifer, eds., *Women Composers: Music through the Ages*

Feminist Aesthetics

I.
Recovering Jouissance: Feminist Aesthetics and Music

Renée Cox Lorraine

Wa-oh-oh-oh . . .

—The Ronettes

Adherents of feminism seek to discover ways that women or the feminine are undermined in various cultures and to identify ways to raise the status of women. Broadly speaking, aesthetics is the philosophy of art. A feminist aesthetician, then, would philosophize about art in ways that would serve feminist ends. An aesthetic experience has traditionally been described as an intense concentration on formal or sensuous properties in art, nature, and beyond. Yet aestheticians have always been concerned to some extent, and are particularly concerned of late, with relationships of aesthetic properties or processes to those of life. In music there is a current interest in relating musical processes to personal, social, or political processes, including gender and sexual practices. These tendencies serve the interests of feminism. While there is at present relatively little work in philosophy that could qualify as feminist musical aesthetics, there is an increasing body of work on women or gender in musicology, music theory, or music criticism that is relevant to this area of study.

Much of this work has dealt with historical and cultural constructions of the masculine and feminine in music—that is, with the relation of aesthetic properties to socially constructed gender characteristics or the musical reflections of such gender characteristics. Such relationships can be discerned even in ancient Greece and in the early centuries of the common era. Authors such as Plato, Aristotle, Clement, Basil, and Boethius associated manly music with reason, restraint, and order, whereas music associated with women or effeminacy was thought to give rise to sensuality, excitement, passion, or madness.[1] Socrates warned that music in the Mixolydian and "intense Lydian" modes, which were associated with women and goddess worship, would give rise to drunkenness, softness, and sloth. He preferred a harmony that "would fittingly imitate the utterances and the accents of a brave man who is engaged in warfare or in any enforced business." Aristotle claimed that professional musicians were vulgar, that performing music was unmanly, except when the performer was drunk or just having fun. He stated that the Phrygian mode, associated with the great goddess Cybele, should not be allowed, "for the Phrygian harmony has the same effect among harmonies as the aulos among instruments—both are violently exciting and emotional." And all agree, Aristotle continued, "that the Dorian harmony is more sedate and of a specially manly character." Boethius (ca. 600 C.E.) relates that the ancient Timotheus angered the Spartans by playing complex rhythms and harmonies and by using the chromatic genus, "which is more effeminate" than other genera. He tells of a youth excited by the Phrygian mode who locked himself in a room with a harlot and planned to burn down the house, and how this youth's fury was reduced to a perfect state of calm when Pythagoras played a melody in an orderly, spondaic rhythm.

These writings had an impact on the early medieval era and beyond. Leo Treitler has identified both ancient and more recent descriptions of Old Roman and Gregorian chants that relate the chants to characteristics of gender. Whereas Old Roman chant tends to be recursive, highly melismatic, and embellished (and is described as soft, charming, elegant, graceful, round, and voluptuous), the simpler and relatively stable Gregorian chant is reported to display a more manly strength, vigor, power, and reason.[2] Linda Phyllis Austern has shown that in the English Renaissance music was often associated with women or the womanly; the "eternal attraction between men and music" was likened to the sacred bond of marriage, and music was often described as dangerously sensual.[3] Both Suzanne B. Cusick and Susan McClary have shown that in the early baroque period, music associated with female characters or the feminine was likely to be more ornamented, exciting, and unstable than the more straightforward and orderly music associated with male characters or with masculinity.[4]

In the eighteenth, nineteenth, and early twentieth centuries, musical resolution within the tonal system often accompanied the defeat of a female character or of unacceptable feminine qualities. Some operatic music associated a sensual or powerful woman with tonal instability, an instability that was resolved only when the woman was killed or reconciled with social norms. In Mozart's *Die Zauberflöte,* for example, most of the music for the dark, powerful Queen of the Night is in minor mode and highly embellished, while the music of the wise and noble Sarastro (and Tamino and Pamina, when they are initiated in Sarastro's brotherhood) is diatonic, simple, and solemn. Catherine Clément has pointed out that in Wagner's *Tristan und Isolde,* chromaticism is associated with a seductive, deadly feminine sexuality. This association is also well exemplified in Wagner's *Tannhäuser:* the music of Venus, goddess of sensual pleasure and delight, is beautiful but unstable, chromatic, and unresolving, whereas that of Tannhäuser, the Pilgrims, and the saintly Elizabeth is predominantly diatonic and stable. Susan McClary has shown how in Bizet's *Carmen* the music of the slithery, slippery heroine is predominantly chromatic and rhythmically syncopated, whereas Don José and the pure, chaste Micaëla sing more diatonically. Because many of us have a conditioned tendency to want the music of these unacceptable women to resolve into clarity and order, we may subconsciously want them to be defeated, appropriated, to die. And it is precisely when the heroines are defeated at the ends of these operas that all the musical tension associated with them is resolved.

In the area of instrumental music, McClary suggests that in the first movement of Brahms's Third Symphony, the second, more "feminine" theme is more trivial and incidental to the work's central Oedipal struggle between the "Law of the Father" (conventional tonality) and the rebellious son Brahms (who seeks to defy conventional norms).[5] Judith Tick and others have considered Ives's notorious comments on what he regarded as the feminine and the effeminate in music: to Ives, for example, Rachmaninoff became "Rachnotmanenough"; Haydn, Mozart, early Beethoven, and Brahms were "too much of the sugar plum for soft ears"; and various European composers were "pussies" or "cherries." Tick stresses that although these comments were extreme, they were not atypical of the times; Ives inherited a "social grammar of prejudice" and an ideology of gender differences in music. She suggests that Ives used his prejudicial statements, written during the time that also saw radical, modernist experiments in music, to effect a break from a European heritage he found overbearing. In any case, the music of the various works and styles discussed above have reinforced stereotypes about women, and can promote fear, hatred, and the subordination of women.[6] Only by making these associations more conscious, by getting them out into the light, can we diminish their power to stigmatize.[7]

The dramatic tendency to associate musical resolution with the defeat of the unacceptable feminine or female character is detectable in recent films, such as *Fatal Attraction, The Crying Game* (in which the unacceptable "woman" is actually a man), and in traditional Walt Disney films, such as *Snow White, Sleeping Beauty,* and *The Little Mermaid.* The antagonist in these more traditional animated films is almost always a woman and may represent the Oedipal mother. In more recent Disney films, such as *Beauty and the Beast, Aladdin, The Lion King,* and *Pocahontas,* a male antagonist is accompanied by unstable music. But these eventually defeated antagonists are likely to have feminine or effeminate characteristics. In *The Lion King,* Scar is a gay stereotype; in *Aladdin,* Jafar might be *Snow White's* Wicked Queen in drag. In *The Little Mermaid,* Flotsam and Jetsam, the slimy eel sidekicks of the independent, sexual, and powerful Sea Witch, are evidently male—but gender-ambiguous and sometimes physically intertwined. In films in which the femmes fatales achieve their nefarious ambitions, such as *Body Heat* and *Basic Instinct,* the chromatic, open-ended, unstable music associated with the unacceptable female characters never resolves.[8]

As Catherine Clément has pointed out, such associations can cause internal conflicts: we may love operas (or films or pieces) that we find ethically troublesome. Other authors have shown how female characters who are eventually defeated can usurp a good deal of power and authority expressly because of (or in spite of) music or musical accompaniment that defies conventional norms. Gretchen A. Wheelock shows that while the minor mode was generally described in the eighteenth century as representing such feminine qualities as melancholy, hesitation, and indecision, Mozart often uses the mode to destabilize the masculine-feminine dichotomy and the tonal order that contains it. Seventeen of Mozart's twenty-three minor-key arias are sung by women, and two are given to castrati. The minor mode, however, not only is used to express feminine weakness or indecision but also is associated with death and the supernatural or with fury and rage (as in the minor-key arias of Zaide, Electra, and the Queen of the Night). These characters' voices, then, can undermine conventional, gendered expression and represent what is out of control or beyond rational control. Although "out of control" has had (and continues to have) unfavorable connotations, in Mozart's music the "feminine" minor mode is powerful in its association with the inner world of passion, fear, and desire.[9]

In her interpretation of Francesca Caccini's opera *La Liberazione di Ruggiero dall'isola d'Alcina* (1625), Suzanne Cusick suggests an example of a "secret victory" of an unacceptable female character. In this work the knight Ruggiero is rescued by the sorceress Melissa from the love spell of the sorceress Alcina. Melissa appears to Ruggiero as a man, Atlante, and Caccini composes characteristically masculine music, according to early seventeenth-century standards, for him/her: that is, diatonic, firmly tonal, with careful text declamation. Melissa's success in liberating Ruggerio may be interpreted as a warning to those who seek power that they must speak in a patriarchal language and repress what is regarded as feminine. In contrast to the music of Melissa/Atlante, the music of Alcina, with its feminine chromaticism and extraordinary tonal range and expressivity, is relatively unstable. Yet although Alcina is defeated, her captivating song lingers seductively, Cusick suggests, in the ear and imagination, subtly exposing the oppression of the political and gender systems that Melissa's triumph affirms. So Caccini, Cusick thinks, has succeeded where the unacceptable Alcina has failed. Seventeenth-century notions of the feminine are affirmed as long as Alcina's music continues to enchant.[10] Cusick's important thesis might also be applied to powerful but doomed operatic characters created by men—the Queen of the Night, Venus, Carmen, Delilah. While some of the composers involved may have felt ambivalent at best toward their characters, they empowered or "envoiced" the characters, perhaps in spite of themselves, by granting them such beautiful or memorable music.

A similar point is made in Carolyn Abbate's recent interpretation of Richard Strauss's *Salome* in "Opera, or the Envoicing of Women" (a wordplay on Catherine Clément's *Opera, or the Undoing of Women*). Abbate suggests that even though Salome is eventually killed, the character manages, by means of her gender mobility, to usurp the authorial voice in the opera. Rather than being a passive object, she renders the audience passive through the sheer volume and force of her sound. It might be added that Salome's music is privileged as well, in that her final music, although accompanied by a repugnant act, is diatonic, ethereal, and beautiful, whereas the music accompanying her death is unstable and dissonant. From a purely musical point of view, the death of Salome is not a triumph but a tragedy, lending weight to the power of her voice. It could be argued here that Clément is well aware of the authority of certain powerful operatic women, that her very point is that the louder the powerful female characters sing, the harder they fall. But just how much authority these characters can establish, especially in eras when women were often regarded as largely voiceless, is important to highlight.[11]

Similar tendencies can be found in film and instrumental music as well as music of popular culture. In some feminist films made and/or scored by women, the narrative and musical closure ordinarily associated with the death of a socially unacceptable female character is resisted or revised to the character's advantage. In the film *Thelma and Louise*, for example, two socially unacceptable women choose death over submission to an oppressive system. Yet the unresolved but appealing nature of the gospel music accompanying their deaths, as well as the increasing dynamism and unresolved quality of the music that accompanies the women's gradual liberation, helps to subvert the narrative closure represented by their destruction (a closure necessary for social norms to prevail). In the film *The Piano* (1993), the heroine Ada is rebellious; she refuses to speak, expressing herself instead through her haunting piano playing. When she eventually finds happiness in domestic life and is learning to speak, her musical accompaniment provides closure to the earlier nervous, unresolving music she has played throughout the film. Among the most memorable aspects of the film, even more than Ada's final, domesticated situation and the musical resolution, are the rebelliousness of Ada's silence and the music that represents her dissatisfaction with oppressive conditions. Here, again, the power of this music subverts the film's musical and narrative closure.[12]

In an example of instrumental music, Cécile Chaminade's Piano Sonata presents an attempt to subvert the appropriation of the musical feminine to the masculine. In the nineteenth century, some theorists considered the first and second themes of a sonata-allegro form to be masculine and feminine, respectively. Musicologist Marcia Citron suggests that Chaminade, in the first movement of her Piano Sonata (1895), seems to avoid the objectification of the feminine by avoiding tonal Otherness. The "feminine" second theme in a sonata-allegro form generally appears in a key other than the tonic, and is eventually drawn back to the masculine tonic in the final section or recapitulation. But Chaminade does not definitively establish an *Other* key for the second theme area; she only hints at other keys. Although the feminine is a major presence in the movement, it is too slippery, dynamic, or shifting to be appropriated or conquered.[13] Although some listeners might interpret Chaminade's sonata as not establishing a feminine presence at all (constructing a concrete being only for the masculine), the second theme is perhaps better heard as a dynamic feminine that defies set definition of boundaries.

Ethnomusicologist Carol Robinson suggests that the study of culture outside the West can empower those who seek to raise the status of women and affirm gender mobility—and can inform and transform music study in general. In two subcultures that Robinson has studied—the *machi* of the Mapuche of Chile and Argentina and the *mahu* of Hawaii—individuals who are different may move back and forth between margin and center, a condition that allows them a certain power within the culture. In both cases, difference is related to gender, spirituality, and music. The *machi* or "life givers" are either women or men who live as women. Although colonization has diminished their influence and they are sometimes subject to discrimination, they are nevertheless recognized as healers and spiritual guides. A *machi,* for example, may contemplate an herb or collection of herbs until a chant arises that reveals the herb's medicinal power. Chant is also believed to have the power to create and change individuals, to give birth to the spirit, and to bring the forces of the universe into open space. Approximately one tenth of (presumably indigenous) Hawaiians are *mahu* or mixed gender individuals. The *mahu* may be hermaphrodites, transsexuals, cross-dressers, men raised as women, gays and lesbians, or flashy dressers, but in all these forms the feminine is particularly valued. Noted as practitioners of the hula, the *mahu* are seen as spiritual, powerful, and having a capacity for healing. They bring a sense of hope and accomplishment in an atmosphere of cultural depression. Through the study of diverse musical practices, Robinson suggests, ethnomusicologists can help move the reality of gender fluidity from the periphery of Western society and consciousness to the center.[14]

Gender fluidity and gay and lesbian studies have also become topics of interest among American musicologists, and are sometimes seen as being means of empowering women and the feminine. Lesbian studies often concentrate on body and voice, important topics in feminist aesthetics and feminist theory in general. Elizabeth Wood relates what she has termed "Sapphonics" (after the poet Sappho of Lesbos) to a particular type of rich female voice of extended range. She describes this "Sapphonic" voice quality as "a mode of articulation, a way of describing a space of lesbian possibility, for a range of erotic and emotional relationships among women who sing and women who listen." Wood finds a Sapphonic voice particularly thrilling.[15] Suzanne Cusick has likened falling in love with a woman to falling in love with a piece of music, and speculates on possible amorous relationships with musical works. (Here, as in earlier times, music is regarded as a sensual woman, but here the sensual nature is affirmed rather than being feared or condemned.)

> Do I respond [to a piece of music] by interrogating her techniques for causing pleasure? By seeking to know her inner processes? Do I analyze her various lovely parts (harmony, structure)? Or do I not, finding the analytical operation reminiscent of the dismemberments enacted on female bodies in, for instance, modernist paintings? When I "perform" her, do I use her as a means to know and thus express myself? Is our public relationship a means to display my "mastery"? Or do I find power in working to enable her to release her own?[16]

Interpreting the female voice as descriptive of a "space of lesbian possibility" in "Sapphonics" raises the philosophical possibility of a women's music in general. Although some studies cited above have considered the expression of traditionally feminine characteristics in the music of women, a discussion of the possibility of what we might call "women's ways of composing" has been largely avoided. This is due at least in part to the diverse nature of women's compositions and to concerns about essentializing female or feminine characteristics. Being able to identify with women's musics, however (and women's musics would always be multiple, subject to time, place, and collective disposition), could empower some women in somewhat the same way that various styles associated predominantly with African Americans (soul, rap) have empowered and united some members of that group. While various styles associated with women are perhaps unlikely to develop in our postmodern age, the possible benefits to some women of such musics—benefits similar to "Sapphonic" music for some Lesbian women—suggests the topic of women's musics is worthy of discussion.

Because both music and writing are process oriented, it is possible that *écriture féminine,* a style of female or feminine writing characteristic of certain French feminists, might be analogous to a possible type of women's music. *Écriture féminine* is well exemplified by this description of female experience by Hélène Cixous:

> Unleashed and raging, she belongs to the race of waves. She arises, she approaches, she lifts up, she reaches, covers over, washes ashore, flows embracing the cliff's least undulation, already she is another, arising again, throwing the fringed vastness of her body up high, follows herself, and covers over, uncovers, polishes, makes the stone body shine with the gentle undeserting ebbs, which return to the shoreless nonorigin, as if she recalled herself in order to come again as never before. . . . She has never "held still"; explosion, diffusion, effervescence, abundance, she takes pleasure in being boundless, outside self, outside same, far from a "center. . . ."[17]

Cixous asserts that feminine writing is impossible to define and cannot be theorized, enclosed, or encoded. Words used to describe such writing are gestural, rhythmic, spasmodic, heterogeneous, process oriented, immediate, fluid, and elastic. A principle of continuous growth, proliferation, and development replaces expression as product or object. Boundaries melt. Frequent repetitions and conjoined phrases produce a cumulative effect. There are backtracking and stumbling, phrases are rephrased, meanings are shifted. There is resistance to the finite, the definitive, the highly structured; to closure, final-state description, and resolutions of ambiguities; to hierarchies; to dualities, the two-term, dialectical process in which "conflict is held in check."

In what sense might such writing be considered feminine? Both Cixous and Julia Kristeva stress that the "feminine" here refers to a mode that disrupts and explodes conventional culture and meaning. Though it can be found in the writing of either sex, it is most likely to occur in the writing of women and in the speech of women when men are not around. Kristeva believes that the source of such writing is the rhythmic, presymbolic play of mother-infant communication in the infant's preoedipal stage of fusion with the mother (a fusion with the other that lovers seek to recapture). Gestation and maternal nurturance break down the oppositions between self and other, subject and object, inside and outside. Once children become familiar, however, with the "Law of the Father"—the symbolic order of language—they learn to distinguish self and other, and the pleasure or *jouissance* of the preoedipal stage is repressed. When traces of this *jouissance* arise from the subconscious and are set against conventional modes of discourse, the "iron grip of the symbolic is broken." This is precisely what happens, Kristeva believes, in feminine writing. Feminine writing is most likely to appear in the writing of women not only because they give birth and are socialized to become mothers but also because they are more likely to have access to the presymbolic world: in not having to develop a gender identity different from that of the mother, a girl can maintain longer the *jouissance* of that connection with her. Luce Irigaray has suggested in *This Sex Which Is Not One* that the continuity and openness of feminine writing also reflect women's experiences in that "individualization and discrimination of form are foreign to female eroticism." While phallocentric culture is based on singularity, identity, and specificity, female genitalia are multiple and contiguous, and women's sexual experience is indefinite, cyclic, without set beginnings and endings. Cixous writes that a woman's "rising" is not erection but diffusion.[18]

The process, continuity, and immediacy of music—music of all kinds and by both genders—seems analogous to the feminine writing discussed here, which seems more lyrical, more musical than traditional prose. Kristeva describes the lyrical noises that mothers and babies make to one another in the preoedipal stage (the source of feminine writing) as "musical" and "rhythmic," and Cixous describes female speech as the echo of the primeval song the woman once heard, the "Voice of the Mother."[19] If music is expressive of this presymbolic stage, it is potentially highly disruptive to the symbolic order of language, the "Law of the Father." The possibility of disruption would be (or has been?) countered by keeping music strongly controlled, highly structured, and objectified. (The term "piece" of music sounds like an object of some kind, and highly structured music such as canons, fugues, sonatas, or serialized pieces have generally maintained a high status.) A music similar to *écriture féminine,* in contrast, would engage the listener in the musical moment rather than the overall structure, would have a flexible form, and might involve continuous repetition with variation, the cumulative growth and development of an idea. Such music would serve to deconstruct musical hierarchies, and the dialectical juxtaposition and resolution of opposites would disrupt linearity and avoid definite closure. In sung music, vocalization would be relaxed and would make use of nonverbal or presymbolic sounds.

Much of what has been written about the possibility of women's music (and much of the music just described as associated with the feminine) is analogous to the concept of *jouissance*. Composer Kay Gardner, who regularly performs at the Michigan Womyn's Music Festival in Walhalla, claims a sort of women's music that is expressive of the sexual experience of women in its tendency toward circular musical form with climaxes in the middle rather than at the end.[20] Or consider the analogies that rock critic Maggie Haselswerdt makes between music and female sexuality:

> The beat of rock and roll may be the beat of sexual intercourse, but for the most part, it's intercourse from the male point of view. Though female sexuality is one of the stronger flavors in the brew when it comes to the blues, soul and dance music, rock's driving beat, piercing guitar lines, pounding keyboards and expansive, stage dominating gestures mark the territory as male. Female sexual response . . . is slow-building rather than immediate, diffuse rather than focused, buzzing rather than pounding, melting rather than hardening, and cyclical rather than constant. . . . The song . . . "Be My Baby" . . . owes its uncanny power to the wholesale appropriation of female patterns of sexual response. Phil Spector and the Ronettes weave a gauzy curtain around the sexual impulse, diffusing and romanticizing it, blurring the focus with walls of vibrating sound, highlighting the drama of the encounter with a series of minute yet heart-stopping pauses. "So c'mon and be . . . be my little baby" leads to the almost unbearably intense moment when Ronnie's famous "Wa-oh-oh-oh" is punctured by a reprise of the devastating opening beat. That's as close to what I mean by melting as mere vinyl can come.[21]

Not all women would identify with the playful description of female sexual experience Haselswerdt offers. Yet her sense that female sexuality is at issue in "Be My Baby" seems appropriate in light of the song's historical context. "Be My Baby" was co-written for the Ronettes in the early 1960s by Ellie Greenwich, Jeff Barry, and producer Phil Spector. Although Spector is white, he was attracted to what he regarded as the expression of feeling and physicality in African-American music; this attraction led at least in part to the "multilayered, multitextural wall of sound" associated with Spector, a sound that was often heard in the black "girl groups" of the period. These groups were designed to appeal to girls and young women, and usually posited a sweet and sensitive boy as an object of desire. The female "voice" in these songs is not usually a passive one; the young woman urging the boy to "Be My Baby," for example, is gently aggressive, somewhat maternal, more choosing than chosen. Greil Marcus has suggested that the songs of the girl groups have "ecologic, mystic, and poetic preoccupations," and present a "utopia of feeling, sentiment, and desire." The physicality of "Be My Baby" is reinforced by the *boom da boom BANG* of the percussion, which is imitative of a heartbeat. The prolonged "ooohs" and "aaahs" of the chorus, along with the end of the song, where Ronnie replaces the text with long and highly embellished "ohhhs," is suggestive of the preoedipal stage. All of this, combined with the Ronettes' sexual appearance and Ronnie's "sexiest voice in Rock and Roll," gives rise to what might be considered a sweet and sensuous feminine aesthetic.[22]

Offering "Be My Baby" as reflective of a female sexual response is problematic, however. What we hear is not the direct experience of sexually liberated women; rather, it is at least partly the conception of a young white male expressed through the voices of young women who were dominated both professionally and personally. Yet it is unfair to these women to suggest that they had no musical voices of their own, and it seems quite likely that their voices reflected their experiences as women (and as African-American women).

Presentations of women's experience in the work of relatively autonomous female musicians, however, are less problematic. Susan McClary has considered the music of Laurie Anderson from a feminist perspective, and shows how she serves, in both her texts and music, to break down patriarchal dualities and to celebrate female or feminine pleasure. An example of a celebration of female *jouissance* can be found in Anderson's "Langue d'amour [The Hothead]," which evokes biblical accounts of creation in its story of a man, a woman, and a "snake with legs" on an island. Charmed by the snake's stories, the woman falls in love with it and becomes bored with the man who, no matter what happens, is "happy as a clam." At the man's bidding, however, the man and woman leave the island; the woman misses the snake then and is restless, a hothead. The conclusion of "Langue d'amour" consists of a prolonged section in which the woman's *jouissance* is expressed more with vocal sounds than words: "Oooo là là là là. Voici. Voilà. Oooo là là là là. . . ." McClary suggests that in the piece's "chromatic inflections that escape diatonic control and in [its] rhythmic pulsations that defy regular metric organization," Anderson sacrifices narrative—in text as well as music—for the sake of sustained pleasure: "Unitary identity is exchanged for blurred, diffused eroticism."[23] In the area of art music, McClary further proposes that composer Janika Vandervelde, in her *Genesis II,* may present a culturally conditioned feminine concept of temporality by contrasting cyclic and timeless music with more masculine teleological or climactic processes.[24]

Marcia Citron includes a section entitled "Is There a Women's Style?" in her *Gender and the Musical Canon.* Citron considers some characteristics that have been associated with various women's musics, and most particularly with composed art music of the Western tradition. She begins by warning of the dangers of essentialism, the idea that women have some essential nature that will impel them to behave or create in certain ways; "There is no style," she asserts, "that issues from inherent traits in female biology." Further, she continues, it is not possible to determine from stylistic considerations alone whether a particular piece was written by a man or a woman; musical elements such as intervals or chords are not inherently gendered. Yet Citron believes women may tend to compose in some ways that grow out of certain social conditions within particular historical periods or cultural contexts: aspects of the prevailing socialization of women, subject positions that women are likely to develop, or ideologies and historical traditions that influence women's creative output. (Eva Rieger is also quoted as suggesting that there are similarities or tendencies among women's compositions from different historical and cultural periods.)[25] Drawing on Rieger and others, Citron discusses proposed tendencies in (some) women's compositions that are reminiscent of *jouissance*: tendencies, for example, to emphasize extensive development of a limited amount of material, compositional flexibility, a fascination with process as opposed to an adherence to set structures or techniques, and a lyricism characterized by long lines and connectedness, communication more than abstraction, substance more than innovation, and holism or organicism.[26]

Many composers who are women prefer to be thought of as composers rather than women composers and find the notion of women's music limiting. And more and more compositions by women are being held in the highest regard, whether or not they conform to current musical traditions and norms.[27] Yet some contemporary composers embrace the idea of composing like a woman or composing within a women's tradition. Most of these composers note the difficulty of drawing generalizations when the sample is relatively small, and some stress that characteristics may be more reflective of their own personal experiences as women than of some generalized female experience. Still, composer Miriam Gideon has suggested that women are more likely than men to be generous in the musical expression of emotion and less likely to employ specific systems or techniques unless related to an emotional impulse. Composer I'lana (formerly Sandra) Cotton suggests that pacing in women's music is likely to be organic, material is likely to evolve, breathing seems longer, and structure is likely to be fluid. Annea Lockwood and Ruth Anderson note a tendency toward holism in the works of women composers.[28] Among other female composers, Pauline Oliveros is preoccupied with circles, cycles, and mandalas.[29] And the cyclic principle and the tendency toward "continuous growth, proliferation, and development" characterize the music of Ellen Taaffe Zwilich, who describes her music as "organic," as concerned with "the elaboration of large-scale works from initial material" that "contains the seeds of the work to follow," works that are subjected to "continuous variation."[30] All of these characteristics are analogous to descriptions of *écriture féminine*.

It should be noted, however, that Pulitzer Prize–winning composer Shulamit Ran, while feeling that there is something distinctive about her voice as a woman and something distinctive about a woman's music, believes that there is far more to personal expression than expression of gender:

"There is also something distinctive about my music as a Jew, an Israeli, a white person, born at such and such a time, who has read and experienced certain things, who looks in a certain way. . . ."[31] This point cannot be stressed too strongly: hearing music as an expression of a woman's or women's experience is not the only way to hear or regard that music.

A difficulty with the idea of a women's music lies in determining how we might distinguish the expression of women's experience from the expression of male or patriarchal constructions of the feminine. Even in music by feminist women, can we distinguish women's experience from patriarchal conceptions of the feminine that women have internalized? Do women have any authentically female experience unconditioned by patriarchal oppression and constraints? Do the female processes or qualities identified earlier arise out of the very social conditions that we are trying to change, such that celebration of these qualities would limit women's personal and social development?

It is understandable that our present descriptions and expressions of the feminine and of women's experience will be similar to constructions of femininity offered by various male-dominated cultures, first because we cannot avoid the influence of these constructions, and second because these constructions are probably not wholly unrelated to the ways women think, feel, and behave. In their proclivities to dominate women, however, men have often cast in a negative light the characteristics they considered feminine, then used these perspectives to silence and oppress women. Rather than attempt to separate themselves completely from male concepts of the feminine, undoubtedly an impossible task, feminists could expose these concepts or images and reformulate them in a positive light. As beautiful and compelling as Wagner's musical conception of femininity or feminine sexuality may be, an examination of his music dramas makes clear that he views feminine sexuality as attractive yet deadly, and that his ideal woman is pure, chaste, and ready to sacrifice herself for her man. In contrast with *écriture féminine* and the music by women cited already, images of femininity and female sexuality that have usually been viewed negatively are instead reconstructed and celebrated. Anderson's "Langue d'amour" takes a social construct that has been most powerful in silencing women—the idea that woman was responsible for the Fall and that this Fall had something to do with her sexuality—and turns it around, posing a female protagonist who combines thought, emotion, and desire and delights in them, refusing to accept shame or guilt. (Though "Langue d'amour" ends with the woman's *jouissance*, the woman on the island is also intellectual in her curiosity, her desire for knowledge.) So even if the presentations of female sexuality offered in *Tristan und Isolde,* "Langue d'amour," Vandervelde's *Genesis II,* and "Be My Baby" are similar in their emphases on nonlinearity or tonal instability, we could distinguish them by saying (whether or not the effect was intended) that Wagner's presentation of the feminine is misogynist, that of "Be My Baby" is nonjudgmental, and that of "Langue d'amour" and *Genesis II* are feminist. It is also possible for feminist musicians to critique or parody traditional notions of the feminine, to express women's experience as distinct from traditional constructions of the feminine, to emulate processes common to humanity in general, or to transcend gender categories by concentrating on absolute music or pure form (if such a thing exists). What is critical is not so much what we call women's experience or the feminine in music, but rather what are a work's or an era's perspectives on women or the feminine, on how what is regarded as feminine is approached and handled in a particular social and historical context. Whether the feminist critic in question finds generalizations about the feminine or women's experience productive or oppressive (they are most likely both), a feminist approach to music might at least identify, interrogate, explicate, and critique such generalizations.

Scholars who take feminist positions in aesthetics or music criticism have met with considerable resistance, both outside the feminist movement and within it. Courage, tolerance of difference, openness, and support are essential for productive work in this area to continue.

NOTES

1. See Oliver Strunk, ed., *Source Readings in Music History* (New York: Norton, 1950), pp. 5, 23, 59–75, 82–83; and Renée Cox Lorraine, "A History of Music," in *Feminism and Traditional Aesthetics*, ed. Peggy Zeglin Brand and Carolyn Korsmeyer (University Park: Pennsylvania State University Press, 1995), pp. 162–69.

2. Leo Treitler, "Gender and Other Dualities of Music History," in *Musicology and Difference: Gender and Sexuality in Music Scholarship*, ed. Ruth Solie (Berkeley: University of California Press, 1993), pp. 23–45.

3. Linda Phyllis Austern, "Music and the English Renaissance Controversy Over Women," in *Cecilia Reclaimed: Feminist Perspectives on Gender and Music*, ed. Susan C. Cook and Judy S. Tsou (Urbana: University of Illinois Press, 1994), pp. 52–69.

4. Suzanne Cusick, "Gendering Modern Music: Thoughts on the Monteverdi-Artusi Controversy," *Journal of American Musicological Society* 46 (1993): 1–25, and Susan McClary, "Constructions of Gender in Monteverdi's Dramatic Music," *Feminine Endings: Music, Gender and Sexuality* (Minneapolis: University of Minnesota Press, 1991), pp. 35–52.

5. Susan McClary, "Narrative Agendas in 'Absolute' Music: Identity and Difference in Brahms's Third Symphony," in Solie, pp. 326–44.

6. Judith Tick, "Charles Ives and Gender Ideology," in Solie, pp. 83–106. Also writing of the early twentieth century, Catherine Parsons Smith has suggested that musical modernism arose partly in response to the first wave of feminism, and that the misogyny of modernistic tendencies suppressed female composers while it encouraged male composers of art music. See Smith, "A 'Distinguishing Virility': Feminism and Modernism in American Music," in Cook and Tsou, pp. 90–106.

7. See Catherine Clément, *Opera, or the Undoing of Women,* translated by Betsy Wing, Foreword by Susan McClary (Minneapolis: University of Minnesota

Press, 1988), pp. 56–58; Susan McClary, "Sexual Politics in Classical Music," in *Feminine Endings*, pp. 53–79; and Lorraine, "A History of Music," 160–85.

8. See Renée Cox Lorraine, *Tendencies and Inhibitions: Reflections on a Theme of Leonard Meyer*, forthcoming from Humanities Press International, Chapter II.

9. Gretchen A. Wheelock, "*Schwarze Gredel* and the Engendered Minor Mode in Mozart's Operas," in Solie, pp. 201–224.

10. Suzanne Cusick, "Of Women, Music, and Power: A Model from Seicento Florence," in Solie, pp. 281–304.

11. Carolyn Abbate, "Opera, or the Envoicing of Women," in Solie, pp. 225–58.

12. See Lorraine, *Tendencies and Inhibitions*, Chapter II. In the area of popular music, Venise T. Berry has demonstrated how black female hip-hop artists are using the often sexist medium of rap to articulate their own conceptions of the feminine and the feminist. See Berry, "Feminine or Masculine: The Conflicting Nature of Female Images in Rap Music," in Cook and Tsou, pp. 183–210.

13. Marcia Citron, *Gender and the Musical Canon* (New York: Cambridge University Press, 1993), pp. 144–59.

14. Carol E. Robinson, "The Ethnomusicologist as Midwife," in Solie, pp. 107–124.

15. Elizabeth Wood, "Sapphonics," in *Queering the Pitch: The New Gay and Lesbian Musicology*, ed. Philip Brett, Elizabeth Wood, and Gary C. Thomas (New York & London: Routledge, 1994), pp. 27–66.

16. Suzanne Cusick, "On a Lesbian Relation with Music: A Serious Effort Not to Think Straight," in Brett et al., 67–84. See also abstract in *Abstracts of Papers* read at the conference "Feminist Theory and Music: Toward a Common Language," Minneapolis, 1991.

17. Hélène Cixous and Catherine Clément, *The Newly Born Woman*, trans. Betsy Wing, Introduction by Sandra Gilbert (Boston: Beacon Press, 1985), pp. 90–91.

18. See *New French Feminisms*, edited and with introductions by Elaine Marks and Isabelle de Courtivron (New York: Schocken Books, 1981); Julia Stanley and Susan Wolfe (Robbins), "Towards a Feminist Aesthetic," *Chrysalis* 6 (1978): 57–76; Julia Kristeva, *Desire in Language: A Semiotic Approach to Literature and Art*, ed. Leon S. Roudiez, trans. Thomas Gora and Alice Jardine (New York: Columbia University Press, 1980), Chapter 5; Luce Irigaray, "This Sex Which Is Not One," in *This Sex Which Is Not One*, trans. Catherine Porter (Ithaca: Cornell University Press, 1985), pp. 99–106; and Cixous and Clément, *The Newly Born Woman*, p. 88.

19. Quoted in Toril Moi, *Sexual Textual Politics* (London: Routledge, 1985), p. 114.

20. Ruth Scovill, "Women's Music," in *Women's Culture: The Women's Renaissance of the Seventies*, ed. Gayle Kimball (Metuchen, NJ: Scarecrow Press, 1981), p. 158.

21. "Let's Talk About Girls . . . ," *Rock and Roll Confidential* 63 (December 1988): 1–2.

22. See Greil Marcus, "The Girl Groups," in *The Rolling Stone History of Rock and Roll*, ed. Jim Miller (New York: Random House and Rolling Stone Press, 1980), pp. 160–61.

23. "This Is Not a Story My People Tell: Time and Space According to Laurie Anderson," in McClary, *Feminine Endings*, pp. 112–31. "Langue d'amour" is from Anderson's *United States*.

24. McClary, *Feminine Endings*, pp. 132–47.

25. Eva Rieger, "Is There a Female Aesthetic in Music?" paper read at the Seventh International Congress on Women and Music, Utrecht, May 1991. For a brief summary, see Citron, p. 264.

26. Citron, pp. 159–64.

27. Honored female composers include Pulitzer Prize-winners Ellen Taaffe Zwilich, Shulamit Ran, and Melinda Wagner, as well as Guggenheim fellow Joan Tower. Thea Musgrave, Judith Weir, Libby Larsen, and Noa Ain are among the women who have had operas produced; works by Tower, Zwilich, Ran, Larsen, Deborah Drattell, and Augusta Reed Thomas are played by major orchestras.

28. See Elaine Barkin's questionnaire about women and music in *Perspectives of New Music* 19 (1980–81): 461–63, and responses to the questionnaire in vol. 20 (1981–82): 288–331; Jane Weiner LePage, *Women Composers, Conductors, and Musicians of the Twentieth Century: Selected Biographies,* vol. I (Metuchen, NJ: Scarecrow Press, 1980), pp. 222–23; Diane Jezic, *Women Composers: The Lost Tradition Found,* 2nd ed., rev. (prepared by) Elizabeth Wood (New York: Feminist Press, 1988), p. 204; and Citron, pp. 161–62.

29. See Pauline Oliveros, *Software for People: Collected Writings 1963–80* (Baltimore: Smith Publications, 1984).

30. Quoted in James Briscoe, ed., *Historical Anthology of Music by Women* (Bloomington: Indiana University Press, 1987), pp. 375–76.

31. See Barkin, *PNM* 20 (unnumbered).

SUGGESTIONS FOR FURTHER READING

In addition to the sources cited in the text or in the footnotes, the following provide information on the issues raised in this chapter.

Blackmer, Corinne E., and Patricia J. Smith, eds. *En travesti: Women, Gender Subversion, Opera.* New York: Columbia University Press, 1995.

Cox, Renée. "A Gynocentric Aesthetic." *Hypatia: A Journal of Feminist Philosophy* 5, no. 2 (1990): 43–62.

Detels, Claire. "Autonomist/Formalist Aesthetics, Music Theory, and the Feminist Paradigm of Soft Boundaries," *Journal of Aesthetics and Art Criticism* 52 (1994): 113–26.

Ecker, Gisela, ed. *Feminist Aesthetics.* Trans. Harriet Anderson. Boston: Beacon Press, 1986.

Green, Lucy. *Music, Gender, Education.* New York: Cambridge University Press, 1997.

Hein, Hilde, and Carolyn Korsmeyer, eds. "Feminism and Aesthetics." Special issue of *Hypatia: A Journal of Feminist Philosophy* 5, no. 2 (1990). Also published separately as *Aesthetics in Feminist Perspective.* Bloomington: Indiana University Press, 1993.

Koskoff, Ellen, ed. *Women and Music in Cross-Cultural Perspective.* Urbana-Champaign: University of Illinois Press, 1989.

Whiteley, Sheila. *Sexing the Groove: Popular Music and Gender.* New York: Routledge, 1997.

Ancient and Medieval Music

II. Women and Music in Ancient Greece and Rome

Ann N. Michelini

Music had a central and widely diffused importance in ancient Greek culture, and it was just this importance that created strong resistance to the notion of music as an art in its own right. A lyric fragment attributed to Pratinas of the fifth century B.C.E. states that "song is queen," while the pipe "should dance after, since it is the servant." Music was an integral part of much Greek poetry, and Greek poetry was the basic raw material of Greek education. Even after Greek prose writing began to become important in the fifth century B.C.E., the works of Homer and Hesiod remained the textbooks for schools; indeed, in the earliest period (700–450 B.C.E.), poetic works were the source of almost all knowledge about history, religion, morality, philosophy, and geography. The word "music" (*mousikê*) was used virtually as a synonym for education, and a painting of a school scene was as likely to feature a lyre as it was a book. The history of Greek women in music is therefore inseparable from the history of Greek poetry.

Investigating the role of Greek women in music is made difficult, however, because we cannot generalize meaningfully about Greek culture. "Greece," never a united nation in the classical period, consisted of many tiny or medium-sized states. These little states differed greatly in their social, political, legal, and ritual life; they were united only by a common language. But that language expressed itself in a common literature, and poetry was thus doubly important because it was the major source of pan-Hellenic culture. Although the roles of Greek women differed widely from city-state to city-state, in most early Greek cultures women and men tended to work, play, and socialize in single-sex groups. On the one hand, this meant rather strict lines of segregation, amounting in some Greek societies to a virtual seclusion of women. On the other hand, this same segregation left room in some areas and periods for a rich cultural life within female society, including the production by women and for women of poetry and its musical accompaniment.

We know of one such group from the fragmentary remains of the poetry of Sappho, who lived in Mytilene on the island of Lesbos at about the turn of the sixth century B.C.E. and was one of the greatest lyric poets of all time. Sappho's work expresses the homoerotic experience among a circle of women; as a result it has often been misunderstood, both in antiquity and in modern times. Marriage may have marked a change in a girl's role in these homoerotic societies. Sappho wrote wedding songs that emphasize the pathos of the bride's separation from family and friends; several times we hear of grief for absent friends or lovers who may have left Mytilene because of marriage. It is also apparent that an older married woman, such as Sappho herself who wrote poems to her daughter Kleis, could continue to function as a poet and self-proclaimed lover.

Sappho, in one of her most famous works, sings that she envies anyone who can sit opposite her beloved and listen to the beloved's enticing words—she herself becomes helpless when faced with such beauty. (The last stanza is missing several lines.)

> To me he seems equal to gods,
> the man who sits facing you
> and listens as you speak
> Softly close by,
>
> and laughs enticingly. That is what
> startles the heart in my breast,
> for, as I look at you an instant, then
> I can no longer speak.
>
> My tongue is broken, and a thin
> fire quickly suffuses my skin.
> My eyes see nothing; my ears
> Are buzzing.
>
> Sweat covers me, and trembling
> possesses me entire.
> I am paler than grass,
> and I seem to myself
> Just short of death.
>
> But all must be endured,
> for [?] even a poor man. . . .

This sophisticated poem points up the paradox of eloquence and emotion, love and writing about love. Just as in Shakespeare's sonnets, in Sappho's poems the poet hopes to win love through the power of her words, while complaining that as a sincere lover she finds it difficult to speak except through her verse.

We know of no other female poetic social groups like the one in Mytilene, but we do hear of other female poets, such as Corinna of Thebes, Praxilla of Sicyon, and Telesilla of Argos. These women all worked in the fifth century B.C.E., and Corinna has left substantial parts of several lyric poems. Her work seems aimed at male society and includes narratives of heroic myth, but the legends are local and the work is striking for its simplicity, compared with the very complex and sophisticated poetry of Pindar, a contemporary Theban male lyric poet. The contrast suggests that after Sappho's day the poetry of women continued to flourish in some areas without taking part in the development of male poetry, which was performed at the great pan-Hellenic festivals from which female poets were excluded.

While Greek male poets had the dominant role in relation to music, women were active as performers on musical instruments and sometimes as singers and dancers in the *choros*. In Sparta in the mid-seventh century B.C.E., the poet Alkman was famous for his "maiden songs" (*parthenia*), designed for performance by a chorus of unmarried girls. Fragments show that members of the chorus described each other's beauty and expressed erotic adoration for their chorus leader. Boys attended school, but, in the fifth century, Greek girls did not; nevertheless, some of them seem to have learned to play the lyre and to recite poetry (such as the songs of Sappho) to the music. Paintings on fifth-century pottery show well-dressed matrons sitting around with lyres, sometimes apparently as part of bridal ritual. Women were also strongly associated with playing the aulos, but here the aspect of class stratification becomes more prominent. A large class of professional, female aulos players, most of whom seem to have been slaves, were hired out to perform at all-male drinking parties; often the piper is depicted nude, suggesting that she functioned as a prostitute as well. Segregation of the sexes meant that women who came into the male world, like those hired to play music, received little pay and were accorded low status. In the classical period, the most famous lyre players and pipers were male, just as all the actors in Athenian drama were male; they wore masks and wigs when playing women's parts. But paintings give us evidence suggesting that women may have been used as pipers for dramatic performances in Greek-settled areas of southern Italy and Sicily at least by the early fourth century.

In the second half of the fourth century B.C.E., the forces of Alexander of Macedon destroyed the great Persian Empire. Greek-speaking Macedonians gained control of the civilized world, and the resulting spread of Greek culture has caused this era to be called "Hellenistic." New styles of poetry turned content away from male concerns, such as war stories of heroic myth, to everyday life and romantic sentiment. At the same time, from the fourth century on, the increasing prevalence of schooling for girls as well as boys led to an apparent increase in female participation in musical and poetic life. An important figure seems to have been Erinna, a young female poet who, probably in the mid-fourth century, wrote a touching poem to a childhood friend taken from her first by marriage and then by early death. Erinna resumed some of Sappho's themes in a new style, apparently influencing such famous third-century B.C.E. poets as Theocritus and Callimachus. Among female poets in this period were Anyte, who wrote epitaphs for pet animals, and Nossis, whose poems reflect a distinctly Sapphic emphasis on female society. By the second century B.C.E. we also hear of female poets who traveled to such pan-Hellenic festival sites as Delphi and won prizes for public recitations there.

In the Roman period (roughly 250 B.C.E. to 300 C.E.), the relation between women and music continued to be centered in poetry, but it was complicated by the ambivalent reaction of Roman culture to Hellenic influence. While trumpets, pipes, and even the lyre were known to the Romans, the great influx of Greek culture, including Greek music, dates from the second century B.C.E., when Rome began to dominate the civilized world. The Romans thought of dancing, singing, and lyre playing as undignified activities, effeminate for men and perhaps corrupting even for women. When the historian Sallust refers to someone who "played the lyre and danced more beautifully than is necessary for a respectable woman," he implies that respectable women were supposed to know and perform Greek music, but that there also was concern about these foreign arts. The ambivalent attitudes toward music guaranteed its importance in one aspect of cultural life: Roman erotic poetry. By definition holding a position in opposition to traditional Roman cultural values, Roman erotic poetry glorifies the *docta puella*, or learned lady, who is both connoisseur and love object. The poet Ovid advised women to use their vocal and instrumental skills to captivate lovers, performing lyrics from the tragic theatre, from Hellenistic Greek poets, or from Sappho. Because Roman women were less segregated, we hear more about them from Roman men but find few female poets who speak of their own experience. Only one, Sulpicia, has left some poems addressed to a male lover.

SUGGESTIONS FOR FURTHER READING

Anderson, Warren D. *Music and Musicians in Ancient Greece*. Ithaca: Cornell University Press, 1994 (describes instruments and gives a historical account of their use, but includes little on women).

Balmer, Josephine. *Sappho: Poems and Fragments.* London: Brilliance Books, 1984.
Fantham, Elaine [et al.]. *Women in the Classical World: Image and Text.* New York: Oxford University Press, 1994.
Groden, Susy Q. *The Poems of Sappho.* New York: Bobbs-Merrill, 1966.
Maas, Martha, and Jane McIntosh Snyder. *Stringed Instruments of Ancient Greece.* New Haven: Yale University Press, 1989 (has material on women as musicians).
Pomeroy, Sarah. *Goddesses, Whores, Wives, and Slaves: Women in Classical Antiquity.* New York: Schocken Books, 1976.
———. "*Technikai kai mousikai.*" *American Journal of Ancient History* 2 (1977): 51–68 (on musical activities of women in the later Hellenistic period).
Skinner, Marilyn. "Sapphic Nossis." *Arethusa* 22 (1989): 5–18.
Snyder, Jane McIntosh. *The Woman and the Lyre: Women Writers in Classical Greece and Rome.* Carbondale: Southern Illinois University Press, 1989 (evidence of women's activities in poetry and songs; includes some poems in translation).
Starr, Chester. "An Evening with the Flute Girls." *La parola del passato* 181 (1978): 401–10.
Taplin, Oliver. *Comic Angels and Other Approaches to Greek Drama through Vase-Paintings.* Oxford: Clarendon Press, 1993 (evidence of female pipe performers in Greek-ruled southern Italy).
West, Martin L. *Ancient Greek Music.* Oxford: Clarendon Press, 1992 (musical terminology and theory).

III.
Women in Music to ca. 1450

J. Michele Edwards

Secular Music

Resources

Developing a portrait of the musical activities of women in western Europe from the first to the fifteenth century is rather like creating a tapestry from a variety of fibers and textures. No single type of resource provides comprehensive information on the range of their participation. We can, however, bring together an array of resources: iconographic and literary references, wills and financial accounts, guild records and religious documents, didactic treatises, travel chronicles, song texts, and music treatises and manuscripts.

Since each type of resource poses problems for understanding and interpretation, the materials can best be used to clarify each other. For example, limiting a study to music manuscripts produces an unrealistic view of musical activity because written preservation for some types of music was irrelevant. Much secular music of this era was easily learned by rote or was of transitory interest, so that notation was unnecessary. Early liturgical music, on the other hand, called for continuity and was preserved in larger quantities. Since women's roles were particularly curtailed in the area of institutional religion, relying on music manuscripts alone distorts our understanding of women's contributions to the music culture. In addition to unjustly emphasizing liturgical music, a bias toward written documentation also gives unwarranted weight to music of the aristocracy, who, along with the clergy, were more likely than working people to be literate or to have access to a copyist. Furthermore, medieval music manuscripts, even when available, omit many details of sound and performance. Coupling the study of manuscripts with other resources, in sum, reveals more clearly the range and nature of activities in which women of various classes made music during these fifteen centuries.

Musical Roles

Women played many roles in music: amateur and professional singers, dancers, and instrumentalists; composers; benefactors; educators; and copyists. In a late fourth-century sermon St. John Chrysostom, patriarch of Constantinople, described the importance of popular song in the lives of working people, specifically mentioning lullabies sung by wet nurses and songs performed by women weavers, "sometimes individually and to themselves, sometimes all together in concert."[1] Music making by women was woven into the fabric of life and especially linked with two important events: birth and death. *Book of the Pious,* by thirteenth-century Rhenish Jews, almost certainly referred to singing by women in condemning the singing of Gentile lullabies to Jewish infants. Women's choirs sang at Christian and other funeral rites.

Women are especially visible in descriptions of social dancing. Their participation in dance-songs is known from the beginnings of Christianity in both liturgical and nonliturgical situations. The two most common forms of medieval dance-song preserved in writing are the *carole* and the *rondeau,* which were enjoyed by workers and nobility alike. Both include a refrain to facilitate participation in the singing by all the dancers. Although neither form has a single defining shape, each dance type can be identified by a common feature. *Rondeaux* include the refrain within the stanzas, and *caroles* utilize a *vuelta* or "turning line" (i.e., the final line of the stanza rhymes with the refrain). Song texts (e.g., those in an eleventh-century manuscript called the *Cambridge Songs* and in *Carmina Burana*) frequently refer to circle dancing, one of the oldest practices. A woman is most often cited as dance leader. For example, in a secular Latin dance-song on the last page of the *Cambridge Songs* manuscript, a woman leads the dance as solo singer in the center of the ring. The verses are a love song, and the refrain is quite simple, yet has interesting dramatic potential: "With ah! and oh!" Most dance-songs were performed with voices only, but the pipe and tabor (a frame drum, often with a snare) as well as the vielle (a bowed string instrument with an oval-shaped body) were also commonly associated with dancing.

Literary scholar Peter Dronke has reconstructed a possible recitation-performance of the dance-song "Tempus est iocundum, O virgines modo congaudete" (The time is joyful; O girls, rejoice now!) from *Carmina Burana.*[2] The narrative presents a social event. In the first strophe the chorus leader calls the young women and men together and introduces the refrain, which the chorus sings at the end of the remaining seven strophes. Women soloists are featured in the second, fifth, and sixth strophes, and men in the others. Each stanza ends with the word *floreo* (I blossom out of love), which rhymes with the refrain's *pereo* (I die of love). This constant element signals the entrance for the chorus.[3]

Another example of music as part of the social exchange between women and men comes from a biography of St. Jón, the first bishop of northern Iceland (d. 1121). "There was a favourite game of the people—which is unseemly—that there should be an exchange of verses: a man addressing a woman, and a woman a man—disgraceful strophes, mocking and unfit to be heard."[4] These love songs retained their popularity despite Bishop Jón's admonition against them. This game of love songs, as they were called by the biographer, probably presented an opportunity for women and men to sing simple improvised dialogues.

Prominent women were frequently benefactors of music, and several connected with French courts during the high Middle Ages were especially important. Eleanor of Aquitaine (1122?–1204) had substantial political power as wife first of Louis VII, King of France, and later of Henry II, King of England. She and two of her daughters, Marie (Countess of Champagne) and Alis (Countess of Blois), influenced their households, shaping the values and behavior of the nobility in various cultural centers. Eleanor supported the troubadours at her court in Anjou and later transplanted their literature to England. While at her court in Poitiers, Eleanor and her daughter Marie disseminated French chivalric manners—including music, singing, and the new vernacular literature—to women and men who became the ruling nobility in various areas of France, England, Sicily, and Spain. With Eleanor's support and encouragement, Marie's household at Champagne was active in the diffusion of the troubadour/trobairitz lyric and became the most active trouvère center in northern France during the last third of the twelfth century and the first half of the thirteenth century. Eleanor's other daughter, Alis (spelled in various ways, e.g., Aelis and Alix), was reported to have inspired the trouvère Gautier d'Arras; Eleanor's granddaughter Blanche of Castile was a trouvère. In southern France during approximately the same time period, Marie de Ventadorn (b. ca. 1165)—herself a trobairitz (i.e., one of the women composer-poets of Occitania, now southern France)—also supported troubadours. Her marriage to the Viscount of Ventadorn placed her in one of the centers of troubadour activity. Among the men receiving her support was Gui d'Ussel, and one of their *tensos* is preserved.

Writings by a fifteenth-century Dominican friar confirm that some women were skilled copyists or scribes. He cites at least a dozen convents with active scriptoria, and singles out two nuns at Colmar in northeastern France who were especially proficient at copying choir books. In his eulogy for Sister Lukardis of Utrecht, the friar praises her work as a copyist:

> She busied herself with . . . writing, which she had truly mastered as we may see in the large, beautiful, useful choir books which she wrote and annotated for the convent and which has caused astonishment among many fathers and priests who have seen the missal she prepared, written in a neat correct script.[5]

His astonishment need in no way imply that women scribes were rare; it is, instead, more a comment on his own misunderstanding of the activities and contributions of women.

Medieval Lyric

The medieval lyric—a song of personal poetic expression—continued traditions that had flourished throughout western Europe for centuries. The lyric was part of a performing-aural tradition rather than a written-visual one, with poetry and music inseparable. During the late Middle Ages the lyric was international in scope and formed a diverse repertoire, making simple definitions impossible. Though women appear to have participated as composers of the medieval lyric in smaller numbers than did men, they were more active than has often been reported: "For each language and culture, we are much at the mercy of the selectors—the predominantly male world of chroniclers and copyists."[6] For example, the fact that trobairitz materials were transmitted in only a few manuscripts suggests that works by women may have been consciously excluded from some medieval *chansonniers*. On the other hand, a few collections from Italy and Catalonia show particular attention to women's lyrics by grouping them together.

Current scholarship about lyric traditions has produced the most information about the trobairitz and troubadours of southern France. Trobairitz lived in the region with the largest concentration of troubadours, wrote lyrics in Provençal (*langue d'oc*), and flourished during the late twelfth and thirteenth centuries. All trobairitz who can be documented historically were members of the aristocracy, and most had various ties with troubadours. To establish a definitive list of trobairitz and the corpus of their work is not possible, as scholars differ considerably on what lyrics were actually composed by women. Some scholars have argued that songs attributed to women were really created by men, but most scholars now accept the existence of the trobairitz. Conflicting attributions, anonymous works, and poetic references to potentially fictional women continue to pose problems. Twenty-one trobairitz are identified by name, but these may not all be real people, and some anonymous works were likely written by women whose names have been lost. The number of lyrics attributed to women in recent editions and catalogues ranges from twenty-three (Meg Bogin) to forty-six (Angelica Rieger) and forty-nine (William Paden). Attributions for *tensos* between a female and male speaker are the most contested, and the women in some of these debate songs are probably *textualité féminine,* that is, fictional creations of male authors. Like the songs by their male counterparts, most surviving lyrics by trobairitz are *tensos* (debate songs or dialogues involving questioning and an exchange of views) or *cansos* (songs or, more specifically, love songs). Presuming a larger corpus, other genres include *sirventes* (a political or moralizing poem), *planh* (lament), *salut d'amor* (a poetic letter), *alba* (erotic dawn-song), *balada* (dance song), and *cobla* (rhymed exchanges or stanzas)—each represented by approximately one to three exemplars. Several manuscripts from the thirteenth and fourteenth centuries offer information through biographical sketches—*vidas* (biographies) and *razos* (commentaries)—for thirteen trobairitz, as well as portrait-like illustrations, including various miniatures of the Comtessa de Dia, Azalais de Porcairagues, and Castelloza.

The music of trobairitz and troubadours was less frequently written down than their poetry. The melodies were short and easily remembered, in contrast with many of the lengthy strophic poems. The modest interest in written preservation of the music might also be attributable to other factors: (1) the medieval lyric was an outgrowth of earlier traditions of improvisation; (2) precise repetition in the musical renditions was not valued; or (3) the participants sometimes lacked notational skill. Only one melody is generally ascribed to a trobairitz: "A chantar m'er de so q'ieu no volria" (I have to sing of what I would not wish) by the Comtessa de Dia. Billie Ann Bonse recently offered a strong hypothesis for attributing one additional melody to a woman: "S'ie us qier cosseill, bell'ami'Alamanda," a *tenso* between Lady Alamanda and Giraut de Bornelh that is almost always credited to the latter. Bonse postulates that the original *tenso* melody may have been borrowed from a *canso* by Alamanda, basing the hypothesis on medieval definitions that predicate a preexisting melody for the *tenso,* plus references to Alamanda in two contrafacta and an identification in one of these contrafacta suggesting the source of its borrowed melody as a "tune of Lady Alamanda."[7] "A chantar" (see HAMW, pp. 11–13) is preserved in more than one manuscript; however, the music appears only in *Le manuscrit du roi,* a collection of songs copied about 1270, possibly for Charles d'Anjou, brother of Louis IX. Literary scholars have particularly high praise for this lyric, which Fredric L. Cheyette and Margaret Switten describe as "a forthright discussion of amorous discord and of expectations deceived, couched in the usual terms of a legal complaint."[8] Their analysis shows the strong connection between the expectations of real women and the woman's voice in "A chantar," as well as the link between the poetic language used to discuss the lover's infidelity and that used in oaths of political allegiance, some of which were sworn to powerful women in France during this time. Even in her complaint, the speaker in "A chantar" affirms her self-worth and makes a rare claim of her own beauty in the first and last stanzas: "ma beltatz" (my beauty).

Given the small sample of trobairitz songs, generalizations are difficult to establish; however, recent scholarship has begun to focus more attention on interpretive analysis of lyric material. Studies have tentatively identified some common themes in the trobairitz corpus as well as variety among the women's voices. Although they retained some elements of the language and imagery from troubadours' *fin'amors* (fine or courtly love), the creativity of the trobairitz goes well beyond a simple role-reversal or inversion of the power dynamics between the aristocratic lady and her male lover of lower rank. In contrast to troubadour songs, the trobairitz lyric most often speaks directly to the beloved, rather than to a general audience, and often deals with disrupted love that has already been initiated. The women's poems articulate sexual desire and the speaker's aspiration for recognition as an individual and for a voice in relationships with men. Vocabulary studies indicate the trobairitz gave special attention to trust and concern for (in)fidelity. Often the women refer to their difficult relationships with language, as if conscious of their outsider status. Castelloza's *cansos* (three or four, depending on which scholar's attributions are used) seem especially preoccupied with the tension between a desire to speak and the social admonition to be silent; see for example her "Amics, s'ie us trobes avinen" (Friend, I have found you charming). Many of the trobairitz poems include intertextual allusions responding to the songs of troubadours and make "a conscious attempt to comment on masculine discourse."[9] The trobairitz rejected traditional portrayals of women; with their work they contested constructions of femininity. For example, the *tenso* "Na Carenza al bel cors avinenz" (Lady Carenza, fair and lovely of form) challenges two important social values of male-dominated medieval society by raising the possibilities of remaining unwed or of having a husband but no children.

Perhaps the most substantial transformation of *fin'amors* is the *canso* by Bietris de Roman (or Bieiris de Romans), who probably lived during the first half of the thirteenth century. "Na Maria, pretz e fina valors" (Lady Maria, the virtue and pure worth) addresses Maria and may be an expression of lesbian love. Scholars' analyses and views of this *canso* vary considerably, reading this as female friendship (Rieger) or as a poem actually written by a man (Schultz-Gora, Poe, Folena, Zufferey). Still other scholars see Bietris as spokesperson for a man (Sainte-Palaye), view the song as a religious poem in which Maria is understood as the Virgin Mary, or postulate an expression of lesbian love (Bec, Bogin, Nelli, Boswell).[10] As the latter, language of the courtly tradition both elevates the beloved through Bietris's words of praise and speaks of physical desire. The tone of this love lyric, however, is more positive than much of the repertoire of either the trobairitz or troubadours: there is no deceit, no infidelity, no bitterness or anger toward the beloved. For example, stanza two reads:

> For this I beg you, please, to let pure love,
> delight, and sweet humility
> give me the help I need with you
> so you will grant me, lovely lady, please,
> what I most hope to enjoy;
> for in you lie my heart and my desire:
> I have all my happiness because of you,
> I'm sighing many sighs because of you.[11]

By the early thirteenth century, love songs in many languages emerged in imitation of the trobairitz and troubadours. Working in northern France, the trouvères wrote in *langue d'oïl* or the medieval language that developed into modern French. Few works by women trouvères have been identified, and fewer still include music. *Le manuscrit du roi,* mentioned above as the source of a *canso* by the Comtessa de Dia, preserves one item (one strophe only) with music by a woman trouvère: "Mout m'abelist quant je voi revenir" (It pleases me much when I see) by Maroie de Dregnau de Lille (*fl.* 13th century). Other works attributed to women trouvères include "Amours, u trop tart me sui pris" (Love, with whom too late I am allied) by Blanche of Castile (1188–1252), granddaughter of Eleanor of Aquitaine and twice Regent of France, and two songs by the Duchesse de Lorraine, including the death-lament "Par maintes fois avrai esteit requise" (Many a time I have been asked). "Jherusalem, grant damage me fais" (Jerusalem, you do me a great wrong) was attributed to two different men—both attributions rejected by modern scholars—but on the basis of textual and linguistic analysis Peter Dronke tentatively ascribes this woman's lament and crusade song to a woman trouvère.[12] Among ten known *jeux-partis*, or debate songs, appearing to have women authors or coauthors, three survive with music: an anonymous work by a woman and her lover (set to music borrowed from a troubadour *canso* by Bernart de Ventadorn); one by Perrot de Beaumarchais and an unnamed woman; and "Je vous pri dame Maroie" (I beg you, lady Maroie), a debate by Dame Margot and Dame Maroie that survives in two manuscripts with very different melodies, presumably by one of the women.

Discussing the documented singing of women at court, Kimberly Marshall suggests that new questions are needed to assess female creativity in an oral culture like that of the trouvères.[13] She counters the general assumption by scholars that women sang music conceived and notated by men, suggesting instead that their monodies might have been their own creations and were probably performed most frequently without reference to written materials. Further, she speculates that some songs attributed to men are actually just the written formalization of songs created and transmitted orally by women.

Most likely, the pregnancy song "Huc usque, me miseram!" was written by a woman and might serve as an example of a Latin lyric, although like most of the poems in *Carmina Burana* it was an anonymous creation. *Carmina Burana,* a thirteenth-century anthology preserving over 200 poems, includes Latin lyrics from many European lands, especially England and France, along with a number of poems in a German dialect. Subjects range from moral questions to satire, from love to drinking and gambling. Dance-songs, parodies of religion, vagabonds' songs, and six religious plays are also included. Although these poems, spanning more than 200 years, were meant to be sung, only a few include music in staffless, unheighted neumes (nondiastematic notation), while others have space above the text for a melody that was never entered. "Huc usque, me miseram!" which resembles poems about pregnancy written in other European languages, is not preserved with musical notation. It is preceded by a brief introduction:

> Here begins a flowery song
> As it rises like a bird so it gives solace.
> Eve, how many are the joys of love?

The poem itself functions much as a response (literally a *reflexus,* or refrain) to this question.

> I loved secretly, but now the pain! My belly is huge, and birth is near.
> Mother yelled, Father slapped me. Both fumed. I'm alone in this room, and can't play outside.
> Neighbors look at me as at a monster. They stare, poke each other, and clam up till I walk by.
> They always point at me with fingers. I'm a wonder. They wink obscenely. They damn me for one sin.
> Why am I talking? I'm gossip in every mouth. Pain grows and now my friend is gone.
> He ran off for good, back to France. Without him I hurt, almost die. I cry for myself.[14]

Available documentation suggests considerable literary and musical activity at the major Spanish courts during the late Middle Ages. Women participated in various ways in this cosmopolitan culture, which integrated Muslims, Jews, and Christians. For example, in Castile at the court of Sancho IV (reigned

1284–1295), palace account books show salaries for twenty-seven minstrels: two Arabic women, twelve Arabic men, one Jewish man, and twelve Christian men. The association of dark skin with *jougleresses* suggests a special prominence of Moors among women minstrels, even beyond the borders of Spain. Frederick II, Holy Roman Emperor and King of Sicily, employed Moorish musicians in his Norman-Saracen court at Palermo. Several medieval romances (e.g., *Aucassin et Nicolette* and *Bevis of Hampton* [*Bueve de Hantone* in Provençal and *Bove d'Ancona* in Italian]) include episodes in which a noblewoman disguises herself as a *jougleresse* by darkening her face and becoming a traveling musician who plays an instrument as well as sings.

From at least the eleventh century onward, women singers at the courts of Andalusia entertained with bilingual lyrics. They concluded *muwashahat* poems (love poems in classical Arabic or Hebrew) with vernacular stanzas using colloquial Arabic or Spanish. These final stanzas, or *kharjas,* talk directly and frankly of complex feelings and present women as active lovers. In these so-called women's songs (*cantigas de amigo* or *chansons de femme*), male authors attempted to write from a woman's subject position. This type of medieval lyric raises interesting questions about authorship, preliterate expressions, and gender systems, and suggests the willingness of men to speak for women or define their feelings.

Accounts of Arabic and Jewish women who wrote lyrics in medieval Spain indicate the importance of being in a creative environment. Most of these women can be linked with other accomplished poets: a father or lover, a woman teacher, or even a slave master. Although not all were noblewomen, they were usually connected with a court. Kasmūnah, daughter of a Jewish poet, studied with her father and was considered an outstanding writer. Her two-part dialogues with her father parallel the form of some Provençal *tensos.* A lyric exchanged between an Arabic woman, Hafsah bint al-Hājj al-Rakūnīyah (d. 1184 or 1190), and her beloved, Abū Ja^cfar, also resembles the *tenso* and similarly was probably sung.

While a resident of Cordova, Zeynab al-Murabiyyah (d. 1009), who never consented to marriage, composed several verses praising al-Mudhfer, a son of Mansūr ibn Abī ᶜĀmir, who eventually usurped the throne of Cordova. Wallādah (d. 1087 or 1091), daughter of the King of Cordova and for a time the beloved of poet Ibn Zaydūn, was among the most famous poets of her day. At least one of her female students, Bahjah, was also well-known for lyric writing. A freed slave, al-ᶜArūdhiyyah (d. eleventh century), learned grammar and rhetoric from her master in Valencia, then was said to surpass him as a poet. Hind, a slave woman in mid-twelfth century Xativa who excelled in poetry and music as an 'ūd player and singer, was praised by a famous Arabic poet in an invitation to his house: "The nightingale, after hearing thy performance, envies thee, and wishes to hear again the deep intonations of thy lute."[15] Unfortunately, neither medieval Arabic music nor secular music attributed to medieval women on the Iberian Peninsula are known to have survived.

Earlier scholars identified three thirteenth-century women as contributors to the Italian secular lyric; however, modern scholars have found no evidence of poetry by Gaia da Camino (mentioned in Dante's *Divina commedia*), and now consider Nina Siciliana a legend. Two sonnets with religious overtones and part of a secular *tenzone* are still tentatively attributed to a woman known only as "the accomplished damsel," or La Compiuta Donzella, almost surely a pseudonym. Her identity has been extensively investigated, although nothing concrete has been established. Variously evaluated in terms of quality, her poetry is now generally accepted as the earliest Italian verse by a woman.[16] Until at least the mid-fourteenth century no music for the Italian secular lyric has survived.

Study of the medieval lyric is revealing about gender systems. Repeatedly, song texts pronounce what it meant to be a woman or a man, and women and men differed in their perspectives. Women's choices and treatments of genre and form also differed from those of their male contemporaries. To gain a more comprehensive understanding of medieval western Europe, the views of women must be added to men's concept of *fin'amors*.

A distinctive tradition of women's participation in music has also been documented in Japan; however, many details about medieval Japanese women singers remain contested by scholars. Yung-Hee Kim Kwon describes a group of women singers (*asobi*) strongly linked with the performance of *imayo,* a popular song genre that emerged in the late tenth century, flourished during the next two centuries, and died out by the late thirteenth century.[17] Superb singing skills distinguished the *asobi* from other courtesans. Barbara Ruch, on the other hand, has challenged the conventional view of these entertainers as a single group of low status and linked with prostitution.[18] She provisionally suggests three types of women as the most significant artistically: the *kugutsu*, who were traditionally associated with puppet theater and especially with *imayo;* the *shirabyoshi,* dancers cross-dressing in white costumes and perhaps originally among the *kugutsu*; and *yujo* (or *asobime*), literally meaning "female entertainer" but often translated as "courtesan" or "prostitute." Regardless of specific details, Ruch claims that women entertainers had a significant impact on "every major vocal and choreographed genre of literature and music from the twelfth century on,"[19] including Noh and later kabuki.

Court diaries and letters from the Heian period (794–1192) establish that singers entertained prominent members of court, including emperors. Emperor Goshirakawa (1127–1192) launched a particularly striking student-teacher relationship in 1157 when he called Otomae (1085–1169) to court to teach him her repertoire of *imayo*. An esteemed singer, Otomae traced her musical ancestry back through four generations of female teachers and required the Emperor to relearn his repertoire according to her musical style. Although the *imayo* collection entitled *Ryojin Hisho* (Secret Selection of Songs that Make the Rafter Dust Dance) is generally attributed to Emperor Goshirakawa, the material was surely Otomae's, whether she composed the songs or passed along earlier material. Compiled over two decades, the anthology was completed in 1179; today 566 texts from this collection are extant. The lyrics juxtaposed a diversity of topics, ranging from Buddhist doctrine to songs about nature. Unfortunately, all of the music is lost and virtually nothing is known about the performance of *imayo* except that singers often accompanied themselves with a small drum (*tsuzumi*) or by tapping a closed fan against their palms.

Performers

The hierarchy in western cultures which today gives elevated status to composers can also be seen, although to a lesser extent, in the Middle Ages. No clear division between composers and performers yet existed, and some social mobility was possible. When the functions of composer and performer were distinguished, traveling performers (minstrels or *jougleresses* in southern France) were accorded less status and were often from a lower social class than composer-poets (e.g., trobairitz). Whether investigating musical performance by women or men, much about the medieval period and earlier is sketchy. Evidence indicates that women engaged in many of the same secular performing activities as their male counterparts. Distinct musical activities appear to be due at least as much to class as to gender. For example, medieval French literary sources identify aristocratic women as singers of dance-songs, troubadour and trouvère chansons, motets, and *lais*. In Cordova during the reign of al-mansūr ibn Abī ʻĀ-mir (939–1002), well-educated women played instruments, such as the organ, to entertain their husbands. Didactic treatises, such as the anonymous fourteenth-century *La clef d'amors,* intended for middle- and upper-class women, encouraged singing and playing some instruments as a pastime. *Del reggimento e costumi di donna* by Francesco da Barberino (1264–1348) addressed dance and music as appropriate components of a noblewomen's education. French treatises do not generally condemn public performance by women, but Barberino's early fourteenth-century Italian treatise seeks to limit women's musical activity to the private sphere. On the other hand, women known to be professional performers, either traveling minstrels or servants at court, were largely from lower social classes.

Provençal, Old French, Spanish, Galician-Portuguese, and Middle English each have words that refer specifically to women minstrels: *jougleresse, menestrelle, juglaresa* or *juglara, jograresa,* and *gliewméden*. In addition to singing and playing instruments, minstrels possessed an array of entertainment skills—tumbling, juggling, recitation, dancing, magic tricks, acrobatics, exhibiting trained animals, and mime. Some minstrels were slaves; others were employees hired by courts. The eleventh-century court of Poitiers in Occitania included hundreds of Moorish *jograresas,* who were received as remuneration for assistance given Aragon in the campaign against the Moors in 1064. Payment records verify the presence of women singers and instrumentalists at various courts, especially in France. For example, in 1239 Louis IX paid Mélanz, a *cantatrix* or woman singer to the Countess of Blois. Mahaut d'Artois employed a woman singer for Christmas 1319 and a woman organist named Jehanne in 1320. Mahaut's granddaughter, a princess of France, employed three female singers and a woman bellringer. The earliest (about 1175) documented organization of musicians was a lay religious guild in Arras, France, which admitted both women and men. In the articles of incorporation for the earliest trade guild of minstrels, organized in Paris in 1321, women and men were treated equally. The articles, which regulated such activities as apprenticeships and hiring until 1773, consistently refer to *menestreus et menestrelles* or *jougleurs et jougleresses*. Seven of the thirty-seven people to sign the original guild articles as registered in 1341 were women.

Instruments

Iconography, French literary sources, and financial accounts of the English court all indicate that a single instrument, rather than an ensemble, most frequently accompanied voice(s) in European monophonic music of the twelfth and thirteenth centuries. Medieval sources represent women as performers on percussion instruments, organ, and especially string instruments. Wind instruments, which were specifically discouraged as not feminine (and not appropriate even for aristocratic men) during the Renaissance, must already have been a rarity for women. Percussion instruments, also viewed as unsuitable for women by the fifteenth century, were linked earlier with two activities in which women were prominent: processionals and dancing. A late-fourteenth-century illuminated manuscript held in Vienna shows five women in a procession. They are singing and playing small drums and handbells, two of the most common medieval percussion instruments.

Women are linked with the organ from very early in music history. In fact, the earliest known organist, Thaïs, was a Greek woman from the third century B.C.E. Her husband is said to have invented the *hydraulis*, an early

FIGURE 3.1. Two women play chess while a slave or servant entertains with lute music. From *Libro de los juegos* (Book of Games), produced in the court of Alfonso the Wise (1221–84); Escorial, MS J.T.6. Reproduced from Julian Ribera, *La Musica de las Cantigas* (Madrid: Tipographia de la Revista de Archivos, 1922), vol. 3.

organ. Depictions of organs on sarcophagi identify several women from the Roman Empire (second and third centuries C.E.) as organists: Aphrodite, Julia Tyrrania, and Gentilla. In Hungary the inscription on the tomb of Aelia Sabina (probably third or fourth century C.E.) reads: "She herself remaining, as she was seen among the people, playing the hydraulis so well."[20] Since the early Christian church rejected the use of instruments in worship as a pagan practice, the organ was not widely used in church services until the fourteenth century. However, wealthy monasteries owned and used organs much earlier, and perhaps this was also true for convents. Beginning in the Middle Ages, small organs—called positive and portative—were signs of accomplishment and deemed appropriate instruments for domestic entertainment by women. A particularly detailed account by Apostolic Protonotary Teodoro da Montefeltro describes organ performances of the fourteen-year-old Bianca de' Medici, who entertained the entourage of Pope Pius II in Florence in 1460. Montefeltro's letters, which indicate that Bianca performed intabulations of well-known polyphonic vocal works by Binchois and others, favorably describe her playing "with fine phrases and proportion and impressive rhythm."[21] In keeping with the largely unwritten performance tradition of instrumental music during the fourteenth and fifteenth centuries, these pieces were more likely of her own invention, rather than arrangements from notated intabulations by another composer. Thus the close relationship among the roles of performer, improviser, and composer for organists during the late medieval period suggests an area in which women may have participated in creating polyphonic music.

According to French romances and recommendations in didactic treatises, medieval women most frequently played strings: vielle, harp, psaltery, gittern, rote, lyre, rebec, and citole. Thirteenth-century French illuminated manuscripts show women playing a similar group of string instruments: vielle, harp, rebec, and gittern. Iconography from the Iberian Peninsula offers some of the richest sources on medieval instruments and instrumentalists, and women are quite visible in these sources. For example, in a Galician-Portuguese manuscript called *Cancioneiro da Ajuda,* twelve of the sixteen miniatures include women performers, most frequently as singers who often accompany themselves with castanets or tambourine. In perhaps the most significant collection, the *Cantigas de Santa Maria,* compiled at the court of Alfonso the Wise (1221–84), every tenth song—singing general praise to Mary—is accompanied by a miniature of performing musicians. Women appear in at least numbers 29, 30, and 33, as well as in the two unnumbered miniatures.[22]

The combination of information from historic-literary documents, paintings, sculptures, clay figures, and archeological sources also provides insight into some facets of women's musical activities in medieval China. The Tang dynasty (618–907), which sustained one of the greatest eras of Chinese poetry, is also considered a peak in music history. Several paintings, created in various eras, depict all-women court orchestras performing for a nobleman and his wife, most likely representing events in the Tang dynasty.[23] Perhaps the earliest and most exquisite of these is a scroll from the Sung dynasty (960–1279) imitating a tenth-century work (in the Art Institute of Chicago) by the famous painter Chou Wên-chü. The nineteen musicians shown conform to general expectations of the *li-yüan* ensemble, which had been introduced by Ming Huang in 714. The illustration shows precisely the instruments used during the Tang dynasty in the ensemble to accompany a genre of refined art songs called *fa-chü:* pairs of four-stringed *pipa* (lute), *konghou* (harp), *zheng* (zither), *sheng* (mouth organ), *di* (transverse flute), *chi-pa* (vertical flute) or *bili* (oboe), *chieh-ku* (side drum), *fangxiang* (gong-chime), and *paiban* (clapper), along with one *ta-ku* (large drum). Although these paintings claim to depict Emperor Ming Huang and his wife, Yang Kuei-fei, the evidence is insufficient to verify this. In any case, the paintings portray a nobleman—emperor, aristocrat, or high-level official—and his wife enjoying the music of their private orchestra. Ming Huang, an exceptionally charitable sponsor of music and dance, doubled China's official music departments by creating two new conservatories. In addition to a training center for his favorite music, *fa-chü,* mentioned above, he established another school primarily for female court musicians, often called singing girls. This institution, called *chiao-fang,* served more than three thousand women performers during this period. Hundreds of the women who were trained at the *chiao-fang* came to teach at the *li-yüan* conservatory. All of the musicians in these departments were government slaves.

Religious Music

Women in Judaism

Women's prayer-songs had a prominent place in the Hebrew Bible (Old Testament), including the songs of Miriam (Exodus 15: 20–21), Deborah (Judges 5), Jephtha's daughter (Judges 11: 34), and Hannah (1 Samuel 2: 1–10). Each of these is a spontaneous acclamation or celebration: for example, Miriam's song celebrates the Israelites' crossing the Red Sea and their escape from Pharaoh when he and his horsemen were swept into the sea. According to biblical accounts, as worship became more formal, women's roles in services diminished. By the early Rabbinic period in the third century C.E., singing by women in worship was often forbidden because a woman's voice was considered a "sexual incitement" (Babylonian Talmud, treatise *Berakot,* chap. 3, para. 24a). The famous rabbinic scholar Maimonides (1135–1204) voiced hostility toward women's singing and even toward secular music in general. Despite many prohibitions throughout the Middle Ages, evidence indicates that the participation of Jewish women in religious music, especially outside the Temple, continued and that practices varied in different geographic and social circumstances.

Miriam and each of the women at the Red Sea played a *tof,* often called a timbrel, the only membranophone (a percussion instrument whose sound is produced by striking or rubbing a stretched skin) mentioned in the Hebrew Bible. Among Egyptians the *tof* was played only by women and eunuchs, and it may have been exclusively a woman's instrument among the Jews. Perhaps its association with women helps to explain why this instrument was excluded from the music of the Second Temple (late sixth century B.C.E. to 70 C.E.). Outside of worship, Jewish women participated in music both as singers and as instrumentalists. Even in the most restrictive situations women sang among themselves; for festivities, banquets, and weddings; and as wailing mourners. Jewish instrumentalists, including women, were highly visible from the second century B.C.E. onward.

Women in Early Christianity

Women's participation in and contributions to early Christianity were extensive. In its earliest days, this new religion primarily attracted people who lacked economic and social privilege—women of all classes and lower-class men. Particularly in the communities of widows and virgins associated with early Christianity, women redefined themselves and rejected traditional gender roles and class divisions. For women, conversion to Christianity meant chastity, defying the traditional definitions of woman as wife and mother. Cross-class participation by women in Christianity brought together slave and slaveholder, challenging the patriarchal Greco-Roman family. By the end of the second century, men within Christianity recognized women's challenge to gender roles and began working to rebuild the system so as to exclude women and give religious authority to men. The growing institutionalization of Christianity, which might have given women a greater voice in an important cultural sphere, instead restricted women's religious activities. The establishment of Christianity as a state religion brought still more extensive participation and control by men. Ironically, women were increasingly excluded from the very institution they had been so instrumental in establishing.

Women's activities in music paralleled their overall opportunities in the early Christian church. During the early centuries of Christianity both women and men sang during worship. Ignatius of Antioch (first-second centuries) spoke in terms of the congregation's singing with one voice, women and men together. In her account of the service at the Church of the Holy Sepulchre in Jerusalem, the pilgrim Egeria (ca. 386) described singing—perhaps in antiphonal style—by monks, virgins, laywomen, and laymen. However, by the late fourth century many church councils and individual churchmen sought to silence women's singing during the worship service. Patristic literature frequently tried to justify the exclusion of women from singing and preaching activities by citing the injunction "Women should keep silence in the churches" (1 Corinthians 14: 34), an admonition which consensus scholarship now identifies as a later insertion to Paul's letter. Many, but not all, early Christian writers continued to encourage extraliturgical singing of psalms by women as a deterrent to singing secular music. However, both Gregory Nazianzen (ca. 329–ca. 391), one of the three principal Fathers of the Greek Church, and Arsillos, an Iberian ruler, advocated that even in private worship at home, only men should sing. From the fourth century, opportunities for women in public churches were further inhibited with the shift from congregational singing to music provided by select choirs, comprised solely of men and boys.

The gradual suppression of singing by Christian women can be linked with various factors: a reaction to the singing among women in other religious groups; the characterization of women musicians as prostitutes and courtesans; the identification of women with the arousal of sexual desire and worldly temptation; and, chiefly, the political victory of the Roman Church over heretics and Gnostics. The Gnostics, who treated women and men in an egalitarian fashion, were the dominant Christian community in Egypt and northern Syria from the third century until the time of Augustine (354–430) and posed the greatest threat to the Roman Church. The subjugation of women by the Roman Church occurred simultaneously with its suppression of the Gnostic community. The exclusion of women from the music of public worship was also deeply rooted in patriarchy: the domination of women was viewed as a means of retaining and enhancing the power of the Latin church fathers and of institutional Christianity as a state religion.[24]

Despite actions that were likely to thwart compositional creativity, some women did emerge as composers, although few names of individual composers during the first millennium of Christianity are known. At least seven women, however, can be identified as composers of Byzantine Christian chant between the ninth and fifteenth centuries: Martha, a ninth-century abbess at Argos; Thekla, a ninth-century abbess near Constantinople known for a *kanon* praising *Theotokos* or the Virgin Mary; Kassia, a well-educated ninth-century poet-composer and the most significant of these Byzantine women musicians; Theodosia, another ninth-century composer and abbess known for her *kanones;* Kouvouklisena, a singer and *domestikena* (or leader) of a women's choir during the thirteenth century; a singer and composer whose name is not known but who is identified as the daughter of Ioannes Kladas, a leading composer of Byzantine chant in the late fourteenth century; and Palaeologina, a nun from the late fourteenth or fifteenth century who probably founded the convent of St. Theodora in Thessalonika.

Women composers contributed to the major genre of Byzantine chant: that is, hymns, including *troparia, stichera,* and *kanones.* Like a *troparion,* a *sticheron* was originally a short intercalation sung between the last few verses of a psalm. Some have unique melodies, while others share melodies with other *stichera.* A Byzantine *kanon* is a verse form of nine sections, each alluding to one of the nine biblical canticles. Each section contains several stanzas sung to a repeated melody. Palaeologina, a cultured and educated member of the Imperial family, composed *kanones* in honor of Saints Dimitri, Theodora, and others. Music by only two of the women is preserved: one song is ascribed to the daughter of Ioannes Kladas, and numerous liturgical compositions are attributed to Kassia, although not all are considered authentic. Many of her known works are *stichera;* however, her most famous piece, "The Fallen Woman" (see HAMW, pp. 4–5), is a *troparion* about Mary Magdalene.

Religious music-drama was one of the most interesting accretions to medieval Christian rituals. The dramas developed largely from the tenth century, or perhaps as early as the reign of Charlemagne (768–814), during an era when there was an impulse to embellish and humanize the rituals of Christianity. During the next several centuries, the dramas grew in length, and some manuscripts provide detailed rubrics about the enactment, indicating costumes and props or giving directions for dramatic gestures and movement. Women characters have especially significant roles in the Easter drama (*Quem quaeritis* or *Visitatio Sepulchri*), the earliest and most popular story. Additional music-dramas recounting other biblical stories may not have been as prevalent at nunneries. For example, at the abbeys of Origny-Sainte-Bénoîte (near St. Quentin, France), Barking (England), and Wilton (England), only the Easter drama with its prominent roles for women was apparently incorporated into their repertoires. Although clerics and choirboys generally took the roles of both female and male characters, nuns also participated, creating more realistic, mixed casts. In at least six different versions of *Visitatio* (Visit to the tomb), women portrayed the Marys (Mary Magdalene; Mary, the mother of James and Joses; and either Mary, the mother of Jesus, or more likely Mary of Bethany, who was the sister of Martha and Lazarus).[25] A late-thirteenth-century manuscript—largely in French—at Troyes documents a performance by the nuns and clergy of Notre Dame. Three nuns took the Mary roles in fourteenth-century performances at the collegiate church at Essen and at Barking Abbey in Essex (England) during the time when Lady Katherine of Sutton was abbess (1363–1376). Participation by nuns is indicated in the rubrics of the Wilton Processional, in the fourteenth-century St. Quentin drama from the nunnery of Origny-Sainte-Bénoîte, and in a fifteenth-century *Quem quaeritis* from Brescia in the Lombardy region of Italy. The St. Quentin drama and the *Visitatio Sepulchri* in the Wilton Processional, a manuscript created for and by Benedictine nuns ca. 1300, led to a rethinking of the traditional conclusion that development in music-drama was accomplished through the inclusion of additional scenes and characters. The story in the Wilton Processional focuses on the single scene of the three Marys and the angel at the tomb, but it is longer and more complex than many other dramas with this plot. That these nuns should have retained the emphasis on women rather than adding scenes in which men predominated is not surprising.

Women's Faith Communities

In both Judaism and Christianity, women found opportunities for musical participation in religious life through women's communities when their participation was limited in municipal houses of worship. Only one community of Jewish women from late antiquity is known, whereas Christian women's communities were more numerous, and their existence was documented at least as early as the second century.

On the Contemplative Life (first century C.E.), by Philo of Alexandria, described a monastic community of Jews: *Therapeutrides* (women) and *Therapeutae* (men). The women and men of this double house on Lake Mareotis, outside Alexandria, prayed, studied scriptures, and composed and sang hymns and psalms. Both sexes participated separately but equally, except on the Sabbath and for the festival of Shavuot, when they worshipped together. The festival music is quite interesting. Prayers, commentary on scripture given by the president, and the first round of singing preceded a meal of bread and pure water. After the president offered a hymn to God, Philo Judaeus notes:

> all the others take their turn as they are arranged and in the proper order while all the rest listen in complete silence except when they have to chant the closing lines or refrains, for then they all lift up their voices, all the men and all the women.[26]

Since the Therapeutic society emphasized equality, the assumption that both women and men sang as soloists during this ritual is reasonable. Philo continues, describing the sacred choral vigil after supper as the peak of the ritual:

> They rise up all together and standing in the middle of the refectory form themselves first into two choirs, one of men and one of women, the leader and precentor of each being the most honoured among them, and also the most musical.

These separate choirs sang both in unison and antiphonally. Then, in what was clearly a rare occurrence, the women and men joined together in one chorus, singing until dawn in an ecstatic state.

Christian women's communities took on new significance from the fourth century, when the nunnery offered women virtually their only opportunity to sing and compose music in praise of God. The convent nourished leadership and creativity among women: "The impulse toward leadership which kept the men in the world sent the women out of it."[27] Between 500 and 1500 the convent was the only acceptable alternative to marriage for European women, and it "fostered some of the best sides of intellectual, moral, and emotional life."[28] Especially during the eleventh and twelfth centuries, Christian convents were among the major centers of culture. Singing liturgical music was the central communal activity in most convents. The education of novices focused on reading and singing, to encourage participation in collective worship. In singing eight Offices plus Mass together each day, making and sharing music was at the very core of women's communal lives. The visions of Mechtild of Hackeborn (ca. 1241–1299) and Gertrude the Great (1256–1302), both nuns at the convent of Helfta in Germany, attest to the power of music, its subversive potential, and its integral position in their theological understandings.[29] In the community of medieval nunneries women had an outlet for creativity in singing and sometimes in musical composition. In addition, one woman provided leadership as *cantrix,* assuming a leadership role not open to medieval women outside the convent. She served as conductor, with responsibilities for choosing repertoire, conducting rehearsals, overseeing the copying of music and illumination work, managing the library, and supervising liturgy. She may have been among those most likely to compose texts and music for religious services.

In addition to the many anonymous nuns who provided religious leadership and who created embroidery, tapestries, sculpture, miniatures, and songs, a few identifiable individuals stand out during the period of intense creative activity in the twelfth century: Héloise, perhaps the most famous nun of the era; Marie of Oignies, the mother of the Beguine movement; Constance of Le Ronçeray, a lyric poet; Abbess Herrad of Hohenbourg, who conceived and planned the impressive illuminated religious encyclopedia, *Garden of Delights;* and Hildegard, who was exceptional in both the depth and the breadth of her intellectual and creative scope.

Hildegard von Bingen

A visionary twelfth-century theologian, Hildegard von Bingen (1098–1179) composed seventy-seven religious songs (a group of eight antiphons form a cohesive narrative relating St. Ursula's story) and a lengthy music-drama, *Ordo virtutum,* which has no medieval parallel. While knowledge of Hildegard's childhood remains uncertain, we know that at age fourteen (on November 1, 1112) Hildegard and Jutta (her *magistra* or abbess) took vows and became recluses in the Benedictine double house at Mount St. Disibod.[30] Her first official position as a leader came in 1136, when she succeeded her mentor as superior at Disibodenberg. Later, against the wishes of the monks at St. Disibod, Hildegard founded her own community at St. Rupertsberg. Construction for the new convent began in 1148, and when she and her sisters moved in two years later, they took with them rich endowments and greater independence for themselves. Hildegard was so successful that by 1167 she had founded a daughter house in Eibingen. Often called a mystic, she chronicled her visions and wrote on medical and scientific matters as well as on the lives of saints. Hildegard almost

FIGURE 3.2. Hildegard of Bingen with the nun Richardis and Hildegard's secretary, Volmar. Biblioteca Statale di Lucca, MS. Cod. lat. 1942. Reproduced by permission.

certainly supervised the large number of detailed illustrations in a famous illuminated manuscript recounting her visions. She was well known throughout Europe, responding to theological questions, making prophecies, corresponding with popes and monarchs, offering spiritual guidance, and speaking out for reform.

Although Hildegard claimed that all her writings and music came to her in visions, and disavowed an educational background, her works reveal familiarity with the writings of two medieval music theorists, Boethius (ca. 480–524) and Guido of Arezzo (eleventh century). Her need to deny human instruction can be understood in the context of medieval gender politics, expectations of monastic life, the visionary tradition of Rhine mystics, and a deep awareness of biblical dreamers. Since she lived in an era that prohibited women from teaching or holding authority over men, according to Barbara Newman, Hildegard's need to deny human instruction

> is no mere topos of humility, but a claim to high authority. . . . Only through visions could a religious or intellectual woman gain a hearing . . . while men might perhaps heed a divinely inspired woman, they would have little patience with a mere presumptuous female.[31]

For Hildegard, music was an avenue of access to mystical experience, composition a way to make palpable God and divine beauty. Her poetry and music, dating from as early as the 1140s, were written largely for Offices and Mass at her convent. A few pieces celebrated saints important in nearby Trier; these were perhaps written on commission. Her chant cycle *Symphonia armonie celestium revelationum* (Symphony of the Harmony of Celestial Revelations) is preserved in two different versions: one manuscript containing fifty-seven chants (1175) and another containing seventy-five pieces (1180s). These chants are distinctive and idiosyncratic, though not without links to the medieval chant repertory. Her texts, modeled on the prayers and songs of the liturgical Office, "contain some of the most unusual, subtle, and exciting poetry of the twelfth century."[32] Their resulting free-verse or prose quality is echoed in her freely spun melodic lines with their irregular, unpredictable gestures. Like her contemporaries, Hildegard built her works from a small number of melodic formulae; however, her development process was different. In comparison with Adam of St. Victor (d. 1192), who used stock musical figures to assemble chants in the fashion of a patchwork quilt, Hildegard's elaboration and embellishment of melodic formulae resulted in more continuous, through-composed musical lines. Musical stability arises from organic melodic unity, rather than from external factors such as strophic form or regular poetic meter. Hildegard's songs often encompass a wide range of two octaves or more, and in some cases reach nearly three octaves. Melismatic elaboration in her responsories reaches exceptional levels, with frequent melismas of thirty to fifty notes on carefully selected words. Her habitual use of ascending and descending leaps of a fifth is also exceptional for chant. Though Hildegard's hymns and sequences are not bound by traditional forms, her works in other genres—the Kyrie (see HAMW, p. 10), an alleluia-verse, eighteen responsories, and many of the forty-three antiphons—have identifiable precedents in Gregorian chant repertoire.

When church officials interviewed the nuns at Bingen to gather evidence for Hildegard's proposed canonization (which was never completed), three nuns claimed to have seen the abbess chanting "O virga ac diadema" (see HAMW, pp. 8–9) while illuminated by the Holy Spirit. Analysis of this chant shows both Hildegard's independence of and her connections with contemporaries and tradition. Textually, "O virga" has ties with the typical formal pattern of sequences from the tenth and eleventh centuries, in which the first and the last verses stand alone while the other verses are paired (a bb cc dd . . . n). Hildegard balances the salutation in the first strophe with a prayer to *Salvatrix* (a feminine savior) in the last. The central strophes are grouped in threes, not twos, by their content, although the melody of "O virga" retains the couplet form common in the sequences of her contemporaries. Hildegard's strophes are neither rhymed nor structurally alike: they do not contain the same number of syllables or the same pattern of stresses. In "O virga" each pair of verses employs a single melodic idea, transformed to fit the differing texts. The resulting sound is unified through recurring melodic fragments, but literal repetition is avoided.

Recent scholarship by Bruce Holsinger positions Hildegard's music and poetry within a female-centered religious experience that includes homoerotic desire; this contrasts with traditional accounts by Barbara Newman and Peter Dronke viewing medieval devotion to the Virgin Mary as asexual.[33] While not suggesting that Hildegard was a lesbian, Holsinger explores how her music "eroticized the entire body"[34] and how the music and poetry, when read in connection with her scientific writings, present a powerful expression uniting body, voice, and spirituality.

Hildegard's awareness of herself as a woman among women seems evident in the texts of her songs. Many of her seventy-seven extant chants honor women: sixteen are addressed to the Virgin Mary, thirteen to St. Ursula and her women followers, and four to various groups of women. Sixteen are addressed to local or individual male saints, leaving only twenty-eight to such traditional Christian figures as God and the Holy Spirit. Her poetic imagery is frequently woman-centered, and women take an active role in the spiritual story of salvation that Hildegard presents. In this way she inspired women to become aware of the power in the material world and to exercise that power. Working within a women's community, Hildegard developed remarkable leadership and extraordinary creativity. Only as a member of a religious community of women could she have brought together her scientific, artistic, and theological creations.

Polyphony

Women's participation in medieval polyphony as singers or composers is a matter of scholarly debate. Three manuscripts of polyphonic music from fourteenth- and fifteenth-century England have slim ties with nunneries but at least suggest the possibility that nuns in England sang in parts. Continental sources, on the other hand, give strong evidence that nuns sang polyphony: sixteen manuscripts from convents span over 300 years, beginning as early as the twelfth century and originating in Spain, France, Germany, Italy, Switzerland, Austria, and the Netherlands. As with other music by women, the repertoire coincides with the primary genres of the era: conductus, motets, Mass movements, sequences, and hymns.

Las Huelgas Codex, containing 136 pieces, is the most extensive source of polyphony known to have been owned by a nunnery. The manuscript, dating from the fourteenth century, was copied from a collection that Maria Gonzalez de Aguero had transcribed earlier in the century. The complex music apparently reflects the skill of the nuns and girls in the choir of Las Huelgas near Burgos, Spain, and consuetudinary records indicate that the nuns sang in three parts. This convent had a trained choir of young girls, similar to boys' choirs in cathedral schools. From 1241 to 1288, the time of Abbess Berenguela, daughter of Beatrix of Spain and Ferdinand III, one hundred nuns sang in the choir and forty girls were in training. A conventional explanation maintains that women did not participate in church polyphony as performers or composers since their education was insufficient. Indeed, education varied considerably, even in convents, and declined for women in the later medieval period. As the intellectual centers shifted in the late twelfth and thirteenth centuries from convents/monasteries to urban universities, which were closed to women, the artistic and intellectual activity of nuns declined. However, even if women's performing polyphonic music was not a common occurrence, the evidence substantiates that it was widespread in terms of time period and geographic range. Paula Higgins notes "the perplexing absence of a single musical composition attributed to a woman between *c.* 1300 and 1566, followed by a proliferation of publications of polyphonic music by women from 1566 on."[35] She concurs with Howard Mayer Brown that women were probably composing music, but not admitting their authorship due to social pressures.

Summary

Throughout the centuries of the Roman Empire and the European Middle Ages, and contemporaneously in China and Japan, music was viewed as a powerful enterprise as well as a source of entertainment and pleasure. The spiritual power and moral suasion ascribed to music gave it special significance and encouraged its regulation. Thus the same institution that proclaimed, "God established the psalms, in order that singing might be both a pleasure and a help,"[36] also suppressed the voices of women. Middle- and upper-class women were restricted from public performance, yet their education and leisure gave them the opportunity to cultivate music as a personal accomplishment. Women musicians among slave and servant groups, in contrast, had considerable visibility as professional performers, but they were subjected to a loss of liberty and were often treated as sexual objects. Because music can articulate status, it is closely connected with both class and gender systems. The presence of skilled musicians at court, along with the creation of elaborate melodies and complex forms, were marks of power and prestige. Gender and class differences contributed to and helped explain differences in musical activities between women and men or among women during the first to the fifteenth centuries.

Special thanks are due to those who provided research assistance for the first edition of this chapter, Jane Lohr (University of Iowa graduate student) and Melissa Hanson (Macalester College, class of 1990), and for this revision, Jennifer Anderson (Macalester College, class of 1998) and Megan Opp (Macalester College, class of 2000). I am also grateful to colleagues and friends who read portions of the manuscript and offered suggestions, especially to Barbara Newman, Calvin Roetzel, Paul Solon, and Dorothy Williams.

NOTES

1. As translated in Oliver Strunk, *Source Readings in Music History* (New York: W.W. Norton, 1950), p. 68.

2. This poem is among those set by Carl Orff in *Carmina Burana* (1936).

3. Peter Dronke, *The Medieval Lyric,* 3rd ed. (Cambridge: D.S. Brewer, 1996; 1st ed., 1968), pp. 192–93, expanding on Joseph Bédier's reconstruction of another early thirteenth-century dance-song.

4. *Biskupa Sögur* (Copenhagen, 1858), I: 165–66, as quoted in translation by Peter Dronke, *Women Writers of the Middle Ages: A Critical Study of Texts from Perpetua (†203) to Marguerite Porete (†1310)* (Cambridge: Cambridge University Press, 1984), p. 105.

5. As quoted in translation by Margaret Wade Labarge, *Women in Medieval Life: A Small Sound of the Trumpet* (London: Hamish Hamilton, 1986), p. 224.

6. Peter Dronke, *Women Writers,* p. 98.

7. Billie Ann Bonse, "El son de n'Alamanda: Another Melody by a Trobairitz?" (paper read at the Midwest Chapter meeting of the American Musicological Society, Madison, Wis., April 1998). Thanks to the author for sharing her abstract via e-mail (June 24, 1998).

8. Fredric L. Cheyette and Margaret Switten, "Women in Troubadour Song: Of the Comtessa and the Vilana," *Women and Music: A Journal of Gender and Culture* 2 (1998): 26–45. This article presents important analysis toward a new interpretation of the woman's voice in trobairitz repertory. Thanks to Margaret Switten for sharing this article in advance of its publication and for other helpful comments about the trobairitz.

9. Simon B. Gaunt, *Gender and Genre in Medieval French Literature* (Cambridge: Cambridge University Press, 1995), p. 165.

10. See Angelica Rieger, "Was Bieriris de Romans Lesbian? Women's Relations with Each Other in the World of the Troubadours," in *The Voice of the Trobairitz: Perspectives on the Women Troubadours*, ed. William D. Paden (Philadelphia: University of Pennsylvania Press, 1989), pp. 73–94; Oscar Schultz-Gora, "Nabieiris de roman," *Zeitschrift für romanische Philologie* 15 (1891): 234–35;

Elizabeth Wilson Poe, "A Dispassionate Look at the Trobairitz," *Tenso* 7 (1992): 142–64; Gianfranco Folena, "Tradizione e cultura trobadorica nelle corti e nelle citta venete," in *Storia della cultura veneta: Dalle Origini al Trecento* (Venice: Pozza, 1976), pp. 453–562; François Zufferey, "Toward a Delimitation of the Trobairitz Corpus," in Paden, pp. 32–33; Jean Baptiste de la Curne de Sainte-Palaye, *Histoire littéraire des troubadours* (Paris, 1774; reprint Geneva: Slatkine, 1967), vol. 3, p. 379; Pierre Bec, ed., *Burlesque et obscénité chez les troubadours: Pour une approche du contre-texte médiéval* (Paris: Stock, 1984), pp. 197–200; Meg Bogin, *The Women Troubadours* (New York: W.W. Norton, 1980), pp. 75, 176–77; René Nelli, ed., *Ecrivains anticonformistes du moyen-age occitan: I. La femme et l'amour* (Paris: Phébus, 1977), pp. 301–5; John Boswell, *Christianity, Social Tolerance, and Homosexuality: Gay People in Western Europe from the Beginning of the Christian Era to the Fourteenth Century* (Chicago: University of Chicago Press, 1980), p. 265.

11. As translated in *Songs of the Women Troubadours,* ed. and trans. Matilda Tomaryn Bruckner, Laurie Shepard, and Sarah White (New York: Garland Publishing, Inc., 1995), p. 33.

12. Peter Dronke, *The Medieval Lyric,* pp. 106–8, including note 1.

13. Kimberly Marshall, "Symbols, Performers, and Sponsors: Female Musical Creators in the Late Middle Ages," in *Rediscovering the Muses: Women's Musical Traditions,* ed. Kimberly Marshall (Boston: Northeastern University Press, 1993), p. 158.

14. As translated by Willis Barnstone, in Aliki Barnstone and Willis Barnstone, eds., *A Book of Women Poets from Antiquity to Now,* rev. ed. (New York: Schocken Books, 1992), p. 61.

15. Ahmed Ibn Mohammed al-Makkari [al-Maqqari], *The History of the Mohammedan Dynasties in Spain,* trans. Pascual de Gayangos, 2 vols. (1840; reprint New York: Johnson Reprint Corp., 1964), 1: 166–67.

16. Paolo Cherchi, "The Troubled Existence of Three Women Poets," in Paden, pp. 197–209.

17. Yung-Hee Kim Kwon, "The Female Entertainment Tradition in Medieval Japan: The Case of *Asobi,*" *Theatre Journal* 40/2 (May 1988): 205–16; reprinted in *Performing Feminisms: Feminist Critical Theory and Theatre,* ed. Sue-Ellen Case (Baltimore: Johns Hopkins University Press, 1990), pp. 316–27.

18. Barbara Ruch, "The Other Side of Culture in Medieval Japan," in *Cambridge History of Japan,* vol. 3, ed. Kozo Yamamura (Cambridge: Cambridge University Press, 1990), pp. 500–543.

19. Ibid., p. 530.

20. Friedrich Jakob, *Die Orgel und die Frau* (Männedorf, Switzerland: Orgelbau Th. Kuhn, 1972), p. 14, as quoted by Jane Schatkin Hettrick, "She Drew an Angel Down: The Role of Women in the History of the Organ 300 B.C. to 1900 A.D.," *The American Organist* 13/3 (March 1979): 40.

21. William F. Prizer, "Games of Venus: Secular Vocal Music in the Late Quattrocento and Early Cinquecento," *Journal of Musicology* 9/1 (Winter 1991): 3–4.

22. Thanks to Mayra Rodriquez for her assistance identifying women in these miniatures—a process that is not intuitive for the untrained. See all forty two illuminations at a Web site maintained by Greg Lindahl: http: //www.pbm.com/~lindahl/ cantigas/.

23. Shigeo Kishibe, "A Chinese Painting of the T'ang Court Women's Orchestra," in *The Commonwealth of Music: In Honor of Curt Sachs,* ed. Gustave Reese and Rose Brandel (New York: The Free Press, 1965), pp. 104–17; idem, *Todai Ongaku no Rekishiteki Kenkyu* (A Historical Study of the Music in the T'ang Dynasty; summary in English), 2 vols. (Tokyo: University of Tokyo Press, 1960–1961).

24. For additional analysis of women's participation and subsequent exclusion from singing in the early Christian church, see Rebecca T. Rollins, "The Singing of

Women in the Early Christian Church," in *Music in Performance and Society: Essays in Honor of Roland Jackson,* ed. Malcolm Cole and John Koegel (Warren, MI: Harmonie Park Press, 1997), pp. 37–57. See also Johannes Quasten, "The Liturgical Singing of Women in Christian Antiquity," *Catholic Historical Review* 27/2 (1941): 149–65; idem, *Music and Worship in Pagan and Christian Antiquity,* trans. Boniface Ramsey (Washington: National Association of Pastoral Musicians, 1983).

25. Thanks to Calvin Roetzel (e-mail communications with the author, September 4, 1998) for discussion of the "three Marys" who appear in music and visual art of the medieval era. The "three Marys" are not exactly biblical but rather a later tradition established on the basis of various biblical accounts. The lack of a singular answer to their identity is probably why music scholarship tends to ignore this question and simply refer to "the Marys" or the "three Marys."

26. As quoted in translation by Ross S. Kraemer, "Monastic Jewish Women in Greco-Roman Egypt: Philo Judaeus on the Therapeutrides," *Signs* 14/2 (Winter 1989): 346.

27. Emily James Putnam, *The Lady: Studies of Certain Significant Phases of Her History* (1910; reprint Chicago: University of Chicago Press, 1970), p. 78.

28. Lina Eckenstein, *Woman under Monasticism* (1896; reprint New York: Russell & Russell Inc., 1963), p. vii.

29. See Bruce Wood Holsinger, "Plainchant and the Everyday: The Nuns of Helfta and the Somatics of Liturgy" (paper presented at Feminist Theory and Music 3: Negotiating the Faultlines, University of California, Riverside, June 1995).

30. For recent scholarship about Hildegard (including a recently discovered twelfth-century biography of Jutta), see Barbara Newman's biographical essay in *Voice of the Living Light: Hildegard of Bingen and Her World,* ed. Barbara Newman (Berkeley and Los Angeles: University of California Press, 1998); see also Margot Fassler's chapter on Hildegard's music in the same volume.

31. Barbara Newman, "Hildegard of Bingen: Visions and Validation," *Church History* 54 (1985): 169, 170.

32. Peter Dronke, *Poetic Individuality in the Middle Ages: New Departures in Poetry 1000–1150* (Oxford: Oxford University Press, 1970), p. 151.

33. See Bruce Wood Holsinger, "The Flesh of the Voice: Embodiment and the Homoerotics of Devotion in the Music of Hildegard von Bingen (1098–1179)," *Signs* 19/1 (Autumn 1993): 92–125.

34. Ibid., 120.

35. Paula Higgins, "The 'Other Minervas': Creative Women at the Court of Margaret of Scotland," in *Rediscovering the Muses: Women's Musical Traditions,* ed. Kimberly Marshall (Boston: Northeastern University Press, 1993), p. 180; see also Howard Mayer Brown, "Women Singers and Women's Songs in Fifteenth-Century Italy," in *Women Making Music: The Western Art Tradition, 1150–1950,* ed. Jane Bowers and Judith Tick (Urbana: University of Illinois Press, 1986), p. 64.

36. St. John Chrysostom, as translated by Oliver Strunk, *Source Readings,* p. 68.

SUGGESTIONS FOR FURTHER READING

For surveys on trobairitz and trouvères, see Matilda Tomaryn Bruckner, Laurie Shepard, and Sarah White, eds. and trans., *Songs of the Women Troubadours* (New York: Garland Publishing, Inc., 1995); William D. Paden, ed., *The Voice of the Trobairitz: Perspectives on the Women Troubadours* (Philadelphia: University of Pennsylvania Press, 1989); Samuel N. Rosenberg, Margaret Switten, and Gérard Le Vot, eds., *Songs of the Troubadours and Trouvères: An Anthology of Poems and Melodies* (New York: Garland Publishing, Inc., 1998), with accompanying CD. For interpretive work, see Matilda Tomaryn Bruckner, "Fictions of the Female Voice:

The Women Troubadours," *Speculum* 67 (1992): 865–91; idem, "The Trobairitz," in *A Handbook of the Troubadours,* ed. F. R. P. Akehurst and Judith M. Davis (Berkeley: University of California Press, 1995), pp. 201–33; Simon B. Gaunt, *Gender and Genre in Medieval French Literature* (Cambridge: Cambridge University Press, 1995); Marianne Shapiro, "The Provençal *Trobairitz* and the Limits of Courtly Love," *Signs* 3/3 (Spring 1978): 560–71; Fredric L. Cheyette and Margaret Switten, "Women in Troubadour Song: Of the Comtessa and the Vilana," *Women & Music* 2 (1998): 26–46.

On Castelloza, see Peter Dronke, "The Provençal Trobairitz: Castelloza," in *Medieval Women Writers,* ed. Katharina M. Wilson (Athens: University of Georgia Press, 1984), pp. 131–52; Matilda Tomaryn Bruckner, "Na Castelloza, *Trobairitz,* and Troubadour Lyric," *Romance Notes* 25/3 (1985): 239–53.

On Hildegard, see Barbara Newman, *Sister of Wisdom: St. Hildegard's Theology of the Feminine* (Berkeley: University of California Press, 1987); and Saint Hildegard of Bingen, *Symphonia: A Critical Edition of the* Symphonia armonie celestium revelationum, 2nd ed., ed. Barbara Newman (Ithaca: Cornell University Press, 1998), which includes text translations and commentary; Joseph L. Baird and Radd K. Ehrman, eds., *The Letters of Hildegard of Bingen,* vol. 1 (New York: Oxford University Press, 1994), which includes translations of ninety letters with commentary. For Hildegard's music, see Prudentiana Barth, Maria-Immaculata Ritscher, and Joseph Schmidt-Görg, eds., *Hildegard von Bingen: Lieder,* 2nd ed. (Salzburg: Otto Müller Verlag, 1992). A modern edition of *Ordo virtutum* has been prepared by Audrey Ekdahl Davidson (Kalamazoo: Medieval Institute Publications, 1985); a modern edition of nine chants is available in Christopher Page, ed., *Sequences and Hymns,* No. MCMI (Newton Abbot, England: Antico, 1983); a modern performing edition of the antiphon "O frondens virga," paired with a chant Magnificat, has appeared in an edition with extensive notes by William T. Flynn (Chapel Hill, NC: Treble Clef Music Press, 1998).

Anne D. Bagnall, "Musical Practices in Medieval English Nunneries," Ph.D. diss., Columbia University, 1975 (University Microfilms, 75–25, 648), includes material on music-drama and polyphony.

Kimberly Marshall, ed., *Rediscovering the Muses: Women's Musical Traditions* (Boston: Northeastern University Press, 1993), includes several relevant articles.

Volume I of Sylvia Glickman and Martha Schleifer, eds., *Women Composers: Music through the Ages* (New York: G. K. Hall, 1996) contains music by Kassia, Hildegard von Bingen, the Comtessa de Dia, and Suster Bertken, as well as essays on anonymous music and women, women and *Trecento* music, and Saint Birgitta of Sweden.

Portions of this chapter appear in a different version in the author's article in *Women in the Middle Ages: An Encyclopedia,* eds. Nadia Margolis and Katharina M. Wilson (Garland Publishing, forthcoming).

The Fifteenth through the Eighteenth Centuries

IV. Musical Women in Early Modern Europe

Karin Pendle

"Did women have a Renaissance?" Answers to this question, posed by historian Joan Kelly-Gadol in her pathbreaking article, have led to significant reassessments of the concepts of periodization that most students absorb from their earliest encounters with the study of history. Until Kelly-Gadol asked her question, most people's ideas about the era bound by the years 1450–1600—which is now most often referred to as the early modern period—were formed by the writings of relatively wealthy, educated men of Christian background that were aimed primarily at readers of similar sex and class. The best known among these scholars was German historian Jacob Burckhardt (1818–1897), whose influential *The Civilization of the Renaissance in Italy* was first published in German in 1860. In a chapter entitled "The Position of Women," Burckhardt put forth his claim that the sexes in Renaissance Italy were regarded as equal, at least among the educated classes. This view reappeared so often in works of subsequent scholars that its truth was never seriously questioned until Kelly-Gadol proposed a new, woman-centered view of these years.

Renaissance. Rebirth. What was reborn in the so-called Renaissance? The learning and literature of classical authors, the ancient Greeks and Romans, though not unknown to scholars of the early Christian era, now came to dominate the education and thinking of wealthy and titled men. Boys learned Latin, even Greek, so that they could study the ancient authors in their original tongues. Classical education's emphasis on the liberal arts became this period's ideal as well: grammar, rhetoric, logic, mathematics, astronomy, and music theory were its central components; physical education, modern languages and literature, and practical skills in music and dance might be added. Such knowledge was not to be acquired for its own sake, however. It was regarded as learning for life: it dealt with man, hence was humanistic, and prepared the young scholar for his duties as a ruler or a citizen. The Renaissance Man was to be not a specialist but a generalist, one who had absorbed the best ideas of classical civilization in order to enhance his own humanity.

Civic and artistic values as well as personal goals were affected by the rebirth of this humanistic spirit. The years 1450–1600 witnessed the emergence of strong European states and of empires acquired when explorers pushed beyond the boundaries of their known world. Throughout Europe, capitalism continued to undermine the earlier manor-based economy. Some of Europe's greatest religious art and music was created under a humanistic aesthetic that encouraged a greater range of individual expression than had been common heretofore, and painting, sculpture, song, and dance adorned brilliant courts and enhanced public spectacles.

Yet this was a time not of unity of spirit but of diversity and contradiction. During the century that saw the discovery of America, most Europeans were born, lived, and died in a single geographical area, for travel within Europe was slow and often treacherous. The humanistic view of life spread broadly throughout the Continent, yet it was shared largely by the monied, the titled, the male—people who valued education and had access to it. Classical learning affected enlightened views of man and society, yet the activities of Inquisition courts and the widespread persecution of witches, most of them women, stained much of the sixteenth century and continued into the seventeenth. The strength of the Roman Catholic church was everywhere to be seen, in both its enlightened and its oppressive aspects, yet reformation movements from without and within threatened its unifying influence in Europe and, eventually, abroad. Despite talk of humanistic education and the accomplishments of some women as creative artists, musicians, and scholars, most European women were illiterate, and even wealthy families might oppose teaching girls to read and write. Though the new Protestant sects encouraged all members to learn reading—the better to study the Bible—much of what passed for knowledge of scriptures, prayers, or hymns must have been a matter of simple memorization on the parts of both women and men. It would be some time before the number of literate European women would rise significantly. The same factors that freed and empowered the ideal Renaissance Man caused the lines of separation to be drawn ever more closely around the ideal Renaissance Woman, and too many experienced not a rebirth but an increasingly confined existence.

Women in Society, 1450–1600

How then did women participate in the society of their time? There is no single answer to this question, just as there is no single answer to the question of men's participation. A woman's experience was influenced at least as strongly by her social or economic class as it was by her sex. Yet there were certain constants that cut across class lines, for gender was of supreme importance in defining a woman's life. In other words, certain things happened to women simply because they were women. The central position of the family in both public and personal spheres of life influenced the degree to which women's positions were subordinate to men's. The fact of this subordination, however, was unquestionable. For what society required of most women in this period, regardless of class, was that they consider marriage, motherhood, and household management their life vocations; the possibility of an independent woman of marriageable age was rarely entertained. Entering a convent was an option open primarily to wealthy Roman Catholics, for a novice was expected to bring with her a suitable dowry, perhaps even her own furniture or clothing. Most titled or wealthy girls married or entered convents by their mid-teens. Thus, although one reads of academically, artistically, or musically talented women during this era, they are almost always prodigies who retreat into obscurity by the age of twenty. Academically or artistically gifted women might be tolerated, accepted, or even praised for their accomplishments, but only as exceptions to the rule of female inferiority.

It is hardly surprising, then, that major studies of European women's history eschew the divisions into periods or countries that organize most general history textbooks, for such divisions have far less significance for women than for men. Bonnie Anderson and Judith Zinsser's two-volume survey deemphasizes chronological organization in favor of categories that span periods and geographical boundaries: "Women of the Fields" (peasant life from the ninth through seventeenth centuries), "Women of the Churches" (from the tenth through seventeenth centuries), or "Women of the Walled Towns" (from the twelfth through seventeenth centuries).[1] Such an organization acknowledges that political and military events affected women's lives in far different ways than they did the lives of their male contemporaries.

More recently Olwen Hufton has viewed women of Western Europe in the years 1500–1800 in terms of their life stages: finding husbands, then living as wives, mothers, perhaps widows.[2] Alongside this central continuity stand women religious, courtesans and mistresses, witches, and creative or politically active women who bore public faces. Women's history plays out not within the standard historical framework but according to considerations of family, class, and station. It would seem, then, that our consideration of women and music in the early modern period should embrace this model, ignoring the male-oriented concept of a Renaissance and exploring categories more relevant to women's actual experiences during the years 1450–1600.

MUSIC MAKING AMONG THE NOBILITY

Music making has never been limited solely by class, race, or sex. Throughout history peasants have improvised their own tunes, women have hummed lullabies, and people have danced to the sounds of pipe and tabor. Yet at various times in the past, restrictions have been placed on women's musical activities that have had the effect of confining them to certain types or spheres of music. Though wealthy or titled women during the early modern period were expected to be able to read music, to sing, to dance, and to

FIGURE 4.1. "Le Concert champêtre: Le chant." Anonymous sixteenth-century painter. Bourges, Musée DuBarry. Photo courtesy of Giraudon/Art Resource, New York.

play at least one instrument, they were also expected to limit their music making to home or court. Musical ability was a social asset for both sexes, but regardless of how well one performed, to sing or play before a paying audience would not have been thought proper for members of the upper classes. Nor did many titled people admit to composing music—Henry VIII of England or Carlo Gesualdo, Prince of Venosa, come to mind as exceptions—although most could probably have improvised melodies to their own lute accompaniments. To have studied composition, a technical skill acquired for vocational purposes, or to publish one's own music would have been unusual, even unseemly activities for a noblewoman.

Yet music instruction within court society must often have been on a high level. Mary of Burgundy was a pupil of Antoine Busnois, while Isabella d'Este studied with Johannes Martini, then with one of his French pupils. Beatrice of Aragon, the future Queen of Hungary, is said to have been a pupil of Johannes Tinctoris.[3] Anne Boleyn attracted notice at the court of Henry VIII in part for her musical skills, and her daughter Elizabeth was an able performer. Elizabeth's half-sister Mary Tudor was a capable singer to the lute, and Isabella d'Este danced and sang to the lute before guests at the festivities surrounding the marriage of her brother Alfonso to Lucrezia Borgia. She is also known to have played keyboard and bowed string instruments and to have studied singing. Lucrezia Borgia herself also performed music and was fond of dancing. J. Michele Edwards has already described Bianca de' Medici's performances for Pope Pius II and his entourage. Such examples could be multiplied with names of patrician women throughout Western Europe during these years.

Musicologist Nino Pirrotta has observed, "Of all the mythical powers of music, only one seems to have been most familiar to the humanists, that of diverting the mind and bringing relaxation."[4] Ancient Greek authors had noted music's ability to move listeners, and repeatedly stressed the intimate relationship between text and tune. The desire to cultivate these ancient properties of music led humanistically educated Italian noblewomen and men to choose singing to the lute as their favorite mode of social music making. This sort of entertainment did not involve reading music from the printed page; rather, it meant improvising an entire composition—at times both the poem and its musical setting. Hence what Claude Palisca calls "some of the most characteristic music of the period" is not music we can study, for it was not written down.[5] Though women like Isabella d'Este and Elisabetta Gonzaga, Duchess of Urbino, were well known for their ability to improvise songs,[6] the practice was so widespread that there must have been scores of other court ladies and gentlemen who could perform at least adequately. In all likelihood their songs were strophic, perhaps based on a reiterated succession of harmonies or even a popular song from the written tradition. Melodies were probably simple, but are likely to have been ornamented; their lute accompaniments would have been essentially linear, though the performer's aptitude would determine the degree of elaboration.

The bowed *lira da braccio,* also popular as an accompanying instrument for improvised song, could have provided a block-chordal accompaniment that might have been made more elaborate by added ornamentation. Both amateur and professional singers performed as *improvvisatori,* and pictorial evidence suggests that some of the professionals might have been women.[7] The importance of improvised song to the emerging frottola, a type of composed song especially popular in the early decades of the sixteenth century, cannot be underestimated, nor can the role played by women in cultivating this native Italian style go unrecognized.

In mid-sixteenth-century Venice, wealthy and noble men took pleasure in meeting with their educated, like-minded peers in informal clubs, called academies, for purposes of discussing literature and the arts and performing and hearing music. One of the best known of these academies was that led by Domenico Venier, an aristocratic poet who, beginning in the 1530s, opened his home to a group of intellectuals whose humanistic concerns about the ideal relationship between words and music influenced developments in the Venetian madrigal around midcentury. Of particular importance here is the interest Venier and his circle took in improvised song as performed by accomplished female singers, even though no women were regular members of the academy. In his poetry Venier lauded Franceschina Bellamano, whose skill in singing both improvised and composed songs to her own lute accompaniment was apparently known throughout Italy.[8] The singer best known to all members of the academy, however, was Gaspara Stampa, whom Martha Feldman pointedly labels a poet—thus emphasizing the intimate connection between poetry and song that lay at the root of the Italian improvisatory tradition. A musician in the group, Girolamo Parabosco, wrote of Stampa's "angelic voice" that "strikes the air with its divine accents, making such a sweet harmony that it . . . infuses spirit and life into the coldest stones and makes them weep with sweetness."[9] Indeed, Feldman speaks of the intensely musical qualities of Stampa's verses, as if they were made specifically for reciting in song.

The musical education of noblewomen also included the study of notation and sight-singing, as evidenced by the many manuscripts and printed volumes of polyphonic music owned and used by these women. A manuscript of motets and chansons in London's Royal College of Music, for example, bears the coat of arms of Anne Boleyn (1507–1536) and seems to have been used by her and her female friends for performance *in camera.*[10] Margaret of Austria (1480–1530), regent of the Netherlands from 1508 to 1530, owned chanson albums that are important sources of the music of Pierre de la Rue.[11] Women of the north Italian courts, including the aforementioned Bianca de' Medici, as well as Isabella and Beatrice d'Este and Lucrezia Borgia, needed a knowledge of music notation to sing the French repertoire then so popular in Italy. Nor did the desire to acquire such skills end with the nobility. In 1518 Tromboncino, due to what is described in a letter from Giacomo de' Tebaldi to Lucrezia Borgia as "his most urgent poverty," had begun teaching lute and singing to the gentlewomen of Venice. Hence, as Prizer remarks, "there must have been a fairly substantial market among the Venetian ladies" for these skills, "additional proof of the wide diffusion of musical literacy" among Italian women of wealth and position.[12]

Noblewomen also fulfilled in important ways the functions of financially sponsoring and encouraging performers and composers. In these areas it is interesting to note in Italy a kind of sexual division of labor or interest that has continued even to the present day. Whereas male rulers, beginning in the fifteenth century, gave substantial support to musicians of the court *cappella* (chapel) and the composers who wrote for them, noblewomen most often focused their attentions on secular music, music of the chamber for individual performers or small ensembles. In both areas the nobility proved to be not only a source of financial support but taste-makers as well. Isabella d'Este's interest in the frottola enabled this type of music to gain greater exposure than it might otherwise have had. Equally important, her interest in the genre contributed to its stylistic development as she encouraged composers to choose texts of high quality, which in turn inspired more varied and skillful musical settings.

If there was to some degree a woman's taste, if not a woman's voice, in Italian secular music around 1500, it is interesting to note that Isabella d'Este, the most noteworthy tastemaker of the time, nevertheless followed the male model of patronage in her dealings with the arts and artists. As a child in Ferrara she, along with her brothers, received a strong humanistic education. "As she grew older," according to Iain Fenlon, "Isabella became increasingly keen to acquire skills which were both socially and intellectually prestigious." Though her Latin was apparently never particularly good, her insistence on studying classical culture demonstrates "her determination to conform to the traditional humanistic image of an educated [male] ruler." She took an interest in painting, sculpture, and poetry, and studied music as a series of practical skills that enabled her to perform as both singer and instrumentalist.[13] After her marriage to Francesco II Gonzaga in 1490, Isabella determined to turn her new court at Mantua into something it had never yet

FIGURE 4.2. "The Lute Player." Andrea Solario (1465–after 1515). Rome, Galleria Nazionale. Photo courtesy of Scala/Art Resource, New York.

been: a center of artistic activity and patronage. The fact of her gender undoubtedly influenced her choice of secular music as an area for special attention, but her methods knew no sex. She hired additional singers, purchased instruments, and cultivated two men—Tromboncino and Cara—who would become leaders in the development of the frottola. Eventually she symbolized the centrality of music in her life by building a music room, the famous *studiolo,* as a place to display her artifacts and art that reflected her cultural interests. Throughout her life as a benefactor of music, Isabella was in charge, and her taste and skills as well as her fortune decisively influenced the course of Italian music in the early sixteenth century.

Other female benefactors could be equally generous and equally insistent on their artistic values. In France, Queen Catherine de' Medici (1519–1589) encouraged both poets and musicians and was responsible for introducing the Italian ballet into France. Later, Catherine de Bourbon's fondness for masques led her to hire a number of musicians, along with artists and tailors, to provide for all aspects of these productions.[14] Somewhat atypical in their support of household chapels were Lady Margaret Beaufort, mother of England's King Henry VII, and Queen Elizabeth I. According to Fiona Kisby, Lady Margaret's chapel rivaled her son's, and her generosity spread further afield to touch musicians from other local foundations and from urban institutions outside her immediate area of influence.[15] As for Elizabeth I, Craig Monson has remarked that "without Queen Elizabeth and her royal chapel there would have been no Elizabethan 'golden age of church music.'"[16]

England's nobility were also exceptional in their employment of Jewish musicians, often whole families, beginning at the time of Henry VIII. By 1540 most of the foreign musicians at Henry's court were Jewish immigrants from Italy who saw in England a refuge from persecution by both Catholics and members of the new Lutheran church. Though only males were formally on the king's payroll, the example of Mantua suggests that women might have performed on special occasions. From 1587–1600 a Jewish singer cited only as Madama Europa was in the pay of the Duke of Mantua, where she performed with other Jewish actors and musicians, including her brother, Salamone Rossi, and her son Anselmo, in festive dramatic entertainments at court.[17] Though Madama Europa and other Mantuan Jews were apparently welcome as writers and performers of court entertainments, their lives were not unrestricted. It is difficult to say how other Jewish women with musical talent fared under these circumstances or whether they performed under similar arrangements at the English court.

Music and the Middle Class

> Renaissance music is not a set of compositional techniques but a complex of social conditions, intellectual states of mind, attitudes, aspirations, habits of performers, artistic support systems, intra-cultural communications, and many other ingredients which add up to a thriving matrix of musical energy.[18]

So Iain Fenlon, quoting an anonymous source, characterizes the period that for women is more aptly labeled early modern. Of the three "major phenomena of social significance" Fenlon cites, the first—the spread of humanism—finds its clearest examples among the activities of Europe's nobility. The third, religious crises of the sixteenth century, will be dealt with later. That leaves the second, the growth of bourgeois culture, to be considered here.

To some extent bourgeois culture was in a trickle-down relationship with the culture of the nobility, for the middle class of the fifteenth and sixteenth centuries was quite unlike our own. The broad-based group of merchants, landholders, professional men, business owners, and scholars occupied the space between the nobility, which existed on unearned income, and the even larger group of people who simply worked for a living. Some members of the middle class were able and willing to support arts and artists on perhaps a lesser, but still significant scale compared to their aristocratic neighbors. Many enjoyed learning and performing music in domestic surroundings, activities that resulted in the great expansion of musical knowledge and practice that occurred in the sixteenth century. Middle-class patrons bought instruments, the instruction needed to play them or to sing to their accompaniment, and the printed music necessary to enlarge their repertoires. Iconographic evidence shows middle-class women singing, playing keyboard or plucked string instruments (lutes or harps, for example), pumping the bellows of portative organs, or making music on flutes, dulcimers, or bowed strings. Everywhere, it seems, the middle class took music making to heart.

In Italy a middle-class Florentine girl, Marietta Pugi, was among the first of her class to own a manuscript of polyphonic music. She may even have tried composing, since the manuscript contains one textless piece that has the look of a composition exercise. Other numbers in the collection—French and Flemish songs and Italian popular genres—date from the late fifteenth and early sixteenth centuries, and together they allow a view of the sort of music a person of Pugi's age and status would find worth owning.[19]

The middle-class city of Lyons, France, provides a bird's-eye view of the ways in which literature and the arts were taken up by members of the bourgeoisie. Italian courtly models influenced the thought and artistic production of Lyons' women. Marie-Catherine de Pierrevive emulated the great ladies of the courts by opening her home to musicians, poets, and artists. Others became creative artists themselves, though most published no music. The best known of Lyons' female poets, Louise Labé, also studied music and saw it as one of the arts whose practice would liberate women from "their distaffs and bobbins."[20] Clémence de Bourges, dedicatee of Labé's poems, was praised for her musical accomplishments in terms that closely resemble those often cited in connection with noblewomen:

> [She] accompanies her voice so well, playing musical instruments with her own hands, [singing] Tuscan as well as French words, and she adds so much grace to the art that it appears that Pallas acclaimed her as a fourth companion to the three Graces.[21]

Still another sixteenth-century Lyons writer, Loys Papon, joined other poets in praise of a woman known only as Panfile.

> But while she wishes, with more active zeal,
> To mingle the sweet sounds that she fingers
> With an angelic voice, in the celestial harmony

That she calls an echo, with the reprise of her verse,
That she herself enraptures on the wings of her airs.
. . . . .
[She] who with her spinet, who with her Tuscan lyre,
Who with a crossed harp with open strings,
Who to get to the bottom of those diverse rumblings
With which the stars above give rhythm to their ecstasy,
With viols sounds a resonant bass,
To fill the low [diapason] strings that she stretches,
The flourishes of others for whom she waits,
This remnant of comfort in this academy,
Highlights and softens not the air of her melody. . . .[22]

Bourgeois women in other European centers found their own musical places in polite society. In Antwerp, by 1560 the richest and perhaps the largest city in Europe, burghers and their families made music in increasing numbers. Elsewhere in the Low Countries, the Belgians were described as "true masters and restorers of music; they have studied it to perfection, having men and women sing without learning, but with a real instinct for tone and measure."[23] As for those women who worked for a living, their musical activities must have had a broad range indeed, from the improvisations of folksong and dance to the composed tunes of psalms, hymns, and devotional songs, which will be discussed in connection with the Reformation movements of the sixteenth century.

Women Religious and Music

Until recently it has been all too easy to consider the women in early modern religious communities as somehow on the margins of their society, women who had retreated or had been forced to retreat from the mainstream to live out their days, cloistered, in the service of God. New research, however, has made clear that these women and their music making were central elements of their societies, at least in Italy.[24] In a world whose social and political relationships were predicated on family ties and family status, the religious communities that provided viable alternatives to marriage for the women who joined them took on a kind of familial status that was often reinforced by close ties of politics and patronage between specific institutions and the leading Italian families.

The sheer numbers of women admitted or consigned to convents or related institutions should have been sufficient indication that such houses had social as well as religious importance. Olwen Hufton reports that in 1563, when the question of women's religious houses was taken up by the

Council of Trent, over one-third of the teen-aged female children of Italy's aristocratic families had entered convents.[25] By 1650 religious orders claimed three-quarters of the female children born to the Milanese aristocracy.[26] Not all these young women willingly moved within the walls. Yet despite the vague and unevenly enforced Tridentine recommendations that strict claustration be the rule at all women's religious houses, family ties and family influence might well result in a reasonable amount of physical and intellectual freedom for the inhabitants of convents where generations of female relatives had gone before.[27]

Many Italian convents of the early modern period were renowned for their music making. By 1699 Milan had forty-one houses for female religious within city walls and several more in the surrounding area. These included not only the traditional convents but also "open" monasteries for women, independent lay communities, and tertiary orders. As early as the latter half of the fifteenth century, several of these institutions gained fame for their liturgical music; by about 1600 most houses had performed polyphonic music. The leading musical houses, which had been founded in medieval times by noble families, belonged to the Benedictine order. The high dowries required to profess full vows as a choir nun at Milan's S. Radegonda and S. Margarita convents, the Monastero Maggiore, and S. Vittore in nearby Meda restricted admissions to those who were high-born and wealthy. Due to reforms intended to preserve the nuns from worldly contacts and influences, convent churches were eventually divided into two separate areas: an external public church and a partly walled-off inner church for the nuns. Hence the sounds of the nuns' choral and organ music reached the lay congregation as if performed by invisible angelic voices.

Despite the post-Tridentine attempts by Archbishop Carlo Borromeo (r. 1560–1584) to curtail the nuns' musical activities, especially those that attracted the public to their external churches, Milanese nuns, like their sisters in Bologna, found ways of resisting. Eventually a successor, Federigo Borromeo (r. 1595–1631), not only lifted former prohibitions but actually promoted music making by the nuns.

It is difficult to know what music the Milanese nuns performed or whether any of the polyphonic numbers were of their own composition, for these sisters published no music until the seventeenth century.[28] Indeed, sixteenth-century reports of the nuns' music refer only to performers and performances, the high quality of which led some male composers to dedicate music to these cloistered singers.[29] Nevertheless, it is worth noting that certain distinctive features set the Milanese convents apart from institutions in Bologna and Ferrara: first, more than one convent was renowned for its music. The Milanese convents, moreover, apparently used no large instrumental ensembles in their music. Furthermore, the nuns' music was a source of urban pride as well as a main method of "asserting the institutions' and [the nuns'] status in the symbolic world of the city."[30] Even though they may have had to perform from within their walled-off inner churches, the nun musicians were an important presence in their urban society.

In Bologna, however, Cardinal Gabriele Paleotti and his successor, Alfonso Paleotti, determined to set stringent conditions on music making in convents, which by 1595 enclosed some 2,480 women in a city of just 59,000. Soon after the Council of Trent adjourned, Gabriele promulgated increasingly strict rules in an attempt to reform musical practices in these houses and "to render the singing nuns invisible." Their music "should be performed down below in the choir where the older nuns stay" and should, even on Easter, be "only in plainchant." The elder Paleotti at first permitted liturgical music sung by a single soloist to organ accompaniment. By 1584, however, he not only prohibited the hiring of lay musicians for the convent's outer chapels but also decreed that "every nunnery, without exception, should have removed the organ that faces the external church."[31] The cardinal, as well as his successor, reckoned without the resourcefulness of the nuns, whose lack of compliance with these orders prompted many later decrees repeating restrictions that had supposedly been imposed earlier. In 1585, for example, Sant'Omobono convent had not only not removed its organ but had enlarged and reinstalled it in the inner church in such a way that, according to a contemporary report, "resounding excellently well, it still creates delightful harmony with those outside."[32] Once again, as in Milan, music had become a vehicle through which nuns retained contact with the outside world. Even in 1605, "despite twenty-five years of prohibitions and restrictions, music still resounded strongly from behind the grills of the nuns' inner chapels and continued to draw the same dangerous and distracting admirers."[33] Italy's post-Tridentine period became in fact "the heyday of convent music."[34]

By the early sixteenth century Bologna's convent of Santa Cristina della Fondazza was already attracting attention for the quality of its music. However, since no music by a sixteenth-century Bolognese nun has been preserved, it is difficult to say exactly what was performed or whether the nuns wrote the music themselves. We do know that their music was considered elaborate; it could involve both vocal soloists and ensembles with the accompaniment of organ and, apparently quite often, additional instruments as well. Most important, we know that this music, though theoretically cut off from the world, was enjoyed and praised by outsiders who were content to hear and not see these famed musicians.

THE NUNS OF SAN VITO

Ferrara was the home of another group of female performers, the nuns of San Vito convent under the leadership of organist and composer Rafaella Aleotti. While Ferrara's court ladies were fascinating audiences with their vocal virtuosity, the nuns of San Vito presented concerts by an instrumental and vocal ensemble of such excellence that one admirer, Ercole Bottrigari, spoke of them as "not human, bodily creatures," but rather "truly angelic spirits."

> When you watch them come in . . . to the place where a long table has been prepared, at the end of which is found a large clavicembalo, you would see them enter one by one, quietly bringing their instruments, either string or wind. They all enter quietly and approach the table without making the least noise and place themselves in their proper place, and some sit, who must do so in order to use their instruments, and others remain standing. Finally the Maestra of the concert sits down at one end of the table . . . with a long, slender and well-polished wand . . . , and when all the other sisters clearly are ready, gives them without noise several signs to begin, and then continues by beating the measure of the time which they must obey in singing and playing. And at this point . . . you would certainly hear such harmony that it would seem to you either that you were carried off to Heliconia or that Heliconia together with all the chorus of the Muses singing and playing had been transplanted to that place.[35]

At first the friend Bottrigari is addressing is unwilling to believe that such music could be made by a group of women, and he is amazed that concerts of this kind have been going on for some time. Even the instruments the nuns play surprise him: not the usual "women's instruments," keyboards or plucked strings, but cornetti and trombones as well. Giovanni Maria Artusi, who also attended the San Vito concerts, notes that the ensemble included cornetti, trombones, violins, viole bastarde, double harps, lutes, cornamuses, flutes, harpsichords, and singers; he opines that the performance was exceptional not just for its being achieved by women: "Most of the people in Italy could not . . . have done more than what was done by these nuns. . . ."[36] The twenty-three nuns in the ensemble, says Bottrigari, worked under the supervision of Sister Rafaella, who also saw to their instruction. Unfortunately, he says nothing about their repertoire, which could have included any sacred or even secular polyphonic vocal or instrumental pieces of the day.

Despite the reformist attitudes of many sixteenth-century church officials, secular music was not entirely absent from convents. A recently discovered manuscript belonging to a Bolognese nun, Elena Malvezzi (1526–1563), sheds new light on the nature of the music that some nuns performed privately for their own entertainment.[37] Malvezzi, a member of

Bologna's Sant'Agnese convent and its prioress from 1561 to 1563, owned and may even have commissioned this manuscript of keyboard transcriptions, primarily of secular vocal pieces from about the years 1542–1560. Though the transcriptions could have been performed as keyboard solos, they may also have served to accompany a singer or a vocal ensemble. Secular works in this manuscript include pieces by Clément Janequin, Giovanni Pierluigi da Palestrina, Vincenzo Ruffo, and especially Cipriano de Rore. The fact that Archbishop Alfonso Paleotti found it necessary as late as 1598 to prohibit nuns from performing "vernacular pieces . . . under penalty of being forbidden ever to sing and play in the future" undoubtedly indicated that, like Sr. Elena, the nuns of Bologna were still well acquainted with the secular music of their day.[38]

Cloistered nuns were also known for their cultivation of nonliturgical devotional songs in both Latin and vernacular tongues. Under the influence of Catholic reformer Girolamo Savonarola (1452–1498), whom Pope Paul IV dubbed "the Italian Luther," three Dominican cloisters in Tuscany (two in Florence, one in Prato) cultivated the lauda. Simple songs, usually with Italian texts expressing personal relationships to God and His saints, laude had been around since the fourteenth century. They had many uses—in daily devotions of religious houses, to accompany processions, for congregational singing outside formal church services, or as music within religious plays (*sacre rappresentazioni*)—and their music was most often borrowed from extant secular or sacred sources. Most laude are preserved in text-only collections; the single source to contain music is Serafino Razzi's *Libro primo delle laude spirituali* (Venice, 1563). This book contains ninety-one musical settings for one to four voices among a total of 146 texts by authors who include the noblewoman Lucrezia de' Medici and the volume's dedicatee, Caterina de' Ricci (1522–1590). It is no coincidence that Caterina was a nun, for the volume's dedication makes clear that it was published with the object of improving the nuns' musical repertoire:

> [T]he practice of singing laude in the convents is no longer what it was, and currently the religious, especially nuns, are given to singing lascivious songs that would even shock guests at secular gathering.[39]

A lauda by Caterina de' Ricci herself demonstrates the personal faith usually expressed in these songs. Caterina, a member of the convent of San Vincenzo in Prato, believed that a vision of Savonarola had cured her from a disabling illness. Her lauda text describes the course of her illness and reveals personal sentiments of devotion to Savonarola himself. The *ripresa* and first stanza are given below.

Since you have shown me such love,
servant of Christ, with that sweet glance,
and with that gift which now is a double dart,
I will have you always in the center of my heart.
I was submerged in torment and pain
and you mercifully came down:
all joy was lost to me,
when you opened to me your mercy.
I called you, and you finally came,
like a tender father to a daughter,
with that shining vermillion face
that glowed with brilliant reddish light.[40]

Caterina intended her song to be performed to the music of a well-known lauda by Feo Belcari, "Da che tu m'hai Dio, 'l core" (Since the time you, O God, seized my heart), printed in Razzi's collection in a two-voice setting.[41] Caterina's convent became a center for the cult of Savonarola, thus helping to keep alive a type of music he encouraged as a vehicle of religious reform.

Sources of information on devotional music used by nuns outside Italy are far less numerous. A Dutch nun, Christina Hospenthal (known as Suster Bertken, 1426/27–1514), published two books of her poetry, including some pieces intended to be sung. One song appeared in the *Utrecht Liederbuch* of about 1500, with a tune by an unknown author.[42] Another source, the *Liederbuch* of Anna of Cologne (ca. 1500), represents the sorts of popular devotional songs cultivated in pre-Reformation Germany by female mystics, women of middle-class origins. These songs, which Walter Salmen calls "geistliche Hauslieder" (spiritual songs for home use), resemble laude in their largely vernacular texts (some are in Latin) and their transmission primarily by text alone.[43] Though Anna of Cologne, a nun in a middle-class sisterhood, was probably only the owner of the songbook that bears her name, she is nevertheless important for having preserved the largest known collection of melodies for this repertoire. The German dialect used in the texts is definitely not a high literary language, but it expresses perfectly the kinds of personal sentiments typical of women religious in their private devotions.

Reformation Movements and Women

It is difficult to think of a single aspect of Western European life in the sixteenth century that was not affected in some way by the movements toward religious reform. Even within the Catholic church, calls for changes that would encourage a more personal relationship between the faithful and God were responsible for expressions of devotion, by way of laude or other devotional songs, that allowed a woman's voice to be heard. Educated Catholic women living outside religious houses responded to calls for reform by publishing personal, even sentimental, writings of faith that included devotional poetry, meant to be sung. Among the best known of these women was Marguerite of Navarre (1492–1549), sister of King Francis I of France, whose *Chansons spirituelles* first appeared in print in 1547 and remained available in France and elsewhere as late as 1602. Though the ideas expressed in these texts often reveal Marguerite's Calvinistic sympathies, she never formally left the Roman Catholic church.

Marguerite's songs are contrafacta, intended to be sung to familiar secular tunes and, in many cases, parody secular texts. In "Le grand désir d'aymer," for example, she has parodied the text of the love song to which she intends her poem to be sung.

Original

Le grand désir d'aymer me tient	[The great desire to love seizes me
Quand de la belle me souvient	when I think of my beautiful girlfriend
Et du joly temps qui verdoye.	and the fine weather that turns all to green.]

Marguerite's parody

Le grand désir d'aymer me tient	[The great desire to love seizes me
Quand de mon Dieu il me souvient;	when I think of my God;
Assez aymer ne le pourroye.	I cannot love him enough.][44]

Marguerite often indicated the titles or *timbres* of the well-known tunes for which her poems were intended. Of these, many were melodies she had learned as a child. Her textual themes are equally familiar: the sinful soul, the sheep and the shepherd, the thirsty soul at the fountain of grace, the death of the old Adam within the human soul. One particularly Protestant-sounding idea that recurs is her insistence that Christ alone, not the saints or our own good works, has the power to save us. In "Sur l'arbre de la croix," for example, she writes:

> From the tree of the cross, with a clear and beautiful voice,
> I heard sung a new song.
> The bird who sang it would move the spirit
> Of all true pilgrims, saying with sweet words:
> I am the Pelican who gives health and life
> To make live those whom I desire to save.
> Death, who thought to make them and me his subjects,
> I have conquered and put to death. . . .
> Hence [Death] no longer has power over my children,
> Who by means of [my] death have perfect joy in life. . . .
> I am the Truth and the Life and the Way,

Death has no more power in any time or place. . . .
Whoever vaunts himself, proud of his labor and pains,
Deeming my torment and my passion vain,
Will know that Hell, Death, and Sin,
And will not be able to conquer evil through his own efforts.[45]

This lengthy poem (94 lines in rhymed alexandrine couplets), sung to the well-known "Sur le pont d'Avignon, j'ouys chanter la belle," alludes to music as Christ invites those who wish to be saved to "learn my song, full of discipline," for "whoever hears my song will be filled with joy." In other poems the use of refrains and dancelike meters makes even clearer the basis of Marguerite's verses in song.

Marguerite's daughter and granddaughter also revealed Huguenot sympathies in their writing. Jeanne d'Albret (1528–1572) embraced Calvinism on Christmas of 1560, probably under the influence of Théodore Bèze, whose versified psalms formed an important part of Calvin's 1562 *Psalter*. Among Jeanne's poems is a sung dialogue between a monk and some Calvinist girls he tries unsuccessfully to persuade to return to the Catholic church. The music for this piece may have been by Jeanne herself.[46] Jeanne's daughter, Catherine de Bourbon (1559–1604), was also a poet and was reported to have been a fine singer and lutenist.[47] Both women ruled areas of France in their own right.

> [N]ext to the Word of God, the noble art of music is the greatest treasure in this world. . . . Our dear fathers and prophets did not desire without reason that music be always used in the churches. Hence, we have so many songs and psalms.[48]

So wrote Martin Luther of music and its place in the lives and worship of believers. His contemporaneous reformer, John Calvin, would likely have disagreed on the style and substance of music suitable for formal worship services. However, their common conviction that neither persons nor institutions need come between a believer and the Deity had at least one musical result favorable to women: the establishment of congregational singing. Calvinist or Lutheran, woman or man, girl or boy, all could sing the praises of God with one voice. Lutherans, however, retained many Roman Catholic practices, including a formal liturgy, the cultivation of polyphonic church music, and in some cases the use of Latin, whereas Calvinists largely avoided any church music more ornate than the unison singing of psalms in the vernacular. Yet the very fact of congregational singing "takes us into a world where written and unwritten traditions, popular and elite cultures meet,"[49] and where the souls of both women and men are worthy to call upon God for salvation.

Another important outgrowth of the Reformation that affected women's music making was the closing of monasteries and convents in areas of Europe that became Protestant. The nuns thus released were now told that marriage and family life provided the only natural mode of existence for women. Whether or not the former nuns chose to marry, they left the musical life of their communities behind. For those who were musically trained, music making took on a private face as they used their abilities in the home to train children or to lead family hymn singing.

Some Lutheran women, however, put on a public face. Katherine Zell (1497 or 98–1562), wife of a Strasbourg pastor, published a series of pamphlets in 1534 containing her translations of Czech hymns into German. Her words in the preface make her purpose clear:

> When so many filthy songs are on the lips of men and women and even children, I think it well that folk should with lusty zeal and clear voice sing the songs of their salvation. God is glad when the craftsman at his bench, the maid at the sink, the farmer at the plough, the dresser at the vines, the mother at the cradle break forth in hymns of prayer, praise, and instruction.[50]

Surely Zell's was a musical activity proper for a woman: family-oriented, intended for the ordinary members of the Christian flock, and having no aspirations to high art. The logo of the printer, Fröhlich of Strasbourg, is similarly appropriate: a swan above a viol and a sheet of music (see Figure 4.3). Zell also published devotional writing and, in 1588, a book of versified psalms probably meant for singing.

Another Lutheran woman, Duchess Elisabeth of Braunschweig (1510–1558), wrote hymn texts which, though not great poetry, "breathe constancy, love, and joy. . . . [T]here pulses through them a resolute spirit" that saw her through a period of painful exile: [51]

> Joyful will I be
> And bless His holy name.
> He is my help and stay
> And comfort in my shame.

The efforts of Norwegian noblewoman Inger of Austråt to assist in the spread of Lutheranism began as early as 1529, when she was said to have introduced the Lutheran custom of psalm singing to her household.[52] Hymn writing by Protestant women became even more common in the seventeenth century, "when the language of hymns shifted from aggressive and martial to emotional and pious. . . ."[53]

Though John Calvin acknowledged that music was a gift of God, capable "of moving and enflaming the hearts of men to call upon and praise

FIGURE 4.3. Publisher's plate from Katherine Zell, *Von Chriso Jesu . . . Lobgesang* (Strasbourg: Fröhlich, 1534).

God with more vehement and ardent zeal," he found it necessary "to be all the more diligent to regulate it in such a way that it will prove useful and not pernicious."[54] Hence he prescribed for use in churches only psalms sung by the congregation and other biblical and traditional texts performed in unison to unaccompanied melodies. So aware was he of the advantage music could bring to the Christian life that all children in Geneva received instruction in music in elementary school and were taught to read notation rather than simply to learn the psalm tunes by rote. At times the children taught unfamiliar tunes to their congregations after having learned them in school.

Calvinist women in mid-sixteenth-century Lyons "found a new involvement in a faith which permitted them to sing hymns and take a more active role in religious rituals."[55] In addition, the fact that polyphonic settings of psalm tunes by Bourgeois or Goudimel were intended for home use meant that women could also play essential roles in domestic music making. Both liturgical and private devotional music used the vernacular—"the language of women and the unlearned"[56]—to promote fellowship and singleness of thought and purpose. In the end, however, though Calvinist reforms were initially liberating "from the rule of priests and doctors of theology,"[57] the new church and its activities, including music, soon settled into the expected pattern of male domination in which women's creativity had little part.

MUSIC MAKING AS A PROFESSION

Outside the domestic sphere, women performers could be found in many circles. The famous courtesans of this era counted music making an indispensable skill. Courtesans were not simply prostitutes, but women who also wined, dined, and entertained their male guests with music and witty conversation. The famous courtesan Imperia (1481–1512) was known for her ability to sing to the lute, and Tullia d'Aragona, a courtesan of the mid-sixteenth century, headed an intellectual salon, wrote and published poetry, and was commended for her lovely singing voice and her abilities as a lutenist. Another published poet, courtesan Veronica Franco (d. 1591), was an accomplished singer and instrumentalist.

Actresses in the professional *commedia dell'arte* troupes that emerged in mid-sixteenth century Italy were also expected to sing and dance. Music was an integral part of a *commedia* presentation, and music and dances were performed before the drama began and between its acts. The typical *commedia* troupe of the sixteenth century included three women and seven men, some of whom became famous even outside Italy for their lively portrayals of the stock characters. Isabella Andreini (b. 1562) was one of the finest. In addition to acting, she wrote poetry and plays and was quite knowledgeable about music. She also led a notably virtuous life, something that could not be said of most of her female colleagues. Another *comedienne*, Vincenza Armani, was both a singer and an instrumentalist.

Italian actresses were performing in London and Paris by the 1560s, though they were not universally accepted. Reports of a *commedia* company in London in 1577 noted that the actresses scandalized many members of the audience, who would not see English women on their own public stages until after the Restoration (1660). The scandal, however, could have been due not simply to the presence of women on the public stage but to the sorts of parts they played. Lovers or saucy maids, these women were not the passive, chaste, obedient ladies described in Renaissance manuals on female behavior. Little wonder that even in Italy respectable women usually stayed away (or were kept away) from the lusty *commedia* shows.

Women performers were not absent from the stages of the courts; dramatic and musical entertainment in connection with private celebrations included women in the casts. However, many of these performers may have been amateurs. France's court ballets were performed by both male and female dancers, and dramas produced at Italian courts included women musicians and dancers, if not actresses. Wolfgang Osthoff tells of an ensemble of men and women who sang a *strambotto* and a *barzelletta* during the production of a comedy, *Trinumo,* in 1499. Later he mentions one Barbara Salutati, who helped organize and performed in the musical interpolations to a 1526 production of Machiavelli's *La Mandragola.*[58] Whereas the women in the 1499 drama were probably amateurs, Salutati and other women who participated in the 1526 production appear to have been professionals. Osthoff also mentions another occasion when Salutati was paid for her services. Elsewhere, amateurs of both sexes were known to have joined the professional performers on many court occasions. Both Ippolita Sforza, Queen of Naples, and Catherine de' Medici, Queen of France, took their places as dancers, while Marguerite of Navarre wrote her own morality plays and farces, all of which contained music.

In the intermedii that graced the celebration of the marriage of Ferdinand de' Medici to Christina de Lorena in 1589, most of the musicians were male, and men took many of the supposedly female roles as well. However, two outstanding women were among the vocal soloists: Lucia Caccini and Vittoria Achilei, both professional artists and both married to men who were composers and performers. "Dalle più alte sfere" (From the most exalted spheres), perhaps written by Antonio Achilei for his wife, gave Vittoria an outstanding vehicle for her vocal virtuosity; and Lucia Caccini improvised her own accompaniment on the lute for the aria composed for her by her husband, Giulio.[59] Later in the entertainment a third woman, Margherita Loro Alleluia, joined the two Achileis for the trio portions of a madrigal. She also sang with Vittoria and Lucia in segments of a *ballo,* where the women accompanied themselves on a Spanish chitarrina, a Neapolitan chitarrina, and a small harpsichord, respectively. Similarly, Cardinal Bibiena's tragicomedy *La Calandria* was performed in 1548 in Lyons by an Italian troupe with musical intermedii in which women took part. The first intermedio, for example, featured Dawn on a chariot, "combing her long golden locks and singing [a] canzona accompanied by two spinets and four flutes." Later Night, also a woman, sang a canzona to the accompaniment of two spinets, four flutes, and four bass viols.[60]

Women had probably been among the hired musicians at some Italian courts in the early sixteenth century. Dalida de' Putti, a singer who entered the service of Lucrezia Borgia in 1507, was to become the mistress of Cardinal

Ippolito d'Este, whose musical establishment she joined in 1512. Even earlier, a Madama Anna, also referred to as Madama Anna Inglese, appeared on the rolls of royal musicians in Naples in 1471, and reappeared there at various times through the end of the century.[61] Though hers is the only woman's name to be specified, there must have been more women singers or musicians at Naples during this time, for special lodgings were built to house them. Wives and daughters of male performers are known to have been hired elsewhere without officially having their names added to the payrolls, so possibly the women were relatives of some of the male musicians at the court in Naples. Virginia Vignoli, for example, worked with her father, also a performer in Venice, where she was considered his "adjunct." By the 1560s she was pursuing the career of professional singer, though she later gave up her music to marry.[62] At Naples one Eufemia Jozola is named as the best of a group of women singers noteworthy for "a simple and affecting manner of delivery that ultimately influenced Giulio Caccini."[63] At Ferrara a 1465 payroll lists as a singer Anna cantarina Angelica Franceschini, but she seems not to have been rehired in subsequent years.[64]

One of the earliest known female professional musicians in Spain was Isabel de Plazaola. She was the daughter of one Isabel Ortiz, who was arrested by the Inquisition in 1564 both for having spread heretical ideas and for receiving too many male musicians in her home. The purpose of the men's visits, however, was professional: they were giving the younger Isabel music lessons. The daughter had built up a good musical reputation locally when she was hired as a house musician by the wife of the new governor of Milan. Before Plazaola could sail for Italy, however, the governor canceled the offer, "saying that the king did not approve of having a young woman just to sing and play on military expedition. . . ."[65] Plazaola was thus forced to confine her career to Spain.

One of the strangest reports of a woman's being hired as a professional musician was connected with the papal court in Rome. Like Ferrara's duchess, the pope supported a *musica segreta* (household musical ensemble) of secular musicians hired to serve his court. Payroll records indicate the presence in this group of Madonna Laura, *musica,* whose name first appears in December 1537. Thereafter, except for a six-month hiatus, she was paid monthly through January 1548—rather, her husband was paid on her behalf. It is difficult to say precisely what duties Laura and the musicians of the *musica segreta* performed, but they may have included singing the sort of improvised songs discussed earlier, since Laura is known to have played the lute.[66]

Though the Venetian *ospedali*—or orphanages—would enjoy their greatest fame in the seventeenth and eighteenth centuries, they were already offering musical training to orphaned and impoverished girls in the 1520s and featuring the girls as church musicians. By 1575 at least one of the *ospedali* also sponsored public concerts. Such activities would not have been possible had not Venice's religious establishment maintained a high degree of independence from Rome's supervision. Though some *ospedali* educated boys as well, their numbers were far fewer than the girls' and they gained no particular fame as musicians.[67]

FERRARA'S *CONCERTO DELLE DONNE*

In Ferrara women singers had been performing at court for some years before Duke Alfonso II established the famous *concerto delle donne* (women's ensemble) in 1580. Anthony Newcomb lists Lucrezia and Isabella Bendido, Leonora di Scandiano, and Vittoria Bentivoglio, along with the bass Giulio Cesare Brancaccio, as court singers active as early as 1577.[68] Since Brancaccio had been brought to court specifically because of his singing talents, the women may also have been professionals. Yet paid or not, these women, all either noble or wealthy, were the kinds of people who could have been members of the court regardless of musical ability. Members of the *concerto delle donne,* on the other hand, had in common with Brancaccio that they were invited to Ferrara specifically to perform vocal music at the court's chamber music concerts. Though members of the *concerto* were given court appointments as ladies-in-waiting to Duchess Margherita, there is no doubt that they were in fact hired as singers.

The first members of the *concerto delle donne* to arrive in Ferrara were Livia d'Arco (d. 1611); Anna Guarini (d. 1598), daughter of poet Giovanni Battista Guarini; and the much honored Laura Peverara (d. 1601). Their first recorded performance took place on November 20, 1580, though only Guarini and Peverara sang at that time. Brancaccio joined the new ensemble in December of 1580, and the group began regular performances during Carnival of 1581. Livia d'Arco was thought to need further training and did not appear with the group until mid-1582. In 1583 the fabled Tarquinia Molza (1542–1617) joined the ensemble, but was forced to leave in 1589 when her affair with the composer Giaches de Wert became known. For nearly two decades the fame of Ferrara's singing ladies spread, and admirers attempted to establish similar groups in Mantua and Rome. By mid-1589 Alfonso's sister Lucrezia, probably envious of the attention paid to performers who had come to be associated with her sister-in-law's private concerts, founded a rival ensemble in Ferrara.

The ladies in Duchess Margherita's *concerto* differed from earlier female singers, whether amateurs or professionals, in the particularly virtuosic

EXAMPLE 4.1. Luzzasco Luzzaschi, "O dolcezze amarissime d'amore," mm. 12–17. From Alfred Einstein, *The Italian Madrigal* (Princeton: Princeton University Press, 1949), vol. 3, p. 311. Used by permission of the publisher.

vocal style they espoused. Performing in the Duchess's *musica secreta* (private music)—for so the nightly chamber music concerts were called—they specialized in music decorated with numerous *passaggi,* trills, and cadenzas, which were probably improvised in rehearsal and then committed to memory. Court composer Luzzasco Luzzaschi's 1601 volume, *Madrigali . . . per cantare a uno, e duo, e tre soprani* (Madrigals to be sung by one, two, and three sopranos), contains examples of the sort of music with which the women astounded their listeners. The trio "O dolcezze amarissime d'amore" (O most bitter sweetness of love), though less virtuosic than some of the solo numbers, gave each singer a chance to display her artistry. In addition, there must have been some music for female voice or voices and bass, for Brancaccio, already well versed in this luxuriant style, performed with the ladies until he was dismissed for insubordination in 1583.

The women of the *concerto* were skilled not only in singing their memorized repertoire, which was extensive, but in sight-reading polyphonic music from partbooks. Each woman also played at least one instrument and was able to accompany herself or the ensemble. The group had few idle hours, for rehearsals and performances occupied from two to six hours a day. In addition, they took part in court *balletti* both as singers and dancers. Perhaps this work was tiring, but rewards could be considerable. Prestige must be counted among them. Laura Peverara was both the subject and the dedicatee of three anthologies of madrigals: a manuscript collection (ca. 1580) and two published volumes, *Il lauro secco* (The dry laurel, 1582) and *Il lauro verde* (The green laurel, 1583). The printed works were compiled by one of Laura's admirers, poet Torquato Tasso, and all three collections contained music by the best and best-known male madrigalists of late-sixteenth-century Italy.

Financially, the women also reaped benefits. Though society would not yet allow them to exist as independent professionals (all except Molza, a widow, married not long after arriving in Ferrara), they were rewarded with good salaries and what we might classify as fringe benefits. Laura Peverara received a dowry, an apartment in the ducal palace, and stipends for her mother and husband, while Tarquinia Molza was given not only an apartment but also a salary more than twice that of Luzzaschi. She later became the first woman ever to receive Roman citizenship. The fate of Anna Guarini was not so fortunate. Despite her enviable position at court, she met a violent end when her jealous husband murdered her.[69]

Though the *concerto* singers were honored and well paid, there can be no question that their status as professionals did not equal that of male musicians at court. Their high incomes were different in kind from men's, who received not just salaries and gifts but independent living quarters as well, suggesting that they were viewed as more nearly autonomous than the women. In addition, the incomes and very careers of the women were managed by husbands or fathers. In fact, "female singers, far from being self-determining professionals, were frequently pawns in the musical power-play of their husbands and fathers." (One thinks immediately of the Caccinis.) One interesting case is that of Caterina Martinelli, whom the duke of Mantua insisted be certified a virgin before he would hire her. This strange demand was an outgrowth of the common belief that women musicians were also prostitutes and of the duke's desire to demonstrate that he was hiring a singer, not a courtesan.[70]

Luzzasco Luzzaschi was not the only composer to write music specifically geared to the virtuosic performing style of the three ladies. The *concerto delle donne* and rival groups drew forth numerous volumes of pieces for accompanied female soloists that appeared well into the seventeenth century. Equally important was the influence of the Ferrarese *concerto* on the polyphonic madrigal for mixed voices. Among the composers who applied the women's manner of ornamented singing to the madrigal, Giaches de Wert produced many madrigals that featured ornamentation in all voices. The idea of women as paid public performers, spurred no doubt by the employment of actresses in the *commedia dell'arte* and the sort of virtuosity associated with women's singing, surely influenced composers like Peri, Caccini, and Monteverdi to give women key roles in their operas.

The death of Duke Alfonso II in 1597 left Ferrara without a ruler, as the duke had no sons. Alfonso's musical establishment, one of the largest and best in Italy, was dissolved along with his court. Yet the position of Ferrara and its music has led one historian to suggest "that the formation of a virtually professional group of [female] madrigal singers at the Ferrarese court . . . was the most important single development in the history of Italian secular vocal music during the last third of the [sixteenth] century."[71]

WOMEN AND THE WRITTEN TRADITION

Women creators of music in the written tradition did not emerge until rather late in the early modern period. Some of the reasons for this are easy to find. The emphasis on improvised singing to lute accompaniment as court entertainment meant that writing down a piece of music had no particular superiority in circles where women with sufficient musical education might have done so. Also, as with classical education, so with musical training: its availability to girls depended in large part on their families' attitudes toward education. Even under the best circumstances a girl's training might not have extended to theory and composition. In addition, one major source of a thorough musical education was completely closed to girls: the *cappella,* the group of musicians employed by a church or court to create and perform music for sacred services, processions, or other ceremonial or civic occasions. Appointment to a court *cappella* at a young age meant a boy would receive a liberal arts education, perhaps even traveling to a distant university at his patron's expense, and be fitted not just to sing and play but also to compose and to take on other court duties as well. As for the church, it remained a major provider of musical training through the eighteenth century. Though members of a *cappella* might also be asked to perform chamber music for court functions, chamber groups like the *concerto delle donne* were never asked to augment the *cappella,* for this institution and its educational opportunities were reserved for boys and men.

Without access to the *cappella*, the budding composer had few outlets for her products and only limited access to the best musicians. Thus the young woman was kept from an important part of any apprenticeship: learning by doing. Unable to hear her music rehearsed and performed, she had little reason to write it in the first place. Music publishing, a growing industry after 1500, might have provided access to audiences, but if there were no demand for a composer's music, the publisher would be unlikely to want to print it; and if the music remained unpublished, there would be no demand.

Musicologist Paula Higgins has pointed to "the perplexing absence of a single musical composition attributed to a woman between ca. 1300 and 1566" as a phenomenon more apparent than real.[72] The documented activity of courtly women involved in creating poetry intended for musical performance is exemplified in the circle of the young Margaret of Scotland (1424–1445), wife of the dauphin, Louis XI, whose enthusiasm for writing verses was said to have contributed to her early death. Though no examples of music have been attributed to the women in this or similar circles, several observations strongly suggest that they must have created some compositions, if only in improvised form. The early modern period was one in which anonymous creativity by both men and women of the European nobility was encouraged; hence improvised songs by women would have been so common as to deserve no particular attention in contemporary sources. In addition, many courtly women had sufficient musical training to enable them to commit their songs to paper, even though it would have been unseemly for them to sign their work. Higgins notes that numerous supporters of courtly music in the fifteenth century also wrote poetry, sang, played musical instruments, and were seriously interested in polyphonic music: Beatrice of Aragon, Marie of Burgundy, Margaret of Austria, Anne of Brittany, and the aforementioned Isabella d'Este, among others.

The many anonymous works in both manuscript and printed sources of this time, particularly those whose texts speak with a woman's voice, increase the likelihood that music by women from about the years 1300–1566 has indeed been preserved and that the circumstances of its composition and preservation have prevented us from identifying it. The first possibly recovered composer is Margaret of Austria (1480–1530), who may have written the chanson/motet "Se je souspire/Ecce iterum," printed in MTA, vol. 1. That women began to write down, sign, and even publish their music during the final decades of the sixteenth century is surely another manifestation of the spirit that moved them to become professionals in other artistic and creative fields—literature, painting, acting, and music performance.

In 1556 Albrecht V, Duke of Bavaria, hired as his *maestro di cappella* the distinguished composer Orlando di Lasso. Since Lasso obtained the position in part because he was knowledgeable in the latest musical styles, it is interesting that as part of the celebration of the marriage of Albrecht's heir Wilhelm V to Renata of Lorraine in 1568, he programmed two motets by women. The first, a five-voice piece, "Nil magis iucundum," was by Maddalena Casulana, soon to become known for her madrigals; the second, "Vas sacrae adeste tonis," was by Caterina Willaert. As both were commissioned works, with texts by Nicolò Stopio, Albrecht's Venetian agent, their composers must already have established reputations for work of high quality.[73] Unfortunately neither work has been preserved. Elsewhere, both Paola Massarenghi and Cesarina Ricci de' Tingoli published madrigals: Massarenghi, a single piece in a 1585 Ferrara anthology; Tingoli, a complete volume in Venice (1597). (Massarenghi's "Quando spiega" is printed in MTA, vol. 1.) Though Rafaella Aleotti is the only sixteenth-century nun whose music remains, other nuns probably wrote music as well.

It is difficult to determine whether two pieces attributed to sixteenth-century noblewomen were actually written by them. Anne Boleyn (1507–1536), to be sure, was capable of writing a piece of the quality of "O Deathe, Rock Me Asleepe" (HAMW, pp. 16–17), and the sadness expressed in both text and music seems to prophesy the fate that awaited her. Italy's Leonora Orsina (ca. 1560–1634) was also capable of writing music. Yet the song "Per pianto la mia carne" (With sobs my body, printed in MTA, vol. 1), which appears in a Modena manuscript, may only have been dedicated to her by an unnamed composer.[74] This piece is one of the first to provide both plain and ornamented versions of its melody. Leonora's mother, Isabella de' Medici, may have written another song in the same manuscript (see MTA, vol. 1). Her name also appears as the dedicatee of the first published book of madrigals by a woman.

THE MUSIC OF MADDALENA CASULANA

Maddalena Casulana (ca. 1540–ca. 1590) is both the first woman known to have published her music and the first to have considered herself a professional composer. Born at Casola d'Elsa near Siena (hence the name Casulana), she received her musical training there and in Florence, the city that also heard her first compositions.[75] In 1566 four of her madrigals appeared in the collection *Il Desiderio,* published by Girolamo Scotto of Venice. (One of these pieces, "Se sciôr di ved'il laccio," appears in MTA, vol. 1.) These four-voice madrigals, sharing a volume with works by such masters as Cipriano de Rore and Orlando di Lasso, were the first known pieces by a woman to appear in print. A third book in the same *Il Desiderio* series (1567) contained another of Casulana's madrigals. It was followed one year later by a volume devoted solely to her music, her *First Book of Madrigals for Four Voices.* This collection was also published by Scotto, and would be reprinted twice in 1583. At about the same time Casulana appears to have moved to Venice, where she gave private lessons in composition. In Vicenza she is reported to have played the lute for a private entertainment. Her next home may have been Milan, for her second collection of madrigals is dedicated to a Milanese government official. Another source, also from Milan, notes that Casulana was making her living as a composer.

Casulana's *Second Book of Madrigals for Four Voices* (Venice, 1570) was followed by a period of more than ten years during which little was heard of her and no new works appeared in print. She apparently married, as documents of the 1580s refer to her either as Signora Maddalena Casulana de Mezarii or Maddalena Mezari detta Casulana, the latter on the title page of her *First Book of Madrigals for Five Voices* (Ferrara, 1583). Her last known madrigal, a piece for three voices, appeared in a collection, *Il Gaudio* (Venice, 1586), now preserved only in its second edition. After this, nothing more of her life is recorded. Though a publisher's catalogue of 1591 lists two volumes of sacred madrigals by someone named Casulana, the composer cited could be another person by the same name or from the same area of Italy.

Maddalena Casulana was a respected and honored composer, demonstrated not only by the fact that her music was reprinted but also that music by others was dedicated to her and poems were written in her praise. Yet she was all too aware of society's attitudes toward women and their accomplishments. In dedicating her *First Book of Madrigals for Four Voices* to Isabella de' Medici, Casulana wrote:

> I truly know, most illustrious and excellent lady, that these first fruits of mine, because of their weakness, cannot produce the effect I would like, which would

> be not only to give some testimony to Your Excellency of my devotion but also to show the world (for all that has been granted to me in this profession of music) the vain error of men, who so think themselves to be the possessors of the high arts of the intellect that they cannot believe themselves to have the least thing in common with women.

Most dedications of music to noble patrons include any number of standard expressions of unworthiness of both the composer and the music being offered to so exalted a person. Casulana's dedication is much more specific: she is publishing her (apparently not so weak) music to show men that a woman is capable of creating such works. Her words also make clear that she considers herself a professional composer, undoubtedly the first woman in the history of music to do so.

Maddalena Casulana's music is finely crafted and worthy to stand beside that of any other composer of her day. The madrigal, her genre-of-choice, engaged the best creative talents of the sixteenth century. Choosing the finest Italian poems of past or present, madrigalists attempted to reflect the imagery of those texts in their music. Casulana was particularly well attuned to the sentiments of the poems she chose, writing music with an expressive content that ranged from simple "madrigalisms" (for example, running eighth notes for such words as "singing," "circling," "flying") to the passionate, declamatory outpourings that begin such pieces as "Morir non può il mio cuore" (My heart cannot die) or "Morte—Che vôi?—Te chiamo" (Death—What is your wish?—I call to you; HAMW, pp. 20–21). In the latter, the separate cries to Death, in the soprano, tenor, and bass voices (the tenor in quite a high range), coupled with Death's "What is your wish?" set to a very disjunct alto line, aptly establish the mood for the rest of the piece. The work is compact, intense, and free of trivial word painting. The intellectual and musical device of setting the syllable *fa* to notes that are *fa* in different hexachords intensifies the poetic dialogue between Death and the supplicant.

VITTORIA/RAFAELLA ALEOTTI

Some confusion still exists over the identities of two published composers of the sixteenth century, Rafaella (ca. 1570–after 1646) and Vittoria Aleotti (ca. 1573–after 1620).[76] Some scholars maintain that the two women were in fact one person, and that Vittoria simply took the name Rafaella upon entering Ferrara's San Vito convent, while others maintain that they are two separate persons. A major source of this confusion is the dedication written by Giovanni Battista Aleotti for his daughter Vittoria's *Ghirlanda de madrigali a quattro voci* (Garland of madrigals for four voices; Venice, 1593). Telling of the musical talents of his five daughters, Signor Aleotti relates that since the oldest girl had already decided to become a nun, he thought it a good idea to provide her with music lessons. "It so happened," he continues, "that while she was learning, my second daughter was always present, along with her sister Vittoria (a child of four going on five). . . ." Though it seems clear from this translation that Aleotti has spoken thus far of a total of three daughters, other translations have muddied the waters by rendering the passage, "my second daughter and her sister who is called Vittoria was always present," assuming that "her sister Vittoria" simply modifies "my second daughter."[77] Most scholars have assumed the oldest daughter to be Beatrice, who did enter the convent for a time, perhaps only as a student, and who later married.

Aleotti goes on to tell how young Vittoria absorbed enough from her sister's lessons that she astonished her parents and the music teacher, whereupon the child was given lessons of her own. At the age of six or seven Vittoria was sent to San Vito convent to continue her education, and by the age of fourteen she decided to become a nun herself. Meanwhile, she had made such progress in her study of music theory that her father asked the poet Giovanni Battista Guarini for some verses, which Vittoria soon set to music as four-voice madrigals; hence the *Ghirlanda,* the work of a composer still in her teens.

Soon thereafter we hear only of Rafaella, and the name Vittoria Aleotti drops from sight. Rafaella, too, brought out a volume of vocal music in 1593, *Sacrae cantiones quinque, septem, octo, and decem vocibus decantande* (Motets for five, seven, eight, and ten voices singing together), the first known sacred music by a woman to appear in print. After that date, all references to Rafaella are consistent with what we know of Vittoria: she is cited as a composer of both madrigals and motets, an exceptional organist and teacher in the convent, and a performer of both vocal and instrumental music in the homes of wealthy citizens of Ferrara. It may not be possible to determine with certainty whether Vittoria and Rafaella are two separate individuals, for the documents uncovered to date are inconclusive. However, existing evidence lends more support to the conclusion that the two women were in fact one. For purposes of discussion, however, we shall use the name Vittoria when referring to the madrigals, and Rafaella when referring to the motets.

Vittoria Aleotti's first published composition appeared in 1591: a single madrigal in an anthology of works by Ferrarese composers, put out by Giacomo Vincenti of Venice. Her complete volume of 1593 contains twenty-

EXAMPLE 4.2. Vittoria Aleotti, "Baciai per haver vita," mm. 13–20. Edited by C. Ann Carruthers. Reproduced by permission of Broude Brothers Limited.

one madrigals, all for four voices. Though written during the years when Ferrara's *concerto delle donne* was helping to change the complexion of the madrigal, Vittoria's pieces do not reflect these or other progressive trends. Instead, they reveal a solid grasp of basic sixteenth-century compositional technique and a youthful exuberance that is contagious. "Baciai per haver vita" (I kissed to have life), one of the pieces with text by Guarini, is typical. Each textual idea is given a musical setting that differs clearly from that which precedes or follows it and yet complements them. The lively imitative texture of the opening gives way to chordal declamation; then a sustained texture introduces the idea of death ("morte," in the first three bars of Example 4.2). Yet this is to be "so welcome a death" that the musical gloom cannot help but lift as the voices ascend, the bass drops out, and the soprano even sings a two-bar ornament. Vittoria's harmonies and rhythms are quite straightforward. Yet though she is not an innovator, her music reveals a lively talent that, given the opportunity, could have risen to new heights.

Most of Rafaella Aleotti's sixteen motets use biblical or liturgical texts associated with Matins services during the Christmas season or on one of the Feasts of the Virgin Mary. Though the specific times and places of their performance are unknown, the motets may have been used by the San Vito nuns in their chapel, with tenor and bass parts either sung at the octave or filled in by the organ. "Facta est cum angelo" (And suddenly there was with the angel), for SAATB choir, uses text from Luke 2: 13–14 relating the conclusion of the angel's announcement of Jesus's birth to the shepherds outside Bethlehem. Like most motets of this period, "Facta est" contains chordal segments that contrast with those in an imitative style. The changes in texture are pictorial, for all voices sing together homophonically when they represent the "multitude of the heavenly host" singing "glory to God in the highest," whereas the narrative portions of the text are most often set imitatively. Other motets in Rafaella's collection are more strictly contrapuntal and less sectional than "Facta est," while still others are polychoral. On the whole, they seem more mature than Vittoria's madrigals. Yet like the madrigals, the motets exhibit a good grasp of technique and style and convey a more than superficial understanding of their subjects.

Vittoria/Rafaella Aleotti cannot be considered a professional composer, since her intention in entering the convent was to lead the life of a nun. Yet she was among the small but growing number of women whose works were published not just as isolated pieces here and there, but in full volumes. In addition, Sister Rafaella was known as a performer, teacher, and conductor, and her activities continued into old age despite the potentially dampening effect of the Counter-Reformation.

Women Musicians and the Concept of the "Renaissance"

If women's status as composers and musicians improved during the final decades of the sixteenth century, the course of this improvement was irregular and its effects seemingly confined to certain geographical and musical areas. By 1600 women could aspire to positions as court musicians or opera singers, but the professions of instrumentalist or church musician would remain almost exclusively male for some time. The field of composition had opened up to women, but only in a restricted way, confined as it was to music for vocal soloists or ensembles. Finally, the necessity to pursue a vocation as wife or nun led most young women to give up their music studies and disappear from recorded history at an early age. Nevertheless, women played an active and influential role in the unwritten tradition of fifteenth- and sixteenth-century music, creating texts, musical settings, and manners of performance that were not only part of the artistic mainstream but were even in its vanguard. Singing to the lute was a pastime that women shared with men, and the vocal virtuosity of such women as the *concerto delle donne* and the anonymous nuns of Milan, Bologna, Ferrara, and other locales influenced performance practice and the written tradition itself. Devotional music of a simpler sort captured the attention of reform-minded women of both Catholic and Protestant faiths.

An overview such as this might lead readers to question Joan Kelly-Gadol's pessimistic view of the negative effect the so-called Renaissance had on women in the years 1450–1600. In fact, one might be tempted to agree with Robert Kendrick that "the remarkable growth in female creativity in early modern Italy, to be found in visual arts, . . . literature, and far from least, music [provides] a counter-example to the idea of the Renaissance as a [period of] decline in women's status."[78] Yet, like it or not, we are dealing here with the exceptional women from, at most, two classes of society and a relatively small number of geographical areas. Perhaps with more time and research we can someday claim that women of early modern Europe had a Renaissance.

NOTES

1. Bonnie S. Anderson and Judith P. Zinsser, *A History of Their Own,* 2 vols. (New York: Harper and Row, 1988).

2. Olwen Hufton, *The Prospect before Her: A History of Women in Western Europe, 1500–1800* (New York: Alfred A. Knopf, 1996).

3. Allan Atlas's comment that Beatrice was probably uninterested in Tinctoris's ideas concerning music theory seems unwarranted given the evidence. In the end, even Atlas concludes that one cannot really judge "either the level at which Tinctoris

may have tutored the princess or the skill at music that [she] . . . may have attained." See *Music at the Aragonese Court of Naples* (Cambridge: Cambridge University Press, 1985), p. 112.

4. Nino Pirrotta, "Music and Cultural Tendencies in Fifteenth-Century Italy," *Journal of the American Musicological Society* 19 (1966): 144.

5. Claude Palisca, *Humanism in Italian Renaissance Musical Thought* (New Haven: Yale University Press, 1985), p. 5.

6. Nanie Bridgman, *La vie musicale au Quattrocento et jusqu'à la naissance du madrigal (1400–1530)* (Paris: Gallimard, 1964), p. 134.

7. James Haar, "*Improvvisatori* and their Relationship to Sixteenth-Century Music," in his *Essays on Italian Poetry and Music, 1300–1600* (Berkeley and Los Angeles: University of California Press, 1987), Figures 3 and 5. In Figure 3 the drape of the singer's costume suggests female attire, and in Figure 5 a *commedia dell'arte* figure is either a woman or a cross-dressed man.

8. Martha Feldman, "The Academy of Domenico Venier, Music's Literary Muse in Mid-Cinquecento Venice," *Renaissance Quarterly* 44 (1991): 499–500. Others in Venier's circle cited Polissena Pecorina and Polissena Frigera as Bellamano's equals.

9. Ibid., p. 500.

10. See Lisa Ann Urkevich, "Anne Boleyn, a Music Book, and the Northern Renaissance Courts: Music Manuscript 1070 of the Royal College of Music, London" (Ph.D. diss., University of Maryland-College Park, 1997).

11. See Martin Picker, *The Chanson Albums of Marguerite of Austria* (Berkeley: University of California Press, 1965).

12. William Prizer, "Games of Venus: Secular Vocal Music in the Late Quattrocento and Early Cinquecento," *Journal of Musicology* 9 (1991): 7–8.

13. Iain Fenlon, "Gender and Generation: Patterns of Music Patronage among the Este, 1471–1539," in *The Court of Ferrara and Its Patronage,* ed. M. Pade, L. W. Petersen, and D. Quarta (Modena: Panini, 1990), pp. 214–15.

14. Sharon Kettering, "The Patronage Power of Early Modern French Noblewomen," *Historical Journal* 32 (1989): 831.

15. Fiona Kisby, "A Mirror of Monarchy: Music and Musicians in the Household Chapel of the Lady Margaret Beaufort, Mother of Henry VII," *Early Music History* 16 (1997): 204.

16. Craig Monson, "Elizabethan London," in Iain Fenlon, ed., *The Renaissance: From the 1470s to the End of the Sixteenth Century* (Englewood Cliffs, N.J.: Prentice Hall, 1989), pp. 304–5.

17. Some reports also claim that Madama Europa played the title role in the premiere of Monteverdi's *Arianna* in 1608, but this is an error. See Eduard Birnbaum, *Jewish Musicians at the Court of the Mantuan Dukes (1542–1628),* English edition, revised and augmented by Judith Cohen (Tel-Aviv: Tel-Aviv University, 1978), pp. 16, 42–43.

18. Fenlon, *Renaissance,* p. 1.

19. Bonnie Blackburn, "Two Carnival Songs Unmasked: A Commentary on MS Florence Magl. XIX, 121," *Musica Disciplina* 35 (1981): 121–78.

20. Frank Dobbins, *Music in Renaissance Lyons* (Oxford: Clarendon Press; New York: Oxford University Press, 1992), pp. 79–83. The Labé quotation appears in the dedication of her *Euvres,* published in 1555.

21. Jean-Baptiste du Four, letter published in Roville's edition of Bocaccio's *Decameron,* 1555, cited in Dobbins, p. 83.

22. Ibid., pp. 84–85.

23. Fenlon, *Renaissance,* p. 361, quoting L. Guicciardini, *The Description of the Low Countries and the Provinces Thereof* (London, 1593).

24. See Robert Kendrick, *Celestial Sirens: Nuns and Their Music in Early Modern Milan* (New York: Clarendon Press, 1996); Craig Monson, ed., *The Crannied Wall: Women, Religion, and the Arts in Early Modern Europe* (Ann Arbor: University of Michigan Press, 1992); and Craig Monson, *Disembodied Voices: Music and Culture in an Early Modern Italian Convent* (Berkeley and Los Angeles: University of California Press, 1995).

25. Hufton, p. 370.

26. Ibid., p. 68.

27. Ibid., p. 375. See also Prudence Baernstein, "The Counter-Reformation Convent: The Angelics of San Paolo in Milan, 1535–1635" (Ph.D. diss., Harvard University, 1993); and Jutta Sperling, "Convents and the Body Politic in Late Renaissance Venice (1550–1650)" (Ph.D. diss., Stanford University, 1995).

28. See Kendrick, passim.

29. In some areas, however, church officials tried to prevent nuns from any contact with the outside world. These prohibitions included the receipt of music and the hiring of music teachers or performers from outside the wall. See Monson, *Crannied Wall,* pp. 193–95.

30. Kendrick, p. 415.

31. Monson, *Crannied Wall,* pp. 191–93.

32. Ibid., p. 194.

33. Ibid., p. 199.

34. Monson, *Disembodied Voices,* p. 2.

35. Ercole Bottrigari, *Il Desiderio; or, Concerning the Playing Together of Various Musical Instruments,* trans. Carol MacClintock (Rome: American Institute of Musicology, 1962), pp. 57–59.

36. C. Ann Carruthers-Clement, "The Madrigals and Motets of Vittoria/Raphaela Aleotti" (Ph.D. diss., Kent State University, 1982), p. 10.

37. Craig Monson, "Elena Malvezzi's Keyboard Manuscript: A New Sixteenth-Century Source," *Early Music History* 9 (1989): 73–128.

38. Ibid., p. 113.

39. Patrick Macey, "The Lauda and the Cult of Savonarola," *Renaissance Quarterly* 45 (1992): 457.

40. Ibid., p. 468; translation used by permission of author.

41. Serafino Razzi, *Libro Primo delle laude spirituale* (Venice, 1563; facsimile edition, Bologna: Forni, 1969), pp. 32v-33r.

42. Printed in MTA, vol. 1.

43. Walter Salmen, ed., *Liederbuch der Anna von Köln (um 1500),* Denkmäler rheinischer Musik 4 (Düsseldorf: Musikverlag L. Schwann, 1954), p. 3.

44. Marguerite of Navarre, *Chansons spirituelles,* ed. Georges Dottin (Geneva: Droz, 1971), p. xv.

45. Ibid., pp. 21–25.

46. Roland Bainton, *Women of the Reformation in France and England* (Minneapolis: Augsburg, 1973), pp. 45–46.

47. Ibid., p. 75.

48. Foreword to Georg Rhau, *Symphoniae iucundae atque adeo breves quattuor vocum* (1538), quoted in Walter Buszin, *Luther on Music* (St. Paul, MN: North Central Publishing Co., 1958), p. 4.

49. Fenlon, *Renaissance,* p. 52.

50. Roland Bainton, *Women of the Reformation in Germany and Italy* (Minneapolis: Augsburg, 1971), p. 72.

51. Ibid., p. 141.

52. Sherrin Marshall, ed., *Women in Reformation and Counter-Reformation Europe: Public and Private Worlds* (Bloomington: Indiana University Press, 1989), p. 51.

53. Ibid., p. 17.

54. Robert Homer Leslie, "Music and the Arts in Calvin's Geneva" (Ph. D. diss., McGill University, 1969), quoting the preface to the Psalter of 1542; my translation.

55. Hufton, p. 412.

56. Natalie Zemon Davis, *Society and Culture in Early Modern France* (Stanford, CA: Stanford University Press, 1975), p. 86.

57. Ibid., p. 78.

58. Wolfgang Osthoff, *Theatergesang und darstellende Musik in der italienischen Renaissance* (Tutzing: Hans Schneider, 1969), vol. 1, pp. 10, 219–20.

59. Archilei's and Caccini's arias are published in D. P. Walker and J. Jacquot, eds., *Les Fêtes du mariage de Ferdinand de Médicis et de Christine de Lorraine* (Paris: Editions du Centre National de la Recherche Scientifique, 1963), pp. 1–8, 156.

60. Dobbins, p. 116.

61. Atlas, pp. 105–6.

62. Anthony Newcomb, "Courtesans, Muses or Musicians? Professional Women Musicians in Sixteenth-Century Italy," in *Women Making Music*, ed. Jane Bowers and Judith Tick (Urbana: University of Illinois Press, 1986), p. 108.

63. Donna G. Cardamone, "Lifting the Protective Veil of Anonymity: Women as Composer-Performers, ca. 1400–1556," in *Women Composers: Music through the Ages*, ed. S. Glickman and M. Furman Schleifer (New York: G. K. Hall, 1996), vol. 1, p. 112.

64. Lewis Lockwood, *Music in Renaissance Ferrara 1400–1505* (Cambridge: Harvard University Press, 1984).

65. Sherrin Marshall, p. 117, n. 88.

66. Alison Sanders McFarland, "Papal Singers, the *Musica Segreta,* and a Woman Musician at the Papal Court: The View from the Private Treasury of Paul III," *Studi Musicali* 24 (1995): 220–30.

67. Jane Baldauf Berdes, *Women Musicians of Venice: Musical Foundations 1525–1855,* revised edition (Oxford: Clarendon Press, 1996).

68. Anthony Newcomb, *The Madrigal at Ferrara* (Princeton: Princeton University Press, 1980), vol. 1, pp. 8–13.

69. Newcomb, "Courtesans," pp. 95–96.

70. Laura Macy, "Women's History and Early Music," in *Companion to Medieval and Renaissance Music,* ed. T. Knighton and D. Fallows (New York: Schirmer Books, 1992), pp. 95–96.

71. Newcomb, *Madrigal,* vol. 1, p. 3.

72. Paula Higgins, "The 'Other Minervas': Creative Women at the Court of Margaret of Scotland," in *Rediscovering the Muses*, ed. K. Marshall (Boston: Northeastern University Press, 1993), p. 180.

73. Fenlon, *Renaissance,* pp. 243, 251–55. Though Caterina may have been related to Adrian Willaert, she was not his daughter, since he had no children.

74. Carol MacClintock, ed., *The Solo Song, 1580–1730* (New York: W. W. Norton, 1973), no. 4.

75. Biographical information from Beatrice Pescerelli, *I Madrigali di Maddalena Casulana* (Florence: Leo S. Olschki, 1979). The dedication is on p. 7; the translation is my own.

76. Most of the information on this controversy is taken from C. Ann Carruthers-Clement. The birth and death dates for Vittoria and Rafaella are those in *The New Grove Dictionary of Music and Musicians,* which treats them as two separate persons. The dedication cited is reproduced in Carruthers-Clement, p. 160.

77. " . . . sempre presente v'era la seconda mia figliuola, & sua sorella Vittoria detta (bambina di quattro in cinque Anni). . . ." The first translation is my own; the

second is from Jane Bowers, "The Emergence of Women Composers in Italy, 1666–1700," in *Women Making Music*, ed. Bowers and Tick, p. 130.

78. Kendrick, p. 426.

SUGGESTIONS FOR FURTHER READING

In addition to the items mentioned in the text or cited in the footnotes, the following sources provide information on women during the period 1450–1600.

Austern, Linda. "'Alluring the Auditorie to Effemanacie': Music and the Idea of the Feminine in Early Modern England." *Music and Letters* 74 (1993): 343–54.

———. "Music and the English Controversy over Women." In *Cecilia Reclaimed*, ed. S. Cook and J. Tsou, pp. 52–69. Urbana: University of Illinois Press, 1994.

———. "'Sing Againe Syren': The Female Musician and Sexual Enchantment in Elizabethan Life and Literature." *Renaissance Quarterly* 42 (1989): 420–48.

Campori, Giuseppe. "La figlia del Guarini [Anna Guarini]." *Nuova antologia* 12 (1869): 321–32.

Castiglione, Baldesar. *The Book of the Courtier.* A number of good editions are available.

Cook, Susan, and Thomasin Le May. *Virtuose in Italy, 1600–1640.* New York: Garland, 1984.

Elias, Cathy Ann. "Musical Performance in Sixteenth-Century Italian Literature: Straparola's *Le piacevoli notti.*" *Early Music* 18 (1989): 161–73.

Hamessley, Lydia. "Lost Honor and Torn Veils: A Virgin's Rape in Music." In *Menacing Virgins: Representing Virginity in the Middle Ages and Renaissance,* ed. Kathleen C. Kelly and Marisa Leslie. Newark: University of Delaware Press, 1999.

Higgins, Paula. "Parisian Nobles, a Scottish Princess, and the Women's Voice in Late Medieval Song." *Early Music History* 10 (1991): 145–200.

Jackson, Barbara Garvey. *Say Can You Deny Me: A Guide to Surviving Music by Women from the Sixteenth through the Eighteenth Centuries.* Fayetteville: University of Arkansas Press, 1994.

Kelly-Gadol, Joan. "Did Women Have a Renaissance?" In *Becoming Visible: Women in European History*, ed. R. Bridenthal and C. Koonz. Boston: Houghton Mifflin, 1987.

Kelso, Ruth. *Doctrine for the Lady of the Renaissance.* Urbana: University of Illinois Press, 1956.

Lea, Kathleen. *Italian Popular Comedy.* 2 vols. Oxford: Clarendon Press, 1934.

Macey, Patrick. *Bonfire Songs: Savonarola's Musical Legacy.* Oxford: Oxford University Press, 1998.

MacNeil, Elizabeth. "Music and the Life and Work of Isabella Andreini: Humanistic Attitudes toward Music, Poetry, and Theater during the Late Sixteenth and Early Seventeenth Centuries." Ph.D. diss., University of Chicago, 1994.

Masson, Georgina. *Courtesans of the Italian Renaissance.* New York: St. Martin's Press, 1975.

Newcomb, Anthony. "The Three Anthologies for Laura Peverara, 1580–1583." *Rivista italiana de musicologia* 10 (1975): 329–45.

Prizer, William. "Isabella d'Este and Lucrezia Borgia as Patrons of Music: The Frottola at Mantua and Ferrara." *Journal of the American Musicological Society* 38 (1985): 1–33.

Rosenthal, Margaret F. *The Honest Courtesan: Veronica Franco, Citizen, and Writer in Sixteenth-Century Venice.* Chicago: University of Chicago Press, 1992.

Treadwell, Nina. "The Performance of Gender in Cavalieri/Giudiccioni's *Ballo 'O che nuovo miracolo'* (1589)." *Women & Music* 1 (1997): 55–70.

MUSIC

Briscoe, James. *Historical Anthology of Music by Women.* Bloomington: Indiana University Press, 1990.

Glickman, Sylvia, and Martha Furman Schliefer, eds. *Women Composers: Music through the Ages.* New York: G. K. Hall, 1996. Volume 1 contains music by Suster Bertken, Margaret of Austria, Maddalena Casulana, Gracia Baptista, Leonora Orsini, Paola Massarenghi, and Vittoria Aleotti/Raphaela Alleota [*sic*].

V.
Musical Women of the Seventeenth and Eighteenth Centuries

Barbara Garvey Jackson

Introduction

Despite the existence of barriers to their success, women participated in most of the major developments of both Baroque and Classical styles in the seventeenth and eighteenth centuries, from composition in new forms and styles to music publishing and instrument building. The period saw the rise of an important new career for women, that of opera singer, because a well-trained soprano or mezzo-soprano was the favored voice for most solo vocal music. Opera was the major new musical genre of the early seventeenth century, one that required women singers. Some women composed operas; Francesca Caccini, for example, who sang in the first operas, was also an opera composer. Despite two centuries of competition with castrato singers and such minor setbacks as the ban on women's appearances on the stages of the Papal States, women opera singers flourished throughout Europe.[1] The great stars had international careers from London to St. Petersburg, and traveling companies (often family enterprises) provided opera to smaller courts and cities.

The contemporary dramatic and virtuoso singing styles also found their way into the music of Catholic, Lutheran, and Anglican church services, and the practice of combining instruments with voices in church music spread from Venice throughout Europe. Particularly in Italy and Austria, Catholic women responded to operatic, and later symphonic, influences when they wrote for the church, just as did their male contemporaries. The only Protestant women active as composers of sacred music were German Lutheran aristocrats, and they wrote mostly devotional music for home use, not service music. A noblewoman might have had time and opportunity for musical training and have been in a position of sufficient authority not to suffer restraint from the composition of sacred music if that was her bent; however, even such a woman would have been discouraged from exposing her music to the general public. Anglican service music by women is practically unknown before the nineteenth century, while in denominations emphasizing congregational singing, women sang as worshipers but were not allowed to participate in choirs.[2] There was never a Protestant equivalent of the musical opportunities afforded Catholic women by the convent.

Musical performances in the convents of seventeenth-century Milan and other northern cities were often splendid. After the Council of Trent in the sixteenth century the enforcement of strict enclosure in all women's religious orders in Italy (except the Ursulines), uneven as it was, nevertheless meant that congregations heard the singing of the nuns coming only from an inner church.[3] The intent was to make the bodies of the singers invisible to the public that worshiped in the external church. In the seventeenth century, however, nuns did publish Masses and other liturgical music as well as paraliturgical motets, although in most cases their initial volumes of music were not followed by additional collections. Much depended on the rigor with which the local authorities treated the nun musicians: in Bologna convent music, which had flourished and been heard by lay worshipers for centuries, was strongly opposed by several seventeenth-century bishops,[4] whereas in Milan, Archbishop Federigo Borromeo was sympathetic to music making by the nuns.[5] During the eighteenth century, however, musical life in the convents declined, and with the dissolution of convents and destruction of their libraries during the Napoleonic wars, much of what had existed was lost.

Outside the convents the secular composers Barbara Strozzi and Francesca Caccini also wrote some works with religious texts. Five sacred pieces by Francesca Caccini are in MTA, among them a joyful, florid setting of the liturgical text "Regina caeli" for soprano and continuo.[6] Elsewhere in Europe some laywomen composed religious music. In the latter half of the eighteenth century, for example, Marianna von Martines wrote several symphonic Masses and other liturgical music in Vienna.[7] However, after the death of Empress Maria Theresa in 1780, her son, Emperor Joseph II, enacted many restrictions that discouraged elaborate musical settings of the liturgy, the use of instruments in church, and the involvement of women in the performance of church music.

In France and England there were some women organists by the late eighteenth century, such as Elisabeth Lechanterie at the church of Saint-Jacques de la Boucherie in Paris. There were a few women soloists in a church in Hamburg, as early as 1716, and at Eszterháza and Salzburg in the late eighteenth century. However, only men and boys were allowed to be members of church choirs, whether Catholic or Protestant.

During these centuries there was an increase in public, secular music making and in more musical careers not directly tied to the church (although not all career venues were open to women). Catholic church musicians were no longer required to be celibate clergy, and the Protestants never had been, so married church musicians began to contribute to the networks of musical families so characteristic of the era. Male and female members of these musical dynasties pursued a wide variety of musical activities and formed support systems fostering the education and employment of their talented children. Families like the Caccinis, the Bachs, the Couperins, and the Bendas usually married within the profession. The daughters of musicians were often professionally trained, usually as singers. They often married other musicians, and their children seemed to inherit musical talent, while the family setting provided professional apprenticeships. In the Bach family the professional activities of most of the women ceased at the time they married (except for J. C. Bach's wife, the soprano Cecilia Grassi, who had a long professional career). Women in families of court singers (like the Caccinis), however, often continued their musical careers after marriage. Professional activities within extended families included the creation and performance of various types of music, instrument building, and music engraving and publishing. There were active and successful women in every one of these activities (although church performance was rare).

No court musical establishment was complete without well-trained female singers, even if it did not maintain an opera house. Female instrumentalists were sometimes court musicians, especially in the musical establishments of women aristocrats such as Queen Marie Antoinette. However, violinist Regina Strinasacchi, who worked in the ducal orchestra at Gotha, was a rare exception to the general pattern that women were not hired as orchestral musicians at court or in the opera house.

Until the mid-eighteenth century, the harpsichord and the organ were the main keyboard instruments, both for solo music and as continuo in virtually all ensemble music. There were renowned women harpsichord players and some important composers for that instrument, but there were few female organists except in convents. In the late eighteenth century the rise of the piano, with its solo role in concertos and sonatas, was accompanied by the rise of women pianist-composers, and some of the best performers were women.

The academies of Italy from the mid-sixteenth century onward were societies of intellectuals, under aristocratic sponsorship, that considered literary, philosophical, and musical matters and often fostered musical performances, especially of works that represented their aesthetic ideas and experiments. Their members were all male, but women performed in their musical presentations. Members of the Caccini family in Florence and Barbara Strozzi in Venice were among the women musicians for whom academy performance was important.

By the eighteenth century the salon, an aristocratic or middle-class gathering of intellectuals and music lovers, had also become a means of fostering new music as well as art and literature in such cities as Paris, Vienna, and Berlin. Unlike the male academies, the salons were often under the patronage of art-loving or intellectual women who gathered brilliant representatives of the culture about them in a sort of private sponsorship, as in the soirées of Marianna von Martines in Vienna. Most of the concert life of eighteenth-century Vienna took place in salons, private homes, and musical instrument shops (like the showroom of the piano builder Nannette Stein Streicher).

The seventeenth century also saw the emergence of public concerts. By 1678 Thomas Britton was holding some in the loft over his London small-coal shop, and these included many women performers. In Venice the girls of the *ospedali* (conservatories) performed orchestral music and oratorios within their institutions for enthusiastic public audiences. By the early eighteenth century the Concert Spirituel series in Paris used male and female musicians, both Parisians and touring artists. Similar series were soon organized in London, Edinburgh, Frankfurt, Hamburg, and even in such American cities as Boston and Charleston.

The mixed chorus—a choir of both men and women—was first established in the eighteenth century. At the beginning of the seventeenth century most sacred choral music was for all-male choirs, with boy choristers and adult male falsettists and castrati singing the treble parts. There were women's choirs, but only in convents or in the Venetian *ospedali.* The church viewed with suspicion the whole idea of men and women singing sacred choral music together in the worship service. Even in convents, much of the polyphonic music that has survived seems to have been sung there by groups of soloists. Since established choral groups existed only for religious music, mixed choral groups could be found only in occasional secular court festivities. But in opera, which grew out of such festivities, the chorus was always mixed—although it virtually disappeared from the Italian stage not long after the opening of public opera houses (Venice, 1637), either for reasons of economy or because the public preferred instead to hear virtuosic solo numbers. Women remained on the stage as soloists, often receiving fabulous reimbursements. In France, where opera was both a public and a court activity supported by the royal purse, the mixed chorus was retained. At the Concerts Spirituels choral works were performed with the same chorus that sang at the Opéra.

Similar choral trends are noticeable in Germany. Johann Mattheson (Hamburg) and Johann Adam Hiller (Leipzig) argued strongly that women's voices should be well trained and used in all choral music, including that of the church, but it was only outside the church that the mixed chorus could develop. Hiller opened a singing school in 1771 in which he trained male and female singers for his public concerts in Leipzig. C. F. C. Fasch organized a *Singakademie* of professional musicians and capable amateurs in Berlin (1790) that demonstrated the viability of a permanently organized mixed chorus and became a model for choral societies throughout Europe and even in America.

The establishment of these choruses was facilitated by the strong musical interests of amateurs from the growing middle class, which was also affluent enough to pay for music instruction, buy instruments (especially pianos and harps), attend public concerts, and purchase printed music. Eighteenth-century amateurs were often very fine performers and sometimes quite good composers; their ranks included both aristocratic and middle-class women and men. There was a wide range of abilities, of course, from young women for whom music was merely a social adornment to make them more marriageable, to such excellent pianists as Barbara von Ployer, Marianna von Grenzinger, and the Archduke Rudolph, for whom Haydn, Mozart, and Beethoven wrote demanding masterpieces. It was the connoisseurs and amateurs who created the vigorous market for widespread domestic and public music making of the late eighteenth century.

THE EARLY SEVENTEENTH CENTURY IN ITALY

Music theorists in the early seventeenth century distinguished between *prima prattica* (the first practice, the old contrapuntal art of Renaissance polyphony) and *seconda prattica* (the second practice, the new text-driven style for solo singers or ensembles in which dramatic effectiveness took precedence over formerly held rules of proper composition). The *prima prattica* had been largely a male art, composed and sung for church, and access to formal instruction in this art was not readily available to women. Nevertheless, some women did learn counterpoint through private study, among them Isabella Leonarda, the most prolific woman composer of the seventeenth century, who apparently studied with Gasparo Casati, the *maestro di cappella* (music director) of the Novara cathedral. Her work shows her sound training in the art, for many of her more than two hundred compositions are written according to the strict rules of traditional counterpoint, as are sections of two of her Masses. She also uses imitative counterpoint freely in instrumentally accompanied choral works, such as the second Kyrie of Messa Prima from Op. 18 (HAMW, pp. 51–53).

The *seconda prattica* was the modern music of the day and the style of the new forms of monody and opera. Although it originated in secular music, it quickly invaded church music and may be seen in devotional music by Francesca Caccini, Barbara Strozzi, and Chiara Margarita Cozzolani (nun at S. Radegonda in Milan) as well. Most women musicians, both performers and composers, cultivated the *seconda prattica* in secular musical works and learned the new art as singers. Their theoretical training emphasized the newly invented figured-bass technique rather than the older contrapuntal style.

The Caccinis

The remarkable Caccini family led in the development of the dramatic style of solo song accompanied by figured bass at the beginning of the seventeenth century. The musically active family members included the father, his two wives, a son, two daughters, and at least one granddaughter. Giulio Caccini, the father, had developed a style of musical declamation that aimed to "almost speak in tones." The "certain noble negligence of song" of this new music required a new manner of singing, which he taught to his first and second wives—Lucia and Margherita—and to his children—Francesca, Settimia, and Pompeo. He also taught his daughters to compose and to play continuo instruments—harpsichord and lute. Mastery of these instruments was a technical tool necessary for composition in the new style, as was the improvisation of vocal ornamentation. When the spectacular virtuosa Vittoria Archilei sang at the Medici court in Florence in 1589, Caccini associated himself with her by proudly claiming that she performed his music, bragging in the preface to his opera *L'Euridice* of "the new manner of passages and redoubled points, invented by me, which Vittoria Archilei, a singer of that excellence to which her resounding fame bears witness, has long employed in singing my works" (although a contemporary witness, Giustiniani, claimed it was Archilei herself who had "almost originated the true method of singing for females").[8]

Giulio's oldest daughter, Francesca Caccini (1587–by 1645), made her professional debut at the age of thirteen in *Euridice,* an opera by her father's rival Jacopo Peri. When the ensemble of family musicians, "il concerto Caccini," traveled to Paris in 1604, Francesca's singing so impressed the French king that he sought to keep the young woman in Paris, but the Florentine court would not release her, and she formally entered the service of the Medicis in 1607. The same year she married the singer Giovanni Battista Signorini. She collaborated with Michelangelo Buonarroti (nephew of the artist), setting his poetry to music for several court entertainments (all of which have been lost). She, her sister, and Vittoria Archilei performed in a trio (now lost) said to have contained splendid contrapuntal passages. In 1616 Francesca and her husband went to Rome to perform in the entourage of Cardinal Carlo de' Medici, and the following year they traveled to other Italian cities. They were thus among the earliest artists to tour, an activity that later became common for professional musicians and in which women were active from the beginning.

At a time when women were generally barred from singing in church, Francesca and her sister Settimia were soloists in the church of San Nicola in Pisa during the Holy Week performances directed by their father. Francesca was described as "singing perfectly in the interpretation of music of every style, sacred as well as secular, and contrapuntal as well as monodic."[9] She also had a number of students among the nobility whom she trained for court performances. The transmission of a new style to a circle of followers and students is an important stage in the development of any art form, and her teaching role is thus an indication of her significance. In 1621 she bore a daughter, Margherita, whom she trained as a singer.

In 1618 Francesca Caccini published her *Primo libro delle musiche a una e due voci,* a collection of seventeen secular pieces and nineteen works on sacred themes.[10] It is a varied group of pieces that she had probably composed over the preceding decade. Most are solo songs, but there are four duets for soprano and bass, perhaps for performance with her husband (see her *madrigale a due voci* "Io mi distruggo" in MTA, vol. 1, pp. 253–58, which also illustrates the care with which she notated vocal ornamentation). The *Primo libro* was dedicated to Cardinal de' Medici, which may explain the inclusion of so many religious pieces. The Italian devotional poetry for twelve of the pieces may have been written by Francesca herself. In the Italian spiritual madrigal "Maria, dolce Maria" (HAMW, pp. 25–34) she uses embellishment for expressive rather than purely decorative effect. She makes five Romanesca variations the basis for a shortened Italian paraphrase of the Reproaches for Good Friday in "Ecco ch'io verso il sangue" (Here I spill my blood), with its insistent refrain, "Rispondi, rispondi ò popol mio" (Answer me, answer, my people; MTA, vol. 1, pp. 240–44).

The music of *Il Primo libro* combines the style of musical declamation Francesca had learned from her father with the virtuoso embellishments practiced by Archilei and the Ferrarese *concerto delle donne*. She uses many musical forms popular in this period: simple canzonettas, completely strophic in form; strophic variations, in which the bass line, though somewhat varied, is repeated while the succeeding stanzas are set to a freely worked melody; and sectional pieces foreshadowing the cantatas of Barbara Strozzi, in which the changing emotions of the text are reflected in contrasting sections. Some pieces are completely through-composed.

The most famous of Francesca Caccini's stage works was *La liberazione di Ruggiero dall' isola d'Alcina* (The Liberation of Ruggiero from the Island of Alcina), the first extant opera by a woman (see "Aria of the Shepherd" from this opera in HAMW, pp. 35–37). It was commissioned by the joint regents, Christina de Lorena and Maria Maddalena de' Medici, mother and widow, respectively, of Cosimo de' Medici. The occasion was the state visit of Prince Ladislas Sigismond of Poland to Florence's Pitti Palace on February 2, 1625. The opera was repeated in Warsaw three years later, the first Italian opera performed outside of Italy. It was also the first opera based on Ariosto's *Orlando Furioso,* earlier a popular source of Renaissance madrigal texts, which remained a literary inspiration for composers and librettists for more than a century.

Caccini's cast for *La liberazione di Ruggiero dall' isola d'Alcina*—six sopranos, two altos, seven tenors, and one bass—exemplifies the seventeenth century's delight in high voices, although the large number of natural male voices and the absence of castrati are unusual. The opera's many short arias commonly bracket the sections in which the singer is accompanied by continuo and alternate with instrumental ritornelli, as in the "Aria of the Shepherd." The choice of three recorders for the ritornelli is an example of the taste for treble ensembles. The opera also contains several short five- and six-part choruses (probably sung by an ensemble of soloists), a brief chorus for six sopranos, and a double-chorus madrigal in eight parts.

In 1626 Francesca's husband died. She left the Medici court in 1627 and married Tomaso Raffaelli, a music-loving aristocrat of Lucca. In her new home she continued to be active in the musical-theatrical productions of her husband's Accademia degli Oscuri. A son was born in 1628, and in 1630 her second husband died. She was quarantined at Lucca during the plague, but in 1633 she returned to Florence and the Medici payroll, serving the grand duchesses by composing, directing entertainments, and singing with her daughter. Although her own two marriages had left Francesca well off and high in social status, when her daughter Margherita was fifteen, she refused to allow her to sing on stage, fearing that it would compromise her chances of a good marriage or convent placement, "would tarnish the social position of her son and break the terms of Raffaelli's will."[11] Eventually Margherita did enter the convent of San Girolamo in Florence. Francesca's son became the ward of his uncle Girolamo Raffaelli in 1645, probably at the time of Francesca's death.

The career of Settimia Caccini (1591–ca. 1638) was centered in Mantua. After two years in the service of Medici, both she and her husband, singer Alessandro Ghivizzani, went to the Gonzaga court in Mantua. Earlier,

Settimia had been in Mantua when she created the role of Venus in Monteverdi's *Arianna* in 1608. Settimia was employed to perform in the cities in which her husband worked, so when he became *maestro di cappella* at Lucca and later went to the court of Parma, she sang professionally in those cities. After she was widowed in 1632, she returned to the payroll of the Medici court in Florence. Later court account books list a Settimia Ghivizzani, who was probably her daughter. Both Settimia and Alessandro composed, and two manuscripts survive that contain their songs.[12] "Già sperai" (Once I hoped; see MTA, vol. 1, pp. 317–21) is strophic, but within the strophes there is a sectional structure, with the meter alternating between common time and 3/2. Although she does not write out ornamentation as her sister so commonly did, there are moments of text painting, such as melismas on *riso* (laugh), although the melismas and word meaning do not fit together as well in succeeding stanzas.

Barbara Strozzi: Cantata Composer outside the Theatre

Barbara Strozzi (1617–after 1664) was a Venetian composer and singer, renowned as the "virtuosissima cantatrice" (most virtuosic singer). She was the adoptive daughter of the poet Giulio Strozzi, who may actually have been her birth father. Although she lived in Venice, the birthplace of public opera, and studied composition with an opera composer (Francesco Cavalli), she herself neither performed nor composed opera. For unknown reasons, she sang only in her father's house for the academy he founded. She made her public career in a quite new way—entirely by publishing her compositions. Eight volumes of her music appeared in Venice between 1644 and 1664. They contain over a hundred works, all vocal music, mostly for solo voice and continuo. There is, however, one volume of ensemble pieces, *Il primo libro de madrigali,* Op. 1 (1644), and a few numbers for more than one voice appear in later collections. The continuo accompaniments could have been performed on lute or chitarrone, and were probably originally played by the composer herself. Although Strozzi did not perform publicly, her published work circulated outside Italy, and decades after her death she still rated an entry in Walther's German *Lexikon.* More than a century after her death, the English historians Charles Burney and John Hawkins both considered her a noteworthy composer.

Barbara Strozzi's was a precocious talent, and she was singing for her father's musical and literary friends by the age of fifteen (when Nicolò Fontei wrote songs for her to texts by her father). Her father's Accademia degli Unisoni (Academy of the Like-Minded) met at the Strozzi house for their witty and rhetorical discussions, at which Barbara sang, often performing her own compositions, and served as their mistress of ceremonies. Her sheltered career may have been an attempt to protect her from the slander to which Venetian women musicians were vulnerable.[13] If so, it was not successful, for association with her father's free-thinking and libertine circle already subjected her to malicious rumors and satire at the tender age of sixteen (although references to her in her adult life do not allude to the earlier, spiteful rumors). Perhaps it was this bitter experience that kept her from a public performing career. Strozzi's early publications were underwritten by her father, and her later volumes were dedicated to high-ranking patrons in Venice and across the Alps. Some of her works also appeared in seventeenth-century collections. Most of her music is secular, except for Op. 5, *I sacri musicali affetti,* which contains settings of fourteen Latin poems with sacred themes, tied to specific seasons of the church calendar.

One of the most prolific composers of secular chamber music in the century, Strozzi ranked above even Giacomo Carissimi, Luigi Rossi, and Marc' Antonio Cesti in numbers of published works. She used many of the forms and vocal styles common in the period, ranging from long works labeled "cantata" or "lamento" to simpler, even strophic, forms. "L'Astratto" from Strozzi's Op. 8 (1657; see MTA, vol. 2, pp. 63–76) illustrates her successful handling of an irregular poetic structure with theatrical emotion. In this long *scena* (173 measures) the singer keeps trying to sing of her love, but breaks off, unable to find the right expression; after a successful two-stanza aria she wants to sing no more, having sung too much already. "Hor che Apollo" (Now that Apollo; see MTA, vol. 2, pp. 77–97) alternates ritornelli for two violins and continuo with vocal sections, also in irregular poetic forms, combining the singer with the violins at the end. At 228 measures it is even longer than "L'Astratto." Expressive melodic style and strong, active bass lines are both illustrated in Example 5-1, an excerpt of "Tradimento!" from Op. 7, *Diporte di Euterpe overo cantate e ariette a voce sola* (Amusements of Euterpe, or cantatas and ariettas for solo voice). The one-word refrain, "Tradimento" (betrayal), opens the piece, appears again before the second stanza, and concludes the work. The martial, trumpet-like melodic figure to which it is set is varied each time it appears. Different musical material is used for each of the three stanzas of the poem, expressing their specific emotional content. In the last stanza, the martial motive from the refrain is used for the words "To arms, my heart." The section shown here, the second refrain and the beginning of the second stanza, illustrates the text painting on the word "legarmi" (to tie me) and the writhing embellishment of "lusinga" (entices).

EXAMPLE 5.1. Barbara Strozzi, "Tradimento!" (mm. 24–31) from *Diporte di Euterpe* (Venice: Francesco Magni, 1659). Copy in the Civico Museo Bibliografico Musicale, Bologna. Used by permission. *Text:* "Betrayal! Hope, to tie me, with great things entices the more I believe."

Women and Music in Italian Convents

More than half the music published by women in northern Italy in the seventeenth century was composed by nuns, especially those of Milan, Bologna, Pavia, and Novara. The nuns wrote psalms, Magnificats, and Masses, as well as motets with extraliturgical texts, often to contemporary devotional poetry they had also written; virtually all their music was intended for use in the church service. The composers were known as far away as Strasbourg and even in Protestant Leipzig, where some of their works were published in seventeenth-century collections. Splendid musical performances took place in the convents despite the strictures of the Council of Trent in its strongly worded decree of 1553:

> [In convents] the Divine Office should continue to be sung by them [the nuns] and not by professionals hired for that purpose, and . . . they should answer in . . . the Mass [only] whatever the choir is accustomed to answer, but they will leave to the Deacon and Subdeacon [male clergy] the office of chanting the Lessons, Epistles, and Gospels. *They will abstain from singing either in Choir or elsewhere the so-called "figured chant"* [polyphonic music]. . . .[14]

Another consequence of the Council of Trent was the possible application of strict enclosure to almost all convents.[15] This affected the nuns' ability to hear music being produced by others and to have music instruction from the outside. Their inner churches were physically separated by walls and gratings from the external church in which the public worshiped, so that when they sang they were invisible to the public and the possibility of collaborating with musicians from the outside was minimal.

In Bologna the post-Trent years saw a series of very strict bishops whose rigorous measures were applied to convents which had previously enjoyed very splendid and active musical lives. Lucrezia Orsina Vizzana (1590–1662), of the Camaldolese convent of Santa Cristina, actually published a volume of motets in 1623.[16] However, well before the end of her life the convent was embroiled with the authorities in internal schisms and a painful series of disputes, often about music. Vizzana published no more and became mentally ill. She had entered the order as a child when the authorities were favorable to music, and her education there was probably supervised by her aunts, including the musician Camilla Bombacci, who was an organist, novice mistress, and eventually abbess of the convent.

Several musical convents flourished in the Milan diocese in the first half of the seventeenth century. There Archbishop Federigo Borromeo (in office 1595–1631) actively supported convent music. He considered that musical training should be part of the novitiate and that music served the spiritual growth of the sisters. In Milan, a high percentage of girls from patrician families were destined for the convent. Convent dowries were lower than those for marriage, and nuns often gave up their inheritance rights, so a girl's entrance into a convent was a way of preserving family estates. The dowry might be even lower if the girl were an organist or otherwise musical. Patrician families therefore had an incentive for giving their daughters some musical training. Claudia Rusca (1593–1676), a nun of the Umiliate order at S. Caterina in Brera, was educated at home (a curriculum that included lessons in composition) before taking her final vows. She served her convent as soprano, organist, and music teacher, and published her *Sacri Concerti* in 1630.[17] Her training and experience demonstrate that the decrees of the Council of Trent and pronouncements by bishops and archbishops concerning music in cloisters were unevenly enforced.

Often there were family members already inside the convent who could continue a novice's musical education. Such was certainly the case for Chiara Margarita Cozzolani, for she had two aunts, a sister, and later two nieces at the Benedictine convent of S. Radegonda, the most musically celebrated Milanese house. Composers Cozzolani (1602–between 1676 and 1678) and Rosa Giacinta Badalla (ca. 1660–ca. 1715) were both nuns there. Cozzolani published more music than any other nun in Milan, although unfortunately two of her four volumes of sacred music as well as a secular aria have been lost. Her style in *Concerti sacri,* Op. 2 (1642) is similar to that of Isabella Leonarda's Novarese teacher Gasparo Casati, and suggests that current, new musical influences reached her from outside the convent despite the enclosure. This collection, edited by Robert Kendrick, is vol. 87 in A-R Editions' series Recent Researches in Music of the Baroque Era. Her other surviving volume includes both old-fashioned but splendid eight-voice settings of psalms and Magnificats and more modern vocal concerti for two or more voices, sometimes combined with violins. There are also dialogues in which single voices or groups of voices answer each other, as in the five-voice motet "O caeli cives" (Oh citizens of heaven; MTA, vol. 2, pp. 117–38), in which three sopranos represent heavenly beings who answer the questions of the shepherds, two earthly tenors. Her publications end in 1650, perhaps because of her added responsibilities, first as abbess and then as prioress. Also, in the 1660s the new archbishop, Alfonso Litta, took a very harsh view of nuns' music, and publication might have been unwise. Cozzolani is now regarded as one of the leading composers of Milan in the seventeenth century, regardless of gender.

Caterina Assandra (fl. 1609–1619), from the Benedictine convent of S. Agata in Lomello, near Milan, was also in touch with the latest developments in musical style and, like Isabella Leonarda later, studied with a male teacher, Benedetto Rè, *maestro di cappella* at the cathedral in Pavia. Her first volume of music has been lost, but her second collection of motets (Milan, 1609) is similar in style to Lodovico Viadana's well-known *Concerti ecclesiastici* of 1602. A motet by Assandra appears in each of Rè's volumes (1611 and 1618), and two motets were reprinted in German anthologies as well. Her motet for two sopranos, bass, and basso continuo appears in MTA, vol. 1, pp. 336–40. The bass voice mainly doubles the continuo line and could be omitted in convent use. The text, expressing love for Jesus in the strongly affective emotions characteristic of much religious poetry of the time, may be by Assandra herself.

There were two Ursuline composers, Isabella Leonarda (1620–1704) and Maria Xaveria Peruchona (ca. 1652–ca. 1709), both from Novara. Peruchona studied with two male teachers before joining the Collegio of Sant' Orsola in Galliate, but she probably also had at least informal studies or contact with her famous townswoman, Isabella Leonarda. Only a single volume of Peruchona's music survives, *Sacri concerti de motetti a una, due, tre, e quattro voci, parte con violini, e parte senza* (Sacred concertos of motets for one, two, three, and four voices, some with violins and some without). Like music of many of the other nun composers, her compositions often call for bass and tenor parts. The motet in MTA (vol. 2, pp. 232–47), "Quid pavemus sorores" (What do we fear, sisters), opens with a long bass solo, which immediately raises the problem of performance in a convent, where male singers were not available. Although a common solution was to play the bass voice on an instrument (and it often follows the continuo line closely), in this work the text is essential as it states the central problem to be answered later in the piece. In this case an alto might have sung the line an octave higher.

Isabella Leonarda published over two hundred works in twenty volumes, making her the most prolific of all the nun composers. The earliest compositions were two dialogues for alto, tenor, and basso continuo, which appeared in 1640 in a collection compiled by Gasparo Casati, Leonarda's teacher and *maestro di cappella* of the Novara cathedral. It was common practice for a teacher to introduce works of a maturing student by including them in his own publication. Although Leonarda's first two independently published volumes have been lost, her printed music from 1670 on is extant. A gap of several years in her published output might indicate that she had ceased composing for a time, but her style gives no evidence of a creative hiatus. Rather, like her younger contemporary Arcangelo Corelli, she probably selected pieces for publication from works she had already composed, a supposition borne out by the neatly balanced arrangement of the works within her volumes. In 1693 she published twelve church sonatas (eleven trio sonatas and one solo sonata), the earliest volume of instrumental works by a woman to have survived complete.

Leonarda's family was of the minor nobility and had strong church ties. Two of her brothers were churchmen at the Novara cathedral, and two or three sisters were nuns in her order. She entered the Company of Saint Ursula at the age of sixteen, and her first music was published four years later. She eventually rose to administrative office, and the title pages of her publications chronicle her successive titles of *madre, madre superiora, madre vicaria* (perhaps a provincial administrator), and finally *consigliera* (counselor). The Company of Saint Ursula (Collegio di Sant' Orsola) was founded to educate girls. In Novara it may have been associated with a school in which the girls could have received musical training, but since it was dissolved during the Napoleonic era, with most of its records destroyed and its library scattered, its actual organization and mission are still unknown. No manuscript music survives. Leonarda's strong personal devotion to the Virgin Mary is indicated in the unusual double dedications of her works to the Virgin and to a human dedicatee (from city officials in Novara to Emperor Leopold I). She may well have written many of her motet texts, as the very personal text of "Quam dulcis es" from Op. 13 suggests. In it she addresses Mary directly:

> How sweet you are, how dear, my loving heart! O holy Mother.
>
> . . . .
>
> If I sing, if I make sounds, they are songs through you.
> With the music I give you, you take me back again.
> I fashion melodious accents so that my harmonies magnify you.
> Therefore my music is always wholly yours, Virgin Mary. Amen.[18]

Like this piece, many of Leonarda's vocal works use two violins and continuo to accompany the voice. This combination, the "church trio," survived to the end of the eighteenth century as a common and practical instrumental grouping in much church music.

All of Leonarda's vocal volumes included pieces that required tenor and/or bass voices. Even the books that are entirely for solo voice (Opp. 12, 14, 15, 17, 20) include works for bass. Leonarda probably revised works originally written for the nuns to make the published volumes useful outside convents. Although it seems possible that the convent hired extra singers for special occasions (a practice also found in other church institutions), church policy strongly opposed such a practice for nuns. Other adaptations, such as using instruments for the lowest parts or transposing bass parts up an octave to be sung in the alto range, were known in other convents.

Most of Leonarda's music is written in the highly expressive dramatic, sectional style favored in the mid-seventeenth century (for her *Messa Prima* from Op. 18, see HAMW, pp. 41–56). In the Credo of this Mass, tempo changes, even within sections, are used for text expression. The word "Crucifixus" (He was crucified) is marked *adagio* and is floridly set, but the next phrase, "etiam pro nobis" (also for us), is marked *spiritoso* (animated), a term Leonarda uses frequently. The syllabic text setting also increases the animation, to express joy that the sacrifice was "for us." The violins echo both emotions. Some dynamics are marked; see the word *piano* at measures 94 and 108. Occasional tutti and solo markings make clear that this is truly a choral work, which seems to be a rarity among the surviving works of seventeenth-century nuns.

Copies of Leonarda's works are to be found in libraries in northern Europe as well as in Italy. Sébastian de Brossard (1655–1730) owned several of her collections (which he gave to France's Bibliothèque Nationale), and he thought highly of them. At the time Beethoven was growing up in Bonn there was a set of partbooks for one of her Masses in the court library inventory, though by then the music was too old-fashioned to be used. Long after her death Leonarda's works were known to Fétis and Gerber, and her name appears in both of their biographical dictionaries.

The Venetian Conservatories

Among the most remarkable institutions in seventeenth- and eighteenth-century Europe were the four *ospedali,* or conservatories, of Venice: the Ospedale della Pietà, dei Mendicanti, degli Incurabili, and dei Derelitti (or l'Ospedaletto). They cared for many persons in need, including orphaned or abandoned boys and girls, as did charitable institutions in other cities. In the Venetian institutions, girls who showed musical talent were given remarkable educations, apparently because music performed by the children had proved useful to encourage the giving of alms. Similar institutions in Naples and elsewhere provided musical training for boys only.

In the seventeenth and eighteenth centuries, money to run the institutions was raised by both private donations and public funds (such as gondola rental fees and the sale of indulgences). Furthermore, the alms collections financed dowries for the girls who married, a remarkably enlightened concern at a time when a respectable marriage without a dowry was nearly impossible. Girolamo Miani (St. Emiliani), the Venetian nobleman who founded the Ospedaletto, believed in teaching the poor and considered the arts important in their education. Thus, by the mid-sixteenth century the girls at the Ospedaletto received sufficient musical training to perform the daily Offices at the institution, and by 1600 about forty girls were admitted into a special program to learn music.[19]

By the early seventeenth century, music had become important in all four institutions, each of which had its own choir and orchestra of girls. Famous musicians (for example, Antonio Vivaldi at the Pietà) were employed as teachers. Each institution presented concerts of both instrumental and vocal music, which visitors from all over Europe came to hear. The rigorous curriculum took ten years to complete. At the end of this time the most accomplished could remain in the institution as licensed *maestrae.* This gave the musically talented woman an alternative to marriage: a teaching (and performing) career in an institution that was not a convent. The teaching was shared between outside masters and the *maestrae*. Sometimes the *maestrae* were celebrated artists, well known to the public through their performances at the *ospedali* concerts, though they never toured in the outside world. Vivaldi wrote at least twenty-two violin concertos to display the virtuosity of Maestra Anna Maria della Pietà, which were heard only in the concerts of that institution. Incidentally, her name illustrates the use of the title of an institution or instrument as a surname for a foundling.

An alternative for a woman of the *coro* (ensemble) who was not a *maestra* was to remain as a permanent member of the group as a singer or instrumentalist. Lists from recently discovered archives of the Pietà give information about the size of the *cori* in the eighteenth century, which ranged from thirty to seventy girls and young women. Even as late as 1807 the Pietà had "thirteen singers, six violinists, three violists, thirteen students of violin, six cellists, five organists, four horn-players, an apprentice vocal soloist, and a copyist."[20]

The central instrumental form cultivated in the conservatory concerts was the concerto: hundreds were written for soloists accompanied by string orchestra and continuo, using almost every instrument of the period (except organ and harpsichord) in solo roles. The performances clearly demonstrated that women could perform on any instrument, a fact mentioned with delight and surprise by many visitors. Choral music was also performed in the conservatories, including much liturgical music, a valuable and virtually unexplored repertoire for treble voices. Some of the music written by Galuppi, Hasse, Porpora, and Vivaldi for the conservatories exists in two versions: one for treble voices only, and another that includes tenor and bass voices. There was music in the conservatory libraries that called for male voices, but it was sung entirely by women, sometimes with the lower parts transposed up an octave and sometimes with instruments performing the low parts. There is no record that men were ever hired to sing at the Venetian *ospedali,* and the markings on many performance parts confirm that the performers were all women. This is another indication of the horror with which the church viewed mixing male and female voices.

Oratorio provided edifying religious recreation in the operatic style during Lent, when the theaters were closed. Although in other parts of Italy oratorios were often performed for audiences of all-male confraternities (religious clubs for laymen), in Venice they were written for the female conservatory students to perform for mixed public audiences. The great popularity of the conservatory oratorios may be judged by the fact that the libretti for more than two hundred of them have survived.

There were restrictions for students educated in these institutions. If a conservatory musician left to marry, she had to agree not to perform in public, at least not in Venice; even if she became a nun, she had to go to a convent outside the Republic of Venice. The violinist Anna Maria della Pietà could continue a performing career only by staying as a *maestra* at the institution. Maddalena Lombardini, who was educated at the Mendicanti, was an exception to this rule. She achieved a distinguished international reputation, performing in Paris, London, Dresden, and as far away as Russia.

Maddalena Lombardini, later Sirmen (1745–1785), was a virtuoso violinist and the most famous composer trained in the Venetian conservatories. Her parents were impoverished aristocrats who had her admitted to the Ospedale dei Mendicanti at the age of seven. During her fourteen-year stay at the conservatory, she was granted special permission to leave occasionally to study with Giuseppe Tartini (1692–1770). An early critical notice she received as an adult performer was from Quirino Gasparini, who wrote:

> She won the hearts of all the people of Turin with her playing. . . . I wrote to old Tartini last Saturday telling him the good news. It will make him all the happier, since this student of his plays his violin compositions with such perfection that it is obvious she is his descendant.[21]

At twenty-one, Lombardini was a licensed *maestra* at the conservatory, so she had to ask permission from the Board of Governors when she decided to marry and to pursue a musical career in the outside world. She married violinist Ludovico Sirmen in 1767, and they toured together. In London she performed her own violin concerti, was a member of the Italian opera orchestra, and even took leading roles as a singer in works by Pergolesi and Gluck. Other successes were as a violin soloist in Paris at the Concerts Spirituels in 1768–1769 and again in 1785, when she performed a concerto by Viotti in which the most modern violin techniques were exemplified. She was enormously successful as a composer. Leopold Mozart considered her concertos "beautifully composed," and her works were published in France, England, the Netherlands, Germany, and Austria. Many of her works were still in print sixty years after her death, some having gone through as many as five editions. The violin concertos and chamber music she composed display the violin with brilliant virtuosity in the new style of the early Classical period. According to family archives, the daughter of Maddalena Lombardini Sirmen married a distant relative of the seventeenth-century composer Isabella Leonarda.

Until recently it was believed that Lombardini Sirmen was the only composer educated at the *ospedali,* but evidence of several other composers has been found, though only a little of their music has survived. Some were foundlings, such as soprano Agata della Pietà, violinist and organist Michielina della Pietà, and violinist and contralto Santa della Pietà (a student of Anna Maria della Pietà and her successor as director of the orchestra in about 1740). Some were day students accepted at the schools, like composers Vicenta da Ponte and Maria Verger at the Pietà. Surely the Pietà was unique in Europe at that time as a place where a foundling could have such a career.

Opera Singers

Except in France, opera in the seventeenth and eighteenth centuries was dominated by Italian singers. The careers of hundreds of women singers are documented, although there was competition from the castrati for high-voice roles. Baroque opera typically used high voices for most of the roles, regardless of gender, so the hero was commonly a mezzo-soprano or an alto, and could be either a castrato or a woman. The contralto Francesca Bertolli, one of Handel's singers, was described in London in 1729 as "a very genteel

FIGURE 5.1. Faustina Bordoni. Portrait by Rosalba Carriera (1675–1757) in the Civici Musei Veneziani d'Arte e di Storia, Venice. Photo by Fotoflash di Zennaro Elisabetta. Used by permission.

Actress, both in Men's and Women's Parts." On the other hand, seventeenth-century Venetian operas often used a male tenor to sing the role of a comic old woman. The gender of characters in opera, as in Elizabethan spoken drama, in which boys played the women's roles, was sufficiently ambiguous to facilitate the disguise plots that the audiences of the time relished.

Women opera singers were usually privately trained, as was the case with Faustina Bordoni (later Hasse, 1700–1781). She was from a noble Venetian family, which was unusual for a female professional musician. Her family background ensured that she did not suffer the moral problems associated with sponsorship by a nobleman (a common pattern for French actresses and singers) or need to worry about her reputation. Her family's position also assured Bordoni an excellent education. Her musical talent was recognized early, and she studied with the singer Antonio Bernachi, the aristocrat-composer Benedetto Marcello, and Michelangelo Gasparini, brother of one of the important teachers at the Pietà. Although part of her education was obtained as a day student at one of the *ospedali,* she was allowed to begin her career in Venice, where she made her debut at age sixteen.[22] She was soon an international star, singing for very high fees in other Italian cities as well as in Munich and Vienna. She went to London in the 1720s, where she sang for Handel for nearly a decade. Although her family name was distinguished, she was often referred to merely as Faustina, a first-name-only form of address common in the theatrical world.

In 1730 Faustina married the composer Johann Adolph Hasse, in whose operas she had been a great success. Both were hired at the court of Dresden, where she was paid twice as much as he. Their two daughters became singers, though they were not superstars like their parents. The Hasses were able to retire with financial security to Vienna and later to Venice.

FROM THE *GRAND SIÈCLE* TO THE REVOLUTION IN FRANCE

The latter half of the seventeenth century in France began the "great century" of Louis XIV, during which Jean-Baptiste Lully was the monarch of French music. Among Lully's innovations was the use of professional female dancers on the stage in 1681, replacing the aristocratic amateurs of earlier French productions. The stunning performances of de La Fontaine, Pasant, Carré, and Leclercq brought women permanently onto the French stage as professional *danseuses.* The French did not care for the castrato voice, so treble roles in French opera were sung by women. As Le Cerf said, "A third of the leading roles in the operas of Lully are those of ordinary tenors; our women are always women; our basses sing the roles of Kings, Magicians, solemn and older Heroes; and our tenors and *hautes-contres* are the young gallant heroes and the amorous gods."[23]

The singing of French nuns at convents like the Feuillants in Paris and the Abbey of Longchamps was much praised, but no French nun composers are known. Nuns also sang outside the convent walls, as soloists in liturgical music at the chapel of Versailles. Even more surprising, laywomen sang sacred solos both in convents and at Versailles, where Anne-Renée Rebel and her two daughters sang regularly for the King's Mass, as did Louise Couperin, a cousin of François Couperin *le grand*. François's eldest daughter, Marie-Madeleine Couperin, was a musical nun, probably an organist, at the Royal Abbey of Maubisson.

The Concerts Spirituels were founded in 1725 to perform instrumental music and sacred choral works at the Salle des Suisses of the Tuileries Palace during Lent and on other religious holidays when the opera was closed (hence the name). The grand motets with Latin texts performed at these concerts were some of the earliest sacred works to enter the concert hall, and the choir included women. Women also performed as solo singers and instrumentalists. Among the performers were harpists Anne-Marie Steckler Krumpholz (who also had a brilliant career in England after the Revolution) and Countess Stéphanie-Félicité de Genlis, violinists Mme. Gautherot and Maddalena Lombardini Sirmen, many harpsichordists (and, later in the century, fortepianists), and singers. Many works by women were also heard in the Concerts Spirituels.

Women were active in the business of engraving and publishing music in France, and young girls could be apprenticed in the craft of engraving. One such businesswoman was Louise Roussel, who married the violinist Jean-Marie Leclair and engraved and published much of his music, as well as works of many other composers. She came under suspicion (though she was apparently innocent) when Leclair was murdered with a sharp object that might have been an engraver's tool. Frequently women were partners in business with their husbands and were therefore quite prepared to take over the shop when they became widows. In the important Boivin firm, publisher François Boivin married Elizabeth Ballard, who worked with him in the shop. Her father was the music printer Jean-Baptiste-Christophe Ballard, who represented the fifth generation of another important publishing house. Women in the family had been active in the Ballard business since its founding, so Elizabeth undoubtedly learned the profession as she was growing up. When her husband died in 1733, she ran the Boivin company for twenty years, during which time the value of the stock skyrocketed. In the Erard family (more noted for piano and harp building), Marie-Françoise Erard and Catherine-Barbé Erard Marcous were active as publishers from 1798 to 1833.

Aristocratic Frenchwomen learned to play the "feminine instruments"—lute, harp, harpsichord, or, later in the century, piano—or to sing. Some reached a high level of artistry; others remained inept. The number of serious amateurs created a market for music teachers (a few of whom were women), however, especially since it was the custom for dedicated, wealthy dilettantes to have daily lessons. Lady amateurs, as well as some professional singers, published numerous songs of varying quality in fashionable collections or in journals such as the *Mercure de France*. The two most impressive women composers in France before the Revolution, in terms of the quality as well as the quantity of their surviving works, were the Parisian Elizabeth-Claude Jacquet de la Guerre and the Italian-born Antonia Bembo, both of whom were writing in the late seventeenth and early eighteenth centuries.

Elizabeth-Claude Jacquet de la Guerre[24]

For four years a wonder has appeared here. She sings at sight the most difficult music. She accompanies herself, and accompanies others who wish to sing, at the harpsichord, which she plays in a manner that cannot be imitated. She composes pieces, and plays them in all the keys asked of her . . . and she is still only ten years old.[25]

The prodigy described in this review is Elizabeth Jacquet (1665–1729), daughter of the French organist Claude Jacquet and his wife, Anne de la Touche. Both parents were musicians from families of performers, teachers, and, in the case of the Jacquets, harpsichord builders. Elizabeth took her first lessons with her father, a harpsichord and organ teacher. By the time she made her Versailles debut in 1673 she was well prepared to accept the offer from Mme de Montespan, the king's mistress, to reside at Versailles. There Elizabeth performed and completed her general education, perhaps with Mme de Maintenon (the governess of Montespan's children by the king and later his secret wife). In 1684, probably aged eighteen, Elizabeth married Marin de la Guerre, an organist and harpsichord teacher, and moved back to Paris. She maintained her contacts with the court without having to live there, enjoying the best of both worlds.

Marriage did not end professional activities for La Guerre. She wrote a ballet (now lost), which was performed at Versailles, and a successful opera, *Céphale et Procris*. A score of this work, edited by Wanda Griffiths, is vol. 88 in A-R Editions' series Recent Researches in the Music of the Baroque Era. In 1687 she published a book of harpsichord pieces that included several suites of French dances, unmeasured preludes, chaconnes, and toccatas. In some movements she exhibits the marriage of French and Italian styles, also found in music of François Couperin *le grand*, her contemporary. An unmeasured Prelude, Allemande, and Chaconne from the A-minor suite in this volume is available in MTA, vol. 2, pp. 293–99. A second set of harpsichord pieces, which appeared in 1707, includes "La Flamande," an elegant allemande. Both the 1687 and the 1707 allemandes are fully marked with the French symbols for little embellishments (*agréments*), and the one from 1707 is followed by a *double,* or variation, on each of the sections (HAMW, pp. 59–62). Both the Chaconne of 1687 (HAMW, pp. 63–65) and that of 1707 are variation dance forms in triple time, in which the first couplet returns between each new statement, combining variation and rondeau principles in a characteristic French manner.

La Guerre also wrote violin solo and trio sonatas in about 1695, within five years of the first such music in France.[26] She published three volumes of cantatas in the first wave of French cantata production (the first printed collections appeared in 1706, La Guerre's first volume in 1708). Her first two books are unique in France in that the texts are based on biblical stories, with three of the twelve on women: *Esther, Susanne et les vieillards* (Susannah and the elders), and *Judith.* The mythological subjects of cantatas in the third volume are more typical of French taste. The first piece in this volume is *Semelé,* based on the Greek myth of Semele, the mistress of Zeus, whose desire to see her lover destroys her (see HAMW, pp. 66–76). The last air, as in most French cantatas, is the moral of the story (often a rather cynical one, although not in this case). The cantata calls for one singer, although the text alternates between the narrator and the protagonist, which is typical of the French form. Although many of La Guerre's cantatas are for singer and continuo only, this one is "avec Simphonie," that is, with an instrumental part (violin or violins in unison, with optional flute in the second air) in addition to the basso continuo. The violin plays the prelude and the interludes between the airs, and forms a duet with the singer in all but the last air. The instrumental pieces in La Guerre's cantatas are often vividly descriptive, as in the agitated prelude to the accompanied recitative "Mais quel bruit étonnant" (But what an astonishing noise), in which the violin and voice alternately portray the thunder and lightning of Zeus's appearance.

Jacquet de la Guerre was widowed in 1704, and her only son, a young musical prodigy, apparently died at about the same time. In her years of widowhood she was professionally active, and many of her publications come from the period after her bereavement. She performed publicly at the popular fair theatres, for which she wrote some songs, and gave concerts in her home. Her last known work (now lost) was a choral Te Deum celebrating Louis XV's recovery from smallpox. Such a work would only have been commissioned from a composer of undoubted importance. At her death in 1729 a medal was struck in her honor, and Evrard Titon du Tillet wrote:

> She had a very great genius for composition, and excelled in vocal music the same as in instrumental; . . . One can say that never had a person of her sex had such talents as she for the composition of music, and for the admirable manner in which she performed it at the harpsichord and on the organ. . . .[27]

La Guerre apparently never left France, but her music was known in Germany. She performed for Maximilian Emanuel II, Elector of Bavaria, when he visited Paris in 1712, and dedicated the mythological cantatas to him (see *Semelé*). Walther's German *Lexikon* (1732) has a longer article for La Guerre than for François Couperin *le grand*. Although her rediscovery took longer than Couperin's, today she is probably the woman composer of the period best known to modern audiences, through performances of her harpsichord works and cantatas and several fine recordings. Many of her cantatas and her trio sonatas, along with her harpsichord music, are now available in modern editions.

Antonia Bembo

Antonia Padoani, later Bembo (ca. 1643–ca.1715), was born in Venice, the child of doctor Giacomo Padoani and Diana Paresco. By 1654 she was a student of Francesco Cavalli, as Barbara Strozzi had been some years earlier. Although she was not of noble birth, she married a Venetian nobleman, Lorenzo Bembo, in 1659. She bore Lorenzo three children: Andrea, Giacomo, and Diana. Sometime before 1676 she left her sons with her husband and her daughter at the convent of San Bernardo of Murano, and went to Paris with an unidentified person or persons. There she describes herself as a Venetian noblewoman, "abandoned by the man [or the person] who drew me from Venice."[28] She continued contacts with Venice in such matters as the debt owed for the care of her daughter at the convent of San Bernardo and the settling of accounts by means of the jewels she had left there. She also corresponded with a friend at the convent, through whom we know that she was given refuge at the Petite Union Chrétienne des Dames de Saint Chaumont, in the parish of Notre Dame de Bonne Nouvelle in Paris.[29]

Five volumes of manuscript scores dating from the late 1690s to after 1707, all but one dedicated to King Louis XIV, are now in France's Bibliothèque Nationale. In the prefaces to these works, Bembo says that the king had heard her sing and, learning of her present distress, gave her a pension and found shelter for her in "a holy retreat until such a time as the occasion presented itself for me to place myself in some more distinguished lodging." This move apparently never happened.[30]

A few pieces of Bembo's music recently became available in a modern publication. "Amor mio" (My love), "Tota pulcra es" (Thou are fair, text from the *Song of Solomon*), and "Ha, que l'absence est un cruel martire" (Ah, absence is a cruel martyrdom) from her first manuscript volume, *Produzioni armoniche,* illustrate her different treatments of texts in three languages, Italian, Latin, and French (see MTA, vol. 2, pp. 205–16). Her music shows the influence on this Italian-trained composer of the French style with which she became acquainted in her exile. In *Produzioni armoniche* she includes forty-one vocal compositions, of which five set Latin texts, a pair of couplets are in French, and the rest are in Italian. Most are songs for soprano (the range is often quite high) and continuo, perhaps written for her own voice; they also include a few duets, a trio (a cantata for the marriage of the Duchess of Burgundy), and a few pieces with added violins. The continuo parts frequently explore low ranges, even descending to a low A, which would indicate a seven-string French viola da gamba as the accompanying bass instrument. Some of the texts are religious, some are in praise of the monarch, and some seem to contain more personal emotions, such as in the da capo aria "Habbi pietà di me, non mi lasciar morir" (Have mercy on me, do not let me die; see Example 5.2). There is an unusual double key signature (F# minor and F minor), apparently so that the performer could choose the key in which she wanted to perform the piece. In the following example only the signature of F# minor appears.

In her last works Bembo used increasingly developed and sophisticated techniques in large-scale pieces. She wrote two Te Deums, one for a *petit choeur* of two sopranos and a bass, accompanied by two violins and figured bass (the church trio instrumentation), one a vast *grand motet* for five-part chorus. Her opera *L'Ercole amante* (Hercules as lover, 1707) is based on the same text her teacher Cavalli had used more than forty years earlier to celebrate the marriage of Louis XIV in 1662. Although a composer of that time would not have written an opera without a performance in view, we do not know why she composed this work, why she set that particular text, or even whether the piece was ever performed.

Bembo's last known work is a setting of French translations of seven Penitential Psalms. The progression from the Italianate style of her first volume to the increasing use of French style traits in the Te Deum and the psalms suggests that Bembo had opportunities to hear music of her contemporaries, either within the convent in which she had taken refuge or through outside performances. French translations of the psalms were very fashionable in the court at this time. The translations Bembo used had been made by the painter and musician Elisabeth-Sophie Chéron (1648–1711). Although Chéron had renounced her Huguenot religion to continue in court life, these serious psalms probably had special meaning for her, and Bembo responded to the intense texts with expressive musical settings.

EXAMPLE 5.2. Antonia Bembo, opening aria from "Habbi pietà," *Produzione armoniche,* MS, pp. 157–58. Bibliothèque Nationale, Paris. Used by permission. Text: "Have pity on me, do not let me die."

EXAMPLE 5.3. Antonia Bembo, Venus's first aria from *L'Ercole amante,* MS score, p. 166. Bibliothèque Nationale, Paris. Used by permission.

COMPOSERS OF THE GERMAN ARISTOCRACY

The musical education of girls in the Lutheran parts of Germany in the eighteenth century was intended to prepare them to sing chorales and other spiritual songs in the church congregation and at home in order to provide a Christian atmosphere for their children. For a daughter of an aristocratic family, musical skills were at the bottom of the list of accomplishments for which her tutor and governess were responsible. The aim was that music should be cultivated just enough so that the girl "could do little airs and Lieder . . . without many runs and variations."[31] Nevertheless, in households in which the family valued music as more than part of good Christian domesticity or a social skill enhancing marriageability, children of both sexes could—and did—receive much better musical educations than this wary minimum.

Anna Amalia, Princess of Prussia

When Anna Amalia, Princess of Prussia, was growing up in the court of her music-hating father, the soldier-king Frederick William I, she received little musical instruction, and formal study was possible only after her father died. Yet thanks to the clandestine aid of Queen Sophia Dorothea, many of the king's fourteen children developed into musicians. The three most musical were Princess Wilhelmina Sophie (later Margravine of Brandenburg, 1709–1758), the son and heir Frederick (later Frederick the Great, 1712–1786), and the youngest princess, Anna Amalia (1723–1787). The king treated all the children with great cruelty, and in his rages even dragged little Anna Amalia across the room by her hair. Music was the children's secret consolation. Frederick and Wilhelmina both learned the flute and played duets away from their father's watchful eyes; and Frederick gave his little sister Anna Amalia her earliest music lessons, which she always remembered with affection. She learned harpsichord, flute, and violin, and turned to the harpsichord for release from the constant family strife around her.

When the old king died in 1740, Frederick came to the throne, bringing a great throng of musicians into the court with him. What had been forbidden was now richly available. Anna Amalia could at last hear Italian opera, study with cathedral organist Gottlieb Hayne, and devote herself to other pleasant pursuits. Alas, she also met a young army officer with whom she fell deeply and unwisely in love. Her brother was furious and imprisoned her lover for ten years. Anna Amalia was made abbess of a religious community in Quedlinburg, although she could live in her own house in Berlin. Her only joy for the rest of her life was music. In 1758, at the age of thirty-five, she finally began systematic and serious study of music theory and composition, and had an organ built in her home. She hired Johann Philipp Kirnberger, a student of J. S. Bach, as her *Kapellmeister* (music director) and teacher. She learned the techniques of four-voice settings of chorales and of old-fashioned counterpoint, at a time when the music around her was in the *style galant*, elegant, and sentimental. She wrote an opening chorale and chorus for the oratorio *Der Tod Jesu* (The Death of Jesus), which Kirnberger used as models in the theory book he dedicated to her; her brother's court composer, Graun, later set the whole libretto. Her chamber music includes a lovely flute sonata (the first movement is in HAMW, pp. 86–87). This work is more *galant* in style than her other works and might have been written before her studies with Kirnberger. The choice of solo instrument for this sonata was a natural one for a composer in a flute-playing family.

Anna Amalia was an ardent collector of the old music she loved, and she preserved more than six hundred volumes of musical treasures by J. S. Bach, Palestrina, Handel, Telemann, and other composers of the past, as well as works by a few moderns such as C. P. E. Bach. Her collection made a significant contribution to European culture. Except for some items lost in storage during World War II, her library has been housed since the reunification of Germany in Berlin's Deutsche Staatsbibliothek, Musikabteilung, and comprises a priceless heritage. Only a small bundle of her personal compositions remains.

Anna Amalia, Duchess of Saxe-Weimar

In contrast to the Princess of Prussia, with her conservative tastes, the Duchess of Saxe-Weimar, also named Anna Amalia (1739–1807), was dedicated to fostering new developments in both literature and music. Her parents were Philippine Charlotte (a sister of Anna Amalia of Prussia) and Duke Karl I of Brunswick; both valued musical training as part of the excellent education they gave their children. When Anna Amalia married the Duke of Saxe-Weimar, she had need of her good education, for by the age of nineteen she was a widow with two sons to raise. For the next seventeen years she was responsible for running the state as Regent. When her elder son came of age, she turned her energies to artistic and intellectual endeavors, so successfully that Weimar came to be known as the "Court of the Muses." While her aunt Anna Amalia of Prussia had preserved the legacy of the glorious Baroque past in her magnificent library, Anna Amalia of Saxe-Weimar pointed to a future thriving German cultural life. Her court circle planted the seeds of literary romanticism, nourished by rich musical activity.

Throughout her life the duchess pursued intellectual interests, composed music, played the harpsichord and the new fortepiano, and encouraged the most brilliant young poets, playwrights, and musicians of Germany to come to Weimar. Twenty-four-year-old Johann Wolfgang von Goethe came to the court as an advisor and minister of state for the duke and remained under the regency of the duchess. Many plays by Wieland and Goethe were first staged in the Weimar court theatre. Anna Amalia's most successful composition was music for the 1776 production of Goethe's Singspiel *Erwin und Elmire,* which Johann André had set a year earlier. The text of one of the songs in the work, "Das Veilchen," is now best known in Mozart's setting of a decade later.

Artists from many of the great musical families came to Weimar. Johann Ernest Bach, nephew and student of J. S. Bach, was the *Kapellmeister* when

Anna Amalia arrived. She hired Ernest Wilhelm Wolf (who had worked with Hiller in Leipzig) to be her sons' music tutor; he later was her own teacher as well as *Kapellmeister.* His wife, Maria Carolina Benda, was a harpsichordist and singer, a sister of composer Juliane Benda (later Reichardt).

Eighteenth-Century Oratorio Composers of Northern Italy and Vienna

During the reigns of Leopold I (d. 1705), Joseph I (reigned 1705–1711), Charles VI (reigned 1711–1740), and Maria Theresa (reigned 1740–1780), oratorios by several women were performed in Vienna. The composers were the Austrian nun Marianne von Raschenau and the Italians Caterina Benedetta Gratianini, Camilla de Rossi, and Maria Margherita Grimani. In the late eighteenth century, the Viennese composer Marianna von Martines also wrote two oratorios. Raschenau was the *Chormeisterin* (choir director) at the convent of St. Jakob auf der Hülben in Vienna, but of her two oratorios and two secular state works, only the printed libretti from the performances survive. Two oratorios by Gratianini[32] have survived in manuscript: one was "sung before the Highnesses of Brunswick and Modena . . . and wondrously received," according to a note on the score. Camilla de Rossi and Maria Margherita Grimani composed the largest amount of surviving music. Nothing is known about the life of either composer: the manuscripts by Rossi identify her as Roman. Grimani, on the other hand, bears the name of a famous Venetian family, although no documentation has yet been found to connect her with it. All we know is that their music was used in the court at Vienna and, from the cast lists on some of the scores, that some of the best singers of the court participated in the performances.

The oratorios of Rossi, Grimani, and Gratianini are large works in the formal scheme used by Alessandro Scarlatti after 1700. They are divided into two large sections, each introduced by a single-movement or a multimovement *sinfonia*. The two sinfonias of Gratianini's *Santa Teresa* are in MTA, vol. 2, pp. 344–51. Within each half of the oratorio itself are a succession of *da capo* arias alternating with *secco* recitatives. There are occasional duets and usually a final ensemble of soloists. Many of the solos are continuo arias with orchestral ritornelli, while others are accompanied by a larger group of instruments. There is no chorus. The dramatic style resembles that used for opera in the same time period. For example, the scene between Erode (Herod) and Salome from Grimani's *La decollazione di S. Giovanni Battista* (The Beheading of St. John the Baptist) shows the composer's use of contrasting affects for the two characters: Herod as vain and bombastic,

EXAMPLE 5.4. Camilla de Rossi, "Quanto, quanto mi consola un oggetto lontananza," mm. 32–40, from *Santa Beatrice d'Este,* MS score, Musiksammlung, Austrian National Library, Vienna. *Text:* "If by itself hope were so beautiful, what then would be the reward?"

portrayed with repeated sixteenth notes in *stile concitato* (excited style), and Salome pretending naiveté, expressed by a simple dance tune (not the one with which she eventually lures Herod to kill the Saint). Rossi's *Il figliuol prodigo* (The prodigal son) is paced so dramatically that one could easily stage it. According to the title page of the manuscript score, Rossi wrote the libretto herself, and the opening and closing scenes show a dramatic interchange of short recitatives and even recitative ensembles with arias.[33]

The orchestra for all these works consists of strings, harpsichord continuo, and a few other instruments, sometimes used adventurously. The Grimani aria in which Salome convinces Herod to kill John the Baptist, for example, adds an oboe to the orchestra for a seductive affect. Rossi's *Il Sacrifizio di Abramo* (Abraham's sacrifice), composed in 1708, calls for two *chalumeaux* (predecessors of the clarinet) to convey the peaceful affect of Abramo's dream. This was just one year after the instrument had been introduced into the opera in Vienna (its first orchestral use). Rossi also uses instrumental color for characterization: the lute is associated with Isaaco's innocence in *Il Sacrifizio di Abramo,* while trumpets are used for the villain, a military man, in *Santa Beatrice d'Este* (1707). Rossi uses striking key relations and chromaticism for expressive effects, as in the chromatic excerpt from *Santa Beatrice d'Este* shown in Example 5.4.

Among the extant works by Maria Margherita Grimani are two oratorios and an opera, *Pallade e Marte* (Pallas Athena and Mars). All that is known of the composer's connection with any particular place is that her oratorios were performed in Vienna. The opera's manuscript is inscribed "Bologna, April 5, 1713," apparently the time and place of the completion of the work. Performed in Vienna later in 1713 to celebrate the emperor's name day (a prestigious occasion for a composer), the opera is her shortest extant work and calls for only two singers, a soprano and an alto. Its Sinfonia (see HAMW, pp. 79–83) is a miniature Italian overture: a short, brilliant flourish of sound in the opening G major allegro; a largo in the relative minor in sarabande rhythm; and a return to major, a binary-form presto movement in a lively 3/8 meter.

SONG COMPOSERS IN BERLIN AND WEIMAR

The confluence of literary and musical talents in mid-eighteenth-century Berlin and Weimar was conducive to the development of the Lied. Berlin was the center for an aesthetic that called for simple, often strophic songs, with unobtrusive accompaniment (usually for piano), many of them deliberately *volkstümlich* or folklike. *Volkstümlich* songs in Berlin, Leipzig, and Weimar were written for intimate private performances, usually by amateur singers. A more sophisticated style developed in Vienna; more Italianate, it placed greater demands on the singer and included more elaboration of the piano part. Lieder were published in collections of all kinds, and music magazines (a development of the eighteenth century) often included the latest new songs. Many women composed and published songs, among them Corona Schröter (1751–1802) in Weimar and Juliane Benda, later Reichardt (1752–1783), in Berlin.

Corona Schröter

Corona Schröter grew up in a musical family. Her father, an oboist, taught music to his children: Corona (a singer), Johann Samuel (a pianist), Johann Heinrich (a violinist), and Marie Henriette (a singer). He took the whole family on concert tours to Leipzig, the Netherlands, and England, as a few years later Leopold Mozart would take his *Wunderkinder* Nannerl and Wolfgang. When Corona was thirteen the family moved to Leipzig. Johann Adam Hiller, a leading figure in the musical life of the city, was distressed about the generally poor training of German singers as well as the exclusion of women from choral singing, especially in church. He argued, "If God primarily gave man the splendid talent of producing a melodic tone with his throat in order to praise Him, then it is highly unfair to exclude the other sex, which has received this gift to a great extent from its creator, from worshiping Him too. . . ." To encourage improvement of choral singing, he advocated, "Concert societies and weekly rehearsals could be established . . . with the main focus directed upon the improvement of singing. One should not again, however, make the mistake to exclude women."[34] Hiller founded a singing school in 1771 to which both sexes were admitted. The curriculum included vocal technique, solfège, diction in choral music from operas and oratorios, aria performance, keyboard playing, and Italian. Corona Schröter was his most famous student. When Goethe went to Weimar from Leipzig, he took Schröter to Anna Amalia's court as an actress and a singer. Her closest friends at the Weimar court were the poets Goethe and Schiller. She acted and sang in Goethe's plays, and she composed the incidental music for Goethe's *Die Fischerin* (1782). She also taught singing and drama there in the last two decades of the century.

Schröter published two collections of Lieder, in 1786 and in 1794.[35] The first composer to set Goethe's "Der Erlkönig," she included it in the 1786 collection. It was a stage song in *Die Fischerin,* and was originally sung by the character Dortchen (played by Schröter) to pass the time as she sits by the hearth. Goethe wanted the piece to be a folklike ballad, as if "the singer [had] learned to sing it somewhere by memory."[36] As a stage ballad Schröter's setting is very successful, aiming at an aesthetic goal totally different from that behind Franz Schubert's more famous setting. Not all of Schröter's Lieder are in the *volkstümlich* style of "Der Erlkönig," however, and the piano has much more independence in the songs of her second volume. In "Das Mädchen am Ufer" (The Maid on the Shore), from her first book, the voice and piano parts are notated together on two staves, the normal convention for the early Lied.[37] The piano usually doubles the singer's line, and in this example, there are additional small notes for the pianist. The soprano clef used in the right hand is the normal convention of the period.

EXAMPLE 5.5. Corona Schröter, "Das Mädchen am Ufer," *Fünf und zwanzig Lieder* (Weimar: The author, 1786), p. 14. From the copy in the Anton und Katharina Kippenberg Stiftung, Goethe Museum, Düsseldorf. *Text:* "The ocean was wildly howling; the storm groaned with woe. There sat the maiden weeping; on the hard rock sat she. Far over the ocean's roar she cast her signs and her gaze. Since naught could still her sighs, the echo came back to her."

Juliane Benda Reichardt

The Benda family was one of the largest and most complicated musical dynasties of the late eighteenth century. Juliane (1752–1783) was one of four musical children of the violinist Franz Benda, concertmaster to Frederick the Great. Her grandmother was from the Brixi family of Czech musicians, her aunt Anna was a singer, and she had at least a dozen musician cousins, several of whom were composers. The Benda family was related by marriage to other musical dynasties of Bohemia and Germany, and Juliane's daughter Louise Reichardt was to be a prolific composer of Lieder in the nineteenth century.

When Juliane was only six, her mother died, and she received her music instruction from her father. A young composer named J. F. Reichardt came to Berlin as court *Kapellmeister* in 1775. His first love had been Corona Schröter, who had refused him (and in fact never married). Reichardt heard Juliane Benda sing and play the piano in Berlin, and fell in love with her. Within a year they were married; both were twenty-three years old. Juliane was already composing songs and piano music.[38] She published Lieder in a collection with her husband as well as in musical magazines. In 1782 she published two piano sonatas and seventeen songs that showed great promise for the future. The normal life of a young married woman of the eighteenth century included frequent pregnancies, with their attendant risks, so the births of three children in the seven years of her marriage were not unusual, nor was her early death in 1783, after the birth of the third child. Juliane Benda Reichardt was buried on her thirty-first birthday.

Late-Eighteenth-Century Vienna

In the latter half of the eighteenth century Viennese women composers cultivated many musical forms: concertos and sonatas for piano, chamber music, oratorios, Masses, operas and other large works, and a few symphonies. Women performed as singers, fortepianists (the piano was gradually replacing the harpsichord), harpists, and (a few) violinists. As the piano gained ground, many of its best players were women, and several were also composers. Vienna was also the workplace of the great piano builder Nannette Stein (later Streicher, 1769–1833), who with her younger brother, André Stein, moved their shop to Vienna from Augsburg in the 1790s.

Although the financial problems of the Empress Maria Theresa led to decreased support for the court music that had earlier dominated the Austrian musical scene, a rich musical life was dispersed throughout the city, and the most glorious period in Vienna's musical history was underway. Noble and middle-class homes alike rang with music, and much of the concert life of the city took place in private houses, from the grand events at Baron Gottfried van Swieten's palace to more intimate evenings at the Martines's house. Concert societies sprang up, beginning with Florian Gassmann's Tonkünstler-Sozietät in 1772, providing public concerts modeled on the Concerts Spirituels in France. In the churches, music for the Mass often used large orchestras, and elaborate settings of religious music appeared all over Austria, not just in the Cathedral of St. Stephen in Vienna.

By the end of the eighteenth century there are scattered references to women as soloists in Austrian church music. At the Esterhazy court, for example, solos in Joseph Haydn's Masses were sung by women, among them Thérèse Gassmann (later Rosenbaum), who was also the soprano soloist for the first Austrian performance of the choral version of Haydn's *The Seven Last Words.* Michael Haydn's wife, Maria Magdalena Lipp Haydn (daughter of the court organist), was hired by the archbishop in Salzburg as a soloist for both sacred and secular music.

Marianna von Martines[39]

The most prolific composer among Viennese women of the second half of the eighteenth century was Marianna von Martines (1744–1812), who left the largest extant body of works. She composed Masses and other liturgical music (mostly in symphonic style), oratorios, cantatas, concertos for piano and orchestra, sonatas, a symphony, arias, and other vocal works—almost every genre of the period except opera. Of her more than two hundred known works, only about seventy survive.

Born into a family of minor nobility, Martines was the daughter of the master-of-ceremonies to the papal nuncio and lived in a house on the Michaelplatz. The building presented an interesting microcosm of Viennese society. On the first floor lived the Dowager Princess Esterhazy (mother of Joseph Haydn's patron). On each higher floor, seemingly, the social level of the occupants declined. The Martines family lived on the third floor in a spacious apartment that also housed the court poet and opera librettist Pietro Metastasio. The attic apartments were rented to poorer tenants, tradespeople, and music teachers. In 1750 a young fellow who had just been dismissed from the choir school at St. Stephen's took an attic room there: his name was Joseph Haydn.

The bachelor Metastasio took a great interest in the Martines family, especially in the education of the children. Struck by Marianna's talent, he arranged, by the time the little girl was ten years old, for her to study singing with the great Italian opera singer and composer Niccolò Porpora; he also paid for harpsichord lessons with Joseph Haydn, the young man in the attic room who also accompanied her singing lessons. Marianna showed talent for composition, which she studied with Hasse (Faustina Bordoni's husband, who had now retired to Vienna) and court composer Giuseppe Bonno. Charles Burney, the English music historian, heard her sing in 1772 and praised both her singing and her compositions. Her cantatas for soprano and orchestra show something of her capabilities as a singer.[40]

By the 1760s Martines was writing large church works. Four symphonic Masses, six motets, and three litanies for choir and orchestra are extant. It has been suggested that the "Christe" of her Mass No. 1 in D Major may have been known to the young Mozart and that his 1768 Mass, K. 139, is modeled on it.[41] One of her Masses, probably her third, was performed at St. Michael's Church, the court chapel, in 1761. It is a large work (more than one hundred and fifty pages of score) with soprano, alto, and tenor solos; four-part chorus; and an orchestra of two natural trumpets, two oboes, two flutes, violins, and organ continuo. She composed her fourth Mass in 1765. When Emperor Joseph II came to the throne in 1780, his "reforms" led to a simpler style of church music, without orchestras, and brought back the old rule against women "speaking" (that is, singing) in church. So Martines wrote no more Masses, although she did make several psalm settings, using Italian translations by the Neapolitan poet who commissioned the compositions. Her *Dixit Dominus* (Latin Vulgate, Psalm 109, The Lord Spake) was written in 1774 for the Accademia Filarmonica in Bologna, which in 1773 had elected her its first female member.[42] *Dixit Dominus* is a large work for orchestra (including two natural trumpets, two oboes, two flutes, violins, and continuo) and five-part (SSATB) chorus. The work breaks the psalm text into seven contrasting sections, with some segments for soloists, and in the second and third parts the bass line (cello/bass) is without organ.[43]

By this time Martines is spoken of as a pianist rather than as a harpsichordist. Mozart probably wrote his Piano Concerto in D major (K. 175) for her to perform in Dr. Mesmer's garden in 1773.[44] Her keyboard music was mostly for piano, although the Sonatas in A Major and in E Major were published in a harpsichord anthology in 1765. The same two sonatas were included in a piano anthology some seventy years after her death, when they were reedited with the dynamics of piano music.[45] The first movement of the Sonata in A Major (HAMW, pp. 90–93) shows rococo embellishment of the thematic material, with a development section that exploits spicy little mordents and trills in bright, idiomatic passages split between the hands and alternating with roulades of triplets (see mm. 16–26).

Martines was active as a performer, particularly as a pianist, and was a prolific composer, but she never held a professional appointment, which would have been unacceptable for a woman of her social class. She and her sister provided a household and care for their family friend and benefactor Metastasio until his death. He wrote the libretti for two of her oratorios, *Santa Elena al Calvario* (St. Helen at Calvary, 1781) and *Isacco figura del redentore* (Isaac, Symbol of the Redeemer, 1792). The latter was scored for an orchestra with a full string section, timpani, and a Classical-period wind section: pairs of trumpets, horns, oboes, flutes, and bassoons. A performance by the Tonkünstler-Sozietät used a large orchestra and a choir of about two hundred singers.

In 1782 Metastasio died, and the Martines siblings inherited his large estate. Their home was a center for weekly musical soirées, with the most distinguished musicians in town as guests and performers. Haydn and Mozart were often there, and Mozart wrote four-hand piano sonatas to perform with Marianna. Foreign visitors, such as the tenor Michael Kelly, made sure to go to these events when they visited Vienna. In 1796 Martines opened a singing school in her home and produced singers of professional quality. Many fine female singers—amateur and professional, choristers as well as soloists—were trained in such private schools.

Martines's last known public appearance coincided with that of her old teacher Haydn; they both came to hear Salieri conduct Haydn's *Die Schöpfung* (The Creation) on March 27, 1808. Martines and her sister, neither of whom ever married, died within two days of each other in 1812. Although Martines held no professional posts, she was a thoroughly trained and serious musician and a significant composer. Her musical evenings were important events in the cultural life of Vienna during its golden age, and her own performances were splendid. She took teaching seriously and in this way promoted the continued vitality of the cultural life she had helped to shape.

In the nineteenth century, when most of her music was forgotten, Martines's creative contributions were downgraded (usually by persons who had neither seen nor heard them) in the fashionable debates about whether women possessed creativity. In 1844 the publication of Caroline Pichler's memoirs provided ammunition for the negative side of the argument, with spiteful criticism of feminine creativity in general and of Martines in particular.[46] Pichler had been a salonnière of the 1780s whose gatherings competed with those of Martines and Paradis, and the biased memories and aesthetic judgments of her old age should be read with skepticism. Modern musicians and scholars have viewed Martines's accomplishments much more favorably, and the many modern editions of her works now available make it possible to hear and judge the music directly.

Maria Theresia von Paradis

Maria Theresia von Paradis (1759–1824) was born into the family of the royal court secretary of Empress Maria Theresa, for whom the little girl was named. When she suddenly became blind at the age of three, various cures were attempted (including efforts by Dr. Mesmer), but she never regained her sight.[47] The empress provided an annual stipend for her (it was stopped during the reign of Joseph II but was restored by Leopold II), and she was given the best musical education possible, perhaps in the belief that her blindness was an impediment to marriage. Paradis studied piano with Leopold Koželuch, singing with Vincenzo Righini and Antonio Salieri, and composition with Salieri, Carl Friberth, and Abbé Vogler. Her theoretical studies included dramatic composition, harmony, counterpoint, and figured bass. By the age of sixteen, Paradis was astonishing the Viennese public with her talent as a piano virtuoso and singer. Mozart composed a piano concerto for her—probably the one in B-flat major, K. 456—and Salieri wrote for her his only organ concerto.

In 1783 Paradis, her mother, and her friend and librettist Johann Riedinger started a three-year concert tour of Europe. Her 1784 visit to Paris was significant for more than musical reasons, for while there she met

Valentin Haüy, an educator who was soon to open a pioneering school for the blind. In his *Essay on the Education of the Blind*[48] he referred frequently to the methods that had been used to teach Paradis reading, mathematics, geography, and music.

In the 1790s Paradis worked with Riedinger to develop a peg board, on which she could set down her musical compositions, which could then be transcribed by a copyist. Her first extant works are the songs written during her concert tour, *Zwölf Lieder auf ihrer Reise in Musik gesetzt* (1784–1786). "Morgenlied eines armen Mannes" (Morning song of a poor man) is a particularly moving song from this collection (see HAMW, pp. 97–98). Her compositions were not limited to the works that she herself performed. She composed at least five operas and three large cantatas (one in memory of the unfortunate Louis XVI of France), and her dramatic works were performed at major theatres in Vienna. Her last opera, the comic magic-opera *Rinaldo und Alcina,* was produced in Prague in 1797. It is based on Ariosto's *Orlando Furioso,* the same literary source used by Francesca Caccini for *La liberazione di Ruggiero* nearly two hundred years earlier.

Unfortunately, much of Paradis's music has been lost.[49] All that survives of her dramatic works is an excerpt from the Singspiel *Der Schulkandidat* (The School Candidate), a very successful work that had six performances at the Marinelli Theatre in Vienna in 1792–1793. Had Paradis published more of her music, more might have survived, but she responded self-deprecatingly when asked why she had not done so, saying, "Would male fellow artists withdraw from me if I, as a woman—and especially as a blind woman—dared to compete with them?"[50] Among the lost works are two piano concertos, several sonatas, songs, and a piano trio. Though much of her music was no longer known, her name was still so illustrious in our own century that Samuel Dushkin borrowed it for a work that he attributed to her, the *Sicilienne* (see HAMW, pp. 99–100).

Paradis's circle of friends included many musicians, such as the Mozart family, and literary figures, including the novelist and poet Sophie de Laroche (one of whose texts Paradis set in *Zwölf Lieder*). Like Martines before her, Paradis opened a music school (in 1808) in which she taught many outstanding women pianists and accepted both blind and sighted students. The school was noted for its Sunday house-concerts. Paradis was buried in St. Mark's Cemetery, where the site of her grave, like Mozart's in the same cemetery, is unknown.

SUMMARY

In the year 1800 one could look back over the two preceding centuries and see increased roles for women in music in many areas. Women were especially active as opera singers, composers, harpsichordists and pianists, teachers, publishers and engravers, and, in a few instances, violinists. Their ranks included an important instrument builder and even a few impresarios and theatre managers. The various activities of women in music are well documented in Italy, France, Germany, Austria, and England (there especially as performers), although they may have been active in other regions where records have been lost or are still inadequately studied.

Women were active as musicians in convents (whose importance was greatest during the seventeenth century but had fallen sharply by 1800), court venues (which declined after the French Revolution), and the new and growing public concert series. The eighteenth century saw early examples of touring artists such as Maddalena Lombardini Sirmen. Extended musical families provided opportunities for training and networks of related professionals. Husbands, wives, and children (as in the Caccini family) might all work in a court; wives and husbands might be partners in musical businesses, especially publishing. Within an extended family one might also find a wide variety of musical professions, as was the case among relatives of Elizabeth Jacquet de la Guerre. Formally organized educational opportunities for women outside the convent were found first in the Venetian conservatories. Singing schools for both sexes were established in Leipzig and Berlin, and private music schools—for example, those of Martines and Paradis—developed in Vienna and elsewhere.

Although some of the most productive women did not have professional careers in the modern sense, their activities helped shape the whole musical society in which they lived. Neither Barbara Strozzi in the seventeenth century nor Marianna von Martines in the eighteenth performed in public or held official positions of any sort, yet both contributed significantly to their societies. The academies of seventeenth-century Italy and the French and German salons of the eighteenth century provided private forums for artistic work, and often women were leaders in the salons. The expanding activities of noble and middle-class amateurs (of both sexes) enriched musical life in many ways, including the fostering of mixed choral organizations at the end of the eighteenth century.

Women composers, from the seventeenth-century nun Isabella Leonarda to the Viennese laywoman Marianna von Martines in the eighteenth century, wrote Masses and other Catholic service music. They also composed devotional music for use outside the service, opera (Francesca Caccini, for example, in the earliest days of the form), oratorio (especially Italians who were active in early eighteenth-century Vienna), harpsichord music (Elizabeth Jacquet de la Guerre), and piano music. Especially as composers of vocal music, they contributed to almost every form in vogue during their lives—the monodies of the Caccini sisters, the French cantatas of Jacquet de la Guerre, the German Lieder of Corona Schröter and Juliane Benda Reichardt, and, of course, operas. Fewer women composed purely instrumental music, although there are chamber works by Leonarda and Jacquet de la Guerre, violin concertos and chamber music by Lombardini Sirmen, symphonic music by Martines, and even military marches by Anna Amalia of Prussia. Despite the barriers that still existed, many doors to music had opened for women during the seventeenth and eighteenth centuries, and the nineteenth century was to see a further blossoming of their activities.

NOTES

1. The practice of preserving boys' high voices by castration in order to provide trained high voices for polyphonic church music flourished from the mid-sixteenth to the nineteenth century, especially in Italy. The injunction by St. Paul that women should be silent in church was interpreted to mean that they should not even sing there, and by extension that men's and women's voices should not be combined in church music. Male sopranos and altos, falsettists or castrati, soon found that their voices were also in demand on the opera stage, with much greater remuneration. When women were banned from the stage in the Papal States by Sixtus V, castrati were available to take female roles, and male sopranos, mezzos, and altos also sang heroic male and other roles in opera throughout Europe, with the exception of France.

2. In the eighteenth century a Miss Steemson was organist at a parish church in Lancaster, England, and Ann Valentine was organist at St. Margaret's, Leicester. No women musicians appear again in English churches until the mid-nineteenth century. About 1795 a Mrs. Wilbraham published an anthem for high voice and treble instrument (probably violin), performed in Westminster Abbey, but the circumstances are not known.

3. The Council of Trent legislated and Pope Pius V tried to enforce enclosure (*clausura*) of the convents in 1566. This meant the physical separation of nuns from the outside world; nuns could not leave the convent, nor could lay people go inside. Often the only outsiders who could visit them were their parents. Even in their legal status they were to be shut off from the external world. However, the regulations were enforced unevenly, and the nuns themselves found many ways to circumvent them.

4. For a fascinating study of the struggles of the nuns at S. Cristina della Fondazza in Bologna and the tragic fate of composer Lucrezia Vizzana, see Craig Monson, *Disembodied Voices: Music and Culture in an Early Modern Italian Convent* (Berkeley: University of California Press, 1995). Seven of Vizzana's motets, with discussion of her expressive text settings, are in MTA, vol. 1, pp. 264–305.

5. For the contrasting world of Milanese convents, especially S. Radegonda where Claudia Sessa, Claudia Rusca, Chiara Margarita Cozzolani, and Rosa Giacinta Badalla were composing, see Robert L. Kendrick, *Celestial Sirens: Nuns and Their Music in Early Modern Milan* (New York: Clarendon Press, 1996). MTA, vols. 1–2, include works of Sessa, Cozzolani, and Badalla.

6. MTA, vol. 1, pp. 234–52.

7. Some of her religious music is now available in modern editions. See "Suggestions for Further Reading" at the end of this chapter.

8. Giulio Caccini, dedication to *L'Euridice* (1600), translated in Oliver Stunk, *Source Readings in Music History* (New York: W.W. Norton, 1950); and Vincenzo

Giustiniani, *Discorso sopra la musica* (1628), ed. and trans. Carol MacClintock, Musicological Studies and Documents 9 (Rome: American Institute of Musicology, 1962), pp. 70–71.

9. Maria Giovanna Mesera, "Una musicista fiorentina del seicento: Francesca Caccini," *La Rassegna musicale* 14/5 (May 1941): 197; *The New Grove Dictionary of Music and Musicians,* s.v. "Caccini [Giulio Romano]," by H. Wiley Hitchcock; and *The Norton/Grove Dictionary of Women Composers,* s.v. "Caccini, Francesca" and "Caccini, Settimia," by Suzanne G. Cusick.

10. Three secular pieces and five works on religious themes, all from Caccini's *Primo libro,* are included in MTA, vol. 1, pp. 234–63.

11. *The Norton/Grove Dictionary of Women Composers,* s.v. "Caccini, Francesca."

12. One copy is in Bologna at the Civico Museo Bibliografico (Q49) and the other in Prague, Music Department of the National Museum (II La 2). Only one song is attributed to her in both places, and a second, "Già sperai," appears only in the Prague manuscript.

13. See above discussion of Francesca Caccini's concern for her fifteen-year-old daughter.

14. Italics added. Quoted in Jane Bowers, "Music in the Italian Convents," *Helicon Nine: The Journal of Women's Arts and Letters* 9 (1983): 69–70, reprinted from liner notes for *Music for the Mass by Nun Composers,* Leonarda LPI 115 (1982).

15. The Company (Collegio) of St. Ursula (the Ursulines) in seventeenth-century Italy was an exception. Its members generally did not live a cloistered life, according to correspondence from Madeline Welch, OSU, Ursuline Bedford Park Convent, Bronx, NY, May 8, 1998. Seventeenth-century Novara, where Isabella Leonarda lived, may have been an unusual case of Ursulines living in a convent but not yet subject to enclosure.

16. Seven works of Lucrezia Vizzana are in MTA, vol. 1, pp. 264–305.

17. The sole surviving set of partbooks (formerly in Milan) was destroyed in August 1943 by bombing during World War II.

18. Isabella Leonarda, "Quam dulcis es" from Op. 13 (1687) for high voice, two violins, and organ continuo, ed. and trans. Barbara Garvey Jackson (Fayetteville, AR: ClarNan Editions, 1984).

19. Jane Berdes, "The Women Musicians of Venice," in *Eighteenth-Century Women and the Arts,* ed. Frederick M. Kenner and Susan Lorsch, Contributions to Women's Studies No. 98 (New York: Greenwood Press, 1988), p. 156.

20. Jane Baldauf Berdes, *Women Musicians of Venice: Musical Foundations, 1525–1855* (New York: Oxford University Press, 1993), pp. 236–37. A revised edition appeared in 1996.

21. *The Norton/Grove Dictionary of Women Composers,* s.v. "Lombardini Sirmen, Maddalena Laura" by Jane L. Berdes, pp. 287–88.

22. Berdes, "Women Musicians," pp. 118, 182.

23. Jean Laurent Le Cerf de la Viéville, *Comparaison de la musique italienne et de la musique françois* (Brussels: n.p., 1704–1706).

24. Two spellings are found for the composer's given name, Elizabeth and Elisabeth. The composer's own practice was usually Elizabeth, which has therefore been used in this chapter.

25. *Mercure galant,* July 1677, pp. 107–9, translated in Edith Borroff, *An Introduction to Elisabeth-Claude Jacquet de la Guerre* (Brooklyn: Institute of Medieval Music, 1966), p. 6.

26. Two movements of the D-major trio sonata are found in MTA, vol. 2, pp. 300–6.

27. Evrard Titon du Tillet, *Parnasse française* (Paris, 1732), translated in Edith Borroff, pp. 17–18.

28. From the Preface to *Produzioni armoniche,* translated in Yvonne Rokseth, "Antonia Bembo, Composer to Louis XIV," *Musical Quarterly* 23 (1937): 149. It is not certain that "man" is correct; at present we know neither the identity nor the gender of the person who brought her to France.

29. Biographical details of Bembo's life have been traced by Claire Anne Fontijn in "Antonia Bembo: *Les Goûts réunis,* Royal Patronage, and the Role of the Woman Composer during the Reign of Louis XIV" (Ph.D. diss., Duke University, 1994), pp. 8–43 and 409–26.

30. Claire A. Fontijn, prefatory remarks to "Antonia Bembo" in MTA, vol. 2, pp. 201–4.

31. F. Guthmann, "Grad der musikalischen Bildung bei Frauenzimmern," *Allgemeine musikalische Zeitung* 9 (1807): 380 ff., cited in Eva Weissweiler, *Komponistinnen aus 500 Jahren* (Frankfurt am Main: Fischer, 1981), p. 114.

32. On one of the scores her name is given as Caterina Benedicta Grazianini, and on the other as Caterina Benedetta Gratianini, the spelling used here.

33. Excerpts of both oratorios are included in MTA, vol. 2, pp. 356–65 and 370–81.

34. Susanne Julia Beicken, "Johann Adam Hiller, *Anweisung zum musikalisch-zierlichen Gesange,* 1780: A Translation and Commentary" (Ph.D. diss., Stanford University, 1980), pp. 9–10.

35. For more information on Schröter's Lieder and on music at the Weimar court during this time, see Annie Janeiro Randall, "Music and Drama in Weimar 1776–1782: A Social-Historical Perspective" (Ph.D. diss., University of Cincinnati, 1994). See also Randall's discussion of the composer and three of her songs in MTA, vol. 4, pp. 184–203.

36. Marcia J. Citron, "Corona Schröter: Singer, Composer, Actress," *Music and Letters* 61 (1980): 23.

37. The same song in modern notation appears in MTA, vol. 4, cited above.

38. One of her keyboard sonatas is in MTA, vol. 3, pp. 44–53.

39. The composer's family name is found variously as Martines, Martínez, or Martinez. Her baptismal name was Anna Katherina, but she chose to use the name Marianna—sometimes found spelled Marianne. Her father was born in Naples of a Spanish father, apparently of minor nobility, which entitled the family to use the nobiliary particle "von." Her own signature was usually Marianna Martines.

40. "Alfin fra le tempeste," from *La Tempestà* for soprano and orchestra, is included in MTA, Vol. 4, pp. 74–93.

41. Bruce MacIntyre, *The Viennese Concerted Mass of the Early Classic Period* (Ann Arbor: UMI Research Press, 1986), p. 81.

42. She was one of three women in the eighteenth century, and the only non-Italian, to achieve this honor. The other two were a Roman, Maria Rosa Coccia, and Rosa Tartaglini Tibaldi from Bologna.

43. Marianna von Martines, *Dixit Dominus,* ed. Irving Godt. Recent Researches in the Music of the Classical Era, vol. 48 (Madison, WI: A-R Editions, 1997).

44. Dr. Franz Anton Mesmer (1734–1815) was famous for his theory that animal magnetism could be used as a cure for many illnesses. Although his theories were rejected, "mesmerism" led to later uses of hypnotism and other practices in what became modern psychotherapy. Maria Theresia von Paradis also worked with Dr. Mesmer.

45. First published in *Raccolta musicale contenente XII sonate per il cembalo solo d'altretanti celebri compositori italiani* (Nüremberg: Haffner, 1756–1765); here the title of the collection makes her an honorary Italian. The word "cembalo" and

the early date show that the works were harpsichord music, although by the end of the composer's life they would have been performed on the piano. Emil Pauer included them in *Alte Meister: Sammlung wertvoller Klavierstücke des 17. und 18. Jahrhunderts* (Leipzig: Breitkopf & Härtel, 1868–1885); here the collection title makes her an "old *master.*"

46. Caroline Pichler, *Denkwürdigkeiten aus meinem Leben,* ed. E. K. Blümml (Munich, 1914), vol. 1, pp. 191, 296, 343, 515. Cited in *The New Grove Dictionary of Music and Musicians,* s.v. "Martinez, Marianna [Anna Katharina] von," by Helene Wessely.

47. A fascinating account of Mesmer's attempted cure is found in the historical novel by Brian O'Doherty, *The Strange Case of Mademoiselle P.: A Novel* (New York: Pantheon Books/Random House, 1992).

48. Valentin Haüy, *Essai sur l'education des aveugles* (Paris: n.p., 1786); trans. ed., *An Essay on the Education of the Blind* (London: Sampson, Low, Marston & Co., 1894). The first volume of this work had embossed letters for the blind to read. Louis Braille, who invented the Braille system, was one of Haüy's students.

49. Two late piano works survive. The Fantasie in G Major was published in 1807 and may be found in MTA, vol. 3, pp. 106–26. In 1966 a rare manuscript of a Paradis work, Fantasie in C Major, was found in the Austrian National Library in Vienna. It is dated 1811 on the title page. The copyist's identity is unknown.

50. "Nachrichten," *Allgemeine musikalische Zeitung* 12 (1810): 471–74; translated in *Women Making Music,* Jane Bowers and Judith Tick, eds. (Urbana: University of Illinois Press, 1986), p. 230.

SUGGESTIONS FOR FURTHER READING

In addition to the items mentioned in the text or cited in the notes, the following sources provide information on women during the seventeenth and eighteenth centuries.

BOOKS AND ARTICLES

Bates, Carol Henry. "The Instrumental Music of Elisabeth-Claude Jacquet de la Guerre." Ph.D. diss., Indiana University, 1978.

Carter, Stewart Arlen. "The Music of Isabella Leonarda (1620–1704)." Ph.D. diss., Stanford University, 1981.

Fremar, Karen Lynn. "The Life and Selected Works of Marianna Martines (1744–1812)." Ph.D. diss., University of Kansas, 1983.

Harness, Kelley. "*Amazzoni di Dio:* Florentine Spectacle under Maria Maddalena d'Austria and Cristina di Lorena." Ph.D. diss., University of Illinois, 1996.

Jackson, Barbara Garvey. "Oratorios by Command of the Emperor: The Music of Camilla de Rossi." *Current Musicology* 42 (1968): 7–19.

———. *"Say Can You Deny Me": A Guide to Surviving Music by Women from the Sixteenth through the Eighteenth Centuries.* Fayetteville AR: University of Arkansas Press, 1994.

Kendrick, Robert L. "The Traditions of Milanese Convent Music and the Sacred Dialogues of Chiara Margarita Cozzolani," in *The Crannied Wall: Women, Religion, and the Arts in Early Modern Europe,* ed. Craig Monson. Ann Arbor: University of Michigan Press, 1992, pp. 211–33.

Laini, Marinella. "Le produzioni armoniche di Antonia Bembo." Ph.D. diss., University of Pavia, 1988.

Larson, David. "Women and Song in Eighteenth-Century Venice: Choral Music at the Four Conservatories for Girls." *Choral Journal* 18 (October 1977): 15–24.

Lorenz, Franz. *Die Musikerfamilie Benda: Franz Benda und seine Nachkommen.* Berlin: W. de Gruyter, 1967.
Matsushita, Hidemi. "The Musical Career and the Compositions of Maria Theresia von Paradis." Ph.D. diss., Brigham Young University, 1989.
Monson, Craig A. "Disembodied Voices: Music in the Nunneries of Bologna in the Midst of the Counter-Reformation," in *The Crannied Wall: Women, Religion and the Arts in Early Modern Europe,* ed. Craig Monson. Ann Arbor: University of Michigan Press, 1992, pp. 191–210.
Raney, Carolyn. "Francesca Caccini, Musician to the Medici, and Her *Primo Libro* (1618)." Ph.D. diss., New York University, 1971.
Rosand, Ellen. "Barbara Strozzi, *virtuosissima cantatrice:* The Composer's Voice." *Journal of the American Musicological Society* 31 (1978): 241–81.
Silbert, Doris. "Francesca Caccini, called La Cecchina." *Musical Quarterly* 32 (1946): 50–62.
Ullrich, Hermann. "Maria Theresia Paradis in London." *Music and Letters* 43 (1962): 19–23.
Whittemore, Joan Margaret. "Revision of Music Performed at the Venetian Ospedali in the Eighteenth Century." DMA thesis, University of Illinois, 1986.

Modern Editions and Facsimiles of Music

ANTHOLOGIES AND COLLECTIONS

Harbach, Barbara, ed. *Eighteenth-Century Women Composers for the Harpsichord or Piano.* 2 vols. Pullman, WA: Vivace Press, 1992. Works by Gambarini, Hester Park, A Lady, and Martines.
Jackson, Barbara Garvey, ed. *Arias and Sinfonias from Oratorios by Women Composers.* 6 vols. Fayetteville, AR: ClarNan Editions, 1987, 1990, 1992, 1996 (2), 1997. Works by Rossi, Gratianini, and Grimani.
———. *Lieder and Other Songs by Women Composers of the Classic Era.* 4 vols. Fayetteville, AR: ClarNan Editions. 1987, 1994, 1997, 2000. Works by Liebmann, Westenholz, Schröter, Paradis, Brillon de Jouy, Cosway, Eichner, and Reichardt (born Benda).
———. *Three Sacred Works for Soprano, Two Violins, and Organ Continuo.* Fayetteville, AR: ClarNan Editions, 1996. Works by Leonarda, Peruchona, and Mrs. Wilbraham.
———. *Two Sacred Works for Three Treble Voices.* Fayetteville, AR: ClarNan Editions, 1990. Works by Assandra and Nascinbeni.
Johnson, Calvert, ed. *Organ Music by Women Composers before 1800.* Pullman, WA: Vivace, 1993. Works by Gracia Baptista, Assandra, and Miss Steemson.
Rieger, Eva, and Kate Walter, eds. *Frauen komponieren: 22 Klavierstücke des 18.-20. Jahrhunderts.* Mainz: Schott, 1985. Works by La Guerre and Martines.

SEPARATE PRINTS

Anna Amalia of Prussia. *Der Tod Jesu* [1760, SATB, strings and organ]. Louisville KY: Editions Ars Femina, 1993.
———. Sonata in F Major for flute and continuo. Ed. Gustav Lenzewski. Munich: Chr. Friedrich Vieweg, 1975.
———. Trio Sonata for Two Violins and Continuo [1748]. Louisville KY: Editions Ars Femina, 1993.

Anna Amalia of Saxe-Weimar. Quartet for Clarinet [violin], Viola, Cello, and Pianoforte [1786]. Louisville KY: Editions Ars Femina, 1995.

Caccini, Francesca. "Aure volante." Ed. Carolyn Raney. In *Nine Centuries of Music by Women*. New York: Broude Brothers, 1977.

———. *Il primo libro delle musiche a una e due voci di Francesca Caccini ne' Signorini* (facsimile). In *Italian Secular Song: 1606–1636,* vol. I: Florence. Introduction by Gary Tomlinson. New York: Garland, 1986.

———. *La Liberazione di Ruggiero.* Ed. Doris Silbert. Northampton, MA: Smith College Archives, 1945.

Coccia, Maria Rosa. *Dixit Dominus Domino meo* [1775, for two four-voice choirs and continuo]. Ed. Irene Hegen. Kassel: Furore, 1997.

Cozzolani, Chiara Margarita. *Laudate Domino* [1650, soprano, two violins, and continuo]. Louisville, KY: Editions Ars Femina, 1993.

———. *Magnificat* [1650, SSAATTBB and continuo]. Ed. Barbara Garvey Jackson. Fayetteville, AR: ClarNan Editions, 1998.

———. *Motets.* Ed. Robert L. Kendrick. Recent Researches in the Music of the Baroque Era, vol. 87. Madison: A-R Editions, 1998.

Grimani, Maria Margherita. Sinfonias to *La Visitazione, La Decollazione,* and *Pallade e Marte* [strings and continuo]. Louisville, KY: Editions Ars Femina, 1991.

Jacquet de La Guerre, Elizabeth [Elisabeth]-Claude. *Céphale et Procis.* Ed. Wanda R. Griffiths. Recent Researches in the Music of the Baroque Era, vol. 88. Madison: A-R Editions, 1998.

———. *Esther* [cantata for voice and continuo]. Ed. Conrad Misch. Kassel: Furore, 1996.

———. *Jacob et Rachel* [cantata for voice, violin, gamba/cello, and continuo]. Ed Conrad Misch. Kassel: Furore, 1996.

———. *Jonas* [cantata for voice, violin, gamba/cello, and continuo]. Ed. Conrad Misch. Kassel: Furore, 1995.

———. *Judith* [cantata for voice, violin, gamba/cello, and continuo]. Ed. Conrad Misch. Kassel: Furore, 1995.

———. *Le passage de la Mer Rouge* [cantata for voice, violin, and continuo]. Ed. Diane Guthrie. Bryn Mawr, PA: Hildegard, 1995.

———. *Pièces de Clavecin* [1707]. Ed. Paul Brunold, 1938, and Thurston Dart, 1965. Monaco: Oiseau Lyre, 1965.

———. *Pièces de Clavecin* [1687]. Ed. Carol Henry Bates. Paris: Le Pupitre, 1986.

———. "Raccommodement comique de Pierrot et de Nicole." Ed. Carolyn Raney. In *Nine Centuries of Music by Women.* New York: Broude Brothers, 1978.

———. Sonata No. l in G Minor for two violins and continuo. Ed. Robert P. Block. London: Nova, 1985.

———. *Susannah* [cantata for high voice and continuo]. Ed. Valerie Macintosh. Bryn Mawr, PA: Hildegard, 1995.

———. *Vier Triosonaten* [for two violins, cello, organ/harpsichord continuo]. 2 vols. Ed. Carol Henry Bates. Kassel: Furore, 1993, 1995.

Leonarda, Isabella. *Ave Regina Caelorum.* Ed. Stewart Carter. In *Nine Centuries of Music by Women.* New York: Broude Brothers, 1980.

———. *Iam du dilecte mi Jesu* from Op. 20 [1700, for soprano, two violins, and continuo]. Ed. Ingrid Müller-Grave. Kassel: Furore, 1997.

———. *Messa Prima* from Op. 18 [1696, for SATB, two violins, and continuo]. Ed. Barbara Garvey Jackson. 2d ed. Fayetteville, AR: ClarNan Editions, 1988.

———. *Quam dulcis es* from Op. 13 [1687, for soprano, two violins, and continuo]. Ed. Barbara Garvey Jackson. Fayetteville, AR: ClarNan Editions, 1984.

———. *Selected Compositions of Isabella Leonarda.* Ed. Stewart Carter. Recent Researches in the Music of the Baroque Era, vol. 59. Madison: A-R Editions, 1988.

———. *Sonata Duodecima* for violin and continuo from Op. 16 (1693) Ed. Barbara Garvey Jackson. Baroque Chamber Music Series, No. 16. Ottawa: Dovehouse Editions, 1983; reprint Hannacroix, NY: Loux Music, 1994.

———. *Sonate Nr. l* from Op. 16 [1693, two violins and continuo]. Ed. Ingrid Grave-Müller. Kassel: Furore, 1997.

Lombardini Sirmen, Maddalena. *Six Duets for Two Violins.* Ed. G. Cooper and K. Clarke. Bryn Mawr, PA: Hildegard, 1997.

———. *Three Violin Concertos.* Ed. Jane Berdes. Recent Researches in the Music of the Classical Era, vol. 38. Madison: A-R Editions, 1988.

———. String Quartet in E Major. Louisville, KY: Editions Ars Femina, 1992.

Martines [Martinez], Marianna [Marianne] von. *Dixit Dominus* [1774, soli, SSATB choir and orchestra]. Ed. Irving Godt. Recent Researches in Music of the Classical Era, vol. 48. Madison, WI: A-R Editions, 1997.

———. *In Exitu Israel de Agypto* [soli, choir, and orchestra]. Ed. Conrad Misch. Kassel: Furore, 1993.

———. *Konzert für Klavier und Orchestra,* A-Dur. Ed. Rosario Marciano. Kassel: Furore, 1977.

———. Mass No. 1 in C Major [SATB choir and orchestra]. Ed. Shirley Bean. Fayetteville, AR: ClarNan Editions, 1998.

———. *Miserere* [SATB and organ continuo]. Ed. Shirley Bean. Fayetteville, AR: ClarNan Editions, 1996.

———. *Quarta Messa* [1765, soli, choir, and orchestra]. Ed. Conrad Misch. Kassel: Furore, 1993.

———. *Three Sonatas for Keyboard* [E major, A major, G major]. Ed. Shirley Bean. Bryn Mawr, PA: Hildegard, 1994.

Paradis, Maria Theresia von. *Lenore* [1789, voice and piano]. Ed. Hidemi Matsushita. Fayetteville, AR: ClarNan Editions, 1989.

———. Overture to *Der Schulkandidat* [1793, orchestra]. Ed. Hidemi Matsushita. Fayetteville, AR: ClarNan Editions, 1992.

———. *Zwölf Lieder auf ihrer Reise in Musik gesetzt (1784–86)* [voice and piano, one also with violin]. Ed. Hidemi Matsushita. Lieder by Women Composers of the Classic Era, vol. 2. Fayetteville, AR: ClarNan Editions, 1987.

Rossi, Camilla de. *Dori e Fileno* [SA soli and string orchestra]. Ed. Barbara Garvey Jackson. Fayetteville, AR: ClarNan Editions, 1984.

———. *Il Sacrifizio di Abramo* [1708, SSAT soli and orchestra]. Ed. Barbara Garvey Jackson. Fayetteville, AR: ClarNan Editions, 1984.

———. *S. Beatrice d'Este* [1707, SAATB soli and orchestra]. Ed. Barbara Garvey Jackson. Fayetteville, AR: ClarNan Editions, 1986.

Strozzi, Barbara. *Cantatas by Barbara Strozzi* [facsimile]. Introduction by Ellen Rosand. New York and London: Garland, 1986.

———. *Cantate, Ariette a una, due e tre voci,* Op. 3 [1654]. Ed. Gail Archer. Recent Researches in the Music of the Baroque Era, vol. 83. Madison: A-R Editions, 1997.

———. "Con le belle non ci voul fretta" and "Consiglio amoroso." Ed. Carolyn Raney. In *Nine Centuries of Music by Women.* New York: Broude Brothers, 1978.

———. *Diporte di Euterpe, overo Cantate e ariette a voce sola, opera settima, Venezia 1659* [facsimile]. Introduction by Piero Mioli. Florence: Studio per edizioni scelte, 1980.

———. *Il Primo Libro de Madrigali* [1644, two voices and continuo]. Ed. Elka Masche Blankenburg, continuo realized by Elisabeth Bussmann. Kassel: Furore, 1997.

———. *I sacri musicali affetti* [facsimile]. Introduction by Ellen Rosand. New York: Da Capo Press, 1988.

———. "Lagrime mie." In *The Solo Song, 1680–1730*. Ed. Carol MacClintock. New York: Norton, 1973.

———. *Vierzehn Arien* from Op. 2 [1651, soprano or tenor and continuo]. Ed. Richard Kolb. Kassel: Furore, 1997.

The Nineteenth Century and the Great War

VI. European Composers and Musicians, ca. 1800–1890

Nancy B. Reich

Introduction

The political, social, and economic events that followed in the tumultuous aftermath of the French Revolution offered women many opportunities in musical life but also presented them with additional problems. Patronage of the arts, formerly a prerogative of the aristocracy, was moving to the middle class. The consequent growth of public concerts; the establishment of music festivals, concert halls, and concert societies; and the increasing numbers of opera houses open to paying audiences enabled musicians, both men and women, to reach an expanding public. The founding of music schools throughout Europe brought a new professionalism to the art. The development of such transportation facilities as railroads and steamships made it possible for touring artists to travel with greater ease. Imperialist expansions encouraged musicians to tour not only on the European continent but throughout the world, and tour they did, journeying by steamer and traveling by carriage, camel, or elephant to bring European music to Africa, Australia, the Americas, and India.

Because of the increasingly prosperous middle class, women in increasing numbers took part in amateur musical activities during the first half of the nineteenth century. Their numbers gave an impetus to all the businesses that served music: the number of piano builders swelled, music publishing houses proliferated, and music journalism became a thriving enterprise. Books, almanacs, and dictionaries of music as well as music magazines designed especially for the needs and interests of "the fair sex" became popular in every European country.

Aspiring bourgeois families discovered that music lessons for their daughters could be an asset in their climb up the social ladder. The leisure created by new technology and industry afforded middle-class girls and women the opportunity to cultivate music (primarily voice and piano) to improve their marriage possibilities as well as to provide entertainment in the home. Although this situation yielded a large group of amateurs, from which some real talents emerged, upper- and middle-class women were discouraged from taking music too seriously. Even the most competent among them were forbidden by husbands or fathers to appear in public, to publish music under their own names, or to accept fees for any teaching they did, lest it reflect badly on the social status of the family. The advice and support of a man was still a necessity in the career of any woman musician, no matter how talented. Men held the important posts in music teaching and publishing, formed the committees making decisions for concert organizations and festivals, and held the power in the musical world despite the entrance of some women into positions of prominence as performers and teachers.

The movement we call Romanticism dominated all the arts in the nineteenth century, although its roots extended well back into the eighteenth. The writings of social and educational philosopher Jean Jacques Rousseau (1712–1778) influenced developments in all the arts in the nineteenth century and shaped attitudes toward women and their place in society. Such pronouncements as "There are no good morals for women outside of a withdrawn and domestic life; . . . the peaceful care of the family and the home are their lot; . . . the dignity of their sex consists in modesty; . . . shame and chasteness are inseparable from decency . . ." or "The whole education of women ought to be relative to men" affected the roles and education of women in every sphere, but were particularly damaging to the development of women composers and performers.[1]

The Romantic ethos idolized the artist-genius (always male) who was seeking self-expression, and composers like Chopin were praised for showing their sensitive, "feminine" sides. Woman was idealized; her function was to serve as a muse for the creator, to inspire and nurture the man; her feminine side was deemed a weakness should it color her music. The women who befriended and inspired Beethoven—Eleonore von Breuning, Antonie Brentano, Countess Marie Erdödy, Dorothea von Ertmann, and Marie Bigot, among others—were skilled, well-educated, and talented musicians, but theirs was always a supporting role. In 1795 Wilhelm von Humboldt, German linguist, statesman, and educator, described the difference between the sexes in these terms:

> Creative force is more attuned to aggressive movement, while receiving force is more attuned to regressive movement. That which animates the former we

> call male; that which inspires the latter—female. All that is male shows more spontaneous activity; all that is female more passive receptivity. . . .[2]

Fortified by the words of these eminent thinkers, most men (and women) accepted this point of view. Women who attempted creative work suffered societal displeasure; consequently, even among professional women musicians who were supported and encouraged by family and friends there were internal and external conflicts about composing. This may explain why a gifted composer like Clara Schumann was ambivalent about her creative work and easily discouraged.[3] The prevailing views on proper feminine behavior (passive and submissive) were so firmly entrenched that she was uncomfortable about her role as a composer; nevertheless, she had no qualms about appearing as a performer, which she considered a re-creative activity. Indeed, newspaper accounts of the work of successful professional women musicians almost always assured the readers that the musician was not only accomplished but also "womanly."

Education

The establishment of largely state-supported music schools to train professional musicians created new environments for women performers. Very few schools, however, accepted women as composition students. Women composers of the first half of the nineteenth century studied privately, just as their forebears had done. By the 1870s, however, conservatory classes in orchestration and composition began to admit women. Only at this point did women trained as professional composers begin to emerge from educational institutions, though opportunities to use such training were scarce.

The forerunners of the nineteenth-century conservatories were the Venetian *ospedali* and the music schools established in Germany and France primarily to train professional singers. By the time the first group of pupils entered the Paris Conservatoire, founded in 1795 to educate musicians who would help preserve and maintain the ideals of the French Revolution, it was understood that women would be among the students. The Royal Academy of Music in London accepted an equal number of boys and girls at its opening in 1823. Conservatories in Milan (founded in 1807), Vienna (1817), Brussels (1832), Leipzig (1843), Cologne (1850), Dresden (1856), Bern (1857), Berlin (1869), and Frankfurt (1878) admitted female students subject to special conditions. In all these schools, boys and girls received instruction in separate divisions and often in separate quarters. In Brussels in 1877, for example, girls and boys attended the conservatory on alternate days. Joint classes for both sexes, such as French declamation and mixed chorus, were held on Mondays, Wednesdays, and Fridays, the girls' days. Although rarely spelled out in the statutes of organization, the policy assumed that women were studying to become performers or teachers rather than composers or conductors, and that they would limit their studies to voice, piano, or harp. By the 1870s more female students began to study violin. Soon women were winning prizes and awards in Paris, Brussels, and Berlin and also serving on the faculties of major institutions.

Policies regarding the study of such subjects as theory, harmony, and composition varied widely. In most conservatories the women were required to study these subjects, but since the sexes were separated, it is doubtful whether the curriculum was equal. In Leipzig, for example, entrance requirements were the same for boys and girls, but male students were required to take a three-year course in theory, whereas women took a two-year course "especially organized for their requirements."[4] In some schools there were no classes in composition for women, and those who wished to study did so privately; in other schools, such as the Brussels Conservatoire, women could study composition with the director himself at designated hours on Wednesday afternoons. By 1883, however, several women at the Hoch Conservatory in Frankfurt were listing counterpoint and score-reading as major studies, and a slow (sometimes grudging) change in attitude could be found throughout European music schools. Regulations regarding participation in student orchestras also varied from city to city. Some schools did not permit women instrumentalists to enroll in orchestra or ensemble classes; others required their participation. Over the years, and after some bitter battles, the restrictions were lifted.

The numbers of female music students swelled in the course of the century. When the Leipzig Conservatory opened in 1843, the first class consisted of 33 male and 11 female students. By 1868, twenty-five years after its founding, this conservatory had graduated 1,420 students: 975 men and 445 women. At the Hoch Conservatory in Frankfurt, which opened thirty-five years later, the numbers of students in the first year (1878) included 97 women and 42 men. How many of the women went on to professional careers and remained in those careers after marriage, however, is difficult to say.

With the openings of the new conservatories, teaching opportunities for professional women musicians were expanded. Some—Marie Pleyel and Pauline Viardot, for instance—joined faculties on retiring from the concert stage. Others—including Louise Farrenc, professor at the Paris Conservatoire for more than thirty years—taught throughout their careers. There were, however, restrictions on these professors: in general, women taught only women, though male professors could teach both women and men. Even though the Brussels Conservatoire boasted of procuring such a star as Marie Pleyel for its faculty, she was restricted to teaching the "classe des jeune filles." Also, as Louise Farrenc discovered, male teachers doing work equivalent to women's commanded larger salaries. Except for such superstars as Clara Schumann, women professors were generally not accorded the respect, ranks, and prestige of their male counterparts.

Despite the discrimination they faced, some women garnered fame and even fortune as teachers. Mathilde Marchesi (1821–1913), a student of Manuel Garcia, passed on the bel canto–based methods of her teacher while on the faculties of conservatories in Vienna, Paris, and Cologne. Her greatest fame, however, came after 1878, when she left institutional teaching for good and opened private studios, first in Vienna, then in Paris. Students (all of them women) flocked to her, and she produced many well-known artists, including Emma Eames, Nellie Melba, and Emma Calvé. Her teachings live on in recordings by her protégées and in the published exercises and vocalises she developed in the course of her sixty-five years of teaching. Her pedagogical writings include a series of columns for the *Ladies' Home Journal* in 1907–1908. Mathilde's daughter Blanche (1863–1940) also enjoyed a long career as performer and teacher, having begun working with students at the age of fourteen to fill in for her ailing mother.[5]

Writers and Scholars

There were few women musical scholars in the nineteenth century; more than most branches of music, the field of scholarship was dominated by men. Nevertheless, several women musician-writers made valuable contributions to music history. The works of Elise Polko (1822–1899), Lina Ramann (1833–1912), La Mara (pseudonym for Marie Lipsius, 1837–1927), Florence May (1845–1923), and Amy Fay (1844–1928), for example, have become standard documents for study of the nineteenth century. Ramann, a teacher, composer, and writer, is best known as the biographer of Liszt; La Mara knew Liszt and Wagner, wrote more than twenty books and many essays, and edited letters of musicians. Amy Fay's book *Music Study in Germany* had over twenty printings and was translated into French and German.[6] Florence May's biographies of Clara Schumann and Johannes Brahms are major sources for these nineteenth-century musicians. Michel Brenet (pseudonym for Marie Bobillier, 1858–1918), a highly respected music historian, was one of the few women musicologists of her time. Under her male pseudonym she wrote many important articles and more than twenty monographs.

Composers

In the early decades of the nineteenth century, a number of women composers achieved professional status—that is, their music was published and performed and they received money for their work. Most were from families of professional musicians: parents of these creative women were composers or performers. In fact, many of the mothers of nineteenth-century musicians, both male and female, were themselves skilled and talented artists, a circumstance long neglected in discussions of composers. It is also interesting to note that the majority of women musicians were also wives and mothers, some bearing as many as eight children. These exceptional women managed family and professional responsibilities and were often the sole support of their families.

Many professional women composers were concert artists who, like the male virtuosi of their day, wrote to display their performing skills. They introduced their own works as well as compositions by others. Some well-known women composers of the nineteenth century who performed their own works in public concerts were Maria (Wolowska) Szymanowska, Clara (Wieck) Schumann, Marie Léopoldine Blahetka, Josephine Lang, Pauline (Garcia) Viardot, Louise Farrenc, Luise Adolpha Le Beau, and Agathe Backer-Grøndahl. A smaller number composed for other groups: some wrote for their students (Louise Reichardt), others for home performance (Fanny Hensel), and still others for orchestras and opera companies (Louise Farrenc, Loïsa Puget, Louise Bertin). Emilie Zumsteeg (1796–1857), Johanna Kinkel (1810–1858), Annette Droste-Hülshoff (1797–1848), Emilie Mayer (1821–1883), and Louise Héritte-Viardot (1841–1918) were also active as composers.

COMPOSERS OF VOCAL MUSIC

Song Composers

The art song (in German, *Lied*) was considered to be a particularly appropriate genre for women composers, partly because it was associated with home music making, thereby remaining within women's domain, and partly because, as a relatively simple form, it did not compete with the more complex, "masculine" genres such as sonatas or symphonies, which required the more intensive study frequently denied to women musicians. Throughout the nineteenth century the great majority of published works by women were art songs and, equally suitable for the female, short pieces for piano (discussed later).

Louise Reichardt (1779–1826) grew up in a musical and literary home and received her education in that household. Her mother, Juliane (1752–1788), a keyboard player and composer who died when Louise was only four, was one of several talented daughters of Franz Benda, concertmaster to Frederick the Great. Louise's father, Johann Friedrich Reichardt, was *Kapellmeister* at the same court and a composer, conductor, and writer. Although he encouraged his eldest daughter in her musical interests, he offered her no formal training in composition. Political outspokenness caused Reichardt to lose his court position in 1794, and the Napoleonic invasions of Germany (1806–1815) brought great financial difficulties to the family, including the temporary loss of their home near Halle. Louise Reichardt, who never married, left home in 1809, moved to Hamburg, and established a private voice studio. She was able to support herself and even assist her family by her teaching, composing, and other musical activities. For the sake of her pupils, she became involved with the Hamburg Gesangverein, a choral group which she helped organize. Reichardt conducted the chorus at rehearsals but not at concerts. Modest, very pious, and holding firmly to traditional patterns of feminine behavior despite her financial independence, she barely acknowledged her own accomplishments as a composer or musician.

The earliest printed songs by Louise Reichardt appeared in a joint collection with her father in 1800, but she published on her own thereafter. More than seventy of her songs, most in the *volkstümlich* (folklike) style popularized by the Romantic poets, are known to have been published, though not all have been found. Her texts were by the leading German poets, whom she knew personally: Wolfgang von Goethe, Ludwig Tieck, Novalis, Clemens Brentano, and Achim von Arnim. Among the best of the early *volkstümlich Lieder* by any composer, most of Reichardt's songs are strophic, and their words are never obscured by the melody or the simple piano accompaniment. The harmonies are diatonic and the phrases regular. Her songs demonstrate an unforgettable melodic gift and were beloved by generations of Germans, who sang them in the belief that they were folksongs. A number were reprinted in collections of German folksongs that proliferated in the nineteenth century. Louise Reichardt also published a collection of more dramatic Italian songs with texts by Metastasio, as well as some religious choral works for women's voices. (Forty-two of her songs appear in *Louise Reichardt: Songs*, published by the Da Capo Press, and five are available in MTA, vol. 4.)

The next generation of song composers—Josephine Lang, Fanny Hensel, and Clara Schumann—wrote in a more sophisticated style. Like their male colleagues, these composers used texts from such prominent contemporary poets as Goethe, Eichendorff, Rückert, and Giebel. Romantic love (often thwarted) and the beauties of nature formed the subjects of the texts; unlike their male counterparts, women generally avoided poetry extolling heroism or war. Piano parts no longer served merely to support the voice but were of greater technical difficulty and formed an integral part of the composition;

chromaticism appeared regularly in both voice and piano parts, and all the elements—piano, voice, and poem—blended into the artistic unity that characterized the mature song style.

Parents, grandparents, and aunts of Josephine Lang (1815–1880) were professional musicians, and in 1836 Lang joined her parents at the Munich court as a singer. Almost entirely self-taught in composition, she attracted the attention of Felix Mendelssohn and Robert Schumann, whose encouragement fueled her determination to continue to compose. During the fourteen years of her marriage (1842–1856) to poet Reinhard Köstlin, she had six children and virtually ceased all creative work. When her husband died, she resumed teaching and composing, producing piano works as well as songs. The support of Ferdinand Hiller, a composer and friend of Mendelssohn and the Schumanns, helped her as a girl and later (during her widowhood) to make the necessary contacts with publishers.

Josephine Lang wrote her first songs at the age of thirteen, and some of her best work stems from her adolescent years. (See "Frühzeitiger Frühling," composed in 1830, in HAMW, pp. 111–13, and other songs in MTA, vol. 6. Da Capo Press published a collection of 52 songs in 1982.) More than 150 of her songs were published during her lifetime, and in 1882 the prestigious firm of Breitkopf & Härtel brought out a two-volume collection.

The older sister of Felix Mendelssohn and the daughter of a prominent and wealthy Berlin family, Fanny Hensel (1805–1847) was heir to a distinguished musical tradition carried on by accomplished women amateurs. Grandmother, mother, aunts, and great-aunts were all skilled musicians, and Fanny, too, had the best training Berlin afforded. Her general and musical education were practically identical to those of her brother, but her father, who encouraged Felix's professional aspirations, forbade her to perform for fees or to have her music published. Her first songs appeared in collections of her brother's and under his name.[7] Both her father and brother held that professional work had no place in the life of a woman of their class and status; they believed that Fanny Hensel's responsibilities were to home and child rather than to art. Nevertheless, Hensel continued composing, and her works were performed at the Sunday musicales she organized and directed in her home. Her mother and her husband, Wilhelm Hensel, an artist whom she married in 1829, encouraged her creative work. At the age of forty she summoned up the courage to defy the strongly held beliefs of father and brother and accepted an offer from a Berlin publisher for her compositions. Only a few works were printed; the composer died at age forty-one, one week before a review of a number of her piano compositions appeared in a leading Leipzig music journal.

Hensel's music was influenced by her study of Bach and her close relationship with her brother, but she developed her own distinctive voice, particularly in her songs and piano miniatures. Her songs have a confidence and melodic ease not always found in Felix Mendelssohn's works in that genre, gifts her brother acknowledged when he wrote: " . . . she has composed several things, especially German lieder which belong to the very best we have."[8] Though numbered Op. 1, No. 1, "Schwanenlied" (HAMW, pp. 115–18) is not an early work; it is, however, a beautiful example of her lyrical style. (Additional songs appear in MTA.)

Exceptionally prolific, Fanny Hensel composed songs (about 300), works for piano (including several sonatas), music for organ, chamber music, choral works with and without orchestra, and an overture for orchestra. The manuscripts remained in the hands of her family, who kept almost all from public view for several generations, but many of her works have been published and recorded in recent years.[9] Still, the greater part of her output is unpublished.

Clara (Wieck) Schumann (1819–1896) was born in Leipzig to Marianne Tromlitz Wieck, pianist, singer, and daughter and granddaughter of a well-known musical family, and Friedrich Wieck, eminent music pedagogue and music merchant. Clara entered the musical world as a child prodigy. Her ambitious father saw to it that she had a superb musical education: she studied piano with him, and theory, harmony, counterpoint and fugue, composition, orchestration, and voice with the best available teachers in Leipzig, Dresden, and Berlin. Following a long and bitter lawsuit against her father, who refused to consent to her marriage to composer Robert Schumann (1810–1856), she and Schumann were wed in 1840, and she continued to compose, teach, and perform despite the births of eight children. After her husband's death (1856) she ceased composing but resumed her career on the concert stage and remained a sought-after teacher and editor.

Almost all of Clara Schumann's songs were composed after her marriage. The first song group was written as a Christmas gift for her husband in 1840; soon afterward he suggested that she join him in writing a collection of songs based on texts by Friedrich Rückert. This publication, called Op. 37/12—that is, his Op. 37 and her Op. 12—was followed several years later by Clara's own collection of six songs, dedicated to Queen Caroline Amalie of Denmark. Her last group, *Six Songs from Jucunde*, was composed in 1853. Of her twenty-five songs, seven remained unpublished during her lifetime, but these have appeared in recent editions.[10] Her oeuvre encompasses songs, choral works, a concerto for piano and orchestra, chamber music with piano, and short piano works. (Examples of her work in three different genres appear in HAMW, pp. 122–42 and in MTA, vols. 6 and following.)

Although her melodies lack the spontaneity of those of Louise Reichardt or Fanny Hensel, the songs of Clara Schumann are powerful and expressive. When appropriate, she employs a brilliant piano style (e.g., "Er ist

FIGURE 6.1. Pauline Viardot. Reproduced by permission of the Music Division, The New York Public Library for the Performing Arts, Astor, Lenox and Tilden Foundations.

gekommen" or "Am Strande"), as befits a concert artist of her rank. Some of the most moving of her songs are in a declamatory mode with a sparse accompaniment; their strength derives from her bold harmonies and sensitivity to the texts, as in, for example, "Ich stand in dunklen Träumen," "Sie liebten sich Beide," or "Es fiel ein Reif in der Frühlingsnacht." Her last songs, Op. 23, are the least known, but their skillfully interwoven voice and piano parts capture the joyful evocation of love and nature so beloved by the Romantics.

Although Pauline (Garcia) Viardot (1821–1910) was best known as an international opera star, she was also a composer, a pianist of concert rank, a great actress, a voice teacher, and a gifted graphic artist. Born into a family of musicians, she was surrounded with singers and opera from her earliest years. Her father, Manuel Garcia, a renowned singer, vocal pedagogue, composer, and impresario, brought the first Italian opera company to the United States in 1825. Her mother, born Joaquina Sitches, was an actress and singer, and her sister was Maria Malibran, the fabled soprano. Pauline studied voice with her father and mother, piano with Franz Liszt, and composition privately with Anton Reicha, famed composition teacher at the Paris Conservatoire. Her career was first guided by her father and later by her husband, Louis Viardot (1800–1883), a writer and theater producer who gave up his own career to support hers. The Viardots had four children; their daughter Louise Héritte-Viardot was a singer and composer. (Her works appear in MTA.)

Pauline Viardot possessed a colorful, compelling personality, and had friends in artistic, theatrical, literary, and musical circles throughout Europe. After hearing two operettas that Viardot had composed, accompanied, and produced, Clara Schumann, a lifelong friend, wrote about her, "She is the most gifted woman I have ever met."[11] Viardot composed German Lieder, French chansons, opera and operettas, short works for piano, and several interesting arrangements for voice and piano. Her songs, like her life, are distinguished by her flair for color and drama. (A brilliant example of her song writing is "Die Beschwörung" in HAMW, pp. 154–57; a number of other works appear in MTA.)

Composers of Opera and Operetta

Only a few women essayed opera and operetta, but of those who did, a surprising number had their works produced. Among the nineteenth-century women who wrote operas were Loïsa Puget (1810–1889), Louise Bertin, Marie de Grandval, Pauline Viardot, and Ingeborg von Bronsart.

Daughter and sister of the editors of the prestigious *Journal des débats,* Louise Bertin (1805–1877) lived her entire life in Paris. Encouraged by her family and her teacher François Fétis, the writer and critic, Bertin wrote four operas, three of them produced at the Opéra-Comique and the Opéra between 1827 and 1836. These were *Fausto,* based on Goethe's *Faust; Le Loup-garou,* with libretto by Scribe and Mazères; and *Esmeralda,* based on Victor Hugo's *Notre-Dame de Paris,* which the author himself adapted as a libretto. However, the young composer found the lack of critical acclaim discouraging, and after the performance of her last opera, *Esmeralda,* turned to other genres. She wrote twelve cantatas, a piano trio, ballades for piano, and a number of chamber symphonies.

Vicomtesse Marie (de Reiset) de Grandval (1830–1907) was a serious and prolific composer with professional skills and accomplishments, but her aristocratic background and social class doomed her to amateur status. She studied with Friedrich von Flotow and later, when she recognized her need for further tutelage, with Camille Saint-Saëns. A number of her operas were produced in Paris, but for the early works she used *noms de plume,* both male and female. By 1869, however, she had enough confidence to use her own name; her compositions—operas, oratorios, a Mass, and other large choral pieces—were published, performed, and favorably reviewed. She also wrote chamber music, symphonies, and other works for orchestra. Her last opera, *Mazeppa* (ca. 1892), was highly praised by contemporary critics. (See Scenes IV and V in MTA.) Her works have been characterized as "essentially French, energetic, vibrant, and melodic."[12]

Ingeborg (Starck) von Bronsart (1840–1913) was born in St. Petersburg to Swedish parents. She was best known as a pianist, although she had been composing since she was a child. While studying with Liszt, she met Hans Bronsart von Schellendorf, a musician, and they married in 1862. She continued her career, but convention decreed that she give up public appearances when her husband took on the position of director of the Hanover Court Theater. Although Ingeborg von Bronsart composed vocal music, works for piano, and chamber and orchestral music, she achieved her greatest success with her operas. Her *Jery und Bätely,* based on a Goethe libretto, was published in 1873 and performed throughout Germany.

Choral Works by Women

Secular choral singing by groups of men or women was a nineteenth-century phenomenon, an outgrowth of efforts by the middle class to participate in the Romantic revival of music from earlier periods. As women singers joined in this activity, women composers took up this genre. Secular choral groups for men had been founded in the late eighteenth century: many were choral societies organized by alumni of the great church choirs in which only men and boys participated. Women's choral groups began to appear in the first decades of the nineteenth century and soon merged with the male choruses. By midcentury almost every city that professed a musical life had a choral society. These large mixed choruses were the mainstays of the two- or three-day festivals, which were particularly popular in England and Germany. It may be of interest to note that Felix Mendelssohn organized, conducted, and wrote his large choral works for performances at these festivals, whereas his sister Fanny conducted her choral works—several cantatas, an oratorio, and shorter works for mixed chorus—at her Sunday home musicales.

Other women who wrote choral music for public consumption include Louise Reichardt, whose compositions are scored for women's voices.[13] Johanna Kinkel (1810–1858), who founded and conducted a mixed chorus that sang an extensive repertoire of old and new works, also composed choruses, secular cantatas, and sacred works. Clara Schumann accompanied the Dresden Gesangverein (conducted by her husband) and composed three *a cappella* choruses for that group. Luise Adolpha Le Beau, who wrote in many genres, wrote secular choral works as well as choruses on biblical subjects. Still other composers of choral music included Pauline Viardot, Agathe Backer-Grøndahl, Ingeborg von Bronsart, and Elfrida Andrée.

COMPOSERS OF INSTRUMENTAL MUSIC

Women and the Piano

The Romantics held instrumental music to be superior to music with words, and the piano seemed best suited to exemplify Romantic ideals. By 1830 the piano had a greater range, bigger sound, and more strength than keyboard instruments of the previous century, and it could express intimate emotion as well as display dazzling virtuosity. It was as suitable a musical vehicle for the great virtuosi as it was for the amateur. The lingering echoes of the sustaining pedal could project "the infinite longing which is the essence of romanticism."[14] The piano, seen and heard in concert hall, palace, and parlor, was considered a particularly appropriate instrument for women to play because of its association with domestic music making.

The women who composed for piano employed, for the most part, the short lyric forms so beloved in that age: songs without words, ballades, etudes, romances, nocturnes, intermezzos, scherzos, and dance forms such as polonaises and mazurkas. Although frequently associated with what was derogatorily called "salon music," these works were, in the hands of the best composers, elegant and expressive pieces. Particularly popular among those concert pianists who performed their own works was the theme-and-variations form in which the artist could demonstrate versatility and brilliance. Among the composers who wrote for the piano were Maria Szymanowska, Louise Farrenc, Léopoldine Blahetka, Fanny Hensel, Clara Schumann, Luise Adolpha Le Beau, Agathe Backer-Grøndahl, Ingeborg von Bronsart, and Elfrida Andrée—all of them successful concert artists as well.

Maria (Wolowska) Szymanowska (1789–1831) was the first Polish pianist to gain a European reputation. As a child, she was given the best musical education Warsaw had to offer. Beginning in 1810 she toured throughout continental

Europe and England. She married in 1810, but her husband was not interested in her career and she left him in 1820, taking her three children with her. Szymanowska supported herself and her family by composing, teaching, and concertizing throughout Europe. In 1822 she was appointed pianist to the Russian court in St. Petersburg. She died in that city during a cholera epidemic.

Szymanowska's published piano works include nocturnes, waltzes, and etudes, which were known and played throughout Europe. She was one of the first composers to write concert music employing Polish dance forms such as the mazurka and polonaise. Polish scholars credit her with having had enormous influence on the young Frédéric Chopin. She also composed songs and chamber works. (Her Nocturne in B-flat Major is published in HAMW, pp. 103–8, and fourteen selections appear in MTA, vol. 3. Six of her songs appear in vol. 4, and two pieces of chamber music in vol. 5.)

Louise (Dumont) Farrenc (1804–1875) was born in Paris, and that city remained the lifelong center of her activities. She studied piano with Anne-Elisabeth Soria, her godmother, and composition and orchestration with Anton Reicha. The Paris of Farrenc's youth was a city where opera reigned supreme, but her interests and those of her husband, Aristide Farrenc (1794–1865), a flutist and music publisher, lay in music of the Classical and earlier eras. Their edition of a multi-volume historical anthology, *Trésor des pianistes,* brought keyboard music of previous centuries to the attention of the French public.

Shy, serious, and essentially conservative, Louise Farrenc devoted herself to composing and teaching piano at the Paris Conservatoire, where she was a professor for over thirty years. Her few public appearances as a pianist were urged on her by her husband, who hoped that her compositions would become better known as a result. Her creative work reflected her activities: she wrote etudes in a wide variety of styles to use at the Conservatoire for teaching purposes. She also composed rondos, variations for piano, sonatas, chamber music, symphonies, and other works in the classical forms. Her contemporaries praised her craftsmanship and erudition, and she was awarded many honors during her lifetime.[15] (A set of variations for piano appears in MTA, vol. 6.)

Léopoldine Blahetka (1809–1885),[16] an Austrian pianist and composer, grew up in an intellectual environment. Her father taught mathematics and history, and her maternal grandfather was the Viennese composer Andreas Traeg. Beethoven heard her perform when she was five years old and convinced her parents that she should study with Joseph Czerny (not related to Carl Czerny). She later studied piano with Friedrich Kalkbrenner and Ignaz Moscheles and composition with Simon Sechter, the highly respected pedagogue who taught Franz Schubert and other eminent Viennese musicians. Between 1825 and 1827 Blahetka performed throughout Germany and was acclaimed by critics both as a pianist and composer.

FIGURE 6.2. Léopoldine Blahetka. Reproduced by permission of the Music Division, The New York Public Library for the Performing Arts, Astor, Lenox and Tilden Foundations.

Blahetka wrote for voice, violin and piano, piano and orchestra, and solo piano. An opera, *Die Räuber und die Sänger,* was produced in Vienna in 1830. For the piano she composed polonaises, many sets of variations, and piano transcriptions of popular operatic arias. Her *Souvenirs d'Angleterre* uses "God Save the Queen" as the basis of brilliant and pianistic variations. Her piano trio is a joyful work with a rollicking polka finale. Her writing, reminiscent of both Beethoven and Mendelssohn, exploits the singing tone of the piano and the brilliant upper range of the keyboard. Blahetka retired from active concertizing and composing at the end of the 1830s, settled in Boulogne-sur-Mer in France, and turned to teaching. (Blahetka's Sonata for Pianoforte and Violin, Op. 15, was published by Hildegard Press in 1997 and her *Variations Brilliantes on a Hungarian Theme,* Op. 18, can be found in MTA.)

Fanny Mendelssohn Hensel's piano works, like those for chorus, were composed for her own Sunday home musicales. Strongly influenced by Bach and

Beethoven and the musical training both she and her brother received, Hensel composed studies, contrapuntal works, sonatas, and character pieces for the piano, including her *Lieder ohne Worte* (Songs without Words). Scholars believe that it was she, not her brother, who gave the name to the genre, but the influence of one sibling on the other was so great that it is impossible to determine the origin of the term. Her brother chose a group of her last *Lieder ohne Worte* for publication after her death. Hensel's experimentation in these works has been described as "an original attempt at elevating the genre to one of greater musical significance."[17] (Several large works, including sonatas for piano and *Das Jahr,* a cycle of twelve character pieces, have been published recently. See also MTA.)

The keyboard works of Clara Schumann delineate the changing styles of piano music in the first half of the nineteenth century. Among her girlhood works are several in variation form—typical of the period—in which popular melodies were employed to demonstrate the prowess of the pianist. At the same time, however, the young pianist was writing short, lyric pieces characteristic of the New Romantic School, a group that included Chopin, Mendelssohn, Robert Schumann, and Clara herself. After marrying Robert Schumann, she chose to write in more traditional forms, reflecting her joint studies with her husband of works by Bach, Mozart, Haydn, and Beethoven. In these years she wrote several romances and some character pieces, as well as a sonata for piano (unpublished until 1989), preludes and fugues (Op. 16), and the *Variations on a Theme by Robert Schumann* (Op. 20), a serious and formal work (HAMW, pp. 130–42) unlike the flashy variation sets of her youth. (Other works, some never previously published, can be found in MTA.)

At a time when Swedish law forbade women from holding appointments as church organists, Elfrida Andrée (1841–1929) worked to change the law, and in 1861 became the first Swedish woman to work in this profession. She was also the first woman in Sweden to write chamber and orchestral works and the first to conduct an orchestra. In addition to a piano sonata and two groups of character pieces for piano, Andrée wrote several chamber works that included piano in their ensembles, as well as some organ pieces (including two organ symphonies) and some songs. Though her opera, *Fritiofs saga* (1899, libretto by the noted Swedish author Selma Lagerlöf) remained unperformed, two orchestral suites, along with her two symphonies, were included on concert programs. She also produced several choral works, among them two Swedish Masses and a ballad, *Snöfrid* (1879), for soli, chorus, and orchestra. Her music, like that of many other Scandinavian composers of the era, shows its roots in the idioms of Mendelssohn and Schumann and of the nineteenth-century French organ school.

Women and Chamber Music

Like art song and piano music, chamber music was considered an acceptable genre for women composers. In the first decade of the nineteenth century it was still associated with private music making rather than with concerts for paying audiences. In fact, public chamber music concerts were not given until the 1820s. Nevertheless, only a few women composed chamber music. Léopoldine Blahetka, who performed with chamber groups in Vienna between 1823 and 1830, composed for chamber ensembles that included piano; Louise Farrenc's best works may have been the pieces she wrote for various combinations of instruments: sonatas, trios, quintets, a sextet, and a very successful nonet for winds and strings. All were performed but not all were published in her lifetime. (The first movement of Farrenc's Trio, Op. 45, for flute [or violin], cello, and piano, can be found in HAMW, pp. 145–51.)

Clara Schumann, who programmed Beethoven's piano and violin sonatas and piano trios in her recitals as early as the 1830s, organized a trio in Dresden for which she was the pianist, and she organized the first public chamber music performances in that city in the 1840s. Her own piano trio, Op. 17, undoubtedly inspired by the works she had played, was well received by reviewers. Many commented on the gender of the composer, and several critics expressed surprise that a woman could write an instrumental work so skillfully and with such effect. "Let us look at this trio," wrote one critic; "the basic foundation has been designed with confidence, the individual parts have been fashioned with taste, and throughout the whole, there is a tender, poetic quality that pervades the entire piece and consecrates it as a work of art."[18] (See HAMW pp. 124–29 for the first movement of the trio.)

For her home musicales Fanny Hensel composed duos, a piano quartet, a string quartet, and a piano trio, her posthumously published Op. 11. This piece demonstrates, in the words of one Hensel scholar, her "formidable compositional skill and inventiveness."[19] Other composers who wrote music for chamber combinations were Bronsart, who wrote a number of duos, and Le Beau, whose chamber works, including sonatas, trios, and a string quintet, were considered to be among her best compositions.

Women and Orchestral Music

Rare was the woman who ventured into the realm of orchestral music in the nineteenth century. There were several reasons for this. First, symphonies and works for large groups were considered to be masculine forms to be performed in public concert halls. Second, writing orchestral works required skills that many women musicians had not had the opportunity to learn. Third, women rarely had access to the groups that could rehearse and perform their works. All composers, male and female, needed (indeed, still need) connections to the men who held power in the musical world. This posed a special difficulty for women: they were less likely to know the right people and might well have antagonized the influential conductors and managers by stepping out of their traditional, submissive female roles.

Because most women composers were pianists, their works for orchestra usually involved the piano as well. Consequently, we find that concertos and fantasies for piano and orchestra, which the composer herself could introduce, were among the most frequently performed orchestral works by women. Clara Schumann's concerto was just such a piece; written as a vehicle for her girlhood concerts, it was first played, to great acclaim, in 1837.

Later in the century, as women had more opportunity to study composition and orchestration, a number of composers had the courage to undertake orchestral music, Farrenc and Le Beau among them. Farrenc's three symphonies (written between 1841 and 1847) were performed but not published. According to Friedland, who has studied the autograph scores, these works are modeled on those of the great classical masters—Haydn, Mozart, and Beethoven—and share with the symphonic productions of her contemporary, Felix Mendelssohn, "the classical ideal of formal and textural lucidity."[20]

Luise Adolpha Le Beau (1850–1927) did not shun large musical forms; indeed, she persevered in her composing despite opposition from the musical establishment in her native Germany. Supported by her parents, who were not professional musicians but were musical and totally devoted to her, she studied piano and composition privately with such eminent teachers as Clara Schumann, Franz Lachner, and Josef Rheinberger. Like other nineteenth-century women composers, she took her first career steps as a pianist, and she earned a living as pianist, teacher, and music critic even though she saw her true vocation to be that of composer. Le Beau wrote an opera and songs as well as works for piano, chorus, orchestra, and chamber groups. Her cello sonata, Op. 17, won first prize in a Hamburg competition in 1882, and she received much critical acclaim for her chamber works. Her compositions tended to be conservative, reflecting her studies with Rheinberger. Among her best works are a piano sonata (1879), a sonata for violin and piano (1882), the cello sonata, Op. 17, and a Symphony in F Minor, Op. 41. Le Beau received praise for the energy and power of her works, which critics found very "masculine." She withdrew from musical life in 1903 but lived until 1927.

PERFORMERS

Singers

Of all the professional women performers in the nineteenth century, the largest number were singers. Most prominent were those who sang opera, but many great vocalists also appeared in public concerts and church music. The opera singers were the great stars of the period: lionized and adored, they had international reputations and appeared in opera houses throughout Europe and North and South America. Most singers were related to professional musicians or actors and continued the family tradition as a matter of course. Few singers from middle-class families went into opera; they feared the opprobrium visited upon women. Aspiring opera singers from professional musical or theatrical families (who were already *déclassé*), in contrast, were not discouraged by such attitudes. Performing in opera was a means to money, fame, and even marriage into the aristocracy, though it was generally understood that they were to relinquish the stage when they married.

The vocation of singer could begin astonishingly early: stars as young as fifteen appeared at the Paris Opéra; they could be used up by the age of twenty-five. Some then turned to provincial opera houses; others taught or made good marriages at retirement, still in their twenties. Among the prominent and influential singers who appeared in opera and concert in the first half of the nineteenth century were Angelica Catalani (1780–1849), who dubbed herself the "prima cantatrice del mondo" (the foremost singer in the world) and managed the prestigious Théâtre Italien in Paris for a brief period; Anna Milder-Hauptmann (1785–1838), who created the role of Leonore in Beethoven's *Fidelio;* and the vocal phenomenon Giuditta Pasta (1798–1865), who sang the title role at the premiere of Bellini's *Norma.*

Henriette Sontag (1805–1854), the first German to have an international reputation in a field dominated by Italian singers, was eighteen when she sang in the first performance of Beethoven's Ninth Symphony. Sontag's husband, Count Rossi, was an Italian nobleman who, an English critic wrote, "did not publicly announce the marriage until after his wife (in 1830) had made a very lucrative concert tour."[21] Sontag returned to the stage in 1848 when Rossi was in financial difficulty. She died a few years later in Mexico while on an American tour.

Wilhelmine Schröder-Devrient (1805–1860), also German, had a particularly colorful career. The daughter of a well-known actress in Vienna, she made her debut at the age of seventeen in that city as Pamina in *The Magic Flute.* Schröder-Devrient created roles in three Wagner operas, including that of Venus in *Tannhäuser,* and was associated with Wagner and

FIGURE 6.3. Jenny Lind's first appearance in America (Castle Garden, September 11, 1850). Reproduced by permission of the Music Division, The New York Public Library for the Performing Arts, Astor, Lenox and Tilden Foundations.

other revolutionaries in the uprising against the Saxon king in 1849. She made fiery political speeches that forced her into exile from Dresden.

Other renowned singers who sang opera but were better known for their activities on the concert stage were the English soprano Clara Novello (1818–1908), a favorite singer of Felix Mendelssohn and Robert Schumann, and Jenny Lind-Goldschmidt (1820–1887), the so-called "Swedish Nightingale." Because of her gifts and popularity and the fact that her personal reputation remained unsullied, Lind was able to dispel to some degree the aura of disrepute associated with the stage. For this, several subsequent generations of singers are indebted to her.

Among the eminent singers who were members of family dynasties and passed the musical tradition down to younger sisters, daughters, nieces, and cousins were Maria Malibran and her younger sister, Pauline Viardot, members of the Garcia family. Malibran, like Viardot, also composed; her brilliant career—the subject of novels, plays, songs, and movies—was cut short by a riding accident. Though Viardot was a more versatile musician than her sister, she never inspired the wild adoration that surrounded Malibran. Yet both Meyerbeer and Berlioz were sufficiently impressed to create leading roles for her: Meyerbeer in his *Le Prophète* (Fidès, 1849) and Berlioz in his edited revival of Gluck's *Orfeo*.

Several notable singers appeared in Paris, the foremost opera center in the first half of the nineteenth century. Laure Cinti-Damoreau (1801–1863), who began her career at the Théâtre Italien at the age of fifteen, is one of the few to have sung leading roles at all three of Paris's opera houses—the Italien, the Opéra, and the Opéra-Comique. In fact, she had the longest career of any French prima donna of her time. Rossini admired her and coached her for important roles in his works.[22] She was also in the original casts of works by Meyerbeer and Auber. After retiring from the stage in 1841 Cinti-Damoreau concertized extensively and made an American tour with violinist Alexandre Artôt. In 1848 she left performing for good but continued to teach at the Paris Conservatoire until 1856.

Marie-Cornélie Falcon (1812? 1814? –1897), a soprano much beloved by Parisian audiences, lost her voice during an 1837 performance of Niedermeyer's *Stradella,* thus ending a career of only five years. Despite remedies ranging from medical treatments to journeys to Italy for retraining, her singing voice never returned to anything near its youthful glory, and attempts to make a comeback were at best disappointing.[23] Before this unhappy end to her career, however, Falcon had created leading roles in Halévy's *La Juive* and Meyerbeer's *Les Huguenots.* The controversial mezzo-soprano Rosine Stoltz (1815–1903), who may have attained stardom as much for her liaison with Opéra director Léon Pillet as for her voice, was nevertheless a leading singer in the 1830s and 1840s, and was particularly admired for her acting ability.[24]

In the latter part of the century the Patti sisters, Carlotta (1835–1889) and Adelina (1843–1919), both coloratura sopranos, were celebrated in Europe and North America. Carlotta had a career as a concert artist; Adelina was considered the successor to Pasta and Grisi as an international star and "Queen of Song." Distinguished for the sweetness and purity of her voice rather than for her dramatic gifts, Adelina Patti nevertheless triumphed equally in opera and concert.

Pianists

A number of women pianists of the nineteenth century were celebrated as world-class artists. First and foremost was Clara Schumann, who had a blazingly successful career as a concert pianist that lasted over sixty years, longer than that of any other musician, male or female, in the nineteenth century. The works she programmed changed the character of the piano recital from a lengthy potpourri of virtuoso works based on popular melodies to a serious composer-centered program concentrating on a few works by such major composers as Bach, Beethoven, Mendelssohn, Chopin, Robert Schumann, and Brahms. Clara Schumann was one of the first pianists to play from memory and to play complete recitals without any assisting artists. Through her teaching she had a direct influence on later generations of pianists: among her outstanding women students who had professional careers in Europe and North America were Fanny Davies (1861–1934), Ilona Eibenschütz (1872–1967), Mathilde Verne (1865–1936), and Natalia Janotha (1856–1932).

Schumann was not without female rivals. As a child she was compared to Léopoldine Blahetka, Anna de Belleville (later Belleville-Oury, 1808–1880), and above all, Marie Pleyel (1811–1875, born Marie Moke). Pleyel, acknowledged as the leading French woman pianist from the 1830s on, headed "a formidable battalion" of pianists which included Louise Mattmann (1826–1861), Sophie Bohrer (1828–before 1866), Victorine Farrenc (1826–1859), and Louise-Aglaé Massart (1827–1887). Their Parisian performances in 1844–1845 provoked a music critic to write, "The year 1845 will mark the beginning of a new era: the reign of the women."[25] Among the outstanding women of a later generation were Wilhelmine Clauss-Szarvárdy (1834–1907) and the English pianist Arabella Goddard (1836–1922). In 1873 Goddard, famous as a Beethoven interpreter, began a three-year world concert tour that took her to North America, Australia, and India; within weeks of her return she gave two London recitals.

Some of the most celebrated women pianists of the latter half of the century were as well known for their tempestuous personalities as for their musicianship and formidable techniques. Among them were Sophie Menter (1846–1918), a student of Carl Tausig and Liszt and later a professor at the St. Petersburg Conservatory, and Teresa Carreño (1853–1917), a Venezuelan pianist and composer who was considered a world-class artist. In the last decades of the century, there were so many outstanding female keyboard artists that it is difficult to single out individuals from among the talented crowd. Anna Essipoff (also known as Annette Essipova, 1851–1914) was a Russian virtuoso who toured throughout the world and was the favorite partner of violinist Leopold Auer. She taught at the St. Petersburg Conservatory from 1893 to the end of her life. Agnes Zimmermann (1847–1925), who was born in Germany but built her career in England, edited sonatas of Mozart and Beethoven, and was considered to be a great classical pianist.

Harpists

Along with the piano, the harp was considered eminently suitable for women. In fact, it was played almost exclusively by women, in part because the movements required to play it were graceful and audiences enjoyed the sight as well as the sound of the players. Johann Friedrich Reichardt reviewed the 1809 Viennese recital of Caroline Longhi in a style typical of that period:

> She played very well, and what is more, looked very well, because she understood how to show off a beautiful figure to its greatest advantage, especially at the harp, where she managed to place herself and deport herself in so many varied and yet still graceful positions that we received a good view of her entire beautiful figure from all sides. Her harp playing itself was quite delicate and pleasing.[26]

The first women to play in orchestras were harpists. Josefa Müllner (1769–1843) was a soloist in the Vienna court orchestra and harp teacher of the archduchesses (sisters and daughters of the Emperor). Dorothea (Scheidler) Spohr (1787–1834) toured with her husband, Ludwig Spohr, the violinist, composer, and conductor; both Spohrs were employed in the orchestra of the Theater an der Wien between 1813 and 1815.

Violinists

String instruments were considered unfeminine in the early nineteenth century in large part because it was thought that the performers did not

FIGURE 6.4. Teresa and Marie Milanollo. Reproduced by permission of the Music Division, The New York Public Library for the Performing Arts, Astor, Lenox and Tilden Foundations.

look attractive while playing. Nevertheless, Italy's very talented and well-trained Milanollo sisters, Teresa (1827–1902) and Marie (1832–1848), were celebrated throughout Europe. After Marie's death, Teresa toured alone until 1857, when she married and retired from the stage.

By 1870 the violin was more acceptable, and many women came to Berlin to study with Joseph Joachim—despite being forbidden to participate in the orchestra of the Hochschule where he taught. Marie (Soldat) Röger (1863–1955), one of Joachim's favorite students, won the prestigious Mendelssohn prize at the Hochschule, as did Gabriele Wietrowetz (1866–1937), another Joachim pupil. These violinists, and many others who studied at the Paris and Brussels Conservatories, went on to have careers as soloists and to play in all-women string quartets in the last decades of the century. Perhaps the best-known European woman violinist of her time was Wilma (Neruda) Norman, later Lady Hallé (1839–1911). Making her debut at the age of seven, she subsequently appeared in all the principal cities of Europe. She married Sir Charles Hallé (her second husband) in 1888, continued with her career, and played an important part in the musical life of London. Lady Hallé was one of the few women who played in chamber groups with male colleagues.

Other Instrumentalists and Orchestra Players

Women were not encouraged to study orchestral instruments in the conservatories until late in the century, but there were a number of instrumentalists, usually the daughters of professional musicians, who studied privately and had professional careers in the early decades of the nineteenth century. Occasionally we find a woman on the roster of a provincial orchestra, but more often women instrumentalists appeared only as soloists. From the programs of the Leipzig Gewandhaus, a renowned concert hall, we learn that between 1781 and 1881 a number of women were featured soloists; they included eighteen violinists, two cellists (1845 and 1875), one flutist (1832), and two concertina players (1851 and 1870). In 1845 Lisa Cristiani gave the first public cello recital by a woman.

Another well-known instrumentalist was Caroline (Schleicher) Krähmer (1794–ca. 1850), one of the few women wind players of the nineteenth century. When her father died, she took over his duties as a town musician and later played in the orchestra of the Duke of Baden. Schleicher, who embarked on a concert tour as a clarinet soloist at the age of twenty-eight, met and married oboist Ernst Krähmer in Vienna. There the couple (who had ten children) gave annual concerts between 1827 and 1837. After her husband's death she continued to perform, appearing with two of her sons.[27]

By the 1870s women instrumentalists who had been denied entry into orchestras began to form their own string quartets and all-women orchestras. Although these musicians had the best conservatory training—many graduating with the highest honors—the women's orchestras were rarely given the same serious attention and respect enjoyed by the orchestras filled with their male colleagues.

Conductors

The art of conducting as we know it developed in the nineteenth century, and the first modern conductors were composers: Mendelssohn, Weber, Berlioz, and Wagner. As far as is known, women of the time were not invited to conduct professional instrumental groups, but a number of women established and conducted choral groups. Because many women musicians held positions as teachers, they may have conducted student groups. In some rare circumstances a composer was asked to conduct her own work, but almost always she faced hostility; Louise Héritte-Viardot, for example, described her difficult experience with a Stockholm orchestra when she conducted her cantata.[28] Women were not admitted to conducting classes nor were they welcomed as apprentices. It was to be many years before a woman would be accepted on the podium.

Summary

Despite social, educational, and economic restrictions, women participated in every aspect of musical life in the nineteenth century. They composed songs, keyboard music, chamber music, symphonies, and operas that were performed and published. Performers were seen and heard on concert stages throughout Europe as women artists traveled to and performed on five continents. Women students flocked to the great conservatories established in the nineteenth century to avail themselves of the professional training now open to them. Women were employed as teachers in the public conservatories and founded their own schools as well. Denied membership in symphony and opera orchestras, women established their own ensembles. Women writers and scholars produced basic studies on music and musical life. As in previous centuries, however, most of the professional women musicians were from families of musicians with a generations-long tradition.

The new prosperity of the middle classes afforded many women the time to study music. A large group of female amateurs developed, some rising to the highest levels of musical proficiency. Nevertheless, because of the prevailing attitudes toward feminine behavior, they were denied the opportunity to work professionally. Most often, well-to-do female amateurs, no matter how talented, were expected to limit themselves to domestic music making. Historians have largely ignored the accomplishments of professional and amateur women musicians of the nineteenth century, and only now are they beginning to be recognize them.

NOTES

1. Jean Jacques Rousseau, *Politics and the Arts: Letter to M. D'Alembert on the Theatre (Lettre sur les spectacles),* trans. Allan Bloom (Glencoe, IL: Free Press, 1960), pp. 82–83, as quoted in Mendel Kohansky, "Introduction," *The Disreputable Profession: The Actor in Society* (Westport, CT: Greenwood Press, 1984); Jean Jacques Rousseau, *Émile,* bk. 5, in *Oeuvres complètes,* ed. Michel Launay (Paris, 1967–1971), vol. 3: *Oeuvres philosophiques et politiques: de l'Émile aux derniers écrits politiques, 1762–1772,* pp. 243–47, as quoted in *Women, the Family, and Freedom: The Debate in Documents,* Susan Groag Bell and Karen M. Offen, eds., 2 vols. (Stanford: Stanford University Press, 1983), 1: 49.

2. Wilhelm von Humboldt, "Ueber der Geschlechtsunterschied und dessen Einfluss auf die organische Natur," in *Die Hören* I, pt. 2 (Tübingen, 1795), p. 111, as quoted in Bell and Offen, 1: 68.

3. See Nancy B. Reich, *Clara Schumann: The Artist and the Woman* (Ithaca, NY: Cornell University Press, 1985), pp. 228–29. Second edition, 2000.

4. *Das Conservatorium der Musik in Leipzig* (Leipzig, 1843), p. 6.

5. Kandie Kearley, "A Bel Canto Tradition: Women Teachers of Singing during the Golden Age of Opera" (DMA thesis, University of Cincinnati, 1998), chapters 3–4.

6. For a recent biography, see Margaret William McCarthy's *Amy Fay, America's Notable Woman of Music* (Warren, MI: Harmonie Park Press, 1995).

7. Hensel wrote numbers 2, 3, and 12 in Mendelssohn's Op. 8 (1827) and numbers 7, 10, and 12 in his Op. 9 (1830). Five pieces are songs; the sixth is a vocal duet, "Suleika und Hatem."

8. Quoted in Victoria Sirota, "The Life and Works of Fanny Mendelssohn Hensel" (DMA thesis, Boston University School for the Arts, 1981), p. 85.

9. Hildegard Publishing publishes or distributes performing editions of many of Hensel's piano works, songs, chamber and choral music.

10. See *Clara Schumann: Sämtliche Lieder,* ed. Joachim Draheim and Brigitte Höft, 2 vols. (Wiesbaden: Breitkopf & Härtel, 1990, 1992); and *Clara Schumann: Seven Songs,* ed. Kristin Norderval (Bryn Mawr: Hildegard Publishing Company, 1993).

11. Berthold Litzmann, ed., *Clara Schumann–Johannes Brahms Briefe aus den Jahren 1853–1896* (Leipzig: Breitkopf & Härtel, 1927), 1: 565.

12. Hippolyte Buffenoir, *La vicomtesse de Grandval* (Paris, 1894), pp. 10–11. I am indebted to Professor Lydia Ledeen of Drew University for the quotation and additional information about Grandval.

13. See Louise Reichardt, *Sechs geistliche Lieder* for SSAA choir and piano (New York: Broude, 1979).

14. E. T. A. Hoffmann, as quoted in *Source Readings in Music History,* ed. Oliver Strunk (New York: Norton, 1950), p. 777.

15. Piano music by Farrenc and Blahetka is published in vol. 10 of *Piano Music of the Parisian Virtuosos 1810–1860,* ed. Jeffrey Kallberg (New York and London: Garland Publishing, 1993).

16. Dates for Blahetka have been established by Freia Hoffmann. See *Instrument und Körper: Die musizierende Frau in der bürgerlichen Kultur* (Frankfurt am Main: Insel, 1991), pp. 352–70.

17. Sirota, p. 177.

18. *Allgemeine musikalische Zeitung* 50 (April 5, 1848): 233. The translation is my own.

19. Sirota, p. 246.

20. Bea Friedland, *Louise Farrenc, 1804–1875: Composer, Performer, Scholar* (Ann Arbor: UMI Research Press, 1980), p. 163.

21. H. Sutherland Edwards, *The Prima Donna* (London, 1888; reprint New York: Da Capo, 1978), p. 237.

22. Austin B. Caswell, ed., *Embellished Opera Arias*. Recent Researches in the Music of the Nineteenth and Early Twentieth Centuries, vols. 7–8 (Madison, WI: A-R Editions, 1989).

23. For more information on these and other Parisian singers, see Karin Pendle, "A Night at the Opera: The Parisian Prima Donna, 1830–50," *Opera Quarterly* 4 (April 1986): 77–89.

24. An interesting study of Stolz and her position in French opera of her day is Mary Ann Smart's "The Lost Voice of Rosine Stoltz," *Cambridge Opera Journal* 6 (1994): 31–50.

25. Quoted by Katharine Ellis in "Female Pianists and their Male Critics in Nineteenth-Century Paris," *JAMS* 50 (1997): 359–60.

26. Johann Friedrich Reichardt, *Vertraute Briefe geschrieben auf einer Reise nach Wien und den Oesterreichischen Staaten zu Ende des Jahres 1808 und zu Anfang 1809*, 2 vols., ed. Gustav Gugitz (Munich: Georg Müller, 1915), 1: 193–95. The translation is mine.

27. Pamela Weston, *Clarinet Virtuosi of the Past* (London: Pamela Weston, 1971), pp. 175–77; and Pamela Weston, *More Clarinet Virtuosi of the Past* (London: Pamela Weston, 1977), pp. 226–28. For more information on Schleicher-Krähmer, see Freia Hoffmann, pp. 370–80.

28. Louise Héritte-Viardot, *Memories and Adventures* (London: Mills and Boon, 1913; reprint, New York: Da Capo, 1978), pp. 224–25.

SUGGESTIONS FOR FURTHER READING

In addition to the sources cited in the footnotes or the text, the following books and articles provide information on women's activities in European music during the nineteenth century.

Bushnell, Howard. *Maria Malibran: A Biography of the Singer.* University Park: Pennsylvania State University Press, 1979.

Citron, Marcia. *The Letters of Fanny Hensel to Felix Mendelssohn.* Stuyvesant, NY: Pendragon, 1987.

Fitzlyon, April. *Maria Malibran: Diva of the Romantic Age.* London: Souvenir Press, 1987; distributed in the United States by Indiana University Press.

———. *The Price of Genius: A Life of Pauline Viardot.* New York: Appleton-Century-Crofts, 1964.

Hensel, Sebastian. *The Mendelssohn Family (1729–1847) from Letters and Journals.* 2nd ed., revised. Trans. C. Klingemann and an American collaborator. 2 vols. New York: Harper and Brothers, 1982; reprint, Westport, CT: Greenwood Press, 1969.

Loesser, Arthur. *Men, Women, and Pianos: A Social History.* New York: Simon and Schuster, 1954.

Mackenzie-Grieve, Averil. *Clara Novello, 1818–1908*. London: Geoffrey Bles, 1955; reprint, New York: Da Capo, 1980.
Metzelaar, Helen. "From Private to Public Sphere. An Exploration of Women's Role in Dutch Musical Life from c. 1700 to c. 1880 and Three Case Studies." Ph.D. diss., Utrecht University, 1996.
Myers, Margaret. *Blowing Her Own Trumpet: European Ladies' Orchestras and Other Women Musicians in Sweden, 1870–1950*. Göteborg [Sweden]: University of Göteborg, 1993.
Öhrström, Eva. *Borgerliga kvinnors musicerande i 1800-talets Sverige* (Music Making by Middle-Class Swedish Women of the Nineteenth Century). Göteborg: University of Göteborg, 1987. With a summary in English, pp. 191–96.
———. *Elfrida Andrée: ett levnadsode*. Stockholm: Prisma, 1999.
Reich, Nancy B. "Louise Reichardt." In *Ars Musica, Musica Scientia: Festschrift Heinrich Hüschen*, ed. Detlef Altenburg. Cologne: Gitarre und Laute Verlagsgesellschaft, 1980.
———. "Women as Musicians: A Question of Class." In *Musicology and Difference: Gender and Sexuality in Music Scholarship*, ed. Ruth Solie. Berkeley: University of California Press, 1993, pp. 125–46.
Smart, Mary Ann. "Verdi Sings Erminia Frezzolini." *Women & Music* 1 (1997): 33–45.
Tillard, Françoise. *Fanny Mendelssohn*. Translated by Camille Naish. Portland, OR: Amadeus Press, 1996.

In addition to those works cited in the text of this chapter, the various volumes of MTA include works of Ingeborg Bronsart [Schellendorf], Josefina Brdlikova, Frances Ellicott, Gabrielle Ferrari, Marie Jaell, Johanna Kinkel, Maria Malibran, Emilie Mayer, Ida Moberg, Helena Munktell, Loïsa Puget, Delphine von Schauroth, Elizabeth Stirling, and Jane Vieu. For songs by Sophia Westenholz see *Six Lieder by Sophia Maria Westenholz (1759–1838)*, ed. Barbara Garvey Jackson (Fayetteville, AR: Clar-Nan, 2000).

VII.
European Composers and Musicians, 1880–1918

Marcia J. Citron

Introduction

The status of European women generally improved between 1880 and 1918. Women benefited from many of the far-reaching political, social, and economic forces that were reshaping the attitudes and conventions of Western society. Politically, nationalism yielded to internationalism, a trend capped by the global reach of World War I (1914–1918). Socially, increased urbanization accompanied a new wave of industrialization. Women entered the labor pool in increasing numbers, and the figures swelled during the war as women filled jobs vacated by men at the front. This proved a very important stage in women's move from supportive to primary work roles. After the war, however, the numbers dropped drastically as Western Europe reverted to more traditional notions of women and work.

In the late nineteenth century, increased industrialization created a need for social reform. Although most reforms focused on the typical laborer, who was male, women figured as incidental beneficiaries. A strong wave of feminism swept through Europe in this period, notably in England, as middle-class women in particular perceived a growing discrepancy between themselves and men. Ironically, this perception arose as a result of women's greater access to education and because increased wealth exaggerated the split between the male world of the public sphere and the female world of the domestic. The various feminist movements culminated in the granting of the vote to women, which generally occurred by 1920. Economic reliance on women during World War I probably played a major role in bringing the long struggle to a successful conclusion. Nonetheless, suffrage functioned more as a symbol than as a barometer of widespread change. With few exceptions, women still lacked such basic legal rights as holding office, owning property, and suing for divorce.

Increased access to birth control devices proved critical in women's expanded array of options. The production of cheap rubber for use in condoms as well as the development of the diaphragm in the 1880s marked an important stage in women's reproductive freedom. Birthrates, especially in the middle and upper classes, dropped markedly by the early years of the twentieth century. With infant and maternal mortality in decline, women felt less of a need to produce large numbers of children in order to ensure familial succession. Industrialization alleviated the necessity for children to work at home for the family's livelihood. These factors gave women greater control in the timing and number of children, a necessary condition for sustained creative work.

Although reproductive freedom was probably the single most important factor in the emergence of the modern woman, other signs were in evidence. The drastic social upheavals during World War I led to radical changes in women's appearance, reflecting their expanding options. Short skirts and short hair, for example, allowed for greater freedom of movement and thus were less restrictive of women's activities. At the same time the stigma of makeup—a sign of "loose women"—began to vanish, and women could enjoy additional possibilities for physical individuality.

What was the typical profile of the European woman composer in this period? In many ways she resembled her prototype earlier in the century. She was likely to come from the middle or upper class and from an artistic home environment, where encouragement by knowledgeable family members helped instill the motivation and self-confidence needed for artistic fulfillment. This was especially important for women. Whereas society still took male success for granted, talented women continued to be viewed as exceptions. Men had the benefit of a long history of role models and support systems; women, on the other hand, due in part to ignorance of their own past, still had few female composers as role models and lacked the support of colleagues or family. They tended to feel isolated and unsure of their group identity. But aspiring female creators, unlike their predecessors, had the advantage of better education, especially in the burgeoning music conservatories. Although women were still a rarity in theory or composition classes, a few of them, such as Ethel Smyth and Lili Boulanger, took advantage of these opportunities.

Women composers were active in various musical cultures. One of the most interesting was *fin-de-siècle* France, with its mixture of the new and the old: the resurgence of a specifically French style fanned by nationalism after the Franco-Prussian War (1871), an interest in instrumental music, and the continuation of academic values as promulgated by the Paris Conservatoire.

Augusta Holmès

Augusta Holmès (1847–1903) flourished in this rich, late-nineteenth-century French atmosphere. Of Irish extraction, Holmès was born in Paris but spent her formative years in Versailles. Although neither of her parents was especially musical, Augusta nonetheless reaped the benefits of a home that attracted leading writers, artists, and musicians. Unfortunately, Augusta's mother discouraged her interest in music; after Mme Holmès's death when Augusta was a young teen, however, her father encouraged the girl to develop her talent. Despite the proximity of Versailles to Paris, the center of French musical life, Augusta studied with local musicians. The poet Alfred de Vigny, her godfather (and possibly her natural father), played a major role as mentor and adviser, a kind of substitute for her mother.

As Holmès approached her twenties, she became an ardent Wagnerian and fought hard to have works by Wagner included on the Concerts Populaires, an important Parisian series. She had the opportunity to meet Wagner at his home on Lake Lucerne, and she corresponded with Franz Liszt, who admired her musical talents. In the mid-1870s Holmès joined the circle of César Franck—it is unclear whether she actually studied with him—and began to compose in earnest. Her lifelong attraction to the grand French vocal tradition and its lofty ideals is exemplified in her early works, including the symphonic poem *Hymn to Apollo* (1872). Many of her large orchestral works are subtitled "dramatic symphony" and include chorus and vocal soloists; other orchestral works, such as *Triumphal Ode,* composed for the Paris Exposition of 1889, also include vocal forces. Among her large works that appeared on programs of major concert series, such as the Concerts Populaires, was *Les Argonautes* (1881).

Like many a French composer, Holmès tried her hand at opera. Strong literary talent, as well as admiration for Wagner, probably influenced her decision to write her own libretti. She completed four operas, but only one was produced: *La montagne noire,* a work in four acts, performed at the Paris Opéra on February 8, 1895. Along with Louise Bertin's *Fausto* (1831) and *La Esmeralda* (1836), it was one of the few operas by women introduced in Paris in the nineteenth century. Unfortunately, *La montagne noire* was poorly received, and Holmès suffered a great disappointment. Some have attributed its lack of success, which contributed to Holmès's physical decline, to the fact that it was actually composed some twelve years earlier, so that by the time the performance materialized its Wagnerian subject matter and musical treatment had become passé.

Holmès's interest in vocal genres extended well beyond dramatic music, however. She composed approximately 130 songs (most of them after

1880), many to her own texts. The large number published attest to her popularity, and Ethel Smyth was one contemporary who greatly admired them. The songs that are readily available exhibit typical traits of the period as well as individual characteristics.[1] Many texts deal with idealized love, heroism ("Ogier le Danois," 1900), or exotic locales ("Garci Perez," 1892). These were conventions among the texts in contemporary French song, although Holmès's attraction to heroism also reflects her strong Irish patriotism. Her musical style displays great variety. The Christmas song "Noël" (1885), for example, features an appropriate folk style. The exotic flavor of Morocco in "Charme-du-jour" (1902) comes through in the drone bass and the improvisatory turns in the vocal line. The ghost of Wagner hovers in "La Haine," from her song cycle *Les sept ivresses* (1882), where the markedly dramatic style builds on the piano part's left-hand pattern—as might an important Leitmotiv in *The Ring*. In contrast, a neoclassical vocabulary found in much French music around 1900 permeates the playful "À Trianon" (1896). Holmès composed only a few small-scale instrumental pieces, including *Fantaisie* for clarinet and piano, written as a competition piece for the Paris Conservatoire in 1900.

Throughout her life Augusta Holmès mixed easily in leading artistic circles. She had a vibrant personality and was described as a real beauty.[2] Although she never married, she had a lengthy affair with the poet Catulle Mendès (1841–1909) and reputedly had three children with him. The typical posthumous assessment dwells on her beauty to the exclusion of her music. Posterity has idealized Holmès's persona and feminine charms and thereby ignored, or at best marginalized, her creative achievements. A truer assessment can emerge only when we peel away the layers of idealization to expose the human characteristic and creative energy of this interesting woman.

Cécile Chaminade

The professional paths of Holmès and Cécile Chaminade (1857–1944) crossed in the 1880s, when the orchestral works of both women appeared on the programs of major concert series. For the most part, however, their careers remained distinct. Chaminade was born in Paris to an upper-middle-class family that valued the arts. Both parents were amateur musicians, and her mother taught her to play the piano. Chaminade's earliest pieces may date from 1865, composed for her first communion. Félix Le Couppey, an important Paris musician, recommended that she study at the Conservatoire. Although Chaminade's father would not permit his daughter to attend the school because of his views on proper female decorum, he allowed her to study piano and theory privately with professors on the faculty.

FIGURE 7.1. Cécile Chaminade. Photo courtesy of the Vicomtesse J. de Cornulier-Lucinière. Used by permission.

By the late 1870s Chaminade began to perform publicly as a pianist in chamber music. Her compositional debut occurred in April 1878 and was well received by the press. Throughout her active career as composer-pianist, which lasted until the outbreak of World War I, character pieces for piano and songs formed her repertoire's mainstay. In the 1880s she produced several large-scale works as well, including *Suite d'orchestre* (1881) and *La Sévillane* (1882), a one-act opéra-comique performed privately in concert version. *Callirhoë*, a ballet, premiered in Marseilles (1888) and probably was Chaminade's greatest success. The decade also included the dramatic symphony *Les Amazones* (1884–1888) and the *Concertstück* for piano and orchestra, both introduced in April 1888 in Antwerp. *Concertstück* proved highly successful and enjoyed numerous performances before World War I. Except for the still-popular Concertino for flute and orchestra, written as a competition piece for the Conservatoire (1902), Chaminade composed no other orchestral works.

About 1890 Chaminade embarked on a parallel career as a concert pianist, performing almost exclusively her own compositions. She toured the European continent and began annual visits to England in 1892. She focused on piano works and songs, and the widespread exposure created a market for their publication. In fact, Chaminade was one of the most published women composers. She became extremely popular in the United States, where her pieces were also printed. The first of many Chaminade Clubs came into existence at the turn of the century, and her growing popularity led her to make the long journey to America. Between October 24 and December 15, 1908, Chaminade gave concerts in twelve cities, traveling as far west as Minneapolis. Audiences flocked to see her, although press reception was mixed. During this period Chaminade won several awards, including the Jubilee Medal from Queen Victoria (1897) and the Chefekat from the Sultan of Turkey (1901). In the summer of 1913 she was admitted into the prestigious Legion of Honor, the first female composer so honored. Advancing years and the outbreak of war curtailed Chaminade's concertizing. The rest of her life was played out in increasing debilitation and isolation, exacerbated by her belief that she was forgotten. Chaminade died in Monte Carlo on April 13, 1944, at the age of eighty-six.

Personally, Chaminade preferred solitude or the company of her family to the broader social or musical scene and enjoyed a close relationship with her mother. Her platonic marriage (1901–1907) to Louis-Mathieu Carbonel, a Marseilles music publisher twenty years her senior, shocked her family yet apparently suited Chaminade, who later declared that "it is difficult to reconcile the domestic life with the artistic. . . . When a woman of talent marries a man who appreciates that side of her, such a marriage may be ideally happy for both."[3] Thus we have Chaminade's views on a classic dilemma facing women.

Chaminade was extremely prolific. Of her approximately 400 compositions, about 200 are piano pieces and about 135 are songs. Like many women she was drawn to these intimate genres, whose expressive potential holds special appeal for female culture. Almost all of Chaminade's piano works are character pieces with descriptive titles that capture the flavor of *la belle époque*. The harmonic language is diatonic and functional, with frequent color chords to add spice. The forms are simple and traditional, while the melodies, their most prominent element, are generally elegant and tuneful. Like many a French work of the period, Chaminade's piano pieces often exploit exoticism, such as the Spanish flavor of "Sérénade" (1884) or "La Lisonjera" (The Flatterer, ca. 1890). Standing apart is the Sonata (composed ca. 1888 and published in 1895), her only work in this genre. Since Chaminade did not perform the complete piece in public, she may have considered it an experimental work.

The Sonata consists of three contrasting movements (the entire piece has been published in a Da Capo reprint, *Three Piano Pieces* [1979]; the second movement is in HAMW, pp. 213–17), with the leisurely pacing typical of Romanticism. The third movement, a virtuosic showpiece, was first published in 1886 as the fourth of *Six Études de Concert*, Op. 35. The first movement takes its cue from Chopin, and in its sweep and grandeur resembles an extended ballade more than a classically structured first movement. The piano writing is bold and idiomatic for the instrument. Built on two ideas that are subjected to various manipulations, including thematic transformation, the movement stands out within Chaminade's piano *oeuvre* on several accounts. First, it emphasizes thematic development rather than melody, the composer's mainstay (melody is supreme in the second movement). Second, it reveals structural experimentation. Third, it deploys fugal procedures, probably attributable to the influence of Camille Saint-Saëns, whom Chaminade greatly admired, and Moritz Moszkowski, the Polish-German composer who would become her brother-in-law.

Chaminade's art largely reflects the culture of the middle- to upper-class woman of *la belle époque*. Despite great success and popularity in her heyday, however, Chaminade has not fared well in music history. If mentioned at all, she is dismissed as a composer of charming salon pieces. Such assessments rest on the assumption of a two tiered hierarchy of music making, the professional and the amateur, in which the former takes precedence. Since the word *amateur* implies the domestic world inhabited by women, critics and historians have thus placed less value on women's activities. In order to evaluate Chaminade we will have to gain a firmer understanding of the sociology of the domestic sphere: its activities, conventions, and value systems.

Agathe Backer-Grøndahl

Another composer-pianist whose music mirrors feminine culture near the end of the century is Agathe Backer-Grøndahl (1847–1907). At the height of her career she told the astonished George Bernard Shaw, then a London music critic, that her artistry grew out of her life as wife and mother. Indeed, Backer-Grøndahl managed to combine a rich domestic life and a fulfilling musical career, a feat that would make her the envy of many a modern woman.

Born near Oslo, Norway, into an artistic home, Backer-Grøndahl showed early talent for the piano. She studied with Theodor Kullak in the mid-1860s, then with Hans von Bülow and Franz Liszt. Her performing career took flight in the early 1870s, and she received high praise for her renditions of Beethoven and Chopin. In 1875 she married, and thereafter immersed herself in composition, producing the majority of her works. In 1898 she returned to concertizing, this time (like Chaminade) emphasizing her own works, and enjoyed great success throughout Scandinavia. She undoubtedly received encouragement from her husband, who became a choral conductor.

Parallels with Chaminade can be seen in the music of Backer-Grøndahl. Both composers stressed piano works and songs, and both were prolific in these genres. The piano music in particular exhibits stylistic similarities to Chaminade's works, as in Backer-Grøndahl's early collection *Trois morceaux* (Three pieces), Op. 15, published in 1882.[4] It features the directness of expression typical of much music by women. The evocation of dance rhythms in various guises represents another feminine connection: women's centrality in ballet, an art form then at its height, and in dance in general. Although considered a leading artistic representative in her country, Backer-Grøndahl did not write in a noticeably nationalistic style. Her music is cosmopolitan and, like many a Chaminade work, betrays its debt to Chopin and Mendelssohn.

Elfrida Andrée

Another Scandinavian composer, Elfrida Andrée (1841–1929), also attained fame as a conductor and organist. Andrée and her sister, opera singer Fredrika Stenhammar, received their first music lessons from their father. Andrée went on to Stockholm, where she studied composition and perfected her organ-playing skills, and then to Copenhagen, where her composition teacher was the respected figure Niels Gade. After influencing Swedish authorities to revise a law that prevented women from being hired as church organists, she accepted a post in Stockholm. In 1867 she became cathedral organist in Göteborg, a position she held for the rest of her life.

Andrée's music reveals her solid grounding in the German Romantic style of the first half of the nineteenth century and in the French style of organ music. She produced two symphonies, chamber music, works for chorus, piano and organ solos, and songs. Her opera, *Fritiofs saga* (1899), with libretto by the distinguished Swedish author Selma Lagerlöf, remained unperformed save for two orchestral suites drawn from its score. Andrée was also associated with Göteborg's Labor Concert series, arranging some 800 programs, and was known for her work toward equal rights for women.

Lili Boulanger

The music of Lili Boulanger (1893–1918), on the other hand, reflects a post-Romantic world. Born two generations after Chaminade and Backer-Grøndahl, Boulanger inhabited the Paris of Fauré and Debussy, Diaghilev and Stravinsky. In her short lifetime this remarkable composer accomplished a great deal, buoyed by a combination of prodigious talent, sheer will, and a supportive family environment. Lili was born in Paris into a family with musical roots. Her paternal grandmother was an opera singer and her mother, Russian by birth, came to Paris to study voice with Ernest Boulanger, a professor at the Conservatoire and a winner of the Prix de Rome in composition (1835).

Boulanger married his pupil in 1877, despite an age difference of more than forty years. Lili was the youngest of their three children, of whom the first died in infancy. Lili's close relationship with her older sister, Nadia (1887–1979), had a profound impact on her musical outlook. Nadia provided a strong female role model, instilling a sense of unlimited possibilities. Among musical siblings, the relationship between this pair of sisters is unique. As a child Lili experienced the death of her father, to whom she was also quite close, and survived a life-threatening case of bronchial pneumonia. The psychological and practical effects of chronic illness would play major roles in molding Boulanger's self-identity and her relationship to the creative process.

Both Lili and Nadia received a wealth of encouragement and support for the development of their musical abilities. In the late 1890s Lili often accompanied Nadia to her classes at the Conservatoire. Her own private training began with solfège lessons and moved on to include instruction in several instruments. She had the good fortune to be exposed to a broad range of historical styles, and her first pieces date from this period. As Lili grew older, frequent bouts of illness prevented sustained music training, and she lived largely in the isolation that Mme Boulanger imposed to protect her daughter from contamination. Catholicism became especially meaningful to Lili and found its way into some of her works of this period.

The year 1910 marked a turning point. The seventeen-year-old, increasingly aware of the likelihood of an early death, decided to devote all her energies to becoming a composer. To Boulanger this included winning the Prix de Rome, the prestigious annual prize in composition awarded by the Conservatoire on the basis of a grueling competition. No matter that the competition had only recently begun admitting women or that she lacked the stamina to survive such an expenditure of effort. Over the next two years Boulanger pursued a systematic course of preparation. She took theory lessons and practiced setting the types of texts given in the competition. More formalized training occurred in early 1912, when she entered the Conservatoire. Boulanger attempted the Prix de Rome that spring, but illness forced her to drop out. The next year, however, she was successful, and she became the first woman to win the prize (Nadia had earned second place in 1908). One wonders whether it is mere coincidence that two "firsts" for French women composers occurred about the same time: Boulanger's winning the Prix de Rome and Chaminade's admission to the Legion of Honor.

Boulanger garnered the honor with her cantata *Faust et Hélène,* which was premiered in November 1913. Although she encountered sexual prejudice in the first months of the fellowship residency in Rome, Boulanger gradually became acclimated and worked on several compositions, including the song cycle *Clairières dans le ciel.* War broke out in 1914, and Boulanger returned to Paris. The next year she and Nadia participated in the war effort by keeping colleagues and friends at the front abreast of musical news. She spent the spring of 1916 in Rome in an attempt to complete her interrupted fellowship. Deteriorating health forced her return to Paris in late June, and over the next two years she was able to work only sporadically. On March 8, 1918, the Paris premiere of *Clairières* took place. One week later Lili Boulanger died. Despite her tragically short life, she was a prolific composer. Of her twenty-nine extant completed works, twenty-one have been published. She also left an incomplete opera, *La Princesse Maleine,* based on a Maeterlinck play. Approximately three-quarters of the extant works are vocal, many with orchestra. This preference places her squarely in the French tradition.

Boulanger's major work during her 1914 residency in Rome was the magnificent song cycle *Clairières dans le ciel* (Rifts in the sky). The thirteen poems come from the larger collection *Tristesses* (1902–1906) by the Symbolist writer Francis Jammes. The poetry elicited a powerful response from Boulanger, who identified with the heroine. Narrated by a male (a tenor voice), the texts speak in delicate floral metaphors of the hope, tenderness, joy, fulfillment, loneliness, and desolation of fleeting love. Boulanger's settings are subdued, almost somber, and the range of contrasts is narrow. A musical expression of the text emerges as the most important element. With suppleness and a responsiveness to the nuances of the French language, the semideclamatory vocal lines approach the rhythms of speech. In this Boulanger is typically French and resembles Debussy. She also shows her nationality in the cycle's emphasis on color and sonority: exploring new combinations, registers, and textures in the piano, and utilizing the Impressionists' harmonic palette of nonfunctional seventh and ninth chords, parallel chords, and modal progressions. Most of the songs are through-composed or in a loose AB form.

The twelfth and thirteenth songs (HAMW, pp. 234–44) exemplify Boulanger's mastery. "Je garde une médaille d'elle" (I keep a medallion of hers), only sixteen bars long, depends for its unity on a one-bar harmonic progression, set in strict contrary motion, juxtaposing the sonorities of the stark open fifth, the major seventh chord, and the minor ninth chord. The vocal line resembles recitative and moves brilliantly to the dramatic setting of "prier, croire, espérer" (to pray, believe, hope). The last song, "Demain fera un an" (Tomorrow it will be a year), is the longest of the set. The poetry is often painful, as it speaks of nothingness and death. Tonally the song begins in D minor, where No. 12 ends. Boulanger matches the retrospective text with retrospective music, namely, three substantial references to earlier songs: a *Tristan* section from No. 6; an accompaniment pattern from No. 11; and, near the end, a quotation of the poetry and music from the beginning of the cycle. Although the song features greater contrasts than do the preceding numbers, Boulanger deploys a repeating bass rhythm (quarter note, half note, quarter note) that provides continuity. Her sense of impending death colors the song and leaves the listener stunned by the final line: "Nothing more. I have nothing more, nothing more to sustain me. Nothing more. Nothing more."

Boulanger grew up in a transitional culture, and many of her works express the changes that were taking place. *Clairières*, for example, hints at the isolation and alienation that were to become hallmarks of modernism; the song cycle displays many of the traits we single out in Debussy as harbingers of twentieth-century style. As a woman, Boulanger ignored confining gender stereotypes in her quest for personal achievement. Her total absorption in her art provides an inspiring model for female creators. One cannot help but wonder what this remarkable woman would have composed had she lived longer.

Alma Mahler-Werfel

Although Paris witnessed many moments of modernism, Vienna lay much closer to the heart of the movement. From 1900 to the end of World War I, the twilight of the old artistic order and the birth of the new intermingled

FIGURE 7.2. Alma Mahler-Werfel. Alma Mahler-Werfel Papers, Department of Special Collections, University of Pennsylvania Library. Used by permission.

in fascinating ways. Gustav Mahler's music, for example, embodied the excesses of post-Romanticism and hinted at the alienation of modernism. It was but a short step to the compositions of Schoenberg and Berg, the artworks of Klimt and Kokoschka. Freud's theories of the unconscious, conceived around 1900, reflect the modernist tendencies of this culture.

Alma Mahler-Werfel (1879–1964) was a product of this fascinating period. Her father, Emil Schindler, was a noted portraitist. Alma adored him and claimed that he always took her seriously. She spent much of her time in his studio and remembered fondly his fine tenor voice singing Schumann's Lieder. Perhaps this early musical association played a part in her creative attraction to that genre. In any case, the Schindler home regularly hosted the leading cultural figures in Vienna, providing the young girl with an invaluable understanding of the artistic world and the artistic personality. Alma found music irresistible and, according to her memoirs, began composing at the age of nine. Her early compositions were for various media, both instrumental and vocal. As a teen she passed through a Wagnerian phase, in which she described herself as "screaming Wagner parts until my beautiful mezzo-soprano had gone to pieces."[5] Alma fed her literary passion by assembling a personal library that ranged from the classics to the avant-garde.

Alma began composition lessons about 1900 with Alexander Zemlinsky, a young composer-conductor who also taught Schoenberg. Zemlinsky introduced her to Gustav Mahler, and Alma was smitten by this temperamental celebrity who was head of the Vienna Opera and nineteen years her senior. Mahler asserted his dominance, whether it concerned what she read or whether she would be permitted to compose. Alma later wrote: "He considered the marriage of Robert and Clara Schumann 'ridiculous,' for instance. He sent me a long letter with the demand that I instantly give up my music and live for his alone."[6]

After their marriage in March 1902 Alma gave up composition and became copyist and helpmate to her husband. Mahler apparently could not brook competition, especially from a woman, which he took as a threat to his fragile ego. As to why Alma agreed to such a marriage, we must remember that she was young and less confident of her own needs and that she gravitated toward a father substitute—in this case a much older man, a famous man, an artistic man. Shortly after a marital crisis in 1910, which prompted Mahler to consult with Freud, Gustav begged her to resume composing and insisted on helping to get her works published. It is difficult to believe that Mahler, who had not even heard Alma's music when he demanded that she stop composing, experienced a sincere change of heart. Rather it was a plea of desperation—the fear of losing his wife to another man. In any case, Alma's *Five Lieder* (1910) resulted.

Mahler died in 1911, and Alma began a relationship with the artist Oskar Kokoschka, once again subordinating herself to a man's work. In 1915, after she broke with Kokoschka, she married Walter Gropius, a young architect who was to found the Bauhaus school of art in 1919. While he was serving in the war, Alma met the poet Franz Werfel, whom she married in 1929. This was her only happy, long-lasting relationship. In the intervening years she published two other collections: *Four Lieder* (1915) and *Five Songs* (1924).

Mahler-Werfel's keen intellectual faculties made her a focal point of leading cultural circles, especially through 1920. She relished the avant-garde. In her memoirs she notes with pride her ability to single out and marry men whom posterity would consider great. She wrote about Gustav Mahler after the successful performance of his Symphony No. 8 at the Hollywood Bowl, "I saw once more how instinctively right I had been to cast my lot with Mahler when people thought of him as just a conductor and opera director and would not believe in his creative genius."[7] In her relationships with artistic greats Alma believed she had a mission to nurture their talent. She did not see herself as some passive Muse, a contemporary gender stereotype, but as an active participant in building artistic fulfillment and success.

What of her own artistic fulfillment? Alma is surprisingly reticent about her own music, except for the period with Mahler. We find a few allusions in her memoirs, but they convey little. She also says little about other musical activities, such as playing the piano. In part this is because her memoirs were intended for a broad readership and best-seller success. Yet the reticence signifies more: deep-seated ambivalence about her own creativity. Her background was ripe for such conflict. On the one hand she had support from her father, her teacher, and her environment; on the other she had few female role models and internalized the debilitating attitudes of her first husband. She implies that Werfel was more supportive, but by the time they were married (1930s) it was probably too late for her musical career. Despite youthful confidence and enthusiasm, and above all great talent, Mahler-Werfel produced a relatively small number of compositions over her eighty-four years. Most were probably early works. Only fourteen pieces in three sets, all Lieder, were published. These and two other songs in manuscript constitute her existing creative output (other musical manuscripts were destroyed in the bombing of Vienna in World War II).

The *Four Lieder* of 1915 exemplify Mahler-Werfel's glorious contribution to the art song.[8] Each song is based on a poem of a contemporary writer and displays her perceptive grasp of literary values, especially declamation, imagery, and symbolism. Musically the songs display a broad stylistic range. One of Mahler-Werfel's main characteristics is the skillful control of dissonance. Her vocal lines often proceed in large leaps, a manner that accords well with dissonance and a harmonic idiom that verges on atonality. Such a daring vocabulary places Mahler-Werfel in the company of such contemporary experimentalists as Schoenberg and Berg. The third song, "Ansturm" (Assault), on a text by Richard Dehmel, is particularly bold. Composed in 1911, it is perhaps the earliest work by a woman set to a text that centers on sexual desire and release. In this flouting of social convention, Mahler-Werfel deploys a fascinating mix of musical styles, including recitative, Brahmsian lushness, sharp dissonance, and an unresolved dominant seventh chord at the end.

"Der Erkennende" (The one who is aware; HAMW, pp. 248–50) was composed in 1915 and published in *Five Songs* (1924). Set to a poem by Franz Werfel, it reveals Mahler-Werfel's brilliant ability to translate poetic imagery into musical terms. The desolation of the text is captured through spare musical language: even rhythms, repeated pitches, ostinato-like patterns, and economic thematic material. This stylistic simplicity, which also includes an ABA form and scalar melodies, contributes to a sense of irony that reflects the *Angst* of the era. Above all, Alma Mahler-Werfel's songs show passion—passion corresponding to the person. The addition of her songs to the repertoire provides singers some wonderful vehicles of expression.

Ethel Smyth

While Vienna and Paris were encouraging experimentation, England was continuing to pursue an insular tradition that perpetuated ideals of the early nineteenth century. In addition, England lacked a native tradition and an institutional structure for music making—it had only a few opera houses, very brief opera seasons, and a handful of operas by English composers. This musical culture formed the backdrop to the indomitable Ethel Smyth (1858–1944).

Of the same generation as Chaminade, Smyth came from a middle-class Victorian family with little artistic bent. From the first she was a nonconformist. Not only did she overcome paternal objections to her attending the Leipzig Conservatory (1877), but after her return she also broke convention by deciding to devote herself to the composition of opera, a bold decision for her time, nationality, and gender. Smyth broke gender conventions in other ways. Her dress was as much masculine as feminine, and she liked to smoke cigars. She participated actively in the suffragist movement in England (1910–1912) and even spent some time in jail. Her "March of the Women" became the rallying call for the movement. Sexually she was a lesbian, a fact she did not attempt to conceal. Through autobiographical writings, including several books and numerous articles, Smyth revealed in a forthright manner her shrewd understanding of gender conventions as they affected women's attempts to attain success in a man's world.

Smyth's student works included chamber music, piano sonatas, and Lieder, genres that reflect the traditionalist Germanic leanings of the Leipzig Conservatory and of her subsequent teacher, Heinrich von Herzogenberg. After writing two successful orchestral pieces in England (1890), Smyth composed one of her best works, the Mass in D. Although the Mass received some very good reviews after its premiere in 1893, it was not performed again until some thirty years later. Smyth identified the work's genre and Germanic style, along with the time's prevailing sexual prejudice, as reasons why the Mass was subsequently ignored:

> Year in year out, composers of the Inner Circle, generally University men attached to our musical institutions, produced one choral work after another—not infrequently deadly dull affairs—which, helped along by the impetus of official approval, automatically went the round of our Festivals and Choral Societies. . . . Was it likely, then, that the Faculty would see any merit in a work written on such a very different line—written too by a woman who had actually gone off to Germany to learn her trade?[9]

Perhaps Smyth found solace in the fact that Sir Donald Francis Tovey included the Mass in his analytic volume on choral music, comparing it to Beethoven's Missa Solemnis and noting that both are spiritual, not liturgical, works. He admired the vocal writing and declared that "the score should become a *locus classicus* for the whole duty and privileges of choral orchestration."[10]

Around the time that her Mass was introduced, Smyth was working on the first of her six operas, *Fantasio* (1892–1894). Dissatisfied with this "fantastic comedy," which was set in German and had been performed in Weimar in 1898, Smyth destroyed all copies in 1916. Her next opera was *Der Wald* (The forest), a one-act tragedy composed between 1899 and 1901. In its Germanic traits—language, symbolism, and compositional technique—the opera betrays her musical roots. In 1902 *Der Wald* was performed in Berlin and London. The next year, with Smyth as conductor, it was staged at the Metropolitan Opera in New York, the first opera by a woman to be performed there.[11]

The Wreckers (1903–1904) is Smyth's best opera. After a personal experience at the caves off the coast of Cornwall, Smyth was inspired to sketch a story and give it to her friend and collaborator Henry Brewster to fashion into a libretto. Smyth, ever practical, assented to Brewster's wish to write in French because she sensed the possibility of a performance under conductor André Messager. This fell through, as did projected performances in Monte Carlo and Brussels. Arthur Nikisch, the opera director in Leipzig, liked the work and engaged it for the 1906–1907 season. It was premiered successfully in November 1906, with the German title *Standrecht* (Martial Law).

Smyth nonetheless withdrew the work by removing the music from the players' stands when the conductor refused to reinstate cuts she opposed, an incident that reveals Smyth's character and her unyielding commitment to principles. The opera, translated into English, was introduced to England in May 1908 in a concert version of Acts I and II, and it received a fully staged performance in June 1909.

Smyth's dual loyalties to English and German traditions are embodied in *The Wreckers*. Its subject matter melds the English people and the forces of nature. In this Smyth laid the groundwork for later English composers, notably Benjamin Britten in *Peter Grimes* (1945). The tonal clarity reflects both English conservatism and Smyth's training in Leipzig. Her powerful orchestration and emphasis on thematic development exemplify the Germanic tradition, and the legacy of Wagner is evident in the absence of traditional divisions into separate numbers. Smyth creates unity by using recurring motifs, although her practice differs from Wagner's full-fledged Leitmotif technique. She does, however, emulate Wagner in the symbolic importance assigned the power of nature. Smyth may have modeled the heroine, courageous and willing to defy conventional morality, on Wagner's Isolde as well as on herself.

The overture, constructed as a medley, introduces many of the important themes of the opera. It opens with the Wagner-like motif that the chorus intones during the storm scene of Act I (HAMW, pp. 222–31). The orchestra is exploited for color and evokes many pictorial effects. The harmonic language is largely functional, although modal progressions provide occasional contrast. Counterpoint is one of the chief compositional devices. In 1910, John Fuller Maitland concluded his enthusiastic assessment of *The Wreckers* with the following statement: "It is difficult to point to a work of any nationality since Wagner that has a more direct appeal to the emotions, or that is more skillfully planned and carried out."[12] This opera, dormant for many years, was revived in London in 1994 in a concert performance led by Odaline de la Martinez. A CD recording of a live performance was released the same year by Conifer Records Limited. As a fine counterpart to Britten's *Peter Grimes,* Smyth's opera could strike a resonant note, especially with English audiences.

In 1910 Smyth suspended her creative activities for a few years to participate in the suffragist movement. World War I forced the cancellation of some planned performances of her music, especially in Germany. Between 1919 and 1940 she concentrated on writing about her life and expressing her views, completing ten books. Her style is direct, perceptive, witty, and practical. She also continued as an activist, for example, persistently attempting to keep women orchestra players in jobs they had held during the war. All in all Ethel Smyth counts as one of the most striking figures in women's history. A pathbreaking composer and feminist, she had the courage to live up to her convictions regardless of consequences. She is the first woman to articulate in so direct a manner the subtle and overt types of discrimination facing women musicians. Even increasing deafness could not dampen the energy and pluck of this iconoclast.

Summary

As we have seen, European women musicians around the turn of the century participated vividly in musical life. Their impressive achievements round out our picture of musical creativity at that time. Taken as a group they might suggest a new model for historical periodization. In any case, these achievements serve notice that factors particular to women's experience—career-marriage relationship, mothering, role models, and access to training and to audiences—must be added to the variables of historical evaluation. Only a very small percentage of compositions by these women is known today. The most obvious reason is that very little of their music is available, but that is a symptom rather than a cause and reflects various attitudes about art music, canon formation, and women themselves. Fortunately, these complex issues are being explored; they hold out the promise of a better appreciation of women's accomplishments in their own right.

NOTES

1. See Augusta Holmès, *Selected Songs* (New York: Da Capo, 1984).
2. For Ethel Smyth's narration of Holmès's attraction to Smyth's friend Henry Brewster see her essay "Augusta Holmès," in *A Final Burning of Boats* (London: Longmans, Green & Co., 1928), pp. 126–36.
3. Interview in *The Washington Post,* November 1, 1908, magazine section, p. 4.
4. Reprinted in Agathe Backer-Grøndahl, *Piano Music* (New York: Da Capo, 1982).
5. Alma Mahler-Werfel, *And the Bridge Is Love* (New York: Harcourt, Brace and Company, 1958), p. 9.
6. Ibid., p. 19.
7. Ibid., pp. 301–2.
8. A modern edition of all Alma Mahler-Werfel's published songs was brought out by Universal Edition of Vienna in 1984.
9. Ethel Smyth, *As Time Went On* (London: Longmans, 1936), p. 172.
10. Donald Francis Tovey, *Essays in Musical Analysis,* Vol. 5: *Vocal Music* (London: Oxford University Press, 1937), p. 236.
11. See excerpts from the review that first appeared in *Musical Courier* (March 18, 1903) in *Women in Music,* rev. ed., ed. Carol Neuls-Bates (Boston: Northeastern University Press, 1996), pp. 225–26.
12. *Grove Dictionary of Music and Musicians,* 2d ed., s.v. "Smyth, Ethel," by J. A. Fuller Maitland.

SUGGESTIONS FOR FURTHER READING

In addition to the items mentioned in the text or cited in the footnotes, the following sources provide information on the chapter's topic.

Citron, Marcia J. *Cécile Chaminade: A Bio-Bibliography.* Westport, CT: Greenwood Press, 1988.

———. *Gender and the Musical Canon.* Cambridge: Cambridge University Press, 1993.

Dopp, Bonnie Jo. "Numerology and Cryptology in the Music of Lili Boulanger: The Hidden Program in *Clairières dans le ciel.*" *Musical Quarterly* 78 (1997): 557–83.

Fauser, Annegret. "*La Guerre en dentelles:* Women and the *Prix de Rome* in French Cultural Politics." *Journal of the American Musicological Society* 51 (1998): 83–130.

Filler, Susan. "A Composer's Wife as Composer: The Songs of Alma Mahler." *Journal of Musicological Research* 4 (1983): 427–41.

———. "Lili Boulanger's *La Princess Maleine:* A Composer and Her Heroine as Literary Icons." *Journal of the Royal Musical Association* 122 (1997): 68–108.

Hyde, Deryck. "Ethel Smythe [*sic*]: A Reappraisal," in *Newfound Voices.* London: Belvedere Press, 1984, pp. 138–206.

Kane, Susan. "Liza Lehmann (1862–1918): Her Times, Roles, and Songs." DMA thesis, University of Cincinnati, 2000.

Kravitt, Edward. "The Lieder of Alma Maria Schindler-Mahler." *Music Review* 49 (1988): 190–204.

The Memoirs of Ethel Smyth. Abridged and introduced by Ronald Crichton. London: Viking, 1987.

Meyers, Rollo. "Augusta Holmès: A Meteoric Career." *Musical Quarterly* 53 (1967): 365–76.

Myers, Margaret. *Blowing Her Own Trumpet: European Ladies' Orchestras and Other Women Musicians in Sweden, 1870–1950.* Göteborg [Sweden]: University of Göteborg, 1993.

Öhrström, Eva. *Borgerliga kvinnors musicerande i 1800-talets Sverige* (Music Making by Middle-Class Swedish Women of the Nineteenth Century). Göteborg: University of Göteborg, 1987. With a summary in English, pp. 191–96.

———. *Elfrida Andrée: ett levnadsode.* Stockholm: Prisma, 1999.

Pasler, Jann. "The Ironies of Gender, or Virility and Politics in the Music of Augusta Holmès." *Women & Music* 2 (1998): 1–25.

Rosenstiel, Léonie. *The Life and Works of Lili Boulanger.* Rutherford, NJ: Fairleigh Dickinson Press, 1978.

St. John, Christopher [Marie]. *Ethel Smyth: A Biography.* London: Longmans, Green and Co., 1959.

Tardif, Cécile. *Portrait de Cécile Chaminade.* Montreal: L. Courteau, 1993.

Wood, Elizabeth. "Lesbian Fugue: Ethel Smyth's Contrapuntal Arts," in *Musicology and Difference: Gender and Sexuality in Musical Scholarship.* Ed. Ruth Solie. Berkeley and Los Angeles: University of California Press, 1993, pp. 164–83.

———. "Performing Rights: A Sonography of Women's Suffrage." *Musical Quarterly* 79 (1995): 606–43.

VIII.
Women in American Music, 1800–1918

Adrienne Fried Block
assisted by Nancy Stewart

Introduction

Music in the New World, except for that of native American tribes, was a transplanted tradition with roots in Europe and Africa. In the United States, as in Europe, the dawn of the nineteenth century found women in music in two separate worlds, those of the amateur who made music at home and of the professional, usually a woman from a musical or theatrical family, who made music outside the home and was paid to do so. An unbridgeable divide separated the middle- or upper-class amateurs from the professionals: respectable women did not perform in public. Under the prevailing American doctrine of domestic feminism, man's sphere was the world and woman's, the home. Victorian middle- and upper-class women were trained for marriage, for playing a supportive yet dependent role in a patriarchal society, not for careers.

However, American middle-class women soon began demanding education, the better to train their children; they wanted training in music in order to bring the beneficent influence of the "divine art" into the home. With time, musical training for girls and women improved, becoming institutionalized and more accessible. Gradually, too, a few American-born women emerged as professional performers and composers of vernacular and parlor music (later of art music as well). Their emergence was aided by the women's movement that developed in the decades following the Civil War, creating an ideology that offered an alternative to domestic feminism, empowering women to move into the public sphere. This chapter will trace the changes in women's participation in music over a dozen decades.

Theater and Concert Singers: From Visitors to Natives[1]

During the Federal period (ca. 1780–1820), professional women performers from England or the continent appeared on American stages as members of touring troupes. Typically the women had grown up in the English theatre, served their apprenticeships under the watchful eyes of parents and siblings who were professional artists, and later married stage people. A singing actress was always under the management of her closest male relative, who signed contracts and collected her wages. Whatever her status, she called herself "Mrs." as a badge of respectability. Despite this, every aspect of her life, from her morals to her finances to her weight, was open to scrutiny by the diverse public that attended her performances. Gender, class, national origin, and mores were all shaping factors in her public and private lives.

English theatre companies first introduced ballad operas (e.g., *The Beggar's Opera,* 1728) into America in 1735. Comic opera soon followed. In 1791 French opera came to New Orleans, and was introduced in the North as well. Roles for women included heroines, fine ladies, chambermaids, old women, and hoydens (ill-bred, demanding, ready-for-fun, out-of-control women). In addition, women dressed as men appeared in trouser roles.

The leading singing actress on the American stage before 1800 was Mary Ann Pownall (Wrighton, 1751–1796).[2] Famous as an opera and concert singer in England, after coming to America in 1792 she performed in cities along the Atlantic Coast as a member of the Old American Theater Company. Pownall's concert repertory included her own compositions, which exhibited the flowing melodies and strophic form typical of English popular song as well as more operatic ornamentation and dramatic climaxes. Eight of her songs appeared in print, three in a joint publication with James Hewitt, English-born concert manager, violinist, publisher, and composer.

Italian opera soon began edging out English opera on American stages. The Garcia troupe, a Spanish family of professional singers, arrived in 1825, presenting Mozart's *Don Giovanni* and some of Rossini's operas among other works. The company gave about eighty performances in a matter of months. In the troupe were Manuel Garcia and his son Manuel, later renowned as a voice teacher; the elder Manuel's seventeen-year-old daughter Maria (1808–1836) was the prima donna and star of the company. New York audiences did not accept Italian opera immediately, and the Garcias experienced a mixed reception. However, Maria Garcia had an outstanding personal success as both a concert and opera singer. After marrying she returned to Paris and a fabled career in opera under her husband's surname, Malibran.

The Garcia troupe was followed by other foreign companies that performed Italian opera in English, a change that turned the genre into popular entertainment. Occasionally husband-and-wife teams ran the companies, among them the Seguin Opera Company that toured the States from 1841 to 1852 and the 100-member Parepa-Rosa English Opera Company that appeared between 1869 and 1871.[3] Because of the growing popularity of Italian opera, publishers began issuing arias and ensembles separately for amateur parlor pianists and vocalists, among whom were large numbers of women. The result was that Italianate stylistic elements were absorbed into the American musical stream.

It is significant that the first American-born professional singer came from America's first family of professional musicians. Eliza Ostinelli Biscaccianti (1824–1896), who made her debut in New York as Amina in *La Sonnambula,* was the daughter of the pianist and organist Sophia Hewitt Ostinelli and the granddaughter of James Hewitt. Thanks to the money raised by a group of Bostonians, Eliza Ostinelli was able to go to Italy to study voice. After her marriage and return in 1847, she became a favorite of American audiences, singing in opera and concert from New York to San Francisco.

In the 1840s opera singers from abroad began touring the United States as solo artists. The most famous was the charismatic Jenny Lind (1820–1867), who in September of 1850 began an eighteen-month tour. She sang all over the United States, and brought enormous numbers of Americans into concert halls for the first time. Her programs included orchestral works, opera arias and ensembles, and parlor songs (e.g., "Home, Sweet Home"), a democratic mix that contributed to her broad appeal. Although she was known as "the Swedish nightingale," a nickname that suggests the mindless singing of a bird, she was a hard-working and first-rate musician. P. T. Barnum, her concert manager for the tour, shrewdly played up Lind's piety and impeccable personal reputation, advertising her as "the musical saint." As a result, Jenny Lind succeeded almost single-handedly in convincing Americans that a woman could go on the lyric stage and still retain her virtue. Lind's visit also was the stimulus for the building of opera houses in many cities across the United States, thus opening up further opportunities for women. Because of her success, first-rank European singers like Henriette Sontag and Marietta Alboni also made American tours.

Lind, who was famous for her generosity, made European study possible for an American singer. The English-born contralto Adelaide Phillips (1833–1882) came to Boston as a singing, acting, and dancing child prodigy. Lind heard Phillips sing and gave her $1,000 to study in London with Manuel Garcia. After a debut in Europe, Phillips become a leading opera, oratorio, and concert singer, and she ran her own opera company for a season. Hers became the typical pattern for singers: early training in the United States followed by study and a debut in Europe and finally a return to the United States, their professional caliber validated by their European success.

This pattern, however, rarely applied to African-American singers. Before Lind's American tour ended, Elizabeth Taylor Greenfield (ca. 1817–1876) made her debut in Buffalo in 1851, singing operatic arias as well as several of the songs Lind had made popular. Greenfield's label as "the black Swan" not only attempted to transfer some of Lind's appeal but also exploited the novelty of a black person singing a classical repertory. Born in slavery, Greenfield was freed while still a child when her owner, a Quaker, moved north to Philadelphia. Although she had a rich voice and an enormous range, poverty and prejudice left her no choice but to teach herself. Following her debut, Greenfield embarked on concert tours, first in the United States, then in England. There she finally found a temporary teacher in Sir George Smart, but was never able to raise enough money for further study in Europe. She returned to Philadelphia in 1854 to teach voice and give occasional concerts. Even though prejudice prevented her from fulfilling her potential, she broke ground for later African-American singers of art music.

Clara Louise Kellogg (1842–1916) did succeed, both in America and Europe, following an all-American education, the first opera singer to do so. She also epitomized the new American vocal artist: born into a white middle-class American family without a tradition of professional performance, she overcame the Puritanical censure of women who went on the stage, finally achieving the highest international stature as well as social acceptance. Kellogg was born in Sumterville, North Carolina, of an educated and musical family who supported her musical aspirations. She displayed musical talent as a young child and soon began lessons in piano, at which she excelled. Later she joined a church choir, and, in a less traditional vein, learned to sing minstrel songs to her own banjo accompaniment. After hearing Lind's first concert in New York in 1850, the eight-year-old Kellogg determined to be a professional singer.[4] Her family moved to New York in 1857, where Kellogg studied with leading voice teachers.

Sensitive to social attitudes about stage people, she called her friends together before her debut to announce that she was going on the stage, and that if they never spoke to her again she would understand and forgive them. Kellogg added that she hoped some day to overcome their rejection and make them proud of her. Her debut in New York in 1861 as Gilda in *Rigoletto* was enormously successful. Two years later she sang Marguérite in the American premiere of Gounod's *Faust* and in London's 1867 production at Covent Garden. In all she sang forty roles, and was in demand for concert and oratorio work as well.

Despite her family's love of music, their attitudes about her career were ambivalent, as Kellogg noted years later:

> My mother hated the atmosphere of the theatre even though she had wished me to become a singer, and always gloried in my successes. To her rigid and delicate instinct there was something dreadful in the free and easy artistic attitude, and she always stood between me and any possible intimacy with my fellow singers.[5]

Her mother accompanied her on tour until Kellogg's marriage to her concert manager and simultaneous retirement at age forty.

Emma Abbott (1850–1891), a protégée of Kellogg, studied in both the United States and Europe. She never relaxed her Victorian moral standards; indeed, her European career ended when she refused on moral grounds to sing the role of Violetta in *La Traviata.* On her return she found a way to continue in opera without violating her moral code: she formed her own opera company and gave abridged—and sanitized—versions of operas in English translation to audiences in America's West, with enormous success and handsome financial returns.

Sissieretta Jones (1869–1933), like Greenfield before her, had to deal with the societal limitations placed on African Americans. However, she had fine training, especially from the famous New York voice teacher Luisa Cappiani. Following her New York debut in 1888, she toured with the Jubilee Singers, the Patrick Gilmore Band, and other groups, and gave solo recitals, including appearances at the White House for President Harrison and in London for the Prince of Wales. Nevertheless, opera was never an option for her because of prejudice. From 1896 to 1916, Jones toured with a troupe of African-American performers called the Black Patti Troubadours. Although her colleagues offered vaudeville-type acts, Jones sang only opera excerpts and popular songs, as had Lind before her.

Among the other black concert singers of the period were Nellie Brown Mitchell (1845–1924), Marie Selika (1849–1937), Anna Madah Hyers (1853–1934), her sister Emma Louise Hyers (1855–1904), and Flora Batson (1864–1904). The Hyers sisters ran their own company, presenting a drama interspersed with songs about the Underground Railroad entitled *Out of Bondage,* the final act of which gave them the opportunity to sing opera arias. Despite this beginning, after 1880 most support for black artists in the United States diminished, and African-American singers found their best opportunities in Europe.

By 1918 many American women had aspired to operatic careers for fame and fortune. Among those who succeeded—as expected, all white singers—in addition to Kellogg and Abbott were Annie Louise Cary (1841–1931), Emma Thursby (1845–1931), Minnie Hauk (1851–1925), Lillian

Nordica (1857–1914), Marcella Sembrich (1858–1938), Emma Nevada (1859–1940), Emma Eames (1865–1952), Louise Homer (1871–1947), Olive Fremstad (1871–1951), Lillian Blauvelt (1874–1947), Mary Garden (1874–1967), Geraldine Farrar (1882–1967), and Alma Gluck (1884–1938). By 1900 divas were lionized as celebrities and cultural heroines, and the doors of high society were open to them. Even without careers in opera, singers found opportunities as church and oratorio soloists, as voice teachers, and as concert artists. The time between 1880 and 1920 was a golden period for singers on the recital stage. These women's lives testified to the changes that had taken place in American society in the late nineteenth and early twentieth centuries. The seeds that Lind had planted bore significant fruit.

There were also opportunities for women in the popular theatre—in vaudeville, musical comedy, and operetta—beginning in the latter part of the nineteenth century. Outstanding performers included Lillian Russell (1861–1922), who sang in all three genres, including Gilbert and Sullivan operettas; Eva Tanguay (1878–1947), a performer of "exuberant sexuality"; and Sophie Tucker (1884–1966), featured, as was Tanguay, in Tony Pastor's vaudevilles; Fay Templeton (1865–1939), who starred in musical comedy, most notably in George M. Cohan's *Forty-Five Minutes from Broadway* (1906); and Fritzi Scheff (1879–1954), who left the Metropolitan Opera to appear in operettas and was famous for her role in *Mlle. Modiste* (1906), written for her by Victor Herbert.

MUSIC TRAINING AND EDUCATION

Before 1830 or so, music making by amateurs was considered a social grace in imitation of English high society. Only wealthy families could offer their daughters music instruction—superficial as it usually was—or buy the harpsichords, harps, guitars, or pianos women played. Women who sang and played in society as part of the rite of courtship or at home to relieve boredom and isolation usually abandoned music after marriage. However, as cities grew in the nineteenth century, the merchant class grew along with them, and musical accomplishment became middle class. Lessons in music, as well as dancing, embroidery, drawing, and rules of deportment, became all but mandatory for well-bred young ladies. Although music continued to play a role in courtship, women also played at home to promote domestic harmony and to uplift and charm their children. Indeed, music was associated with the ideal of woman as "angel in the house." The abundant literature about women in music included advice about maintaining the image of the "angel"—modest, patient, sober, unselfish, and submissive—who sang only parlor songs with chaste words. If she played piano for others, she was counseled to avoid long and complex works. As Judith Tick wrote, "Tradition simultaneously encouraged [women] to take up music, yet discouraged them from aspiring to any meaningful standards and repressed artistic ambition."[6]

Music was first taught at seminaries as an ornamental course along with embroidery. In the early nineteenth century a typical music curriculum consisted of instruction in piano, harp, guitar, and voice. However, training gradually improved at female seminaries and academies where middle- and upper-class teenagers studied. The curriculum began to include violin and organ also, especially in better schools like the Moravian Seminary in Bethlehem, Pennsylvania, the Cherry Valley Seminary in New York, and Music Vale in Connecticut. As a result of young women's widespread participation in amateur music making, schools offered better training in music for girls than for boys. Troy Seminary in New York progressed from having an ornamental curriculum for amateurs to developing a rigorous music program for professionals during the course of sixty years. By 1900 its music department had become a conservatory, and its catalog stipulated that the curriculum was suitable not only for aspiring professionals but also—and apparently secondarily—for amateurs. These changes also reflected the increased professionalization of women in music.

As music teaching became a preferred field for women during the second half of the nineteenth century, the need for better teacher preparation became apparent. Music Vale at some point became Salem Normal School, enjoying a national reputation. It offered training in notation, harmony, thoroughbass, counterpoint, and composition. At its peak the Salem Normal School drew students from a wide geographical area, and its graduates fanned out all over the country, effectively raising the level of music teaching.

The Crane Normal Institute of Music of Potsdam, New York, founded in 1886, was the first music school in the country to become affiliated with a teacher-training college. Its aim was to offer thorough training to future public school music teachers, primarily women. Founded and directed by Julia Ettie Crane (1855–1923), the school is now known as the Crane School of Music of the State University of New York at Potsdam.[7] Schools like Crane helped professionalize the field for women: by 1910 women constituted 60 percent of all music teachers, their highest percentage in this country's history. However, men occupied the more prestigious teaching positions, were better paid, and were considered more qualified to teach advanced students.

The establishment of American conservatories after the Civil War was an important development for women, who predominated as students. Oberlin College-Conservatory opened in 1865; the Cincinnati, Boston, and

New England conservatories followed in 1867; Peabody in 1868; the National Conservatory of Music in New York in 1885; and the American Conservatory in Chicago in 1886. The music schools offered high-caliber training, often with European-educated teachers. Because many parents would not send their daughters abroad without a chaperone—usually the mother—yet were loath to disrupt family life, American conservatories provided an alternative. The year after the New England Conservatory opened, its student body consisted of 1,097 females and 317 males. But its two violin scholarships were reserved for boys between eight and fourteen. On the other hand, the Boston Conservatory opened its string classes to women, an action that forever changed prospects for women as instrumentalists. Founded by Louis Eichberg, Boston's curriculum was modeled on that of the Brussels Conservatory, renowned for training violinists.

Two women, Clara Baur (1835–1912) and Jeannette Thurber (1850–1946), were among those setting up American conservatories. Before leaving Germany at the age of fourteen, Baur had studied piano and voice at the Stuttgart Hochschule für Musik. In 1867 she founded the Cincinnati Conservatory in its image. Offering training to both amateurs and aspiring professionals, the conservatory drew students from all parts of the country. After Clara Baur's death, her niece Bertha Baur (1858–1940) directed the school. Jeannette Thurber, who founded the National Conservatory of Music in New York, had studied violin at the government-supported Paris Conservatory. Noting that no such support existed for comparable American conservatories, Thurber determined to establish a school on the Parisian model. In 1885 she opened the New York school, but had to assume the role of patron herself: the government support she actively sought was never granted. Like Baur, she included a number of women on her faculty. Because she believed, as did Antonin Dvořák, who led the school 1892 to 1895, in the importance of the music of African Americans for the future of American music, the school offered scholarships to talented black students.

However, many believed that nothing took the place of European training. Amy Fay (1844–1928) left Cambridge, Massachusetts, in 1869 to study piano in Europe. Her letters from Germany, written to her sister during her six-year stay and published in her *Music Study in Germany*,[8] are especially valued for the vivid descriptions of Franz Liszt's piano "classes." At the same time she painted a picture of student life and the marvelous opportunities such a sojourn offered for absorbing music and European culture. Fay's book inspired hundreds, perhaps thousands, of women to go and do likewise.

Almost two generations later, in 1905, another American woman, Mabel Wheeler Daniels (1878–1971), told of her experiences as a music student in *An American Girl in Munich*.[9] Like Fay, Daniels began her studies in Boston and completed them in Europe, at the Munich Conservatory. Unlike Fay, she had gone to study composition, and there she met long-standing prejudices against admitting women to composition classes. Fortunately, she had the preparation and courage to overcome those obstacles, at the same time paving the way for women who followed her. Daniels' compositions consisted mainly of songs and choral music, but her orchestral works, such as *Deep Forest* (1933), were performed throughout America. Her best known piece, *The Desolate City* (1914) for baritone solo and orchestra, was the first in a series of works written at the MacDowell Colony, where Daniels befriended Amy Beach, Mary Howe, Helen Hopekirk, and Marion Bauer.

RELIGIOUS MUSIC

Most women who studied music—at home or abroad—remained amateurs who played and sang at home. But for both black and white women, religious rituals offered opportunities for music making outside the home: singing in the congregation or the choir, or playing the organ. In the late eighteenth century, women and men attended singing schools in New England where they learned the rudiments of musical notation using shape notes. The practice of shape-note, or "fasola," singing soon spread to the South and West. In using shape notes for singing hymns, the tenors sang the melody, the women the two upper parts. Of the many tune books that contained the fasola repertory, the first to include hymns by women was the famous *Southern Harmony* compiled by William Walker (1835). In it are several hymns composed by women, including the shape-note piece for three voices given in Example 8.1.

As religious activists and guardians of society's morals, it was natural that women become important as hymnists—that is, authors of hymn texts—and occasionally as composers of the music. Most of these women were amateurs, but because the texts were religious, they could allow their names to appear in print with impunity—something that amateur composers of secular music tended to avoid.

Woman in Sacred Song, the first retrospective collection of hymn tunes and texts by women, reflects the extent of activity by women in this field.[10] In it are about 2,500 religious poems and about 103 hymn tunes by fifty composers. Phoebe Palmer Knapp (1839–1908), an outstanding writer of gospel hymns, is represented by several tunes, most notably her "Blessed Assurance," with text by the leading poet of Gospel hymnody, Fanny Jane Crosby.

While women contributed heavily to Evangelical hymnody, their participation in more traditional churches was limited. In the more ritualistic

EXAMPLE 8.1. Miss M. T. Durham, "The Promised Land." Reprinted from Judith Tick, *American Women Composers before 1870* (Ann Arbor: UMI Research Press, 1983), p. 117. Reproduced by permission of the author. *Text:* "On Jordan's stormy banks I stand, And cast a woeful eye, To Canaan's fair and happy land, Where my possessions lie. I am bound for the promised land, O, who will go with me?"

Protestant churches, for example, only males sang in the choirs. Many women served as church organists, but often for little or no pay; the large churches tended to hire men, and concert organists were almost invariably male. One notable exception to this was Lillian Frohock, whose concert career in the 1860s and 1870s extended to Boston, New York City, and even to Germany.

Choral singing for amateurs was initially a male activity in the eighteenth and nineteenth centuries. Eager to perform major choral works by leading European composers but frustrated by the musical limitations of church choirs, men organized private singing societies. The Handel and Haydn Society of Boston became the model for many later groups. It was run by an all-male membership, and women sang by invitation. At the Society's first concert, in 1815, the chorus numbered ninety men and ten women.[11] Usually men sang the alto, tenor, and bass parts, and women, reinforced by a few male falsettists, sang the soprano. Beginning around midcentury, German and Scandinavian men newly arrived in the United States also formed singing societies, inviting women to join them in performances of Haydn's *Creation* or Handel's *Messiah*.

With the formation of women's music clubs, however, women were able to organize and run their own choruses. Some all-women choruses, such as the St. Cecilia Society of New York (founded in 1906), became polished performing organizations. Composers—many of them women—responded to the increased demand for music for women voices, building up a substantial repertory issued by publishers in special series. During the 1909-1910 season, the ninety-five-member chorus of the Rubinstein Club of Cleveland gave a program that featured violinist Maud Powell as soloist and presented *The Mermaid,* a cantata by Fannie Snow Knowlton. Women also functioned as conductors of these female choruses: in 1900, for example, the Dominant Ninth Chorus of Alton, Illinois, assisted by a male chorus, gave a concert at which Mrs. C. B. Rohland conducted Coleridge-Taylor's *Hiawatha's Wedding Feast.*

Although these choral singers were all amateurs, around midcentury a few talented women were able to assume public roles while remaining—literally—in the bosom of the family as members of professional singing families. These familial groups brought professional polish to the performance of vernacular music. As usual, their model was European: the Rainer Family from the Tyrolean Alps. As a result of the Rainers' tour in the early 1840s, several American singing families became active, among them the Baker Family of New Hampshire and the Luca Family Singers, a black family from New Haven, Connecticut. The most famous, however, was the Hutchinson Family Singers: three brothers and their sister, Abby Hutchinson. She composed, arranged, sang, and sometimes accompanied the group on the guitar. Their repertory included glees, sentimental songs and ballads, and the yodeling Tyrolean songs the Rainer Family had popularized. But the Hutchinsons also presented topical songs in support of equal rights for women, for temperance, and for the abolition of slavery.

The Fisk Jubilee Singers, organized in 1871 to raise funds for Fisk University in Nashville, Tennessee, eventually became a professional touring group. They began with four men and seven women, a conductor, and an accompanist, Ella Shepherd, who trained but did not conduct the choir. The Jubilee Singers offered concert arrangements of spirituals at the World Peace Jubilee in 1872, singing for President Grant as well as for Queen Victoria, who became a patron. The group thus brought spirituals into the mainstream of American concert music, and became the model for other black choirs.[12]

The Music Club Movement

The first women's amateur musical club, the Rossini Club, was organized in Portland, Maine, in 1868. Its purpose, which set a pattern for the many clubs formed in the late nineteenth century, was to provide members a place outside the home where they could share their music. Their aims were broadly educational: women members learned organizational skills, and musically trained amateurs performed for and with each other and occasionally for invited guests. Out of this modest beginning a large and influential movement grew.

By 1893 there were forty-two women's amateur musical clubs, thirty-five of which sent representatives to the National Convention of Women's Amateur Musical Clubs. This took place June 21–24 in the Music Hall at the World's Columbian Exposition held in Chicago. Rose Fay Thomas, leader of the Woman's Amateur Musical Club of Chicago and wife of famed conductor Theodore Thomas, suggested that the clubs' aims be broadened to include the support and encouragement of music in their communities.

This community-service aim became a reality when, in 1898, 225 club representatives met again in Chicago and formed the National Federation of Music Clubs. The Federation's record has been impressive: its members have educated the general public about music, set up concert circuits (local and, eventually, national), championed women composers, organized women's choral clubs and provided performance venues for them, supported young performers and composers, advanced the cause of American music, and organized competitions for composers. Strong advocates for music in the schools, the member clubs continue to give crucial support to local music organizations. A particular concern historically has been to increase children's access to musical training. In 1902 the first junior music club joined the federation (and in 1919 the NFMC established a Junior Division, greatly increasing the membership of children).

The NFMC was not the only amateur organization to promote music. The General Federation of Women's Clubs (GFWC), established about 1890, from its beginnings included some clubs devoted to musical activities. However, in 1910, the GFWC set up a specific Music Department. According to Karen J. Blair, "the GFWC was no less successful than the NFMC in its campaign to musicalize America,"[13] publishing instructional books to improve members' musical education, as well as collections of music for community singing, among them *Indian Music Programs for Clubs and Special Music Days* (1926), which was accompanied by a guidebook for its use. These were part of a program to bring a broad range of music, including folk and ethnic as well as art music, to members through performances at meetings by their choral groups, promising young musicians, and professionals.

PIANISTS AND VIOLINISTS

A few American women emerged as concert artists by the latter part of the nineteenth century. The special conditions that fostered their development included an active feminist movement that supported women's aspirations for professional careers and improved opportunities for high-quality training, and a wave of visiting virtuose, women soloists from overseas who served as models. Later the music clubs aided in the support of women artists.

The mother of singer Eliza Biscaccianti, Sophia Hewitt (1799–1845), was an exception in the early history of women instrumentalists: she was one of the first American women to become a professional keyboard player. James Hewitt's eldest child, Sophia Hewitt first appeared in New York and Boston as a seven-year-old prodigy. Later she taught piano, harp, organ, and singing, and served as organist at two churches in Boston. In September of 1820 Sophia Hewitt was appointed organist of the Handel and Haydn Society, a position she filled for ten years. Her husband, violinist Louis Ostinelli, had to collect her pay; according to the law, married women had no economic independence.

Beginning in midcentury, instrumental virtuose began to appear, at first foreign-born and later American-born and -bred. Teresa Carreño (1853–1917) emigrated to the United States with her family in 1862.[14] Within a month of their arrival in New York the child was presented to the public as a piano prodigy. Audiences were entranced with her. So too was pianist Louis Moreau Gottschalk, whom she worshiped as a performer and composer, and who gave her lessons when he was in town. Following a concert with an orchestra in Boston, the conductor called Carreño the "grandest prodigy . . . since the days of Mozart."[15] A creative as well as a performing talent, Carreño regularly included her own works on her programs. After two years of American tours, her family took her to Paris, where she captivated Rossini with one of her piano pieces and where Liszt, in a symbolic laying on of hands, declared her a genius. Carreño's frequent tours of the United States allowed the American public to watch her development from a performer of somewhat slapdash brilliance to a mature but always intensely energetic pianist of acknowledged greatness.

In the 1870s a number of eminent European pianists toured the United States, playing solos with the famous Theodore Thomas orchestra. Among them were the German pianists Anna Mehlig and Marie Krebs, and the English pianist Madeleine Schiller. During that decade Julie Rivé-King (1854–1937) became the first American-born woman to succeed on the concert stage.[16] Harold Schonberg states that she "was to the piano what Theodore Thomas was to the orchestra, and she helped to establish a new standard in repertoire and performance."[17] Rivé-King was born in Cincinnati to parents who had come from France in 1850; because of their professional involvement in the arts, they were important models for their daughter. She displayed her prodigious gifts at the piano early, and soon after her mother began to give her lessons. In 1871 Rivé studied in New York; later she studied in Europe where she delighted Liszt with her playing. Shortly after she made her debut in Leipzig, her father died quite suddenly; Rivé cancelled her projected European tour and sailed for home, never to return.

In 1874 she began a series of concert tours of the United States and Canada, including several with Theodore Thomas, one with conductor Anton Seidl. Many of her concerts were arranged by her husband, Frank King, whom she married in 1877 and who managed her career until he died in 1900. Thereafter, unused to being her own manager, she gave up touring and took a position at Chicago's Bush Conservatory, where she taught for the rest of her life. Her playing was notable for its clear, precise, facile touch and technical perfection.

Fannie Bloomfield Zeisler (1863–1927), who as a child came to America from Austria, fused strong European influences with an equally strong sense of identity as an American.[18] Zeisler grew up in the Midwest and studied in Chicago. At fourteen she played for the touring Russian pianist Annette Essipoff, who urged her to study in Vienna with Essipoff's husband, the famous Theodore Leschetitzky. After studying in Europe, Bloomfield Zeisler returned to make her American debut in 1884. During her long and brilliant concert career, Zeisler struggled to overcome stereotypes: for example, many people assumed that women lacked men's physical power at the keyboard, all the while branding women who did exhibit such power and energy as boisterous Amazons. Zeisler projected an image to Americans of a woman who could "play like a man" yet remain a woman concerned with husband, home, and family. Indeed, women felt impelled at the time to assure their audiences that they were "real women" as well as artists.

Until the late nineteenth century, women were told they should not play orchestral instruments other than harp because they did not look good playing them (e.g., the flute) or did not have the required strength (e.g., lower woodwinds and brass). Violins were considered instruments of the devil that no self-respecting woman would play. But thanks primarily to the influence of Camilla Urso, the violin became not only an accepted but even a preferred instrument for female musicians.

Urso (1842–1902) arrived in New York from Paris in September 1852, just a few months after Jenny Lind had ended her American tour. Then a ten-year-old prodigy, Urso was the first professional female violinist to perform in the United States, and soon became an inspiration and role model for others. Born in Nantes into a family of professional musicians, Urso decided at age five to study violin. Her father objected because he believed that no respectable girl played violin. She insisted, and finally he agreed to find her a teacher. After fighting her way into the Paris Conservatoire, where she was a scholarship student, she graduated two years later with highest honors. Her New York debut was the start of a series of American concert tours, interrupted by a hiatus of eight years (1855–1863) when she returned to Europe for further study. While there she married the man who became her concert manager. During her many years of touring, she also gave concerts in Europe, Australia, and South Africa.

In 1867 Urso, who performed frequently in Boston, received an extraordinary honor: the members of the Harvard Musical Association presented her with a written testimonial that declared her the equal of the best male violinists. Yet as a woman she could not play in that orchestra, a discriminatory practice she later attacked.[19] Urso had qualities that resembled Lind's, including dignity and an artistic integrity that generated respect from audiences, and a warmth that communicated itself both to the musically sophisticated and the untutored. Her extensive repertory included concerti by Beethoven, Mozart, Mendelssohn, and many of the now-standard solo works by Paganini and Vieuxtemps. She never lowered her standards. As a result she was an effective educator of the American public.

Urso's artistry and personality may have influenced Julius Eichberg in 1867 to open string classes to female students at the Boston Conservatory. By 1894 *Freund's Weekly* could report that between 400 and 500 young women were studying violin in Boston, and that many had already gone beyond the student level. The writer also noted that this also was of great benefit to professional [male] "fiddlers," who as a result could find all the students they wanted. Several of Eichberg's students went on to work with Joseph Joachim in Europe and later became solo or ensemble players. Geraldine Morgan, who played quartets with Joachim, and Lillian Shattuck, who returned to teach at the Boston Conservatory, both formed their own string quartets. Another of Eichberg's students, Olive Mead (1874–1946), later became a protégée of Franz Kneisel, whose string quartet was the most famous in the United States. Mead had a distinguished career both as soloist and as leader of the highly regarded Olive Mead Quartet.

The outstanding American woman violinist of the late nineteenth century was Maud Powell (1867–1920).[20] As a girl she had heard Urso play, and because of Urso's example Powell became a violinist. Born in Uniontown, Pennsylvania, Powell grew up in Aurora, Illinois, and went to Europe to study at the Leipzig and Paris Conservatories and with Joachim, with whom she made her debut in 1885. But like many concert artists, she and her family paid a high price for her European training and career. At fourteen she terminated her general education to concentrate on the violin. Her mother accompanied her to Europe on a tour of duty as chaperone that ended only seventeen years later and all but destroyed the elder Powells' marriage. Like many other professional women of the time, Maud Powell believed that she must choose between marriage and family and a career. Like others as well, when she finally married, at thirty-seven, it was to her concert manager. During her intensely hard-working yet gratifying life, she played with leading orchestras in Europe and the United States, toured the world, and organized and led her all-female string quartet and later her own trio.

Female string players at the Boston Conservatory also learned orchestral skills in the Eichberg Lady Orchestra (organized in 1884), a string ensemble that played both classical and popular music. By training women, their male teachers were in a sense creating competition for professional jobs. That competition, however, was not yet actual but potential, since women were effectively barred from all-male orchestras. Black and white women found other solutions, among them all-women orchestras and bands, segregated by color and, almost without exception, marginal and underpaid even when fully professional.

True to pattern, the first such group was an imported one, the Vienna Ladies Orchestra: this *Damen Orchester* was formed in 1867 and toured in the United States beginning in 1871. Although its members were concert artists, they found it necessary to play in beer halls and restaurants. In 1880, Marion Osgood of Chelsea, Massachusetts, organized her own Ladies' Orchestra to play at dances and parties. Four years later Caroline B. Nichols, one of Eichberg's violin students, formed the outstanding and long-lived Boston Fadette Lady Orchestra. By about 1920, some six hundred women had played in the Fadettes, and some of them went on to form their own orchestras.

Of course, women's orchestras needed more than strings. Some employed men to play the missing instruments. Others made do with whatever women instrumentalists they could find: the New York Ladies' Orchestra, active in 1888, included strings, guitars, mandolins, harp, kettle drum, banjo, piano, and organ. Such a combination was appropriate for a light-classical and popular repertory, which all the orchestras found they had to offer—whether or not they also played more serious music—in order to get work. Indeed, some, like the Fadettes, included not only a mixed repertory but vaudeville acts as well. The number of women's orchestras continued to grow: in 1908 there were thirty such orchestras active in the United States.

In 1917–1918, when many men were in uniform, women trained in all-women orchestras were hired and paid union wages to play in hotel orchestras, but they had to give up their jobs to men at the war's end. Maud Powell noted at the time the persistence of discrimination against women in orchestras: "When I first began my career as a concert artist, I did pioneer work for the cause of the woman violinist, going on with the work begun by Camilla Urso. . . . A strong prejudice then existed against women fiddlers, which even yet has not altogether been overcome."[21] With few exceptions, women only began to have opportunities as orchestral musicians during World War II.

WOMEN AS COMPOSERS

Women were publishing songs as early as the 1790s. For the next several decades most of their songs and dances, some with variations, marked them as accomplished amateurs with minimal training in music. Often the pieces were attributed to "A Lady" or "Mary," thus preserving their anonymous status as amateurs while making clear that the composer was a woman. Whereas composing concert music was beyond most women's skills and such genres as minstrel songs were too vulgar, the parlor song, that quintessential musical expression of the Victorian era, occupied a central position in women's amateur music making.

Most parlor songs are about love—romantic, filial, maternal, sisterly, platonic, or unrequited. Most call for a woman's voice, employ a limited range, are set in a strophic form with regular phrases, and are simple enough to be sung by an amateur. An occasional parlor song from early in the century had a fairly demanding piano accompaniment, and vocal lines in more elaborate songs showed the influence of Italian opera. Mrs. Townshend Stith, one of the first women to sign her music, published "Our Friendship" (1830), a quasi-operatic song with an elaborately ornamented *bel canto* melody (see Example 8.2).

EXAMPLE 8.2. Mrs. Townshend Stith, "Our Friendship." Reprinted from Judith Tick, *American Women Composers before 1870* (Ann Arbor: UMI Research Press, 1983), p. 97. Reproduced by permission of the author.

Inspired by the examples of several Englishwomen whose songs first circulated in the 1830s, a few American women emerged from behind the veil of anonymity, using their names under the protective canopy of music for the home. Parlor songs by women were printed in *Godey's Ladies' Book* and other women's journals. At first their songs were unaccompanied or were harmonized by men, since women were almost always self-taught in composition and harmony was considered a "scientific" skill that women were incapable of learning.

By midcentury, however, a few composers emerged who were both more skillful and more professional than earlier composers of sentimental songs. Jane Sloman, born in England in 1824 to parents in the theatre, first became known as a solo pianist at age seventeen. Yet she felt compelled to embrace Victorian standards of ladylike behavior, modestly informing her audiences that only after the most strenuous urging by others did she consent to appear in public. Sloman's song "The Maiden's Farewell" (1842) has a highly ornamented, chromatic melody for its sentimental subject, a young woman's conflicts upon marrying and leaving her mother. Yet the words also express the close bond between mother and daughter that was typical of the Victorian era.

Susan Parkhurst (1836–1918), a member of the next generation, had an active career in the 1860s. Widowed in 1864, she supported herself and her daughter by performing and composing. Her works, published under the name Mrs. E. A. Parkhurst, include variation sets for piano—among them sets on the tunes of "Yankee Doodle," "Blue Bells of Scotland," and her own "Sweet Evalina"—and a "Funeral March to the Memory of Abraham Lincoln." In addition to piano music, Parkhurst wrote gospel hymns, parlor songs, and topical songs on abolitionist, patriotic, and temperance themes, including "I'll Marry No Man If He Drinks."

Faustina Hasse Hodges (1822–1895) came from a more elite tradition. The daughter of Edward Hodges, an organist and church composer who came to America from England in 1838, she also worked as a church organist and taught organ, piano, and voice at Troy [New York] Seminary. Her works included keyboard music and sacred and secular songs. Like other composers of her day, Hodges wrote many of the song texts herself. Two of her most successful songs were "Dreams" and "The Rose Bush," both with sentimental texts. Tick explains that "fading roses and fading dreams were typical conceits of parlor culture in the 1850s," and calls Hodges "a gifted musical genre painter."[22]

Marion Dix Sullivan (fl. 1840–1850) was the first American woman to write what today would be called a hit song, her ballad "The Blue Juniata" (1844). Often reprinted, the song was mentioned by Mark Twain in his *Autobiography,* and it inspired variation sets by at least two other composers. In addition to individual songs, Sullivan published two collections, *Bible Songs* (1856) and *Juniata Ballads* (1870), the latter a book of fifty simple, unaccompanied school songs.

Augusta Browne (1821–1882) was both the most professional and the most prolific of the midcentury composers: her compositions number about two hundred. She supported herself by performing on organ and piano and by her own writings, both musical and literary. Her articles on music appeared frequently in popular periodicals of the day; later she also championed equal rights for women. Having married late and been widowed soon after, Browne was acutely aware of the hardships women faced when trying to make a living. She was a skillful composer, writing most of her music between 1840 and 1855. One of her best-known works, "The War-Like Dead in Mexico," was published in 1848 and dedicated to Henry Clay. It is atypical in its masculine subject and its dramatic martial rhythms.

The songs of Carrie Jacobs-Bond (1861–1946), the most successful song composer of the late nineteenth and early twentieth centuries, blend two traditions, the parlor song and the art song.[23] Born in Janesville, Wisconsin, Carrie Jacobs was a precociously talented child who played by ear at the age of four, learned Liszt's Second Hungarian Rhapsody by ear at nine, and decided to become a serious student at fourteen after hearing Rivé-King play the Rhapsody. Because of family setbacks Jacobs's musical training was restricted to lessons on piano. In addition, her childhood was clouded by poor health that dogged her throughout life. Her twenties were marred by a failed marriage and a financial struggle to support herself and a son. Her second marriage, although a happy one, was troubled by economic disaster in the panic of 1893 and ended with her husband's premature death.

Torn between expectations of a traditional woman's role and her musical ambitions, Jacobs-Bond decided in 1893 to bring some money into the household through her music. She arranged with a Chicago publisher to issue two of her songs, launching her career as a composer. Most of her 200 works are songs that she published herself, painting the decorative title pages and promoting them by her own performances. "A Perfect Day" (1910), her biggest hit, sold eight million copies and five million records and appeared in sixty editions. Jacobs-Bond said that her aim was to write "the home songs . . . that touch the heart."[24] Although originally intended for the recital stage, her music became part of the popular culture.

Mary Turner Salter (1856–1938) began as a concert and oratorio singer, but after marriage she retired from performance and became a successful writer of parlor songs. Her most famous was the sentimental "The Cry of Rachel," a favorite encore of the contralto Ernestine Schumann-Heink, who measured the song's success by the number of listeners it moved to tears.

Although women were widely accepted as composers for the parlor, creating art music was a skill considered more appropriate for men. Women, critic George Upton wrote in 1880, should be content to function as men's muses or inspirations. Furthermore, a prevailing theory, social Darwinism, placed women lower on the evolutionary scale than men, incapable of creating high art because they lacked the necessary intellectual ability. Hence there was serious doubt that women could create art music of real value even under the most favorable conditions. Yet support from the women's movement and the long and slow rise of women as composers in the nineteenth century prepared the way for the emergence of women as composers of art music. Among them were Clara Kathleen Rogers (1844–1931), Helen Hopekirk (1856–1945), Margaret Ruthven Lang (1867–1971), and Amy M. (Mrs. H. H. A.) Beach (1867–1944).

These four women were accepted members of Boston's Second New England School of composition, led by composer-teachers John Knowles

FIGURE 8.1. Clara Kathleen Rogers. Billy Rose Theatre Collection. Reproduced by permission of The New York Public Library, Astor, Lenox and Tilden Foundations.

Paine (1839–1906) of Harvard and George Whitefield Chadwick (1854–1931) of the New England Conservatory of Music. All four women lived in Boston, where support came from the dozens of extraordinary Boston women active as abolitionists, suffragists, social activists, educators, poets, writers, painters, physicians, lawyers, and architects. Boston's intellectual and social elite was proud of its own composers—whether male or female—and regularly turned out to hear their music. Additional support came from publisher Arthur P. Schmidt, who issued many of their works soon after they were composed.[25] Most important, ensembles such as the Boston Symphony Orchestra, the Handel and Haydn Society, and the Kneisel String Quartet performed their works, often more than once.

Rogers was the first of the four to have her music published and performed. Born Clara Kathleen Barnett, she was the youngest child of England's leading opera composer, John Barnett. At the age of twelve she was already admitted to Leipzig Conservatory as a student because of her musical gifts as a singer and a pianist. She was also gifted in composition—during her student years she wrote a string quartet—but was refused entry into the composition class because she was female. Because of her example, however, the Conservatory later established a composition class for women.

After graduating with honors when she was sixteen, Clara Barnett faced choosing between voice and piano; she chose opera, as many multitalented women before and after her have done. At once highly competitive and demanding, opera nevertheless was a preferred field for women. First and foremost—and unlike instrumental performance—opera *required* the participation of women. As members of opera companies, women were part of a community of artists and had a certain continuity of work. Those who made it to the apex as prima donnas collected higher fees than any other performing musicians.

Rogers spent ten years as a prima donna in Italy, singing under the name of Clara Doria; she was chaperoned the entire time by her mother. Then she returned to England, sang in concerts and oratorios, and finally toured the United States with the Parepa-Rosa Opera Company. She married Henry Munroe Rogers, a lawyer from Boston, and settled there, finally having time not only to sing and teach but also to compose songs and an occasional instrumental work. Most of her compositions were published by Schmidt, beginning in 1883.

Her music shows a substantial lyric gift. Indeed, she described the process of composition as "a supreme delight—amounting at times almost to intoxication." Yet she believed that with training in composition she would have tackled the larger forms as well:

> As I look back, I cannot help deploring that when I was a student in Germany there were no facilities accorded to women for learning orchestration, or in

> fact, for obtaining any guidance whatever in original composition. Had I obtained early in life a good technique in writing for instruments I really think I might have accomplished something worth while in orchestral composition.[26]

Like many other American composers, Rogers was fond of poems by Shakespeare; Example 8.3 gives an excerpt from a dramatic art-song, one of her settings of his poems.

Helen Hopekirk wrote songs, piano solos, chamber music, and music for piano and orchestra. She was first a successful concert pianist, having toured England, continental Europe, and the United States for a number of years, playing both in solo recitals and with leading orchestras. Like Rogers, Hopekirk had studied in Leipzig, making her debut there in 1878. More and more drawn to composition, Hopekirk twice interrupted her performing career to study and compose. With her husband, who was also her concert manager, she settled in Boston in 1897, where she lived for the rest of her

FIGURE 8.2. Helen Hopekirk. Reproduced from Constance Huntington and Helen Ingersoll Tetlow, eds., *Helen Hopekirk 1856–1945* (Cambridge: privately printed, 1954); image copyright C. H. Hall.

EXAMPLE 8.3. Clara Kathleen Rogers, "She Never Told Her Love" (Boston: Arthur P. Schmidt, 1882).

life, teaching piano, playing, and composing. Her interest in folk songs from her native land led to her collection *Seventy Scottish Songs* (1905), which she arranged for voice and piano. That interest also was reflected in her original compositions, many of which, like the song in Example 8.4, show a distinct Scottish folk influence.

In 1893 the Boston Symphony Orchestra gave the first performance of Margaret Ruthven Lang's *Dramatic Overture*—the first time a major American orchestra played a work by a woman. This was the first of seven works for orchestra—now lost—that were performed in the 1890s by the Boston Symphony and other orchestras. This same year her *Witichis,* an orchestral

EXAMPLE 8.4. Helen Hopekirk, "The Bandriudh" (Song of Spring), from *Five Songs* (New York: G. Schirmer, 1903).

FIGURE 8.3. Margaret Ruthven Lang. Billy Rose Theatre Collection. Reproduced by permission of The New York Public Library, Astor, Lenox and Tilden Foundations.

piece, was performed three times at the World's Columbian Exposition in Chicago. Lang, like Rogers, was the daughter of musicians. Her mother was known as an "exquisite singer." Her father, Benjamin Johnson Lang, also was a leading musician in Boston—a teacher, a frequent soloist on piano and organ, an organist with the Handel and Haydn Society and the Boston Symphony Orchestra, and a conductor of choruses and instrumental ensembles. B. J. Lang taught his daughter, and later sent her to Munich to study violin and composition. On her return, Margaret continued composition studies with Chadwick and Paine. Her father was also her mentor, whose approval of her works she regularly sought before submitting them to Schmidt for publication. He presented many of her works at his own concerts. But Lang had other sources of support, among them some leading singers and conductors as well as members of music and women's clubs. Her song "Ojala" was sung on a program of representative American works given in Paris during the Exposition of 1889. Although Lang stopped composing many years before her death at the age of 104, singers and choral groups continued to perform her music for many years, often giving entire programs of her works.

Like others of the Boston School, she composed under the primary influence of German Romanticism. On the other hand, her most famous song, "An Irish Love Song," Op. 22 (1895), is among a number of her works written in a folk idiom. It also exemplifies the widespread interest in folk song among contemporary American composers of art music. Some of her late works show French influence too, especially *Wind,* her beautiful and atmospheric double chorus for women's voices (see Example 8.5).

Amy Marcy Beach (1867–1944) (née Cheney), an outstanding composer of the period, was born the same year as Lang. As a child she came to Boston from Henniker, New Hampshire. The Marcy side of the family was quite musical, and her mother, Clara Imogene (Marcy) Cheney, had performed as a singer and pianist before her marriage. Thus she was well qualified to recognize her infant daughter's remarkable talent: "Her gift for composition showed itself in babyhood—before two years of age she would, when being rocked in my arms, improvise a perfectly correct alto to any soprano air I might sing."[27]

At four years the child played by ear any music she had heard and composed her first pieces for the piano—in her head and away from the instrument. Two years later she began piano with her mother, and studied

EXAMPLE 8.5. Margaret Ruthven Lang, *Wind,* Op. 53 (Boston: Arthur P. Schmidt, 1913).

FIGURE 8.4. Amy Marcy Cheney Beach. Elizabeth Porter Gould Collection, Division of Rare Books and Manuscripts, Boston Public Library. Used by permission.

successively with two German-trained pianists, the second a student of Franz Liszt. By the time she was sixteen, she had made an eagerly awaited debut with a Boston orchestra. At least fifteen local critics covered the concert, and all agreed that she was an outstanding talent with technical ability to match. For the next two years she played regularly in Boston and its environs, and was as regularly admired by the critics. By the time she made her debut with the Boston Symphony Orchestra in 1885, the critics were calling her a master musician.

Her training in composition had not been totally neglected. In 1882 Amy Cheney studied harmony and counterpoint with an outstanding Boston teacher. After her debut, she sought advice from Wilhelm Gericke, conductor of the Boston Symphony, about a composition teacher. He recommended that she teach herself. Such a suggestion may have been influenced by public perceptions that although men wrote out of their intellects, women wrote from their feelings and therefore would not respond to training. Following that advice, Amy Cheney (Beach) taught herself—very well indeed—by studying the scores of the masters. Throughout her youth she had continued to improvise and compose, and two of her songs were published under her maiden name: "The Rainy Day" (Oliver Ditson, 1883) and "With Violets," Op. 1, No. 1 (1885), the first piece of hers issued by Arthur P. Schmidt.

The year 1885 marked the beginning of her long association with Schmidt, her exclusive publisher for twenty-five years. That year also saw her marriage at eighteen to Dr. Henry Harris Aubrey Beach, who was then forty-three and clearly delighted to have as his wife such a promising creative talent. They agreed that she would concentrate on composition, curtailing performing to an occasional recital, proceeds of which would go to charity. This arrangement was in some ways ideal for a composer. During the next twenty-five years, Beach turned out dozens of art songs, among them "Elle et moi," Op. 21, No. 3 (1893; see HAMW, pp. 161–65). In it the piano figurations depict the fluttering of the butterfly's wings, imitated as well in the voice's florid passages. Beach also wrote compositions for piano and for chamber ensemble, choral works, and several major works involving orchestra, including her Mass in E-flat, Op. 5 (1890), her Symphony in E Minor *(Gaelic),* Op. 32 (1897), and her Piano Concerto, Op. 45 (1900).

The "Gaelic" Symphony (first movement printed in HAMW, pp. 166–203) was an important landmark in music, for it was the first symphony by an American woman to be performed anywhere. Indeed, during her lifetime it had multiple performances by over a dozen orchestras in the United States and Europe. Its importance lies also in being the first symphony by an American composer that quotes folk songs as themes. This work, and many others that followed, placed Mrs. Beach within the nationalist movement in music (ca. 1893–1950), characterized by the use of folk and traditional music of the many native and immigrant groups in the United States.[28]

Following the deaths of her husband in 1910 and her mother in 1911, Beach again became active as a pianist, though she continued to compose. Major works from the latter half of her life, composed in Beach's chromatic post-Romantic style, include the *Theme and Variations for Flute and Strings,* Op. 80 (1920); her String Quartet in One Movement, Op. 89 (MS, 1929); a large number of choral works for the Protestant liturgy, among them her *Canticle of the Sun,* Op. 123 (1928) for chorus and orchestra; and many songs, including the superb *Rendezvous,* Op. 120 (1928), with violin obbligato (see Example 8.6).

Her numerous piano works include two written during her first residency at the MacDowell Colony in 1921, "The Hermit Thrush at Eve," and "The Hermit Thrush at Morn," Op. 92, Nos. 1 and 2 (1922), based on bird calls that Beach heard and notated at the Colony (see HAMW, pp. 204–10). Like the use of folk songs, bird calls offered composers a fresh vocabulary that contributed to the changes in compositional style that took place in the twentieth century.

EXAMPLE 8.6. Mrs. H. H. A. Beach, "Rendezvous," Op. 120, for voice, violin, and piano (Boston: Oliver Ditson, 1928).

During her lifetime Beach's works had wide currency: in addition to the popularity of her symphony, her songs were sung by leading opera stars, her chamber music was featured by many ensembles, and her choral music occupied an important place in church repertories. Despite her many successes, much critical commentary during her lifetime dwelt on the fact that she was a woman, insisting hence that her works could not be compared with those of mainstream, male composers. At the same time, her colleagues in New England believed her to be the most gifted composer of their group. Her compositions crowned a century of progress by American women in music. Beach became a heroine to American women, her example a beacon to light the way for the coming generation of female composers.

NOTES

1. Information in this section was generously provided by the late Susan L. Porter from her book, *With an Air Debonair: Musical Theatre in America, 1785–1815* (Washington, DC: The Smithsonian Institution Press, 1991).

2. Information on composers is summarized from Judith Tick, *American Women Composers before 1870* (Ann Arbor: UMI Research Press, 1983), passim, and from Porter, passim.

3. Information on opera troupes summarized from Katherine Preston, "Traveling Opera Troupes in the United States, 1825–1860" (Ph.D. diss., The City University of New York, 1989); revised and published as *Opera on the Road: Traveling Opera Troupes in the United States, 1825–1860* (Urbana: University of Illinois Press, 1993).

4. Information about Kellogg is from her autobiography, *Memoirs of an American Prima Donna* (New York: G. P. Putnam, 1913; repr. 1938).

5. Ibid., p. 30.

6. Tick, *American Women Composers before 1870*, p. 30.

7. Information about Julia Crane and Crane Normal Institute comes from the Archives of the Crane School of Music, SUNY-Potsdam.

8. Amy Fay, *Music Study in Germany,* ed. Mrs. Fay Pierce (New York: Macmillan, 1880; repr. 1979).

9. Mabel Daniels, *An American Girl in Munich (Impressions of a Music Student)* (Boston: Little Brown & Co., 1905), quoted in *Women in Music: An Anthology of Source Readings from the Middle Ages to the Present,* Carol Neuls-Bates, ed. (New York: Harper and Row, 1982), pp. 219–222.

10. Eva Munson Smith, ed. *Woman in Sacred Song. A Library of Hymns, Religious Poems and Sacred Music by Women.* Foreword by Frances E. Willard (Boston: D. Lothrop, 1885). The collection also includes temperance and suffrage songs.

11. *History of the Handel and Haydn Society,* vol. 1, ed. Charles C. Perkins (1883; reprint New York: DaCapo Press, 1977), pp. 50–51.

12. *The New Grove Dictionary of American Music,* s.v. "[Fisk] Jubilee Singers," by Geneva H. Southall.

13. Karen J. Blair, *The Torchbearers: Women and Their Amateur Arts Association in America, 1890–1930* (Bloomington: Indiana University Press, 1994), p. 55. In 1936 a Student Division was added to the National Federation of Music Clubs. Today there are thousands of clubs, and members number in the hundred thousands. Although membership is open to all, regardless of gender, the overwhelming majority of members, as well as the leaders, continue to be female. The clubs also support members attempting to develop as performers and to learn organizational skills and concert management, helping some to move from amateur to professional status. In pursuit of these aims, members themselves benefit: they have space to develop as performers, and to learn organizational skills and concert management; some are then able to move from amateur to professional status.

14. See Marta Milinowski, *Teresa Carreño: "By the Grace of God"* (New Haven: Yale University Press, 1940).

15. Ibid., p. 45.

16. Information on Julie Rivé-King is from M. Leslie Petteys, "Julie Rivé-King, American Pianist" (D.M.A. thesis, University of Missouri-Kansas City, 1987).

17. Harold Schonberg, *The Great Pianists* (New York: Simon and Schuster, 1963), p. 249, quoted in Petteys, pp. vii-viii.

18. Information from Diana Ruth Hallman, "The Pianist Fannie Bloomfield Zeisler in American Music and Society" (M.M. thesis, University of Maryland, 1983).

19. See Susan Kagan, "Camilla Urso: A Nineteenth Century Violinist's View," *Signs: Journal of Women in Culture and Society,* 2 (1977): 727–34.

20. Information from Karen A. Shaffer and Neva Garner Greenwood, *Maud Powell, Pioneer American Violinist* (Arlington, VA: The Maud Powell Foundation, 1988; distributed by Iowa State University Press).

21. Henry Roth, "Women and the Fiddle," *The Strad* 83 (March 1973): 557.

22. Tick, p. 171. Also see Tick, pp. 94–98, 188–95, and 199–216 for information on Stith, Sloman, and Parkhurst.

23. Information on Jacobs-Bond comes from Phyllis Ruth Bruce, "From Rags to Roses: The Life and Works of Carrie Jacobs-Bond, an American Composer" (M.A. thesis, Wesleyan University, 1980).

24. Carrie Jacobs-Bond, *The Roads of Melody* (New York: D. Appleton, 1927), p. 4.

25. On Schmidt's support of women composers, see Adrienne Fried Block, "Arthur P. Schmidt, Music Publisher and Champion of American Women Composers," in *The Musical Woman: An International Perspective,* vol. 2 (1984–1985), ed. Judith Lang Zaimont et al. (Westport, CT: Greenwood Press, 1987), pp. 145–76.

26. Clara Kathleen Rogers, *The Story of Two Lives: Home, Friends, and Travel* (Norwood, MA: Plimpton Press, 1932), p. 81.

27. Copy of letter from Clara Cheney to "Cousin Anna" dated 27 April 1898, from 28 Commonwealth Avenue, Boston, in Box 4, F. 25, Beach Collection, University of New Hampshire at Durham.

28. For more information on the relation of this work to the nationalist movement in the United States, see Adrienne Fried Block, "Dvořák, Beach, and American Music," in *A Celebration of American Music: Words and Music in Honor of H. Wiley Hitchcock* (Ann Arbor: University of Michigan Press, 1990), pp. 256–80.

SUGGESTIONS FOR FURTHER READING

In addition to items mentioned in the text or cited in the footnotes, the following sources provide information on women in American music, ca. 1800 to ca. 1918.

Blakesly, Melissa. "Mabel Wheeler Daniels: Her Life and Works." M.M. thesis, University of Cincinnati, 1999.

Block, Adrienne Fried. *Amy Beach, Passionate Victorian: The Life and Work of an American Composer, 1867–1944.* New York: Oxford University Press, 1998.

Handy, D. Antoinette. *Black Women in American Bands and Orchestras.* Metuchen, N J: Scarecrow Press, 1981.

Loesser, Arthur. *Men, Women and Pianos: A Social History.* New York: Simon and Schuster, 1954.

Morath, Max. "May Aufderheide and the Ragtime Women." In *Ragtime: Its History, Composers, and Music,* ed. John Edward Hasse. New York: G. Schirmer, 1985, pp. 154–65.

Smith, Jewel. "Music, Women, and Pianos: The Young Ladies' Seminary in Antebellum Bethlehem, Pennsylvania (1815–1860)." Ph.D. diss., University of Cincinnati, 2001.

Tawa, Nicholas E. *Sweet Songs for Gentle Americans: The Parlor Song in America, 1790–1860.* Bowling Green, Ohio: Bowling Green University Popular Press, 1980.

Whitesitt, Linda. "Women as 'Keepers of Culture': Music Clubs, Community Concert Series, and Symphony Orchestras," *Cultivating Music in America: Women Patrons and Activists since 1860,* ed. Ralph P. Locke and Cyrilla Barr. Berkeley: University of California Press, 1997, pp. 65–86.

Modern Music around the Globe

IX.
Contemporary British Composers

Catherine Roma

During the early years of the twentieth century an unusual number of British women composers were born. The first decade alone saw the births of Priaulx Rainier, Elizabeth Poston, Grace Williams, Elisabeth Lutyens, Elizabeth Maconchy, Imogen Holst, and Phyllis Tate. Most of these composers attended the Royal College of Music (RCM) in the twenties, and many were students of Ralph Vaughan Williams or Gustav Holst. They reacted to and were affected by the English Musical Renaissance and seemed more open than many in their generation to musical currents from the Continent. All struggled with their careers, not only because they were forward-looking composers but also because they were women. None felt she had experienced discrimination at the RCM. However, once out in the professional world, many felt the need to band together and to organize performances where their works could be heard. Anne Macnaghten, in collaboration with conductor Iris Lemare and composer Elisabeth Lutyens, established the recently disbanded Macnaghten-Lemare series as a platform for performances of modern British music.[1] Distinguished soloists were approached for help; voices were solicited for a chorus; and Lemare conducted a chamber orchestra made up of amateurs and students.[2] By the 1960s, when a favorable musical climate in London and the momentum of their past efforts and successes came together, these women had become well known. In fact, the Society of Women Musicians, an organization founded in 1911 to deal with the problems of invisibility among women composers and performers, disbanded in the early 1970s, believing it had met its objectives.

Thea Musgrave (b. 1928) stands alone in the next generation of composers. Not until the 1960s and early 1970s, when London emerged as one of the international centers of new music, did the RCM and the Royal Academy of Music (RAM) see another generation quite like the one nearer to the beginning of the century. Women composers, including Nicola LeFanu, Erika Fox, Judith Bingham, Diana Burrell, Eleanor Alberga, Rhian Samuel, Sally Beamish, and Judith Weir have benefited from the groundbreaking work of their predecessors. Yet Nicola LeFanu, the daughter of Elizabeth Maconchy, strongly believes that the 1980s saw a rapid decline in opportunities for women in music because of the growing conservative political climate.[3] As a result, in 1987 musicians organized Women in Music to address many of the problems created by that decline. The goals of the new organization were to raise the profile of women working in music, alert the media of discrimination against women in all aspects of musical life, organize performances, list upcoming events, review recent triumphs, educate, inform, and network with other women musicians. This organization continues to support women composers to attain their goals.

THE FIRST GENERATION

Elisabeth Lutyens

Elisabeth Lutyens (1906–1983) was born in London, the fourth of five children of the distinguished architect Edwin Lutyens and Lady Emily Lytton. Though theirs was not a musical family, they did not actively disapprove of their daughter's interest in music. Lutyens studied both piano and violin, practiced many hours a day, and began to compose in secret. Strongly impressed by "the exciting flavor of new music from France—Debussy and Ravel—that was beginning to filter through the fog of English programmes,"[4] she persuaded her parents to let her go to Paris to study at the École Normale. She then entered London's Royal College of Music and was assigned to Harold Darke—though she might have been placed with Ralph Vaughan Williams or John Ireland, composers whom, in retrospect, she relegated to "the cowpat school of composition."[5] Darke's encouragement was central to the eventual development of her own highly individual compositional style.

In the 1930s Lutyens had two experiences that influenced her greatly: she was introduced to Purcell's contrapuntal string fantasias, which, she said, led her to discover serial composition; and she heard a performance of Webern's "Das Augenlicht," which she found unforgettable. Lutyens turned permanently to serial technique with her Concerto for Nine Instruments (1940). Her new musical language developed naturally out of the rigor of her compositional attitudes, and her fascination with mathematical relationships placed her outside Britain's musical mainstream. Life for Lutyens was extremely difficult during and after World War II. In 1933 she married Ian Glennie, with whom she had three children, but she later left him for Edward Clark, a well-known champion of contemporary music. Though Clark played many roles in her life, he did not provide financial support. At first Lutyens made a meager living copying music, but writing music for documentary films eventually became a major source of her income, and she produced more than one hundred such scores.

O Saisons, O Châteaux! (1946) for soprano, mandolin, guitar, harp, solo violin, and strings presages Lutyens's mature style. Setting a poem from Rimbaud's *Les Illuminations,* Lutyens creates an extraordinary atmosphere, expressed directly in beautiful, highly articulate melodic writing. Another side of Lutyens can be seen in her Stevie Smith songs of 1948; light and humorous, these cabaret songs capture the essence of Smith's poetry. During the 1950s Lutyens solidified elements in her compositional style and emerged a mature composer in such works as her *Concertante for Five Players* (1950) and String Quartet No. 6 (1952). Marks of her style included the use of palindromic structures and a progressive paring down of materials and gestures. Her harmonic language became consistent, her musical structures more tightly organized. Despite her rigorous approach to composition, she had an instinct for keeping the music varied.

Her vocal music is most impressive—both solo and choral works are characterized by a wide-ranging choice of texts and sensitive musical reactions to the words themselves. *Motet (Excerpta Tractati-Logico-Philosophici),* Op. 27 (1953), is one of Lutyens's most remarkable compositions. For her text she selected a series of statements from Ludwig Wittgenstein's *Logisch-philosophische Abhandlung* (1912), a tract that poses the questions: How is language possible? How can a person, by uttering a sequence of words, say something? And how can another person understand? The formal, abstract nature of the text freed Lutyens from any necessity to interpret words. Hence her motet is not a setting of words so much as a realization of Wittgenstein's philosophical ideas through her technique of musical composition. Though the motet uses twelve-tone aggregates, combinations, and serial techniques, it is not dodecaphonic in the strict sense of the word. This taut, complex, lyrical work, full of choice and craft, is not without the performance difficulties typical of all Lutyens's works.

Two important works from the 1960s are *And Suddenly It's Evening* (1966) and *Essence of Our Happinesses* (1968). The earlier work is scored for tenor voice and eleven instrumentalists: an ensemble of brass instruments as well as two trios: one of harp, celesta, and percussion; the other of violin, horn, and cello. Lutyens creates a universe of sound in her distilled and economic use of material in this twenty-five-minute work. *Essence of Our Happinesses,* whose title is taken from Donne's Devotion XIV, is built on texts by three different poets from different periods, nationalities, and traditions. The central movement, "Their Criticall Dayes," is the spiritual core of the work. The opening uses four-part SATB choir; thereafter the choir alternates with the tenor soloist. Simple vertical sonorities are employed, and the texture is sparse. The work achieves a timeless effect through the subtlety of its musical events, the sparseness in the layout of the melodic and harmonic incidents, and the repetition of musical material.

In the 1970s, after focusing on dramatic and vocal works, Lutyens wrote a series of instrumental pieces entitled *Plenum* (*Plenum I:* piano; *Plenum II:* solo oboe and thirteen instrumentalists; *Plenum III:* string quartet; and *Plenum IV:* organ). In them Lutyens increased the flexibility of her notation and continued to reduce musical events. *Plenum I* (CAMW, p. 179) represents a departure in Lutyens's piano compositions, indicated by such immediately visible features as the lack of bar lines, many pauses, and phrase markings followed by commas for breaths. The tone rows stated in the first half of the piece are restated in retrograde from the work's central point, an example of the palindrome form Lutyens frequently uses.

Lutyens always had a loyal following, and during the last decade of her life her closest friends were avant-garde musicians younger than she. These were the people who appreciated her work, her uncompromising spirit, her fearlessness, and her commitment to new music.

Elizabeth Maconchy

Elizabeth Maconchy (1907–1994) was born in Broxbourne, Hereford, north of London. Although both her parents were Irish, the family lived in Buckinghamshire for several years before moving to Dublin after World War I. When her father died, the family returned to England. In the same year, when she was sixteen years old, Maconchy was accepted into the Royal College of Music, where she studied composition with Charles Wood and Ralph Vaughan Williams. She worked with the latter for many years and acknowledged the central influence on her music of both Vaughan Williams and the Hungarian composer Béla Bartók.

During her six years at the RCM, Maconchy won the Blumenthal and Sullivan scholarships. In 1929, on being awarded the Octavia Traveling Scholarship, she visited Vienna and Paris and then spent two months in Prague studying with Karel Jirák. Her music aroused much interest, and she returned in 1930 when her piano concerto was premiered by the Prague Philharmonic. Maconchy later (1935) traveled to Prague, Cracow, and Warsaw

(1939) for performances of her works by the International Society for Contemporary Music (ISCM). Her first major performance in London had already occurred in 1930, when Sir Henry Wood conducted her suite, *The Land,* at the Prom Concerts. Yet despite favorable press notices and recognition from people in important places, her early career did not flourish as one might have expected. Maconchy remained a private person, with a strong, quiet nature, and her hard-fought struggle with tuberculosis restricted her activities. However, in her solitude she was able to develop her own way of thinking, and she never stopped composing. She focused on chamber music, concentrating specifically on the string quartets that form the core of her output.

Between 1933 and 1984 Elizabeth Maconchy wrote thirteen string quartets, thus becoming the modern English composer most closely associated with this medium. Like the quartets of Bartók, Maconchy's reveal highly contrapuntal textures, short chromatic motives, and canonic procedures. However, her compositions are not derived from folk music, as are those of Bartók, Vaughan Williams, and Janácek—composers with whom she is constantly compared. For Maconchy, the string quartet is the perfect vehicle for dramatic expression, as if four characters were engaged in statement and comment: "the clash of their ideas and the way in which they react upon each other."[6] Her early quartets, those most often compared to Bartók's, follow a classic multimovement format, but the later ones tend to be more compact, often in one continuous movement, with a very economical use of material.

In the mid-1950s, after having experienced what she called a creative block, Maconchy began to write operas, and she produced three one-act works in a ten-year period (1957–1967). She also wrote several pieces for children's voices: operas, extravaganzas, *scenas,* and musical theatre works. Her interest and enthusiasm for setting text also led to a rich outpouring of choral music and music for solo voice and instrumental ensemble, including *Ariadne* (1970), for soprano and orchestra, and *The Leaden Echo and the Golden Echo* (1978), for mixed chorus, alto flute, viola, and harp. Her integrity as a composer came from knowing current trends, supporting other musicians, participating in contemporary music organizations, and quietly writing because she had to. Maconchy achieved a balance of craft and control with insight. She was named Commander of the British Empire (CBE) in 1977. The Arts Council of Great Britain sponsored a film in 1984 documenting her lengthy and prolific career, examining the struggles she had to endure as a female composer in what until very recently was predominantly a male world. In 1987 Maconchy received the title Dame of the British Empire, only the second woman composer to be recognized with this honor. The music which Maconchy continued to produce until she was in her late seventies showed an untiring determination to explore new ground without losing the lyricism and expressive qualities of her maturity.

Grace Williams

In the history of Welsh music, Grace Williams (1906–1977) occupies a position of first importance, and her reputation is undisputed. She came from a musical family and fondly remembered the days when she played violin in a family trio. After studying music at the University of Cardiff, she went on to the Royal College of Music, as did her friend Elizabeth Maconchy; there she studied composition with Ralph Vaughan Williams. Upon completing her degree, she traveled to Vienna to study with Egon Wellesz. Back in London, Williams taught at the Camden School for Girls and composed music. She remained in London a total of twenty years (1926–1946) before returning to Wales, where she spent the rest of her life. Highly self-critical, she later purged many of her earliest, highly experimental pieces: her journal of May 10, 1951, reads, "DAY OF DESTRUCTION. Examined all my music manuscripts and destroyed nearly all which I considered not worth performing." Yet this early period also saw the creation of two of her most frequently programmed works, the *Fantasia on Welsh Nursery Tunes* (1941) and *Sea Sketches* (1947), a suite of five pieces inspired by the coastline near her home. *Fantasia,* which quotes eight traditional melodies, immediately became popular and was soon recorded. The work did much to make Grace Williams known, and for this it occupies an important position in her output.

The years between 1955 and 1961 were richly creative and productive. *Penillion* (1955), a suite for orchestra, is closely related to an indigenous, improvisational form of singing in Wales known as *cerdd dant;* it retains the recurring form ABAB, the narrative style, and the rhythmic and melodic characteristics of the traditional *penillion.* Most of Williams's compositions written in the last ten years of her creative life involved voice in some way. At the age of sixty she wrote an opera, *The Parlour* (1966), adapting her own libretto from Guy de Maupassant's short story *En famille.* In *Missa Cambrenisis* (1971) she incorporated nonliturgical material into the Latin rite. The sound of bells and the interval of the tritone color the score, and the work as a whole shows the influence of Benjamin Britten's *War Requiem.*

The Marian hymn *Ave Maris Stella* (Hail, Star of the Sea, 1973) for unaccompanied mixed chorus is perhaps her most impressive work. The first three words of the hymn form a refrain that opens every stanza, and the plastic rhythms reflect the ebb and flow of the sea, as do the undulating melodic lines and the skillful changes in vocal color. Williams was a communicator whose command of orchestral writing and skilled handling of voices made her contribution to Welsh music inestimable.

Priaulx Rainier

Priaulx Rainier (1903–1986), born in South Africa, was largely a self-taught composer. Her musical language combines twentieth-century forms with the sounds she heard on the borders of Natal and Zululand during her childhood. In 1920 Rainier was awarded a Cape University Overseas Scholarship to study violin at the Royal Academy of Music. After graduation she remained in London, where she taught and performed. While recovering from a serious car accident she composed her first work, a duo for piano and violin, which was performed at Wigmore Hall in 1936. This successful premiere was followed by *Three Greek Epigrams* for soprano and piano (1937) and a string quartet (1939). Trademarks of Rainier's early style are apparent here: a wide variety of textural contrasts and ostinato-like rhythmic structures reminiscent of African music and dance.

In the autumn of 1937 Rainier studied for several months with Nadia Boulanger; these were her only formal composition lessons. Though composing did not come easily to Rainier, she found her own way and was able to forge a refined, disciplined, meticulously crafted, highly personal idiom. By the mid-1940s she had become a professor of composition at the RAM.

In 1953 Peter Pears commissioned the first of two works from Priaulx Rainier: *Cycle for Declamation* for unaccompanied tenor voice on fragments from John Donne's *Devotions*. Pears's second commission produced *Bee Oracles* (1970), Rainier's largest chamber work. This accessible and attractive piece, written for voice, flute, oboe, violin, cello, and harpsichord, is frequently performed; its text by Edith Sitwell draws on Indian philosophical thought. Rainier's only choral work is a powerful and prophetic Requiem (1955) for unaccompanied chorus and tenor solo. The text, by David Gascoyne, is a warning for future victims, a requiem for the ideals and hopes of the world. Rainier's choral writing is homophonic and stark in its rhythmic strength. The incantatory tenor solo acts at times as an integral part of the chorus, while at other times it provides a connection between choral sections and dramatic recitative.

The Requiem was the culmination of Rainier's early work. A change can be detected in her style during the early 1960s, when her compositions became more abstract, compressed, and chromatic, with many semitones and minor ninths. A strong rhythmic energy, employed with great sophistication, continued to pervade her music. Rainier's mature style can be heard in *Pastoral Triptych* (1960) for solo oboe, and *Quanta* (1962) for oboe and string trio. The title of *Quanta,* the first of her BBC commissions, refers to the quantum theory of energy existing in space, independent of matter. Though Priaulx Rainier's output is not large, it is meticulously crafted, and her music is complex, with highly charged dissonance and fragmented rhythms.

THE MIDDLE GENERATION

Thea Musgrave

Thea Musgrave was born in Barnton, Midlothian, near Edinburgh, Scotland, on May 27, 1928. Though music was an essential part of her childhood, not until she had begun a premedical course at Edinburgh University did she choose to make it her life's work. A postgraduate scholarship enabled her to work with Nadia Boulanger, from whom she learned the fundamental principles of discipline and economy and "the importance of every bar."[7] In 1952 Musgrave received the coveted Lili Boulanger Memorial Prize in composition, the first Scottish composer to be so honored. The next year she fulfilled her first commission—from the Scottish Festival at Braemar—with *A Suite o' Bairnsangs* for voice and piano. Her first major success came with *Cantata for a Summer's Day* (1954), a work commissioned by BBC Scotland and scored for chamber ensemble, narrator, and small chorus. Thereafter, Musgrave's works show a gradual movement toward serial technique. Her first fully serial piece is a setting for high voice and piano of "A Song for Christmas," a declamatory *scena* written in 1958.

The period 1961–1965 marks a break in her development. Without commission or prospect of performance, Musgrave embarked on her first full-length opera, *The Decision,* and worked on it for two years to the virtual exclusion of everything else. Its successful world premiere in 1967 at Sadler's Wells in London led Musgrave in a new direction as a composer. She became preoccupied with an instrumental style she describes as dramatic-abstract: dramatic in the sense that certain instruments take on the character of dramatic personae; abstract because there is no program. In several of the twenty-seven instrumental compositions written between 1964 and 1972, soloists are required to stand and move around the stage, engaging in musical dialogue or confrontation with other performers. While all the parts are fully notated, they need not be exactly coordinated with other parts or with the conductor; such a piece is described as asynchronous music. The first of Musgrave's dramatic-abstract works is the Chamber Concerto No. 2 (1966). This piece in homage to Charles Ives uses the character of Rollo, represented by the viola, to disrupt the general calm with phrases from popular melodies.[8] The concerto, in one uninterrupted movement divided into six short sections, is written for five players performing on a total of nine instruments.

A natural outgrowth of Musgrave's interest in the dramatic aspects of instrumental music was her return, in 1973, to operatic composition. In *The Voice of Ariadne,* a three-act chamber opera, the asynchronous techniques of the concerti are carried over into the vocal ensembles. During the late 1970s Musgrave wrote two operas, *Mary Queen of Scots* (1977), one of her most significant works to date, and *A Christmas Carol* (1979), her most frequently performed work. The musical idiom of *Mary* is accessible and often tonal. The orchestral textures are always inventive, and the chorus is used very resourcefully, on and off the stage. The title character's soliloquy (see HAMW, pp. 367–74) provides powerful insight into her strength and determination. A drama of conflict and confrontation, *Mary* highlights Musgrave's keen sense of dramatic timing and her rich theatrical imagination.

Musgrave's opera *Harriet, the Woman Called Moses* (1985) is based on the life of Harriet Tubman, whose exploits as a conductor on the nineteenth century's Underground Railroad, leading African-American slaves to freedom, made her a major heroine in American history. As the librettist, Musgrave embroidered the details of Harriet's life and utilized a flashback technique, unusual for opera, to portray Harriet as she plots her return to free other slaves. Musgrave uses authentic folk songs and spirituals as she tells of Harriet's escape from slavery and of the many people who helped her. The work opens and closes with a thundering chorus built around two chords that carry the "Freedom" motif of the opera, and the chorus is almost always on stage to observe, comment on, or participate in the action. *Harriet* was revised in 1986 as *The Story of Harriet Tubman.* While the original version was scored for full orchestra, the later edition uses only flute, clarinet, horn, piano (doubling on synthesizer), percussion, violin, viola, and cello. In addition to changes in the orchestration, there are significant changes in length (the new version, in one act, is one and one-half hours long, as opposed to the two-act original, which takes three hours in performance).

Simón Bolívar (1995) has proved to be the strongest of Musgrave's eight operas to date. Bolívar, an important nineteenth-century Venezuelan idealist and liberator, freed six Latin American countries from the yoke of colonialism. His story and the historical context of the struggle to unify South America provided the theatrical urgency necessary for Musgrave's dramatic presentation. Though the original libretto (by Musgrave) was written in English, the premiere run, in Richmond, Virginia, was sung in Spanish. In two acts, comprising fourteen scenes, *Bolívar* subtly combines twentieth-century style with folk material. To prepare the libretto, Musgrave read more than a dozen biographies of Bolívar—some strongly pro-Bolívar, others highly critical—and his letters, several of which became the bases for arias. She immersed herself in various indigenous musics of the Caribbean region and of Central and South America. Musgrave succeeds, as she did earlier in *Mary* and *Harriet,* in incorporating music borrowed from various sources into her own distinctive style with authenticity and integrity. Her scoring in *Bolívar* provides a palette of musically distinctive colors. Musgrave utilizes a prepared harp (a brown bag is threaded through the strings) to sound like a banjo, and a synthesizer to produce mandolin and guitar sounds. The chorus is engaging throughout.

In choosing Harriet Tubman and Simón Bolívar as operatic subjects, Musgrave has deliberately made historical connections from the nineteenth century to the final decades of the twentieth. She has chosen larger-than-life, charismatic figures: "Harriet is every woman who dared to defy injustice and tyranny; she is Joan of Arc, she is Susan B. Anthony, she is Anne Frank, she is Mother Theresa."[9] Writing about Bolívar, Musgrave adds:

> Each generation needs its heroes: those people who can conceive of a new world and who also have the charisma, commitment and skill to bring it to reality. Thus Bolívar. Though in his own eyes he was not successful (those who serve a revolution only plough the sea), for us he is a source of insight and understanding of the difficulties of achieving the goals he aspired to. No struggle of this nature is in vain: we find renewal of his spirit in a few rare and wonderful people of our own time.[10]

Musgrave has not lost her fascination with the concerto-style works for which she was so well known in the sixties and seventies. Her most recent interest lies in two neglected instruments of the orchestra: the marimba, featured in *Journey through a Japanese Landscape,* and the bass clarinet, which plays protagonist in *Autumn Sonata*. In the earlier work the marimba is mixed in with a wind orchestra (rather than blended), and presents the four seasons through a connected series of haiku, each introduced by the soloist who produces evocative sounds of the seasons with glissandi on wind chimes made of different materials: bamboo, wood, metal, and glass for spring, summer, autumn, and winter, respectively. (This work is one of the many major percussion pieces inspired by the musicianship and virtuosity of Evelyn Glennie.)

In *Autumn Sonata* an extramusical inspiration is apparent. Musgrave, still haunted by the poetry of Austrian writer Georg Trakl, places fragments of his work at the beginnings of each of the five movements and the coda. The poetic lines serve to inspire and set the tone for the piece—they are not read but are only printed in the score for effect. In *Wild Winter,* the piece written just prior to this sonata, Musgrave used one of Trakl's poems in a setting for vocal quartet and viol consort. That earlier work, a moving protest against the horrors of war, was premiered by the British ensemble Fretwork. In this "autumnal dream landscape" Musgrave abandons one aspect of her earlier dramatic concerto style—solo players do not move around the stage to illustrate the dialogue visually or to project the role of protagonist.

However, the solo bass clarinet is shadowed by an offstage orchestral bass clarinet. Beethoven's Moonlight Sonata (for piano, Op. 27, No. 2), hinted at early in this work, adds to the dark colors of her orchestral writing, especially in the concluding *Adagio sostenuto*. In a program note Musgrave writes of "the three musical elements that open this famous sonata (the dotted rhythm of the melody, the accompanying triplet figure, and the low resonant bass)." She concludes her comments with a statement that "neither *Autumn Sonata* nor *Wild Winter* are intended as direct descriptions of war, but rather a memory, alternating between dream and nightmare."[11]

In addition to her accomplishments as a composer, Musgrave has become a welcomed lecturer and a respected conductor of her own works. She was the third woman to conduct the Philadelphia Orchestra since its inception in 1900 and the first to conduct one of her own compositions, the Concerto for Orchestra, with that symphonic ensemble. She has directed the New York City Opera, the Los Angeles Chamber Orchestra, the San Diego and San Francisco Symphony Orchestras, the St. Paul Chamber Orchestra, the BBC Symphony Orchestra, and London's Royal Philharmonic Orchestra. Musgrave is fortunate to have had almost all of her works performed soon after they were written. She recognizes what a valuable lesson this is for any composer, for only then can the writer gain confidence and begin to explore new and individual paths.

The New Generation

Nicola LeFanu

Nicola LeFanu, the daughter of Dame Elizabeth Maconchy, was born in Essex in 1947. She remembers that her mother would play the piano every evening and compose music; thus, "It never entered my head that to be a woman composer was unnatural."[12] LeFanu studied composition with Egon Wellesz at St. Hilda's College, Oxford, from which she graduated in 1968 with a Bachelor of Arts (and honors) degree in music. Her other teachers included Goffredo Petrassi, Peter Maxwell Davies, and Earl Kim.

The music of Nicola LeFanu covers a broad range of genres. She has written for orchestra, chamber ensemble with and without voice, solo voice, chorus, and solo voice accompanied by one instrument. Many people think of her as primarily a composer of vocal music, and indeed her works for solo voice are popular with singers. Since poetry, theatre, and opera have fascinated LeFanu since childhood, it is no surprise that during the last decade four of her operas have been premiered.

The Same Day Dawns (1974), one of LeFanu's most-performed works, is scored for soprano and five players and uses texts drawn from Tamil, Chinese, and Japanese poems. The work is a cycle of very short, atmospheric songs that reflect the moods and colors of the words with a conciseness reminiscent of Asian art. Though only eleven pieces are written, the set in fact includes fifteen, since four of the first five songs are repeated in reverse order toward the end of the cycle. *The Old Woman of Beare* (1981), a dramatic dialogue for soprano and thirteen instruments, is based on a medieval Irish poem in which a tenth-century retired Irish courtesan, who is ending her life in a convent, compares her current physical state with that of earlier years. The work was written to celebrate the fiftieth anniversary of the former Macnaghten Concerts (earlier called the Macnaghten-Lemare Concerts). The score alternates highly dramatic, narrative lines with sung lines requiring a wide range and an agile singing voice. Shifting colors in the instruments support the texture and timbre of the old woman's story as it is presented in song (see CAMW, p. 130).

In 1989 the BBC broadcast *The Story of Mary O'Neill,* a commissioned radio opera with libretto by Sally McInerney. It tells of a young Irish woman who leaves her homeland during the potato famine of 1860 and heads for South America. There she marries an indigenous man and gives birth to twin sons. As adults, one son seeks his fortune in Buenos Aires and the other remains in touch with his native roots and environment. In old age, the two brothers reconnect and reflect on their fates. As in *The Old Woman of Beare,* LeFanu cleverly integrates speech and music; solo and ensemble passages alternate with lyrical and angular writing.

LeFanu collaborated with medieval scholar and poet Kevin Crossley-Holland for two operatic enterprises, *The Green Children* and *The Wildman.* The first retells one of Britain's oldest folk tales, dating from the twelfth century. The story, which at its premiere featured more than two hundred children, tells of the inexplicable appearance of two children from another—green—world. Though the setting is medieval, the opera addresses such issues as society's attitudes toward difference, color, acceptance, and rejection. These are universal themes that interest LeFanu and to which she would return.

For *Blood Wedding* (1992), LeFanu, Deborah Levy (librettist), and Anne Manson (conductor) were approached by Jules Wright (theatre director of the Woman's Playhouse Trust) to collaborate on an opera. The venture showcased the work of prominent artistic women working together on a single project. The plot, adapted from a play by Federico Garcia Lorca, provides strong roles for the women characters. Defying operatic conventions, the two main male characters in the opera die. Instead of a solitary prima donna role there are several roles of sustained depth and significance for women. Critic Claire Messud made this observation:

> That the opera should close with all its women—full, human characters—singing together is a symbolic departure in a new direction. I don't think it's an accident that the composers Thea Musgrave, Judith Weir, and Ethel Smyth all felt that [opera] was a suitable form of expression for them. If there is some way in which women view the world differently, then perhaps it is a kind of overall, integrative view which might mean there is a connection between women and opera.[13]

Blood Wedding is the largest operatic commission ever undertaken in Britain outside the great opera houses. The work, in two acts, is scored for a seventeen-piece orchestra. Its premiere, though highly successful, received a lukewarm reception from much of the mainstream press.

LeFanu's most recent opera, *Wildman* (1995), not unlike the children's opera, deals with an outsider who both distracts and attracts—and sometimes liberates the townspeople he encounters. The libretto, by Kevin Crossley-Holland, derives from a twelfth-century Suffolk legend: the fishermen of Orrford capture a creature—half man, half beast—who terrifies them with his strangeness and lack of human speech. The townsfolk lock him away, but the local sheriff's wife and children learn to respond to his strangeness. As he regains his speech, he tells his story, then swims back to sea, leaving the people to ponder how he changed their lives. The cast consists of eight singers, with some doubling of roles. The orchestra, only twelve players strong, subtly captures the sound and mist-enveloped bleakness of the coastal marsh, and the dissonant writing for the winds is particularly evocative.

LeFanu's article "Master Musician: An Impregnable Taboo?" written in 1987, challenged and changed the discourse in Britain with regard to women composers. The staid music establishment and the press took notice of her well-documented inequities, but they have yet to make any tangible changes. Her plea for balance in programming and commissioning and for equal opportunities, while not having fallen on deaf ears, has fallen on resistant ones. At the conclusion of her introduction to the *Contemporary Music Review's* special issue on British women composers, LeFanu writes:

> The bibliography which completes this volume does not try to be comprehensive. . . . It should provide a useful introduction; a first guidebook through territory which ought to be completely familiar, yet in fact is hardly ever visited. We all have received a view of West European music history from which the woman composer has been excluded. . . . Which is more unsatisfactory for a composer: to appear in a reference book which segregates by gender? Or not appear in a reference book at all? Very few artists know how passionately many of them have called out for rescue from it. Let us all make sure that the next generations of young women composers do not vanish like their predecessors.[14]

Judith Weir

Born in Cambridge in 1954, Judith Weir grew up believing that music was something spontaneous and homemade. Her family, originally from Scotland, included enthusiastic amateurs who often played Scottish folk music. Weir began composition lessons while still in high school, and her experience as an oboist in the National Youth Orchestra influenced and inspired her. Before going to Kings College, Cambridge, in 1973, she spent six months at the Massachusetts Institute of Technology, where she sat in on computer music classes with Barry Vercoe. She also benefited from study with Gunther Schuller at Tanglewood.

The catalogue of publicly performed works by Judith Weir begins in 1972, though she has already withdrawn pieces she feels are not up to standard. Until her extremely successful opera, *A Night at the Chinese Opera,* most of her compositions were for small forces, and almost half of them used voice. From the start of her career Weir has preferred to fashion her music for specific performers (often her friends), for she feels that this is a natural, organic way of working and thinking. She has found the music of Stravinsky and the ever-surprising elements in the music of Haydn to be rich sources of inspiration. Restrictions and parameters inspire her and set her going, as in *King Harald's Saga* (1979), composed for soprano Jane Manning. This unaccompanied, ten-minute *scena* is a colorful portrayal of the Norwegian king's unsuccessful invasion of Britain in 1066. Weir captures the essences of eight colorful characters, all depicted by the soprano, through economy, clarity of text setting, and a keen sense of the sung word.

The Consolations of Scholarship, a music-drama based on two Chinese or Yuan plays of the seventeenth and eighteenth centuries, has received frequent performances. The work is for a mezzo-soprano, accompanied by nine instrumentalists who play all the characters in this drama about court intrigue, politics, and revenge. Again, clarity of text setting, light-textured harmony, sparse instrumental accompaniment, and an economy of gesture demonstrate Weir's inventiveness and musical wit.

Although Weir is thought of primarily as an opera composer, she always emphasizes the significance of her instrumental and orchestra works in her output. She calls her *Airs from Another Planet* (1993) a suite of traditional music from outer space. This chamber piece in four movements ("Strathspey and Reel," "Traditional Air," "Jig," and "Bagpipe Air with Drones") is playful, bright, and Pierrot-like. In *Moon and Stars,* for choir and orchestra, Weir sets Emily Dickinson's three-stanza poem "Ah, Moon and Star!/You are very far" about the wonders of the universe and the impossibility of comprehending them. Weir likens her use of the chorus in

Moon and Stars to Debussy's in *Nocturnes,* where the voices add another layer of color to the instrumental palette.

Judith Weir catapulted to international prominence with *A Night at the Chinese Opera* (1986–1987), commissioned by the BBC for Kent Opera. Already intrigued by the Chinese music-dramas of the thirteenth century, she constructed her own libretto and created a three-act opera for eleven singers and a modest orchestra. The outer acts are fully scored, staged, and sung, whereas Act II is a fast-moving, musically stylized reconstruction of a Yuan play (*The Orphan of the Chao Family*). In the play Weir reduces her instrumentation to more or less authentic Yuan proportions. The plot traces the adventures of a young canal builder in Kubla Khan's China who sees his career mirrored in the play. The opera moves at a very rapid pace, for Weir has cut her text to a minimum. The orchestral forces in the central act are greatly reduced and the sound is starkly oriental, whereas the orchestral writing in the outer acts is vivid and striking. Weir makes use of minimalist techniques, and her thematic economy and precision illuminate the situation on stage.

For her third opera, *Blond Ekbert,* Weir again fashioned her own libretto, this time from a short story by nineteenth-century German writer Ludwig Tieck. Commissioned in 1993 by the English National Opera, *Blond Ekbert* presents a story within a story. The first act is the retelling by the protagonist's wife, Berthe, of the fairytale circumstances of her childhood. The psychotic Eckbert finds himself reliving these incidents in the second act, where he learns, after her death, that his wife was also his sister. When the truth is revealed, Eckbert is destroyed. Weir calls her work "a story of psychological discovery and a detective story." The few characters are sketched skillfully, their moods and psychological complexities painted with fresh sounds and ever-changing orchestral doubling. Though the orchestra is substantial, Weir's lightness of touch and chamber-like approach are again evident in this work.

Weir believes that the labels "minimalist" and "eclectic" certainly capture some aspects of her work, although she believes the minimalist label is a "loaded" word these days. She does not rule out any musical device, and sees each piece as a fresh beginning. Her work is a diary of what happens to her, and she remarks, "Should I meet people I want to work with, I will. I don't like to get too scheduled up too long in advance, because you change."[15]

Diana Burrell

Diana Burrell was born in 1948 in Norwich, and studied music at Cambridge University. There she concentrated more on viola performance than on composition. For a time after her studies she taught at an all-girls high school, where she gained practical experience writing music. Later she traveled as a freelance violist. Burrell has seen a steady stream of commissions since she gained recognition for her 1980 *Missa Sancte Endeliente*. Self-taught in composition, she has struggled to forge her own musical language.

Burrell feels challenged to create music that is bold, imaginative, and challenging. In her Arthur Batchelor lecture, "Open Wide the Windows, or Cower under the Duvet?" she argues that our visual sense is more developed than our aural sense. We have learned to assimilate a lot of visual stimuli, exercising our visual faculties more than our hearing. She posits that our aural abilities have not kept pace with film, pop-videos, and ballet images; hence much popular music strives to be inoffensive; it is ubiquitous; it is easy-listening and user-friendly. When asked what inspires her, she replies:

> The combination of timeless and contemporary. The combination of forms that seem half human, half landscape or rock formation; and the sense that humanity is part of something much bigger. Above all, the constant vertical nature of the forms, humans striving to gain awareness of their place in the cosmos—creatures that look upwards and outwards beyond everyday experience.[16]

Since 1980 Burrell has seen a steady stream of commissions in all genres. In her music she combines both practical and imaginative elements, which sound new, fresh, and bold. Lately she has started to introduce her music to audiences immediately before performances in order to guide listeners through the landscapes of sounds that unfold in her works. She has accepted residencies, working in community with groups, and she maintains a close association with Contemporary Music Making for Amateurs. She is a composer in community, and the sounds of everyday life attract her:

> I can truthfully say that church bells are my favorite sound in the universe! Steel pans and shrieking of seabirds are not far behind, and the clanging of metal in a building-site or scrapyard is slightly further down the list again.[17]

Resurrection (1992), a work for chamber orchestra, casts the English horn as the outsider who appears from within the music's texture and addresses the other players. It seems that the outsider is not accepted, as the listener hears an aural attack, swooping sounds in the instrumental lines that seem to silence the English horn. The metaphor here is not that of Christ's death and resurrection, but rather that of a representative of a new artistic or musical experience in our lives. Burrell's palette of percussion sonorities often drives the elemental energy of her rhythms. Wind chimes, marimba, bells, and rainstick add to the wailing brass and scampering strings, as if the whole ensemble is in conversation, argument, and resolution.

In *Landscape* (1988), steel drums, with their usual sonorous decay, and various metal objects find their way into the imaginative environment, part seaside and part cityscape. What might seem disparate sounds yield the curious, exciting, riveting character of Burrell's pieces. Having an appetite for unfamiliar sounds, she is always conscious of an underpinning of elemental energy.

In her Viola Concerto, composed in 1994, Burrell includes a subtitle, " . . . calling, leaping, crying, dancing," to reveal the entire realm of human expression the music evokes through its physicality and strength. In one overarching movement she employs the concerto principle of solo instrument against group. She captures the "vertical nature of the forms" using expansive vertical sonorities, dark and dissonant, against the excitement and conversational lyricism of the viola. Other works for orchestra include *Das Meer, das so gross und weit ist, da wimmelt's ohne Zahl, grosse und kleine Tiere* (The Sea, that is so long and wide, where numberless large and small creatures swarm; 1992), *Landscape with Procession* (1988), and *Symphonies of Flocks, Herds and Shoals* (1995–1996). Her significant works for chorus range from the short *Hymn to Wisdom* to extended works like *Missa Sancte Endeliente* and *Io Evoe*. There are also works for chamber ensemble, along with duo and solo works. Burrell summarizes her aims:

> I want my music's building-blocks to be the old ones of melody, harmony, and rhythm and I want (I imagine like many composers) to attempt the impossible, and find a musical language that works at all levels, and for all people, and is of today.[18]

Rhian Samuel

Rhian Samuel (b. 1944) was born in Aberdare, Wales, and was educated in Britain and the United States. She received her doctorate in composition from Washington University in St. Louis, where she taught from 1977 to 1983. Samuel's first large-scale published work was *Elegy-Symphony* (1981), written for the St. Louis Symphony Orchestra (Leonard Slatkin, conductor). Many of Samuel's pieces use or are inspired by texts. Some of her most successful works are written for female voices, where "women speak for themselves." In *White Amaryllis*, for example, she sets three poems by May Sarton. Samuel says she likes to interact with the poet herself, and appreciates dramatic scenarios. Her assured command of compositional technique and her poetic sensitivity make her works for voice and instruments among her finest.

Samuel currently teaches at the City University, London, and recognizes that teaching has been an important part of her growth as a composer. When she was a student, female composition teachers were a rarity—women seldom received the experience she herself finds so valuable. Though Samuel was the sole female composition student in both her American and British universities, this situation has changed. She notices many more female students now and is aware of her role as a teacher to those young women, as well as to her male students. Samuel, along with Julie Anne Sadie, is coeditor of an invaluable, long-overdue resource, *The Norton/Grove Dictionary of Women Composers.*

Sally Beamish

Sally Beamish (b. 1956), born in London, now resides in Aberfoyle, Wales. She entered the Royal Northern College of Music as a violinist in 1974. Though she studied composition intermittently with Anthony Gilbert and Sir Lennox Berkeley, Beamish considers herself self-taught (she wrote notes at a young age before she wrote the alphabet). For practical reasons during her school years she moved her area of concentration from composition to viola in 1979. For the next ten years Beamish was a professional freelance violist in a variety of ensembles—she held the post of principal violist in the London Mozart String Players and the Scottish Chamber Orchestra. She also performed in the Rachel Quartet, the London Sinfonietta, and Lontano. These performance experiences, especially in the latter two groups, have given her opportunities to hear and absorb influences from contemporary composers. The theft of her viola in 1989, however, caused her to slow down and reassess her life. She realized she was lacking solitude and time for her deep Christian faith. At this time Beamish's career as a composer began to flourish, and she moved to Scotland, where she and her husband, cellist Robert Irwin, founded the Chamber Group of Scotland.

The BBC commissioned *in dreaming,* a composition that Beamish wrote for a concert series celebrating both the Purcell tercentenary (1995) and Sir Michael Tippett's ninetieth birthday. Beamish used a text from Shakespeare's *The Tempest* and wrote for tenor and viol consort. The early-music group Fretwork was recording a series of pieces with specific limitations, and wanted to juxtapose the seventeenth-century Fantasias and In Nomines of Purcell with newly commissioned works for the ensemble. Beamish was one of several composers, and the only woman, invited to write for this project.

No, I Am Not Afraid (1988), written at about the time she was expecting her first child, is a setting of poems by Irina Ratushinskaya for spoken voice, strings, oboe, and harp. Ratushinskaya wrote the poetry on scraps of paper and had them smuggled out of a Russian prison during her incarceration for anti-Soviet agitation and propaganda. In Beamish's work the six poems alternate with five instrumental interludes. She insists that the movements are not meant to be in a Russian style, though they have references to Russian folk and church music, but are composed in a musical language that is strictly her own.

Commedia (1990), on scenes of the *commedia dell'arte,* is a theatre piece without actors, an imaginary Italian comedy of the seventeenth or eighteenth century. She composed this piece about the time her second child was born. The Viola Concerto (1995), described by Beamish as an impassioned response to the Apostle Peter's agonized denials after the arrest of Jesus, is intended also as a story with which her audience can identify: "It is a story of human weakness and betrayal in the face of the true cost of commitment, and the agonizing remorse of failure."[19] The work is a single, continuous sixteen-minute movement. The three denials are structural pillars, heard as quasi-cadenzas, in which the texture is thinned down to represent a single questioner (clarinet, cello, horn) and Peter (viola).

Poetry has played a part in many of Beamish's compositions. Her first Cello Concerto, subtitled *River* (1997), was inspired by natural landscapes and four poems about rivers by Ted Hughes; the titles of the poems correspond to the four movements of the work. Cellist Robert Cohen, a long-time friend, commissioned the piece, and he and Beamish chose the texts together. They agreed that "a stretch of river is in itself a variation form, the same but constantly changing."[20] Divided strings and a variety of colors from percussion instruments (rainstick, crotales, chocho, a Mexican bean shaker) add to the watery and transparent textures of the music.

Priti Paintal

Priti Paintal (b. 1960) was born in New Delhi, India, and received strong training in both Western and Indian classical music from her parents. At a young age she studied sitar and tabla, improvised at the piano, and wrote little pieces at the keyboard.

> There was nothing wrong with listening to Indian music and then immediately playing through a Beethoven sonata. I was very lucky, as it all seemed so normal. I'd play Brahms by ear or fiddle around with a Chopin melody. . . . I hadn't thought at any stage I'd be able to live off this.[21]

Paintal studied anthropology at Delhi University, and followed up with a master's degree in ethnomusicology, doing fieldwork on the tribal and folk music of villages in the Himalayas. In 1982 she won a British Council scholarship to study composition at York University. After one year she transferred to the Royal Northern College of Music to study with Anthony Gilbert; there she received a master's degree in composition.

FIGURE 9.1. Priti Paintal. Photo by Judith Hurst. Printed by permission of ShivaNova.

Paintal's early works were performed in India, but more recently her compositions have had performances in Britain. An early piece, *Gandharva Music I* (Celestial Music I), based on secret mantras used by Brahmin priests, transports the performers and listeners into a state of exaltation. The song was premiered in 1984 at a concert of the Society for New Music at St. John's Smith Square. Paintal comments about this composition:

> In India, the female sex is banned from either listening to or reciting these mantras which are exclusively used by male priests: thus I decided to use them. . . . This particular setting is of a mantra based on the phenomena of birth and growth, using the analogy of a cucumber (a phallic symbol, perhaps?) seed. Based on the gapped scale of a northern Indian raga and two derived harmonies, the song alternates very fast and very slow passages, each associated with one of two mantra-groups.[22]

In 1988 Paintal began to receive more frequent commissions. *Survival Song,* a chamber opera set in South Africa, with libretto by Richard Fawkes, was commissioned and performed by Garden Venture of the Royal Opera House. That year also saw the formation of Shiva Nova, an eclectic ensemble of Western and Asian musicians. In part, Paintal's aim was to create her own musical language using musicians from diverse traditions. Her works involve a certain degree of improvisation, and this group, after years of working together, has developed ways to make that language work. Shiva Nova features a vast array of world instruments to create new sound frontiers: sitar, santoor, cello, African kora, Chinese dulcimer, pipa, mbira, marimba, piano, and many more. Paintal observes:

> My interest in working with instruments from different cultures, and the special experiences accumulated through my anthropological work in tribal and folk music of India, are the driving forces which inspire me to write the kind of music I do. . . .[23]

Priti Paintal calls herself a music explorer rather than a composer.

Eleanor Alberga

Jamaica-born Eleanor Alberga's musical experiences and training are diverse. She studied classical piano from the age of five, taught herself to play the guitar, and composed her first music at the age of eight. She performed with the internationally acclaimed Jamaican Folk Singers while attending a convent school in Jamaica, and for three years she was a dancer with a semi-professional African dance company, Fonton From. Later she joined the London Contemporary Dance Company as its pianist. Alberga had formal training at the Royal Academy of Music, where she studied piano and voice. Her music is characterized by exciting, driving rhythms, and her style is versatile and evolving still. She has received commissions from the Chard Festival of Women in Music, the European Woman's Symphony, Lontano, the London Mozart Players, and the Dahl Foundation. Often Alberga teams up in performance with her husband, Thomas Downes (viola), who has commissioned works from her.

Katherine Norman

Katherine Norman (b. 1960) studied composition at Bristol University, and later received a Fulbright Fellowship to complete a Ph.D. in composition at Princeton University. A composer of both instrumental and electronic music, Norman's recently commissioned works include *Squeaky Reel* and *Transparent Things*. She describes a CD of her works as a digital *soundscape*: recognizable sounds are juxtaposed, hidden, decontextualized, or colored by digital processing techniques and editing, but the sounds remain familiar and tell a tale. One work on the CD, *London E17*, features a recognizable London soundscape created out of such entertaining audio materials as the subway, cars in traffic, children playing, jackhammers, human voices in an open-air food market, trucks shifting gears, birds, clips of classical music, rain on a tin roof, and a weather report that chimes in as the rains clear away.

In another work, *In Her Own Time,* Norman uses taped interviews with her mother about early childhood experiences in World War II, and bases her piece on the words, emotions, and personality of her mother. The impetus for the work came during the Gulf War (1991), when Norman herself remembered her mother's tales as bedtime stories. The stories began to haunt her as she realized for the first time how life must have been during the second World War. The piece is about "the temporal nature of sound itself, and the important legacy that stories provide."[24] Norman teaches at the Guildhall School of Music and Drama.

Sadie Harrison and Diedre Gribbin

Sadie Harrison was born in South Australia in 1965 and now lives in South London. She graduated from the University of Surrey, continued studies at King's College, London, and completed doctoral work under the guidance of Nicola LeFanu. Recent compositions that were written on commission include *Quintet for a Winter Solstice* for the New Macnaghten Concerts, *Hoploits and Anthems* for string orchestra, and *Architechtonia* for cello and ensemble. Harrison is lecturer in composition at Goldsmith's College, London.

Diedre Gribbin (b. 1967) studied composition at Queen's University in Belfast, Northern Ireland, and at the Guildhall School of Music and Drama. In 1992 she received awards from the Arts Councils of the Republic and of Northern Ireland that enabled her to complete a residency in Denmark. Five years later, in 1997, she was appointed Northern Arts Composing Fellow. Her most recent work, *Hey Persephone* (to a libretto by Sharman MacDonald), was commissioned by the Almedia Opera. Its premiere at the Aldeburgh Festival drew rave reviews. Gribbin is composer-in-residence at Pimlico School, London, and lecturer in composition at Bath College for Further Education.

Rebecca Clarke

Rebecca Clarke (1886–1979) has a special place in this chapter because, though British by birth, she wrote her major works while a resident of the United States. She was born in Harrow, England, to an American father and a German mother. Her earliest training in composition came from 1903 to 1905, when she attended the Royal Academy of Music. Her studies there were cut short when her harmony teacher, Percy Miles, proposed marriage to the teen-aged Clarke. Her father, known to be abusive and dictatorial, withdrew her from the Academy when he learned of the proposal. In 1907 she returned to London and entered the Royal College of Music (RCM), where she became the first woman to study composition with Charles Stanford.

During her early years and up through her time at the RCM, Clarke composed songs and chamber music, primarily for strings. She also became a consummate violist and was in demand by ensembles specializing in contemporary music. She was one of the first women to play in Sir Henry J. Wood's Queen's Hall Orchestra, and she played in an all-female string quartet with Nora Clench and in an all-female piano quartet called the English Ensemble. Her extensive concertizing took her to the United States, where she taught viola and harmony, coached and performed chamber music, and played frequently with cellist May Mukle. She continued to compose and won recognition for songs performed by Gervase Elwers in a New York recital. Another success was *Morpheus* for viola and piano, which she signed with her pseudonym, Anthony Trent.[25]

In 1916 she met the American arts patron Elizabeth Sprague Coolidge. Several years later, at Coolidge's urging, Clarke entered her Viola Sonata in a juried competition. The six members of the adjudication panel received seventy-three entries and found themselves unable to decide between the top two compositions; hence the sponsor, Coolidge, had to cast the tie-breaking vote in favor of Ernest Bloch's Suite for Viola and Piano. To the surprise of the jurists, the second place went to a woman, Rebecca Clarke. It was this work that established Clarke as a composer of the first rank. Influences of Debussy and Ravel as well as Bloch are heard in this expressive, lyrical, and passionate work. In 1921 her piano trio, another of Clarke's acclaimed compositions, won second place at America's Berkshire Festival. Performed in New York and London, the piece won immediate recognition as a great achievement in chamber music literature of the day. In 1923 the Rhapsody for Cello and Piano was commissioned by and dedicated to Elizabeth Coolidge. It was premiered by May Mukle and Myra Hess at the Berkshire Festival. Other works were forthcoming during the following years, especially 1939–1942, but her compositional output decreased partly due to the necessity for taking a job as a governess to support herself. In 1944 she married pianist James Friskin, whom she had met when a student at the RCM. The couple settled in New York, and Clarke, for reasons unknown, ceased composing and performing. She died there in 1979. Despite her relatively small compositional output, Clarke is considered one of the greatest British composers of the inter-war years.

NOTES

1. In spring of 1998 the last New Macnaghten Series Concerts took place at the British Music Information Centre, London.

2. Ernest Chapman, "The Macnaghten Concerts," *Composer* (Spring 1976): 13–18.

3. Nicola LeFanu, "Master Musician: An Impregnable Taboo?" *Contact* 31 (Autumn 1987): 8.

4. Elisabeth Lutyens, *A Goldfish Bowl* (London: Cassell and Co., Ltd., 1972), p. 9.

5. Elisabeth Lutyens, unpublished article, July 2, 1971.

6. Elizabeth Maconchy, "A Composer Speaks," *Composer* 42 (Winter 1971–1972): 28. All thirteen quartets have been recorded by Unicorn Kanchana under the supervision of the composer.

7. Donald L. Hixon, *Thea Musgrave: A Bio-Bibliography* (Westport, CT: Greenwood Press, 1984), p. 3.

8. Musgrave notes in the score: "Rollo was an imaginary character invented by Ives and represented the Victorian Conservative; 'one of those white-livered weaklings' unable to stand any dissonance."

9. Allen Shaffer, "*Harriet, the Woman Called Moses* by Thea Musgrave," *The Opera Journal* 18 (1985): 31–37.

10. Note by Musgrave in publicity from Chester Music Limited/Novello and Company Ltd. about the premiere of *Simón Bolívar,* British Music Information Centre, London, [1995].

11. Thea Musgrave, liner notes from the CD, *Autumn Sonata* [and other works], Cala Records CACD 1023, 1997.

12. Nicola LeFanu, interview with Catherine Roma, London, England, February 27, 1989.

13. Claire Messus, "New Blood," *Guardian,* March 11, 1992.

14. Nicola LeFanu, "Introduction," *Reclaiming the Muses,* whole issue of *Contemporary Music Review* 11 (1994).

15. Judith Weir, interview with Catherine Roma, London, March 8, 1989.

16. Quoted from "Open Wide the Windows, or Cower under the Duvet?" her Arthur Batchelor Lecture, University of East Anglia, February 15, 1994, British Music Information Centre, London.

17. "Diana Burrell," *Contemporary Music Review* 11 (1994): 56.

18. Ibid., 57.

19. Sally Beamish, in a program note written about the Viola Concerto, British Music Information Centre, London.

20. Susan Nickalls, "Premiere of the Fortnight," *Classical Music,* September 20, 1997, p. 11.

21. Karin Brookes, "They Thought I Was Pulling Their Legs," *Classical Music,* June 9, 1990, p. 35.

22. Priti Paintal, in a program note written about *Gandharva Music I*, British Music Information Centre, London.

23. "Priti Paintal," *Contemporary Music Review* 11 (1994): 229.

24. Katherine Norman, liner notes from *London, Trilling Wire,* NMC Recordings Ltd., NMC DO34.

25. She used the name in New York when, for a program, two of her works were to be performed.

SUGGESTIONS FOR FURTHER READING

In addition to the items mentioned in the text or cited in the footnotes, the following sources provide information on contemporary British composers.

Baxter, Timothy. "Priaulx Rainier: Study of Her Musical Style." *Composer* 60 (1977): 19–26.
———. "Priaulx Rainier." *Composer* 76–77 (Summer–Winter 1982): 21–29.
Boyd, Malcom. *Grace Williams.* N.p.: University of Wales Press, 1980.
Bradshaw, Susan. "The Music of Elisabeth Lutyens." *Musical Times* 112 (1971): 563–66.
———. "Thea Musgrave." *Musical Times* 104 (1963): 866–68.
Carner, Mosco. "Phyllis Tate." *Musical Times* 105 (1964): 20–21.
Doctor, Jennifer. "Intersecting Circles: The Early Careers of Elizabeth Maconchy, Elisabeth Lutyens, and Grace Williams." *Women & Music* 2 (1998): 90–109.
Dreyer, Martin. "Judith Weir, Composer: A Talent to Amuse." *Musical Times* 122 (1981): 593–96.
East, Leslie. "The Problem of Communication—Two Solutions: Thea Musgrave and Gordon Crosse." In *British Music Now,* ed. L. Foreman, pp. 19–31. London: P. Elek, 1975.
Fuller, Sophie. *The Pandora Guide to Women Composers—Britain and the United States 1629 to the Present.* Hammersmith, London: Pandora, 1994.
———. "Calls of the Wild." *The Musical Times* 138 (1997): 12–17.
Halstead, Jill. *The Woman Composer—Creativity and the Gendered Politics of Musical Composition.* Aldershot, England: Ashgate Press, 1997.
Kay, Norman. "Phyllis Tate." *Musical Times* 116 (1975): 429–30.
Macnaghten, Anne. "Elizabeth Maconchy." *Musical Times* 96 (1955): 298–302.
Opie, June. *Priaulx Rainier: A Pictorial Biography.* Penzance: Alison Hodge, 1988.
Pendle, Karin. "Thea Musgrave: The Singer and the Song." *Journal of the National Association of Teachers of Singing* 43/2 (November–December 1986): 5–8, 13.
Roma, Catherine. "The Choral Music of Twentieth-Century Composers Elisabeth Lutyens, Elizabeth Maconchy, and Thea Musgrave." D.M.A. thesis, University of Cincinnati, 1989.
Routh, Francis. *Contemporary British Music.* London: Macdonald & Co., 1972.
Saxon, Robert. "Elisabeth Lutyens at 75." *Musical Times* 122 (1981): 368–69.
Wright, David. "Weir to Now?" *Musical Times* 134 (1993): 432–36.

X.
Composers of Modern Europe, Israel, Australia, and New Zealand

Karin Pendle and Robert Zierolf

The writing of history is always a selective process, and with selection comes a certain amount of bias. Never is this statement more true than when writing about the twentieth century. Not only are we temporally closer to the music and its creators than we have been up to this point, but we are living at a time when opportunities for women to compose, perform, and teach music have expanded beyond anything that history has experienced. During this century women have received such awards as the Prix de Rome, the Pulitzer Prize, and Guggenheim Fellowships in composition, recognition which had been closed to them in years past. They have become college and university professors in the various subdisciplines of music; they are members of most of the best orchestras worldwide; they stand before choruses and orchestras as conductors; they are highly paid soloists. They write operas, stage operas, and manage opera companies. Discrimination still exists, but at the same time opportunities are more plentiful.

Yet with expanded opportunities comes the necessity, in a survey such as this, to decide which women have achieved the most, have risen the highest, have become exceptional in fields where, not long ago, a successful woman was by definition an exception. Those women whose names appear in this chapter have achieved distinction that ranks high not just among women but among all who have aspired to greatness. They are worthy of mention now and are worthy of being remembered by future generations.

Twentieth-century Europeans have experienced the hardships of war, political turmoil, and dislocation. Twice in this century the world has exploded in near-general warfare, which also involved fearful events in local and world politics. The rise of communism in Europe eventually cut off the so-called Eastern Bloc nations from contact with the West, and its fall introduced both halves of Europe to music and musical creators they knew nothing of. The destructive power of the Holocaust and the rise of the state of Israel affected music and musicians as much as they affected world politics. The story of women's music has taken on multiple dimensions as women have been oppressed or freed, have kept silent or been allowed to speak, have remained in place or emigrated in search of artistic and political freedom.

Space does not permit us to follow up on all these threads of history, but some examples will at least help define the issues. Both World War I and World War II profoundly affected the lives of all the people of Europe. Many women in music chose self-imposed exile as the only response that would allow them to continue to practice their art. Germaine Tailleferre, Betsy Jolas, and Nadia Boulanger are examples of the many artists who sought safety in the United States rather than accept the wartime disruptions of the 1940s. People in the United States were beneficiaries of these temporary relocations, in that the musicians' talents could be observed at close range. Personal and artistic associations were formed that otherwise would have been unlikely.

Many women composers chose deliberately to stay in their homelands regardless of conditions. At the beginning of World War I, for example, Lili Boulanger returned home from Italy, suspending her Prix de Rome privileges, and did volunteer work with her sister, Nadia, in hospitals and elsewhere. At the beginning of World War II, Nadia donated her conducting and performing talents to the French Relief Fund before she finally found it necessary to set sail for America. Ilse Fromm-Michaels also remained in her country even though the Nazi government would make her life as an artist untenable. Because her husband was Jewish, he was fired from his government job; Fromm-Michaels was blacklisted beginning in 1933, forced to put her career as a pianist on hold and to watch ineffectually as her works were banned from public performance. She did not resume composing or teaching until 1946, when she was appointed professor of piano at the Musikhochschule in Hamburg. Grażyna Bacewicz chose to stay in Poland during World War II despite dangers and hardships endemic to her native country. It was not that she lacked contacts elsewhere, since she had just returned from Paris as the war broke out. (Paris, of course, would soon become inhospitable as well.) Bacewicz's performing and composing were curtailed during the war, and her creative efforts were less fruitful than would have been the case had the war not intervened.

War was not the only factor that caused women to leave their homes, however. While the Iron Curtain was still an invisible but significant factor in Eastern Europe, some of this area's finest composers chose (when they could) to move to the West. The distinguished Russian composer Sofia Gubaidulina, Romania's Violeta Dinescu and Adriana Hölszky, Czechoslovakia's Viera Janácekova, and Poland's Joanna Bruzdowicz resettled in Western Europe. Others, such as Poland's Marta Ptaszyńska, Russia's Sophie-Carmen Eckhardt-Gramatté, or Germany's Ruth Schonthal, made their ways to North America. All expected and found greater artistic freedom in their newfound homes than they had enjoyed before. On the other hand, many women developed strategies that allowed them to live and create music uncompromised by the limitations governments placed on their work. In Romania, for example, Myriam Marbé and her colleagues learned of musical developments in the West by studying smuggled-in scores and recordings; Marbé emerged as an avant-garde composer with a distinctive voice.

In September 1991 the Soviet Union, by vote of the Congress of People's Deputies, was dissolved, creating a situation that has had ramifications in all of Europe and the Middle East, but especially in the countries of the former Eastern Bloc. One by one these governments toppled or reformed themselves, usually along more democratic lines. The rest of the musical world beyond their borders became aware of the many composers and performers whose work had been inaccessible. There is still much to be learned about the women who, often against great odds, created a life in music for themselves under communist rule.

Not all migration was due to political instability and oppression, however. In the twentieth century we became a mobile society, whether within our own countries or within the world as a whole. There were times when only the very adventurous would move far from home to seek their fortunes; today many people think nothing of traveling half-way around the world in search of congenial working conditions or to supervise performances of their music. The fact that most people can now return to their first homes via convenient airlines makes adjusting to relocation somewhat easier. So, for example, Marta Ptaszyńska spends some months each year in Poland, Shulamit Ran holds dual citizenship in the United States and Israel, and Australia-born Jennifer Fowler and Alison Bauld now live primarily in England.

The establishment of support groups internationally and in individual countries might make relocation still easier for women in music. The largest such group—the result of a recent merger of two smaller groups—is the International Alliance of Women in Music, which, though based in the United States, draws its membership from all over the world and sponsors two journals and regular conferences. In Europe some active support associations include Women in Music (Great Britain), Mujeres en la música (Women in Music, Spain), Stichtung Vrouw en Muziek (Women in Music Foundation, Netherlands), Internationalen Arbeitskreis: Frau und Musik (International Forum: Women and Music, Germany), and Italy's Donne in musica (Women in Music). Similar organizations exist in Switzerland, Denmark, Sweden, and Finland, and most sponsor concerts and festivals of women's music too numerous to mention. Since the 1980s information on music by women, along with scores of recordings, has circulated freely.

Regardless of nationality or even generation, this past century's women composers have moved far beyond the gender's stereotypical genres of piano pieces and songs. The greatest growth seems to be in chamber music, either multimovement or single-movement works, but concertos and large-scale symphonic works are well represented, and operas and ballets appear far more frequently than in earlier times. The growth in chamber music plays out in unique ensembles more often than in the traditional groups of string quartet or piano trio, and composers most often give picturesque, even programmatic titles to their instrumental music, even for quartets and trios.

And so we return to our beginning, the matter of selectivity. Though many composers born in the nineteenth century had careers that stretched into the twentieth century, we will be looking almost exclusively at women born after 1890. Then other factors enter in: How many works have these women written? What kinds of works? Were any of the compositions prize-winners? How often were these works performed? Where? Did the composer teach at a prestigious institution? Are one or two particular women of a given generation illustrative of the whole? Are their works available in scores and recordings? These are some factors that influenced which women are included in this chapter and which are omitted; all of these composers could profit from the attention of an able performer or an interested scholar.

FRANCE

Over the centuries France has seen a number of talented and well-trained women taking prominent roles in music as both composers and performers. At the end of the eighteenth century the Paris Conservatoire had opened its doors to both male and female students, and women composers of songs and piano pieces were not uncommon. Just after the turn of the twentieth century women were allowed to enter the contest for the prestigious Prix de Rome in composition; in 1913 Lili Boulanger (1893–1918) became the first woman to win the first prize. She would not be the last.[1]

Nadia Boulanger

Though she began her career as a composer, in the mid-1920s Nadia Boulanger (1887–1979) decided to turn from composition to teaching, and the world may well be better for this decision. An accomplished conductor and organist,[2] she became famous for her uncompromising standards and the ability to nurture creativity in composers as stylistically diverse as Elliott Carter, Aaron Copland, Thea Musgrave, Philip Glass, and Peggy Glanville-Hicks. Her command of traditional subjects—harmony, counterpoint, form—was never the impediment to learning and teaching modern music that plagued so many of her colleagues at the Paris Conservatoire and elsewhere. Her suspicion of atonal music—"There are dangers in atonal music. There is nothing to surprise one"[3]—did not extend to all its composers. She claimed that "Stravinsky's use of twelve-tone elements in the *Canticum Sacrum* is not an experiment. It is an accomplishment."[4] Her humanistic attitude toward life and art, combined with enormous talent, directly inspired hundreds of students and thousands more through her legacy. Her composition classes often included extraordinary numbers of women, although it is curious that few became as well known as her most successful male students. It could be that history has simply ignored them. Boulanger's eyes and ears for talent were acute, and her ability to encourage compositional ability in her women students was one of the most valuable, if most overlooked, attributes of her long service to the arts. For this, as well as for many other reasons, one cannot overestimate Nadia Boulanger's contribution to twentieth-century music.

Given the long history of distinguished musicians in her family, Boulanger's musical talent might be seen as a birthright. Most of this lineage was Parisian, going as far back as her grandmother Marie-Julie Boulanger, née Hallinger, who enjoyed a long career as a singer for the Opéra-Comique. Her father, Henri-Alexandre-Ernest Boulanger, also attended the Conservatoire, where his winning the Grand Prix de Rome supported his travels to Rome and Florence. After his return to Paris, Boulanger composed operas while teaching at the Conservatoire. There he met the talented eighteen-year-old Russian singer Raisa Mychetskaya, whom he married when he was sixty-two; Nadia was born ten years later.

A fluent talent and a penchant for work were evident early; by the age of sixteen Nadia had won every prize available at the Conservatoire. Composition came easily; two years after her first composition, *La lettre de mort* (1906), she won second place in the Prix de Rome competition with a cantata entitled *La Sirène*. Composition study with Gabriel Fauré, Louis Vierne, Charles-Marie Widor, and others was combined with organ lessons. She excelled in the latter as well as in classroom subjects, and she succeeded the brilliant Fauré as organist at the Madeleine Church in 1924. By this time Boulanger had decided to forego composition. Despite some success and prominent performances, she believed her composing had weaknesses: "If there is anything of which I am very sure, it is that my music is useless."[5]

Whether this would have proved true is impossible to ascertain, but what is sure is that Boulanger would have needed one masterpiece after another even to approach the brilliant career she enjoyed as a pedagogue.

In the early 1920s Boulanger began not only a career as an organist but also her long tenure at the American School at Fontainebleau and, often concurrently, professorships at the Paris Conservatoire and the École Normale. Indefatigable, she combined performance, touring, and writing criticism with teaching. From 1921, her first year at Fontainebleau, she attracted an international class. But it was the talented young Americans who made her reputation so quickly: George Antheil, Aaron Copland, Roy Harris, Walter Piston, and Virgil Thomson studied with her in the 1920s and, along with Walter Damrosch, brought their enthusiasm for her musicianship back to the United States.

By the late 1930s Boulanger was conducting major orchestras in important performances. In 1937 she conducted the Royal Philharmonic in London; in 1939, the Boston Symphony, the New York Philharmonic, and the Philadelphia Orchestra. She was probably the first woman to conduct these distinguished ensembles, but she seems not to have paid much attention to that fact. Instead she made music with her usual magnificent ease. Like many others, Boulanger spent some of the war years in the United States, conducting, performing, and teaching at Juilliard and other prestigious institutions. Her associations were with the best musicians of the times: Walter Damrosch, Leopold Stokowski, Serge Koussevitzky, Darius Milhaud (then at Mills College), and, most of all, Igor Stravinsky. Her reputation with Americans had been made in Paris in the 1920s; it was solidified and extended in the United States in the 1930s and 1940s.

Perhaps because she was not a composer in her later years, or because she was not flamboyant or eccentric, Boulanger was more highly regarded by composers outside of France than by those in her native country. Rosters of students show far fewer French than other nationalities, a curious fact given the nationalistic enrollment policies of the Paris Conservatoire. It can be fairly said that the American School at Fontainebleau was where she ruled; in Paris she was overshadowed first by Fauré and Ravel, then by Olivier Messiaen and Pierre Boulez. It probably did not help that Boulanger promoted American music, especially that composed by former students, but it seems also that many were jealous of her reputation and talents. In addition, her skepticism of dodecaphonic technique was at odds with postwar fervor for Schoenberg and Webern as promoted by Boulez and René Leibowitz; twelve-tone technique had a brief but potent hold on young French composers. Boulanger was exegetical in her thinking about all music, believing that thorough study was the only way to proper criticism. In the end, she was no different with regard to serialism.

Whatever the demands of her profession, Boulanger frequently made time for worthy social causes. In addition to her wartime activities she was active in the French League of Women's Rights, and gave benefit performances for this and similar organizations. Her favorite cause was her sister's music, the preservation and dissemination of which was one of her life's projects. From the early 1950s until her death in 1979, Boulanger devoted herself primarily to teaching at Fontainebleau and the Paris Conservatoire. She accepted an amazing diversity of talent and held seminars in major music centers throughout Europe. She was honored and decorated in public and private by the leading musicians of the 1970s, and her reputation as the greatest teacher of the twentieth century—perhaps of any century—is unassailable.

Prix de Rome Winners

In addition to the Boulangers, other women entered the Prix de Rome competitions once it became the policy of the Académie Française to allow them to do so.[6] The first, Hélène Fleury (1876–after 1917), was unsuccessful in 1903 but was awarded the *deuxième* (second) prize in 1904. After Lili Boulanger took first prize in 1913, more women were encouraged to try. René Dumesnil cites Marguerite Canal (1890–1978), grand prize winner in 1920, Jeanne Leleu (1898–1979) in 1923, Elsa Barraine (b. 1910) in 1929, Yvonne Desportes (1907–1993) in 1932, Odette Gartenlaub in 1948, Adrienne Clostre in 1949, and Evelyne Plicque in 1950.[7]

Like others of his time (and even today), Dumesnil voiced a kind of grudging respect for many of these composers as long as they were content to remain feminine in their music. Jeanne Leleu, for example, he described as having "a vigor that one rarely encounters in works by women." In her *Sonnets de Michel-Ange,* however, he found "grace, a contained and delicate sort of emotion," and he cites composer Florent Schmitt's opinion that her *Transparences,* a three-movement orchestral suite, was "a marvel of freshness, of precision, of feminine grace."[8] Elsa Barraine, another prizewinner, he considered as "the writer of prettily orchestrated melodies," and Yvonne Desportes' *Trifaldin* was "a charming ballet." Henriette Roget, winner of a *deuxième* prize, received somewhat more neutral praise for the symphonic poem, *Montanyas dell Rosello:* "She knows how to get the most original impressionistic effects." Her Cello Concerto, however, which had "solid architecture, developments of precise concision," joined "the feminine grace to qualities that ordinarily pass for virile."[9]

Germaine Tailleferre

Surely the most feminine and graceful of all, however, was Germaine Tailleferre (1892–1983), whose early ballet *Le marchand de oiseaux* (1923), like much of her later music, was described as "charming," "fresh, *spirituelle,* and transparent."[10] Turning such patronizing evaluations rather on their heads, Ravel would later remark that her music was "full of feminine charm, not at all an unworthy quality in music."[11] Yet throughout her life the talented Tailleferre would have to endure flippant refusals to take her and her music seriously, as in Deems Taylor's evaluation:

> One thing is certain, after beholding Mlle Tailleferre last night and remembering the portraits of the Six, whatever the talents of the others, she is decidedly the best looking.[12]

Germaine Tailleferre, if she is mentioned at all in studies of twentieth-century music, is highlighted as the only woman in *Les Six,* a group of influential French composers of the post–World War I era.[13] Then she disappears from view, despite the fact that she was a prolific composer who was still writing music into her eighties, long after the few common projects of *Les Six* were all but forgotten. In fact, the individuals in *Les Six* actually had little in common aesthetically; their work covered the gamut from Poulenc's cabaret-influenced style to Milhaud's exoticism to Tailleferre's classicistic conservatism.

Over her father's objections, but encouraged by her mother, Tailleferre entered the Paris Conservatoire in 1904 and remained there until 1915, winning several prizes for her prowess in harmony, solfège, counterpoint, and accompanying. After meeting Erik Satie, she came into contact with the young composers under his influence—Georges Auric and Darius Milhaud. Eventually she also met the other composers who constituted the group first labeled *les nouveaux jeunes* by Satie and eventually *Les Six* by the critic Henri Collet, who was attempting to establish a corollary to the Russian Five. Unlike the Five, however, *Les Six* sought a new mode of expression in opposition to the romanticism of Wagner, which most French musicians detested, and in reaction to the impressionism of Debussy. As a group they produced an album of individual piano pieces and one collaborative score (without Durey), the incidental music for Jean Cocteau's *Les Mariés de la Tour Eiffel.* For personal, musical, and sociological reasons the group ceased to exist after a couple of years, although several members maintained contact and supported one another's efforts even as each took a separate musical direction.

Given Tailleferre's excellence as a pianist, it comes as no surprise that most of her composing involved the keyboard in some way. Her earliest piece to gain public notice was the fresh, energetic *Jeux de plein air* (Outdoor Games, 1917; published, 1919) for two pianos. *Jeux de plein air* has two movements: "La tirelitentaine" (a card game) and "Cache-cache mitoula" (literally, a fox hunt; here probably a type of hide-and-seek). Both are lively, witty pieces with catchy rhythms that breathe the air of the new.[14] Even before meeting the other composers with whom she would soon be linked, Tailleferre caught the ear of Erik Satie with this clean-textured, anti-Romantic suite. Satie promptly dubbed her his "musical daughter" and asked that she contribute some pieces to be performed in conjunction with an art exhibit in one of Paris's bohemian cafes.[15] Meeting Satie would prove decisive for her career.

However, Tailleferre's many works for duo pianists are rather the tip of an iceberg that rests on a foundation consisting of her whole compositional process. According to Janelle Gelfand, when Tailleferre was not composing in her head, she "composed virtually everything first in a two-piano version, whether it was a concerto, an orchestral work, a ballet, or a film score, and then she orchestrated it appropriately. . . . She composed at a table next to her piano, and she went back and forth between the two. . . ."[16] The two-piano framework is clearly audible in her unique Concerto Grosso for two pianos, eight singers, and four saxophones (1932).[17] This engaging three-movement piece distinctly recalls the circus-like atmosphere at the beginning of Stravinsky's *Petrushka*. There is an exuberance, a sense of excitement in something that was probably familiar to most listeners but is humorously turned aside as the unexpected sounds of the wordless vocal ensemble and the quartet of saxophones arise from the texture. Throughout this piece Tailleferre does not so much work with motives or themes as she repeats, spins out, juxtaposes, and abruptly contrasts them within a harmonic fabric that creates its own logic through ostinato-like repetitions or an anchoring in one or more pedal points. Dissonance abounds, but it is countered by each movement's own sense of a definite tonal center.

The slow movement brings the vocal ensemble to the foreground in a sinuous intertwining of lines that at times takes on a Near Eastern quality and at other times the suave music of the thirties' Palm Court. The opening fugue of the final movement, featuring both voices and instruments, forges links with the baroque concerto grosso. Even though an emphatic cadence brings the fugue to a close, bits of contrapuntal writing pop up here and there, as if to remind us not to take things too seriously, even when they are presented in formal counterpoint. This intriguing piece deserves to be revived.

Tailleferre's anti-romantic, anti-impressionist musical language is, in the years between the World Wars, an up-to-date neoclassicism, taking in elements of modality, pentatonicism, and polytonality as aspects of her individual voice. Her Sonata No. 1 for Violin and Piano (1921; published, 1923; first movement in HAMW, p. 262 ff.) is smoothly polished and facile in the best sense of the word. The texture is largely melody-and-accompaniment, accommodating some dialogue but little that could be called counterpoint. Bitonality and a pandiatonic, "wrong note" technique add spice without overbalancing the carefully wrought structure, a clearly audible sonata-allegro form poised with minimal conflict and maximum spontaneity. Other neoclassical chamber works include the Second Violin Sonata (1951), *Sonatine* for violin and piano (1973), and Piano Trio (1978).[18] These are from the postwar years, when much of the classical-music world had moved on to serialist, electronic, aleatory, and other techniques that would themselves be replaced in time. Tailleferre's late works were in a style no longer appreciated for the values it represented: a clean neoclassicism with undertones of wit, *esprit,* polish, and art. Ultimately even Tailleferre realized her position as an anomaly:

> My music doesn't interest me anymore [she told her friend, violinist Hélène Jourdan-Morhange], and dodecaphonic and *concrète* music, which attracts me, represents such work that I would not have the strength to undertake it. It would be as if I would want to express myself in Chinese! It is a little late to learn.[19]

Nevertheless, her music is fine—well crafted, balanced, attractive—and it communicates a sense of well-being, a knowledge that even in a fast-changing world some things remain true. Tailleferre died on November 7, 1983, the last of *Les Six* to be laid to rest.

Claude Arrieu

Claude Arrieu (a pseudonym for Louise Marie Simon; 1903–1990) was one of the most prolific French composers of the twentieth century. Her more than 200 compositions, including both sacred and secular music, range from solo pieces, chamber and vocal music, and instrumental works to opera and incidental music for stage productions. Arrieu composed in classical forms—sonata, concerto, suite, and symphony—as well as in programmatic and modern idioms. In general, her style is best described as personal neoclassicism. She learned much from the French neoclassic tradition prevalent during her formative years, but her music is not so much a reminiscence of Ravel or Poulenc as it is a corollary to their styles.

Along with most other well-known composers of her generation, Arrieu studied at the Paris Conservatoire. Even as a student she won several important prizes in composition; eventually she would be named to the prestigious Legion of Honor. In 1946 she began a long relationship with French radio and television studios, and she was one of the first composers to work with Pierre Schaeffer at Radiodiffusion français. Schaeffer is usually credited with inventing *musique concrète,* an early phase of electronic music in which acoustic sounds are manipulated electronically. Arrieu quickly lost interest in this experimental music, composing but one piece, *Fantastique lyrique* for *ondes Martenot* (1959), as her contribution to the electronic genre. Nevertheless, the studio experience was ultimately valuable as an apprenticeship for composing scores in other media. At least thirty film scores and more than forty radio scores attest to Arrieu's interest in and facility with the media. The most widely recognized was the score for the radio drama *Frédéric Général,* which won the Italia Prize in 1949, the year of its composition. Her many commissions, most notably the one from the French government for the opera *Les deux rendezvous* (1947), suggest a high degree of respect for Arrieu as a composer.

Yvonne Desportes

A somewhat younger contemporary of Arrieu, Yvonne Desportes (1907–1993) was also a product of the Paris Conservatoire, where she studied with Paul Dukas and Marcel Dupré. Her Prix de Rome financed a four-year sojourn in that city (1933–1937), but by 1943 she was back in Paris, where she taught solfège, counterpoint, and fugue. Her more than 500 works include operas, symphonies, concertos, ballets, a great deal of chamber music, and music for solo voice and for guitar.

Jeanne Demessieux

Jeanne Demessieux (1921–1968), a disciple of French organist and composer Marcel Dupré, was best known as an organist, but composed some outstanding music for her instrument as well. She made her professional debut as a recitalist in 1946; by the year of her death she had presented over 700 recitals in Europe and North America and had taught at conservatories in Nancy (France), Liège (Belgium), and Haarlem (Netherlands). Her Etudes for Organ, Op. 8 (1946), have been called "six of the most daunting pieces in the entire [organ] repertoire. . . ."[20] These pieces were designed with the aim of building virtuoso pedal technique, and their difficulty led Olivier Messiaen to remark that "Demessieux demands from the feet what Chopin demanded from the hands."[21] Other organ works include *Sept méditations sur le Saint-Esprit* (Seven Meditations on the Holy Spirit, 1945–1947), which are often compared with music by Messiaen due to their harmonic language. Her *Douze chorals-préludes* (Twelve Chorale Preludes, 1947; published, 1950) are settings of Gregorian chant melodies, and her *Répons pour le temps de Pâques* (Responses for the Easter Season) was published in 1968.

Ida Gotkovsky

The daughter and sister of professional violinists, Ida Gotkovsky (b. 1933) is an interesting and highly skilled composer who is little known outside her own country. Her teachers at the Conservatoire included Messiaen and Nadia Boulanger; in 1967 she was awarded the Prix Lili Boulanger for her compositions. Her expansive list of works includes nearly every medium, from operas and ballets to orchestral and chamber works, pieces for wind ensembles, and teaching pieces for various solo wind and brass instruments and piano. In fact, wind and brass players are particularly well served by Gotkovsky, whose works for saxophone, horn, trumpet, trombone, and tuba fill a real need for solo literature in these areas. Her three-movement Suite for Tuba and Piano (1959) reveals compositional techniques resembling those of Hindemith, and her Concerto for Trombone and Orchestra (1978) has at times the flavor of Messiaen and uses his idea of modes of limited transposition. The work is virtuosic and requires stamina, but is also very idiomatic for the trombone. Among her more recent works are *Or et lumière* (Gold and Light, 1993) for wind ensemble, *Hommage à Jean de la Fontaine* (1995) for multiple choirs and full orchestra, and a Quartet for Clarinets (1998).

Betsy Jolas

Betsy Jolas (b. 1926) has combined composition with simultaneous careers as conductor, editor, and writer. Hers is an excellent example of the French-American connection in twentieth-century music, but in ways different from those of Nadia Boulanger or Germaine Tailleferre. Born in France to American parents, Jolas moved to New York City with her family at the outbreak of World War II. She completed high school and college in the United States, earning a Bachelor of Arts degree from Bennington College before returning to France in 1946. She attended the Paris Conservatoire and studied composition with Darius Milhaud and Olivier Messiaen, subsequently becoming the latter's assistant. Currently on the faculty of the Conservatoire, she is greatly admired for her teaching and musicianship. The prizes she has received for conducting and composing have been rewarding, and her multidimensional career has brought much acclaim. Her eclectic techniques of composition range from Renaissance-style polyphony to atonality and aleatory.

Jolas makes no secret of her affinity for the human voice, which possesses qualities that are fundamental to her work. However, this does not mean that she writes mostly vocal music, but rather that she has a vocal quality in mind as she writes instrumental, especially chamber, music in which she can mentally transform instrumental style by means of vocal inflections.[22] The best examples of this quality occur in her operas for instrumental ensembles. In *O Wall* (an allusion to the tradesmen's rehearsal in Shakespeare's *Midsummer Night's Dream*) we find in the woodwind quintet "five well-defined characters in a sort of puppet opera, the imaginary action of which should be perceived only through the music."[23] In fact, the instruments take on their own personalities as we follow them playing alone or in solos with chordal accompaniment, in dialogues or arguments with one another, and even in a kind of fugue on dissimilar subjects. The instruments are instructed to play quarter and three-quarter steps in addition to normal pitches. A similar work, *D'un opéra de poupée en sept musiques* (A Puppet Opera in Seven Movements, 1982, rev. 1984), involves a larger ensemble (flute, clarinet, horn, violin, cello, piano, percussion, and two *ondes Martenots*) portraying in each of the *musiques* a different character or mood (e.g., "Avant-garde," "Lyric," "American," "Feminine"). Despite the seeming difficulty of this wispy, discontinuous score, Jolas seems to be one of the few ultra-modernists who has a sense of humor.

In all her works Jolas reveals herself as a supreme colorist. The ending of *J. D. E.* for fourteen instruments (1966) has harp and winds drifting upward until they disappear into the ether. *Points d'Aube* (1968, rev. 1971) for viola and thirteen winds (eight of them brasses) combines the full, Romantic sound of the viola with the sharp, precise, argumentative brasses and the more lyrical woodwinds. Her set of variations *E.A.* (the letters are the initials of one of the dedicatees) puts forth the unlikely combination of trumpet and vibraphone. Finally, her series of *Episodes* for unaccompanied solo instruments take color one step further by drawing all the changes of hue possible from a single instrument. Jolas's is not an easy or particularly accessible style, but her thoroughly polished craft is obvious in every work.

Germany and Austria

Lists and other sources of information on twentieth-century women composers in German-speaking lands indicate that they still seem to be less well represented both quantitatively and qualitatively on the international scene than one might expect, given the long and glorious tradition of German art music. No woman here has achieved the status of a Lili Boulanger, a Thea Musgrave, a Marta Ptaszyńska, or a Joan Tower. There has, of course, been noteworthy activity in research on women and music and in such organizations as the Internationalen Arbeitskreis: Frau und Musik. Until recently Germany itself has been a politically divided nation. The collapse of the Berlin Wall in 1989, however, surely means that women in the former Eastern sector will become better known internationally.

Although one may argue the point, it seems that sexist prejudice in the performing and other arts is still more pervasive in German-speaking lands than in similarly developed countries. For example, a tremendous row ensued when the late Herbert von Karajan, music director of the Berlin Philharmonic, chose a woman clarinetist for the orchestra. Although she was clearly the best player who auditioned, her gender was unacceptable to many members of the orchestra. (In general, European orchestras hire fewer women than do American orchestras.) Karajan threatened to cancel concerts and lucrative recording sessions until the woman was hired, but she did not take the job after all. More recently the International Alliance of Women in Music has undertaken a picketing and letter-writing campaign in the hope of persuading the venerable (and nearly all-male) Vienna Philharmonic Orchestra to open positions in the orchestra to women. So far, the results of this campaign have been less than encouraging: the orchestra has merely given an official position to the one woman who has been playing harp with the group for some years on an unofficial basis. Perhaps the voices of women and their male supporters will be able to convince the players and their management that women must be allowed to audition for open positions and expect to be taken seriously.

Grete von Zieritz

As is almost always the case in any country, a few women have managed to invade the compositional arena, often through their own performance skills. Born in Austria, Grete von Zieritz (b. 1899) studied piano and composition in Graz before honing these skills in Berlin. After winning the Mendelssohn Prize in 1928, Zieritz toured as a pianist and taught at music schools in Germany and Austria. Approximately half of her large output is vocal—choral or solo; the other half is orchestral or chamber music. Her *Zehn Japanische Lieder* (Ten Japanese Songs, 1919, premiered in 1921) for soprano and piano are particularly interesting and colorful; other songs are based on Dutch, German, Portugese, or Spanish texts. In 1958 Zieritz was awarded a government prize for composition, the first woman of her country ever recognized for this sort of creativity.

Zieritz was a respected concert pianist who nevertheless felt that composition was really her calling. Even after the favorable reception of the *Japanische Lieder* she continued to study composition, attending Franz Schreker's composition classes for five years (1926–1931). Still, she remarked, if she was to be a composer, the piano would have to finance that part of her career.[24] So great was her desire to compose that, taking her young daughter with her, she left her husband, seeing this as the only way she would be able to continue writing music.[25]

World War II, of course, delayed her once more. She trained as a plane spotter (*Feuerwehrmann*), though she served only during the last days of the war. In the meantime, her composing fell off markedly. In her extensive list of works,[26] forty-five pieces are from the years 1916–1940, and sixty-nine from 1945–1991; only seven, however, appeared during the war years of the early 1940s. Among her later creations one finds some strongly political works: *Drei Lobgesänge polnischer Dichter* (Three Songs of Praise by Polish Poets), written for the closing concert of a 1981 conference entitled Frauenkomponieren für den Frieden (Women Composing for Peace); *Cassandra-Rufe* (The Cries of Cassandra) for eight solo voices and a nonet (1986); *Ein Mensch erinnert sich* (A Person Remembers, 1991) for clarinet, commemorating the fifth anniversary of Chernobyl; and various works having gypsies or gypsy music as their themes.

As picturesque as the gypsy images must seem at first glance, all were in several senses political statements. Zieritz's *Zigeunerkonzert* (Gypsy Concerto) for violin and orchestra in six scenes (1984), the most striking of the lot, is a work of great beauty and deep expression. Each movement's title describes a scene from gypsy life or history:

1. Gassed in Auschwitz, still pursued
2. Procession for Sara la Kali to Saintes-Marie-de-la-Mer[27]
3. Phuvusche, Nivaschi, and Urmen[28]
4. Fire before the tent of a baby boy[29]
5. We are the kings of the fields and meadows, the forests, the mountains, the rivers, and the streams
6. Witches' Sabbath in the Grotto of Zugarramurdi in the year 1610[30]

Hitler's treatment of the gypsies is well known, though it was only the worst example of the continuous persecution of the gypsies over the centuries. Zieritz, in treating this subject musically, introduces the cimbalom as a color foreign to the orchestra and includes some gypsy-style themes and rhythms. As the titles of the movements suggest, this piece is far from being a portrayal of gypsy life for pops-concert performance.

One might well ask why Zieritz felt so drawn to the gypsies. Beate Philipp has suggested that, since Zieritz's grandmother was Hungarian, she equated the folk music of this nation with the music of the gypsies, as Liszt had done a century before. Zieritz herself tells another story:

> I felt bound to the gypsies as well as to all underclasses, for I, a woman composer, was oppressed all my life, and this oppression has run through my whole existence like a red thread and has left deep scars behind.[31]

Zieritz was determined to become a composer, regardless of the sacrifices and compromises along the way; hence she, like the gypsies, had no choice but to spend her life on the margins of society.

Ilse Fromm-Michaels

Ilse Fromm-Michaels (1888–1986) was, according to German scholar Eva Weissweiler, "a classicist of the modern age."[32] A successful concert pianist and a composition student of Hans Pfitzner, Fromm-Michaels is a link between the late German Romanticism of Brahms or Reger and the conservative modernists of post–World War I Europe. Her *Variations on an Original Theme,* Op. 8 (1919) for piano develops a set of seven variations on a pleasant character piece that has the ring of familiarity about it; it is straightforward, nonthreatening, and Romantic in style. The figure of Reger haunts the early variations, but by Variation 4 the theme has become a musical pile-driver that alternates threateningly with a more lyrical segment that seems to remain unbowed. In Variation 6, however, the frightened theme appears in a dry staccato with the superscription, "totally without expression." The piece that started out with one foot in the past century also foresees the discontinuity of the future. A similarly complacent opening marks the Suite for Cello, Op. 15 (1931), but in this piece, too, the comfort of a long and admirable tradition (here symbolized by recalling Bach's Suites for Unaccompanied Cello that are Fromm-Michaels's model) butts up against contemporary reality (here, the long-breathed, chromatically intense "Aria" of the fourth movement).

Fromm-Michaels's unfortunate circumstances during World War II and her husband's death in 1946 were difficult to bear. In 1957 she accepted a position as professor of piano at Hamburg's Hochschule für Musik. She died in a retirement home.

Ruth Zechlin

Like Fromm-Michaels, Ruth Zechlin (b. 1926) felt strongly drawn to German musical traditions. Born in Leipzig, she felt the presence of J. S. Bach as a model: she once stated, "Bach is my center."[33] Zechlin went often to hear music at Bach's Thomaskirche and, like Bach, studied harpsichord, organ, and composition. She lived without persecution in East Germany (until the fall of the Berlin Wall in 1989 made her country's division obsolete), where she became a professor of composition at the Academy of Music in Berlin in 1969. Never an advocate of avant-garde compositional techniques, she was the right sort of tradition-respecting musician to fit well with an ideology that sought to bridge the cultural gap between the average person and the intelligentsia, in part by censoring art that was ultra-modern. At the same time she listened to avant-garde music on the radio and became a friend of Henze, Lutoslawski, and Penderecki. The high quality of her music was obvious enough that even a West German publication could declare, "Zechlin is one of the most significant and most important women composers in Germany."[34]

Ruth Zechlin has written a great deal of chamber music, along with concertos and symphonies—that is, all instrumental music and all in traditional genres. Among her works, however, one also finds songs, ballets, incidental music for stage productions, and an opera for actors. Her *Music for Orchestra* (1980) is a study in tones and tone colors. Frank Schneider has described it as follows:

> [T]he strings initially weave a delicate, pulsating fabric of sound . . . [with] striking interjections from the woodwinds. . . . [Then] brass finally create a tense situation from which the strings . . . finally liberate themselves. . . .[35]

This sort of musical dialogue between instrumental groups is reminiscent of the sorts of effects one can get on a large organ through contrasting registrations. The imitative counterpoint played by four solo violins points to Bach as its model. So, too, does Zechlin's String Quartet #6 (1977), which is based on a twelve-tone row consisting of permutations of the motive BACH.[36] It is significant that on a recently issued set of nine CDs filled with music by East German composers, Zechlin's are the only pieces by a woman.

Siegrid Ernst

The expressive and carefully wrought music of Siegrid Ernst (b. 1929) is becoming better known through recordings and by way of the women composers' network in which she has been an active presence.[37] Ernst, one of the founders of Germany's Internationalen Arbeitskreis: Frau und Musik, has been involved in other societies as well for the support of modern music and women in music. She was instrumental in bringing an international conference on women in music to Germany in 1988. Ernst is a multi-talented person who has concertized as a pianist and has taught piano and various composition and musicianship courses at German conservatories. Her quest for an individual style led her to investigate serialism and various experimental techniques, including aleatory, before settling into what she has called a free tonality. One of her early dodecaphonic works, *Variations for Large Orchestra* (1965), presents the row clearly and melodiously in several incarnations, in which some series of three or four adjacent pitches suggest a tonality. This work is also a model of skillful orchestration in its play of colors between and among contrasting orchestral groups.[38]

Another twelve-tone work, *Seven Miniatures on Japanese Haiku* (1961) for alto, viola or cello, and piano, uses the row freely to create a lyrical, evocative cycle that is challenging but accessible to performers and audiences alike. Another chamber work, *Quattro mani dentro e fuori* (Four Hands within and without, 1975), uses two pianists playing one piano—one on the keys, the other on the strings and soundboard of the instrument. What emerges is a rainbow of instrumental color that projects inventive sonorities of great beauty in distinctive, often catchy rhythms.

In 1993 Siegrid Ernst decided that she would cut back her other musical activities, including accepting new commissions, and devote herself solely to attaining her own creative goals. Two very different works exemplify this stage of her development: *Triade* (1993–1994) for ten instruments and *Peace Now* (1996) for orchestra. *Triade* finds its inspiration in numbers—specifically the number three—in all aspects of the work, including the number and placement of the players. There are three movements and three groups of instruments of three players each (winds, high strings, low strings), who sit at the points of three intersecting triangles. The tenth player, a percussionist, moves to each of three positions outside these triangles in the course of the piece.[39] *Peace Now* is intended "as a reaction to the unending military conflicts—as well as to the newly erupting wars—of our time, . . . a testimonial to those who speak out for peace." Though neither simple nor facile, the work "avoids complicated structures and avant-garde techniques . . . to reach out directly to a broader public."[40] There are three movements: *Klage* (Lament), *Aufbruch* (Awakening), and *Huldigung* (Homage), tracing the grief of those hurt by the war, the renewed strength that comes with rebuilding, and the return of peace and the resolution of war's tensions. Siegrid Ernst's music, says one reviewer, "is clearly structured, well crafted, and varied in its expression. It is consistently absorbing and beautiful."[41]

Barbara Heller

The service Barbara Heller (b. 1936) has dedicated to the cause of German women in music has been exceptional. A teacher and a pianist as well as a composer, she has lived in Darmstadt since 1963. That year, however, began a fifteen-year hiatus in her composing: "During my marriage and parenthood (starting in 1963) I gave up my profession."[42] Heller had to start again to build her confidence, a process helped along by her introduction to the women's movement and her subsequent work on behalf of Frau und Musik.

Heller's skill as a pianist spills over into her work as a composer. Not only has she written many works for solo piano or groups that include piano, but her thorough knowledge of the instrument's sonority affects the content of the music. For example, a short piece from her piano collection *Scharlachrote Buchstaben* (Scarlet Letters, 1983) has no melody to speak of but only a series of block chords with one or more notes in common, which are stated, then arpeggiated slowly, then quickly. Another piece, *Piano Muziek voor Anje van Harten,*[43] punctuates segments of broken texture with swirls of thirty-second-note scale fragments. The second movement of *Tagebuch für Violine und Klavier* (CAMW, 45–49) uses a single chord in the piano to accompany a simple melody. This provides the essential basis of the structure, although "in between is the 'imprisoned melody,' going back and forth."[44]

Recently Heller has been collaborating with women visual artists on "joint compositions, sound installations, and experiments with environmental noises and graphic notation."[45] She has described aspects of her creative process in organic terms:

> It often fascinates me to find in my own creative process something curious over the long haul—days, weeks, years. That is, when I have found a particular seed that grew and unfolded, but I still don't know what sort of plant it will be, so I nurse and care for it particularly attentively.[46]

By working at her own speed on projects that interest her, Heller is making a place for herself in the world of modern German music.

It is difficult to evaluate the contributions of younger composers, perhaps because World War II and, more recently, reunification have consumed our attention, perhaps because emigration to Germany from the countries of Eastern Europe has called into question just who can be considered a German composer. Adriana Hölszky, for example, though born in Romania, is of German ancestry and lives now in Germany. America's Gloria Coates and Nancy Van de Vate, Poland's composer Grabiela Moyseowicz, Britain's Caroline Wilkins, and Korea's Younhi-Pagh-Paan spend all or sizable parts of every year in German-speaking areas. Some German composers now in their thirties have shown great promise: for example, Annette Schlüna (b. 1964), Isabel Mundry (b. 1963), Christiane Pohl (b. 1964), or Olga Neuwirth (b. 1968). Finally, people have yet to evaluate the place technology and advanced mathematics-based approaches to composition will play in the future of music by women. In general, German composers appear to have cultivated these features of the "most avant" of the avant-garde more thoroughly than women composers in other lands, at a time when many are returning to neoromantic or neoclassic techniques that are more audience-friendly than, say, computer-generated sounds. Of course, no technique can be better than the person who applies it, and a truly gifted composer is able to move audiences regardless of method.

The Low Countries

In the course of the centuries the boundaries between what we now call the Netherlands and Belgium have not remained constant, nor have their people or languages remained separate. Hence it seems convenient to do as many others have done and group these women under the blanket title "Low Countries."

Helen Metzelaar, writing of the Dutch, has noted the paucity of women composers in the Netherlands even during the best of times.[47] The same could be said of Belgium. Yet there were a few outstanding women in music even in the worst of times. The career of Dutch composer and conductor Elisabeth Kuyper (1877–1953) spanned the late nineteenth and early twentieth centuries and included the founding of four women's symphony orchestras (Berlin, 1910; The Hague, 1922; London, 1922–1923; and New York, 1924–1925), which included her works in their repertoires. Somewhat later, Henriette Bosmans (1895–1952) graduated with honors from the Amsterdam Conservatory and began a career as a concert pianist. Though she had been composing for some years, only in the 1920s did she study composition formally, including among her teachers the distinguished Dutch composer Willem Pijper. She wrote both orchestral and chamber music but was particularly attracted to songs with piano accompaniment. Brussels-born Lucie Vellère (1896–1966) was trained in piano and violin as well as composition and won several prizes for her works, but she chose to keep music as a hobby and make her living as a pharmacist.

Jacqueline Fontyn

Born in 1930 in Antwerp, Jacqueline Fontyn has become a respected figure in the field of composition. After music studies in Brussels, Paris, and Vienna, she returned to Belgium and took teaching positions, first at the Antwerp Conservatory, then at the Royal Conservatory in Brussels, where she was professor of composition from 1971 until 1990. In addition, she has held short-term appointments in Egypt, Korea, Taiwan, Israel, and the United States.[48] Fontyn's progress as a composer has led her into free serialism and atonality and experiments with free or unconventional rhythms and tone colors to her current eclectic style. As early as 1964 Fontyn stood out as the only woman in a field of prominent Belgian composers. She has been called "the most remarkable personality of the younger generation . . . because she has something to say and can communicate it in a lucid and purely musical fashion."[49]

Tera de Marez Oyens

One of the finest composers of her generation, Tera de Marez Oyens (1932–1996) was also an outstanding pianist and, as one of the founders of the Dutch Stichting Vrouw en Muziek in 1985, an advocate of women's activities in music. Her studies at the Amsterdam Conservatory included techniques of electronic music, which she put to good use in one of her strongest and most meaningful works, the *Sinfonia Testimonial* (1987) for chorus, orchestra, and prerecorded tape.[50] The three movements of this work are based on three poems (two by Ariel Dorfman, the centerpiece by Rosario Castellanos) that portray the conditions of political prisoners in Chile and Mexico. The acoustical forces (chorus and orchestra) deliver their messages in thick, panchromatic textures that have ties to both tradition and innovation; but the tape in *Sinfonia Testimonial,* which suggests the closing of doors, the howls of pain, and the cries of despair, projects not just imprisonment but the prison itself, a three-dimensional representation of terror. Other works (among her more than two hundred compositions) that have political overtones are *Litany for the Victims of War* (1985), for orchestra only, and the oratorio *The Odyssey of Mr. Good-Evil* (1981). The text is by her husband, a survivor of Auschwitz. His attempted suicide in despair after having revisited the camp inspired Marez Oyens's *Charon's Gift* (1982) for piano and tape. In *Odyssey* (for two choirs, four soli, two narrators, and orchestra), the horrors of war are described from the point of view of an inmate of a concentration camp who always exists "on the continuous borderline between life and death."[51] In a lighter vein, *A Wrinkle in Time* (1994), for flute, violin, cello, and piano, plays on the idea that by folding the present so that one perceives the time before and after the pleat as continuous one creates a "wrinkle in time." In the music the composer plays with "the parameter of duration and stepping as it were over some motives, going on as if nothing had happened in between, stretching and shortening time" in "a kind of fake waltz" (although 3/4 meter appears only four times in the piece, the longest being only three bars).[52]

Hilary Tann has characterized Marez Oyens's music as "strong, somewhat stark, writing, with clear formal distinctions and, often when least expected, almost heartbreaking surges of lyricism.[53] Tera de Marez Oyens played her last concert in Göteborg, Sweden, on April 30, 1996. She died shortly after of cancer.

SCANDINAVIA

It is difficult to trace a tradition of women's music in the Scandinavian countries any further back than the mid-nineteenth century, for so much music remained unpublished and even unperformed. Sweden's Elfrida Andrée (1841–1929), who was her country's first female church organist, was able to publish many of her songs and her chamber, organ, and piano works, but the only parts of her opera, *Fritiofs Saga* (1899, libretto by Selma Lagerlöf) to be performed were two orchestral suites drawn from this score. Her pupil Sara Wennerberg-Reuter (1875–1959), who was organist at Stockholm's Sofia Church for nearly forty years, also produced a number of choral works, vocal quartets, and cantatas that attained some popularity during her lifetime. The songs of Andrée's contemporary Helena Munktell (1852–1919) were well received at home and abroad. Indeed, Munktell's opera, *I Firenze* (The People of Florence, 1889), counts as the first opera by a Swedish woman.[54]

Norway's Signe Lund (1868–1950) spent some of her most productive years in Chicago, and Mon Schjelderup (1870–1934), a student of Agathe Backer Grøndahl (1847–1907), was admired for her songs. Ida Moberg (1859–1947) counts as Finland's first woman composer,[55] and Hilda Sehested (1858–1936) and Tekla Wandall (1866–1940) made their reputations in Denmark. It would seem, then, that by 1900 most Scandinavian countries could point to at least a few women composers whose music was performed and admired. Space does not permit an extensive historical survey of women's music in Scandinavia, but the following discussion of selected composers, most of them now living, will provide a sample of the varied and vital creative powers in the north of Europe.

NORWAY

Signe Lund and Mon Schjelderup fall into the transition period over the turn of the twentieth century that produced few but fine composers in Scandinavia. The next generation brought multi-talented Pauline Hall (1890–1969), known as "one of the most outstanding, active, many-sided personalities in Norwegian musical life."[56] A skilled composer, particularly of music for the stage, Hall was also the Berlin correspondent for music and theatre news from 1926 to 1932, then music critic for the Norwegian *Dageblatt* (Daily Newspaper) for some thirty years (1934–1963).[57] One of the founding members of the Society of Norwegian Composers and of Norway's arm of the International Society for Contemporary Music (she was president from 1938 to 1960 or 1961), Hall was a tireless advocate for Norwegian music, though she "strongly opposed reactionary nationalism" and favored a more international perspective. Another of her activities involved translating the librettos of foreign stage works into Norwegian, Milhaud's *Le pauvre matelot,* Stravinsky's *Histoire du soldat,* and Poulenc's *La voix humaine* among them. She also conducted and directed several productions.

Hall's earliest works grew out of the late Romantic tradition of Germany, but a year of study in Paris in 1912–1913 exposed her to musical Impressionism and the music of Stravinsky, both influential on her emerging compositional voice. Each of the four movements of her *Verlaine Suite* for orchestra (1929) is inspired by a poem and calls upon not so much a French style of music as a Frenchified style, with an individual stamp and a touch of Stravinsky's *Petrushka* (movement 4, *Markedsgjøg* or Fair). Her favorite compositional genre, music for the stage, is represented in a sense by this suite, which is strongly picturesque. Excerpts from Hall's incidental music for Shakespeare's plays *Julius Caesar* (1947) and *As You Like It* (1958) became an orchestral suite (1949) and a five-movement *Little Dance Suite*, respectively. Both reveal the clean neoclassical style with its "wrong note" pandiatonicism that emerged at the beginning of the 1930s. One of her last works, the *Four Fooleries* (*Tosserier*) for soprano and winds (1961), demonstrates the good humor and sense of irony that also typifies the lighthearted music of Poulenc or Milhaud.

The next generation of Norwegian women composers is represented by Anne-Marie Ørbeck (1911–1996), who studied piano and composition in Oslo and Berlin, and in Paris with Nadia Boulanger and Milhaud. Though her songs are most numerous of all the genres in which she composed, her orchestral works have attracted more attention. She was soloist in the premiere of her Concertino for Piano and Orchestra (Berlin, 1938); the first performance of her symphony occurred in Bergen, Norway, in 1954. Despite Ørbeck's study of twelve-tone composition, she finds tonality more compatible with the expression of her musical personality.

Quite different in this regard is Cecilie Ore (b. 1954), who has won several prizes for her electroacoustic compositions and for some other works. In 1988 the Norwegian Society of Composers chose her *Porphyre* for orchestra (1986) as the composition of the year. A series of four pieces under the general title *Codex Temporis* (1989–1992) is concerned with aspects of musical time. Though each of these pieces involves a different ensemble, all use amplified acoustic instruments and all are related by considerations of time: "The time structure of the first work [is] applied to a computer model . . . [and] then used to generate related time-structures in the three other works."[58] In 1988 Ore was awarded the Norwegian State Guaranteed Income for Artists.

SWEDEN

One of the most interesting and expressive of Sweden's living composers is Carin Malmlöf-Forssling (b. 1916). Though she has written for many performance media, she is particularly skilled in solo vocal and choral music. Malmlöf-Forssling studied at the Royal Academy of Music in Stockholm from 1938 to 1943, after which, according to Aaron Cohen, she began her musical career as a piano teacher in the Swedish mining town of Falun.[59] By 1957 her wish to develop her technique of composing more fully led her to Paris and study with Nadia Boulanger. For many years after her election in 1970 to the Society of Swedish Composers she was its only woman member. Yet despite a growing reputation, it was 1984 before her music appeared on a commercial recording. With this CD she became Sweden's first woman to have an entire recording devoted to her music. In 1987 she also became the first woman composer to win the Royal Academy of Music's medal for the Promotion of the Art of Music in Sweden, and in 1988, the first woman to win the Kurt Attenberg Prize.

Among Malmlöf-Forssling's finest solo vocal works is the cycle *Songs of Light and Darkness* (1975), set to poetry by Nobel Prize–winner Harry Martinson. The long-breathed, wandering melody of "Night," which opens the cycle, rests over an ostinato-like succession of random thirds, familiar in their idiom (or sonority) but individual in their progress. Similar procedures occur in other songs, where the seemingly random harmonies create their own logic. Elsewhere, vocal lines may be disjunct, incorporating wide leaps intended to be sung lyrically. In this cycle, as elsewhere, the composer sometimes interjects spoken lines to put ideas in relief against the rest of the setting. This technique is particularly effective in "Painful Memory," which recalls the Holocaust in sung text but backs off into speaking for the starkest statement, "So the slaughter-house rests even today in my memory, although a lifetime has nearly passed." The quick, treble-oriented depiction of "Sunshine," the next song, is as ironic as it is welcome, and turns to a double irony when the poet equates a hailstorm with "a volley of bullets of false wheat."

"Orizzonte" (1981) for solo horn is a technical and emotional tour de force. Malmlöf-Forssling features various techniques in this piece: open tones echoed by hand-stopped tones, multiphonics created by simultaneously sounding sung and played notes, and bent notes produced by gliding upward or downward a semitone or a tone. Somewhat in the same mode, in *Aum* (1987) for solo soprano she plays on the many shadings of the Sanskrit word in the song's title. The music itself is based on the *Bhairava* scale of Indian music, and the voice circles around an initial minor second, enlarging the still-restricted vocal range as if chanting a meditation. Similar effects occur in *Shanti shanti* (1990) for soprano and orchestra and *Ahimsa* (1992) for a cappella choir. *Ahimsa* (Nonviolence) has no actual melody. Instead, block chords build up and recede in third-based sonorities with parallel streams of extended tertian harmony and polytonal effects where one triad clearly jars another. The way is long but never dull, placid but strongly affirmative. The composer denies that she means *Ahimsa* or *Shanti shanti* (Peace, peace) as protest music: "I do not compose in order to protest."[60] Nevertheless, the three

Sanskrit pieces do reflect her beliefs in nonviolent solutions to world problems and "a universal feeling of affinity with all living [things]."[61]

Born in Stockholm in 1957, Karin Rehnqvist has emerged as one of Sweden's most distinctive musical voices of the last decades of the twentieth century. The best examples of her individuality are the vocal pieces in which she exploits the practice of *kulning,* a type of Swedish folk singing associated with the women who tend herds of farm animals in the countryside. This high-pitched, vibratoless singing not only calls the animals but also communicates with other herders in the area. Both the work and the song that goes with it, being associated exclusively with women, might be interpreted as a feminist feature of Rehnkvist's music. Two of her best-known pieces to use this technique are *Davids nimm* (1983) and the song cycle *Puksånger-lockrop* (Timpanum Songs-Herding Calls, 1989) for two sopranos and percussion.[62]

In *Davids nimm,* for three unaccompanied female voices, the singers face away from each other and develop a counterpoint of dissimilar lines that nevertheless turns on their commonalities: the particular tone color of the voices, the quick ascending appoggiaturas that end a note or phrase, and the integrity of each vocal line. Starting from a point of calm (that in a harmony emphasizing seconds, fourths, and fifths recalls medieval organum), the dynamic level builds to a high, challenging shout before retreating into a calmer coda. *Timpanum Songs* apparently "caused a considerable stir at the ISCM World Music Days in Stockholm in 1994."[63] It consists of five songs in which both the singers and the percussionist build to truly hair-raising climaxes. Among the texts are two traditional Swedish poems, some lines from William Blake, and a series of anti-woman proverbs (e.g., "The woman has long hair and a short mind"; "One laughs at women's advice, but never at men's"; "When a woman whistles, the devil laughs"). Both *Davids nimm* and the third of the *Timpanum Songs* are essentially vocalises on phonetic texts that have no literal meaning.

Perhaps most important in evaluating the feminist content of these works is the fact that *kulning* is representative of real women—strong, earthy, unafraid, working—rather than of girls exhibiting the supposedly feminine qualities of conventional beauty, weakness, and dependency. In 1996 Karin Rehnqvist was honored by the Läkerol Arts Award "for her renewal of the relationship between folk music and art music."[64]

Finland

One author has suggested that musical developments in Finland can be divided into three periods: pre-Sibelius, Sibelius, and post-Sibelius.[65] Though meant ironically, this suggestion does contain a certain amount of truth: Ida Moberg is almost an exact contemporary of Finland's musical giant, and Kaija Saariaho, who has emerged as Finland's best-known woman composer, was born in 1952, just five years before Sibelius's death. Saariaho received her early musical training at the Sibelius Academy in Helsinki under the tutelage of Paavo Heininen. After further study in Freiburg, Germany, with Brian Ferneyhough and Klaus Huber, she began to work at several of Europe's electroacoustic studios, including the Finnish Radio Experimental Studio, the Electronic Music Studio in Stockholm, and Paris's IRCAM (Institut de Recherche et de Coordination Acoustique-Musique), which has been her musical home since 1982.

Most of Kaija Saariaho's major works combine electronic procedures with sounds from live performers. *Lichtbogen* (Arc of Light, 1985–1986), for example, uses nine live instrumentalists whose parts are heard both directly and by way of electronic manipulation. *Lichtbogen* is the first piece for which Saariaho used the computer as a tool for composing. A larger performing force, though similarly set off by electronic manipulation, appears in *Verblendungen* (Bedazzlement, 1982–1983) for full orchestra, live electronics, and prerecorded tape. Saariaho's first major work after having finished her study at the Sibelius Academy, *Verblendungen* conveys the sounds of crystalline and high, nearly imperceptible tones resembling wind chimes of glass. Saariaho herself describes the work:

> *Blindingness,* various surfaces, textures, weaves, depths. Metaphorical dazzling. Interpolation, *contre-jour*. Death. The sum of independent worlds. Shadowing, the refraction of light.[66]

A more recent work, *Stilleben* (Still Life, 1987–1988), combines the sounds of speaking (Kafka in three languages), singing, acoustic instruments, and electronically generated pitches in what Saariaho labels a "radiographic composition." This piece, she says, is

> about journeying, distance, communication between people when parted from their own country. How can people communicate with one another when they are apart? When the medium most important to all those in love, the eyes, cannot be used?[67]

Saariaho is kept busy with commissioned works, including a violin concerto, *Graal Théâtre* (1995), for Gidon Kremer and two song cycles—*Château de l'âme* (1996) and *Lohn* (1996)—for American soprano Dawn Upshaw. Her cello octet, *Neiges*, dates from 1998, and her first opera, *L'Amour de loin*, was written for the 2000 Salzburg Festival.

Saariaho is often impatient with those who ask her about living as a woman composer in what they see as a man's world. She has alluded to this impatience:

> I'm so tired of this aspect of women composers: tired and tired. I'm not sure the profession of composer is one you want to propose to your child, boy or girl. Only if it's the only thing you want to do, then you better do it.[68]

Possibly conditions under which Finnish composers work have led her to assume all are as well off as she has been. Eero Richmond reports:

> [T]he lot of Finnish composers in general is much envied by other countries. Government support, given as awards, scholarships, tax-free grants . . . , and "art professorships," which pay full professional salaries with no strings attached other than that the artist pursue his or her art, is remarkable for such a small country. . . . At concerts in Finland, Finnish works are commonly programmed, including works by women (with virtually no attention drawn to gender).[69]

ICELAND

Though Karólina Eiríksdóttir (b. 1951) began her musical training at the Reykjavík College of Music with every intention of becoming a piano teacher, she seemed to gravitate naturally to the composition classes of Thorkell Sigurbjörnsson as well. And when, in 1974, she entered the University of Michigan as a piano student, she emerged with two Master's degrees, one in musicology, the other in composition. Returning to Iceland, she became not only a prolific composer and teacher but also, for a time, head of the Icelandic Music Information Center (1983–1988) and a member of the governing board of the Society of Icelandic Composers. All her works have been performed in Iceland and other Scandinavian venues, but have also appeared on programs in other European cities and at festivals of women's music (e.g., that sponsored by Mujeres en la Música in Spain). Though the majority of her works are instrumental—she particularly enjoys chamber music—Eiríksdóttir seems more individual in her song cycles *Ljódnámuland* (Land Possessed by Poems, 1987) and *Six Poems from the Japanese* (1977) for mezzo-soprano, flute, and clarinet; and in her opera *Nagon har jag sett* (Someone I Have Seen, 1988).

Eiríksdóttir's works of the 1970s and early 1980s tend to be very economical, with movements that are almost aphoristic, but later works, while not losing their expressive edge, are more expansive. *Land Possesed by Poems,* for example, is a cycle of nine songs on poems by Sigurdur Pálsson for bass-baritone and piano. Demands are great on all parts of the singer's range, and the performer may be required to move quickly from pedal tones in his lowest range to near falsetto above the staff. In the fourth song, which deals with the first sighting of land, we hear one of Eiríksdóttir's musical thumbprints: a precise, disjunct melody set to a series of equal notes, rather like clockwork. Another thumbprint appears in a recorded aria from Act II of *Someone I Have Seen:* a series of melodic figures that repeat irregularly the same few pitches.[70] Though she seems to cultivate no obvious, overreaching compositional method, economy and precision in pitches and rhythmic gestures are characteristic, and her sureness of technique is everywhere apparent.

Denmark

Birgitta Alsted (b. 1942) is interested especially in multi-media productions that involve music (both acoustic and electronically generated) with dance and image projections. Her *Sorgsang II* (Lament II, 1995), inspired by the Old Testament story of Job, for example, involves photo images, extended vocal techniques, and *concrète* sounds used in their original form or as basic material for computer manipulation. Bells, birdsongs, vocal wails and moans, and texted sung phrases create a dark and wrenching mood to which even the bright tone of the tenor must succumb, as electronic manipulation turns his textless cries into sounds of lament that can only end in quiet despair.

Another Danish composer, Anne Linnet (b. 1953), has feet in two musical camps: one in classical music, the other in pop/rock. She has performed with her current band, the Bitch Boys, at women's music festivals, including Donne in musica in Fiuggi, Italy, and in the process has questioned whether the division between classical music and rock is more apparent than real.[71] The first woman to graduate in composition from a Danish music school (Aarhus), Linnet has written, performed, and recorded her own music in both categories. Her philosophy is that rock and classical music "both aim for a direct and intense personal expression and make equal use of her technical abilities."[72]

Spain

Though not much music by Spanish women is known outside their country, the support group of Mujeres en la música has taken noticeable strides forward, especially by sponsoring international congresses featuring music of their own members alongside that of some of the most interesting figures from other countries. In addition, research has brought to light many little-known but talented women from earlier in the twentieth century. Historian Alicia Casares, for example, has discussed women's activities in music as components of Spanish history and culture. She also continues to include performers and teachers along with composers in her research. Among women composers of the first half of the twentieth century, she cites Narcisa Freixas (1859–1925), Maria Teresa Pelegri (b. 1907), Maria Rodrigo (1888–1967), Rosa García Ascot (b. 1906), and Maria Teresa Prieto (1908–1982). The Spanish civil war affected women artists as well as men, and some composers—Ascot and Rodrigo, for example—felt the need to go into exile due to the turmoil in their homeland.[73]

Elena Romero (1908–1996)[74] was both a concert pianist and a composer; she also became the first woman in Spain to conduct a symphony orchestra. Though women far outnumbered men in Spain's music schools in the 1920s, when Romero would have received her education, her generation's women only exceptionally continued in music as a career. Daughter of a wealthy Madrid family, Romero was a child prodigy whose real career did not start until after her husband's death, when she supported herself and her sons as a performer, piano teacher, conductor, and composer. Her ballet *Titeres* (Puppets) and her *Ensayo para orquestra sobre dos canciones sudafricanas* (Essay for Orchestra on Two South African Songs) won prizes, and she included her own piano works on recital programs: for example, *Canto a Turina* (Song to Turina, 1950), a Spanish-flavored piece in honor of her composition teacher, or *De noche en el Albaicin* (The Albaicin by Night, 1955).[75]

Maria Luisa Ozaita (b. 1939), one of the founders and active workers in Mujeres en la música, is a harpsichordist as well as a composer and teacher. Her compositions for harpsichord include *Módulos canónicos* (Canonic Modules, 1981) and *A modo de improvisación* (In the Style of Improvisation, 1982), while among her piano works one finds the intriguing title *Que fue de Bach* (What Happened to Bach). Her style is eclectic, encompassing Spanish and French Impressionistic elements alongside formal counterpoint. A chamber piece, *Aleluyas* (1982) for flute, clarinet, and soprano, is based on a Gregorian chant but includes aleatory elements that exploit the timbral possibilities of each member of the ensemble, alone or in combination with others. The form alternates short instrumental segments and vocal interludes using the text "Alleluia."

Italy

It is surprising that so few works by modern Italian women have been heard in Western Europe and America, though some have appeared on programs of women's music in Spain and Italy. The best-known woman composer of Italy appears to be Teresa Procaccino (b. 1934), currently a professor of composition at the Santa Cecilia Conservatory in Rome, where she herself studied. She has written operas, orchestral works, and chamber music. Her elegant *Serenata notturno* for horn and harp has been recorded.[76]

The subdued voice of Ada Gentile (b. 1947) is well exemplified by her *In un silenzio ordinata* (1985),[77] a delicate, pastel-shaded piece for violin, flute, clarinet, two percussionists, and piano that never moves beyond a *piano* dynamic. Gentile describes her style, saying, "I work with subtle sonorities and favour the *pianissimo*. The resulting effect is a very light musical fabric at the limits of the audible, a kind of miniaturization of sound."[78]

Another individual voice belongs to Giovanna Marini (b. 1937), whose specialty has been music for films. Her Requiem, successfully premiered in Hamburg in 1986, has been recorded.[79] Elisabetta Brusa (b. 1954) has won many prizes for her music outside of Italy, including three residencies at the MacDowell Colony in New Hampshire. She currently teaches at the Milan Conservatory. Of the youngest composers, Sonia Bo (b. 1960) is promising.

Israel

Though the state of Israel is only a half-century old, this small and often embattled country has produced several world-class women composers. Typical of the early twentieth century is Verdina Shlonsky (1905–1990) who, like so many of the older residents of Israel, emigrated from her country of birth—in this case, Ukraine—to Israel, where she lived from 1929 until her death.[80] Like many composers of the older generation, Shlonsky was strongly grounded in the styles, forms, and traditions of Western European music. Starting with piano lessons at age five, Shlonsky studied piano in the 1930s in Berlin with such luminaries as Arthur Schnabel and Egon Petri. She also spent time in Paris developing her skills as a composer under Nadia Boulanger, Edgard Varèse, and Darius Milhaud. Her earliest works were in genres standard for Western Europe: piano suites and character pieces, a string quartet, a piano concerto, Lieder for solo voice and piano. After 1964, however, attending Darmstadt's Festival of New Music motivated her to try new techniques and even to experiment with electronic music. "Introduction" for piano, from the same year, is an aphoristic study on major and minor seconds which, while some steps beyond the bounds of traditional tonality, is representative of her work at the time.[81]

Two of Shlonsky's younger contemporaries, both born and raised in Israel, have tried in their own ways to redirect compositional procedures of the Western tradition toward the styles, modes, and rhythms of their homeland.

The daughter of Polish immigrant parents, Tsippi Fleischer (b. 1946) was born in Haifa and studied music theory and composition at the Rubin Academy of Music in Jerusalem. Her interest in all phases of music and the complex history of the Middle East led her to seek a master's degree in music education from New York University (1975) and a Ph.D. in musicology at Israel's Bar-Ilan University (1995). She also studied Arabic language and literature, Hebrew, and Middle East history at Tel Aviv University. Fleischer has made a conscious effort to create a musical idiom that combines features of mid-Eastern style with traditional Western musical idioms and forms. She often uses texts in Hebrew or Arabic, as in her work for children's chorus "The Clock Wants to Sleep" (1980), which alternates refrains on the onomatopoeic syllables "tick tock" with verses in Hebrew, or in the song cycle *Ballad of Expected Death in Cairo* (1987), which uses an Arabic text.[82]

Most of Fleischer's instrumental works are programmatic and reveal the melodic and rhythmic colors of the Middle East within an essentially Western framework. Her earliest orchestral work, *A Girl Called Limonad* (1977), is a symphonic poem that takes its inspiration from the surrealistic verses of Lebanese poet Shawqi Abi-Shagra. In its four sections we find the metamorphoses of several modal, folklike themes, accompanied by Arabic drumming and growling *bassi ostinati*. Alongside these are found triadic, neoromantic harmonies and lush orchestral textures.[83] Fleischer's typically deft orchestration, her freely spun-out melodies, and her use of parallel motion in two or more voices on any intervals (from triads or fifths to seconds or sevenths) are already apparent in this early work.

In a more recent symphonic poem, *Salt Crystals* (1995), Fleischer's favorite sonorities are more skillfully developed. Cascading parallel seconds or tone clusters "verticalize" the chromatic melodic lines; sharply contrasting sonorities, rather than blending, simply coexist as they build to a climax. An ostinato on Arabic drums and the other-worldly sound of triangle and bowed cymbal provide some consistency and are perhaps the most direct reflections of the salt crystals on the shore of Israel's Dead Sea, the inspiration for this work. *Masks and Pipes,* a ballet of the same year, is inspired by aspects of life in ancient Egypt. It is a study in intervals of seconds and microtones, carried out by Fleischer, dancer/choreographer Ruth Eshel, and sculptor Dalia Meiri. Fleischer's program celebrates the ages of woman:

> Three pictures are suggested: Old Woman, evoking dryness, boniness, a moving skeleton, a network of facial wrinkles carved out of the desert; Sensuous Woman, suggesting sexuality, fertility and the joy of openness, the search for communication, forging ahead in yearning; and Mighty Woman, evoking muscularity, flesh, self-adornment, physical strength, pride, power.

FIGURE 10.1. Tsippi Fleischer. Photo courtesy of the composer.

A single recorder-player, Naomi Rogel, provides the music, playing along with her own pre-recorded sounds. Each woman is represented by a particular range and color of recorder, after which the three identifying textures sound together. However, "It is the Old Woman/Age that brings everything to a close."[84]

Fleischer's *Oratorio 1492–1992* (1992) uses full orchestra, SATB chorus, and an ensemble of guitars and mandolas to commemorate "the expulsion, dispersion, and resettlement in the twentieth century of the Jewish people in Israel."[85] In its five movements Fleischer takes us on a musical journey of five hundred years' duration, starting with "Of Wine and the Delights of Love" in fifteenth-century Spain and ending with "The Return to Zion." Throughout this varicolored work Fleischer's musical fingerprints—unaccompanied, spun-out melodies; ornamental and microtonal inflections; writing in parallel sonorities of all kinds; a vital rhythmic sense; and a gift for orchestral color—effect an individual synthesis of East and West.

Though nearly contemporary with Fleischer in age, Shulamit Ran (b. 1949) is very different in outlook and style and, for some listeners, less accessible. Yet there is in her music a flavor of the Middle East, especially in melodies that turn in ornamental inflections around single pitches or groups of pitches.[86] Born in Tel Aviv, Ran—like Fleischer—is the daughter of European immigrants and received her early musical training in Israel. In 1963 she entered New York's Mannes College of Music, where she studied composition with Norman Dello Joio and piano with Nadia Reisenberg. After graduation she continued to study—composition with Ralph Shapey and piano with Dorothy Taubman. Though she had already made her mark as a performer, she stopped concertizing in 1973 to devote more time to composition. In 1973, at the age of 24, she joined the faculty at the University of Chicago, where she still teaches. In 1990 she became Composer in Residence for the Chicago Symphony Orchestra. She has also served as Composer in Residence at the Chicago Lyric Opera, a position that resulted in her first opera, *Between Two Worlds* (*The Dybbuk*), in 1997. Though her main residence is now the United States, she still maintains steady contact with Israel.

Shulamit Ran has written in nearly every standard genre: music for piano or solo instruments, chamber and orchestral pieces, songs, and electronic works. She premiered her first significant piece, *Capriccio* for piano and orchestra, in 1963 with the New York Philharmonic. In the 1970s she began an association with the Da Capo Chamber Players that led to several strikingly different works. *For an Actor: Monologue for Clarinet* (1978) is a virtuosic drama involving a variety of clarinet sounds, including multiphonics, "bent" pitches, flutter-tonguing, and extremes of range and dynamics. Another Da Capo commission, *Private Game* (1979) for clarinet and cello, is a somewhat whimsical duo in which the order and return of specific sections of the piece in the order ABA CBC plays on the name of the commissioning ensemble by incorporating two da capo forms.

In 1990, for the twentieth anniversary of the Da Capo Players, Ran created *Mirage* for clarinet, violin, cello, piano, and flute doubling on piccolo and amplified alto flute. The possible colors and sonorities for these instruments are exploited to excellent effect, though the alto flute (amplified for tone color, not for balance) is featured somewhat more than the others. That same year Ran completed a commission from the Philadelphia Orchestra for the symphony that won for her the 1991 Pulitzer Prize in music and the 1992 Kennedy Friedheim Award.[87]

Shulamit Ran's craft relies on no particular system or method, other than the general approach she described in a recent interview:

> The challenge is to take one idea and then really work with it and employ everything that I have by way of imagination and inventiveness to take it as far as I can take it. In any creative act, there needs to be a fine balance between the element of the intuitive—the fantasy—which is really subconscious, with discipline, which is to a large extent a conscious thing. . . . I find myself always engaged in a search, trying to tune into what needs to happen next, where the music wants to go—as though trying to probe its deep secrets. It is as though to every phrase I compose there are powerful consequences as to what is to happen next.[88]

Still young, Shulamit Ran has already made her mark as a composer of the twentieth century whose reputation will last well into the twenty-first and, one hopes, beyond.

EASTERN EUROPE

Until the collapse of the USSR in 1991 and the subsequent dissolution of communist governments in other nations of Eastern Europe, finding information, scores, and recordings of music by women in these areas was difficult. The task became somewhat easier when certain individuals emigrated westward to other countries of Europe or to the United States, but getting materials on those women composers who remained in their countries of birth was still not easy. Living behind the Iron Curtain had limited the international exposure these composers received—and their exposure to Western music as well. Though conditions are much better now, it will take time before we learn of more than a few outstanding women from Russia and the former Eastern Bloc.

RUSSIA

Composers in the former Soviet Union have had experiences vastly different from those of their Western counterparts. From the revolutions in the first decades of the twentieth century, through the Stalin era, World War II, and the Cold War, tribulations unimaginable to most Westerners have placed before them burdens as well as unique opportunities. For many years, what was published and performed was controlled by the Soviet Composers Union, with style and taste often arbitrated by lesser talents, even by nonmusicians.

Information on new music and composers, especially those censured as "formalist" for their progressive or avant-garde works, was very difficult for outsiders to obtain. Much modern music, including everything by Bartók, Hindemith, and the Second Viennese School, was banned during the 1930s and 1940s. The first serial piece by a Soviet composer was Andrei Volkonsky's *Musica stricta* (1956), but composers were strongly urged to compose music for the common people under the guidelines of "socialist realism." Under Gorbachev, exchanges of information, composers, and performers finally allowed outsiders a good view of music from a group of countries, both ethnic Russian and others, with long, colorful musical heritages. Women composers are still few, but their numbers are increasing.

Sofia Gubaidulina

One Soviet woman, Sofia Gubaidulina (b. 1931), stands as the leader, at least with respect to the international scene, and her music is remarkable for its stunning originality. The progress of her style extends from early tonal pieces (most Soviet composers and their immediate predecessors wrote tonal music as students), to atonality (serial and free), to electronic music, to eclecticism. A strong spiritual element is evident in Gubaidulina's music, whatever its method or idiom. She achieves powerful effects through the utterances of humans manifest in the cries, screams, whispers, and other nonmusical sounds in her sonic palette. She considers Bach, Webern, and Shostakovich to have exercised the greatest influence on her and her work. Gubaidulina has said that the last two "taught me the most important lesson of all: to be myself."[89]

Perhaps the reason that the music of Sofia Gubaidulina has struck such a responsive chord with audiences around the world is that she connects where our stressful modern existence does not: with the spiritual, the powers that are higher than self—in short, with God. She uses every property of music possible, from a simple chant to a special way of playing a familiar instrument, to formal or rhythmic elements worked out in accordance with abstract mathematical theories in service of personal expression. *Seven [Last] Words* (1982) for solo cello, bayan (a type of accordion), and string orchestra, and *In Croce* (On the Cross, 1979) for cello and organ, both of which deal with the crucifixion of Christ, illustrate this statement. The latter, a relatively short piece, incorporates the meaning of its title in lines that cross within the musical fabric—the cello starting at a low pitch, using sustained tones, the organ beginning with birdlike motifs in a high range. By the end of the piece the two lines will have reversed themselves, in the process depicting the agony of the crucifixion in wrenching tone clusters and improvisatory string glissandos and melodic material that scurries over the full range of the instrument. In this piece and in *Seven Words,* her most frequently recorded work, the cello itself, its bow positioned at right angles to the body of the instrument, becomes symbolic of the cross. In *Seven Words* each movement bears as a title one of the short phrases Jesus uttered as he hung on the cross. The cellist's bow moves from its normal position above the bridge to play on the bridge, then below it, as a symbol of the soul's leaving the body at the time of death.

A second characteristic that *Seven Words* shares with another of Gubaidulina's instrumental works, the violin concerto *Offertorium* (1980, rev. 1982, 1986), is the use of borrowed music in a symbolic manner. In *Seven Words* she quotes a phrase from Heinrich Schütz's seventeenth-century work of the same title (the melody sung to Jesus's words, "I am athirst"), which eerily haunts the twentieth-century fabric of her piece. *Offertorium,* the first of Gubaidulina's works to find an international audience, draws on material from J. S. Bach's *A Musical Offering,* which in the course of the concerto is taken apart and reassembled as yet another offering.

One of Gubaidulina's very finest works is her largest: *Alleluia* (1990) for vocal soloists, large SATB choir (usually singing *divisi*), expanded symphony orchestra, and a projector of varicolored lights.[90] There are seven large movements, the first five of which set only the word "Alleluia." In the sparse, chantlike beginning or in the fullest, most forceful expression in movement five, Gubaidulina reveals noteworthy qualities of her style. Her building blocks are motives consisting of three to five notes sounded in successive or intertwined whole or half steps within a small interval (a major or minor third, a perfect fourth). Using these materials she builds up imitative or, more often, heterophonic textures that begin low in the orchestra or chorus and eventually fill the entire available range of both forces. Along with this expansion comes an unerring sense of instrumental and vocal color that creates combinations and progressions that are uniquely hers. In *Alleluia* musical (or aural) color combines with visible color as the projectors bathe the scene in one or more of the hues that the composer has noted in the score.

The sixth movement introduces a few new words ("I believe, endlessly," a kind of symbolic Credo) as chorus and orchestra build to an overwhelming, even terror-filled, climax that gives way to a solo by a boy soprano who brings hope and fulfillment:

> Let my mouth be filled with your praise, O Lord,
> That I may sing of your glory.

In the end all voices rise and are taken up into one, as if merged on a single higher plane—redemption. Uncompromising, dedicated to her art both professionally and spiritually, Sofia Gubaidulina teaches hard but transforming lessons about the expressive power of music. Not without cause has she been called "the most important living woman composer."[91]

Galina Ustvolskaya and Elena Firsova

Two other Russian women, older and younger contemporaries of Gubaidulina, have deservedly attained positions of honor, both within and without their country: Galina Ustvolskaya (b. 1919) and Elena Firsova (b. 1950). Ustvolskaya was a student of Shostakovich, who had great respect for her music and even sought her opinions about his own. Her individuality is evident in her symphonies and piano works. The symphonies all have titles that suggest a religious orientation: Symphony No. 2, *True and Eternal Bliss* (1979); No. 3, *Jesus Messiah, Save Us* (1983); No. 4, *Prayer* (1985–1987); or No. 5, *Amen* (1989–1990). Like the other symphonies, the fifth is scored for what most would regard as a chamber ensemble: violin, oboe, trumpet, tuba, percussion, and reciter. However, Ustvolskaya is a composer who thinks big, and she has said, "My music is never chamber music, not even in the case of a solo sonata."[92] In Symphony No. 5, a ten-minute, single-movement work, the instruments introduce and return to a small number of musical ideas, including a violin theme marked *fervido* that recurs like a refrain over a well-articulated accompaniment supported by percussion and filled with detailed indications for performance. The speaker, "a man with a microphone in a black shirt and black trousers," declaims the Lord's Prayer expressively in units separated by periods of rest. Ustvolskaya writes, "The soloist must recite the text as if he were fervently praying to God."[93]

Ustvolskaya has written six piano sonatas, only the first of which has anything in common with traditional sonata structure and sound. Textures are lean, and the composer explores all registers of the instrument. All but the first of the sonatas have no bar lines, though this does not rule out the use of regular rhythms within a given segment. Harmonies exploit seconds and fourths, and dynamics are extreme and highly contrasted, from *ffff* to sudden *ppp* in the second movement of Sonata No. 4 (1957), for instance. In Sonata No. 5 (1986) dynamics at levels from *f* to *ffffff* contrast with a few passages marked *p* or *pp*, and accents abound. *Espressivo* and even *espressivissimo* often define the characters of these works. Ustvolskaya frequently repeats textual passages, as in Sonata No. 5, rehearsal number 5, where tone clusters rise slowly in sequence, all the time preserving a steady quarter-note rhythm. Passages like this, along with long-phrased melodies in even quarters or eighths, immediately call to mind the techniques of the minimalists, but Ustvolskaya really recalls, if anyone, the Impressionists or her countryman Scriabin. Her sonatas need to be played, not just studied, to appreciate their intense expressive qualities. As their composer has said, "All who really love my music should refrain from theoretical analysis of it."[94] This music, of great beauty and emotion, deserves a wider audience.

Representing a new generation, Elena Firsova was in the prime of her career when the Soviet Union collapsed, and she and her family fled to London in April 1991. There she and her composer-husband began writing film music and commissioned works to maintain a steady income. One of these works, the result of a commission from the BBC National Orchestra of Wales, resulted in a piece of which Firsova writes:

> I named it *Cassandra* [Op. 60, 1992–1993], the images being not only connected with the Trojan prophetess but also with the situation in Russia today, where an apprehension for the country's future leads to concern for the fate of the world.[95]

Nevertheless, her public face, at least in Russia, had already appeared during her student days in Moscow with the works of Opp. 1–13 (Op. 3 is for chorus; Op. 7 is an opera; Op. 12 contains songs; the rest are instrumental). Her cello sonata, Op. 5 (1971), pits soloist against pianist in "an unremittingly competing, sometimes even aggressive . . . dialogue. . . ."[96] Since then, Firsova has been a prolific composer, as the extensive list of her works in the *Norton/Grove Dictionary of Women Composers* demonstrates. Among her long string of vocal works are songs to texts by Russian poets Osip Mandelstam, Anna Akhmatova, and Boris Pasternak. Her *Three Poems by Osip Mandelstam* (1981)[97] for high voice and piano challenge the singer to make the text clear while negotiating a wide range and leaps of a seventh or more. Though Firsova appears to compose with ease, the expressive content of her work is high.

POLAND

Poland, for centuries beset by war and civil strife, its borders changed forcibly by more powerful nations, remains a country with a vibrant artistic presence in the international community. Despite the repressive political climate and economic deprivation of the past few decades, Poles have retained their great love of music. Polish music has often been on the leading edge of progressive trends. Advanced electronic music facilities are available, and composers' organizations support their members as best they can. Today, opportunities for women in Poland may be better than for their counterparts in many Western European countries. Their music is heard frequently at the Warsaw Autumn Festivals and in other venues. Styles and compositional procedures range from neoclassic to avant-garde, but on the whole they are more progressive than reactionary.

This relatively happy situation was not always the case. Wanda Landowska (1879–1959) left Warsaw in the early 1920s for Western Europe and the

United States, where she lived for the remainder of her life. She was the most highly acclaimed harpsichordist of her generation, with recordings of much of Bach's keyboard music to her credit. Prominent composers, including Poulenc, composed especially for her, and she was in constant demand as a performer and lecturer. However, her compositions remain largely in obscurity. Her Serenade for Strings and *Bourrées d'Auvergne* are particularly worthy of rediscovery.

Grażyna Bacewicz

For a time Grażyna Bacewicz (1909–1969) was better known as a violinist than as a composer, and she performed regularly into the 1950s. Her musical training (she also studied philosophy seriously) had always included equal parts of composition and performance. Even after her undergraduate years in Warsaw, Bacewicz continued both disciplines at a very high level, studying composition with Boulanger and violin with Carl Flesch, a famous pedagogue and author of method books on violin playing. From the early 1940s through the mid-1950s, Bacewicz performed solos with major orchestras and was a frequent judge of major violin competitions, including the Wieniawski International in Poland. She served for two years as concertmaster of the Polish Radio Orchestra. Also an accomplished pianist, she played the premieres of several of her compositions, including the Sonata II for Piano.

It was probably her ability as a violinist that led Bacewicz to compose so much for strings. Seven string quartets, two piano quintets, and five violin sonatas constitute the bulk of her chamber music; four symphonies, several concertos, other orchestral music, and choral pieces with orchestral accompaniment are the heart of her large works. *Music for Strings, Trumpets, and Percussion* (1958), one of several prizewinning compositions, is also one of her most frequently heard works in Europe.

Clearly delineated structures are a prominent feature of all of Bacewicz's scores, regardless of style or medium. Her music through the early 1950s is tonal to varying degrees—and in many ways has been considered to be her strongest music. Her experiments with atonality and other modern idioms have met with less critical success, but a reappraisal of these notions is definitely in order. The quartal harmony in the last movement, Toccata, of her Sonata II for Piano (1953; see HAMW, pp. 300–18) sounds confident in context, if a bit derivative of Bartók and Hindemith. The opening of the third movement of her String Quartet No. 7 exhibits quartal harmony less pervasively, and the first movement contains some dodecaphonic sections in a larger tonal setting. This quartet and other late works are more difficult to perform and comprehend than her earlier, neoclassical compositions. But normal growth, unfettered by external, nonmusical influences, was not Bacewicz's lot. This unusual dichotomy of style and the abrupt changes coming late in her creative life may be explained by the social and political difficulties that Bacewicz, along with most other Europeans, encountered during World War II, obstacles that continued in Eastern and Central Europe long after the war.

Bacewicz returned to Warsaw from Paris at the outbreak of World War II. She and her family left the city immediately, taking refuge in rural areas and smaller cities. Although her music making did not stop completely, survival amid the horrors of war interrupted her creative efforts to an appreciable extent. Returning to Warsaw after the war, she found the city in rubble and artistic organizations in disarray. It was soon obvious that rebuilding would be supervised by Soviet bureaucrats and the military, and that the arts would come under close supervision. This was to be true of all Soviet-bloc countries, and it is the reason that composers such as Bartók and Ligeti left Central Europe for the relative freedom of Western Europe and the United States. Composers of music considered by authorities as too "modern" (read dissonant, atonal, discontinuous) were labeled "formalist" and were often harshly censured. Much progressive new music was banned from public performance, as it had been by Hitler during the war, and what little was heard in private settings lacked either adequate performance or, worse, a context for critical evaluation. Polish musicians banded together to promote composition and the dissemination of new ideas, and their efforts led eventually to magnificent festivals such as the Warsaw Autumn. But the youthful energy of an international Darmstadt, for example, was not available to Poles.

Bacewicz composed prolifically, but it is a mistake to label her progressive music reactionary when in fact she came late to others' new musical styles and absorbed whatever she found valuable only when it was considered passé by those who had no such disadvantage. In other words, it is quite likely that Bacewicz would have contemplated atonality and some other, newer idioms much sooner had she been able to avoid the suffocating political situation. Serious analytical study and repeated high-quality performances will show that Bacewicz was in fact progressive in an intuitive, contemplative sense. Bacewicz's later music is vigorous, well crafted, and confident, and it deserves study. It might very well be added to or even supplant her better-known earlier pieces and bring her music more to the forefront of midcentury compositions.

Marta Ptaszyńska

Marta Ptaszyńska (b. 1943) is often cited along with Witold Lutosławski and Krzytof Penderecki as one of the most significant Polish composers of her time. Ptaszyńska is a multi-talented woman. An accomplished percussionist,

FIGURE 10.2. Marta Ptaszyńska. Photo courtesy of the composer.

she often plays her own or others' percussion pieces. Although she specializes in contemporary techniques, she has been a regular member of the Warsaw Philharmonic percussion section.

After study at the Warsaw Conservatory and in Poznan, Ptaszyńska studied with Nadia Boulanger in Paris and with Donald Erb at the Cleveland Institute of Music, where she also earned an Artist Diploma in percussion. Her skill as a performer is reflected in the compositions written especially for her. She appears frequently as a featured artist, and is represented as a composer at international concerts and festivals, including World Music Days of the International Society for Contemporary Music, the Aspen Music Festival, and of course, the Warsaw Autumn. Since the early 1970s Ptaszyńska has lived both in Poland and abroad. She maintains residences in Pennsylvania and Chicago, where in 1998 she joined the music faculty of the University of Chicago. Often sought as a composer-in-residence, she has spent all or substantial parts of years on the faculties of Bennington College, the Berkeley and Santa Barbara campuses of the University of California, the University of Cincinnati, and Indiana University.

The sensual quality of Ptaszyńska's music arises in part from her pictorial imagination and interest in the fine arts. In this area she is attracted both to exotic art (that of the East) and to European surrealism because of this school's use of forms and colors in conjunction with unusual, fantastic moods and feelings. Ptaszyńska creates this pictorial/atmospheric quality in interesting, refined ways. Perhaps the best example of her merger of musical and artistic interests is her one-act opera, *Oscar of Alva* (1972), which she wrote specifically for television and which makes good use of the medium's unique capabilities.

Ptaszyńska's fascination with surrealistic art is also revealed in her Concerto for Marimba, in which each movement refers to a specific picture: I, "The Echo of Fear" (a painting by Yves Tanguy); II, "The Eyes of Silence" (by Max Ernst); and III, "The Thorn Trees" (by Graham Sutherland). This last movement displays sharp and aggressive expression and rough sonorities; it is strongly marked by rhythms that contrast strikingly with preceding movements. The writing for marimba is difficult but idiomatic, testifying to the composer's own skill as a solo percussionist. (A score of this movement is in CAMW, 244–59.) One of her most striking and often performed works is the *Holocaust Memorial Cantata* (1993), commissioned by the Lira Singers of Chicago and conducted in several performances during its first year of life by Sir Yehudi Menuhin.[98]

Ptaszyńska's many pieces for children are especially welcome at a time when little worthwhile contemporary music is being written for young people. Her *Musical Alphabet* for two pianos (1993), intended for children who have studied piano for a year or two, provides an excellent introduction to the sounds of twentieth-century music in its use of both traditional and modern genres (baroque dances, nineteenth-century character pieces, Eastern European folk dances, and twentieth-century pop). An opera for children, *Mister Marimba,* was a great success when premiered in Warsaw, receiving twenty-eight performances in the course of the 1998–1999 season. Her plans for the year 2000 include a concerto for percussion, commissioned by the percussion virtuosa Evelyn Glennie, and a piano concerto for Jeremy Menuhin, son of the late violinist and conductor Yehudi Menuhin.

Other Polish women are also emerging as world-class composers. Elzbieta Sikora (b. 1943),[99] for example, composed a musical theatre piece, *Wyrywacz sere* (Heart Snatcher), that was favorably received at the 1995 Warsaw Autumn. She has also written two operas, three ballets, and chamber and orchestral music. In 1968 Sikora traveled to Paris to explore electroacoustic techniques, studying with Pierre Schaeffer, François Bayle, and

Betsy Jolas. Since 1981 she has lived in France, where she, along with three Polish men composers, has formed a new music collective, Grupa KEW.

> Together they have played an important role in the cultural life of the country, introducing novel compositional issues, as well as original forms of concert life, including happenings and performances in unusual concert locations.[100]

Another expatriate, Joanna Bruzdowicz-Tittel (b. 1943), also studied in Paris, where her teachers were Nadia Boulanger, Olivier Messiaen, and Pierre Schaeffer. Since 1975 she has lived in Belgium. In 1972–1973 she premiered two operas in Tours, then in Paris. She has also written ballets, concertos, film scores, and orchestral music. In her role as music journalist and critic she has proved a fine advocate for modern composers. Other living Polish composers who have produced music of fine quality are Krystyna Moszumanska-Nazar (b. 1924), Bernadetta Matuszcak (b. 1937, another Boulanger pupil), and Bettina Skrzypczak (b. 1963).

THE CZECH REPUBLIC

World War II left Czechoslovakia, now divided into the Czech Republic and Slovakia, with the task of rebuilding; since the collapse of communistic rule in 1989, the country has been plunged more than once into political turmoil of major proportions. One might ask, then, whether the time would ever be right for the emergence of composers of classical music who are also women. Indeed, of two such women born in the 1940s—Viera Janáceková and Ivana Ludová—the former moved to Germany in 1972, and the latter, though still living in the Czech Republic, went abroad to Paris to study. Though she has written for several media, Ludová seems particularly drawn to chamber music and various kinds of vocal works, rather typical fare for women composers of most eras and nations.

Among women of the next generation, the one who has achieved the strongest international reputation is Silvie Bodorová (b. 1954). Bodorová received her earliest music instruction in her homeland, but traveled to Siena, Gdansk, and Amsterdam for additional study. In the 1980s she taught composition at the Janáček Academy and served for a short time as composer-in-residence at the University of Cincinnati. She currently lives in Prague and devotes all her energies to composition, almost always on commission.

Bodorová's concern that modern music reach and communicate with its audience led her to join with three male colleagues (Lubomir Fiser [b. 1935], Otmar Macha [b. 1922], and Zdenek Lukás [b. 1928]) in a group named *Quattro*. Though of different ages and backgrounds, these artists have a single vision:

FIGURE 10.3. Sylvie Bodorová. Photo courtesy of the composer.

> At a time when avant-garde art . . . is undergoing a crisis and when all attempts at overcoming it in a positive way have become condensed under the single term of post-modernism, the members of Quattro are convinced about music's communicative and emotional power, and share the desire to convey to their audiences a message of beauty, not fearing to resort to traditional or quasi-traditional means of expression.[101]

To say that Sylvie Bodorová is a supreme melodist is still to understate the obvious. Her long-breathed, often unaccompanied lines take on lives of their own as they spin out, now in widely spaced intervals, now freely turning around a small number of adjacent pitches. These qualities appear in works early (e.g., *Plankty* for viola and orchestra, 1982) and late (e.g., *Dona nobis lucem* for female voice, violin, guitar, and string orchestra, 1994). It seems that a composer so committed to pure melody would logically gravitate toward contrapuntal textures, but Bodorová's counterpoint is generally one of coexistence and complementarity rather than imitation or obbligato. In *Magikon* (1987), a concerto for oboe and strings, for instance, imitation of three melodic themes at the distance of an eighth note complements the soaring oboe line, but the texture also verges on heterophony. In *Dignitas homini* (The Dignity of Humankind, Bodorová's String Quartet No. 1), for example, one segment contains four different but similar lines that build up a texture of complementarity (see Example 10.1). Balkan rhythms and modes also characterize her writing, and their differences from Western-style metrical rhythms and scales give her music a freedom that is characteristically her own. With her distinctive treatment of melody and rhythm, it is hardly surprising that texture is more important to her than harmony, which can be traditionally triadic or built in clusters of seconds but never seems to be a driving force in the music.

EXAMPLE 10.1. Sylvie Bodorová, *Dignitas Homini* (String Quartet No. 1). Used by permission of the composer.

Among Bodorová's recent works, two compositions speak to modern anxieties and events. *Dona nobis lucem* (Grant Us Light), a concerto movement for woman's voice, violin, guitar, and strings, appeared in 1994. The light is prefigured in the opening bars, which offer permutations of the note C# at pitch, in octave doublings, and in string harmonics. Like the melodies of *Dignitas homini,* those given the soloists here form a counterpoint of complementarity. While the singer has only open vowels during most of the piece, near the end she presents three statements of "Dona nobis lucem," a variation of the final phrase of the Latin Requiem Mass, "Dona nobis pacem" (Grant us peace). The final statement of this text occurs on a dramatic high C#.

The *Terezin Ghetto Requiem,* written on commission from England's Warwick and Leamington Festival, saw its premiere in 1998. This work, for baritone and string quartet, was inspired by a historical fact: twenty performances of Verdi's Requiem took place in the concentration camp at Terezin, in the Czech Republic, in 1943–1944. Here Bodorová symbolizes this seeming anomaly by combining texts from the Latin Requiem with Hebrew synagogue chants, an approach that suits her technique of sounding together different but complementary music. She describes the purpose of the work as the honoring of "those who, under the most extreme conditions and in the face of death, found the courage to protest against torture by means of something as ultimately human as Verdi's Requiem."[102]

Romania

The people of Romania endured almost unthinkable oppression under the dictatorial rule of Nicolae Ceauşescu, yet some of the most talented creative artists enjoyed support from the government for their education and professional activities. Three talented and productive women, all born in Bucharest, took advantage of this support to develop in different ways as first-class composers: Myriam Marbé (1931–1997), Violeta Dinescu (b. 1953), and Adriana Hölszky (b. 1953). All three began their formal education in music at the Porumbescu Conservatory in Bucharest, and all came to be known internationally for the quality and originality of their music.

Myriam Marbé

Permitted to travel outside Romania—notably to the Darmstadt Festivals in 1968, 1969, and 1972 and the Gaudeamus seminars in the Netherlands—Marbé chose always to return to Bucharest and to her position as professor of composition at the Porumbescu Conservatory, which she held from 1954 to 1988. Her thirst for news of avant-garde music had been whetted in her student days, when a teacher at the conservatory taught from scores and recordings of Western music that had been smuggled into the country. Marbé and other students—referred to as the Golden Generation of Romanian composers—worked together, out of official sight, to experiment with new approaches to composition that at the same time would somehow use native Romanian music as a resource and inspiration. Marbé herself introduced some elements of folk music and ritual into such pieces as *Ritual for the Thirst of the World* (1968) for chorus and percussion, which combines sung and spoken texts drawn from the Romanian rain ritual, a ceremony of great antiquity. Writing about her Requiem *Fra Angelico—Marc Chagall—Veroney* (for mezzo-soprano soloist, SATB choir, and fourteen instruments, 1990), Thomas Biemel states:

> All the [musical] languages join in the act of mourning: fragments of the Latin Requiem are combined with songs from the traditional Romanian ritual for the dead, portions of the Jewish Kaddish, the Byzantine resurrection hymn, and single works from Greek antiquity.[103]

Yet censorship was a way of life, and finding ways to escape it, he adds, "was one of the minor occupations for that generation of Romanian composers."[104]

Mathematical factors often influence structural elements of Marbé's music. In *Incantatio* (1973) for solo clarinet, Marbé allows a series of prime numbers dictate the note values of the piece, while in *Zyklus* (1973–1974) for flute, guitar, and percussion she uses the Fibonacci series as a point of departure.[105] However, these pieces are not just dry mathematics, for Marbé uses these structural foundations as points of departure and as the bases on which to construct expressive musical statements.

Despite being to some extent cut off from the Western world, Marbé developed a musical language that was anything but conservative. Her concerto composed for Romanian saxophonist Daniel Kientzy (1986), in four movements played without pause, is a compendium of saxophone techniques—multiphonics, bent pitches, rhythmic effects using keys on the instrument, glissandos, contrasts of extreme ranges, and the like. In the course of the piece Kientzy plays two saxophones at once, combines singing voice with saxophone (third movement), and changes among types of saxophone—from baritone (movement 1) to soprano (movement 2), to alto (movement 3).[106] Throughout the work Marbé contrasts free, improvisatory writing (e.g., the beginning of the first movement) with more strictly measured material (movement 3). She also introduces elements stylized from the folk idiom—for example, frequent use of heterophonic textures that circle around a central pitch or repeat a set of pitches in various orders. This circling technique provides a feeling of tonal center without ever being conventionally tonal. This is kaleidoscopic music in which the saxophones are central and other voices move in, out, and around this principal color. Some similar writing appears in her *Piesa pentu* (1997) for piano and harpsichord, which effectively alternates and combines two instruments that are simultaneously similar and dissimilar in an often sparse texture that makes every note count.

Violeta Dinescu

> Strictly speaking, there is nothing in music that hasn't already been said in some way.[107]

One of a relatively small number of women to have studied composition with a woman, Violeta Dinescu was a pupil of Marbé at the Porumbescu Conservatory in Bucharest. Unlike her teacher, however, Dinescu eventually emigrated to Germany, where she has lived since 1982. She is currently professor of composition at the University of Oldenburg.[108] A thoughtful composer, she has arrived at a personal style that, while acknowledging that there is little new under the sun, maintains its own integrity in the face of other trends. In fact, she says, "I feel myself still on the same path as the one I began in Romania."[109] Her vast repertoire includes operas, ballets, and orchestral, chamber and vocal music.

Like Marbé, Dinescu has created an avant-garde idiom that reveals careful attention to organic structure and a thorough knowledge of the possibilities and limitations of performing media. Also like Marbé, Dinescu relies on mathematics to derive certain basic features of a piece of music. She explains her method, in specific connection with *Figuren II* for two guitars:

> In the beginning of every composition, I try to find a sphere, an imaginary space, where the flood of imagination can meet the rigor of thought. It is necessary to control the different dimensions of the musical language in the microstructure as well [as] in the macrostructure. . . . The numbers [are] used in the music in different ways—as different intervals, directions, proportions—but remain without the limits given by the order, appearance, and importance of certain members. The music tries to dominate this strength of succession and priority of numeric symbols, discovering new spaces which have their origin in the same structures. My aesthetic necessity is at the same time to know better the infinite universe of sound and to discover new relations between thought and its multitude of spiritual projections.[110]

Other examples of works in which mathematics determines the overall structure are the *Echoes* series and *Satyras I–IV,* for solo instruments or chamber ensembles.

Dinescu's works seem to unfold organically, growing beyond the musical boundaries one might expect of the particular media. For example, the piano tremolos in *Tautropfen* (Tightrope, 1991) for clarinet and piano "have an orchestral scope that almost threatens to overwhelm its partner." Elsewhere, her use of silence in *Lichtewellen* (Wells of Light, 1991) for solo clarinet "creates a spatial, almost three-dimensional sound world . . . the music seems to be enlarged beyond normal boundaries, and we tend to experience this . . . piece as though it were a solo symphony."[111] An earlier work, *Scherzo da fantasia* (1985) for violin and cello, presents transformed versions of the Romanian folk music she studied in the 1970s on a grant from the Romanian government.

Adriana Hölszky

Another Bucharest-born composer, Adriana Hölszky also received early musical instruction at the Porumbescu Conservatory. Unlike Marbé and Dinescu, however, Hölszky was of Austro-Hungarian stock and had a somewhat easier time moving to Germany in 1976. She continued her study of composition, including electronic and experimental music, in Stuttgart, where she currently lives and works as a freelance composer and teacher. Since she has spent her professional life entirely in Germany, many consider her to be German rather than Romanian.

Though Hölszky has written dramatic and orchestral pieces, she seems drawn more to chamber and vocal music. Her outlook has been formed by principles of serialism, in that her precompositional process involves organization of contrasts, tone colors, and other parameters—length or dynamics, for instance—and in that levels of construction repeat elements on higher, lower, or parallel planes of structure. She has also attempted to transfer formal principles of literature to music. For example, *Nouns to Nouns,* a piece for solo violin, is based on a poem by e. e. cummings, and *Omaggio a Michelangelo* draws formal principles from two of his sonnets.[112]

A publicity brochure from Breitkopf and Härtel describes her work as "chaos under control."[113] Her *Hängebrücken* I and II (Suspension Bridges) for double string quartet was composed in 1989–1990 and first performed in 1991 (excerpt in CAMW, 52–59). In effect, each of the *Hängebrücken* exists separately for a single quartet, and the two together created *Hängebrücken III.* Part of the fabric of the piece draws on Schubert's String Quartet in D minor, D. 810. According to notes in the score, the underlying concept of this piece is that a kind of horizontal, "endless" Schubertian time can be vertically transformed. In this way the structure is enhanced with a great concentration of structural fields that emit a "pulsating" or "vibrating" sound energy.[114] One of Hölszky's most admired works is the music-theatre piece *The Screens,* based on the play by Jean Genet, which "received its much remarked premiere" in 1995 at the Vienna Festival.[115]

Roswitha Sperber described Hölszky's music as follows:

> Meticulous workmanship, where no chance elements have any place, characterize her (almost impenetrably complex) scores, which are also calligraphic documents of great artistic charm. . . . Most . . . are quasi-spatial and actionistic, and thus latently stageable.[116]

AUSTRALIA AND NEW ZEALAND

Australia is a fascinating country in many ways: geographically closer to Asia than to Europe, yet largely British in manners and culture; home to one of the most interesting indigenous populations anywhere, but a population only recently acknowledged and accommodated in all its richness; the location of great modern cities, yet also some of the most desolate, unpopulated, vast expanses of open land on this planet.

Australia's art world is similarly dichotomous. Development of conditions conducive to concert life did not take place in Australia until the latter half of the nineteenth century. (In this, Australia and the United States are somewhat comparable.) European music, primarily English, was programmed sporadically, and schools of music patterned after British models opened in the few major cities. In the 1890s two songs for women's chorus by a Miss Woolley from Sydney were published (by Novello) and performed; at about the same time, Mona McBurney's *The Dalmatians* became the first opera by a woman to be performed in Australia. In the second half of the twentieth century a semblance of what might be called Australian music has developed, and several composers enjoy national and international reputations. However, much instructional material in music is still very British, and many composers, even the younger ones, still travel to London for advanced musical studies.

One of Australia's most eminent composers, Peggy Glanville-Hicks (1912–1990) exemplifies this eclecticism. She traveled widely and lived in Europe and the United States. Studies with Vaughan Williams at the Royal College of Music in London, with Egon Wellesz in Vienna, and with Nadia Boulanger in Paris provided a broad background for her fertile musical imagination. Eastern Mediterranean culture was a further, if less noticeable, influence. The widely discussed opera *The Transposed Heads* (1953) is indicative of Glanville-Hicks's unique style. Her music is forged of diverse materials and techniques built on the conceptual foundation of her belief that music should exploit the components of melody and rhythm, with harmony as an incidental factor that, while usually present in some way, is not to be structurally important. In *The Transposed Heads* the influence of Indian music can be heard clearly in vocal and percussion parts. Other works call on idioms from Spain, Africa, South America, and Ancient Greece.[117]

Discussing the life and works of Peggy Glanville-Hicks brings up two interesting topics: the place of women composers in history and the place of Australia in the lives of its women composers. Peggy Glanville-Hicks frequently voiced her opinion that she was the only woman ever to succeed as a composer. She also said that women composers—she called them "ladies" though she professed to hate the term—had to be twice as good as men to succeed, suggesting either a gigantic ego on her part or something of a realization that she did have predecessors.[118] The problem of finding traditions, of sensing a usable past—"roots," as it were—has plagued women in all walks of life. At least writers can point to books, and visual artists to portraits, as concrete evidence of women's work in the past, whereas music must be performed in the here and now before it can be considered to exist. One might celebrate with Peggy Glanville-Hicks that she believed she was successful—and at the same time note the distortion of the past that left her feeling so isolated.

The career of Peggy Glanville-Hicks also prompts the question: Who is an Australian composer? Glanville-Hicks was born in Australia, received her early training there, and returned in retirement. The bulk of her professional life, however, was spent elsewhere: in London and Paris for advanced study, in the United States (1942–1959) as a composer and music journalist (she became a U.S. citizen in 1948), and in Greece, from 1959 until her return to Australia in 1976. Other Australian expatriates include Jennifer Fowler (b. 1939) and Alison Bauld (b. 1944), both currently living in England. Dulcie Holland and Miriam Hyde (both b. 1913), though they spent the bulk of their careers in Australia, studied at London's Royal College of Music and enjoyed some success in England before returning home. Mary Mageau (b. 1934), on the other hand, was born in Wisconsin but has lived and worked in Australia since 1974; her music is included on a CD entitled *I Am an American Woman,*[119] while elsewhere she is referred to as Australian. It would seem that, in the mobile and technology-saturated society of the late twentieth century, to set divisions between composers solely on the basis of national boundaries is to falsify the conditions under which women live and work today.

Returning to Peggy Glanville-Hicks, her most productive years began in the late 1940s, when she was living in New York and supplementing her income as a composer by reviewing concerts for the New York *Herald Tribune.* (She produced over five hundred columns for this newspaper.) In addition to writing *Transposed Heads,* she composed her best song cycles

(*Profiles from China*, 1945; *Thirteen Ways of Looking at a Blackbird*, 1947, publ. 1951; *Thomsoniana*, 1949; and *Letters from Morocco*, 1952) along with the well-known Sonata for Harp (1951), Sonata for Piano and Five Percussionists (1952), and the *Etruscan Concerto* (1954) for piano and orchestra in the United States.[120] In the concerto we see a fine demonstration of her conviction that melody and rhythm should be the building blocks of music. Here rhythms are marked and melodies, many with exotic touches, are irregularly repetitious and bedecked with ornamental flourishes. The second movement, "Meditation," declares its exotic, pseudo-ancient character in static, kaleidoscopic beauty. Here and elsewhere Glanville-Hicks has had to invent a kind of generically exotic language that suggests a foreign world, since she could not know the music of a people living so long ago. Given the nature of the piano part and its relationship to the orchestra, the work is more *concertante* in style than *concerto*.

In 1976, having been diagnosed with a brain tumor, Peggy Glanville-Hicks traveled from Greece to New York for surgery. Although she lived far longer than her doctors expected, she was no longer able to compose. After spending a few more years in Greece, she retired to Australia, but there was no more music.

Margaret Sutherland

Despite a very different sort of musicality and lifestyle, Margaret Sutherland (1897–1984) shared with Glanville-Hicks some elements in the area of education. After attending the Albert Street Consortium in Melbourne, Sutherland won scholarships to study with Sir Arnold Bax in London. After a brief period in Vienna, she returned to Melbourne determined to enhance dramatically the quality of Australian concert music and to build the facilities and administrative apparatus necessary for performance at an international level. She succeeded, as is evident by the well-appointed arts complex on the banks of the Yarra River. The Spoleto Festival is but one of many major international arts attractions to make use of this facility. In addition, Sutherland maintained an active teaching schedule and a career as a chamber music pianist. In recognition of her eminence in Melbourne's cultural life, she was awarded an honorary doctorate from the University of Melbourne in 1969.

Sutherland's best music is post-tonal, with synthetic scales, polytonality, and quartal harmony employed in a personal, engaging style. Sophisticated imitative counterpoint occurs in her two string quartets; the second, entitled *Discussion* (1954), is interesting for presenting modern techniques in an accessible language.

Sutherland's contribution to Australian art music goes beyond her high standards and her advocacy efforts, however. Among her traditional sonatas, concertos, fantasies, and suites is a single opera, *The Young Kabbarli* (1965), which uses a tale from Australia's history for its plot and includes in the score a native Maori singer and music for a Maori instrument, the didjeridu.[121] Described as "an opera of ideas rather than of action,"[122] the work concerns missionary Daisy Bates (1863–1959) and her efforts to Christianize the Australian natives. In contrast to the Maori music, Daisy's music reveals the style of Irish folksongs she has brought with her to Australia. The opera includes music for dance as well as vocal set-numbers, though the latter may be interrupted or otherwise divided in ways that make them difficult to perform out of the opera's context. In bringing together native music and the music of some of the white immigrants who settled in Australia, Sutherland took a step forward in creating something truly Australian.

Betty Beath

Another composer interested in using native materials and ethnic music from the Pacific Rim, Betty Beath (b. 1932) has written several orchestral works inspired by music she heard in Bali and Java when doing research there. Unfortunately, some of these works are given rather Hollywood Western-style accompaniments.[123] On the other hand, it is very difficult to dislike Beath's songs. Though not without challenges, they are truly vocal in idiom, with piano parts that are created equal to the voice. The group *River Songs* (1990–1992; some orchestrated in 1992), with texts by Australian poet Jena Woodhouse, are excellent, varicolored pieces. A piano piece, *Didjeridu,* transfers the sound and playing style of this Maori instrument to the keyboard. Beath has also created music for children, including *Abigail and the Bushranger* (1974), a musical story for children's voices and percussion, and its companions, *Abigail and the Rainmaker* (1976) and *Abigail and the Mythical Beast* (1985).

Jennifer Fowler and Alison Bauld

Both Jennifer Fowler and Alison Bauld currently live in London. Their styles and interests are quite different, however. Fowler, since completing university courses in Australia and additional study at the University of Utrecht's Electronic Music Studio, has maintained a respected position among Britain's progressive composers. Her music, as James Briscoe has observed, is "written for performing groups that are either unconventional or at times flexible in instrumentation. . . ." For example, the 1983 version of *Echoes from an Antique Land* is for five percussion instruments, whereas its 1986 incarnation uses an irregular ensemble of five or ten instruments. *Ravelation* (1971, rev. 1980), more conventional, is for a cello quintet (two violins, viola, and two cellos), while the ensemble for *We Call to You, Brother* (1988, composed nearly two decades after Fowler left Australia) includes a didjeridu. Briscoe's preface to her *Blow Flute, Answer Echoes in Antique Land Dying* (1983; see CAMW, 17ff.) contains some interesting comments by Fowler on her compositional process and her life as a composer.[124]

Alison Bauld's life has been marked by the effects of drama and dance. In fact, she considered an acting career and attended Australia's National Institute of Dramatic Art before music came to occupy more of her life. In England she studied with Elisabeth Lutyens and Hans Keller, and composed for several theatre productions. In 1975 she became music director of the Laban Centre for Dance at London University. Dramatic works involving solo voice(s) also emerged as an important compositional interest: *Dear Emily* (1973), *Mad Moll* (1973), and *Farewell Already* (1993) are dramatic scenas for soprano, and *In a Dead Brown Land* (1972) is a theatre piece set in colonial Australia. *Banquo's Buried* (1982) and *Richard III* (1985) draw texts from Shakespeare. *Banquo*, the mad scene from *Macbeth*, for mezzo-soprano and piano, involves sung declamation and both rhythmicized and free speech over an evocative piano accompaniment. British soprano Jane Manning, whose promotion of music by living composers is well known, has premiered several of Bauld's works, including *Dear Emily, Mad Moll, One Pearl* (1973), and *I Loved Miss Watson* (1977).

Mary Mageau

Mary Mageau's Triple Concerto (1990) for violin, cello, piano, and orchestra shows her to be a particularly adept orchestrator as well as an imaginative writer for solo instruments (alone and in relation to others).[125] Hers is a rich, varicolored sound that, especially in *The Furies* (1995) for piano and orchestra, has a Prokofiev-like character. Given this quality, some might dismiss her, along with any number of twentieth-century composers, for lack of originality. Such an evaluation is largely irrelevant for, as Violeta Dinescu has pointed out, there is nothing in music that has not been done before. Nor was originality considered an important criterion of music's value before the nineteenth century. Rather, supreme skill was a decisive factor in evaluating art. Mary Mageau writes with supreme skill, and she and her music deserve to be better known outside Australia.

Gillian Whitehead

Gillian Whitehead (b. 1941) was born in New Zealand to musical parents, and studied music in Auckland and Wellington. She moved to Australia and then to London for graduate study with Peter Maxwell Davies (no graduate programs in music composition are available in New Zealand). Her many grants and commissions have come from foundations in New Zealand, England, and Australia. She held a series of fellowships and temporary appointments in England and Australia before taking a permanent position at the New South Wales Conservatorium in Sydney in 1982.

Whitehead, who is one-eighth Maori, has absorbed influences from the Maori people and from many twentieth-century composers, from Debussy to Webern. This prolific composer is a gifted listener, and she exhibits a plethora of styles resulting from her diverse experiences. *Okura* (1979) for violin and piano begins a series of works that draws on her Maori heritage.[126] The list includes her three string quartets (*Bright Forms Return,* 1980, which includes a female voice; *Moon, Tides, and Shoreline,* 1990; and *Angels Born at the Speed of Light,* 1990). The score for the highly virtuosic *Journey of Matuku Moana* (Journey of the White Heron, 1992) for solo cello is available in CAMW, 371–86. Her recent opera, *Bride of Fortune,* is set in Australia.

* * *

It is difficult to assess at such a close range which of these composers or works will touch the most listeners, and which will fall by the wayside for no other reason than that they were written by women. There can be no doubt, however, that this music is worthy of study and that it offers performance possibilities too numerous to count.

NOTES

1. For more information about women and the Prix de Rome, see Annegret Fauser, "*La Guerre en dentelles:* Women and the *Prix de Rome* in French Cultural Politics," *Journal of the American Musicological Society* 51 (1998): 83–129; and Ruth Robertson, "Women Winners of the *Prix de Rome:* A Chronological Analysis," *ILWC* [International League of Women Composers] *Journal* (February 1993): 4–7.

2. When Stravinsky was unable to conduct the premiere of the Dumbarton Oaks concerto because of illness, he chose Boulanger as his replacement.

3. Donald Campbell, *The Master Teacher* (Washington, DC: Pastoral Press, 1984), p. 80.

4. Ibid.

5. Ibid., p. 31. A number of works by Nadia Boulanger are available on CDs: *In memoriam Lili Boulanger* (Marco Polo 8.223636 [1993]) and *Nadia Boulanger: Lieder und Kammermusik* (Troubadisc TRO-CD01407 [1993]) are just two.

6. See Fauser, "*Guerre.*"

7. No prizes were awarded during World Wars I and II.

8. René Dumesnil, *La musique en France entre les deux guerres, 1919–1939* (Paris: Editions du milieu du monde, 1946), pp. 192–93 and passim.

9. Ibid., pp. 196–97, 214–15.

10. Ibid., p. 182.

11. Arbie Orenstein, *A Ravel Reader* (New York: Columbia University Press, 1990), p. 432.

12. Deems Taylor, review in *The World,* March 25, 1925.

13. Other members of *Les Six* were Georges Auric, Louis Durey, Arthur Honegger, Darius Milhaud, and Francis Poulenc.

14. Recorded as part of *Germaine Tailleferre: Music for Two Pianos and Piano Four Hands,* the Clinton-Narboni Duo, Elan CD82278 (1997).

15. Later, pianist Arthur Rubinstein would engage her to play *Jeux de plain air* with him in London; still later, desperate to find money to pay her mother's medical bills, she created an orchestral version that Serge Koussevitsky programmed on the Boston Symphony's 1926 season. Tailleferre claimed that the idea for orchestrating the pieces and showing them to Koussevitsky came to her in a dream. See Janelle Gelfand, "Germaine Tailleferre (1892–1983): Piano and Chamber Works" (Ph. D. diss., University of Cincinnati, 1999), pp. 52–53.

16. Ibid., p. 97.

17. Recorded by the Clinton-Narboni Duo, Elan CD82298 (1997).

18. Recordings of the first two pieces are on *Germaine Tailleferre: Musique de chambre,* Cambria CD-1085 (1994); of the trio, on *Piano Trios,* Clementi Trio Köln, Largo 5112 (1988).

19. Hélène Jourdan-Morhange, *Mes amis musiciens* (Paris: Les Editeurs Français Réunis, 1955), p. 160. Translations by Gelfand, p. 92.

20. Peggy Jane Johnson, "The Organ Compositions of Jeanne Demessieux" (DMA thesis, University of Cincinnati, 1994), p. 17.

21. Ibid., p. 22, quotes the review.

22. Jolas sometimes combines solo voices and instruments in chamber works: for example, in the String Quartet II (1964) for singer and three strings and in *Plupart du temps II* for tenor, tenor saxophone, and cello (1989; CAMW, pp. 63–70).

23. Composer's note in the score of *O Wall* (Paris: Heugel, 1980).

24. C. Mayer, ed., *Annäherung VI an sieben Komponistinnen* (Kassel: Furore, 1995), p. 7.

25. Ibid., p. 8.

26. Ibid., pp. 12–15.

27. Kali, the patron saint of gypsies, was an Egyptian slave girl who accompanied Mary Magdalene and the other Marys across the Mediterranean Sea to France (hence the place name Saintes-Marie-de-la-Mer, an area holy to Catholics).

28. The first two are demons, the last a sort of angel.

29. Urmen defends a newborn child and drives the demons away with fire.

30. Zugarramurdi is a site in the Basque country (near the border between France and Spain) that is associated with black magic.

31. Grete von Zieritz, liner notes for her *Zigeunerkonzert für Solo Violine und Orchester in sechs Bildern,* recorded on Polyphonia POL 63015 (1984).

32. Claudius Reinke, notes from the CD *Komponistinnen des 20. Jahrhunderts,* translated by Micheline Sauriol and Scott Swope, Bayer BR 100200 (1994).

33. B. Sonntag and R. Matthei, eds., *Annäherung I an sieben Komponistinnen* (Kassel: Furore, 1986), p. 57.

34. Ibid.

35. Frank Schneider, notes for *Musik in der Deutsche Demokratische Republik,* vol. 1, translated by Janet and Michael Berridge, Berlin Classics 009071213C (1995), p. 25.

36. Webern's String Quartet, Op. 28, also uses the BACH motif as the basis for a twelve-tone row.

37. Recordings include *Siegrid Ernst: Kammermusik,* Vienna Modern Masters VMM 2018 (1994); *Variations for Large Orchestra* on *Music from Six Continents,* 1996 series, VMM 3035 (1996); *Peace Now* on *New Music for Orchestra,* VMM 3040 (1997).

38. For a more detailed discussion of this piece see Beate Philipp, "Siegrid Ernst," *Annäherung VIII an sieben Komponistinnen* (Kassel: Furore, 1997), pp. 57–60.

39. Ibid., pp. 60–62 for a detailed discussion of this piece.

40. Siegrid Ernst, notes for VMM 3040.

41. June Ottenberg, Review of *Siegrid Ernst: Kammermusik, IAWM* [International Alliance of Women in Music] *Journal* 3, #1 (February 1997): 40.

42. B. Sonntag and R. Matthei, eds., *Annäherung I,* p. 12.

43. Available in E. Rieger and K. Walter, eds., *Frauen komponieren: 22 Klavierstücke* (Mainz: Schott, 1985), p. 62.

44. CAMW, p. 43.

45. Roswitha Sperber, *Women Composers* (Bonn: Inter Nationes, 1996), p. 53. See the cover of CAMW for a graphically notated piece by Heller.

46. B. Sonntag and R. Matthei, eds., *Annäherung I,* interview by Klarenz Barlow, July 3, 1986.

47. Proceedings, 8°congresso internacional de Mujeres en la Música (Bilbao, Spain, March 18–22, 1992), pp. 72–77.

48. B. Sonntag and R. Matthei, eds., *Annäherung III an sieben Komponistinnen* (Kassel: Furore, 1987), p. 60.

49. Centre Belge de Documentation Musical, *Music in Belgium. Contemporary Belgian Composers* (Brussels: A. Manteau, 1964), p. 63.

50. Recorded on Composer's Voice CVCD8702 (1988).

51. Anne Gray, "Tera de Marez Oyens: In Memoriam," *Women of Note Quarterly* 5, #1 (February 1997): 4.

52. Composer's preface, *A Wrinkle in Time* (Kassel: Furore, 1995).

53. Hilary Tann, "Tera: A Personal Reminiscence," *IAWM Journal* 3 #1 (February 1997): 6.

54. Biographies of these and other Swedish women are available online from the Swedish Music Information Center <http://www.mic.stim.se>. Eva Örström's *Elfrida Andrée–ett levnadsöde* was published in 1999 (Stockholm: Prisma).

55. See Pirkko Moisala and Riita Valkeila, *Musiikin toinen sukupuoli: Naissaveltajia keskiajalta nykyaikaam* (*The Other Sex in Music: Women Composers from the Middle Ages to the Present*) (Helsinki: Kirjayhtyma Oy, 1994) and Pirkko Moisala, "Can Women's Studies Change the World of Music?" *Finnish Music Quarterly* (April 1997): 18–23.

56. Siri Haukenes, notes for *Pauline Hall,* Simax CD PSC3105 (1990).

57. Aaron Cohen, *International Encyclopedia of Women Composers* (New York: R.R. Bowker, 1980; 2d ed., 1987), p. 298, gives the dates 1934–1942, then 1945–1963.

58. Halljerd Aksnes, biography of Cecilie Ore, available online from the Norwegian Music Information Center at <http://www.notam.uio.no>.

59. Cohen, p. 443. Per-Anders Hellqvist, notes for *Flowings,* Bluebell ABCD 069 (1997), says she went to Paris in 1953; the online biography from the Swedish Music Information Center (<http://www.mic.stim.se>) gives the year 1952.

60. Aksnes, p. 12.

61. Ibid.

62. Both appear on the CD *Karin Rehnkvist: Davids nimm,* Phono Suecia PS CD85 (1996).

63. Unsigned biography of Rehnkvist, online from the Swedish Music Information Center (see footnote 59).

64. Ibid.

65. Eero Richmond, "Finnish Women Composers," *The Musical Woman: An International Perspective,* ed. J. L. Zaimont et al. (New York: Greenwood Press, 1991), vol. 3, p. 444. Sibelius was born in 1865 and died in 1957.

66. Ibid., p. 452, quoting Risto Nieminen, "An Interview with Kaija Saariaho," translated by Susan Sinisalo, *Finnish Music Quarterly* (1985): 24. Both pieces are on Finlandia Records, FA CD 374.

67. Ibid., p. 453, quoting Risto Nieminen, "Kaija Saariaho Gains New Ground," translated by Susan Sinisalo, *Finnish Music Quarterly* (1988): 64.

68. Benjamin Ivry, "Kaija Saariaho," *BBC Music Magazine,* May 1996, p. 35.

69. Richmond, pp. 453–54. However, Pirkko Moisala might disagree. See "Can Women's Studies Change the World of Music?"

70. The opera, in three acts, has a libretto by Swedish poet Marie Louise Ramnefalk. Both the aria and the song cycle appear on *Karólina Eiríksdóttir: Portrait,* a CD issued by the Icelandic Music Information Center.

71. See the abstract of her paper, "Comporre per due mondi diversi: quello del pop/rock e quello classico," proceedings of the first conference of Donne in musica (Fiuggi, Italy: September 17–21, 1996), pp. 46–47.

72. Julie Ann Sadie and Rhian Samuel, eds. *Norton/Grove Dictionary of Women Composers,* s.v. Linnet, Anne, by Inge Bruland.

73. Alicia Casares, "Women in Spanish Music, 1900–1939: An Approach to the State of Matters," paper delivered at 8° congresso internacional de Mujeres en la Música (Bilbao, Spain: March 18–22, 1992), Proceedings, pp. 101–21.

74. Many sources cite her birth year as 1923. Even her sons did not know until shortly before her death that she was born in 1908, since she had a very youthful appearance.

75. The Albaicin is the gypsy quarter in Granada, Spain.

76. *Horn and Harp Odyssey,* BIS CD-793 (1996).

77. UMMUS 102 (1990).

78. Ibid., liner notes.

79. Gema 880248–230 (1986).

80. Antje Olivier and Karin Weingartz-Perschel, eds., *Komponistinnen von A–Z* (Düsseldorf: Tokkata, 1988), pp. 296–97.

81. This piece is available in Rieger and Walter, eds., *Frauen komponieren,* p. 58.

82. Recorded on *Around the World with Tsippi Fleischer,* Vienna Modern Masters VMM2023.

83. Recorded on *Music from Six Continents,* 1991 Series, Vienna Modern Masters VMM3004.

84. Recorded on Vienna Modern Masters, VMM2023. The description by the composer is from the notes to this album.

85. Clyde Smith, notes for *Music from Six Continents,* 1992, Vienna Modern Masters VMM3013.

86. See, for example, the opening flute melody in *Mirage* (1990).

87. Ran was the second woman to win the Pulitzer Prize in music; Ellen Taaffe Zwilich had earlier won the award (in 1983) for a symphony. The second movement of Ran's work is in CAMW, pp. 260–80.

88. C. B. White, "Equilibria: Shulamit Ran Balances," *ILWC Journal* (October 1994), quoted in CAMW, p. 261.

89. Online biography from IRCAM—Centre Georges Pompidou, <http://mactextier.ircam.fr/textes/C00000915/note/html>. Gubaidulina's "Garden of Joys and Sorrows" for flute, harp, and viola is in CAMW, pp. 28–42.

90. Recorded on Chandos CHAN9523 (1997).

91. Dorothea Redepenning, "Staccato Existence," in R. Sperber, ed., *Women Composers in Germany* (Bonn: InterNationes, 1996), p. 101.

92. Online biography maintained by her publisher, Sikorski, at <http://www.sikorski.de/autoren/ustwo_ve.htm>.

93. Composer's preface, Symphony No. 5 (Hamburg: Hans Sikorski, 1993).

94. Ibid.

95. Notes for Grammofon A-B BIS-CD668 (1994), p. 9.

96. Ibid.

97. Published by G. Schirmer, 1981.

98. See Philip Hong Chan, "A Study of Marta Ptaszyńska's *Holocaust Memorial Cantata*" (D.M.A. thesis, University of Cincinnati, 1996).

99. Sikora's birth year is listed in various sources as 1944 or 1945. Her IRCAM biography says 1943.

100. Maria Anna Harley, "Composers' Corner: Notes on Polish Women Composers," *IAWM Journal* 2, #2 (June 1996): 12–15.

101. Jiri Stilec, notes for *Prague Guitar Concertos,* Supraphon CD SU3272–2 031 (1996).

102. Sylvie Bodorová, program notes for the premiere.

103. Thomas Biemel, trans. Andrea Leonhardt, "New Ways Despite Censorship: Romanian Composer Myriam Marbé," *IAWM Journal* 4, #2 (Summer 1998): 22.

104. Ibid., p. 21.

105. The Fibonacci series is a sequence of numbers in which each is the sum of the two numbers before it: 1, 1, 2, 3, 5, 8, 13, 21, etc.

106. See *The Romanian Saxophone,* Olympia OCD410 (1986).

107. Gabor Halasz, quoting Violeta Dinescu, notes for the recording *Internationales Festival Komponistinnen: Violeta Dinescu,* CPO 999016–1 (1984–1985).

108. There are a number of inconsistencies in her *Norton/Grove Dictionary of Women Composers* biography.

109. B. Sonntag and R. Matthei, eds., *Annäherung II an sieben Komponistinnen* (Kassel: Furore, 1986), p. 50.

110. Emma Lou Diemer, "Works by Violeta Dinescu Recorded on Two CDs," *IAWM Journal* 2, #1 (February 1996): 30.

111. Gabriela Lena Frank, "CD Review," *IAWM Journal* 4, #3 (Fall 1998): 36.

112. Sonntag and Matthei, eds., *Annäherung II,* pp. 20–21.

113. CAMW, p. 108.

114. Ibid., p. 51.

115. Parts of this complex score can be found on the cover and p. 107 of Sperber, ed., *Women Composers in Germany.*

116. Ibid., p. 108.

117. See, for example, her "Greek" opera *Nausicaa* (1961) and the unperformed *Sappho* (1965).

118. *Peggy Glanville-Hicks: A Modern Odyssey,* video from Juniper Films, Sydney, Australia (1991).

119. Vienna Modern Masters VMM3028 (1994).

120. The concerto is named for the people who inhabited parts of Tuscany (Italy) from ca. 700 to ca. 200 B.C.E.

121. A didjeridu is an end-blown straight natural trumpet without a separate mouthpiece, used by the Australian aborigines.

122. James Murdoch, liner notes for *The Young Kabbarli,* EMI-Australia Records, SOX LP7654 (1973).

123. For example, *Lagu Lagu Manis II* and *Indonesian Diptych,* recorded, respectively, on Vienna Modern Masters VMM3036 and VMM3031.

124. CAMW, pp. 17–19.

125. Recorded on *Music from Six Continents,* 1990 Series, Vienna Modern Masters VMM3001 (1991).

126. "Okura" is a Maori word for the fifth day of the new moon.

SUGGESTIONS FOR FURTHER READING

In addition to the items mentioned in the text or cited in the footnotes, the following sources provide information on women in modern Europe, Israel, Australia, and New Zealand.

"Alison Bauld." *Contemporary Music Review* 11 (1994): 21–22.

Antheil, George. "Peggy Glanville-Hicks." *Bulletin of the American Composers Alliance* 4, #1 (1954): 2–9.

Bebbington, Warren. *Oxford Companion to Australian Music.* Melbourne: Oxford University Press, 1997.

Beckett, Wendy. *Peggy Glanville-Hicks.* Pymble, New South Wales: Angus and Robertson, 1992.

Best, Michael. *Australian Composers and Their Music.* Adelaide: Elder Music Library Series, 1961.

Brooks, Jeanice. "The *Fonds Boulanger* at the Bibliothèque Nationale." *Notes* 51 (1994): 1227–37.

———. "*Noble et grande servante de la musique:* Telling the Story of Nadia Boulanger's Conducting Career." *Journal of Musicology* 14 (1996): 92–116.

Callaway, Frank, and David Tunley, eds. *Australian Composers in the Twentieth Century.* Melbourne: Oxford University Press, n.d.

Fleischer, Robert Jay. *Twenty Israeli Composers: Voices of a Culture.* Detroit: Wayne State University Press, 1997.

Ford, Karrin. "Jeanne Demessieux." *American Organist* 26 (April 1992): 58–64.

"Gillian Whitehead," *Contemporary Music Review* 11 (1994): 305–14.

Harley, Maria Anna. "Bacewicz, Picasso, and the Making of *Desire.*" *Journal of Musicological Research* 6 (1997): 243–81.

Hayes, Deborah. "New World Inspiration and Peggy Glanville-Hicks's Opera *Nausicaa.*" *Vistas of American Music: Essays in Honor of William K. Kearns,* ed. S. Porter and J. Graziano. Warren, MI: Harmonie Park Press, 1999.

———. *Peggy Glanville-Hicks, a Bio-Bibliography.* New York: Greenwood Press, 1990.

———. "Peggy Glanville-Hicks: A Voice from the Inner World." In Judith Lang Zaimont et al., eds., *The Musical Woman: An International Perspective,* 3: 371–409. Westport, CT: Greenwood Press, 1991.

Hanning, Herbert. "A Woman's Destiny Will Be Danced: An Interview with Violeta Dinescu." *IAWM Journal* 4, #2 (Summer 1998): 6–17.

"In memoriam Myriam Marbé (1931–1997)." *IAWM Journal* 4, #2 (Summer 1998): 21–23.

"In memoriam Tera de Marez Oyens (1932–1996)." *IAWM Journal* 3, #1 (February 1997): 3–8.

"Jennifer Fowler," *Contemporary Music Review* 11 (1994): 95–108.

Kendall, Alan. *The Tender Tyrant: Nadia Boulanger.* London: MacDonald and Jane's, 1976.

Kerr, Elizabeth. "Women Composers in New Zealand in the Nineteenth and Twentieth Centuries—An Ancient Culture and a 'Young Country'?" *Contemporary Music Review* 11 (1994): 325–32.

Kratsewsa, Iwanka. "Betsy Jolas." *Schweizerische Musikzeitung* 114 (1974): 342–49.

Libby, Cynthia Green. "Report from Sweden: The Music of Karin Rehnqvist." *Women of Note Quarterly* 7, #1 (February 1999): 1–5.

Lili and Nadia Boulanger. Special issue of *La Revue musicale* (1982).
"Marta Ptaszyńska." On-line biography at <http://www.presser.com/Ptaszyńska.html>.
McCredie, Andrew D. *Catalogue of 46 Australian Composers.* Canberra: Australian Government Printing Office, 1969.
Mitgang, Laura. "Germaine Tailleferre: Before, During, and After *Les Six.*" In Judith Lang Zaimont et al., eds., *The Musical Woman: An International Perspective,* 2: 177–221. New York: Greenwood Press, 1987.
Monsaingeon, Bruno. *Mademoiselle: Conversations with Nadia Boulanger.* Trans. Robyn Marsack. Manchester, England: Carcanet Press, 1985.
Moulder, Earline. "Rediscovering the Organ Works of Elsa Barraine." *Women of Note Quarterly* 3, #2 (May 1995): 21–29.
———. "Jewish Themes in Elsa Barraine's Second Prelude and Fugue for Organ." *Women of Note Quarterly* 3, #3 (August 1995): 22–31.
Newman, Richard, with Karen Kirtley. *Alma Rosé: Vienna to Auschwitz.* Portland, OR: Amadeus, 2000.
Norton, Kay. "Musical Emissary in America: Nadia Boulanger, Normand Lockwood, and American Musical Pedagogy." *Vistas of American Music: Essays in Honor of William K. Kearns,* ed. S. Porter and J. Graziano. Warren, MI: Harmonie Park Press, 1999.
Öhrström, Eva, and Märta Ramsten, eds. *Kvinnors Musik.* Stockholm: Sveriges Utbildningradio AB and Svenska Rikskonserter, 1989.
Philipp, Beate, et al., eds. *Komponistinnen der neuen Musik: Alice Samter, Felicitas Kukuck, Erna Woll, Ruth Bodenstein-Hoyme, Ruth Zechlin, Eva Schorr, und Siegrid Ernst: Ein Dokumentation.* Kassel: Furore, 1993.
Plaut, Linda. "Grażyna Bacewicz." *Women of Note Quarterly* 2, #3 (August 1994): 1–5.
Polin, Claire. "Interviews with Soviet Composers II: Firsova, Gubaidulina, Loudova, Smirnov." *Tempo* 151 (December 1984): 13–16.
Robinson, Suzanne. "Composers' Corner: Unmasking Peggy Glanville-Hicks." *IAWM Journal* 2, #2 (June 1996): 4–7.
Rosen, Judith. "Grażyna Bacewicz: Evolution of a Composer." In Judith Lang Zaimont et al., eds., *The Musical Woman: An International Perspective,* 1. Westport, CT: Greenwood Press, 1987.
Rosenstiel, Léonie. *The Life and Works of Lili Boulanger.* Cranbury, NJ: Fairleigh Dickinson University Press, 1978.
———. *Nadia Boulanger.* New York: Norton, 1982.
Shapiro, Robert. *Germaine Tailleferre, a Bio-bibliography.* Westport, CT: Greenwood, 1994.
Stevens, Elizabeth Mruk. "The Influence of Nadia Boulanger on Composition in the United States." D.M.A. thesis, Boston University, 1975.
Tailleferre, Germaine. "Memoires à l'emporte pièce," ed. Frédéric Robert. *Revue International de la musique française* 19 (February 1986): 6–82.
Thomas, Adrian. *Grażyna Bacewicz: Chamber and Orchestral Music.* Los Angeles: Friends of Polish Music, University of California School of Music, 1985.
Trickey, Samuel Miller. "Les Six." Ph.D. diss., North Texas State University, 1955.
Wilk, Wanda. "An Online History of Women Composers in Poland." On-line at <http://www.usc.edu/dept/polish_music/essays/womenww.html>.

Forthcoming volumes in the series *Women Composers: Music through the Ages,* ed. Sylvia Glickman and Martha Furman Schleifer (New York: G. L. Hall) will include music by Elfrida Andrée, Nadia Boulanger, Jeanne

Demessieux, Ilse Fromm-Michaels, Pauline Hall, Wanda Landowska, Helena Munktell, Margaret Sutherland, Germaine Tailleferre, and Lucie Vellère.

A number of people contributed to this chapter in various ways: Frank Pendle was research assistant and proofreader, and Melissa Blakesly was a tireless editorial assistant. The following provided information, scores, or recordings: Betty Beath, Sondra Bell, Janelle Gelfand, Darrell Handel, Robert Johnson and the University of Cincinnati Libraries, Olga Komarnitskaya, Maria-José Martin, Marta Ptaszyńska, the Swedish Music Information Center, and Vienna Modern Masters. I am grateful to all of them for their help and encouragement.

XI.
North America since 1920

J. Michele Edwards,
with contributions by Leslie Lassetter

American Voices

Ratification of the Nineteenth Amendment to the United States Constitution on August 20, 1920, marked the culmination of decades of work by women activists. However, with the right to vote secured, the intensity of collective activity among American women diminished. According to historian Sara M. Evans, "The twenties formed an era when changes long under way emerged into an urban mass culture emphasizing pleasure, consumption, sexuality, and individualism."[1] These traits were present in the popular music, e.g., jazz and the Charleston, which emerged from black culture and spread into the dominant white culture. Perhaps even the plurality of styles within American music was an outgrowth of a social context focused on individuality and diversity within American life. Consider, for example, the various piano styles represented among the following performers and composers: Lovie Austin's accompaniments for blues singers, Lil Hardin Armstrong's performances and recordings with many leading jazz artists, *From the New Hampshire Woods* by Marion Bauer, and the piano preludes of Ruth Crawford Seeger.

Marion Bauer and Mary Howe

The musical language of Marion Bauer (1882–1955) and Mary Howe (1882–1964) remained strongly rooted in the Western European harmonic tradition. Rather than followers of the Second New England School, which favored abstract instrumental forms, Bauer and Howe are descendants of

Edward MacDowell's emphasis on coloristic harmony, programmatic titles, and narrative, through-composed forms. Both women traveled in Europe during the early twentieth century, and Bauer was among the first American composers to study with Nadia Boulanger. In exchange for harmony lessons in 1906, Bauer provided English lessons to both Nadia and Lili Boulanger as well as to the daughter of Raoul Pugno, Bauer's violin teacher.

Bauer's *From the New Hampshire Woods* (1921) is firmly grounded in periodic rhythm, tertian harmony, and an integrated melodic-harmonic unit, yet it is colored with tints of impressionism. Written three years later, *Turbulence* for piano (1924) moves further away from functional tonality with more complex harmonies. Rhythmic energy, more than harmonic seduction, propels this work. Giving it a feminist reading, Ellie Hisama analyzes Bauer's Toccata from the *Four Piano Pieces* (1930) in terms of gender, sexuality, and shifting power relationships, based on the changing physical relationship of the pianist's hands.[2] Characterized in the 1920s as the work of a left-wing modernist, by the 1940s Bauer's music was viewed as conservative, yet well-crafted.

Bauer was well recognized during her lifetime with publications and many performances, including those by such prominent soloists as Ernestine Schumann-Heink (alto) and Maud Powell (violin), as well as by the New York Philharmonic under Leopold Stokowski for a 1947 performance of *Sun Splendor* (1926; orchestrated 1944?). This was the only work by a woman the Philharmonic had performed for a quarter of a century. Mary Howe's orchestral tone poem *Spring Pastoral* (1937) was originally a setting of a poem by Elinor Wylie for women's chorus. In the orchestral version, lush string writing supports the soloistic treatment of French horn and woodwinds. Howe also composed character pieces for piano as well as other orchestral tone poems, including *Dirge* (1931), *Stars* (1927?), *Sand* (1928?), and *Potomac* (1940).[3]

Both Howe and Bauer produced many of their compositions at the MacDowell Colony in Peterborough, New Hampshire. Howe spent summers there almost every year from 1927 onward. Bauer, who visited twelve times between 1919 and 1944, expressed her gratitude to Mrs. Edward MacDowell for founding "a haven where many other composers, writers, and painters have shared with me the extraordinary opportunity and privilege of doing creative work in peaceful, stimulating, and beautiful surroundings."[4] Along with a supportive atmosphere, the Colony also offered Bauer an opportunity to meet other important women composers such as Amy Beach, Ruth Crawford, and Miriam Gideon. For Howe, Bauer, and others, the MacDowell Colony was a very stimulating "room of one's own"—a necessary component for creative activity by women, according to Virginia Woolf.

Howe and Bauer also made substantial contributions to American musical life beyond composition. Howe, one of the founders of the Association of American Women Composers, was active in many artistic and philanthropic organizations. Bauer, a champion of American music, was active in many musical organizations and was frequently the only woman in a leadership position in groups that included America's most prominent composers. She was editor of the *Musical Leader*, author of many articles and five published books, and, for twenty-five years, professor of music history and composition at New York University.

Florence Price

In a self-conscious effort to find an American voice and to establish artistic independence from the Central European tradition, some composers in the 1920s and beyond cultivated musical nationalism, incorporating elements from vernacular or ethnic music. Florence Price (1887–1953)[5] had ties with the Harlem Renaissance, which sought "the elevation of the Negro folk idiom—that is, spirituals, blues, and characteristic dance music—to symphonic form. This elevation could be accomplished through the fusion of elements from the neo-romantic nationalist movement in the United States with elements from their own Afro-American cultural heritage."[6] Price was the first black woman to gain recognition as a major composer. Her Symphony in E Minor (1931) was among the earliest by an African American to be performed by a major orchestra, receiving its premiere at Chicago's World's Fair Century of Progress Exhibition concert in the Auditorium Theatre (not at Orchestra Hall). While this symphony does not quote preexisting tunes, it promotes racial pride and awareness. It uses various Afro-American characteristics: incorporating a pentatonic scale, call-and-response, syncopated rhythm, altered tones (or "blue notes"), and timbral stratification, as well as the more obvious inclusion of a juba dance (in the third movement) and African drums (especially prominent in the second movement). Similar characteristics are found in many of Price's art songs, piano pieces, organ music, and the Piano Concerto in One Movement (1933–1934).

G. Wiley Smith

G. Wiley Smith (b. 1946), an active flutist and teacher as well as a composer, grew up in Sapulpa, Oklahoma, and received her bachelor's and master's degrees from the University of Central Oklahoma in Edmond, Oklahoma, where she is currently professor of flute. A member of the Muskogee Creek Nation, Smith is also active in the Indian Education Program in the

Edmond Public Schools. She has performed her music at the Indian Education Exposition in Norman, the Red Earth Artist Presentation, and the Seminole Nation Student Honor Reception. Smith's music preserves the sounds of traditional Native American flute playing while adding contemporary influences from her training as a Western flutist. The style of the opening and closing sections of *Whisper on the Land* for Western flute and piano is especially reminiscent of Native American flute playing. Smith says about this work, written to honor her father:

> The piece reflects Native American music and is particularly reminiscent of the native flute. There gradually begins a battle between the cultures as more and more contemporary Western influences are introduced.
>
> This conflict, which many generations of Native Americans have experienced, continues today. I personally have lived with many conflicting values and traditions. Although the Indian culture has all but been eliminated, it still remains a "whisper," as heard in the closing measures.[7]

Smith's composition *Legende,* like *Whisper on the Land,* shows respect for the land as an important cultural value for her people, the Creek Nation. Smith offers the following description of *Legende,* written for alto flute (or flute) solo:

> Whether passing information by spoken words, through paintings, or through music, Indians are natural storytellers. The story of *Legende* begins near water where an Indian flutist begins to describe the nearby scenery. The teller continues, reflecting on cultural heritage. One can imagine the wealth of proud experience from which the story unravels and fades in quiet melancholy.[8]

Depicting the American Scene

Works by white composers also included the experiences and music of African Americans. Mary Howe's *Chain Gang Song* (1925) for chorus and orchestra (originally for piano) was her first major composition to be performed publicly. It incorporates three tunes sung by a crew of black prisoners in the mountains of western North Carolina. In her autobiography, *Jottings,* Howe describes the experience that prompted this composition:

> [I was] rounding a bend on horseback . . . and coming on a gang of twenty or so black convicts in striped clothes . . . iron ball and chain on many feet, and they sang while they drilled the hole for the dynamite charge. One man held and aimed the iron drill, and two more slugged at it with heavy shoulder weight iron hammers, rhythmically, so the three could know inevitably when the hammer blows would fall.[9]

White composers from other regions of the United States also participated in the American music movement through conscious inclusion of American themes in musical materials. Two Texans, Julia Smith (1911–1989) and Radie Britain (1899–1994), incorporated musical idioms typical of the rural West and Southwest—hoedowns, songs of the rodeo and range, Spanish-American elements, and desert themes. Smith's *American Dance Suite* (1936, rev. 1963), an orchestral work, sets folk tunes; it was later arranged for two pianos (1957, rev. 1966).[10] *Cynthia Parker* (premiered 1939), an opera based on the fascinating and tragic story of a young white girl lovingly raised by Comanches and forcibly "repatriated" by whites, quotes Native American melodies. The descriptive titles of several of Britain's works for orchestra bring to life her native Texas: for example, *Drouth* (1939, also for piano); *Red Clay* (1946, later versions for piano and a ballet), which employs Indian rhythms; *Cactus Rhapsody* (1953, also for piano; 1965 arr. for two pianos; 1977 arr. for trio); and *Cowboy Rhapsody* (1956). Spanish-American rhythms are prominent in *Rhumbando* (1975) for wind ensemble.

Mary Carr Moore (1873–1957), active as an organizer of several societies to promote American music, employed materials from the Northwest and California, areas in which she spent most of her adult life. Two of her operas, *Narcissa* (1909–1911) and *The Flaming Arrow* (1919–1920), make extensive use of American themes and Native American materials. Moore and her mother, who prepared these librettos, worked hard to understand Native Americans—their music, their culture, and the shameful ways in which white Americans had treated them. *Narcissa,* based on the 1847 massacre of missionaries Marcus and Narcissa Whitman in the Pacific Northwest, is original in presenting the drama through a woman's eyes. Both dramatically and musically, Narcissa's character is the most fully and deeply drawn within the opera. In Moore's opera *David Rizzio* (1927–1928), another strong woman is the focus: Mary, Queen of Scots.

American Experimental Music

Ruth Crawford Seeger

Ruth Crawford Seeger (1901–1953) took a different yet thoroughly American path: on the surface she separated her compositional activity from her work with folk materials. Yet as Judith Tick demonstrates, Crawford Seeger wove together the strands of her multifaceted careers with a process of "cultural mediation."[11]

FIGURE 11.1. Ruth Crawford Seeger sings folk songs with children at a cooperative nursery school in Silver Spring, Maryland, ca. 1941–1942. Photo courtesy of Michael Seeger and the Estate of Ruth Crawford Seeger.

> Because she [Crawford Seeger] remained first and foremost a composer, no matter what she did, all of her various activities as transcriber, editor, and arranger of folk materials reflected that sensibility. I began to see how she understood tradition through a modernist perspective, finding affinities that linked the very old with the very new. An ideology of opposition pervaded her work. Just as modernism flouted conventional practice, so did tradition. Just as modernism rejected Romantic excess, so did tradition. Decoding the ways opposition as a value informed her musical choices integrated the two parts of her musical identity.[12]

The ambiguities and tensions between the "stratosphere" of classical music and the "solid well-traveled highway" of folk song—as Crawford described them in a 1948 letter—were real but not insurmountable for this experimental composer, wife, mother of four children, transcriber and arranger of folk music, piano teacher, and music educator. During the late 1920s and early 1930s Crawford was one of the most innovative, ultramodern American composers, along with Henry Cowell, Edgard Varèse, and Carl Ruggles. Then, from the mid-1930s she concentrated on folk music, setting high standards of transcription with her work from field recordings. She worked with Alan and John Lomax, transcribing American folk songs found at the Library of Congress (*Our Singing Country,* 1941); created piano arrangements and accompaniments for folk songs (*Folk Song U.S.A.,* 1947, with the Lomaxes and Charles Seeger); and compiled and edited materials for children (*American Folk Songs for Children,* 1948; *Animal Folk Songs for Children,* 1950; *American Folk Songs for Christmas,* 1953). In one composition Crawford did utilize folk melodies: *Rissolty, Rossolty* (1939) was written for a radio series on folk music, and it was her only concert piece composed between the birth of her first child in 1933 and her final composition, Suite for Wind Quintet (1952). Carrying on her legacy, two of Crawford's children, Michael and Peggy, became professional folk singers.[13]

Crawford's compositions from the 1920s show influences from Scriabin's music, which she had studied with Djane Lavoie-Herz, her piano teacher and a Scriabin disciple. In nine preludes for piano, written between 1924 and 1928 (see HAMW, pp. 271–75 for Prelude No. 2), Crawford's use of melodic cells, dissonance, and irregular phrasing forecast her later stylistic directions. Suite for Five Wind Instruments and Piano (1927, revised 1929), an intense and dramatic work, is rhapsodic, presenting divergent musical ideas and a wide emotional spectrum. Crawford's demanding piano writing suggests her technical skill as a pianist and demonstrates her understanding of the piano's expressive capabilities.

Crawford's eight years of study in Chicago offered many opportunities for an emerging composer: participation in the new music circle that gathered at Madame Herz's salons, acquaintanceship with Carl Sandburg, and, perhaps of greatest impact, her professional relationship with Henry Cowell. Cowell published several of Crawford's works in his influential series, *New Music.* He is also credited with arranging her move to New York in 1929 and her year of study with Charles Seeger, whom she later married.

From 1930 Crawford's compositions realized in sound the ideas and theories that Charles Seeger articulated primarily with words. He called for a procedure that would reverse or negate tonal organization to allow greater importance for nonpitch parameters. Crawford first cultivated this approach, called dissonant counterpoint, in four *Diaphonic Suites* for one and two instruments and in *Piano Study in Mixed Accents,* all composed in 1930. Employing Seeger's principles, Crawford created independent musical lines, described by Seeger as "'sounding apart' rather than 'sounding together'—diaphony rather than symphony."[14] Her innovative structures employed an economy of melodic material to create organic wholes; elevated the importance of rhythm, dynamics, accent, and timbre; and enacted a role reversal between consonance and dissonance. In parameters other than pitch, Crawford and Seeger defined dissonance (or "dissonating") as the avoidance of patterns established through repetition and predictability.

Crawford used a serial rotation with a ten-note set in the fourth movement of String Quartet 1931 (see HAMW, pp. 285–90 for the third and fourth movements), coupled with a layered pattern of long-range dynamics and a palindrome structure. Dynamics are also the primary organizing element in the third movement, which Crawford described as a "heterophony of dynamics."[15] String Quartet 1931, which she considered her most representative work, was composed during the productive year she spent in Europe on a Guggenheim Fellowship, the first ever awarded to a woman.

Three Songs (1930–1932), for contralto, oboe, piano, and percussion (see HAMW, pp. 276–84 for "Rat Riddles"), is one of Crawford's most innovative works and employs experimental techniques that only decades later became widely used. In addition to her continued use of dissonant counterpoint and palindromic structures that govern the rhythm and dynamics, Crawford's compositional techniques include vocal performance in "somewhat (though not too much) of the 'sprechstimme' mode of execution"[16] for the declamatory vocal line; tone clusters in the piano part; and optional instrumental ostinatos spatially separated from the primary performers. The level of independence among the four *concertanti* performers is remarkable, yet Crawford created an expressive musical whole consistent with the poems by Carl Sandburg that she set.[17]

Vivian Fine

Vivian Fine (1913–2000) continued in the experimental vein of her first theory teacher, Ruth Crawford. Fine studied with Crawford for four years, beginning at age twelve, and began composing at thirteen. *Four Pieces for Two Flutes* (1930) and *Four Songs* for voice and string quartet (1933) show an affinity with compositions by Crawford. In each of these early works Fine skillfully employs dissonant counterpoint. The third song, "She Weeps over Rahoon," involves carefully planned serialized pitch sets that are not related to twelve-tone technique. According to Steven Gilbert, this song "shows a remarkable degree of pitch and timbral control—this in addition to its being a very moving piece."[18]

Fine, an accomplished concert pianist, received a scholarship to study piano at Chicago Musical College with Djane Lavoie-Herz, one of Crawford's teachers, when she was only five years old. In 1931 she moved to New York to begin her career. In addition to premiering much new music, she earned her living as a dance accompanist. Her experience and success in this area led to collaborations with many leading modern dancer-choreographers, including Doris Humphrey, Charles Weidman, Hanya Holm, and Martha Graham. Between 1937 and 1944, when Fine was most actively composing for dance, her writing moderated to display a more diatonic style, as in *The Race of Life* (1937), a humorous and popular ballet score, and *Concertante* for piano and orchestra (1944).[19] Fine identified this move toward tonal writing as an influence from her study with Roger Sessions, as well as a partial response to changing social conditions and a desire to communicate with listeners. Subsequent scores returned to atonality but with less sharp dissonances and an expanded expressive range. In the fourth movement of a 1960 ballet score, *Alcestis* (see HAMW, pp. 347–54), a prominent melodic motive rises in a succession of perfect fourths. Here an intervallic consistency and a rhythmic motive (a fanfare-like triplet) replace the hierarchical structure of tonality in providing unity to the composition. *After the Tradition* (1988), commissioned and premiered by the Bay Area Women's Philharmonic in celebration of Fine's seventy-fifth birthday, honors her Jewish origins, although the composer calls this a nonreligious work. The first movement is a Kaddish in memory of cellist George Finkel; the second movement takes its title ("My Heart's in the East and I at the End of the West") from Yehuda Ha-Levi, a twelfth-century Spanish poet; and the final movement exhibits much vitality.

Several of Fine's compositions highlight feminist issues: for example, *Meeting for Equal Rights 1866* (1976) and the chamber opera *The Women in the Garden* (1977). *Meeting,* for chorus, soloists, narrator, and orchestra, sets excerpts from nineteenth-century debates on women's suffrage. Although the work is highly complex (it requires three conductors), it still received favorable audience response. One reviewer described it as

> a stirring and timely piece devoted to the unhappily still struggling cause of Equal Rights. Taking a feminist viewpoint that is full of righteous rage—which is understandable—and compassion—which is more important—*Meeting for Equal Rights 1866* . . . augments and dramatizes the conflicts and hopes of countless generations.[20]

Fine's libretto for *The Women in the Garden* brings together on stage Emily Dickinson, Isadora Duncan, Gertrude Stein, and Virginia Woolf (quoting from their writings) to create an evocative drama through their interaction.

After her retirement from Bennington College in 1987, Fine remained an active composer and generally wrote on commission. The following works suggest the variety of mediums for which she composed and exemplify the importance of lush string sound in Fine's compositions: *Asphodel* (1988) for soprano and chamber ensemble; *Madrigali Spirituali* (1989) for trumpet and string quartet (revised for string orchestra in 1990); *Portal* for violin and piano; *Songs and Arias* for French horn, violin, and cello; *Hymns* (premiered in 1992 for two pianos, cello, and French horn); and the chamber opera

Memoirs of Uliana Rooney (1992–1994). Fashioned as a newsreel and including film sequences, *Memoirs* traces the long life of a woman composer who changes husbands several times as her musical style changes. In this chamber opera, which quotes extensively from her own earlier scores, Fine brings humor and satire to a feminist work.

Serial Music

Many American men composers who reached prominence before World War II produced at least some serial compositions during the postwar years (e.g., Roger Sessions, Arthur Berger, and Aaron Copland), and many men composers of the mid-1950s and 1960s established their reputations using serial procedures (e.g., Milton Babbitt, Charles Wuorinen). In composer Jacob Druckman's assessment, "not being a serialist on the East Coast of the United States in the sixties was like not being a Catholic in Rome in the thirteenth century. It was the respectable thing to do, at least once."[21] However, as the twentieth century waned, many composers who began as serialists abandoned this process, and few young composers now take up this approach.

Louise Talma

Louise Talma (1906–1996) was among the composers who shifted to the path of twelve-tone writing.[22] Talma, whose early compositions were neoclassical and tonal, first adopted twelve-tone serialism in *Six Etudes* (1953–1954). In a general way, she perhaps took her cue from Igor Stravinsky's gradual incorporation of twelve-tone procedures after the death of Arnold Schoenberg (1874–1951). As a long-time student of Nadia Boulanger and as the first American to teach at Boulanger's Fontainebleau School in France (1936–1939), Talma was strongly influenced by Stravinsky's music. Like Stravinsky's twelve-tone works, Talma's music retains tonal qualities, and serialism is absorbed as an additional unifying factor. Further, Talma indicates she was influenced by Irving Fine's handling of twelve-tone materials in his String Quartet, composed in 1952, the same year that Stravinsky made his first move toward serialism in *Cantata*. Stylistically, music by Talma and Stravinsky share other common elements: melodies created from short motives, establishment of tonal centers by assertion, nonfunctional harmony, ostinatos, and shifting accents.

Initially, Talma's handling of the row was quite strict. After *The Alcestiad* (1955–1958), an opera written in collaboration with Thornton Wilder, her approach to twelve-tone ordering procedures became increasingly flexible, and her music often exhibited focus through an emphasis on subsets, intersecting rows, and combinatoriality. She utilized this process in various mediums: the choral work *La Corona* (1954–1955; see HAMW, pp. 321–32), *The Alcestiad*, and *Textures* (1977) for piano. Typical of the writing in her late style, she based *Seven Episodes* for flute, viola, and piano (1987) on a twelve-tone row, yet also employed traditional tonal relationships. In an analysis of *The Tolling Bell* (a cantata for baritone and orchestra, 1967–1969) Elaine Barkin concluded that:

> Although the work may indeed be "freely serial" [Talma's description], it is not casual, not "indeterminate"; very carefully determined junctures are articulated, critical constraints have been imposed upon all dimensions of the work at "initiating moments" and "points of arrival," the text-music associations are quite clear—neither overstated nor concealed.[23]

The text of *Have You Heard? Do You Know?* (1974–1980), like the libretto for *The Alcestiad,* offers ample opportunity to critique gender stereotypes and to raise larger feminist issues. During its seven scenes, we meet Della and Fred (a white, middle-class, suburban couple) and their neighbor Mildred. Analogous musical treatment for Fred's concern about the ups and downs of the stock market and Della's similarly moving hemlines gives parity to traditional male and female experiences. Their desire for a "quiet place" is also handled nonhierarchically, with closely related music. However, the work as a whole reinforces gender stereotypes, seems uncritical of the emptiness of the characters' conversations, and glorifies the desire for material things. Accompanied by a mixed chamber ensemble, *Have You Heard?* returns stylistically to neoclassicism with melodic recurrence, tonal referents, and ostinatos reminiscent of Stravinsky.

Joan Tower

Before 1974, the music of Joan Tower (b. 1938) employed various serial procedures. *Prelude for Five Players* (1970) opens with twelve pitch classes, subsequently handled as an unordered aggregate. According to Tower, Prelude "is divided into six sections which are differentiated by changes in tempo, texture, register and dynamics which, for the most part, are associated with various hierarchizations of the twelve-tone set structure."[24] During the early 1970s Tower gradually moved away from serial procedures: *Hexachords* for flute (1972) is based on a six-tone, unordered chromatic series, and *Breakfast Rhythms I* and *II* for clarinet and five instruments (1974–1975) complete the shift. Many of the works that follow are more lyrical and accessible, carrying image-related titles to "open a tiny window into the piece"[25] for audiences. For example, *Amazon I* (1977) reflects on the almost constant flow and motion of the music and the Brazilian river; *Wings* (1981) draws on the flight patterns of a large bird, paralleled in the hovering and swooping lines of the solo clarinet; and *Night Fields* (1994) has a title selected to provide a setting consistent with some of the moods of this string quartet. Tower rarely begins with a title or image, but rather allows the title to emerge from events and gestures in the music. Her music is often characterized by vivid orchestration and energetic rhythms, which Tower attributes to eight years of growing up in Bolivia, Chile, and Peru. After focusing on sonority during the 1970s, Tower gave more attention to rhythmic aspects of music in the 1980s. *Petroushkates* (1980), for example, not only quotes from Stravinsky's ballet but paraphrases the very fabric of his score, much in the manner of a sixteenth-century parody Mass.

Tower's early works were primarily chamber music, and many were composed for the Da Capo Chamber Players, which she founded in 1969 and in which she performed as pianist for fifteen years. In 1981 the American Composers Orchestra under Dennis Russell Davies presented the premiere of *Sequoia* (1979–1981), a commission by the Jerome Foundation. It was subsequently performed by the San Francisco Symphony under Davies, by the New York Philharmonic under Zubin Mehta, and by several major orchestras under Leonard Slatkin. After the St. Louis Symphony (directed by Slatkin) recorded *Sequoia* in 1984—the first of several recordings of her compositions—Tower was named composer-in-residence with this orchestra (1985–1988).[26] Her increased visibility since 1981 demonstrates the career importance of writing symphonic works that receive performances by major orchestras led by established conductors. Since the success of *Sequoia,* her first orchestral composition, Tower has focused on this arena in such works as *Music for Cello and Orchestra* (1984); concertos for piano (*Homage to Beethoven,* 1985), flute (1989), and violin (1992); *Concerto for Orchestra,* a joint commission with premieres in 1991 (St. Louis), 1992 (Chicago), and 1994 (New York); and *Duets* (1994), premiered by the Los Angeles Chamber Orchestra in 1995. Tower won the 1990 Grawemeyer Award, a $150,000 prize for a large orchestral work, *Silver Ladders* (1986). Tower's *Fanfare for the Uncommon Woman* (1986) began as a tribute to Aaron Copland and is now generally perceived to be a feminist response to his *Fanfare for the Common Man.* In less than a decade its popularity spawned four additional fanfares, including one for the centennial of Carnegie Hall (No. 3, premiered by the New York Philharmonic in 1991). By 1997 more than two hundred ensembles had performed the first fanfare. According to Tower, the series of fanfares aims "to honor women who are adventurous and take risks."[27] In May 1998 Tower herself was honored with induction into the American Academy of Arts and Letters for her outstanding achievements in music.

Barbara Kolb

Barbara Kolb's (b. 1939) handling of serial techniques in *Appello* (1976) for piano shows how a personal style can emerge from this compositional procedure. Each of the four movements of *Appello* is based on a series from Book 1a of Pierre Boulez's *Structures* (1952), and the third movement "involves a strict time-point organization for control of the rhythmic acceleration that progresses throughout the movement."[28] *Appello,* however, stands in sharp contrast to Boulez's *Structures.* Kolb's composition is a rich, often dense, expressive work in comparison to the sparsely pointillistic *Structures.* Kolb integrates serialism into a larger stylistic repertoire that combines the performer's freedom (in dynamics, pedaling, and indeterminate clusters) with the composer's control. As in many of Kolb's compositions, texture and timbre in *Appello* remain extremely important expressive means. Her choice of title, which means "call" in Italian, and the poetic references at the beginning of each movement suggest a focus on expressive import, while Boulez's title and subdivisions are pointedly abstract. According to Kolb, each movement is a different call—one that is "reaching and enticing, rather than insistent or demanding."[29]

Sound-Mass

During the first several decades of the twentieth century the domination of music by functional tonality was challenged in a number of ways. Initially these procedures preserved pitch as the foreground compositional element, but gradually compositions refocused attention on other parameters. Sound-mass minimizes the importance of individual pitches in preference for texture, timbre, and dynamics as primary shapers of gesture and impact. As part of the exploration and expansion of sonic materials, sound-mass obscures the boundary between sound and noise. Emerging from tone clusters in piano works of American experimentalists in the early twentieth century, sound-mass moved into orchestral composition most noticeably by the late 1950s and 1960s. Many works that involve sound-mass also include other aspects of sonic exploration, such as the extensive use of muted brass or strings, flutter tonguing, wide vibrato, extreme ranges (especially highs), and glissandos (a form of microtonal writing). Early choral explorations of sound-mass occur in *Sound Patterns* (1961) by Pauline Oliveros and *From Dreams of Brass* (1963–1964) by Canadian composer Norma Beecroft (b. 1934). Beecroft blurs individual pitches in favor of a collective timbre through the use of vocal and instrumental clusters, choral speech, narrator, and a wash of sounds from an electronic tape. Both Barbara Kolb and Nancy Van de Vate have written compositions that rely heavily on sound-mass; however, their compositions also include an array of sources melded into personal stylistic syntheses.

Barbara Kolb

Continuing the American experimental tradition, Kolb has focused her more recent compositional activity on unconventional ensembles as much as on unorthodox styles. Although she has written for solo piano (*Appello,* see above) and occasionally for full orchestra, many of her compositions are for nontraditional chamber ensembles, some with voice. She has also created a series of works combining prerecorded (nonelectronic) sounds with various instruments: for example, *Spring River Flowers Moon Night* (1974–1975), for two live pianists and a tape that involves an unusual group—mandolin, guitar, chimes, vibraphone, marimba, and percussion; *Looking for Claudio* (1975), with guitar and tape of mandolin, six guitars, vibraphone, chimes, and three human voices. Stylistically, both her stimuli and her creations are diverse. *Three Place Settings* (1968) offers unusual wit and humor in a three-movement work for violin, clarinet, string bass, percussion, and narrator; *Trobar Clus, to Lukas* (1970) borrows a repeating structure from the eleventh or twelfth century; *Solitaire* (1971) uses quotations from Chopin; *Homage to Keith Jarrett and Gary Burton* (1976) draws on jazz and improvisation; *Cantico* (1982) is a tape collage for a film about St. Francis of Assisi; and *Millefoglie* (1984–1985)[30] combines computer-generated tape with chamber orchestra.

In *Crosswinds* for wind ensemble (1968) Kolb makes extensive use of sound-mass as she explores the metaphorically loaded title. The work unfolds after the opening segment presents the principal gestures of the whole. Relatively stable blocks of sound (later with more flutter and motion) alternate with soloistic lines suggesting chamber music. The use of mutes creates greater unity between brass and woodwind timbres, contributing to the indistinct plurality of the sound-mass and highlighting timbre and density as the primary compositional elements. The release after the first major climax exposes a single saxophone, reminiscent of the opening bassoon solo in Stravinsky's *The Rite of Spring.* Here again Kolb writes for an ensemble outside the musical establishment.

During the 1990s Kolb has composed more frequently for larger ensemble, and her style is sometimes more accessible—a shift common to many composers in the United States. In *Voyants for Piano and Chamber Orchestra,* premiered by Radio France in 1991 and subsequently revised and expanded for publication, Kolb creates a musical narrative with the piano functioning as the seer or prophet mentioned in the title.[31] *All in Good Time,* commissioned for the 150th anniversary of the New York Philharmonic in 1994, was premiered under the baton of Leonard Slatkin, who has led subsequent performances with major orchestras. Texture and timbre remain important elements, along with rhythmic development and a hint of jazz, especially apparent in the central section for saxophone solo decorated by vibraphone and bass clarinet. Coupled with minimalism, jazz elements are more apparent in the ballet score *New York Moonglow* (1995), premiered by jazz notable Lew Tabackin on tenor sax and flute, along with five other musicians. Kolb's dense textures in the outer sections were supported by multilayered choreography, and Tabackin's improvised solo was matched by choreographer-dancer Elisa Monte's own improvisation. Music for the ensemble is fully notated, whereas Tabackin's part is both notated and left to improvisation.

Nancy Van de Vate

Nancy Van de Vate (b. 1930), whose catalogue is large and varied, has pursued an active career as a composer, educator, and promoter of contemporary music. In the mid-1950s she redirected her plans to be a professional pianist when she moved to Oxford, Mississippi, with her husband and child. She felt performance opportunities were limited there and that she could not commit to the necessary daily routine of practice: "I changed to composition, then became so totally engrossed in it that I never again wished to direct the major part of my time and energy to any other aspect of music."[32] Van de Vate taught piano privately and then at several colleges and universities throughout the southern United States and in Hawaii. After leading the Southeastern Composers League for a decade, she founded the League of Women Composers in 1975 (renamed the International League of Women Composers in 1979) and served as its chair for seven years. While living in Hawaii and then in Indonesia for nearly four years (1982–1985), Van de Vate developed an enthusiasm for Asian musics, which can be heard in the colorful orchestrations of works such as *Journeys* (1981–1984) and *Pura Besakih* (Besakih Temple, Bali; 1987). In addition to massive textures, *Journeys* combines minimalist aspects, a melodic focus of the soloists' lines, extended string sonorities, an enlarged percussion battery (especially mallet instruments), and the development of motivic material (C, B, C, D^b). Like Kolb, Van de Vate integrates many different techniques and styles. Van de Vate, who in 1985 took up residence in Vienna, Austria, has expressed a desire to communicate with a broad public and has worked toward this not only in her compositions but also through her involvement as artistic director for Vienna Modern Masters, a recording company that produces an extensive catalog of contemporary music.[33]

Chernobyl (1987)[34] and Concerto No. 2 for Violin and Orchestra (1996) are among Van de Vate's works for orchestra that utilize sound-mass. According to Van de Vate, *Chernobyl* was written "to express universal feelings about that event [an explosion at the Soviet nuclear power plant at Chernobyl] and its meanings for all peoples. . . . [It] is not intended to tell a story, but rather to evoke images and feelings."[35] The first half of the composition layers coloristic, dense, static clusters; the second half is more diatonic and conventional in the treatment of harmony, rhythm, and melody. A descending minor second, which Van de Vate calls a "weeping motif," is prominent during the second section. It evokes the closing of the Revolution Scene in Modest Mussorgsky's *Boris Godunov,* where a similar string figure of repeated pairs frames the short conclusion sung by the Simpleton. In a prophetic lament, the Simpleton, alone on stage, warns of the impending disaster of war for the Russians. The affinity between these musical gestures is strengthened through the similarity of timbre, rhythm, pace, and range along with contextual links: the setting in Russia and the potential devastation. Van de Vate's Violin Concerto is a virtuosic work based on a symmetrical four-note cell (G, A♭, B♭, C♭) and reveals much contrast within the unified one-movement form. During the late 1990s Van de Vate has concentrated her compositional activities on opera, another large form.

In addition to her commitment to large-scale works, Van de Vate has composed for other mediums. Two trios offer considerable contrast with the orchestral works just discussed: *Music for Viola, Percussion and Piano* (1976) and *Trio for Bassoon, Percussion and Piano* (1980, rev. 1982). Timbre remains an important compositional consideration—occasional clusters occur in the piano parts, the bassoon's upper range is explored, and percussion batteries add coloristic elements. However, tuneful melodies and periodic metrical organization also play important roles, and texture is not a primary component.

Reshaping Traditions

Julia Perry

Julia Perry's extensive catalogue reveals her familiarity with two worlds: the vernacular music of her African-American heritage and Western (neo)classical practices. Born in 1924, Perry linked her early works with their roots in spirituals and blues to the rural past of a colonized people (e.g., the vocal solo "Free at Last" [pub. 1951] and Prelude for Piano [1946, rev. 1962]).[36] During the 1950s, while Perry lived in Europe, she abandoned the outward signs of African-American identity and shifted her artistic attention to European models, especially that of her teacher, Luigi Dallapiccola. Perry avoided the twelve-tone system but followed Dallapiccola's focus on motivic unity and the transformation of small melodic cells, using them as her central organizing principles (e.g., in *Short Piece* [1952, reorchestrated in 1962 and 1965] and Symphony No. 1 for violas and double basses [1961]).

With growing racial awareness emerging from the Civil Rights struggles of the 1960s, Perry returned to a focus on conspicuous issues of the black experience, transformed and reshaped to reflect her social reality. Contemporary urban referents are found in her programmatic titles and in the incorporation of rock 'n' roll and rhythm and blues styles. In the explicit racial components of *Bicentennial Reflections* (1977) for tenor and six instrumentalists, for example, she draws the audience's attention to race with visual and textual elements, which seem to be supported by the musical gestures. For example, Perry's manuscript prescribes that the three percussionists should be an "American Negro (dark complexion)," a "Chinese American," and an "American-Aryan or Jew." In the closing moments of this piece the percussion parts suggest the potential for violence and self-destruction in U.S. race relations, following the final line of text: "By the fountain of dreams flowing in red."

Hailed as an individual of great promise, Perry was favorably recognized during her twenties with major awards, international study opportunities, publications, and favorable reviews. The 1960s, perhaps her most productive decade in terms of the quantity of large-scale compositions, brought Perry distribution of her music by established publishers and the release of three works on separate recordings by CRI. Although she had some major performances, including one by the New York Philharmonic, her public visibility and press coverage seem to have diminished. Sometime during the 1960s Perry developed serious physical health problems including acromegaly and later, probably in 1971, was struck by another grave tragedy: a paralytic stroke affecting her right side. Although she learned to write with her left hand and continued to compose, she lived her last years in seclusion and with diminished ability to work.

Ellen Taaffe Zwilich

In the midst of much experimentation and a proliferation of styles in the late twentieth century, the music of Ellen Taaffe Zwilich (b. 1939) continues the American symphonic tradition, with ties to neoclassicism and the great American symphonists of the 1930s and 1940s. Zwilich updates this tradition, yet she retains a primary focus on pitch, relies on recurring and predictable patterns, and employs developmental forms. Discussions of her music frequently mention both her craft and the music's appeal to concert audiences and musicians. Although handled conventionally, Zwilich's orchestration is often vivid, as heard in *Celebration for Orchestra* (1984), and her string writing virtuosic, as in *Prologue and Variations* for string orchestra (1983). Describing her recent works, K. Robert Schwarz wrote that Zwilich's "music has become increasingly tonal and consonant. Today it is neo-Classic in concision but neo-Romantic in intensity."[37]

After completing a master's degree in composition at Florida State University, Zwilich moved to New York and worked as a freelance violinist. A year later, in 1965, she began a seven-year tenure with the American Symphony Orchestra, gaining important experience for her compositional activity. In 1975 she became the first woman awarded a doctorate in composition from Juilliard, where she studied with Roger Sessions and Elliott Carter, the most important influences on her music. Zwilich has developed a high-profile career with numerous commissions from large, prestigious musical institutions and performers. In 1995 she became the first appointee to the Carnegie Hall Composer's Chair.

In 1983 Zwilich won the Pulitzer Prize for music for her Symphony No. 1 (1982), becoming the first woman to receive this important recognition. The first movement of Symphony No. 1 (see HAMW, pp. 377–401), an organic elaboration of the initial fifteen measures, establishes tonal stability through motivic reiteration, decorated tertian harmony, and pedal points. The intervallic persistence of thirds (especially minor thirds) also contributes to its coherence. String Trio (1982), written at the same time, is noticeably more angular, abstract, dissonant, and virtuosic. A similar contrast between a large-scale public work and a more intimate composition is also apparent in a comparison between *Symbolon* (1988) for full orchestra and *Double Quartet* (1984) for two string quartets. *Symbolon* unfolds in broad, simple gestures, in contrast to the darker, more intense *Double Quartet,* which explores the concept of duality. Tension between D minor and D major persists until the final moments of the work, when D major is finally confirmed.

Since the mid-1980s Zwilich has created a substantial series of concertos, both for the standard instruments (piano in 1986; the Triple Concerto for piano, violin, and cello in 1995; violin in 1997) and for instruments infrequently featured as soloists with major symphonies (trombone in 1988; bass trombone, strings, timpani, and cymbals in 1989; flute in 1989; oboe in 1990; bassoon in 1992; French horn in 1993). According to Zwilich,

> the concerto is an inherently dramatic situation with many analogies to the theatre. For instance, a soloist (protagonist) may have a cadenza (soliloquy) in which to voice his or her essential nature, but the full development of a character requires a dialogue with other strong characters. For this reason, I very much enjoy choosing a special orchestration for a particular solo instrument, aiming for strong but complementary orchestral forces.[38]

Her approach to the solo writing has been to work closely with each of the soloists—often prominent performers—who would premiere these works in an effort to combine virtuosity and idiomatic capabilities of each instrument and performer.

Libby Larsen

In the past twenty years, Libby Larsen (b. 1950) has become one of the most important and successful composers in the United States, with works for orchestra, dance, opera, chorus, theater, chamber ensembles, and soloists. Larsen, whose works are widely written about and commercially recorded, studied at the University of Minnesota with Dominick Argento and co-founded the Minnesota Composers Forum (now the American Composers Forum) in 1973. In addition to giving many performances throughout the United States and Europe, Larsen has served as composer-in-residence with the Minnesota Orchestra (1983–1987) and with a consortium of musical organizations in Denver, including the Colorado Symphony Orchestra (1997–1999). She won a 1994 Grammy for the CD *The Art of Arleen Augér* on which Larsen's song cycle *Sonnets from the Portuguese* (1989) for soprano and chamber ensemble is featured.[39] Larsen, who claims Gregorian chant, rock 'n' roll, stride boogie piano, and music from radio and television are all among her musical influences, has frequently sought to update the traditions and sounds of the concert hall through the inclusion of vernacular music. For example, in *Ghosts of an Old Ceremony* (1991) for orchestra and dance, written in collaboration with choreographer Brenda Way, Larsen focuses on migration, from the physical westward movement of American pioneer women to the migration of sound between the early 1800s and the late twentieth century. This composition not only challenges the expectations of orchestral players and audiences, but it also contests stereotypic, romanticized views of westward expansion and brings to attention the particular hardships and losses faced by these courageous women. According to Larsen,

> Sound, and the groups of musicians who represent it, have migrated as surely and strongly as all the other aspects of our culture. Sound, which began in monodirectional presentation in the concert hall, is now heard mixed through

> speakers coming from multi-directions. Noise has migrated into the domain of musical sound by means of the sampler. At the end of the 1800s, sound was dominated by the high registers of the violin sections. Throughout this century sound has relocated to the bass . . . with the proliferation of speakers, electric basses, electric drums and digital mixing.[40]

The dancers take center stage, while members of the orchestra perform from both sides of the stage, the side tiers, and the back of the hall. Some of the musicians remain in place, others relocate, and some disappear amid sounds that range from an old hymn tune to readings from diaries of pioneer women to electronic music.[41] *Piano Concerto: "Since Armstrong"* (1990), premiered in 1991 by pianist Janina Fialkowska and the Minnesota Orchestra, is another example of Larsen's blending of styles. She describes this piece as a dinner party whose guests include Louis Armstrong, Maurice Ravel, Igor Stravinsky, Arnold Schoenberg, Jelly Roll Morton, and blues guitarist Robert Lockwood.

In a 1996 interview Larsen discussed the importance of rhythm for her style: "I believe that music springs from language of the people. I am intensely interested in how music can be derived from the rhythms and pitches of spoken American English."[42] Although applicable for all mediums, this approach is especially relevant for her vocal and choral works, many of which are settings of texts by women or about strong females. Some examples include *The Settling Years* (1988) for mixed chorus, woodwind quintet, and piano;[43] *Songs from Letters (after Calamity Jane)* (1989) for soprano and piano; *Eleanor Roosevelt* (1996), a dramatic cantata for mezzo, speaker, mixed chorus, clarinet, cello, piano, and percussion; and *Mary Cassatt* (1994) for mezzo, trombone, and orchestra.

Chen Yi

Like the other composers in this section, Chen Yi (b. 1953) is committed to composing music that people wish to hear and musicians wish to perform. In addition to fusing music of the East and West, her main goal has been described as "the desire to create 'real music' for society and future generations."[44] Chen,[45] the daughter of two medical doctors, began piano and violin lessons at age three. During the Cultural Revolution of the 1960s she practiced in secret and then spent two years doing forced labor in the countryside as part of her "re-education." When Chen was allowed to return to her home city of Guangzhou, China, at age seventeen, she became concertmaster and composer with the Beijing Opera Troupe, which specialized in westernized socialist-realist style. She also began studying Chinese traditional music and music theory. Finally, in 1977, Chen was able to enroll as a student at the Beijing Central Conservatory, and in 1986 she became the first woman in China to receive a Master of Arts degree in composition. That year she also arrived in the United States as a participant in the Center for United States–China Arts Exchange at Columbia University, which composer Chou Wen-Chung directs.

In 1993 Chen received her D.M.A. from Columbia and was appointed composer-in-residence with three San Francisco musical organizations: the Women's Philharmonic (which she helped overcome a serious fiscal crisis), Chanticleer, and the Creative Arts Program at Aptos Middle School. In addition to having a busy schedule of composing, Chen taught composition at Peabody Conservatory (1996–1998). In the fall of 1998 she joined the faculty at the Conservatory of the University of Missouri at Kansas City as the Lorena Searcey Cravens Missouri Endowed Professor in Composition.

Discussing her compositional style, Chen stated:

> I want to speak in a natural way in my own language, and that is a combination of everything I have learned from the past—what I learned in the conservatory, and what I learned in the field collecting folk songs. It's all a source for my imagination. . . . If you just put them together as Eastern and Western, then it sounds artificial—they don't sound together. But if you can merge them in your blood, then they sound natural together.[46]

Reviewers consistently cite her success in bringing these musical traditions together and the exciting timbres she achieves. *Duo Ye No. 2* (1987) for orchestra draws on pentatonic material and was influenced by a traditional song and dance form of the Dong minority in the Guangxi Province. After it was performed at Avery Fisher Hall by the Central Philharmonic Orchestra of China, JoAnn Falletta became the first American conductor to program Chen's work with her performance of *Duo Ye No. 2* at the Kennedy Center in Washington. Other works that demonstrate Chen's vivid orchestrations include *Sparkle* (1992) for a mixed octet; *Ge Xu (Antiphony*, 1994) for orchestra; and *Golden Flute* (1997) for flute and orchestra. *Chinese Myths Cantata* (1996) for male choir, orchestra, and Chinese dance—a joint project between Chanticleer and the Women's Philharmonic—emerged as the culmination of Chen's residency program. A poignant and theatrical setting of three Chinese creation myths, it includes four traditional Chinese instruments: erhu (fiddle), yangqin (dulcimer), pipa (lute), and zheng (zither). During the second movement, the audience is encouraged to participate with nonsense syllables to contribute to the climax.[47]

SONIC EXPLORATION

The expansion of sonic resources during the twentieth century can be viewed as an intersection of events, including the enrichment of instrumental and vocal resources throughout the Western European tradition and the century's craving for newness. Further, independence of timbre as a primary compositional parameter emerges from what George Rochberg has described as the shift from a temporal to a spatial concept of music, and it is closely tied to the move away from a melodic-harmonic treatment of pitch material.[48] By defining "acceptable" musical material, women have found resources to challenge cultural norms and the ideology of dominant culture, to reformulate gender constructions, to confront the gender identification of specific instruments, and to destabilize musical and social hierarchies.

Annea Lockwood (b. 1939) often challenges the line between music and noise in her compositions. While working in many genres, her compositions consistently focus on timbral exploration and performance, including spatial concerns. A native of New Zealand, Lockwood came to the United States in 1973 after living in England for twelve years. In the mid-1960s she moved away from instrumental music and synthesized electronic materials to work more with acoustic sound sources from nature. Her imaginative *Glass Concert,* performed many times from 1966 to 1973, uses diverse sizes and shapes of glass, which are struck, rubbed, bowed, and snapped:

> I began to feel that electronic timbres, that is, the classic studio timbres, were simplistic by comparison with acoustic timbres and spectra, and not satisfying, not intellectually stimulating, not interesting to work with. . . . I needed to refine my hearing and my audio sensitivity. . . . What fascinates me still about acoustic phenomena is the large area of unpredictability about them.[49]

During the 1970s and early 1980s Lockwood focused on works for tape and pursued explorations of performance, including theatrical elements, ritual, and improvisation. *Tiger Balm* (1970) for tape effectively combines the acoustic sounds of a cat purring, a heartbeat, gongs, jaw's harps, tigers mating, a woman making love, and an airplane. Here, and typically, Lockwood's arrangement and selection of sounds are crucial since she uses the sounds unmodulated.

During the 1970s and early 1980s she also gave increased attention to events and installations, such as in *The River Archive* (recordings of rivers from around the world were collected over a period of years and presented in 1973–1980) and in *A Sound Map of the Hudson River* (1983), in which the musical parameters of rhythm, pitch, counterpoint, texture, and form are all apparent in the natural sounds of the fifteen locations along the Hudson. Since the mid-1980s Lockwood has returned to composition for acoustic instruments and voice. She has composed a number of solo works, including *Amazonia Dreaming* (1988), *For Richard* (1992), and *Ear-Walking Woman* (1996), plus chamber music such as *Thousand Year Dreaming*

(1990) for four didjeridus, frame drums, conch shells, winds, and projections; and *Monkey Trips* (1995), developed with the California E.A.R. Unit.[50]

The range of timbres on acoustic instruments has multiplied during the second half of the century, and the literature mentioned here gives only a hint of the scope and breadth of activity. Lucia Dlugoszewski (b. 1934), whose *Fire Fragile Flight* (1974) was the first work by a woman to win a Koussevitzky International Recording Award (1977), invented the "timbre piano" in 1951. She has consistently worked with expanded acoustic sounds, using conventional and invented instruments. She composed *Suchness Concert* (1958–1960), which is concerned with Zen immediacy, and *Geography of Noon* (1964) for an ensemble of one hundred of her newly invented percussion instruments, built by sculptor Ralph Dorazio. *Her Space Is a Diamond* (1970) for solo trumpet virtually catalogues extended technique for this instrument.

Composer Anne LeBaron (b. 1953) is also an internationally recognized harpist who pioneered extended techniques, prepared harp, and electronic extensions of harp timbres. She breaks the stereotypes of harpists and harp music in works such as the solo improvisation *Dog-Gone Cat Act* (recorded in 1981) for prepared harp and in *Blue Harp Studies* (1991) with electronic processing. Whether for the unusually constituted LeBaron Quintet (trumpet, tuba, electric guitar, harp, and percussion) or for conventional ensembles, LeBaron's compositions consistently use evocative, colorful timbres. During the 1980s her vocabulary expanded through an increased use of microtones, world music, sounds from nature, electronics, and new instruments, for example, in *Lamentation/Invocation* (1984).[51]

Although some timbral exploration moves in the direction of noise and high intensity, other compositions highlight quiet, refined effects. *Translucent Unreality No. 1* (1978) by Darleen Cowles Mitchell (b. 1942), for prepared piano, flute, and wind chimes, unfolds slowly and calmly, like the ephemeral flowers mentioned in its epigraph. Relative, nonproportional rhythmic durations contribute to the mood of fluid impermanence. *From My Garden No. 2* (1983) by Ursula Mamlok (b. 1928), another delicate piece, is scored for oboe, French horn, and piano, with subsequent versions for viola or violin. The piano part includes pizzicato effects inside the instrument, and each performer also plays a crotale (a thick metal cymbal with definite pitch) by bowing as well as striking it.

At the beginning of the twentieth century, both percussion and the allied parameter of rhythm were largely untapped resources in music of the Western European tradition. Percussion now enjoys prominence through its own ensembles as well as an expanded role in orchestras and chamber groups. Before composing *Amazonia Dreaming* (1988), for solo snare drum, Annea

Lockwood thought of this medium as limited; however, she discovered it is capable of making "wonderful, animal-like sounds . . . as well as great beauty in its own natural resonances."[52] Julia Perry's *Homunculus C.F.* (1960; see HAMW, pp. 335–44), scored for harp, celesta/piano, and an ensemble of eight percussionists, creates a precarious balance between pitch (melodic and harmonic) and rhythm. Although percussion is the principal timbre, the macrostructure is based on a single harmonic unit rather than on rhythm. And although the pitched instruments offer melody and create chords, the chosen instruments (harp, timpani, vibraphone, and even celesta) do not produce sounds with a particularly clear pitch focus. Further, harmonic gestures are virtually nonexistent despite the generation of pitch material from a single chord: a chord of the fifteenth (the "C.F." of the title) rising from an E. Perry's title also derives from the scene in Goethe's *Faust II* in which Wagner, Faust's apprentice, brings Homunculus (literally "little man" in Latin) into being in a vial via alchemy. Perry described the work in figurative terms: "Having selected percussion instruments for my formulae, then maneuvering and distilling them by means of the Chord of the Fifteenth (C.F.), this musical test tube baby was brought to life."[53] Like the alchemy process, Perry's musical materials unfold gradually, and only the final phrase (mm. 171–180) builds in density to include all ten performers and all eight pitches. Homunculus "becomes" in a sharp flash. In addition to this surface narrative, *Homunculus C.F.* can also be analyzed in terms of a narrative focused on instability and on ambiguous roles, perhaps mirroring the insecurity of the experimental artist in contemporary society—particularly true in the case of an African-American woman during the early years of the Civil Rights movement.

Performers as well as composers have been active participants in extending sonic resources, particularly in cases of close collaboration (e.g., Bethany Beardslee and Milton Babbitt; Jan DeGaetani and George Crumb; Cathy Berberian and Luciano Berio). Interestingly, the leading vocalists of contemporary music and especially music with extended techniques are almost exclusively women, including performance artists Laurie Anderson, Joan La Barbara, and Meredith Monk. Many of the compositions exploring vocal resources also call for virtuosic performance skills and a reevaluation of text and the human voice as components of musical expression.

Jan DeGaetani (1933–1989), noted for both technical skill and artistic performances of contemporary music, surely influenced and shaped composition for voice. Jacob Druckman, Peter Maxwell Davies, György Ligeti, and Pierre Boulez composed works for her. The link between DeGaetani and composer George Crumb is particularly striking, covering more than two decades. She premiered and recorded most of his music for voice, including *Madrigals*

(1965 and 1969) and *Ancient Voices of Children* (1970). As professor of voice at the Eastman School of Music and Artist-in-Residence at the Aspen Music Festival for many years, DeGaetani was influential on the next generation of performers.

Like DeGaetani, Cathy Berberian (1925–1983) was a virtuosic performer. Born in the United States of Armenian parents, she developed strong theatrical abilities, and her dramatic presence remained powerful even when illness forced her to perform from a wheelchair. Her vocal skills influenced compositions not only by Luciano Berio, her husband from 1950 to 1966, but also by John Cage, Igor Stravinsky (the final version of *Elegy for JFK*), and numerous Europeans (Sylvano Bussotti, Henri Pousseur, Bruno Maderna, Hans Werner Henze). A large portion of Berio's output was written for Berberian: *Chamber Music* (1953), *Circles* (1960), *Sequenza III* (1960s), and *Recital I (for Cathy)* (1972). Berberian's voice is also crucial in Berio's dramatic electronic works, *Thema (Omaggio a Joyce)* (1958) and *Visage* (1961), which both link violence and the erotic in disturbing ways. Even after their divorce Berberian and Berio continued to collaborate musically. Berberian's own compositions—*Stripsody* (1966), *Awake and Read-Joyce* (1972), and *Anathema con VarieAzioni* (1972)—were also written with her own voice in mind. *Stripsody,* which deals with comic strips as cultural discourse, is a collage verbalizing onomatopoeic words from the comics. Inserted into this witty texture are very short scenes from comic strips (e.g., "Peanuts") or stereotypic movie scenes.[54]

Performance Art and Experimental Music*

Pushing the boundaries of performance and composition still further, performance art unites the roles of composer and performer and generally incorporates a variety of media. Theatricality, vocal experimentation, multimedia events, Eastern philosophy, dance, and storytelling are among the elements included in its stylistic and musical diversity. Performance art, along with minimalism and neotonality, was one of the new directions of the 1980s that sought to reengage the public. A performance artist par excellence, Laurie Anderson has been especially active in this field. Composers Pauline Oliveros and Meredith Monk both have created numerous pieces that fall under this heading. Joan La Barbara, not a performance artist per se, has been active as a collaborator with avant-garde musicians and has developed an extended vocal technique that earns her the title of experimental musician/composer.

*This section, except for the material on Diamanda Galás, is by Leslie Lassetter.

Diamanda Galás

The work of composer–performance artist Diamanda Galás (b. 1955) transgresses many norms, and its unconventional timbres are meant to provoke and to challenge the ideology of dominant culture. Her work is guerilla art. Galás's extraordinary *Plague Mass* (1989) is an anguished cry of outrage for persons living with AIDS. Bathed in red stage lights and covered with a bloodlike substance, Galás appropriates almost earsplitting screams—high, sustained, and raw—to condemn the treatment of people with HIV and AIDS and to denounce U.S. policy and the response to the AIDS crisis. Her performance is riveting and pushes the boundaries of music or any art form. In the words of Richard Gehr, "She demonstrates how an activist artist can push the limits of acceptable social responses, challenging the status quo."[55]

In her music Galás utilizes an extensive personal background: keyboard prodigy, jazz singer, and avant-garde vocalist for European composers such as Vinko Globokar and Iannis Xenakis. She also draws on her Greek heritage through the use of gestures and sounds of Maniot women's mourning. The Maniot, like Galás, used their mourning incantations, called *moirologi,* as a political force: these Greek women would scream and pull out their hair in order to incite people to revenge. Galás acknowledges that these women were considered a threat to the authority of patriarchal society,[56] their incantations "a form of empowerment for the women—an enactment, an assumption, of the power of death."[57] In *Plague Mass,* the shocking sounds of Galás's lamentation push us as listeners to share her outrage and spur us to political action. In other works Galás has undertaken further wrenching topics in equally compelling ways. *Vena Cava* (premiered in 1992) explores themes of psychological claustrophobia and solitary confinement as manifest in people with mental illness or AIDS-related dementia. Performed in total darkness, *Schrei 27* (1994) and *Schrei X* (1995), whose titles mean "shriek/scream" in German, address the interior isolation experienced by a person who is tortured or subjected to sensory deprivation. These two works juxtapose high-intensity vocal sounds with absolute silence.[58]

Pauline Oliveros

Theatricality, humor, feminism, meditation, audience participation, and experiment all are important aspects of the music of Pauline Oliveros (b. 1932). Her family was musical: her mother and grandmother taught piano, and her grandfather collected musical instruments. After studying piano with her mother, Oliveros took up her brother's instrument, the accordion. Later she learned tuba and French horn, but her lifelong affinity with the accordion has remained central to her compositions and improvisations. Her studies at the University of Houston (1949–1952) included accordion and composition. From Houston she transferred to San Francisco State College to study composition with Robert Erickson, and received her B.A. degree there in 1957.

Oliveros's early works show a tendency toward experiment. Her Trio for Flute, Percussion, and String Bass (1963) has a Webern-like texture but uses nontraditional notation, with and without indicating exact pitches. In contrast, *Aeolian Partitions* (1970) has approximately one page of notated music and several pages of instructions, including a list of the required performers and their props (a broom for the cellist, a newspaper and flashlight for the pianist, etc.) and a very detailed scenario. *Aeolian Partitions* also calls for telepathic improvisation.

> Each performer concentrates on another single performer. When he hears an interval or a chord mentally, he plays one of the pitches and assumes that he is sending the other pitch or pitches to the other performer by mental telepathy.[59]

Aeolian Partitions is one of many theatre pieces Oliveros has written. Her earliest work in this genre was *Duo for Accordion and Bandoneon with Possible Mynah Bird Obbligato* (1964). She added her pet mynah bird because it joined in during rehearsals; since the bird added a visual element, Oliveros asked Elizabeth Harris to design stage sets. Harris created a wooden seesaw with revolving chairs, which made reading a score impossible; so Oliveros replaced her original music with a set of simple instructions. The instructions for *Pieces of Eight* (1965) are more elaborate, calling for stage movement, costumes, cash register, skull and crossbones, and a bust of Beethoven with flashing red lights for eyes. Other theatre pieces include *George Washington Slept Here, Participle Dangling in Honor of Gertrude Stein, Double Basses at Twenty Paces,* and *Link* (renamed *Bonn Feier*).

Oliveros has also experimented with electronic music. In 1961, along with Morton Subotnick and Roman Sender, she founded the improvisation group Sonics, later renamed the San Francisco Tape Music Center. When the Center, now called the Center for Contemporary Music, relocated to Mills College in 1966, Oliveros became its director. Her commitment to electronically produced sound has influenced even her music for traditional performance forces. *Sound Patterns* (1961), which won a Gaudeamus prize, calls for an a cappella choir, yet it mimics tape devices such as white noise, filtering, ring modulation, and percussive envelope. *Bye Bye Butterfly* (1965) is an improvised piece realized by Oliveros with two oscillators, two live amplifiers, a turntable, a recording of Puccini's *Madama Butterfly,* and two tape recorders in delay setup. In 1966 Oliveros experimented with compositions whose fundamental tones were outside the range of human hearing, so that the only musical sounds perceived were the overtones. This use of subaudio and supersonic oscillators to create music was so unprecedented, says Oliveros, that "I was accused of black art."[60] Her *I of IV* is based on the very nature of electricity.[61]

In the early 1970s Oliveros became involved with T'ai Chi, karate, dreams, mandalas, and Asian culture. Through a synthesis of her study of consciousness, martial arts, and feminist sociology she developed a theory of sonic awareness in which the goals of music are ritual, ceremony, healing, and humanism; beauty, rather than the goal, is the by-product. Using a parallel to Jung's viewfinder archetype based on sound—sound actively made, imagined, heard at present, or remembered—Oliveros created twenty-five *Sonic Meditations*. The three most suited to beginners appear in HAMW, pp. 364–66. The first, "Teach Yourself to Fly," is an exercise in tuned breathing; Meditation XIV, "Tumbling Song," calls for descending vocal glissandi beginning at any pitch. "Zina's Circle" (Meditation XV) is more complex and involves hand signals between the performers. All three of these *Sonic Meditations* call for the participants to stand or sit in a circle formation; there is no separate audience.

Though Oliveros wrote her *Sonic Meditations* for participants only, she incorporated some of their elements into pieces intended for public performance. In the ceremonial mandala piece *MMM, a Lullaby for Daisy Pauline* (1980), for instance, she invited the audience to participate with humming sounds and audible breathing.[62] Still later works hark back to earlier compositional techniques. At a 1985 performance of *Walking the Heart,* the hall illuminated only by candles, the whirling dancer, and the digital delay device recalled both the theatrical aspects and the electronically manipulated sounds of her early works. *The Roots of the Moment* employs not only an interactive electronic environment but also an accordion tuned to just intonation.

In 1985 Oliveros established the Pauline Oliveros Foundation, based in Kingston, New York. This nonprofit organization supports creative artists worldwide via residencies, international exchanges, the creation of new works, and an active performance schedule.[63] Its mission is to explore new technologies and new relationships between artists and audiences.[64] Prominent performers on the Pauline Oliveros Foundation's concert schedule are the Deep Listening Band and the Deep Listening Chorus. Aligned with Oliveros's *Sonic Meditations,* the Deep Listening pieces are intended to help musicians, trained and untrained, to concentrate on closely listening to one another. Oliveros explains, "Deep Listening is listening in every possible way to everything possible to hear. . . . [It] includes the sounds of daily life . . . one's own thoughts . . . musical sounds. Deep Listening is a life practice."[65] In 1992 the National Endowment for the Arts supported the composition of

Epigraphs in the Time of AIDS for the Deep Listening Band. The same year Tokyo hosted a five-hour, multimedia Deep Listening marathon.

Deep Listening also underlies the collective improvisations of Oliveros (accordion and voice), Stuart Dempster (trombone and didjeridu, an Australian aboriginal trumpet of wood or bamboo), and Panaiotis (voice, found percussion) in music recorded in the Fort Worden Cistern in Port Townsend, Washington. Oliveros describes the process:

> Each composer [Dempster, Panaiotis, and Oliveros herself] has a very individual style of composition. As we improvise together, and listen intensely to one another, our styles encounter in the moment, and intermingle to make a collective music. . . . Listening, not only to one another but to the transformative spatial modulations, is an essential process in the music. The cistern space, in effect, is an instrument played simultaneously by all three composers. . . . The tonal qualities produced by each performer are constantly changed by interaction with the cistern acoustics, making it seem as if many more instruments are present.[66]

Lear, one of the pieces created by this process, was used in Act V, iii, of Shakespeare's play as produced by Mabou Mines.

Oliveros has won a respectful following, among composers and audiences, as an experimenter and a forerunner in the now widely accepted field of electronic music. Through her many residencies at colleges and universities she has spread to a younger generation of composers her ideas about creating a music based on listening. Her concern with meditation and Eastern philosophies recalls the ideas of John Cage, though her music does not. Most poetically stated, Pauline Oliveros is, in her commitment to feminist principles and her exploration of new language of sounds, a musical Gertrude Stein.[67]

Laurie Anderson

Laurie Anderson (b. 1947), unlike the other musicians in this section, never had to give up a preconceived style of composition. As a young adult she was a student not of music but of art history and sculpture, though she had studied violin throughout her youth. In reaction to her sculpture and performance art, with its great emphasis on music and sound, her teachers at Barnard College and Columbia University used to ask her if she were in the wrong department. One early sculpture looked like a mere table. With elbows resting on the table and hands cupped over the ears, however, the viewer could hear music. Anderson began making her own instruments in 1974.

Both sound and the art of the storyteller have always been integral parts of Anderson's work, and her music has very often served a story. To this end the visual element is ever important. As is true of some of Meredith Monk's work, Laurie Anderson's performance art can be appreciated most fully when one sees her perform. With the magical-elfin quality of the spectacle she creates, Anderson is truly an entertainer. In *O Superman,* a video, a light placed inside her mouth shows eerily through closed lips and glows when she opens her mouth to sing. In live performance her charm, wit, inventiveness, and intellectual sarcasm—when at its best—captivate audiences. By means of slide projections, film, video, altered vocal sounds, and various self-invented instruments, Anderson and her concerts have taken on the alternating qualities of comedy club, rock concert, and magic act. In the sophistication of her stories Anderson is a modern minstrel or "Multi-Mediatrix."[68] Many of her tales are partly autobiographical.

In the 1970s Anderson performed throughout the United States and Europe in art galleries and museums, including Berlin's Akademie der Kunst, settings where she could use intimate lighting effects. For example, she once projected a slide out of sight onto a ceiling. When she whisked her violin bow through the beam of light, for an instant the image came into view. She also created haunting music using a violin equipped with a tape-recorder head. Music sounded when her bow, strung not with horsehair but with prerecorded magnetic tape, touched the head. The song "Juanita" uses such a violin. Still another self-invented instrument, a white electric violin, sounds like thunder when played with a neon bow.

Anderson's magnum opus, the four-part, two-evening *United States I-IV,* was given its premiere in 1983 at the Brooklyn Academy of Music. This set of "visual songs" took several years to create and was intended "to make a portrait of a country," says Anderson. "At first I thought it was just the United States, but it's not turning out to be that way. It's a portrait of any highly technological society."[69] The work was inspired by the many questions people asked Anderson about her country while she was on tour in Europe. It is documented both on record and in book form.[70]

Anderson has also written music for choreographers, such as *Long Time No See,* which was made into the dance *Set and Reset* (1983) by Trisha Brown. Anderson's work often has a very feminine, even feminist, undercurrent. The lyric from *Example #22,* sung in a pathetically painful tone of voice, provides one instance:

> The sun is shining slowly,
> The birds are flying so low
> Honey you're my one and only,
> So pay me what you owe me.[71]

In her 1989 *Empty Spaces* concert at the Brooklyn Academy of Music, Anderson sang "Beautiful Red Dress," in which the lyrics symbolized menstruation.

To support the verbal imagery (red wine, red dress, etc.), the white tile walls became redder and redder as the song progressed.[72]

In 1994 Anderson went on a tour that promoted her book *Stories from the Nerve Bible: A Retrospective 1972–92.*[73] The performance contained autobiographical numbers, such as "My Grandmother's Hats," a story about her fundamentalist grandmother's confusion over whether to wear a hat at the moment of death, and a monologue about the comedian Andy Kaufman, who once coaxed Anderson to wrestle with him as part of his act. *Nerve Bible,* however, also continued her turn toward political content, begun in the national-anthem piece, *Empty Spaces.* Anderson had poked fun at national anthems, especially those that could be translated: "We're the best. We're the best in all the world." With satirical humor she juxtaposed such lyrics in a paraphrase of the American anthem:

> Q. Hey? Do you see anything over there?
> A. I dunno . . . there's a lot of smoke.
> Q. Say! Isn't that a flag!
> A. Hmmm . . . couldn't say really, it's pretty early in the morning.
> Q. Hey! Do you smell something burning?
>
> I mean, that's the whole song![74]

Nerve Bible continues this political bent and takes it further. In "Night in Baghdad" Anderson presents the aesthetics of the news media that treat the Gulf War as a cross "between grand opera and the Superbowl."[75] The biggest change apparent in her works of the 1990s is the stripping away of spectacle. In the *Nerve Bible* performance at the Lied Arts Center in Lawrence, Kansas, in 1994, for example, the technical wizardry and laser/video effects were gone.

Despite the multifaceted aspects of Anderson's work—the humor; the homemade violins; the songs, monologues, and toy saxophone; the video, film, and light shows; and the lessening of such theatrical visuals in her work of the 1990s—the central point of it all is the texts. As she says:

> I've never been a filmmaker or musician in the classic sense. . . . I use film and music . . . to be a subtext for the stories. The real subject, the real work, is the spoken words. I feel that's what I'm best at.[76]

Joan La Barbara

Joan La Barbara (b. 1947), a noted interpreter of new music and champion of avant-garde vocal technique, has premiered the works of John Cage, Charles Dodge, Philip Glass, Steve Reich, Alvin Lucier, David Behrman, Roger Reynolds, Morton Feldman, and her husband, Morton Subotnick, among others. Her own music exploits the virtuosity she has developed in her vocal practice. One of her most celebrated pieces, *Circular Song* (1975), demonstrates a vocal technique inspired by (though not technically identical to) the circular breathing used by wind players. Following a graphic score (Example 11.1), La Barbara vocalizes on both the exhalation and the inhalation of breath. The effect is a series of siren-like glissandi on different vowels and vocal timbres, that is, the production of more than one pitch at a time. *Voice Piece: One-Note Internal Resonance Investigation* (1974) takes

EXAMPLE 11.1. Joan La Barbara, "Circular Song," copyright 1975 (Wizard Records, RVX 2266). Used by permission of the composer.

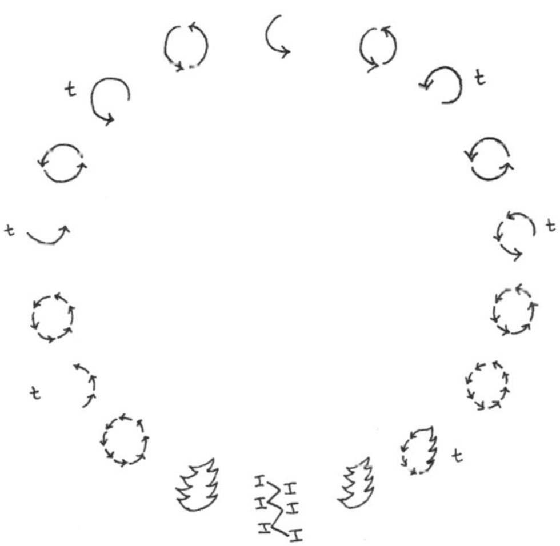
CIRCULAR SONG
Instructions:
· beginning at top center with first exhaled descending glissando from comfortable top to bottom of range, change breath at bottom of range and ascend on inhale to top.
· repeat figure until too exhausting or no longer musically interesting.
· use transition figure t to move to next repeating pattern in which breath changes occur at midpoints of vocal range. repeat as before.
· use next transition figure to move to repeating figure with 3 breath changes per range sweep, alternating inhale/exhale.
· after 3, move on to 4 changes per range sweep.
· then move to one step/half back figure in which one inhales upward then exhales halfway back down, changing at top to exhaling down and inhaling halfway back up.
· One has now arrived at the central figure, the midpoint: alternating inhaled and exhaled multiphonics, one moves from the lower to upper part of the range and then swoops down into the step/half back figure and proceeds through each repeating figure, in reverse, until arriving again at the beginning.
©1975 Joan La Barbara

its substance from the various ways in which La Barbara creates multiphonics from a single pitch. The composer calls such early works tightly controlled studies on specific ideas.

Aurally more intriguing in its greater musical variety is *Vocal Extensions,* written in 1974. La Barbara calls this work a

> stretching [of] the voice, using sounds I've discovered in earlier experiments and expanding these possibilities by feeding the voice signal through a phase shifter, pitch modulator, and echo unit to shape a sound fabric based on the natural rhythmic flow of thought.[77]

Cathing (1977), which begins with a scathing interview of another singer (Cathy Berberian) who does not use some of the new, extended vocal techniques, has similar electronic elements and multitrack sound. In places La Barbara's vocal effects have the sound of various jungle animals responding to the droning, mantra-like chords of an oriental priesthood. One can also hear the influence of different cultures—Hebrew cantillation, Native American wailing, and Japanese Kabuki speech.

La Barbara's works of the 1980s tend toward larger performance forces than the earlier, accompanied and a cappella solos and taped pieces. *Vlissingen Harbor* (1982), for amplified voice and seven instruments, was premiered in Los Angeles, as was *The Solar Wind,* for amplified voice and ten instruments, which was supported by a grant from the National Endowment for the Arts. One critic calls this piece a one-movement concerto for voice and orchestra in a minimal style. In *Chandra* (1983) La Barbara expands her tonal palette further to include solo voice, chamber orchestra, and male chorus.

From ensembles featuring vocal solos, La Barbara has gone on to compose for other kinds of ensembles in works that include the large-scale choral piece *to hear the wind roar* (see CAMW, p. 99) and *tree of blue leaves* (recorded in 1993) for solo oboe and computer-generated sound. Several choreographers have created dances to her music, among them John Alleyne, Martha Curtis, and Merce Cunningham. Her youngest audience members can hear La Barbara's vocal and electronic music behind Steve Finkin's signing alphabet animation on "Sesame Street" (created in 1977 and still being broadcast).[78]

Meredith Monk

Meredith Monk (b. 1942)[79] is an artist in the broadest sense of the word. Her work breaks the dividing lines among dancer-choreographer, singer-composer, actress-stage director, and filmmaker-storyteller. Some of her titles have an anthropological ring: *Dolmen Music* (1981), *Recent Ruins* (1976), *Quarry* (1976), or *The Plateau Series* (1978), for example. Others sound like something from medieval history—*Our Lady of Late* (1973), *Book of Days* (1989)—or modern whimsical fantasy—*Needle-Brain Lloyd and the Systems Kid: A Live Movie* (1970) and *Candy Bullets and Moon* (1967). In the tradition of other contemporary New York artists, she named the company that performs her theatre pieces The House.[80] The program for "Tour 8: Castle" in 1971 describes this company as follows:

> "The House is a group of artists, actors, dancers and a scientist who are committed to performance as a means of expression and as a means of personal and hopefully social evolution. We seek to unite our life and our work without losing our . . . individuality. Our work is full of remembered things and felt things that aren't seen and things that are seen outside and things that are only seen inside. . . ." That description of The House still holds . . . and The House, itself, is still standing. . . . Meredith is the director, the hub.[81]

Today The House is The House Foundation, complete with a paid staff and an illustrious board of directors who raise funds, promote, market, commission, and support the artistic endeavors of Meredith Monk.

As a child Monk studied piano, and at boarding school she sang in the chorus. Her career as a dancer and choreographer began after an intensely creative training period at Sarah Lawrence College. There she studied dance (with Bessie Schoenberg, Judith Dunn, and Beverly Schmidt), music, acting, writing, and literature. Speaking of her college days, Monk says:

> I was encouraged to work with a feeling, an idea . . . and let the medium and the form find itself. It seemed that finally I was able to combine movement with music and words all coming from a single source . . . a total experience.[82]

If Wagner approached the *Gesamtkunstwerk,* or total artwork, from the vantage point of a composer, Monk created what she has called composite theatre from the vantage point of a dancer steeped in all the creative arts. In her work, "the total art experience becomes more important than the significance of a singular message."[83]

In the 1960s critics labeled Monk's work *Blackboard* (1965) as anti-dance and her *16 MM Earrings* (1966) as mixed media. Like Oliveros, Monk experimented with music beyond the range of human hearing. Part of the score for *Duet with Cat's Scream and Locomotive* (1965) included sound waves perceived by the brain but inaudible to the human ear. In her theatre pieces *Juice* (1969) and *Vessel* (1971) Monk experimented with moving the audience to different geographic locations instead of changing the sets on a stage.

Education of the Girlchild (1973) is among Monk's most celebrated theatre pieces. Nancy Goldner, writing for the *Christian Science Monitor,* calls *Girlchild* a theatre piece about movement and stillness. A video of the work reveals just how still and motionless much of *Girlchild* is. The beginning of Part

I is like an extended exercise in staring, and there are no words or dialogue to break the stillness. Goldner interprets a synopsis as follow: In Part I, a girl is born; she is educated by her female companions. By eating at table with them she becomes socialized. Next she studies bricks and learns about the world. Finally she experiences initiation into the cult of the ancestress. Part II is a long vocal solo in which Monk evolves from old age into youth. Her solo's "running vocal commentary of strange animalistic sounds" is a type of "sound-singing [that] draws one back to a pre-linguistic state."[84] Goldner's synopsis is referred to here as an interpretation because *Girlchild* has few words. In Part I, Monk and her mostly female cast do not create a simple pantomime that makes the story line self-evident; in this sense there could exist as many synopses for Part I as there are viewers. In contrast, Part II, the seminal portion of *Girlchild,* first performed in 1972, is universally recognized as a backward movement through time beginning from the protagonist's old age. Monk performed *Girlchild* several times in New York, then in Paris; she revived it in 1979 and again in the 1991–92 season. A few years after *Girlchild* she created *Quarry* (1975–76), which received an Obie award; this time she added film as one more element in her theatrical toolbox.

Nearly two decades after *Girlchild, Atlas* was premiered in 1991 by the Houston Grand Opera. Inspired by the travels of explorer Alexandra David-Neel, *Atlas,* with its continuous musical score and adventuresome, lifelike narrative, is an opera in the traditional sense of the term except for the near-absence of words. (One scene, "Airport," can be found in CAMW, p. 206.) Monk's nonverbal libretto is made up largely of nonsense syllables, siren sounds, melodic melismas, and ensemble sonorities that range from glorious cacophony to ethereal harmonies, with the accompaniment sometimes of exotic instrumental timbres arising from the pit orchestra's ostinato-like foundations.

In *Atlas,* the adolescent Alexandra dreams of traveling the globe. Her parents watch her yearnings with worried eyes, not comprehending her wanderlust. At adulthood, Alexandra sets out to see the world. She chooses traveling companions at the outset of her journey and takes on others along the way. This small band encounters a primitive farm community, desert caravans, tropical climes, militarized cities, cold mountains, and colorful characters in the places they visit. Passing beyond Earth, the travelers reach the realm of invisible light. Here, where Earth's landscapes are seen in miniature, a contemplative, almost heavenly host sings sublime harmonies. Finally, an aged Alexandra sips coffee as she reflects on her life. As in *Girlchild,* Monk treats woman in the entirety of life: girlhood, adulthood, and old age.[85]

After *Atlas,* Monk returned to solo dramatic writing with the intimate *Volcano Songs* (1994, recorded 1997). By contrast, *American Archeology #1: Roosevelt Island* (1994) included seventy performers. Here Roosevelt Island, linked by cable car to Manhattan, became both the historical inspiration and the actual stage of this open-air theatre piece.[86] *The Politics of Quiet* for twelve performers (1996) marked a return to indoor staging while continuing Monk's personal traditions of ritual, dance, multimedia conceptions, and sparse yet graceful repetitive orchestrations.[87]

In her vocal music Monk is interested in exploring the voice as an instrument, allowing it the same flexibility as a dancer's spine. Asserting that music is a universal means of communication, she hints at the reason most of her music is without words: "People can respond directly, without having to go through language. I'm trying to approach a vocal music that's both primordial and futuristic. Maybe there won't be language differentiation in the future."[88] In addition to her concert appearances, Monk has made several recordings, among them *Key* (1970); *Our Lady of Late* (1974); *Dolmen Music* (1981, recipient of a German Critics award for best recording); *Turtle Dreams* (1983); *Facing North* (1992); *Monk and the Abbess* (1996, including selections by Hildegard von Bingen); and *Volcano Songs* (1997).

Monk has not confined her collaborations to the worlds of modern dance (including various projects with Ping Chong since 1972), concertizing, and avant-garde theatre. In 1987 she and popular singer (now conductor) Bobby McFerrin sang a concert together at the Next Wave Festival at the Brooklyn Academy of Music. Monk's works of the late 1980s include the film score *Fayum Music* (1988) for voice, hammer dulcimer, and double ocarina; the music-theatre piece *The Ringing Place* (1987), first presented at the Brooklyn Academy of Music; and her feature-length film *Book of Days* (1989), which played at the New York Film Festival and, in a shorter version, on the PBS series "Alive from Off Center." Monk presented a short, live version of *Book of Days* at the Minnesota Opera in 1988.

John Rockwell has called Meredith Monk "the archetypical multi-media artist, having managed to work—one art at a time or in combination—in dance, theatre, film, and video"[89]—not to mention composing for her own vocal ensemble and maintaining her solo concert and recording career. Monk dislikes being labeled a performance artist, as she considers herself first and foremost a composer. Though some of her theatre pieces fall under the performance art umbrella, she is actually an artist from whose brush flow music, song, theatre, film, sound, dance, saga, humor, ritual, and much more. Indeed, Monk stands apart, and shoulders above, many other personalities in the performing arts by the very breadth of her creative activities.

ELECTROACOUSTIC MUSIC

The gender stereotype that suggests women tend to avoid technology and machines is quickly dispelled by looking at the number of women actively involved in electronic music. Historically, Bebe Barron (b. 1927) and her husband, Louis (1920–1989), in 1949 established one of the earliest electroacoustic music studios. They had experimented with the manipulation of taped sounds since 1948, simultaneously with and independent of Pierre Schaeffer, who is usually named the innovator of *musique concrète*. *Heavenly Menagerie* (1951), the Barrons' first composition using the electronic oscillators they had built, employed collage techniques like those later used by John Cage. The Barrons are better known for their electronic film scores, such as *Bells of Atlantis* (1952) and *Forbidden Planet* (1956), an MGM science fiction movie that helped establish the early association of electronic music with science fiction and outer space. The Barrons also prepared approximately 600 recorded sounds used by John Cage in *Williams Mix* (1952), which involved extensive tape splicing.

Currently, women are involved in virtually every aspect of electronic music. In the early 1980s Beverly Grigsby (b. 1928), herself a composer of electronic music, identified forty women in the United States composing with "electronically generated, processed, or manipulated music (using both analog and digital computers),"[90] and the list continues to grow. About half of these composers teach electronic music at colleges and universities; others work independently. Several of the women founded studios: Ruth Anderson (b. 1928) designed the Hunter College studio in 1968 and served as its director until her retirement in 1988. Jean Eichelberger Ivey (b. 1923) established the studio at Peabody in 1969 and made important contributions to the development of an electroacoustic music curriculum. Judith Shatin (b. 1949), who often combines electronic and acoustic instruments, is director of the Virginia Center for Computer Music, which she founded in 1987 at the University of Virginia. Shatin's *Kairos* (1991) for flute, computer, and effects processing (adding elements [e.g., various types of reverberation] to a sound electronically) is a musical exploration of the Greek title meaning "most propitious time" or the "now" moment.[91] Women have also developed computer hardware and software (see the work of Laurie Spiegel, Mara Helmuth, Carla Scaletti) and created electronic instruments (see the work of Laurie Anderson, Brenda Hutchinson, Jin Hi Kim). Trained as a traditional musician in her native Korea, Kim (b. 1958) has an electric komungo that extends the potential of the Korean zither (whose origins may go back to the sixth century). Since coming to the United States in 1980, Kim has worked extensively with improvisation and views her music as bicultural.[92]

Stylistically, women's works in the electroacoustic media cover a wide range. Their styles range from the extended neoclassicism in Emma Lou Diemer's (b. 1927) Trio for Flute, Oboe, Harpsichord, and Electronic Tape (1973) to the experimental collages by Ruth Anderson in *DUMP* (1970) and *SUM* (*State of the Union Message*) (1973); from the integration of nature sounds in *Beneath the Horizon I* (1977–1978) by Priscilla McLean (b. 1942), for processed whale sounds and tuba quartet, to computer voice synthesis in compositions by Brenda Hutchinson and Pamela Z; and from the meditative, minimal sounds of Laurie Spiegel's *The Expanding Universe* (1975) to the multilingual electronic opera *Apocalypse* (1990) by Alice Shields (b. 1943), which draws on styles from heavy-metal rock and Indian classical music.[93]

Most composers have combined electronic music with live performance, either with acoustic sounds or with other media, such as film (Pril Smiley), dance (Laurie Spiegel, Daria Semegen), or video (Elizabeth Hinkle-Turner). Aesthetic approaches vary radically. For example, Ivey moved to electronic music because she considered the unpredictability of live performance a drawback; Spiegel (b. 1945) claims that machines are nonsexist and therefore politically liberating. Diemer wished to incorporate conventional melodic and rhythmic patterns into electronic music as well as to revitalize her acoustic style; Pauline Oliveros saw "live electronics" as a way to get "noise" into her works. Strategies for musical expression also range widely, from a dramatic presentation of text, as in Joyce Mekeel's tape score for Gertrude Stein's *Yes Is for a Very Young Man* (1965), to the metaphorical and veiled approach of Carla Scaletti (b. 1956) in *sunSurgeAutomata* (1987), whose technical processing of sounds mirrors a scientific theorem about the development of life on earth.[94]

The emergence of electronic music at midcentury may be viewed as the convergence of interests in composer control (as seen in serialism), virtuosity, and timbre used for its expressive potential. However, it has also provided flexibility for composers who wish to explore improvisation (e.g., Spiegel's compositions created with her Music Mouse software) or indeterminacy (e.g., Hinkle-Turner's *Antigone's Peace,* 1994, rev. 1995, for mezzo-soprano, percussion, and live electronics, which allows for active audience participation in the creative decision-making process).[95]

Jean Eichelberger Ivey, who wants the immediacy of visual stimuli, often combines live and electronic media in dramatic ways. She has sometimes chosen texts with prominent roles for women. In *Testament of Eve* (1976?), for mezzo-soprano, orchestra, and tape, the composer reinterprets the biblical temptation story: in Ivey's text, Eve's actions are a conscious choice for knowledge and growth. In the program notes for the premiere by the Baltimore Symphony Orchestra, Ivey points out the bias of traditional interpretations: "[Eve] is very like Prometheus; and yet while Prometheus is usually seen as heroic, Eve in a patriarchal culture was often dismissed as silly, sensual, bad."[96] Earlier, in *Hera, Hung from the Sky* (1973), Ivey completed another composition dealing with a woman's quest for equality with a male deity.

Music of Religion and Ritual

The diversity of religious practice and belief in the United States provides a rich musical resource. African Americans have consistently drawn on the music of their church roots—spirituals and gospel music—and contributed to the repertoires of church and school choirs as well as vocal soloists. Florence Price, Margaret Bonds (1913–1972), Julia Perry, Undine Smith Moore (1904–1989), Evelyn Pittman (1910–1994[?]), Betty Jackson King (1928–1994), and Lena McLin (b. 1929) acknowledged their religious-musical heritages in choral and vocal settings. As teachers in public schools and leaders of various musical groups, Pittman, King, and McLin composed large quantities of music focused on practical, accessible compositions for church choirs and school ensembles, often for immediate performance. McLin, whose music incorporates gospel as well as spirituals, found early influence from her mother, a church musician, and from her uncle, Thomas A. Dorsey, who

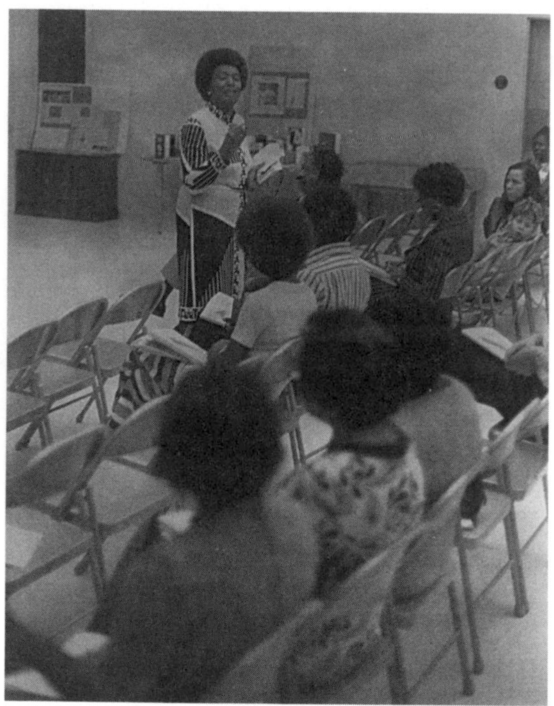

FIGURE 11.2. Undine Smith Moore teaching during a summer festival, "The Black Man in American Music," at Virginia State University, ca. 1972. Photo courtesy of Mary Easter.

is also known as the blues singer "Georgia Tom" and as the "Father of Gospel Music." She acknowledges that gospel music has not always been accepted within black church communities and among classically trained African-American musicians, but believes that it is an important part of her cultural heritage and should be respected—just as spirituals came to be honored.[97] Bonds, Price's most famous student, fused influences from her training in European styles and from the vernacular elements of her African-American heritage. Like Price, who often set poetry by significant black writers such as Paul Laurence Dunbar and Langston Hughes, Bonds retained the spirit of the New Negro Movement. For example, her *Three Dream Portraits* (1959), "while structurally and materially European-derived, is also unequivocally African American in subject matter and treatment." In it, Bonds freely but subtly uses ring-derived procedures (i.e., the African, and later African-American, ring shout that is the source for many cultural and musical practices) to set texts by Langston Hughes.[98]

Undine Smith Moore drew conspicuously on her African-American heritage in many of her compositions. Asked what made her music uniquely black, she responded:

> Musically, its rhythms; its choice of scale structures; its use of call and response; its general use of contrapuntal devices . . . ; the choice of timbres; melody as influenced by rhythms, timbres, scalar structure. When the harmony is non-tertian, it is apt to use the 4ths and 5ths so often sung by black people in the churches of my youth; the deliberate use of striking climax with almost unrestrained fullness.
>
> Philosophically . . . I have often been concerned with aspiration, the emotional intensity associated with the life of black people . . . [and] the capacity and desire for abundant, full expression as one might anticipate or expect from an oppressed people determined to survive.[99]

Moore, whose favorite medium was a cappella choir, is best known for choral compositions and spiritual arrangements. One of her most frequently performed spirituals, "Daniel, Daniel Servant of the Lord" (1952), is more a theme and variations than an arrangement. "Mother to Son" (1955), which sets a Langston Hughes poem for alto solo and mixed chorus, was one of Moore's own favorites and an example of her providing "music of good quality, interesting and fresh"[100] for performers in amateur, church, and school ensembles. "Lord, We Give Thanks to Thee" (1971), written for the hundredth anniversary of the Fisk Jubilee Singers, employs African-American melody and rhythm and builds to intense climaxes. *Scenes from the Life of a Martyr* (*to the Memory of Martin Luther King, Jr.*) (1982), an oratorio for narrator, chorus, and orchestra, was nominated for a Pulitzer Prize in 1982; Moore called this her most significant work.

Not all of Moore's vocal music is overtly rooted in black styles, nor are all of her instrumental works. "Love Let the Wind Cry . . . How I Adore Thee" sets a poem by Sappho in the tradition of Western European art song, celebrating love between women in a dramatic and affirming voice. *Afro-American Suite* (1969) for flute, cello, and piano presents spirituals and includes syncopation typical of black musical traditions. Moore's harmonic practice is generally rooted in tonality, although it is sometimes freely treated or extended through modal references. However, the first and third movements of *Three Pieces for Flute (or Clarinet) and Piano* (1958) explore twelve-tone writing.

Moore, a graduate of Fisk University, continued her musical studies at the Juilliard, Eastman, and Manhattan conservatories and at Columbia University. She contributed to the education of many musicians during her forty-five years as a faculty member at Virginia State College (1927–1972); among her students were such notables as jazz pianist Billy Taylor and opera singer Camilla Williams. Moore's commitment to education was deep; even after her retirement, she continued lecturing, giving workshops, and teaching as a visiting professor at various colleges. Moore was also cofounder and then codirector (1969–1972) of Virginia State's Black Music Center, which was established to spread information about and cultivate appreciation for black music of all types.

Music for worship, once the province of professionals and arena for stylistic innovation, is often performed now by amateur choirs, thus necessitating conservative melodic-harmonic writing. For example, the choral writing and arrangements of Gena Branscombe (1881–1977) and Alice Parker (b. 1925) rely on triads and tuneful melodies. In addition to writing literature appropriate for Protestant services, both women have also composed much secular choral music. Branscombe, a native of Canada, came to the United States as a teenager to study and became a citizen in 1910. A proponent of American music and women composers, she often focused composing activities around amateur music making, such as her women's chorus (1933–1954, called the Branscombe Choral) or women's music clubs. Her last composition was a commission for a special service at Riverside Church, New York: *Introit, Prayer Response, and Amen* (1973). Parker set approximately 400 hymns, carols, and folk songs (from various ethnic and racial traditions) for the Robert Shaw Chorale between 1949 and 1968, and many have received widespread performance. Parker's first opera, *The Martyrs' Mirror* (1971), recounts the lives of four Swiss Anabaptists executed for their religious beliefs. It was written for church performance and is partially based on Mennonite hymn tunes. Since these earlier works, Parker's musical language has become more cosmopolitan.[101]

Louise Talma, born a Protestant, was an atheist when she began her studies with Nadia Boulanger. After hearing Boulanger identify "priest" as the top profession, Talma read extensively about religion, and at the age of twenty-eight she converted to Roman Catholicism. This remains a foundation for her life. Although Talma has not composed much liturgical music (*Mass in English,* 1984), her convictions are revealed by her choice of texts from the Bible and poems that address religious issues, including *The Divine Flame* (1946–1948), *La Corona* (1954–1955; see HAMW, pp. 321–32), *The Tolling Bell* (1967–1969), and *Diadem* (1978–1979), which primarily sets medieval lapidaries.

Miriam Gideon (1906–1996) holds a special place in Jewish music.[102] She joined the faculty at Jewish Theological Seminary in 1955, and was the first woman to receive a commission for a complete synagogue service, *Sacred Service (for Sabbath Morning)* (1970). Although she did not want to be limited by such labels as "Jewish" or "woman" composer, Gideon acknowledged that some of her most interesting commissions came from synagogues and temples. She was consistently active in Jewish musical life as well as in a broad range of compositional spheres throughout her long and busy career. Gideon spent her teen years with an uncle, Henry Gideon, music director at the largest reform temple in Boston, and learned much about that tradition by playing organ at Temple Israel. Twenty years after completing undergraduate school, she received her master's degree in 1946; she was awarded a doctorate in composition from Jewish Theological Seminary in 1970. As a professional she successfully combined teaching in several academic institutions with her work as a composer.

Gideon is not a "Jewish music literalist," but in *Sacred Service* she infused her personal, freely atonal style with "shofar calls, pentatonicism, asymmetrical rhythms, melodicles, and chantlike effects, all reminiscent of numerous aspects and essences of genuine Jewish musical materials from a variety of traditions."[103] Many of her compositions have specific Jewish links, including *How Goodly Are Thy Tents* (1947), a setting of Psalm 84 for chorus; *Adon Olam* (1954), whose rhythms emulate the accentuation of the Hebrew text in this setting for soloists, mixed chorus, and chamber orchestra; and *Three Masques* (1958), using cantillation motives. Another such work, *Shirat Miriam L'Shabbat* (1974) for Sabbath evening, shifts away from dissonance through quartal harmony and freely uses cantillation, prayer modes, and Palestinian shepherd songs. *The Resounding Lyre* (1979), a song cycle, includes a poem by Gideon's husband; *A Woman of Valor* (1981) uses Hebrew texts from Psalms and Proverbs. Even in *The Hound of Heaven* (1945; see HAMW, pp. 293–97), which sets a poem about conversion to Catholicism, Gideon selected verses with particular reference and timeliness for Jewish people. In Gideon's opinion the lines she sets tell how "we must suffer or be charred, as the poem says, in order to live deeply."[104]

In keeping with a general tendency in the twentieth century, some composers and their work remain outside religious institutions yet are still connected with spiritual issues and values. This is not surprising, since institutional religion has often been hostile to women's active participation. Vivian Fine described her *Missa Brevis* (1972) as a personal religious statement:

> Preserving a traditional sense of ritual, it uses both Latin and Hebrew texts. The voice sections—a collage of four separate tracks previously recorded by Jan DeGaetani—are a counterpoise to the parts played by the four cellists.[105]

Women's spirituality, concerned in part with holistic healing, meditation, and environmental issues, has stimulated production of music specifically for the recording medium, such as Kay Gardner's *A Rainbow Path* (1984), *Sounding the Inner Landscape* (1990), and *Musical Massage* (1995). On the other hand, Annea Lockwood's verbal-visual score for *Singing the Moon* (1981) is strictly a participatory sonic meditation.[106] Heidi Von Gunden's *Whistle Music: A Sonic Exorcism* (1980) infers performers in more traditional terms, yet the "performance" involves meditative focusing of attention on the removal of evil spirits from the people present and from the performance space.[107]

Post–Avant-Garde Synthesis

Increasingly in the twentieth century, plurality has been expanding not only through successive and concurrent styles, but also through the coexistence of diverse styles within the output of a single composer—and even within a single composition. While this repertoire of synthesis does not focus on the most radical idioms, it also does not reject traditional materials. This fusion focuses on expression—often dramatic in nature—and has been especially hospitable to compositions on social themes or consciously feminist works.

. . . to piety more prone . . . (1983, revised 1985) by Elaine Barkin (b. 1932) is a powerful "assemblage" for four live speakers plus taped voices and musicians, including blues singers Bessie Smith, Ida Cox, Ma Rainey, and Ethel Waters. In addressing society's response to violence committed by women, this hybrid work discloses gender stereotypes. *Susanna Does the Elders* (1987), by Susan McClary, reworks Alessandro Stradella's seventeenth-century oratorio *La Susanna,* whose central scene is itself an erotic revision of the apocryphal story of Susanna. In Stradella's oratorio, listeners may well imagine a striptease as they hear the seductive singing used to justify

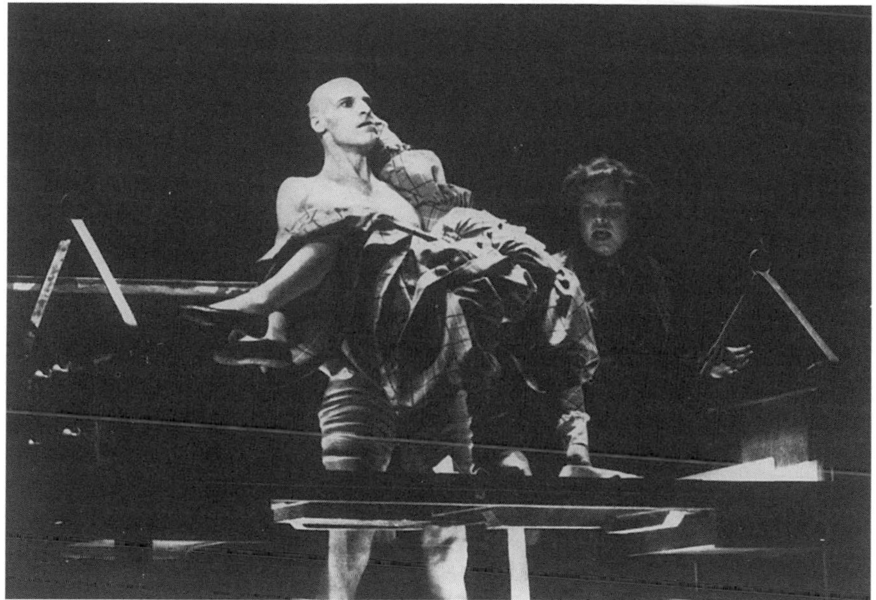

FIGURE 11.3. A silent monster is only one of the innovations in Libby Larsen's high-tech music drama *Frankenstein, the Modern Prometheus*. Photo by Susan Nelson. Reproduced by permission of the Minnesota Opera Company.

attempted rape. McClary's music-theater piece offers a feminist critique by placing seventeenth-century music—it is all Stradella's—within a new theatrical context. McClary asks:

> What do you do with music of theatrical power but which is antifeminist? . . . I want the dilemma to be thrown out to the audience. I'm opposed to censorship, but how do we deal with intolerance, of this or any sort, in "great art"?[108]

Frankenstein, the Modern Prometheus (1990), a multimedia opera by Libby Larsen, revitalizes this traditional genre with extensive and essential video as well as audio technology. The video presents multiple visual and emotional viewpoints, including the monster's perspective and intense close-ups. Larsen's compelling drama, based on Mary Shelley's novel, probes the dilemmas of technology. It is concerned, according to Larsen, with human beings "who, by succumbing to intellectual egotism and ambition, become aliens in the society they wish to enrich."[109] Premiered in 1998 by Opera Omaha, *Eric Hermannson's Soul* (1996–98), based on a story by Willa Cather, is another example of Larsen's setting of strong texts by women authors. Like the characters in the story who inhabit "distinct cultural environments,"

Larsen has used "three distinct pallets of music, including seven Norwegian hardanger fiddle tunes, the Intermezzo from *Cavalleria rusticana* [opera by Pietro Mascagni], and five fundamentalist hymns, to intertwine the three worlds." She continues, "These are all filtered through my own harmonic language full of augmented chords and Lydian scale tones to create the tonal world in which the opera operates."[110] Cather "creates landscapes of the mind and soul which operate in relation to their surroundings." Thus, in contrast to *Frankenstein,* which depends on technology, Larsen uses simple, stark production values for *Eric Hermannson's Soul* to give focus to the interior, psychological dimension.

In recent compositions Anne LeBaron shows postmodern tendencies by adding popular music influences to her style, resulting in an integrated approach and more accessible sound. Her opera *The E. & O. Line* (1991), with libretto by Thulani Davis, reinterprets the Orpheus and Eurydice legend from Eurydice's point of view and mixes elements of the oral traditions of bebop and blues music with her own structured, contemporary classical style. *Story of My Angel* (1993) for female soloist, women's chorus, piano, and optional live electronics incorporates gospel and jazz elements, while *American Icons* (1996), written for and premiered by the National Symphony Orchestra, references jitterbug, cartoon riffs, and Latin dance music.

The music of Joyce Mekeel (b. 1931) also melds an array of resources and often emerges from a dramatic or linguistic catalyst. Several of her works include multilingual texts: *Corridors of Dreams* (1972), *Serena* (1975), and *Alarums and Excursions* (1978), the latter working with material in eight languages. In *Corridors,* mostly sung or spoken in German or English, the execution of the text is an integral part of the composition. The first words are spoken partially through the flute, linking its timbre with the *shakuhachi* and the following Japanese Noh-style recitation by mezzo-soprano. Later the conductor declaims a marching song in counterpoint with dense instrumental gestures and the singer's stage whisper. Reaching back to earlier musical and literary eras, Mekeel also incorporates simpler materials. *Alarums and Excursions,* which refers to an Elizabethan stage direction, includes a tonal, Elizabethan-style tune, interrupted by an insistent twentieth-century violin gesture and a Gregorian chant–style recitation tone in stacked perfect fourths. These coexist with gamelan-like sounds produced from prepared piano and with dense microtonal string glissandi. *Planh* (1975) for solo violin, whose title refers to a lament from the troubadour/trobairitz lyric tradition, suggests improvisation through short-term melodic repetitions and the avoidance of regular phrasing. Among Mekeel's instrumental works, the sound of words remains a part of her timbral resources, as in *Rune* (1977) for flute and percussion and in *An Insomnia of Owls* (1984, revised 1985) for woodwind quintet. Mekeel's stylistic synthesis is well matched by her reliance on media outside primary institutional music organizations (such as the orchestra), which are more amenable to innovation.[111]

ORCHESTRAL PERFORMERS

In the first half of the twentieth century, especially during the 1930s and early 1940s, women's orchestras in the United States offered skilled female players and conductors experience and employment in the symphonic world. Women created their own opportunities because they could not obtain positions in all-male ("standard") orchestras. The Woman's Symphony Orchestra of Chicago and the New York Women's Symphony Orchestra were the best known nationally. The first white women—often harpists—were admitted to professional American symphonies in the mid-1920s, and a handful more were hired during the 1930s. Many major orchestras hired no full-time women players until quite recently: the Boston Symphony in 1945 and the New York Philharmonic in 1966 were among the earliest examples of top-tier orchestras to employ women. In 1964, when pianist Patricia Jennings joined the Pittsburgh Symphony, she became the first black woman under contract with a major orchestra in the United States. After more than two decades of impressive freelance work, timpanist Elayne Jones won a principal position with the San Francisco Symphony in 1972 and became the first black person to hold a first chair with a major American orchestra. However, at the end of two seasons Jones was denied tenure by the players' committee of the orchestra. She agreed to drop her lawsuit against the orchestra in exchange for another audition with a new committee of players. She was again dismissed, and has subsequently performed only on a part-time basis with the San Francisco Opera.[112]

Because of labor shortages caused by World War II, the 1940s brought increased employment opportunities for women. Consistent with this national trend, major orchestras hired increasing numbers of women beginning with the 1942–1943 season. Although women were generally viewed as temporary replacements, musicians—unlike women in many other professions—retained much of their gain after the war. Because women found positions with mixed orchestras, many of the all-women symphonies disbanded during the war years. In 1947, 8 percent of the players with major American orchestras were women. Since the 1940s women have made substantial progress in gaining access to professional symphony positions. In 1964–1965, 18.3 percent of the players in the eighteen largest-budget orchestras were women. In 1974–1975, nearly one-quarter (24.9 percent) of the performers in thirty-one major symphonies were women, and by 1983 the figure was 27.8 percent. Gains for women orchestral players in the late 1980s appear to have reached a plateau in terms of percentages: in 1986–1987 women constituted 30.8 percent of players; in 1987–1988, 30.1 percent; and in 1988–1989, 30.8 percent.[113] During the 1990s, the percentage of women performers has risen a little; however, data from 1996–1997 shows very little difference from information for 1994–1995. For the forty-four orchestras with the largest budgets, women constituted 37.9 percent in 1994–1995 and 34.7 percent in 1997–1998. The publication of vacancy notices, legislation against discrimination practices, and blind auditions behind a screen have contributed to the increased numbers of women hired.

Participation of women in orchestras is in inverse proportion to orchestra budgets: the bigger the budget, the fewer the women engaged. Among the "Big Five" orchestras (Boston, Chicago, Cleveland, New York, and Philadelphia) in 1972, only thirty-eight (7.2 percent) of the players were women; there were fifty-one (9.7 percent) women players in 1977; and one hundred (19.4 percent) in 1988. On the other hand, the percentage of women in regional and metropolitan symphonies (with budgets in the 1987–1988 season of $1 million to $3.6 million and $280,000 to $1 million, respectively) is larger, reaching 46.3 percent and 47.1 percent for the 1988–1989 season. By the 1996–1997 season this gap had closed somewhat: the "Big Five" (now made up of the symphonies in Boston, Chicago, Los Angeles, New York, and San Francisco) had 28 percent women players; those orchestras with budgets over $3.75 million had 34.7 percent women; and those with budgets of $1.1 million to $3.75 million had 46.7 percent women.

In the 1970s and 1980s women again formed alternative musical organizations, such as the now-defunct New England Women's Symphony and the Women's Philharmonic (formerly the Bay Area Women's Philharmonic). In these decades, however, a different motivation underlay the organizations than had the all-women orchestras of the 1920s and 1930s: to foster women conductors and to provide a forum for performance of compositions by women. The Women's Philharmonic is working to change the orchestral repertoire through the recovery of music by women of the past, commissioning new works by women, and promoting performances of those repertoires. In 1998 an anonymous woman was spurred to contribute a $1 million gift to the Women's Philharmonic after seeing a woman conduct for the first time: Eve Queler leading the Opera Orchestra of New York. These funds will support an advanced training and career development program for women conductors.[114]

CONDUCTORS

According to a 1996 interview with Beverly Sills, opera diva and former general director of the New York City Opera, "the barriers have mostly broken down for women composers, stage directors, and designers. Conducting is the last barrier."[115] Why has the field of conducting opened so slowly to women? Why is it often called "the last male bastion"? What factors contribute to the "maestro myth" and its exclusion of women? The orchestral conductor—leader of what is perhaps the most prestigious musical organization in Western culture—is an authority figure in the public spotlight. Visually, the conductor is elevated on a podium at center stage, taking the bow for all. These cultural characteristics conflict with traditional views of women and, along with historical discrimination against women, have contributed to the paucity of women as conductors.

During the 1920s and 1930s, increased conducting opportunities for women were linked with the peak in activity for all-women orchestras. Conductors such as Frédérique Petrides (1903–1983) developed careers by leading women's orchestras but were unable to establish themselves with all-male orchestras.[116] Petrides founded the Orchestrette Classique (later called Orchestrette of New York, 1932–1943), a women's orchestra, and later devoted herself to outdoor concerts, which attracted large audiences as well as critical and popular acclaim. In order to gain conducting opportunities, a significant number of women have founded ensembles, including Ethel Leginska, Antonia Brico, Margaret Hillis, Sarah Caldwell, Eve Queler, and Marin Alsop.

Both Ethel Leginska (1886–1970) and Antonia Brico (1902–1989) established prominent conducting careers during the 1920s and 1930s. They appeared with major orchestras in the United States and Europe, as well as with various all-women symphonies. Brico received rave reviews for her debut with the Berlin Philharmonic in 1930; after the threat of war forced her to return to the United States, however, she received few opportunities. By the late 1930s, the novelty of women conductors had declined, and most of the conducting opportunities for these women disappeared. Leginska moved to Los Angeles and taught piano. Brico moved to Denver, where she taught and coached privately. She also conducted a semiprofessional orchestra, eventually named the Brico Symphony, for more than thirty years. After the release of *Antonia: A Portrait of the Woman* (1974), a documentary film about her life, Brico received some renewed conducting opportunities with major orchestras.

Although Margaret Hillis (1921–1998) conducted the Elgin (Illinois) Symphony beginning in 1971, as well as other orchestras, she is best known for her work as a choral director. During her undergraduate days at Indiana

University, Hillis conducted her first choral performance. Because of her success, she was encouraged to pursue a conducting career—specifically one in choral music, which was deemed possible for a woman. Hillis recalled her composition teacher's assessment:

> "You are a conductor, but there is no place for a woman in orchestral conducting." . . . So [Bernard Heiden] advised me to go into choral conducting. [He said,] "There a woman is acceptable. Otherwise, you're going to go down the drain." I almost had a nervous breakdown, almost a complete functional breakdown. All of a sudden my world fell apart, this world I had lived in and lived for.[117]

In the end, however, Hillis took Heiden's advice and began her studies of choral music at Juilliard with Robert Shaw and Julius Herford.

After attending a rehearsal of her American Concert Choir and Orchestra of New York in 1954, Fritz Reiner employed Hillis and her ensemble with the Chicago Symphony during the next three seasons. In 1957 Hillis founded the Chicago Symphony Chorus at Reiner's request, and she led this ensemble until her retirement in 1994. Through four decades Hillis contributed extensively to the stature of choral music and to raising its performance standards through her leadership in the American Choral Foundation as well as her conducting.

Other women known for their work as choral conductors include Elaine Browne (d. 1997), Gena Branscombe, and Ann Howard Jones. In 1948 Browne founded Singing City Choir (Philadelphia), a multiracial, multicultural, and multireligious ensemble dedicated to achieving peace and harmony among diverse people. She continued as its director until the summer of 1987 and remained active as a guest conductor and workshop leader until 1990. Browne was also director of choral activities at Temple University, one of the sponsors for Singing City, in 1944–1956 and again in 1975–1981.

In addition to choral conducting, women are also found more commonly in opera than in orchestral conducting. Having women conduct operas might initially seem odd, given the substantial responsibility of opera conductors and the large financial costs of opera productions. Yet opera conductors do not take center stage. They lead from the pit and are far less visible than orchestral conductors, who are elevated on a podium and consistently in the spotlight. Perhaps women have been more acceptable to audiences or management in this pit location. Further, the route to being an opera conductor often begins with a stint as rehearsal pianist and coach, a position frequently held by a woman, at least in the United States. Women whose conducting careers have focused on opera include Sarah Caldwell (b. 1924), founder of the Opera Company of Boston in 1957 and, in 1976, the first woman to conduct at the Met; Judith Somogi (1937–1988), whose career was centered in Europe with the Frankfurt Opera (1981–1987) after early success at the New York City Opera; and Eve Queler (b. 1936), who has received international acclaim for her concert versions of rarely performed operas.

Eve Queler was hired as rehearsal accompanist and coach at New York City Opera in 1957, just six months after the birth of her first child. The time demands of these two areas of her life created conflicts, and her contract was not renewed for the following year. Queler returned to school to study conducting, then spent the next several years coaching and doing studio work. Her desire to conduct led her to found the New York Opera Workshop, later called the Opera Orchestra of New York.

In the 1960s and 1970s, Judith Somogi also moved through the ranks from rehearsal pianist and coach to become a conductor at New York City Opera. She was hired in 1966 and conducted her first production in 1974. After establishing her reputation with this company, Somogi conducted at the Pittsburgh Opera and served as principal conductor of major opera companies across the United States, including live telecasts with New York City Opera. After her orchestral debut with the Los Angeles Philharmonic in 1975, she also appeared as guest conductor with various American orchestras.

Much of the visibility for women conductors is recent history, a string of "firsts." The situation is clearly improving for women, but, as with women orchestral players, the participation of women conductors is in inverse proportion to orchestra budgets. No woman has yet held a conducting position with a major orchestra in the United States with the exception of a one-year appointment for Rachel Worby as Youth Concerts Conductor for the Los Angeles Philharmonic. Catherine Comet, associate conductor of the Baltimore Symphony from 1984 to 1986 and originally from France, was the first woman to hold even an associate conductor position with a major symphony in the United States or Canada. A year later JoAnn Falletta became the second, when she was appointed associate conductor of the Milwaukee Symphony. Falletta resigned that post at the end of the 1988 summer season. In 1986, Comet also became the first woman in the principal conducting position of a fully professional orchestra when she was appointed music director of the Grand Rapids Symphony, where she remained until the spring of 1997.

In 1988 twenty-four women held conducting posts with professional orchestras that are members of the American Symphony Orchestra League (ASOL); even in 1990 few women held conducting positions with the ninety-nine U.S. and Canadian orchestras whose annual budgets exceeded one million dollars. Only three women (3 percent) were principal conductors: Iona Brown, leading the Los Angeles Chamber Orchestra from the principal violin seat; Catherine Comet, music director with both the Grand Rapids Symphony and the American Symphony Orchestra; and JoAnn Falletta, conductor of the Long Beach Symphony Orchestra. Three more women held secondary positions: Marin Alsop (associate conductor, Richmond Symphony); Dianne Pope (music advisor, Des Moines Symphony Orchestra); and Tania León (conductor of community concerts, Brooklyn Philharmonic). By 1990 several women held assistant conductor positions with major orchestras (e.g., Dallas, Houston, and Calgary), and others were music directors with smaller-budget professional orchestras: e.g., Victoria Bond (Roanoke Symphony) and Rachel Worby (Wheeling Symphony). Since the late 1980s women in the early stages of their conducting careers have become more visible, and they constitute a growing percentage in conducting workshops sponsored by the ASOL, in the summer program at the Tanglewood Music Festival in Massachusetts, and in important events such as the Stokowski Conducting Competition.

At the end of the 1997–1998 season, women held 47 orchestral conducting positions among the more than 600 member orchestras of the ASOL (excluding youth and college ensembles). However, within the top 25 orchestras by budget size (above $10.8 million total expenses), no women held music director or principal conductor posts; five women held various other conducting positions. In the next tier of 23 orchestras (those with budgets above $4 million)—still considered "majors" by the American Federation of Musicians (union)—two women were music directors, and three held secondary posts. Thus, just over 4 percent of the principal conductors were women. In the next two budget groups, including 64 orchestras (with budgets above $1.2 million), generally comparable to the former category of "regional" symphonies, three music directors (4.7 percent) were women: Falletta at Long Beach and Virginia and Gisele Ben-Dor with the Santa Barbara Symphony. The assistant conductor at Santa Barbara is also a woman—the only orchestra to have more than one woman on its conducting staff—and eight additional women hold secondary positions among the regional symphonies. In the 150 orchestras that are roughly comparable to the "metropolitan" symphonies, many have only one conductor. Women are music directors for 2 orchestras (4.5 percent) with budgets over $700,000 and for 7 orchestras with budgets over $300,000 (7.3 percent). In the final cluster of 359 orchestras, many of which are volunteer organizations or include unpaid personnel, women held thirty-three top posts (9.2 percent).

Direct comparisons over the past eight to ten years are difficult due to inflation, changes in relative budget sizes, and the reorganization of categories used by the American Symphony Orchestra League. The data, however, indicate a slight improvement over the past decade, but apparently the "glass ceiling" remains largely intact. Few women have reached principal positions with the majors, and women are better represented in secondary positions and smaller-budget ensembles. Beginning with the 1998–1999 season, two women stand out for their achievements, visibility, and current positions: Marin Alsop (b. 1957) and JoAnn Falletta (b. 1954).

Marin Alsop

Prior to Alsop's appointment with the Richmond Symphony, she was already conductor of Concordia, a New York chamber orchestra, which she founded in 1984. In 1990 Alsop joined the small group of women music directors with her appointment at both the Long Island Philharmonic and the Eugene (Oregon) Symphony, both of which she conducted until the end of the 1995–1996 season. She has gained considerably more responsibility with several recent appointments: principal conductor and then music director of the Colorado Symphony beginning with the 1993–1994 season; music director of the Cabrillo Festival in California; and an appointment to the Creative Conductor chair with the St. Louis Symphony beginning in the fall of 1996. Alsop grew up surrounded by music, as both of her parents are members of the New York City Ballet Orchestra. When she was about twelve years old, she declared that she wanted to be a conductor, and one of her teachers at Juilliard's Preparatory Department, where she studied violin, told her, "Girls don't do that." Fortunately, her father's response was to buy her a box of conducting batons.[118] After undergraduate study at Yale University, private conducting study, work as a freelance violinist, and two summers of study with Leonard Bernstein at the Tanglewood Music Festival, Alsop was the first woman awarded the Koussevitzky Conducting Prize at Tanglewood. She also won the Leopold Stokowski Conducting Competition in 1989, both awards clearly important recognitions for career development.

JoAnn Falletta

In May 1998 JoAnn Falletta was appointed music director of the Buffalo (New York) Philharmonic Orchestra, a second-tier orchestra, where she began assuming some responsibilities in the fall of 1998. This is the highest orchestral appointment for a woman in the United States. Falletta, music director of the Women's Philharmonic in San Francisco from 1986 until 1996, was the first American woman to lead regional orchestras, as music director for the Long Beach Symphony (since 1989) and the Virginia Symphony (since 1991)—positions she expects to retain at least through the 1999–2000 season. Earlier Falletta held positions with the Denver Chamber Orchestra and the Queens (New York) Philharmonic, and received considerable acknowledgment of her skill on the podium with a first prize in the

FIGURE 11.4. JoAnn Falletta is part of a new generation of orchestra conductors. Photo by Niel Erickson. Reproduced by permission of JoAnn Falletta.

Leopold Stokowski Conducting Competition (1985) and the Toscanini Conductors Award. Since joining the (Bay Area) Women's Philharmonic, about 80 percent of whose repertoire is by women composers, Falletta has learned many scores by women and has programmed some of the music with other orchestras she conducts.

At age seven Falletta began her musical training with guitar lessons because her family's apartment did not have enough room for a piano. When she was about twelve, her immigrant parents began taking JoAnn and her sister to concerts. From this time forward she knew she wanted to be a conductor, although as a teenager she was told this was impossible because no woman had previously worked as a conductor. In spite of this misrepresentation, Falletta continued to pursue her career plans. Her comments in interviews reveal her awareness of gender in relationship to conducting. On the subtlety of gender issues, she claims, "The more I got into conducting, the more I had to come to terms with how I was raised as a young Catholic girl. We were taught to be supportive, nurturing, gentle, kind."[119] Falletta discovered that traditional socialization led women to apologize for making demands, and that this was a problem for a conductor. During her doctoral study with Jorge Mester at Juilliard she learned to avoid phrases and a tone of voice that could sabotage her on the podium. Falletta, who married in 1986, acknowledges the tension between career and family. Although many men have had both with the help of a support system from their wives, only a few women conductors, such as Catherine Comet and Simone Young (an Australian), have been able to sustain both an active career and motherhood. In a 1991 interview Falletta, who has been the first woman on several European podiums, discussed her perception that many European orchestras were eager to have women as guest conductors, but still quite reluctant to consider them for music director positions.[120]

Women and Music in Mexico and Latin America

Even in the twentieth century, women's participation in concert music has emerged only gradually in Mexico and Latin America. Speaking about Mexico, Esperanza Pulido claims that *malinchismo* (an inferiority complex) and *machismo* (an exaggeration of masculinity or male pride) have hampered women as performers and composers.[121] Self-taught composer-poet-singer María Grever (1885–1951), the first Mexican woman to achieve fame as a composer, moved to the United States in 1916 and later composed for Hollywood films and Broadway shows. Among her hit songs were "Bésame" ("Kiss Me," her first published song, 1921), "Júrame" (recorded by José Mojica in 1927), "What a Diff'rence a Day Made," and especially "Tipitín" (the latter two songs recorded by both Frank Sinatra and Bing Crosby). The number of Mexican women active in commercial music has increased during the second half of this century. By 1982 at least forty-seven women had contributed regularly in this area and played an important role in shaping both the musical style and topics or content, among them, Emma Elena Valdelamer and Laura Goméz Llanos.

Mexico

Mexico became home to European-born composers Emiliana de Zubeldia Inda (1888–1987) and Mariá Teresa Prieto (1896–1982), both from Spain, and a temporary haven for Ruth Schonthal (b. 1924), who studied there after fleeing the Nazis in 1941 and before moving to the United States in 1946. During her long life Zubeldia Inda worked as a concert pianist (1928–1936) and composer, then spent forty years in Hermosillo at the university as a teacher, choral conductor, broadcaster, and composer. After meeting Augusto Novaro in 1930, Zubeldia became the sole disciple of this acoustician and instrument builder. She adopted his harmonic theories and used his acoustical principles in her *Sonatine* for two pianos and *Once Tientos* (pub. 1963) for piano. In contrast, Mariá Teresa Prieto moved to Mexico at the outbreak of the Spanish Civil War in 1936. Romantic nationalism, prominent in her early works, is evident in such symphonic compositions as *Chichén-Itzá* (1944) and *Sinfonía breve* (1945). Later she adopted extended tonality and harsh dissonances, creating expressionistic works such as *Odas celestes* (Celestial Waves, 1947) for voice and piano. Subsequently Prieto took up twelve-tone technique in *Doce variaciones seriales* (Twelve Serial Variations, 1961) for piano and *Tema variado y fuga* (Varied Theme and Fugue, 1968) for orchestra. Schonthal, who supported herself and her family by playing in nightclubs, composed some works with Hispanic titles during her years in Mexico: *Concerto romantico* (1942) for orchestra and *Capriccio español* (1945) for piano.

In the field of classical music, Mexican women, like their counterparts in the United States, have often combined composition with teaching and performing. Rosa Guraieb Kuri (b. 1931), for example, who studied in Mexico and Lebanon, is involved in all three areas. She began composing after studying with Carlos Chavez, writing primarily for voice and chamber ensemble as well as for her own instrument, the piano. Her chamber music includes two string quartets (1978, 1982); *Canto a la paz* (Song for Peace, 1982) for oboe, bassoon, and piano; and *Reencuentros* (Reencounters, 1985) for violin, cello, and piano. Marta Garcia Renart (b. 1942) is an accomplished pianist, choral conductor, and composer. Her compositions include choral works, music for a children's play, and *Tres momentos* (Three Moments, 1978) for piano.[122] Graciela Morales de Elias (b. 1944) and Graciela Agudelo Murguia (b. 1945) compose primarily for chamber ensemble and reveal an interest in more experimental paths. For example, Agudelo's *Arabesco* for one recorder player (playing alto and tenor recorders) explores extended techniques such as multiphonics, and her *Navegantes del crepúsculo* (Sailing in the Twilight, pub. 1992) for clarinet, bassoon, and piano also includes avant-garde techniques.[123] Marcela Rodriguez (b. 1951), Lilia Vázquez (b. 1955), and Ana Lara (b. 1959) are among a younger generation of composers. Rodriguez, a guitarist as well as a composer, has written much chamber music. Among her larger works are *Religiosos incendios* (Religious Fires) for orchestra, the opera *La Sunamita* (1991), and Concerto for Recorders and Orchestra (1993). Vázquez, a bassoonist and pianist, received a positive reception for her orchestral work *Donde habita el Olvido* (Where Oblivion Lives, 1984). Lara, who studied in Mexico and Poland, has given particular attention to timbre in her music, as in *Vitrales* (1992) for viola, cello, and double bass and *Icaro* for solo recorder.

Alicia Urreta

Mexican composer Alicia Urreta (1933?–1987?) began her musical studies as a talented young pianist. She attended the National Conservatory of Mexico; however, financial difficulties forced her to discontinue her education and earn a living. While pursuing a career as a concert pianist she worked as an accompanist for a dance troupe, which introduced her to music by many contemporary Mexican composers. Her strong sightreading ability was essential in the dance studio, and led to her strong reputation for performances of difficult avant-garde European and American piano repertoire. Urreta began composing in 1964, writing music for a theatre work, and she continued her involvement with theatre, film, and dramatic works throughout her career.

Urreta utilized several of the more experimental compositional approaches discussed earlier in this chapter (sound mass, sonic exploration, improvisation, noise, and electroacoustic elements) to create a personal style synthesizing many influences. She is among a generation of Mexican composers whose nationalism is no longer linked with folkloric music. *De natura mortis o La verdadera historia de Caperucita Roja* (The True Story of Little Red Riding Hood, 1971) is for a narrator who also uses a synthesizer to distort the voice, an improviser on prepared piano, and an electronic tape. It is a takeoff on the story of Little Red Riding Hood, focusing on the seduction and erotic elements between the girl and the wolf. *Homenaje a cuatro* (Homage to Four, 1975) for string orchestra, calling for extended techniques, and *Salmodia I* (Psalmody, 1978) for piano are important works and among her first to bypass a surface story line. The conceptual origin of *Arcana* (1981), a concerto for prepared and amplified piano and orchestra, was an interesting tarot card reading that used only the twelve major arcana cards. According to Urreta,

> The music is like a chain of events which happen without transitions. It is written like reading the cards. This provokes at times very violent contrasts within the work, while at other times there is a very logical sequence that lends toward a musical development.[124]

Arcana, involving precise notation of complex rhythms, features sound mass and timbral variety.

Considered her most important work, *De la Pluma al Angel* (From the Feather to the Angel, 1982) is a dramatic secular cantata scored for three soloists, narrator, chorus, two organs, harmonium, and percussion. The story concerns angels expelled from heaven who seduce humanity, leaving them without love or passion but with a longing for the angels that have disappeared. Urreta developes her narrative using a wide range of poetic sources, orchestrating each text with a different instrumentation. In addition to having significance as a composer, Urreta also contributed to contemporary musical life through her performances and by organizing annual festivals of contemporary Mexican and Spanish music in Mexico City and Madrid.

Central America and the Caribbean

Roció Sanz (1933–1993) was born in Costa Rica but pursued a career in Mexico from 1953 onward. Known for children's compositions and stories as well as instrumental works and various types of theatrical music, she devoted much of the last two decades of her life to a radio program called Children's Corner, which broadcast music of various composers. Her settings of texts by the outstanding seventeenth-century Mexican poet Juana Inés de La Cruz (Sor Juana), *Sucedió en Belén* (It Happened in Bethlehem), won first prize in a 1976 choral music competition in Costa Rica. Sanz's *Hilos* (Threads) for string orchestra and *Canciones de la muerte* (Songs about Death) for soprano were performed at the International Congress of Women in Music in Mexico City in 1984. Panamanian Marina Saiz (b. 1930) studied extensively with Roque Cordero, first in Panama and then in the United States, where both composers later resided. Her Sonata for Piano uses a free, atonal approach with some complex rhythms suggesting the influence of Panamanian dance.

Ninón de Brouwer Lapeiretta (b. 1907) and Margarita Luna de Espaillat (b. 1921) are both from the Dominican Republic. Brouwer Lapeiretta has become known at home and abroad for her ballet score *La reina del Caribe* (The Queen of the Caribbean), works for piano, two capriccios for wind ensemble, and *Absominación de la espera* (Expecting Freedom from Submissiveness) for soprano and orchestra. A professor of music history and theory, Luna de Espaillat has created chamber music, piano pieces, an oratorio called *Vigilia eterna* (Eternal Vigil), and *Elegie* for choir, narrator, and orchestra.

Esther Alejandro (b. 1947), born in New York City of Puerto Rican parents, returned to Puerto Rico with her family during childhood. After graduating from the University of Puerto Rico in 1968, she also studied with Nadia Boulanger at Fontainebleau (1972) and at the Conservatory of Music in Puerto Rico. On a commission from the Conservatory of Music Alejandro composed *El zapatero prodigioso* (The Marvelous Shoemaker, 1980) for orchestra and narrator, a work based on Hans Christian Andersen's story "The Elves and the Shoemaker" and intended for an audience of children. The piece was later performed by the Puerto Rico Symphony Orchestra, their first performance of a composition by a Puerto Rican woman. Unlike many of her works, this composition is tonal and poses only limited technical demands. In *Intercambio* (Interchange) Alejandro combines a Puerto Rican folk instrument of the guitar family, the *cuatro*, with a violin and explores the sonorities of this combination. Other works include *Claves para una obsesión* (Keys for an Obsession, 1980) for voice, bassoon, and piano; *O grande jogo/El gran juego* (O Large Gamble/The Big Game, 1982) for two actors and tape (*musique concrète*); and *Gratitud, danza puertorriqueña* (Gratitude, a Puerto Rican Dance, 1983) for piano.

Cuba

As a pianist, Cecilia Arizti Sobrino (1856–1930) concentrated on composing for her instrument. Arizti's Piano Trio (1893), the first known chamber music by a Cuban woman, uses a Romantic harmonic vocabulary. Working together, Olga de Blanck Martín (b. 1916) and Gisela Hernández Gonzalo (1912–1971)—both composers as well as teachers—implemented significant changes in Mexico's music education system. Both also worked at the Hubert de Blanck Conservatory, founded by Olga's father. Blanck published several musical comedies: *Vivimos hoy, Hotel Tropical, Rendezvous de tres,* and *Un cuento de Navidad* (Today We Live, Tropical Hotel, A Rendezvous for Three, A Christmas Story). For Hernández, nationalism became an increasingly important stylistic element in her compositions. She therefore used Afro-Cuban melodies, typical Cuban rhythms shifting between 3/4 and 6/8 meters, and texts by Cuban poets (e.g., in the choral cycle *Tríptico* [1967]).

Cuban-born Odaline de la Martinez (b. 1949) left her homeland at age nine because of the revolution and was raised by her aunt in the United States. After studying as an undergraduate at Tulane University, she moved to Britain for graduate study at the Royal Academy of Music, and has been based in London since 1972. The first woman to conduct a BBC Promenade Concert at the Albert Hall (1984), Martinez is founding musical director of the Lontano chamber music ensemble, which has toured extensively and recorded works by British women composers. Conductor of the European Women's Orchestra, which she helped found in 1990, Martinez has also led major British orchestras and appeared internationally in countries such as Columbia, New Zealand, and Canada. As director of the Cardiff [Wales] Music Festival in 1994 she included a significant number of works by women on her programs: Clara Schumann, Fanny Mendelssohn Hensel, Ethel Smyth, Judith Weir, and a new production of Nicola LeFanu's opera *Dawnpath* (premiered in 1977). Although perhaps best known as a conductor, Martinez is also a composer whose eclectic works show the influence of George Crumb, electronic-music composers, and her own heritage. In an interview describing her origins in a rural Cuban community, where her musical experiences were exclusively Afro-Cuban, Martinez said: "My earliest memory of music was falling to sleep to the hypnotic sound of the drums and waking up at five in the morning when they stopped. Music even then was a joy to me and that is where I gained my love of strong rhythms."[125]

Tania León

Tania León (b. 1944), whose family background includes French, Spanish, Chinese, and African elements (her grandmother was a slave in Cuba), received two degrees in music from the Peyrellade's Conservatorio de Música in Havana. She began her career as a pianist while continuing her education in accounting. Later she studied in the United Sates, where she settled and where she has been associated with the Dance Theater of Harlem since 1968. With her involvement as musical director for *The Wiz* on Broadway, *Godspell,* and musical theatre works by Robert Wilson during the late 1970s and early 1980s, American idioms such as gospel and jazz became influences on León's compositional style. Beginning in the 1980s she explicitly incorporated textual and rhythmic elements from her African and Cuban cultural heritage alongside contemporary classical techniques (e.g., in *De-Orishas* [1982] for voices and percussion and *A la Par* [1986] for piano and percussion). Her works feature dense textures, angular melodies, dissonant harmonies, and colorful orchestrations, as heard in *Batá* (1985) and *Pueblo mulato* for soprano and chamber ensemble (1987). Rhythmic energy, polyrhythms, and unexpected accents are often prominent, as in *Carabalí* for orchestra (1991), which draws on Cuban rhythms. Her compositions are technically challenging, whether for the piano, as in *Momentum* (1984)[126] or *Rituál* (1987); for orchestral instruments, as in *Indígena* (1991); or for voices, as in *Batéy* (1989).[127] León received a commission from the city of Munich for her first opera, *Scourge of Hyacinths,* which was premiered by the New Music Theatre under her baton at the 1994 Munich Biennale. Her multifaceted career has included being music director for television in Havana (1965–1966), teaching at Brooklyn College, and giving support as new-music advocate-adviser for various organizations, including the New York Philharmonic (1993–1996).

WOMEN AND MUSIC IN CANADA

In the early part of the twentieth century, music by Canadians revealed its heavy reliance on the study and compositional styles of England and France. During the second and third decades, Canadian composers generally followed one of two traditions: French as exemplified by Claude Champagne, or English as exemplified by Healey Willan. Since the late 1940s most Canadians have studied composition in the United States or in Europe and have participated more in the so-called international styles of music.[128]

Although Violet Archer (1913–2000) began composition studies with Champagne, her early works are linked with the English late-Romantic tradition. After studying with Béla Bartók in New York in 1942, her compositions, which she designated as being in "a neo-classic, perhaps neo-baroque style,"[129] became more dissonant. They presented a new tonal language, juxtaposing and combining various modes but avoiding functional tonality. Following coursework with Paul Hindemith at Yale University between 1947 and 1949, Archer became more austere in her compositions, but they still retained their clarity and reserve. Archer identified her Sonata for Horn and Piano (1965) as a turning point toward greater abstraction and economy of materials. By the 1960s her compositions became more dramatically heightened as she included a new expressionism, and some works from the 1970s incorporate electronic elements.

Archer was a prolific composer, writing for many different media and for performers ranging from young amateurs to highly skilled professionals. Her interest in *Gebrauchsmusik* and her desire to contribute to the literature for various solo instruments and piano show some of the many influences stemming from her association with Hindemith. Sonata for Alto Saxophone and Piano (see HAMW, pp. 357–63), which Archer identified as a work that pleased her very much, is one of her most popular instrumental pieces. A 1994 retrospective of her work held in Toronto included one of her major compositions, *Evocations* (1987) for two pianos and orchestra.

Jean Coulthard (1908–2000) first studied piano with her mother, a professional musician, and later absorbed the English tradition from Ralph Vaughan Williams in London. Her music focuses on lyrical melody with an extended tonal vocabulary, showing commonality with French Impressionism. Among her major works for piano are Sonata for Piano (1947), *B-A-C-H Variations* (1951), *Aegean Sketches* (1961[?]), *Requiem Piece* (1968; arr. for two pianos, 1974), *Sketches for Western Woods* (1970), and *Ecology Suite* (1974). Many of her works draw on the Canadian countryside: *The Pines of Emily Carr* (1969 [?]) for soprano, narrator, string quartet, timpani, and piano, for example, is a title that refers to the landscapes of the famed Canadian painter.

Barbara Pentland (1912–2000) became a composer despite the objections of her parents and her problems with a serious heart ailment. In addition to working with Aaron Copland, three years at Juilliard, and an important summer's study in Darmstadt, Pentland studied with several women musicians: Cécile Gauthiez (in Paris, 1929–1930), Eva Clare (in Winnipeg, 1930s), and Dika Newlin (at the MacDowell Colony, 1947 and 1948). Pentland's style evolved significantly during her long career. Her early compositions, from the late 1930s, were in a neoclassical style, whereas Octet for Winds (1948) was her first work to utilize aspects of twelve-tone technique. *Symphony for Ten Parts* (1957), a concise and transparent work, reveals the influence of Anton Webern's music subsequent to her study at Darmstadt in 1955. By the late 1960s Pentland employed aleatory elements and microtones. She became interested in unusual timbral combinations through her study of Webern, and sonority became the organizing element in her music by the late 1970s.

Dramatic works, especially on topics of social concern, also emerged during the 1970s. *News* (1970) for voice and orchestra is a deeply felt response to the casual reporting and public acceptance of the violence during the Vietnam War. In *Disasters of the Sun* (1976) for mezzo-soprano, chamber ensemble, and tape, Pentland set a poetic cycle by Dorothy Livesay that critiques male domination. In its scenario, the Sun (man) is defeated by the Moon (woman), and Pentland's treatment of woman's victory is calm and understated, as if inevitable. Pentland, who claimed that she had difficulty finding suitable texts, returned to poetry by Livesay in her setting of *Ice Age* (1986) for voice and piano.

Each of these women—Archer, Coulthard, and Pentland—has played an important role in Canadian musical life and, through teaching, has had a strong influence on younger musicians. Archer chaired the music theory and composition area at the University of Alberta from 1961 to 1978; Coulthard taught composition and theory at the University of British Columbia from 1947 to 1973; and Pentland was a university professor there from 1939 to 1963. In addition to their compositions for advanced players, both Archer and Pentland have written teaching pieces for piano.

Electronic music appears to be an important medium for many women composers in Canada. Norma Beecroft (b. 1934) was active in diverse areas of music: as flutist; programmer, producer, and commentator for CBC radio; cofounder and administrator for New Music Concerts; and composer. Since the 1960s she has frequently written electroacoustic music, especially in combination with live performers: for example, *From Dreams of Brass* (1963–1964) for narrator, soprano, mixed chorus, orchestra, and electronic tape; *Two Went to Sleep* (1967) for soprano, flute, percussion, and tape; an electronic piece for the puppet show at Expo '67 in Montreal; *Hedda* (1982–1983), a ballet with orchestra and tape; and *Evocations: Images of Canada* (1991) for digital MIDI synthesizer and mixer. During the 1970s Ginette Bellavance (b. 1946) composed a large number of electronic works for film and theater. She was also involved in music as perception and with Yul, a pop-music research group. Micheline Coulombe Saint-Marcoux (1938–1985) studied electronic music with the Groupe de Recherches Musicales de l'O.R.T.F. in Paris and composed for electronic tape alone and with live performers. Earlier works for acoustic instruments are atonal and employ aspects of sound-mass, such as in *Hétéromorphie* (1970); later works focus on sonic elements, as in her incidental music for marionettes, *Comment Wang-fô fut sauvé* (How Wang-fô Was Saved, 1982–1983), for flute, french horn, *ondes Martenot*, cello, piano, percussion, and tape. Timbral exploration also led Bellavance to use the *ondes Martenot* in *Modulaire* (1967) for orchestra and in *Séquences* (1968, rev. 1973) for two *ondes Martenots* and percussion.

Ann Southam (b. 1937) is best known for her electroacoustic music, especially her lyrical scores for dance, such as *Against Sleep* (1969), *Seastill* (1979), and *Goblin Market* (1986). Her compositions for acoustic instruments give particular attention to the piano, her own instrument: *Spatial View of Pond* (1986) for piano and tape and *In a Measure of Time* (1988) for two pianos. Southam and another pianist-composer, Diana McIntosh (b. 1937), cofounded the new-music organization Music Inter Alia. McIntosh has composed music in various styles and for many different combinations of performers, including multimedia. Both women have contributed significantly to Canadian musical life: Southam as the first president of the Association of Canadian Women Composers (1980–1988) and McIntosh through her premieres and performances of contemporary Canadian music and her role as composer-in-residence at the University of Manitoba.

Alexina Louie (b. 1949), a third generation Chinese-Canadian, is among the most prominent Canadian composers of her generation and was named Composer of the Year in 1986 by the Canadian Music Council. She studied music at the University of British Columbia and then with Pauline Oliveros and Robert Erickson at the University of California, San Diego, where she was a member of the Female Ensemble doing sonic meditations led by Oliveros. While in southern California, Louie began studying world music, especially that of China, Japan, Korea, India, and Indonesia. She returned to Canada in 1980 and continues to compose full time, receiving many awards and commissions. In October 1996 Louie was appointed composer-in-residence with the Canadian Opera Company, and she is composing an opera based on a seventeenth-century Kabuki play that she has described as "an erotic ghost story."[130] Tony Award–winning playwright David Henry Hwang (*M. Butterfly*) prepared the libretto, and *The Scarlet Princess* (working title) is scheduled to premiere during the 1999–2000 season.

Louie's expressive style effectively blends musical elements from the East and West: the influence of Asian instrumental timbres, minimalism,

Asian philosophy (especially the complementary duality of yin and yang), bitonality, quartal chords, nonmetrical rhythm, and traditional Western multimovement forms. In *Music for a Thousand Autumns* (1983) for a mixed ensemble of twelve instrumentalists, Louie writes directions for pitch bends, exaggerated vibrato, and harmonics to create an Asian atmosphere with Western instruments. An array of percussion instruments adds further color. *The Ringing Earth,* a fanfare written for the opening of Expo '86 in Vancouver, has been described as "majestic sounds—beginning with a dazzling flourish of brass and percussion . . . [and ending with] a rousing finish with full orchestra."[131] Canadian pianist Jon Kimura Parker, who commissioned *Scenes from a Jade Terrace* (1988), describes this work as follows:

> Compositional techniques, including the use of semi-chromatic scales, bitonality, exotic timbres, minimalist rhythmic patterns, and right and left hand mirroring are woven together into this work. Through a unique manipulation of the timbral possibilities of the piano and a carefully hewn structure, Louie has succeeded in creating an original and significant piano composition.[132]

Love Songs for a Small Planet (1989, rev. 1992), Louie's first choral composition, brings together the composer's interests in poetry and world spiritual traditions with her humanitarian and environmental concerns.[133] Each section of *Love Songs* presents poems by indigenous peoples of the world that Louie found inspiring. In the final section, entitled "Earth," which sets a text from the North American Lakota tradition, extended choral techniques and a quartet of blown glass bottles add to the evocative texture of the accompaniment by harp, strings, and marimba. Although definitely using a contemporary vocabulary, Louie's music is repeatedly described as accessible and communicative.

Hope Lee (b. 1953), the youngest of the Canadian composers discussed here, was born in Taiwan, although her parents came from mainland China. After completing her formal composition study at McGill University and the Staatliche Hochschule für Musik in Freiburg, Germany, Lee pursued additional studies of Chinese traditional music and poetry and computer music in Berkeley, California. Lee's music is generally atonal and rhythmically complex, and uses extended techniques. In describing her creative process, Lee said:

> Things change constantly and continuously . . . therefore each work should be approached from a fresh angle. Growth is a natural phenomenon reflected in my compositional technique. Not unlike disciplined organic growth—a most fascinating phenomenon—it is the secret of life, the source of true freedom.[134]

The diversity of instrumentations, including electronic works and several compositions using Chinese instruments, is certainly consistent with this viewpoint. Among her principal works are *Nabripamo* (1982) for piano and marimba; *Liú Liú* (1984) for pipa, percussion, baritone, and small string orchestra; *. . . . I, Laika. . . .* (1988–1989) for flute, cello, and piano;[135] *Voices in Time* (1992–94) for large ensemble, tape, and electronics; and *arrow of being, arrow of becoming* (1997) for string quartet with optional live electronics. Like Alexina Louie, Lee works toward integrating Asian—specifically Chinese—ideas and sounds into a Western framework.

FOR FUTURE CONSIDERATION

This chapter focuses primarily on women composers and performers; however, women have been active during the twentieth century in virtually every area of music. They work within traditional institutions and they create their own organizations and venues. They are teachers, music therapists, philanthropists, arts administrators, publishers, and members of the recording industry. For a comprehensive understanding of the scope and breadth of women's contributions and influence in music, additional research in these and other areas is needed. As we grasp more fully the activities of women, we will gain a deeper understanding of the shape of North American music history.

NOTES

Special thanks are due to those who provided assistance for this chapter: research for the original edition, Jane Lohr (University of Iowa graduate student), Melissa Hanson (Macalester College, class of 1990), Lia Gima (Macalester College, class of 1990), and Jill Edwards (Macalester College, class of 1991); research for this revision, Jennifer Anderson (Macalester College, class of 1998), Catherine Davies (Macalester College, class of 2000), and Megan Opp (Macalester College, class of 2000); the American Symphony Orchestra League (Victoria O'Reilly and Christina Mitchell); Sonya Sezun (Macalester College, class of 1990) for translations from Spanish; Elizabeth Hinkle-Turner for sharing research from her forthcoming book on women and electroacoustic music; and the staff of DeWitt Wallace Library at Macalester, especially Jean Beccone and Terri Fishel. I am also grateful to colleague and friend Dorothy Williams for her suggestions and support.

1. Sara M. Evans, *Born for Liberty: A History of Women in America* (New York: The Free Press, 1989), p. 176.

2. See chapter 6 in Ellie M. Hisama, "Gender, Politics, and Modernist Music: Analyses of Five Compositions by Ruth Crawford (1901–1953) and Marion Bauer (1887 [*sic*]–1955)" (Ph.D. diss., City University of New York, 1996; UMI #9618075).

3. For a sample of seven works, see *Mary Howe,* Composers Recordings CRI American Masters CD785 (1998); for a recording of *Sand,* conducted by JoAnn Falletta, see *The Virginia Symphony, Music and the Arts* 2/2 CDR0497 (1997), available directly from the Virginia Symphony (550 E Main Street; Norfolk, VA 23510-2201); for four songs, see *From a Woman's Perspective: Art Songs by Women Composers,* Vienna Modern Masters VMM2005 (1993).

4. Madeleine Goss, *Modern Music-Makers: Contemporary American Composers* (New York: E. P. Dutton & Co., 1952), p. 125.

5. Thanks to Rae Linda Brown (e-mail communication with the author, July 26, 1998), who confirmed the revised birth date of 1887 along with new information about the premiere of Symphony in E Minor.

6. Rae Linda Brown, "William Grant Still, Florence Price, and William Dawson: Echoes of the Harlem Renaissance," in *Black Music in the Harlem Renaissance: A Collection of Essays,* ed. Samuel A. Floyd, Jr. (New York: Greenwood Press, 1990), p. 71. This article (pp. 71–86) provides extended information about Price's Symphony in E Minor.

7. As quoted in CAMW, p. 92. The anthology presents another work by Smith for flute and piano, *A Distant Dream. Whisper on the Land* was published by Medici Music Press in 1988.

8. Private communication by the composer.

9. Mary Howe, *Jottings* (Washington, D.C., privately published, 1959), p. 89, as quoted in Christine Ammer, *Unsung: A History of Women in American Music* (Westport, CT: Greenwood Press, 1980), p. 119.

10. For a CD including the composition's revised version for two pianos (movements 1, 3, and 4), see *Music by American Women Composers,* Bravura Recordings BR-1001.

11. Judith Tick, *Ruth Crawford Seeger: A Composer's Search for American Music* (New York: Oxford University Press, 1997), p. 356; see also her Web site at http://music.dartmouth.edu/~rcs/.

12. Tick, p. ix.

13. Michael and Peggy Seeger are joined by their late sister, Penny, and four of Crawford's grandchildren in a recording of fifty-three songs from Crawford's *American Folk Songs for Christmas,* Rounder CD0268/0269. For *Animal Folk Songs for Children,* Rounder CD8023/24, these performers are augmented by the fourth sibling, Barbara, and two additional grandchildren.

14. Charles Louis Seeger, "On Dissonant Counterpoint," *Modern Music* 7 (June-July 1930): 28.

15. Ruth Crawford to Edgard Varèse (letter and analysis), January 8, 1948, Ruth Crawford Seeger Collection, Library of Congress, Item 8m.

16. Crawford, "Notes" to "Rat Riddles" in *Three Songs,* New Music Orchestra Series, No. 5 (San Francisco: New Music Edition, 1933).

17. For this and other works on CD, see especially *Ruth Crawford Seeger: Portrait,* Deutsche Grammophon DG 449 925-2. See also *Ruth Crawford Seeger: American Visionary,* Musical Heritage Society MHS 513493M, and *Ruth Crawford,* Composers Recordings CRI CD658.

18. Steven E. Gilbert, "'The Ultra-Modern Idiom': A Survey of *New Music,*" *Perspectives of New Music* 12/1–2 (Fall/Winter 1973–Spring/Summer 1974): 310.

19. For this and other works, see *Vivian Fine,* Composers Recordings CRI CD692.

20. Byron Belt, *Long Island Press,* May 21, 1976, as quoted by Jane Weiner LePage, *Women Composers, Conductors, and Musicians of the Twentieth Century,* vol. 2 (Metuchen, NJ: Scarecrow Press, 1983), p. 86.

21. Jacob Druckman, interview, *Soundpieces: Interviews with American Composers,* ed. Cole Gagne and Tracy Caras (Metuchen, NJ: Scarecrow Press, 1982), p. 156.

22. For the Louise Talma Society Web site by Luann Dragone (Ldragone@email.gc.cuny.edu), see http://www.omnidisc.com/Talma.html.

23. Elaine Barkin, "Louise Talma: 'The Tolling Bell,'" *Perspecitves of New Music* 10/2 (Spring/Summer 1972): 151.

24. Joan Tower, liner notes for *Prelude for Five Players,* Composers Recordings CRI SD 302.

25. Joan Tower, as quoted by Michael Redmond, "Towering; Uncommon; Composer," *Cleveland Plain Dealer,* June 2, 1994, p. 30.

26. Elektra/Nonesuch 79245-2 (CD). Other CD recordings include *Joan Tower Concertos,* d'Note Classics CNC 1016; *Joan Tower Music for Clarinet,* Summitt DCD 124; chamber music on CRI CD582 and New World Records, NWR 80470; and *Fanfare* (No. 1) on *The American Album,* RCA Victor Red Seal 60778-2-RC.

27. Joan Tower, as quoted in *Showcase* [program for Minnesota Orchestra], September 1991, p. 29.

28. Barbara Kolb, Program Notes to *Appello* ([New York]: Boosey & Hawkes, [1978]). Further, Boulez had borrowed his series from an unordered pitch set in Olivier Messiaen's pioneering work *Mode de valeurs et d'intensité* (1949). The pitch-class set used is: E^b, D, A, A^b, G, $F^\#$, E, $C^\#$, B^b, F, B.

29. Ibid.

30. For a score excerpt and additional commentary see CAMW, pp. 71–90; see also the CD *Barbara Kolb: Millefoglie and Other Works,* New World 80422-2.

31. For score excerpts and additional commentary see CAMW, pp. 71–73, 91–96.

32. Nancy Van de Vate, as quoted in an interview by Jane Weiner Lepage, *Women Composers, Conductors, and Musicians of the Twentieth Century* [vol. 1] (Metuchen, NJ: Scarecrow Press, 1980), p. 257.

33. CDs of many Van de Vate compositions are available from Vienna Modern Masters and other labels.

34. For score and additional commentary see CAMW, pp. 319–53.

35. Nancy Van de Vate, liner notes for *Chernobyl,* Conifer Records CDCF 168, pp. 3–4.

36. For "Free at Last," see *Watch and Pray: Spirituals and Art Songs by African-American Women Composers,* Koch 3-7247-2H1 (CD). For Prelude, see score in *Black Women Composers: A Century of Piano Music (1893–1990),* ed. Helen Walker-Hill (Byrn Mawr: Hildegard Publishing, 1992), p. 43; *Kaleidoscope: Music by African-American Women,* Leonarda LE339 (CD).

37. K. Robert Schwartz, "Classical Music: A Composer Who Actually Earns a Living Composing," *New York Times,* March 22, 1998, sec. 2, p. 38.

38. Ellen Taaffe Zwilich, as quoted by Peter Laki, *Stagebill Carnegie Hall* (February 1991), p. 20A.

39. Koch 3-7248-2 H1.

40. Libby Larsen, *Showcase* [Minnesota Orchestra's program book], 23/8 (April 1991), p. 27.

41. See Edie Hill, "Larsen Challenges Orchestral Frontiers," *Minnesota Composers Forum Newsletter,* June 1991, p. 4.

42. As quoted by Matthew Balensuela, "Composer Emphasizes Rhythm in Her Music," *Terre Haute Tribune-Star,* September 5, 1996, pp. D1–2.

43. See *Dale Warland Singers: Choral Currents,* Innova MN110 (CD). See also Web sites maintained by her publishers at http: //www.ecspublishing.com/larsen/larsen.htm and http://www1.oup.co.uk/music/repprom/composer/larsen/.

44. Information on the Web site maintained by her publisher at http://www.presser.com/chen.html (July 25, 1998).

45. Chen Yi's family name is Chen; her personal name is Yi. In Chinese practice, the family name is given first.

46. Chen Yi, *San Francisco Chronicle,* as quoted at http://www.presser.com/chen.html (July 25, 1998).

47. Among her CDs are *The Music of Chen Yi,* New Albion NA 090 CD, with the Women's Philharmonic, JoAnn Falletta, and Chanticleer; *Wondrous Love, A World Folk Song Collection,* Teldec, 16676-2, on which Chanticleer performs Chen's arrangements of five Asian folk songs. Videos of her music are *Sound And Silence (Chen Yi and Her Music)* (Paris: International Society for Contemporary

Music, Adamov Films and Polish TC, 1989); *Overseas Artists (New Concept in Creation)* (Taipei: Taiwan Public TV, 1991).

48. George Rochberg, "The New Image of Music," *Perspectives of New Music* 2/1 (Fall/Winter, 1963): 1–10.

49. Tony Coulter, "[Interview with] Annea Lockwood," *Ear Magazine* 13/4 (June 1988): no pagination.

50. For CDs devoted to Lockwood's music, see *The Glass World,* ¿What Next? Recordings WN0021; *A Sound Map of the Hudson River,* Lovely Music LCD 2081; *Thousand Year Dreaming,* ¿What Next? Recordings WN0010.

51. For CDs including LeBaron's music, see *Rana, Ritual, and Revelation,* Mode 30; *Jewel Box,* Tellus 26; *Urban Diva,* CRI CD654; *The Musical Railism of Anne LeBaron,* Mode 42; *Newband,* Music & Arts CD-931. See also her Web site at http://home.earthlink.net/~lebaron/.

52. Coulter, n.p.

53. Julia Perry, liner notes for *Homunculus C.F.,* CRI SD 252 (LP).

54. For CD, see *"Magnificathy": The Many Voices of Cathy Berberian,* Wergo WER 60054-50.

55. Richard Gehr, "Mourning in America: Diamanda Galas," *Artforum* 27, no. 9 (May 1989): 117.

56. Andrea Juno and V. Vale, *Angry Women* (San Francisco: Re/Search Publications, 1991), pp. 11–12.

57. Richard Gehr, "Mourning in America," 118.

58. For CDs, see *Plague Mass* (from live performances at Cathedral of St. John the Divine, New York, 1990), Mute (Elektra) 9-61043-2; *Vena Cava,* Mute (Elektra) 9-61459-2; *Schrei X* (includes *Schrei* 27), Mute 9037-2. See also video of concert performances recorded in Chicago and New York in 1992 (52 minutes), *Judgement Day: Diamanda Galás,* H-Gun Labs Production in conjunction with Mute Records (Chicago: Atavistic Video, 1993). See Galás's Web site, http://www.brainwashed.com/diamanda/Diamanda.shtml, for many links and articles.

59. Pauline Oliveros, *Aeolian Partitions* (Bowdoin: Bowdoin College Music Press, 1983), p. 59.

60. Pauline Oliveros, "Some Sound Observations," *Source,* January 1968, p. 79; quoted in Heidi Von Gunden, *The Music of Pauline Oliveros* (Metuchen, NJ: Scarecrow Press, 1983), p. 59.

61. For a thorough discussion of this work, see Von Gunden, pp. 59–63.

62. For a description of how moving this lullaby can be, see Tom Johnson, "Two Transcendental Experiences," *Village Voice,* June 23, 1980, pp. 66, 68.

63. People: Pauline Oliveros, "Longer Bio," http://www.artswire.org/Artswire.www.pof/peo_po.html, p. 5.

64. Fename Homepage, "Pauline Oliveros," http://www.gvn.net/fenam/oliveros.html, p. 1. Pamela Z's Web site is http://www.sirius.com/~pamelaz/welcome.html.

65. People: Pauline Oliveros, "Artistic Statement," http://www.artswire.org/Artswire.www.pof/peop_po.html, p. 1.

66. Liner notes, Pauline Oliveros et al., *Deep Listening,* New Albion Records NA 022 (1989).

67. For a stream-of-consciousness comparison of Oliveros, Gertrude Stein, and Sappho, see Jill Johnston, "Dance Journal: The Wedding," *Village Voice,* January 14, 1971, pp. 33–34.

68. Pamela McCorduck, "America's Multi-Mediatrix," *Wired* (4 Ventures USA, 1993), http://www.maths.lth.se/matematiklu/personal/apas/laurie/pl.html, p. 1.

69. David Sterritt, "Laurie Anderson Multimedia Blitz," *Christian Science Monitor,* January 31, 1983, p. 17.

70. Laurie Anderson, *United States Live* (Warner Bros., WB 25 192-1, 1985); and *United States* (Harper and Row, 1984).

71. Laurie Anderson, *Big Science* (Warner Bros., WB 3674-2, 1982).

72. Laurie Anderson, *Strange Angels* (Warner Bros., WB 4-25900, 1989).

73. Laurie Anderson, *Stories from the Nerve Bible: A Retrospective 1972–92* (New York: Harper Perennial, 1994).

74. McCorduck, p. 2.

75. Laurie Anderson, *Nerve Bible,* p. 276, as quoted in Woodrow B. Hood, "Laurie Anderson and the Politics of Performance," *Postmodern Culture* 4 #3 (May 1994), http://www/maths.lth.se/matematklu/personal/apas/laurie/lap.html, p. 3.

76. David Sterritt, "Laurie Anderson Considers the Heart of Her 'Performance Art' to be Storytelling," *Christian Science Monitor,* October 24, 1983, p. 26.

77. Joan La Barbara, *Voice Is the Original Instrument* (Wizard Records, RVW 2266, 1975).

78. Joan La Barbara, "Lovely Music Catalogue by Artist: Joan La Barbara," http://www.lovely.com/bios/labarbara.html>.

79. Monk was born in 1942 in New York, not in 1943 in Peru while her mother was on a performance tour, as stated in *The New Grove Dictionary of American Music,* s.v. "Meredith Monk."

80. The Kitchen, formerly located on Broome Street in New York, is a gallery and performance space where Robert Ashley, Laurie Anderson, and others performed early in their careers. The Living Room is the recording studio partially owned by Philip Glass.

81. Lanny Harrison, p. 1 of a two-page typescript, written September 19, 1975. New York Public Library, Lincoln Center, clipping file.

82. L. K. Telbert, "Meredith Monk: Renaissance Woman," *Music Journal,* September-October 1979, p. 9.

83. Sue Snodgrass, "Meredith Monk: Solo Performance," *New Art Examiner,* March 1985, p. 59.

84. Nancy Goldner, "Stillness Becomes Movement in Monk's 'Education of the Girlchild,'" *Christian Science Monitor,* November 14, 1973, p. 18.

85. For more information see Leslie Lassetter, "Meredith Monk: An Interview about Her Recent Opera, *Atlas,*" *Contemporary Music Review* 16 (1997): 59–67.

86. Jack Anderson, "Roosevelt Island as a Stage," *New York Times,* September 26, 1994.

87. Gerald Brennan, "To see the next stage of musical theater, see Monk," *Ann Arbor News,* October 7, 1996; and Kyle Gann, "Monkless Chants," *Village Voice,* October 29, 1996.

88. David Sterritt, "When Meredith Monk Sings, the Whole World Understands," *Christian Science Monitor,* January 19, 1982, p. 14.

89. John Rockwell, quoted in *Current Biography Yearbook,* 1985 edition, s.v. "Monk, Meredith."

90. Beverly Grigsby, "Women Composers of Electronic Music in the United States," in *The Musical Woman* [vol. 1] (Westport, CT: Greenwood Press, 1984), p. 151; Gavin Borchert, "American Women in Electronic Music, 1984–94," *Contemporary Music Review* 16 (1997): 89–97.

91. Available on CD, *Musgrave: Narcissus/Shatin: Kairos,* NEUMA 450-95. See also her Web site at http://www.people.virginia.edu/~jsa.

92. For CDs, see *No World Improvisations,* O.O. Records, O.O. #2; *No World (Trio) Improvisations,* O.O. #4; *The Aerial* [A Journal in Sound] #2 (Santa Fe: Nonsequitur Foundation, 1990).

93. For CDs including works by Hutchinson, see *Vocal Neighborhoods: A Collection from the Post–Sound Poetry Landscape,* vol. 3 (1993) of *The Leonardo*

Music Journal CD Series; Mini-mall, Tellus, no. 27; *The Aerial* [A Journal in Sound] #4 (Santa Fe: Nonsequitur Foundation, 1991). Pamela Z's music is found on these CDs: *Emergency Music Collection,* CRI CD770; *Dice 2 [she sways]: A Collection of Contemporary Women Composers,* Ishtar CD002; *Sonic Circuits. IV,* Innova 113. For recordings of Spiegel's music, see her Web site at http://www.dorsai.org/~spiegel. For music by Shields, see *Apocalypse,* CRI CD647; *Pioneers of Electronic Music,* American Masters, CRI CD 611. For an interview of Laurie Spiegel, see Joanna Bosse, "Creating Options, Creating Music: An Interview with Laurie Spiegel," *Contemporary Music Review* 16 (1997): 81–87.

94. For CD, see Centaur CRC 2045, CDCM Computer Music Series, vol. 3; see also discussion by Elizabeth Hinkle-Turner, "Recent Electro-Acoustic Music by Women," *International League of Women Composers Journal* (October 1992): 8–14.

95. See Spiegel's *Cavis Muris* (1986) on *The Virtuoso in the Computer Age—III,* Centaur CDCM Computer Music Series, vol. 13; also *Unseen Worlds,* which offers a dozen works composed during 1987–1990, originally on Scarlet Records Infinity Series #88802-2 (1982) and rereleased on Spiegel's own label, Aesthetic Engineering, in 1994. Both CDs are available from the Electronic Music Foundation (http: //www.emf.org). Excerpts of Hinkle-Turner's works are available at her Web site (http: //www.smu.edu/~ehinkle/).

96. As quoted by Jane Weiner LePage, *Women Composers, Conductors, and Musicians of the Twentieth Century* [vol. 1], p. 96.

97. See CD of McLin's choral music, *Music for My People,* Neil Kjos Music NN9617C, available from Kjos.

98. Samuel A. Floyd, Jr., *The Power of Black Music. Interpreting Its History from Africa to the United States* (New York: Oxford University Press, 1995), p. 162.

99. As quoted by Herman Hudson, with David N. Baker and Lida M. Belt, "The Black Composer Speaks. An Interview with Undine Smith Moore," *Helicon Nine* 14–15 (1986): 175.

100. Ibid., p. 184.

101. See her Web site at http://members.aol.cim/alicep16/index.html.

102. For a survey of recordings of Gideon's music, see J. Michele Edwards [Recording Reviews], *American Music* 14/2 (Summer 1996): 244–47.

103. Albert Weisser, "Miriam Gideon's New Service," *American Jewish Congress Bi-Weekly* (New York, June 30, 1972), p. 23.

104. Albert Weisser, "An Interview with Miriam Gideon," *Dimensions in American Judaism* 4 (1970): 40.

105. Vivian Fine, liner notes for *Missa Brevis,* CRI SD 434.

106. Annea Lockwood, *Singing the Moon* (score), *Ear Magazine East* 6/3 (April-May 1981): 20.

107. Heidi Von Gunden, "Whistle Music: A Sonic Exorcism" [verbal instructions], *Heresies* 3/2 No. 10 (1980): 45.

108. Susan McClary, as quoted by Carla Waldemar, "Looking at Women and Great Art: Oh, Susanna." *Twin Cities Reader,* July 8, 1987, p. 17.

109. Libby Larsen, notes for the premiere program, Minnesota Opera, May 25 to June 3, 1990, p. 11. For more information on this and other operas by women, see Karin Pendle, "For the Theatre: Opera, Dance, and Theatre Piece," *Contemporary Music Review* 16 (1997): 69–79.

110. All quotations by Libby Larsen are from e-mail to the author, August 23, 1998.

111. For CD, see *Premiere Performances by Boston Musica Viva,* Delos D/CD 1012.

112. For additional information, see D. Antoinette Handy, "Black Women and American Orchestras: An Update," in *New Perspectives on Music: Essays in Honor of Eileen Southern,* ed. Josephine Wright with Samuel A. Floyd, Jr. (Warren, MI: Harmonie Park Press, 1992), pp. 451–61.

113. Statistics from the American Symphony Orchestra League.

114. For further information about the Women's Philharmonic and conductor JoAnn Falletta, see J. Michele Edwards, "All-Women's Musical Communities: Fostering Creativity and Leadership," in *Bridges of Power: Women's Multicultural Alliances,* ed. Lisa Albrecht and Rose Brewer (Santa Cruz, CA: New Society Publishers, 1990), pp. 95–107.

115. As quoted by Anthony Tommasini, "Music Rarity: One Woman Wielding a Baton," *New York Times,* April 9, 1996, p. C13.

116. For more information, see Jan Bell Groh, *Evening the Score: Women in Music and the Legacy of Frédérique Petrides* (Fayetteville: University of Arkansas Press, 1991), which includes annotated facsimiles of all thirty-seven issues of *Women in Music* (1935–1940) plus relevant photographs.

117. Interview with Hillis, February 23, 1982, as quoted by Kay Donahue Lawson, "Women Orchestral Conductors: Factors Affecting Career Development" (M.M. thesis, Michigan State University, 1983), p. 59.

118. Recounted by Richard Dyer, "Tanglewood Music Center's Star Student Conductor," *Boston Globe,* September 3, 1988, p. 9, Living/Arts (available from LEXIS-NEXIS database on-line).

119. Stephanie von Buchau, "JoAnn Falletta at the Podium of the Women's Philharmonic," *San Francisco Magazine,* November 1987, p. 58.

120. Interview by Sara Jobin, "Maestra: Five Female Orchestral Conductors in the United States" (B.A. honors paper, Harvard University, 1992), p. 114.

121. Esperanza Pulido, "Mexican Women in Music," *Latin American Music Review* 4/1 (Spring-Summer 1983): 120.

122. For CDs of *Tres momentos,* see *Sonoric Rituals,* Albany TROY 242; and *Mexico: 100 Years of Piano Music. Romanticism, Ethnicity and Innovation,* North/South Consonance N/S R 1010. For *21 rondas mexicanas* performed by the composer, see *Primer Concurso de Composicion Musical de Queretaro* ([Queretaro, Mexico?]: Egracom Queretaro, 1996?).

123. For Agudelo's Toccata on CD, see *Clavecin contemporaneo mexicano* ([Mexico?]: Fonca, 1996); for *Arabesco,* see *Musica mexicana para flauta de pico,* Serie siglo XX; vol. 8 ([Mexico City]: INBA/CENIDIM, 1992).

124. As quoted from an interview by Jeannine Wagar, "Stylistic Tendencies in Three Contemporary Mexican Composers: Manuel Enriquez, Mario Lavista and Alicia Urreta" (D.M.A. final project, Stanford University, 1985) (Ann Arbor: University Microfilms, 1987), p. 145.

125. Martinez, as quoted by Joanna Pitman, "Take the Cue from Her," *Times* (London), October 11, 1994, Features section (available from LEXIS-NEXIS database on-line).

126. For score and commentary see CAMW, pp. 155–63.

127. For five works on CD, see *Tania León,* CRI CD 662; see also works as part of the *Louisville Orchestra: First Edition Recordings,* LCD010; and *The World So Wide,* Nonesuch 79458-2.

128. Biographical information and a list of selected works are available for each of the Canadian composers at the Canadian Music Centre Web site (http://www.culturenet.ca/cmc/); the CMC lending library catalog of perusal scores is also at the Web site.

129. Interview by Harvey Don Huiner, quoted in "The Choral Music of Violet Archer" (Ph.D. diss., University of Iowa, 1980), p. 217.

130. As quoted by Steven Mazey, "Composer Thrilled by Date with NACO," *Ottawa Citizen,* August 5, 1998, p. E2 (available from LEXIS-NEXIS database on-line).

131. Roxanne Snider, "Celebrating the Nation's Composers," *Maclean's* May 19, 1986, p. 44, Music section (available from LEXIS-NEXIS database on-line).

132. Jon Kimura Parker, "The Solo Piano Music of Alexina Louie: A Blend of East and West" (D.M.A. thesis, Juilliard, 1989), p. 58. The thesis includes considerable formal analysis and reprints complete scores for *Scenes* and *Music for Piano* (1982).

133. See *Love Songs for a Small Planet,* Centrediscs/Cetredisques CMC-CD 4893. This and several other CDs are available from the Canadian Music Centre.

134. Hope Lee, as quoted in her "Bio" (1998) on the Canadian Music Centre Web site (http://www.culturenet.ca/cmc/).

135. For this and another work on CD, see New Concert Discs NCD 0294.

SUGGESTIONS FOR FURTHER READING

In addition to the items mentioned in the text or cited in the footnotes, the following sources provide information about twentieth-century women in music in North and Central America.

Ardito, Linda. "Miriam Gideon: A Memorial Tribute." *Perspectives of New Music* 34/2 (Summer 1996): 202–14.

Armer, Elinor. "A Conversation with Vivian Fine: Two Composers Talk Shop." *Strings* 5/5 (March 1991): 73–78.

Art Performs Life: Merce Cunningham/Meredith Monk/Bill T. Jones. Minneapolis, Walker Art Center, 1998.

Britain, Radie. *Ridin' Herd to Writing Symphonies: An Autobiography.* Lanham, MD: Scarecrow, 1996.

Brown, Rae Linda. "William Grant Still, Florence Price, and William Dawson: Echoes of the Harlem Renaissance." In *Black Music in the Harlem Renaissance: A Collection of Essays,* ed. Samuel Floyd, Jr., pp. 71–86. New York: Greenwood Press, 1990.

———. "The Woman's Symphony Orchestra of Chicago and Florence B. Price's Piano Concerto in One Movement." *American Music* 11/2 (1993): 185–205.

Callahan, Moiya. "Mary Carr Moore's *Narcissa.*" M.M. thesis, University of Cincinnati, 1999.

Contemporary Music Review 16/1–2 (1997), special issue, *American Women Composers,* ed. Karin Pendle.

Edwards, J. Michele. "All-Women's Musical Communities: Fostering Leadership and Creativity." In *Bridges of Power: Women's Multicultural Alliances,* ed. Lisa Albrecht and Rose M. Brewer, pp. 95–107. Philadelphia: New Society Publishers, 1990.

Flanagan, Michael. "Invoking Diamanda." In *Life Sentences: Writers, Artists, and Aids,* ed. Thomas Avena, pp. 161–75. San Francisco: Mercury House, 1994.

Gagne, Cole, ed. *Soundpieces 2: Interviews with American Composers.* Metuchen, NJ: Scarecrow Press, 1993.

Gagne, Cole, and Tracy Caras, eds. *Soundpieces: Interviews with American Composers.* Metuchen, NJ: Scarecrow Press, 1982.

Hilferty, Robert. "The Avenging Spirit of Diamanda Galás." *High Performance* 13 (Spring 1990): 22–25.

Jowitt, Deborah, ed. *Meredith Monk.* Baltimore: Johns Hopkins University Press, 1997.

Kielian-Gilbert, Marianne. "Of Poetics and Poiesis, Pleasure and Politics: Music Theory and Modes of the Feminine." *Perspectives of New Music* 32/1 (Winter 1994): 44–67.

Lochhead, Judy. "Joan Tower's *Wings* and *Breakfast Rhythms I and II:* Some Thoughts on Form and Repetition." *Perspectives of New Music* 30/1 (Winter 1992): 132–56.

McClary, Susan. *Feminine Endings: Music, Gender, and Sexuality.* Minneapolis: University of Minnesota Press, 1991.

Mockus, Martha. "Sounding Out: Lesbian Feminism and the Music of Pauline Oliveros." Ph.D. diss., University of Minnesota, 1999.

Moss, Linell. "An Interview with Composer Libby Larsen." *IAWM Journal* 5, #1 (Winter 1999): 8–10.

Nicholls, David. *American Experimental Music, 1890–1940.* Cambridge: Cambridge University Press, 1990.

Pappas, Elizabeth Helen. "Contemporary Performance Art Composition: Post-modernism, Feminism, and Voice (Diamanda Galás, Meredith Monk, Joan La Barbara, Pauline Oliveros, Laurie Anderson)." Ph.D. diss., University of California, San Diego, 1996.

Parker, Jon Kimura. "The Solo Piano Music of Alexina Louie: A Blend of East and West." D.M.A. thesis, Juilliard School, 1989.

Peters, Penelope. "Deep Rivers: Selected Songs of Florence Price and Margaret Bonds." *Canadian University Music Review/Revue de musique des universités canadiennes* 16/1 (1995): 74–95.

Pope, Rebecca A., and Susan J. Leonardi. "Divas and Disease, Mourning and Militancy: Diamanda Galás's Operatic *Plague Mass.*" In *The Work of Opera: Genre, Nationhood, and Sexual Difference,* ed. Richard Dellamora and Daniel Fischlin, pp. 315–33. New York: Columbia University Press, 1997.

Schwarz, David. *Listening Subjects: Music, Psychoanalysis, Culture.* Durham, NC: Duke University Press, 1997.

Smith, Catherine Parsons, and Cynthia Richardson. *Mary Carr Moore, American Composer.* Ann Arbor: University of Michigan Press, 1987.

Sordo Sodi, Carmen. "Compositoras Mexicanas de Musica Comercial." *Heterofinia* 15 (1982): 16–20.

Straus, Joseph N. *The Music of Ruth Crawford Seeger.* Cambridge: Cambridge University Press, 1995.

Tick, Judith. "Dissonant Counterpoint Revisited: The First Movement of Ruth Crawford Seeger's String Quartet 1931." In *A Celebration of American Music: Words and Music in Honor of H. Wiley Hitchcock,* ed. Richard Crawford, R. Allen Lott, and Carol Oja, pp. 405–21. Ann Arbor: University of Michigan, 1990.

———. *Ruth Crawford Seeger: A Composer's Search for American Music.* New York: Oxford University Press, 1997.

———. "Ruth Crawford's 'Spiritual Concept': The Sound-Ideals of an Early American Modernist." *Journal of the American Musicological Society* 44/2 (Summer 1991): 221–61.

Wilding-White, Ray. "Remembering Ruth Crawford Seeger: An Interview with Charles and Peggy Seeger." *American Music* 6/4 (Winter 1988): 442–54.

Zelenka, Karl. *Komponierende Frauen: Ihr Leben, ihre Werke.* Cologne: Ellenberg Verlag, 1980.

XII. American Popular Music

S. *Kay Hoke*

Since the end of World War I the history of popular music in America has been one of interplay between musical styles and technological advances in sound reproduction. Of the many influences affecting the popular music scene, two are especially noteworthy: the introduction of microphones and amplifiers, allowing performers to project their sound without mastering the same techniques used by performers of art music; and the movement of mainstream popular music from a European-inspired written tradition to a vernacular style derived from oral tradition.

Until the 1920s the primary consumers of popular music were the literate middle and working classes, who had both the ability to read music and the means to buy a piano on which to reproduce it in the home. The emergence of affordable electronic sound reproduction made popular music accessible to a broad audience unconstrained by geography or the necessity for formal musical training. By 1925, control of the popular music industry had begun to shift from publishing houses to radio stations, record companies, and manufacturers of sound reproduction equipment. Popular music in the United States has always been dominated by styles directed toward and listened to by the so-called mainstream audience: urban, middle-class whites. In the first half of the century that music was the product of Tin Pan Alley; in the second half it has been rock. But styles particular to other groups in the population have sometimes attracted broad-based audiences as well—for example, the music of rural whites, first known as hillbilly and later as country, and the music of African Americans, which includes blues, jazz, and gospel.

The study of popular music, whatever its style, provides a rich source of information about women. They have excelled mainly as compelling singers, but have also made significant contributions as instrumentalists and composers. Unlike art music, which is known primarily through its composers, popular music is known primarily through its performers; therefore, the number of preeminent women in the field has been exceptionally large.

TIN PAN ALLEY

What music historian Charles Hamm identifies as the "golden years of Tin Pan Alley" are those bounded by the United States's participation in the two world wars. The songs of Tin Pan Alley, written primarily by Jewish Americans living in New York City and grounded in the European classical tradition, maintain important links with European art music. Some of the people who composed these songs—Irving Berlin, Jerome Kern, George Gershwin, Harold Arlen, Kay Swift—continue to be revered. Throughout the Big Band Era, many bands featured female singers who performed the best of this repertoire. One classic type of singer, referred to as a "canary," was a consummate stylist, cultivating a distinctive stage persona. Beautifully coifed and made-up, costumed in an elegant gown, she performed in clubs, lounges, and, at the peak of her career, in concert halls. The heyday of the canary was ca. 1940–1955; among the many songbirds achieving commercial and artistic success were Jo Stafford (b. 1920), Patti Page (b. 1922), Dinah Shore (1917–1994), Kay Starr (b. 1922), Rosemary Clooney (b. 1928), Margaret Whiting (b. 1924), and Peggy Lee (b. 1920).

Peggy Lee

Dubbed America's "premiere *chanteuse*" by Peter Reilly and "the Queen" by Duke Ellington, Peggy Lee is unarguably the most successful popular singer of her generation. Born Norma Dolores Engstrom on May 26, 1920, in Jamestown, North Dakota, she was encouraged by church choir directors and high school teachers to pursue a career in music. When she began to work as a radio singer, the station manager of WDAY in Fargo gave her the stage name Peggy Lee. Lee went on to perform in Minneapolis, St. Louis, Palm Springs, and Chicago, where Benny Goodman offered her a job as vocalist with his band. In 1942, still with Goodman's band, she recorded "Why Don't You Do Right?" a song that sold more than one million copies. "Why Don't You Do Right?" "Fever," "Baubles, Bangles, and Beads," and "I'm a Woman" are considered her standbys, songs associated with her for over thirty years.

Despite a lack of formal musical training, Lee has either written or collaborated on hundreds of songs. Some of the best known are "It's a Good

FIGURE 12.1. Peggy Lee in the 1940s. The Frank Driggs Collection. Used by permission

Day," "I Don't Know Enough about You," and "Mañana," a song with a distinctive Latin beat. Although she has received many accolades throughout her career, true recognition as a serious artist came only in 1962, when she was invited to appear in Philharmonic Hall at Lincoln Center. For this concert she wrote an entire program entitled "The Jazz Tree," tracing the development of jazz as an American art form. Although plagued by bad health, Lee has continued to perform, record, and write in the 1990s.

Lee's professionalism and perfectionism are well known. She prepares for each performance meticulously, recording every aspect of the event in a large black notebook. For a major performance she culls approximately thirty songs from a list of over one hundred by her favorite writers. Lyrics, arrangements, notes on instrumentation, observations about the songs and the gestures she will use to convey their meaning are carefully entered, along with directions for lighting, her entrances and exits, and her wardrobe and hairstyle. Nothing is left to chance; improvisation, musical or otherwise, is not her style. The result is a refined performance by a woman of queenly bearing. Because her voice is small and its range limited to about an octave and a half, Lee has perfected the subtler aspects of her art. One might call her a sculptor of song, a musical artist who works delicately with color, inflection, emotion, and clarity of enunciation.

Rosemary Clooney

Rosemary Clooney (b. 1928), who came to national attention with such hit tunes as "Come on-a My House" and "Botcha Me," has enjoyed a resurgence in popularity during the 1990s that has made her the toast of the cabaret circuit and the recipient of Grammy nominations for her albums *Do You Miss New York* and *Girl Singer.* Clooney began her rise to fame at the age of seventeen, when she and her younger sister, Betty, appeared on WLW Radio in Cincinnati. The act soon signed on to tour with Tony Pastor's big band, an engagement that lasted until 1949, when Betty left the show and Rosemary struck out on her own. The 1950s brought numerous top-selling records, including "Mambo Italiano" and "Hey There," some well-received movies (e.g., *White Christmas* with Bing Crosby), and her own television show. These years also saw her marriage to José Ferrer and the birth of the first of five children.

But the work also took its toll on Clooney in stress and an overreliance on prescription drugs, and a breakdown on a Reno stage in 1968 seemed the end of her already waning career. Following a stay in a psychiatric hospital, Clooney found that the top-of-the-line clubs and halls she had been playing during the good years were unwilling to hire her. This time the path to success was harder to climb, but climb it she did—first taking many offers she would have dismissed earlier, then cultivating a new kind of material that gradually established her as an artist of real depth and expressive strength. The ballads and up-tempo standards of jazz, pop, and Broadway formed the meat of her acts in cabarets and concerts, bringing her to the forefront of a group of mature artists that includes such luminaries as Julie Wilson, Barbara Cook, and Tony Bennett.

Now in her seventies, Clooney still spends much of her time on tour, drawing appreciative audiences across the country. In 1998 she married Dante de Paolo, with whom she had lived for over twenty years, in a joyous family celebration in her hometown of Maysville, Kentucky. Her recent album, *Still on the Road,* sums up in its title the current state of her career. Clooney's voice has mellowed from the bright, eager sound of her early days, and the richer quality of the 1990s surrounds and subtly shades such songs as "Moonlight Becomes You" and Duke Ellington's "Nothin' but the Blues," alongside the inevitable "Come on-a My House" and a newly glowing "Hey There." Rosemary Clooney is again on top.

Country Music

Country music is a commercial arm of folk music of the rural South that was originally handed down through oral tradition in the nineteenth and early twentieth centuries. Although its origins are in the folk music of British settlers, the evolution of country music has been shaped through contact with African-American and various other types of ethnic and urban commercial music. The roots of country music as an industry reach back to the 1920s, when barn dance programs began to be broadcast on radio. The most important of these shows, originating in Nashville, Tennessee, was *Grand Ole Opry*. Recordings date from 1927, when the Carter Family and a former railroad worker from Mississippi, Jimmie Rodgers, made their first discs for Victor.

The Carter Family

A country music trio composed of Alvin Pleasant Carter (1891–1960), his wife, Sara Carter (1898–1979), and their sister-in-law, "Mother" Maybelle Carter (1909–1978), the Carter Family became one of the most influential and popular country music groups in America. Their repertoire of Anglo-American folk songs, country ballads, religious songs, and sentimental parlor songs was very large. Their musical style—three-part harmony sung to simple chordal accompaniments on Maybelle's guitar and Sara's autoharp—was known and respectfully imitated by other groups. Maybelle, with her distinctive technique of playing the melody on low strings and strumming chords on upper strings, helped to popularize the guitar as a country music instrument. Although the trio did not perform together after 1943, its influence continued into the 1960s, when such singers as Joan Baez learned and performed the group's songs. Mother Maybelle continued to perform with her three daughters, Helen, June, and Anita, on *Grand Ole Opry* and with singer Johnny Cash, June's husband, on television and in road shows.

Because population shifts in the 1940s necessitated by the war effort brought people from the rural South and West together with people from the urban North and Midwest, traditional rural styles fused with urban popular styles. By 1950 Nashville was established as the commercial center of the now-national entertainment of country music. From the 1970s to the present, country music has mirrored the growing homogeneity of American life and represented the way changes take place within the framework of a strong tradition. The lyrics of the songs remain traditional: familial love and traditional values, disappointed love, hard work, hard times, the man who leaves his woman, and old-time religion; the story is still the focal point of the song, and its accompaniment should not be too sophisticated. The change over the years is reflected in the mixture of country with popular and rock styles and the attraction of an international audience. Originally the instrumental ensemble comprised a fiddle, a five-string banjo, and a guitar; a mandolin, a string bass, and a steel guitar were added later. In the 1930s drum and piano were incorporated, and, over time, electric instruments appeared. By the 1970s electric instruments had largely replaced acoustic ones.

Kitty Wells and Patsy Cline

For most of its history country music has been men's music performed by men. Traditionally, women singers sang the sad songs, and few women emerged as top performers until Kitty Wells (b. 1919) made a decisive statement with "It Wasn't God Who Made Honky-Tonk Angels," a pointed reply to Hank Thompson's "Wild Side of Life." Though Thompson's song held women responsible for the fall of man, Wells countered by blaming men for their own downfall and for dragging women down with them. Her song, which made a new statement in country music, marked the turning point in her career and made her the first "Queen of Country Music." With a career spanning some three decades, Kitty Wells served as an inspiration to later stars. She fashioned the singing style that most women country singers have adopted—twangy and nasal, but clear and subtly ornamented. Her later hits, "Release Me" and "I Can't Stop Loving You," were made famous for the mainstream audience by rhythm-and-blues singer Ray Charles.

The other country queen of the 1950s, Patsy Cline (1932–1963), reached her audience in part through the new medium of television. Her singing style, influenced by contemporary popular music, helped her gain a crossover audience. She is best remembered for her song "I Fall to Pieces." Cline, whose life ended tragically in a plane crash in 1963, provided a powerful model of strength and self-sufficiency for women who wanted solo careers apart from male partners or family groups.

The 1960s and 1970s ushered in new trends for women performers. Many of them broke with their male partners and became stars with independent identities. They began to sing about subjects formerly taboo to them: divorce, female adultery, contraception, the experience of sex, and womanly independence. The singing itself was sometimes strongly influenced by mainstream popular styles. Some women began wearing clothes that in earlier times would have caused a scandal. What is true for the best-known stars, however, is not the norm. Most country women still sing about the long-suffering woman who tolerates the weaknesses of her man and whose place is still at hearth and home, caring for the children—the public and lyrical myth of domesticity.

Loretta Lynn

Loretta Lynn has lived the life of the women depicted in many country music songs. Born one of twelve children to a coal-mining family in Butcher Hollow, Kentucky, in 1935, Loretta Webb married Oliver Vanetta "Mooney" Lynn, a veteran and former coal miner, at the age of fourteen and was the mother of four by the age of eighteen. Like most mothers, Lynn sang lullabies she remembered from her own childhood. Mooney Lynn was so impressed with his wife's singing ability that he bought Loretta an inexpensive guitar. It may have been the most prudent investment he ever made. Loretta taught herself to play basic chords and began making up simple songs of her own. These early attempts at songwriting convinced Mooney all the more of her exceptional talent. His boasting that Loretta was a better singer than any country queen except Kitty Wells led to her first opportunity to perform professionally, an invitation in 1960 to sing with a country band on a local radio show in Bellingham, Washington. She was an immediate success.

Lynn taught herself to "compose" in the age-old manner of learning others' songs and respectfully imitating their styles. Over time she developed a style of her own and recorded a demonstration disc of a song she wrote, "I'm a Honky Tonk Girl." In order to promote the song, she and her family drove over 75,000 miles from radio station to radio station, persuading disc jockeys to play it. Their unorthodox scheme worked. The Lynn family was able to move to Nashville, and Loretta was engaged to appear on *Grand Ole Opry*. She also performed on the Wilburn Brothers' syndicated television show and was paired with Conway Twitty to form one of country music's most popular duos. No female country singer before her had been able to gain such national recognition.

A key element of Lynn's tremendous success was her talent for writing honest, direct lyrics about the realities of the lives of women who, like herself, married young, became mothers sooner and oftener than they had intended, and knew daily life in all its tedium and drudgery. Hers are earthy songs emanating from the heart but revealing in their plain language and often outspoken and courageous manner a kind of homespun philosophy. Among her best-known songs are "Don't Come Home a-Drinkin' with Lovin' on Your Mind," "One's on the Way," "You Ain't Woman Enough to Take My Man," "The Pill" (banned from many radio stations because of its stand favoring birth control), "Bargain Basement Dress," "I'm Gonna Make Like a Snake," and "Your Squaw Is on the Warpath" (Lynn is part Cherokee). Because she cannot read music, Lynn sings her songs into a tape recorder and writes the lyrics on whatever paper is available. Her melodies are shaped to fit the mood of the lyrics.

Though Lynn modeled her early vocal sound on that of Kitty Wells, she has since developed her own style, making her strong but touching voice slide like a steel guitar. As she has become one of country music's most prominent crossover artists, her voice has lost some of the twangy harshness that was a part of its early charm. Today one might better describe it as warm and vibrant. After winning top honors in three categories at the Country Music Association Awards in 1972, she appeared on the cover of *Newsweek*, and her life story was told in the film *Coalminer's Daughter*. Country music had finally been absorbed into mainstream popular culture in America.

Dolly Parton

Like Loretta Lynn, Dolly Parton (b. 1946) was one of twelve children whose family lived in a two-room wooden shack. Her childhood in Locust Ridge, Tennessee, revolved around singing and the church where her grandfather was a preacher. At the age of eight she was given a guitar on which she learned to accompany herself when she sang alone in church and with her uncles on the *Farm and Home* television show in Knoxville. Determined to become a country music star, Dolly boarded the bus for Nashville the day after her high school graduation.

Although she was able to find singing jobs immediately, Parton was not allowed to sing "hard" lyrics because of her high, childlike voice; she therefore began recording a country-rock blend known as rockabilly. Her career began to flourish when she joined Porter Wagoner's band and became his protégée. Her seven years on his television show (1967–1974) and concert appearances with his band gained her national exposure. Even after Parton left his band for a successful solo career, Wagoner continued to produce and arrange for her.

In 1977 Parton began a conscious attempt to appeal to a wider audience. She traded a back-up band consisting entirely of relatives for one composed of eight professional Nashville musicians experienced in pop, rock, and country, and she replaced her Nashville manager with a Hollywood firm. By the time she and the new band, Gypsy Fever, opened at the Bottom Line in Greenwich Village, they were playing to enthusiastic houses with such prominent rock stars as Mick Jagger and Bruce Springsteen in attendance. In a review for the *New York Post* (May 14, 1977), Carl Arrington referred to the show as "the hottest ticket in New York" and observed that media people had been "gobbling up seats." A successful crossover album released in the same year, *New Harvest, First Gathering*, reached the top of the country chart and placed near the top of the popular chart. Parton has also had success as an actor and as a host of television variety shows.

A gifted songwriter, Parton often draws on her Tennessee heritage for inspiration. Among the autobiographical songs, "Coat of Many Colors" (in CAMW, pp. 239–40) stands out as a particularly poignant memory of her impoverished childhood. The song, filled with biblical imagery, tells of a coat her mother pieced together for her from scraps of fabric. Other widely known songs with references to her childhood are "In the Good Old Days (When Times Were Bad)," "Daddy Was an Old Time Preacher Man," and "My Tennessee Mountain Home," a beautiful evocation of the sounds and senses of the Great Smoky Mountains. John Rockwell accurately noted that Parton's music is often shaded by the modalities and rhythmic idiosyncrasies of English folk song, a link to the music she learned as a child. Like Loretta Lynn, Parton cannot read music. Her method for writing songs is to sing the tunes and lyrics into a tape recorder. Describing her compositional process as "trancelike," Parton feels that she is spiritually inspired.

A soft Appalachian twang is distinct in Dolly Parton's pure, accurate soprano voice. The voice itself is childlike, shivering with a rapid, controlled vibrato, but it can also be made to sound sheer, delicate, sweet, tender, or passionate. Parton displays a wide range of emotions in her songs, from the haunting "Falling Out of Love with Me" to the raucous, knee-slapping "Muleskinner Blues." The surprising flexibility of her voice has allowed Parton to perform many types of music, from mountain ballads to religious songs to rock-influenced popular tunes, and to elicit deep emotional responses from her audiences.

Because of her impoverished background, Parton thinks of her current life as a fairy tale, an escape from all the ugly things in life. Her stage appearance is flamboyant—even gaudy—yet appealing. She is a pretty, dimpled woman with an hourglass figure who likes to wear elaborate makeup and shiny, glittering, suggestive costumes in vibrant colors. But behind the frothy appearance, which she considers a kind of in-joke with her audiences, is a shrewd and very wealthy businesswoman with her own theme park, Dollywood, in Pigeon Forge, Tennessee.

Country Singers: The Current Generation

For the younger generation of women in country music, image is more important than ever because of video and cable television. The performers of the 1980s and 1990s have succeeded in presenting stunning images both visually and aurally, and they are confident and in control of their careers. At the heart of this group are Mary Chapin Carpenter (b. 1958), Kathy Mattea (b. 1959), Suzy Bogguss (b. 1956), and Wynonna Judd (b. 1964). Although most closely associated with country music, they are also the spiritual daughters of

Joan Baez, Joni Mitchell, Linda Ronstadt, and Bonnie Raitt. Wynonna Judd, whose vivid songs are inspired by the music of Joni Mitchell and Bonnie Raitt, began her career as lead singer in a duo with her mother, Naomi (b. 1946). The Judds were the most successful women in country music for nearly a decade, garnering both top sales and awards. In 1991 Naomi Judd's battle with a debilitating liver disease forced her into early retirement. The following year, Wynonna began her solo career by releasing an album tellingly entitled *Wynonna*. An eclectic mixture of country, rock, blues, and gospel, the album sold over a million copies and was a success on both the country and popular charts. She has released two subsequent albums, *Tell Me Why* (1993) and *Revelations* (1996).

GOSPEL

Although gospel music originated in both black and white fundamentalist churches of the rural South, the more compelling musical style has been that of black congregations. Like ragtime, blues, and jazz, black gospel emerged at the end of the nineteenth century, transforming staid Protestant hymns through the rhythmic techniques of syncopation and reaccentuation, the melodic techniques of note-bending and blue notes, the harmonic techniques of quartal and quintal chords, and performance techniques that called on performers to "sing" with their entire bodies.

Modern gospel style, which dates from the 1920s, continues an older tradition of singing, shouting, and preaching. There are two discrete practices: quartet, dominated by male performers and characterized by singing in precise harmonies, often *a cappella,* by voices ranging from deep, resonant bass to falsetto; and gospel, dominated by female performers and making use of soloists, groups, and choirs. Gospel is sung with full voice and can sound strained, rasping, or guttural. The performers seek emotional power by singing at the extremes of their ranges, though performers in the 1970s and 1980s began to use the middle range more extensively. Long melismas by the soloist alternate in responsorial fashion with brief, staccato exclamations by the background group. In one special technique, originated by Mahalia Jackson and called the *vamp*, the soloist improvises while the accompanist and background group repeat the chord progression of a phrase in ostinato fashion. The piano, the main accompanying instrument from the 1920s on, was replaced by the electric organ in the 1950s. Accompanists, who are viewed as virtuosos in their own right and often have long-standing relationships with particular singers, play in a style that combines syncopations derived from ragtime with the left-hand octaves of stride technique and hymnlike chords in the right hand.

With few exceptions, the greatest individual artists in gospel music have been women. Outstanding among them are Willie Mae Ford Smith (1906–1994), Sallie Martin (1896–1988), Roberta Martin (1907–1969), Clara Ward (1924–1973), Marion Williams (1927–1994), and the undisputed "Queen," Mahalia Jackson (19ll–1972). Most of these performers were also leaders of well-known groups, but it is as individuals that they shaped their performances idiosyncratically in every aspect, from ornamentation to stage deportment.

Women also attained eminence in gospel recording. Gospel recordings date from the mid-1920s, and the initial hit was made in 1938. "Rock Me," a blues-inflected version of an earlier song, "Hide Me in Thy Bosom" by Thomas A. Dorsey, was performed by Sister Rosetta Tharpe (1915–1973), the first gospel performer to achieve a national reputation. Nine years after Tharpe had demonstrated the commercial potential of gospel, Mahalia Jackson's "Move On Up a Little Higher" (1947) became the first such recording to sell a million copies. Jackson's deep, rich voice conveyed the music's message in a way that spoke meaningfully to both black and white audiences. Throughout her enormously successful career, Jackson remained essentially a church singer, but she freely acknowledged a stylistic debt to the "Empress of the Blues," Bessie Smith, whom she called her favorite.

The 1950s: Rock 'n' Roll

American popular music changed markedly when two musical styles, one black and one white, came together. Black rhythm and blues had in common with white country music strong, insistent instrumental backgrounds that urged listeners to dance; the prominent use of the guitar—acoustic, electric, or steel; and a down-home vocal style proud of its rough edges. This new music, which we now know as rock, was known in its early history as rock 'n' roll and was the first American music to cut across cultural and racial lines. The term "rock 'n' roll" was a black euphemism for sexual intercourse; the connotative meaning was lost on neither the white male performers who dominated the early history of the style nor on their youthful audiences.

Most of the well-known performers who shaped early rock 'n' roll were male: Bill Haley, Elvis Presley, Jerry Lee Lewis, Buddy Holly, Chuck Berry, and Little Richard. There was, however, one woman, a black rhythm-and-blues singer named Big Mama Thornton, who deserves special mention as a powerful influence on rock 'n' roll's most successful star, Elvis Presley. The daughter of a Montgomery, Alabama preacher, Willie Mae Thornton (1926–1984) was weaned on gospel before moving on to blues. Throughout the

1940s she sang in clubs and theaters in the South. By the early 1950s she was touring the entire United States. In 1952 she recorded the song "Hound Dog," which so appealed to black audiences that it reached No. 1 on the rhythm-and-blues chart in 1955. With the emergence of rock 'n' roll in the same year, Thornton's career went into a brief decline, while Elvis Presley's "Hound Dog," recorded in 1956 and clearly modeled on Big Mama's earlier version, reached No. 1 on the popular, rhythm-and-blues, and country charts. Of the two recorded versions, Presley's pales in comparison to Big Mama's.

Thornton revitalized her career during the blues revival of the 1960s. Again she served as model for a young white singer, this time rock star Janis Joplin, whose version of Big Mama's "Ball and Chain" helped propel her to stardom. Thornton herself achieved national recognition, appearing at the Monterey and Newport jazz festivals and at other jazz, blues, and folk festivals throughout the country. Her singing style comes out of the tradition of Ma Rainey and Bessie Smith—an earthy, somewhat coarse sound, which could be wrenchingly expressive.

The music industry resisted promoting early rock 'n' roll for several reasons. The music was linked with societal problems ranging from juvenile delinquency and sexual promiscuity to racial unrest. It emerged at the same time as serious consideration of the issue of desegregation in American society and attracted racially mixed audiences. More important, however, it brought on a power struggle between music publishers and recording companies, which the recording companies ultimately won. American popular song had always belonged to a written tradition, whereas rock 'n' roll sprang from two oral music traditions and depended on technological advances that made the shift in power irrevocable.

Rock 'n' roll became an umbrella term for numerous styles in the late 1950s, including popular ballads, love songs, dance music, jazz, gospel, and even California surfing music. Much of the music was performed by squeaky-clean whites, women and men, who became teen idols. Most of these "idols" were boys intended to appeal to adolescent girls, but the two most important female performers of the late 1950s and early 1960s, Connie Francis (b. 1938) and Brenda Lee (b. 1944), were women whose appeal was primarily musical. Francis's strong contralto voice was ideal for rich romantic ballads such as "Who's Sorry Now?" and "My Happiness," but it was also effective in the novelties "Stupid Cupid" and "Lipstick on Your Collar." Though Brenda Lee's roots were in country music, her repertoire ranged from rock to ballads to country. Among her better-known songs are "Dynamite," "Rockin' around the Christmas Tree," "I'm Sorry," and "The Cowgirl and the Dandy." Her powerful voice and diminutive size earned Lee the moniker "Little Miss Dynamite."

By the late 1950s, the Brill Building in the center of New York's music district housed a group of songwriters attempting to bridge the gap between the coarse music of rock 'n' roll and the sophisticated songs of Tin Pan Alley. This successful attempt, which came to be identified as the "Brill Building sound," began as the brainchild of Al Nevins and Don Kirshner, the founders of Aldon Music. The Brill Building writers were talented professionals who believed a good song could carry the singer, and their songs set a new qualitative standard in rock 'n' roll.

Carole King

It seems as if Carole King (b. 1942) has had two separate and successful careers in popular music. In the 1960s she wrote teen-idol music, rhythm and blues, soul, and rock; during the 1970s she helped to develop, write, and perform a style called "soft rock," which emphasized the lyrics rather than the beat. Her first career began when she dropped out of Queens College to marry Gerry Goffin, who was also interested in popular music and wrote lyrics for fun. They began almost immediately to turn out hits, especially ballads sung by black vocal groups and marketed for urban teen audiences. "Will You Love Me Tomorrow?" (recorded by the Shirelles in 1960) and the sophisticated "Up on the Roof" (recorded by the Drifters in 1962) exemplify their best and most famous early songs. In the mid-1960s they wrote a soul tune entitled "Natural Woman" that became one of Aretha Franklin's biggest hits. By the time King and Goffin dissolved their writing partnership and their marriage in 1968, they were probably the most popular and prolific of all the Brill Building teams.

King's second career began on the West Coast, where she moved with her two daughters. She began performing with a rock group called the City, which she formed in Los Angeles in 1968. The group was not successful, but other sides of her career flourished. King began to work with lyricist Toni Stern, who wrote biting, realistic, and not particularly optimistic texts. This change in the sort of texts King set to music proved beneficial to her writing. Another boost to her career was an invitation to tour with James Taylor, who encouraged her as both performer and writer and added some of her songs to his repertoire. She recorded two solo albums in rapid succession. The second, *Tapestry* (1971), which was still on the charts in 1977 and eventually sold some fourteen million copies, was one of the greatest successes in the history of recorded music. In it the new Carole King revealed herself as a gentle balladeer, singing about home, lost youth, friendship, painful separations, and the pleasures of physical love. In the same year she and Taylor made a tour that ended at Carnegie Hall. Writers began referring to King as the "Queen of Rock" and successor to Janis Joplin. In 1972 *Tapestry* won the Grammy Award for "Best Album," King won "Best Female Vocal Performance" for her song "It's Too Late," and James Taylor won "Best Male Vocal Performance" for his version of her song, "You've Got a Friend." The albums that followed could never measure up to the success of *Tapestry,* although several—*Music, Fantasy, Diamond Girl,* and *Simple Things*—were gold albums and *Carole King Thoroughbred* received a Grammy award. Her career then went into a decline, but King attempted a comeback with a new album, *City Streets* (1989), her first in nearly a decade. In 1994, she made her Broadway debut in the musical *Blood Brothers.*

King's songs are characterized by a dominating bass line, simple harmonic progressions with gospel inflections, and shapely melodies with their roots in Tin Pan Alley. As a performer, King is an effective interpreter of her own material. Her plain, rather small voice is deceptively strong but lacks the energy and edge provided by the young black singers who made her earlier songs hits. She compensates somewhat for these deficiencies with good technique.

The 1960s: Urban Folk Revival

By the beginning of the 1960s early rock 'n' roll had vanished, and new trends—among them folk-derived music—recalled musical and social elements of the American past. Bob Dylan (b. 1941) was one of the first prominent figures in the urban folk revival to compose most of his own material. Among those who followed Dylan's new direction were three women—Judy Collins, Joan Baez, and Joni Mitchell—whose careers began in the coffeehouses and intimate nightclubs that were urban sanctuaries for folksingers. Collins (b. 1939) composed some of her own music, but she also sang songs by Dylan and the Canadians Joni Mitchell and Leonard Cohen. She also expanded her repertoire to theatre songs, popularizing Stephen Sondheim's "Send in the Clowns" from *A Little Night Music.* Baez, the first woman folk singer to become a star, began her career in the late 1950s and always remained true to folk music. Mitchell, who composes most of her own material, is a product of the late 1960s and has been able to adapt creatively to the times.

Joan Baez

The original folk madonna, Joan Baez has always viewed her musical career and her political life as one. In 1967, when the Daughters of the American Revolution would not allow her to perform in Constitution Hall because they viewed her protest of the Vietnam conflict as unpatriotic, she gave a free concert at the Washington Monument that drew ten times as many people. Baez has been allied with the civil rights, antiwar, and antinuclear movements, and much of the income from her concerts has gone to these causes.

Baez began to sing in coffeehouses in the Boston area after dropping out of Boston University. She had no formal training in singing and had taught herself to play guitar. In 1959 she was invited to appear at the Newport Folk Festival, where she met and befriended the black folk singer Odetta Gordon (b. 1931), who also became one of the prominent figures in American folk music. Although Baez's name did not even appear on the festival program, her performance made a tremendous impact. In 1960 Baez returned to Newport as a star. Her first album, *Joan Baez,* the most popular folk album ever recorded by a female singer, also dates from 1960. By November 23, 1962, she was *Time* magazine's cover story.

Audiences for some four decades have been attracted to her supple soprano voice, described as pure and haunting. Its range of about three octaves allows her to perform some songs, notably Spanish ones, in an alto range. Her approach to performance has always been spare and informal. Assured and self-contained, she wears comfortable clothing, little or no makeup, and a simple hairstyle. Unlike most stars, Baez placed self-imposed limits on her career, refusing to record more than one album a year (her practice even at the height of her popularity). Anglo-American folk songs constituted her early repertory; soon after, she added protest songs. One of the first established folk singers to promote Bob Dylan's songs, Baez felt his music spoke to her social consciousness, clarifying for her what political action to take. Baez has dedicated herself to political activism while continuing to perform (often at benefit concerts), record, and tour. In 1979 she established Humanitas International, an organization committed to peace and world unity that operated for thirteen years.

Although Baez has written some songs throughout her career, she does not consider composition a particular strength. Ironically, as her popularity faded in the 1970s, she composed some quite effective songs, several of which appeared on her important album, *Diamonds and Rust* (1975). No longer considered a folk madonna, Baez is now called the matriarch by a new generation of women with whom she often performs. Baez's 1995 recording *Ring Them Bells,* a collaboration with several rising folk stars—Dar Williams, the Indigo Girls, and Mary Chapin Carpenter—represents a kind of passing of the torch to these young women. Dar Williams's "You're Aging Well," a song about passing on the wisdom of one's experience to younger people, might well be the theme for Baez at the end of the millenium.

Joni Mitchell

The most innovative woman songwriter to emerge in the late 1960s, Joni Mitchell, with her penchant for minor-mode melodies and texts with multilayered images, grew stylistically over three decades from folk to rock to jazz to jazz fusion. Now a mature artist, she can shift easily among these styles. Born Roberta Joan Anderson (1943) in Fort MacLeod, Alberta (Canada), Mitchell first performed in Toronto and then Detroit. After the breakup of her first marriage to Chuck Mitchell, also a folk performer, she moved to New York, determined to make her way. Here she met David Crosby (of Crosby, Stills, and Nash fame), who was impressed by her artistry and taught her the method of guitar tuning that makes her folk accompaniments unique. In 1968 the album *Joni Mitchell* (later renamed *Song to a Seagull*) was released; like many of her subsequent albums, it was a critical but not a commercial success. *Clouds,* released the following year, included "Both Sides Now," which in a version by Judy Collins sold over one million copies; the album, with Mitchell's interpretation of the song, won the Grammy in 1970 for Best Folk Performance.

By the early 1970s Mitchell was beginning to earn a reputation as a songwriter of uncommon ability. Her songs, often experimental and self-consciously artistic, were critically acclaimed for their beautiful melodies and transparent imagery. Some of her more complex, introspective works have been compared favorably to art songs. Examples of her striking originality as a composer and lyricist appear on the album *Blue* (1971). The title song is about the pressures put upon youth in a world filled with dangers—drugs, alcohol, guns, and sex. The indecisive Dorian-mode melody, blue notes in the harmonies, and varied line lengths intensify the meaning of this "foggy lullaby . . . your song from me." In the touching song "Little Green," Mitchell uses the word *green* to symbolize the child who has been born too soon to parents who are themselves still children. The child, named "Green" so that "the winters cannot fade her," is encouraged to be a nonconformist over the nervous percussive beat of a music that implies such a path is rocky and sometimes filled with sorrow.

In 1978 Mitchell began a collaboration with jazz bassist and composer Charles Mingus (1922–1979) in which she was to write lyrics to his jazz tunes. The project as envisioned was never completed because of Mingus's untimely death, but her next album, *Mingus,* dedicated to him, was in a jazz style. The album also had her paintings of the jazzman on the cover. Her work in the 1980s, marked by its social consciousness, takes a pessimistic look at the political system in America and addresses the problems of aging. *Turbulent Indigo* (1994), her best artistic statement since the 1970s, is a poetically sad album intended to reflect the madness of the contemporary world. For the cover Mitchell painted a self-portrait in the style of Van Gogh, whose turbulent brush strokes were said to be associated with madness. Her "Heijira" from the album of the same name is printed in CAMW.

The 1980s and 1990s: New Urban Folk Revival

The 1980s witnessed the rise of a new generation of urban folk musicians, some of whom refer to their styles as folk-rock, alternative folk, or acoustic rock. Among these groups, Indigo Girls, a duo from Atlanta, reached national prominence and won the Grammy for Best Contemporary Folk Recording in 1989 for their album *Indigo Girls*. Emily Saliers (b. 1964) and Amy Ray (b. 1965), both songwriters and guitarists, began performing together in 1983. Saliers, a soprano whose voice has been described as soft and honeyed, plays a skillful lead guitar and is the more sophisticated writer. Ray's rough-hewn alto voice matches her intense rhythmic playing and visceral songs. Since they produce most of their own material, the writer of a given song usually sings lead. The duo then works by trial and error, building the song by experimenting with passages in call-and-response, unison, and harmony. Until the mid-1990s they worked at blending their contrasting but complementary sounds and styles of playing. In *Shaming the Sun* (1997), they began instead to emphasize the differences in their sounds; they also substituted electric for acoustic guitars and shifted the focus of their songs from the personal to the political.

Rock

From the outset, the new popular music called rock represented a cluster of styles connected by a common ideology, audience, and milieu. Rock belongs to the American political and societal upheavals of the 1960s, when individuals and groups organized into movements to overcome political, social, cultural, racial, and sexual repression. Rituals, among them rock concerts and festivals of various types, arose to replace those deemed outdated and no longer viable, and the music itself became an instrument for change.

There are three particularly striking ironies concerning the rise of rock. The first is that music attached to emancipation movements and liberal ideology should attract a predominantly white middle-class audience and become mainstream music. The second is that the music industry did not cry out in moral outrage, as it had during the emergence of rock 'n' roll, against music that celebrated anti-establishment values, but rather capitalized on its vast commercial potential. The third is that the reinvigoration of American popular music came from an unexpected source: the invasion from the British Isles of groups such as the Beatles and the Rolling Stones, both of which paid homage to the roots of early rock 'n' roll and gave a needed infusion of raucousness and rhythmic drive to the genre.

Bands emerged by the hundreds in the early 1960s from San Francisco's then-obscure Haight-Ashbury district. The music of these early bands, while rooted in the past, was electric and used distorted, heavily amplified instrumental sounds, distinguishing it from rock 'n' roll. As the music grew more sophisticated, it began to assimilate elements of Eastern music, especially Indian ragas. The music and dancing captured a seeming formlessness and spontaneity. The song lyrics, the technique of sound distortion, and the light shows at dance concerts were intended to re-create the psychedelic experience, and audiences were intensely involved with the music. The year 1967 was the heyday for San Francisco rock, and by 1971 the local scene had all but disintegrated; but the musical style that arose there became a national phenomenon and provided the foundation for rock in the 1970s, 1980s, and even 1990s.

Electronic tone generation and amplification are the hallmarks of rock. The core instruments are electric guitars, supplemented by electronic keyboards (piano, organ, and, later, synthesizers), bass, and drums, and a lead singer with backup group. Each performer has a separate microphone and amplifier, and the sound is normally fed into a central mixing board and out through powerful loudspeakers, electronically filtered and distorted through feedback. In recording studios it was possible to manipulate the music still further through splicing, overdubbing, and multitrack taping.

Rock was at first the strict province of males: exclusive, fraternal, misogynistic. The Grateful Dead, a group with a large following even today, represents the quintessential San Francisco rock band of the mid-1960s: all male, psychedelic (under the patronage of Owsley Stanley, an LSD chemist), with a full sound dominated by Jerry Garcia's guitar runs and some twenty-three tons of sound equipment. Women who entered the rock fraternity had to be tough "bad girls" who could compete equally with the boys. Only two women emerged from the San Francisco rock scene as superstars, Janis Joplin and Grace Slick (b. 1939). Lead singer and guitarist of Jefferson Airplane, Slick was responsible for the group's rise to national prominence with her song "White Rabbit," a drug-influenced variation on the theme of *Alice in Wonderland*. She wrote songs uniquely suited to her penetrating voice—bitterly contemptuous songs that made her seem to be both man- and woman-hater.

Janis Joplin

Janis Joplin (1943–1970), whose celebrity no other female rock star approached, projected vulnerability beneath a veneer of toughness. An alienated teenager growing up in a conservative small town in Texas, she preferred reading, painting, and listening to the recordings of Bessie Smith, Odetta, and Leadbelly to typical teenage activities. In 1966 she joined the band Big Brother and the Holding Company in San Francisco. Universally acclaimed as the only white crossover artist to perform the blues convincingly, Joplin turned millions of white, middle-class rock fans into blues enthusiasts. It was in fact her show-stopping rendition of Big Mama Thornton's "Ball and Chain" at the Monterey International Pop Festival in 1967 that made Joplin a national star.

Joplin created an onstage image to please herself. Her eccentric costumes were of feathers, fur, sequins, odd hats, and an equally odd array of jewelry. The counterculture image extended to her stage deportment. Janis

FIGURE 12.2. Janis Joplin. Photo by Doug Fulton. The Frank Driggs Collection. Used by permission.

swaggered onto the stage drinking Southern Comfort, her language peppered with profanity, as she talked to her audiences at length about war and peace, love and brotherhood. When she sang, she was totally unrestrained, gripping. Her powerful, anguished voice, welling up out of deep personal pain, worked in extremes—from whispers and moans to howls, groans, and shrieks—in a single song. Her renditions of the blues had a frenetic, driven quality. Although she usually performed others' songs, she had the rare ability to make those songs hers in a way that few singers have equaled. Joplin was at the peak of her brief career when she died of a drug overdose in 1970. The album she was in the process of recording, *Pearl,* contains her final best-selling song, "Me and Bobby McGee," written by Kris Kristofferson, and two of her own songs, "Mercedes Benz" and "Move Over." It is, however, the last song on the album, "Get It While You Can," that serves as a timely epitaph for Janis Joplin and the counterculture she represented.

Soul

The rise of the musical style known as soul, often described as rhythm and blues with gospel fervor or secular gospel, coincided with civil rights activism and the awakening of black pride in the early 1960s. The musicians who performed it succeeded in breaking down the barriers between white and black, making this black vernacular style a dominant force in popular music. Soul was about sincere feelings, compellingly expressed in music; it carried a message of promise, of expectations. It was music for dancing. Most of the singers had Southern roots and had once sung in black churches. Many of the musical characteristics and vocal techniques of soul are rooted in gospel but applied to secular lyrics in a highly stylized manner. A solid rhythm section provides an anchor for the often fluid vocal lines.

There were two prominent styles in soul. The first, referred to as Southern, "raw," or Red Clay soul, was harsh, aggressive, visceral music with heavy blues inflections, a pulsing rhythm, and a sense of spontaneity. The studio musicians, working without written arrangements, took a sketch of a song from a writer or producer and shaped it with their own ideas as the rehearsal progressed. When they began to "feel" the music, the recording commenced. Because the music was recorded in Southern studios, the house bands were racially mixed and composed of authentic blues and country musicians.

Northern, also called "soft" or "sequin" soul, was the disciplined, polished style usually associated with Motown Records in Detroit. Rhythm was the driving force of this formulaic music. The meter was invariably 4/4 with emphasis on the percussion section. The baritone saxophone figured prominently in arrangements. A slightly later manifestation, called the soul ballad, was a romantic love song, elaborately arranged and indebted to Tin Pan Alley. Motown had a resident composing team—Brian Holland, Lamont Dozier, and Eddie Holland—who came to define Motown's style and produced twenty-eight "top-twenty" hits between 1963 and 1966. Although men produced the recordings and must be credited with developing both styles, women were the most important and successful artists. Many began their careers as gospel singers, standing in a line extending back from Sister Rosetta Tharpe, Bessie Smith, and Ella Fitzgerald, through Dinah Washington, to Aretha Franklin.

Aretha Franklin

The prima donna of Red Clay soul, Aretha Franklin (b. 1942) belongs to a female vocal tradition that mingles the sanctified with the worldly. Child of a Baptist minister and gospel singer, she grew up surrounded by musicians who came to stay at her family's home in Detroit when visiting or performing in her father's church. James Cleveland taught her gospel piano techniques; Mahalia Jackson, Clara Ward, Marion Williams, Dinah Washington, Lou Rawls, and Sam Cooke taught her about singing; and Dinah Washington, Sam Cooke, and Ray Charles served as crossover models for her career.

John Hammond, who had recruited Bessie Smith and Billie Holiday for Columbia Records, signed eighteen-year-old Aretha to a contract. Columbia wanted to mold her into a singer of torch songs and popular standards, but the plan failed miserably. After Jerry Wexler persuaded her to record for Atlantic, Aretha began to find her niche. She was allowed to choose her own material, which ranged from songs by Sam Cooke and Otis Redding to Carole King's "Natural Woman." Wexler took her to record in Muscle Shoals, Alabama. Here she worked out arrangements with studio musicians who, like her, had grown up in gospel music. The result was electrifying. Five of her recordings were No. 1 hits, and her forceful version of Otis Redding's "Respect" won a Grammy award in 1967. She had become one of the most successful singers in America and a powerful symbol to African-American audiences, who referred to the summer of 1967 as the time of "'Retha, Rap, and Revolt." The following summer, Franklin's soul interpretation of the national anthem opened the tempestuous Democratic National Convention in Chicago.

Soul, like the blues of an earlier era, went out of fashion in the 1970s, but Franklin proved her ability to reach beyond its limits with her introspective album, *Young, Gifted, and Black* (1972). Her powerful mezzo-soprano voice, with its range of about two-and-a-half octaves, is vibrant, natural, and expressive. She exhibits great flexibility in register shifts and can change color and intensity as the lyrics demand. Her eloquence is best revealed when she is singing gospel. Franklin's *Amazing Grace* (1972), described by Paul Evans as her magnum opus, returns to the source of her earliest inspiration. The title song displays the range of her vocal techniques: impeccable phrasing, tasteful ornamentation, beautifully styled melismas, an effortless alternation of falsetto with full voice. An arrangement combining Thomas A. Dorsey's "Precious Lord, Take My Hand" with Franklin's sanctified version of Carole King's "You've Got a Friend" [in Jesus] further testifies to her powerful command of the genre.

The 1980s witnessed a new blossoming of her career. In addition to attaining commercial and critical success with new recordings, she starred in a television special for Showtime and was the subject of a PBS broadcast in the *American Masters* series (1989). Franklin also released a second gospel album, *One Lord, One Faith, One Baptism* (1987).

Diana Ross and the Supremes

The pinnacle of Motown success, the epitome of "sequin" soul, and the most famous of the many female singing groups of the 1960s, the Supremes had record sales of over twelve million—second only to those of the Beatles—and were the only group ever to have six consecutive gold records in a single year (1964). The Supremes were a true American success story—a group of three friends growing up in the Detroit housing projects who were recruited out of high school by Berry Gordy and then fashioned into a sleek, sophisticated, professional group. They were a perfectly polished act from their appearances, choreography, and stylized hand gestures to their onstage conversation. Mary Wilson (b. 1943), Florence Ballard (1943–1976, replaced by Cindy Birdsong [b. 1939] in 1968), and Diana Ross (b. 1944) made up the famous group. The Supremes began to generate interest when they were paired with the writing team of Holland-Dozier-Holland, who tailored music to their voices. Their first hit, "Where Did Our Love Go?" provided the model for subsequent songs—simple structures in 4/4 meter with steady rhythm and accents on all four beats, and a soft, velvet vocal sound scored in close harmony with Ross's plaintive little-girl voice singing vapid lyrics about teenage love. Among their most prominent successes were "Baby Love," "Stop in the Name of Love," and "Come See About Me." The Supremes sang their last song as a group, "Someday We'll Be Together," at a farewell performance in 1970, for Diana Ross had decided to begin a solo career. After her departure the group achieved only moderate success and finally disbanded in 1979.

Diana Ross soon sought to change both her feline image and her singing style. With gowns designed by Bob Mackie, she transformed herself into a glamorous vision. Her voice became more refined and the songs she recorded, while verging on the sentimental, were no longer about teenage love but rather about women whose independence had been obtained at a heavy cost. A number of these songs were commercial successes: "Reach Out and Touch (Somebody's Hand)," "Ain't No Mountain High Enough," "Remember Me," and "Do You Know Where You're Going To?"

As a nightclub performer Ross has a wonderful stage presence, and she has been able to command top fees as an entertainer. She received critical acclaim for her portrayal of Billie Holiday in the film *Lady Sings the Blues* (1972). More recently she has worked closely with her former protégé, Michael Jackson, who has produced several of her albums and with whom she often performs. Early in 2000 Ross announced that The [New] Supremes (Ross along with Scherrie Payne and Lynda Laurence) were planning a summer tour. (Payne and Laurence had joined the original trio after Ross left, but the tour was eventually canceled due to lack of public interest.)

Rock since the 1970s

Since the 1970s rock styles have mushroomed to include folk rock, blues rock, hard rock, soft rock, Southern rock, soul, jazz rock, art rock, punk rock, funk, disco, and New Wave. While the basic language of rock has undergone little alteration in this period, it has taken on a new rhythmic vitality that has come from influences without and within. Hispanic immigrants, especially those from the Caribbean basin, have brought their music alive with exciting rhythms. A second enlivening source has been a style of improvised rhymes with rhythmic accompaniment called rap, first developed by streetwise black youths in New York City. Both influences represent the continuing movement away from melody and toward rhythm that began in early rock 'n' roll. Rapid technological progress has been responsible for the most significant modifications in the production and transmission of rock: groups have added sophisticated electronic equipment, particularly synthesizers and digital sequencers.

Despite the shifting fashions in rock, there has always been a desire for songs that speak to the human condition, with the human voice as messenger. Clear evidence of this need shows up in musical trends that thrive outside mainstream rock. One is the persistence of Tin Pan Alley styles—updated arrangements of older songs or new compositions based on models from the past. Among those who have fashioned successful careers by performing this style are Barbra Streisand (b. 1942) and Linda Ronstadt (b. 1946), who began her career in rock. Streisand, known for her emotionally exaggerated singing style, is considered an outstanding interpreter of popular standards.

Ronstadt is an accomplished stylist who, in the recent past, has performed popular standards, operetta, opera, and songs by Philip Glass. Her three 1980s recordings of Tin Pan Alley songs were critical and commercial successes, as was her album of *rancheras,* songs sung to mariachi music, made as a tribute to her Mexican-German father. *Trio,* Ronstadt's 1987 collaboration with Emmylou Harris and Dolly Parton, reaffirmed her love of country music; in *Dedicated to the One I Love* (1996) she restyled popular songs from the past four decades as lullabies for her infant daughter.

A second type of music somewhat outside the rock mainstream, called women-identified music, arose out of the Women's Movement. A number of women musicians began to respond in creative ways to the misogyny expressed in rock music's lyrics and to the nearly total control of the popular music industry by men. Strengthened by the Women's Movement, they began writing "women-identified music" or "women's music" as a conscious expression of the singular experience of a musician as a woman. That it is feminist music implies a political end—the redefinition of the status of women in popular culture and in the mass media.

The audience for this music consists of people who believe in a strong female ideal and in more expansive roles for women in society, and who support women's issues and humanist causes. The performers reach their audiences through recordings, concerts, and women's music festivals. The more traditional ways of communicating with an audience—recordings and concerts—have taken on nontraditional aspects. At concerts, for example, child care and signing for the deaf may be provided and the concert sites made accessible to the disabled. Women's music festivals, which have proliferated since the first one in 1974 at the University of Illinois, are sometimes entirely closed to men.

The male-dominated music industry has resisted change on the question of equal rights for women. Women learned, as had African Americans in the early 1960s, that the best way to transmit new or different musical ideas was to take control of both artistic and business aspects of the industry. Since the early 1970s, women-identified music has grown from several grassroots organizations to sophisticated enterprises controlled entirely by women. Blossom Dearie and Betty Carter had formed their own labels in an earlier era, but their motives were entirely artistic. More recently, women have produced recordings for ideological reasons. Of these, which have record-label names such as Ova, Urana, and Sweet Alliance, the most important is Olivia Records. Founded in 1973 as a women's collective, Olivia's purpose is to control the process, from writing the music to its production and engineering. Olivia's first entirely women-produced album was Meg Christian's *I Know You Know.* Women's Independent Label Distributors (WILD) formed as a collective in 1978 to promote record distribution and concert tours of the recording artists nationally. Today there are a number of promotion companies, among them Women on Wheels and Once in a Blue Moon.

Although the message is often radical, the style of women-identified music is mainly that of the mainstream idiom inspired by Tin Pan Alley. Performers' distinctive musical sounds derive more often from the way instrumental texture, vocal quality, and particular techniques are blended than from innovations of form. Lyrics, then, assume maximum importance; many are directed to a lesbian audience.

A pioneer musician who recorded on her own Cassandra label before the latest revival of the Women's Movement, Malvina Reynolds began writing music in the 1940s that spoke to humanistic causes and was consciously political. Reynolds encouraged the use of her songs as advocacy pieces and allowed them to be performed without payment of royalties. The messages of some of the songs are evident from the titles: "Rosie Jane (Pregnant Again)" or "We Don't Need Men." The song for which she is best remembered, however, is "Little Boxes"; it describes the poorly constructed, look-alike housing developments of the post-1945 era, for which she coined the term "ticky tacky."

Performers of women-identified music who emerged in the late 1960s include the New Harmony Sisterhood, the New Miss Alice Stone Ladies' Society Orchestra, Deadly Nightshade, the New Haven Women's Liberation Band, Meg Christian, Holly Near, and Margie Adams. Meg Christian and Cris Williamson both record for Olivia; Holly Near records on her own Redwood label.

ROCK AT THE END OF THE CENTURY

From the vantage point of the late 1990s, one can look back over some forty-five years in which rock has dominated popular music in the United States. Rock stars lead lives of great affluence and astonishing celebrity, and have become role models for the young. The culture is saturated with rock music. Expensively produced videos serve as the audio-visual equivalents of the 45 rpm records that represented the most current technological advance in the early days of rock 'n' roll. MTV, cable television's most successful rock video channel, has been on the air since 1982. Madonna, arguably the most successful rock star of the 1980s, owes her meteoric rise in popularity in large part to a skillful use of the new technology.

Madonna

A combination of brains, hard work, driving ambition, talent, and timing have made Madonna Louise Veronica Ciccone (b. 1959) the epitome of the late-twentieth-century success story. A shrewd linking of the new—slickly produced music videos—and the old—an album of dance singles—helped bring about her leap to stardom in the early 1980s. Music video was the perfect vehicle for Madonna, who considers videos to be little movies in which she stars. Knowing that she must create an arresting visual image that will film well, she uses as her models glamorous female stars of an earlier era: Judy Holliday, Carole Lombard, Marlene Dietrich, and Marilyn Monroe. The result is an image that is both brazenly sexy and delicately feminine, with the veneer of a Catholic "bad girl" who wears the symbols of her church—rosaries and crucifixes—as jewelry to adorn her revealing costumes. Madonna has said that she is her own experiment, a work of art in progress. Her canny ability to reinvent herself, to embody social change, has been the linchpin to her fame.

The success of her debut album, *Madonna* (1983), was largely due to an aggressive promotional campaign using music videos. Of the two singles to reach *Billboard* magazine's top ten, one was aptly titled "Lucky Star." Madonna's second album, *Like a Virgin* (1984), contained three songs that became best-selling singles, including "Material Girl," the tongue-in-cheek lyrics disdaining romantic love in favor of "cold, hard cash." By 1985 the album had sold over six million copies, earning Madonna some cold, hard cash of her own. The music on the first two albums and on *True Blue* (1986) is light, girlish, fresh, and hip. Madonna's thin, breathy, slightly nasal, and nervously energetic voice drives the music forward and is ideally suited to the dance tunes of these early albums.

Like a Prayer (1989), her most ambitious musical endeavor, reveals a more sophisticated approach. Her voice is lower, darker, fuller, and truer to pitch. The songs, while retaining much of the tunefulness of her earlier work, are serious and self-revelatory. "Till Death Do Us Part" speaks to the painful and very public breakup of her 1985 marriage to movie idol Sean Penn. In "Promise to Try" Madonna attempts to deal with poignant memories of the mother who died while the singer was still a child. The music in some of the songs is referential; "Cherish," a song about lasting love, bows to the Association's song of the same name. Throughout the album Madonna draws effectively on her Catholic background. In the title song she skillfully alternates music of prayerful petition with a more typically Madonnaesque refrain of hard-driving dance music. She rounds out the album with "Act of Contrition," a compelling song that begins with her quiet recitation of the rosary. In the early 1990s Madonna turned her attention to Hollywood. She starred in several films, including *Dick Tracy* and *Evita,* and her image off screen was informed by transvestism. *Ray of Light* (1998), Madonna's first album since the birth of her daughter Lourdes, exemplifies her latest metamorphosis. The woman who once taught us about sexuality, materialism, social ambition, and androgyny now studies sacred texts and seeks to link popular music with metaphysics.

It remains to be seen whether Madonna will come to occupy a place in popular music comparable in status to that of the female singers whom she most admires: Ella Fitzgerald, Joni Mitchell, and Patsy Cline. Still, she has clearly earned a niche in history as "Rock Queen of the 1980s."

Women Rappers

Though at first it seemed as if the world of rap was to be inhabited solely by male performers, the mid-1980s brought several young African-American women to the fore. The three-woman group Salt-n-Pepa brought out its first album, *Hot, Cool, & Vicious,* in 1986. Since then, with new albums appearing about every three years and a Grammy nomination for "Push It," the group has made good on its aim to be the top women on the hip-hop scene. Queen Latifah's first album, *All Hail the Queen* (1989), revealed her lyrics as actively pro-woman and pro-African American, as, for example, in her "Ladies First" (with British rapper Monie Love), "Fly Girl," and "Latifah's Had It Up 2 Here." Owner of her own management company, Latifah has also promoted herself as an actress in films and on television.

Rock's Individualists

Canadian Alanis Morissette cuts a significant figure on today's rock scene. Morissette made her American debut in 1995 with her album *Jagged Little Pill.* Her in-your-face manner won her four Grammys and the knowledge that the album was the greatest commercial success of any rock disc by a female performer. Another Canadian personality, k. d. lang has aroused controversy both for her music and her coming-out as a lesbian. Her earliest albums marked her as a rising star of country music, and her 1989 CD *Absolute Torch and Twang* won her a Grammy in the country music category. However, her next Grammy winner, *Ingénue,* secured the award for best female pop vocalist and established her as a mainstream artist.

Far from most ideals of the musical mainstream, Courtney Love has attacked ubiquitous female stereotypes in her song lyrics and in intense performances that embody the physicality of punk rock. Songs from her albums *Pretty on the Inside* (1991) and *Live Through This* (1994) cry out the painful aspects of growing up female; the latter won several "Best Album" awards. Since the suicide of her husband, rock star Kurt Cobain, Love has established herself as an actress (Althea Leasure in *The People vs Larry Flynt*) and has resumed her musical career.

An Alternative Style for the 1990s: Tori Amos

A prodigy who began playing piano at the age of three, Tori (Myra Ellen) Amos was born in North Carolina in 1963. Her parents moved the family to Baltimore so that their young daughter could study at Peabody Conservatory. Amos, however, was not suited to conservatory study, preferring to create her own music and play by ear. After touring for several years as a teenager in a lounge act, she recorded a debut album, *Y Kant Tori Read,* that was a miserable commercial flop. Success came only after several years of concentrated dedication to songwriting. The reception of *Little Earthquakes* (1991) proved her singular artistic vision was commercially viable.

Amos views her piano as a live, female orchestra and a friend to whom she talks. In concert, sitting at the edge of the bench, her left foot working the sostenuto pedal and her torso turned toward the audience, she appears to be caressing the instrument as she sings to her fans in an intense, confessional whisper. Mainly through extensive touring, she has achieved a cult following among college students and the gay population. Amos's loyal fans are attracted to the disturbing honesty of her lyrics and to her dynamic yet intimate singing style. *Under the Pink* (1994) and *Boys for Pele* (1996), which she describes as "a woman's journey into the hidden parts of the feminine unconscious," are piano-driven albums. A newer album, *From the Choirgirl Hotel* (1998), integrates the piano into an overall sound; all the songs were recorded with bass, guitars, drum, and a programmer. Amos sees this new album as a reflection of her growth as a musician.

Conclusion

The popular music tradition embodies a multiplicity of styles, and though styles may change over time, nothing from the past ever goes away entirely. Today the most creative musicians often speak to contemporary concerns while enlivening their music by reinterpreting or evoking the best ideas from the past. One element that has greatly contributed to enlivening popular music in the twentieth century is the talent of women musicians, vocalists, instrumentalists, and composers. The idea persists that women are incapable of making significant contributions except as singers or pianists. Historical facts, however, document quite dramatically that women instrumentalists and composers have been neither welcomed nor encouraged by the men inside the tradition or by society. Even singers, though always considered more acceptable, were stereotyped—as canaries, bad girls, folk madonnas, and the like. The handful of women who overcame such arbitrary obstacles must be perceived as grand exceptions to the rule. Nevertheless, since the so-called liberation movements of the recent past, much progress has been made in discrediting long-held sexual stereotypes in American society. Although today's world of jazz and popular music is far from providing equal opportunity, women's chances for success are much greater than ever before.

SUGGESTIONS FOR FURTHER READING

In addition to the items mentioned in the text, the following sources provide information on American popular music.

Baez, Joan. *And a Voice to Sing With: A Memoir.* New York: Schirmer Books, 1987.

Bufwack, Mary A., and Robert K. Oermann. *Finding Her Voice: The Saga of Women in Country Music.* New York: Crown Publishers, 1993.

Franklin, Aretha, with David Ritz. *Aretha: From These Roots.* New York: Villard, 1999.

Gaar, Gillian. *She's a Rebel: The History of Women in Rock and Roll.* Seattle: Seal Press, 1992.

Hamm, Charles. *Yesterdays: Popular Song in America.* New York: W. W. Norton, 1979.

Heilbut, Anthony. *The Gospel Sound: Good News and Bad Times.* New York: Limelight Editions, 1985.

Hirshey, Gerri. *Nowhere to Run: The Story of Soul Music.* New York: Times Books, 1984.

Kerstetter, Rich. "Joan Baez: From Folk Madonna to Folk Matriarch," *Sing Out* 41/2 (Aug. 1, 1996): 36–43.

Lee, Peggy. *Miss Peggy Lee: An Autobiography.* New York: Donald I. Fine, Inc., 1989.

Lewis, Lisa. *Gender Politics and MTV: Voicing the Difference.* Philadelphia: Temple University Press, 1990.

Lynn, Loretta, with George Vecsey. *Loretta Lynn: Coal Miner's Daughter.* Chicago: Regnery, 1976.

Malone, Bill C. *Country Music, U.S.A.* Rev. ed. Austin: University of Texas Press, 1985.

Mellers, Wilfrid. *Angels of the Night.* Oxford: Basil Blackwell, 1986.

Metz, Allen, and Carol Benson, eds. *The Madonna Companion: Two Decades of Commentary.* New York: Schirmer Books, 1999.

Miller, Jim, ed. *The Rolling Stone Illustrated History of Rock and Roll.* Rev. ed. New York: Rolling Stone Press, 1980.

O'Brien, Lucy. *She Bop: The Definitive History of Women in Rock, Pop, and Soul.* New York: Penguin Books, 1995.

O'Dair, Barbara, ed. *Trouble Girls: The Rolling Stone Book of Women in Rock.* New York: Random House, 1997.

Pavletich, Aida. *Rock-A Bye, Baby.* Garden City, NY: Doubleday, 1980.

Peraino, Judith. "PJ Harvey's 'Man-Size Sextet' and the Inaccessible, Inescapable Gender." *Women & Music* 2 (1998): 47–63.

Pleasants, Henry. *The Great American Popular Singers.* New York: Simon & Schuster, 1974.

Roy, D. "The Patsy Cline Discography." *Journal of Country Music* 9/2 (1982): 47–115.

Scovill, Ruth. "Women's Music." In *Woman's Culture: The Woman's Renaissance of the 70s,* ed. C. Kimball. Metuchen, NJ: Scarecrow Press, 1981, pp. 148–62.

Steward, Sue, and Sheryl Garratt. *Signed, Sealed, and Delivered: True Life Stories of Women in Pop.* Boston: South End Press, 1984.

Walser, Robert. *Running with the Devil: Power, Gender, and Madness in Heavy Metal Music.* Hanover, NH: University Press of New England, 1993.
Whitesell, Lloyd. "A Joni Mitchell Aviary." *Women & Music* 1 (1997): 46–54.
Winer, Deborah. *The Night and the Music: Rosemary Clooney, Barbara Cook, and Julie Wilson, Inside the World of Cabaret.* New York: Schirmer Books, 1996.

Rolling Stone magazine is an excellent source for articles, interviews, and reviews. The Internet yields interesting, though not entirely reliable, information (audio clips, photographs, "fanzines," etc.) on popular musicians.

Women in the World of Music: Three Approaches

Introduction

Robert Whitney Templeman

Our knowledge of the musical roles, participation, and visibility of women from around the globe has grown considerably since the initial publication of *Women and Music*. This is due in part to the enormous increase of ethnographic and historical studies being carried out among women worldwide, and following this, the publication and availability of articles and books treating the subject. This section, in part new to the second edition of *Women and Music,* consists of a chapter by L. JaFran Jones covering music in parts of Tunisia, North Africa, and Malta; one that I am contributing on music in Latin America; and a final chapter by Michael J. Budds on blues, jazz, and gospel music in the United States.

In labeling this section "Women in the World of Music," I follow the lead of such textbooks as *Excursions in World Music* and *Worlds of Music,* introducing students to the diversity of popular, traditional, and art musics from around the globe.[1] I prefer the qualifiers *world music* and *worlds of music* to "non-Western music" because the subject itself is not beyond or peripheral to Western music, but rather subsumes a great part of it. As Jones wrote in the first edition of *Women and Music,* the problem with "non-Western" is not merely one of scope but also one of marginalizing connotations:

> "Western" music receives the affirmative tag, as if taken as the norm. "Non-Western" tends to place all other musics on the negative side of the equation. This is something like discussing race in terms of "white" and "non-white."[2]

Far from being that which is left over after Western music has been accounted for, world music encompasses most of the music made by people.

The study of world music is closely aligned with the field of ethnomusicolgy, which is a sub-field of both musicology and cultural anthropology. For me, the essential difference between ethnomusicology and musicology lies in its research methodology and, related to this, the types of data researchers collect. While scholars in both fields do archival research and musical analysis, a distinguishing methodology for ethnomusicology is carrying out ethnographic fieldwork. Ethnography entails observing practices and participating with people in their daily activities—as they make music, for example. Ethnographers interpret and document, among other things, the values and relationships that people express through language, art, kinship, religion, and social organization.

In the chapters that follow, the authors explore the musical creativity and participation of women in Middle Eastern, North African, Mediterranean, and North and South American societies. The methodologies, interests, and conclusions are quite different for these authors. While Jones and I base the majority of our findings on our own ethnographic fieldwork, our focus and methods of interpretation differ. Jones posits an approach in which understanding broad cultural patterns and drawing generalizations about music and society are central:

> In pursuing the music, it is only marginally fruitful to look for specific compositions or performances. Individual pieces and events seem less important than the continua of which they are a part. One attends to repertoires and contexts in which music is made. Thus, if one collects a particular song at a specific wedding and "wedding songs" are a valid primary category, one might err by dealing with them on a more atomic level.[3]

This approach is especially useful for surveys and synopses that enable comparisons between people from different regions and histories. By contrast, I focus primarily on individuals, specific compositions by and about women, and the abilities of individual women to foster change within rural villages and urban migrant communities. This challenges the construction of generalizations by demonstrating the continuous reinvention of tradition and a lack of homogeneity among villages, communities, ethnic groups, and "cultures." By focusing on the everyday life of people and the types of leadership, action, and dissent that might be overlooked by generalizations, one can gain insight into the power of music through the multiple and diverse ways people use it, and how they draw upon it as a resource toward specific social, political, or economic ends. Michael Budds focuses on the contributions of individuals within this survey of women in blues, jazz, and gospel; however, unlike my own ethnographic approach and that of Jones, his is a study in historical musicology. By including his study in this section, I hope to promote both a broader understanding of the boundaries of world music—one that recognizes a world of music as much within any one country as around the globe—and the far-reaching musical manifestations of the African diaspora. The scope of world music is ultimately all music that is practiced and consumed by people worldwide, regardless of the problematic labels, including folk, popular, traditional, and art music, that recording industries and academic institutions might impose upon them. Western art music represents only a small fraction of the totality of people's music from around the globe, and it has its counterparts in the art musics of Eastern, Middle, and Southern Asia, Africa, South America, Eastern Europe, and Australia.

NOTES

1. See Bruno Nettl and others, *Excursions in World Music,* 2d ed. (Upper Saddle River, NJ: Prentice Hall, 1997); and Jeff Todd Titon, *Worlds of Music: An Introduction to Music of the World's Peoples* (New York: Schirmer Books, 1996).
2. L. JaFran Jones, "Women in Non-Western Music," in *Women and Music,* ed. Karin Pendle (Bloomington: Indiana University Press, 1991), p. 315.
3. Ibid., p. 316.

SUGGESTIONS FOR FURTHER READING

Bowers, Jane. "Women's Lamenting Traditions around the World: A Survey and Some Significant Questions." *Women & Music* 2 (1998): 125–46.

Moisala, Pirkko. "Tribute to Marcia Herndon, Pioneer in Gender Studies in Ethnomusicology." *Women & Music* 2 (1998): 123–25.

Walton, Susan Pratt. "Singing against the Grain: A Javanese Composer Challenges Gender Ideologics." *Women & Music* 2 (1998): 110–22.

XIII. Women and Music around the Mediterranean

L. JaFran Jones

Introduction

The music dealt with in most of this book constitutes a magnificent repertoire, a monument to human intelligence and creativity by any standards. It is important to understand, however, that it is still only a small part—not necessarily the best part—of a global phenomenon: the music produced by people in all different regions of the world. This is a difficult concept to grasp, because most people who love the music of their own culture—as we do, under the umbrella of European tradition and its extensions in the new worlds—have too little experience with the music of other cultures. It is also difficult because no adequate terminology has been developed to discuss the phenomenon. Cultural bias can be diminished by consciously seeking out the musics of other peoples and endeavoring to appreciate them on their own terms. This is certainly a prime directive for anyone who wishes to become musically literate in today's world. The problem of clarifying terminology and concepts is more difficult. It depends ultimately on a joint effort of music scholars throughout the world. It demands mutual understanding, mutual tolerance, and mutual agreement among diverse people united by their love for music as a human, not merely a national, heritage. Music is only in part a universal language, as humans are only in part a single race. Both appear at first a universe of diversity. Moving beyond this depends to a large extent on the future. It is a future toward which students of "Western" music should seriously consider contributing.

"Music" is a term at once too broad and too narrow to serve us without reservation. On the one hand, it encompasses a range of phenomena that few other cultures would crowd together under a single rubric. The gamut extends from natural sounds to certain events of the mind that no ear can perceive, and it includes activities in specially reserved spheres, such as religion. On the other hand, it may exclude everything that goes against our particular prejudices. Nevertheless, it is a term we have not learned to do without. Nothing more adequate has gained currency.

Until we have refined our conceptual tools, we must continue to use "music" with multiple caveats and awkward qualifiers. Thus the reader is advised to examine the context every time this word occurs and attempt to redefine it accordingly. Frequently the *ad hoc* definition will be more closely linked to presuppositions of the person using the term than to the subject at hand. Some help comes from the rough-shod qualifiers "Western" and "non-Western." They allow at least an initial distinction between musics, yet they fail to shed the trappings of chauvinism. "Western" music receives the affirmative tag, as if taken as the norm. "Non-Western" tends to place all other musics on the negative side of the equation. This is something like discussing race in terms of "white" and "non-white."

It must suffice here to point out some pitfalls in conventional terminology and to put the reader on guard. This is not the place to attempt a remedy. Thus the very terms we have found wanting appear in this chapter and will continue to be used hereafter. Our concern is "non-Western music." Far from being that which is left over after "Western music" has been accounted for, it encompasses most of the music made by people on Earth. The genres that have grown out of the European art-music tradition constitute just one variety of music making among many others. We must be prepared for the realization that "non-Western" music is a vast sea within which the lovely vessel of our own music floats.

Among the new disciplines to emerge in the twentieth century, one is devoted to exploring the global phenomenon of music without the burden of occidental prejudices. English-speaking scholars call it "ethnomusicology." Like musicology, it deals with the technical details of music, intervals, rhythms, and structures. But it must approach these matters from the broadest point of view, for the canons of Western music theory constitute only a special case in the way people organize sound. It also studies instruments and genres, attempting to understand them on their own terms, without establishing hierarchies across cultural boundaries. Thus, the West African *kora* receives the same serious attention as our harp, and the Indonesian *gamelan* has all the respect accorded to a symphony orchestra.

Like ethnology, ethnomusicology focuses its attention on the cultures within which music is produced. Music making is an extremely culture-sensitive activity. It is an error to abstract music from its context. This does not mean that we cannot approach the music of another culture without delving into mountains of ethnographic detail. There are certain universal qualities to music that have appeal across cultural boundaries, and music is an open door to cultures we may otherwise find difficult to appreciate. It does mean that a serious study of any music requires an equally serious study of its specific culture. Ethnomusicologists must usually approach their target music as outsiders, a difficult position. For this reason, they must understand the culture as thoroughly as the music and must endeavor to hear a music through the ears of the culture that fosters it. Music is made by people; it does not exist by itself.

In pursuing the music, it is only marginally fruitful to look for specific compositions or performances. Individual pieces and events seem less important than the continua of which they are a part. One attends to repertoires and contexts in which music is made. Thus, if one collects a particular song at a specific wedding and "wedding songs" are a valid primary category, one might err by dealing with them on a more atomic level. The field researcher asks, "What types of events involve music making?" and "What repertoires are associated with them?" Musical material is analyzed in generic terms—interval structure, range, cadenza types—and coordinated with conventional components of their events.

Beyond cultural background, event type, and musical characteristics, social functions of a repertoire must be considered. Sometimes music has a serious duty to perform, which is not apparent in its immediate context: training youth, reinforcing culturally prescribed roles, passing information, facilitating social transactions, and avoiding confrontations. Here it is important to consider texts as well as music. In addition, the music of one group may be directed at or variously affect another. For example, the study of women's music cannot ignore courtship songs sung by men, or the prohibitions attached to men's repertoires or to men's instruments.

WOMEN AND MUSIC

Our knowledge of world music remains severely limited by lack of data. Ethnomusicology is a young discipline, still seeking valid theories and methods. Yet its subject matter is as old and as vast as human life on Earth. Specific studies on women's music are few and scattered. Thus it is too early to answer most of the questions that might puzzle us. Nevertheless, a few tentative generalizations may be suggested. Women make music, and men make music. Both can sing and play instruments. There is no evidence that one sex possesses more musical ability than the other or gains more enjoyment from music. Nor is there evidence that one sex produces more music makers. We know of no instruments or musical systems that one of the sexes is inherently incapable of mastering. We are not dogged by the question debated in Western music—why are there so many men and so few women?

There are, indeed, differences virtually everywhere between men's music and women's music. There are repertoires, instruments, and musical contexts exclusive to one gender and forbidden to the other. There are other societies besides our own where more men than women are seen making music in public. Perhaps no cases have been studied in sufficient depth to account unequivocally for the differences, but the bulk of evidence from ethnomusicology points to culture as the source of gender distinctions in music. Each culture defines "men" and "women" and prescribes the behavior (including musical behavior) appropriate to each. These unwritten cultural codes typically take only incidental account of the concrete, physical differences between the sexes. Thus it is valid to deal separately with women's music, whereas dealing with women's musicality may be motivated by prejudiced presuppositions.

SURVEY

This overview is not intended to be comprehensive, but suggestive. Likewise, categories are informal and may not be rigorously drawn. Any scheme for breaking down a cultural continuum is necessarily artificial and must admit rough edges as well as troublesome crossover items that refuse to be neatly pigeonholed. The survey framework demands that things be taken out of their rich cultural context, from which they are, in principle, inseparable. The reader must indulgently assume the ample background of detail that would be needed in order to present each item adequately. Consistent with the prime importance of firsthand experience, I draw generously on my own extensive fieldwork in Tunisia, North Africa, and Malta, with some supplementary references to other scholars' work.

The printed page is far removed from real-life music. Yet it is the medium we must use here. Only a few musical examples are provided to stimulate the reader's appreciation of sound in relationship to culture. Time and key signatures are added to help the reader: most of the examples are modal, and there is flexibility within measures.

Making Music

Most music is made by people who are not musicians and whose attention is not focused on the music itself. It is not a matter of performing/listening, but of making music in the course of life's activities. If asked, "What are you doing?" someone who happens to be singing, humming, or whistling will probably not mention the music, but something else: just thinking, waiting, washing clothes, celebrating a wedding, worshipping. The repertoires used may well have been composed by individuals, but they are usually perceived as part of the cultural heritage. At any rate, one does not normally think in terms of composers and poets when they are in the shower, around the campfire, at a celebration: one sings or plays what comes to mind, what one likes, what is appropriate for the occasion. In music making one focuses on the context, the event, the activity, the mood. The music "goes along."

Music making is a basic and satisfying human activity. Everyone can do it. People often make music just for the fun of it, because they feel good, to while away the time, to soothe a troubled mind. Although they may not be doing anything else, they do not concentrate on the music, as in practicing an instrument or in singing someone a song. They are living their lives, and music happens in the process. This may be the underlying perception behind our verb "play," as it applies to music. Other terms express the same thing more consciously. The Sicilian name for jaw's harp is *cacciapensiri*—care chaser (a typically "male" instrument, incidentally).

Women make music in this way at least as much as men do, although rarely outside the family. Many cultures have restrictions on what women may do in public, and such impromptu music making frequently falls under the ban. At home, however, women do more singing and instrument playing than one might expect, particularly in societies where women appear generally repressed. Unlike other music situations, there is no fixed repertoire for this usage. Thus, considerable crossover into men's music may occur. Women sing songs that are normally forbidden them and play instruments that would be inappropriate for them in more formal contexts.

Obviously this sort of music is especially difficult to study and record. It requires an intimacy with family life that most ethnomusicologists are unable to achieve. One normally finds out about it from informants or from published memoirs. It is equally obvious, however, that female scholars have a better chance of penetrating the inner sphere of music life than do their male colleagues. Within a society, this "incidental" music, heard from mothers and female relatives, forms part of everyone's childhood memories. Its importance in transmitting musical traditions to both girls and boys will be stressed below.

"Whistle while you work" is proverbial in our culture. Music helps make work lighter, quicker, and more pleasant. Although it is generally uncommon for women to whistle, there are sizeable repertoires of work songs for both women and men in most societies we study. They provide the most concrete examples of how music may be tailored to suit its context. Our study of this music must perforce center on traditional work, where tasks for women and men are clearly divided by the rules of the culture, where the activities are most conducive to music, and for which long-standing repertoires exist. Music appears to have lost currency in the modern workplace, and traditional repertoires are in danger of being forgotten. No doubt it is the workers—everyone—who stand to lose the most.

In Tunisia, for example, women work mostly in the home or in the company of other women. Their jobs are heavy and demanding: preparing food, making and maintaining clothing, taking care of the home compound, and raising children. Rural women have such additional burdens as fetching water, collecting firewood, processing grain, and tending domestic animals. Except in wealthy families it is rare to find any woman or girl completely idle. When there seems to be nothing else to do, a woman will take up her spindle and make yarn. Except for formal celebrations or ceremonies, when women get together, they work. Men may be rigorously excluded from women's work sessions, under penalty.[1]

FIGURE 13.1. Women in southern Tunisia spinning wool and singing. From André Louis, *Douiret, étrange cité berbère* (Tunis: Société Tunisienne de Diffusion, 1975), p. 73. Reproduced by permission.

EXAMPLE 13.1. *Bormliża* (Malta)

The music women make while working depends largely on what the task is. Pounding food in a mortar and grinding flour are heavy, rhythmic tasks. The songs have a strong beat, with short, simple, often repetitive texts. The grain staple *kuskśī* is often prepared in groups. Movements are still rhythmic, but slower and gentler. This affords the accompanying songs more latitude for melodic and textual elaboration. Often material from religious, ceremonial, or popular repertoires enters in. This music is more social and enjoyable. Often one woman or girl will keep time with traditional drumming patterns on a *darbūka* (vase-shaped clay drum) or a handy household utensil. Songs for spinning have an element of incantation. With charming melodies, the texts address the wool, the yarn, and the spindle, and they express wishes about the clothes to be made and the good fortune of those who will wear them.

Malta offers an example of free-rhythm, improvised work songs. Women often work on the flat roofs of the houses, washing and hanging clothes, for example. Roof repair is also a traditional women's task. The women hold singing "conversations" with each other from roof to roof. They elaborate on a few traditional (modal) melodic patterns with considerable ornamental improvisation. The texts, in verse, are also partly improvised and depend on the subject of the day's conversation. The singing involves an element of contest, where women try to surpass each other with clever turns of melody and phrase. This music belongs to the genre *bormliża*[2] and corresponds in some respects to the popular male "joust" singing, *spirtu pront*. In Example13.1, note the descending lines of *bormliża*. The range is usually between a seventh and a ninth. Extreme melisma in descending patterns is the most striking characteristic of the genre. Voices are tense and must produce a considerable volume of sound.

This calls to mind a variety of improvised conversational singing practiced by the youth of some Bedouin tribes in eastern Libya.[3] It may more accurately be called "social singing," although it occurs in the context of work, at wells. Young women come to fetch water, and young men bring their animals to drink. Although normal social interaction between young men and women is frowned on, they may have singing exchanges in this context. The words are improvised within a body of conventional rules. They must correspond to accepted standards of poetry in a rivalry of taunting and teasing. It is very important to be good at this type of singing. In this semiritualized framework, young people are allowed to become acquainted, to measure each other's qualities and, no doubt, marriageability.

Lullabies constitute a special category of women's work songs. Because of their very specific purpose, they display striking resemblances across cultural boundaries. This has given rise to a plethora of gratuitous theories about cross-cultural influences on the one hand and the "true nature" of women's music on the other. Marius Schneider displayed more ambition in contending that the use of "ra-ra-ra" as opposed to "na-na-na" vocables corresponded to the anthropologists' distinguishing between brachycephalic (short- or broad-headed) and dolichocephalic (long-headed) peoples.[4]

Beyond their immediate function and their pleasing musical qualities, lullabies have important roles in the lives of mother and child. They allow the mother to express hopes and dispel fears, and they constitute the child's first musical experience. Their effect also reaches older children in the family. Lullaby words reinforce cultural values and prejudices. Although the melodies may remain essentially the same, there are often striking differences between the texts sung to boys and to girls. Tunisians traditionally congratulate a woman when she has a boy and console her if she has a girl. This valorization is reflected in the lullabies she will subsequently sing.

Play songs for girls share the musical characteristics typical of children's songs, which, like lullabies, appear to have less culture specificity. The games girls play and the words they sing, however, are significantly different from those of boys. They center on domestic concerns, marriage aspirations, and women's place in society. They may be seen as powerful media for training and acculturation, as some interesting examples collected in Tunisia demonstrate.[5]

Crucial events in individuals' lives are typically solemnized with ceremonies and celebrations. These may involve only the family or include the broader community and possibly the religious establishment. They provide occasions for considerable music making, with many events where women play a leading or exclusive role. Each society has its own set of ritual occasions, but universally prominent for virtually all peoples are birth, marriage, and death. Rich musical repertoires and elaborate customs exist for these crucial celebrations, the proper execution of which may affect the good fortune of the individual feted or of the entire community. Cultural heritage is here most evident and music most prominent.

EXAMPLE 13.2. *Taʿshīqa,* a melodic (modal) invocation of blessing and good fortune (Tunisia)

Birth celebrations in Tunisia are typically restricted to family and close friends and are not elaborate, although they may be more so in the case of a first child. The sexes are quite naturally segregated. Men wait outside for the women's signal and generally have little to do with the affair. As mentioned, the birth is celebrated more joyously if the child is male. The principal actors in the parturition (besides the mother) are the childbirth professionals, a *shaddāda* to hold the mother steady and a *qābla* (midwife) to receive the child. They are not outsiders but are experienced women from the community who contribute to the success of the event by their concern for the mother and by the particular importance of their persons. There should also be an *ʿashshāqa,* whose role it is to chant or shout certain conventional formulae that invoke blessing, protection, and good fortune on mother and child. She is armed with an incensor and, at specific points of juncture, circles it above the mother three times and pronounces her *taʿshīqa* (Example 13.2; this is also used on other propitious occasions and to ward off evil). The *ʿashshāqa,* who may earn a few much-needed coins for her service, is also a woman distinguished by experience, piety, or other powers.

As important to the event as any conventional singing are the attendant women's *zaghrīṭ* and *tarḥība. Zaghrīṭ,* usually described as ululation, is an exclusively female vocalization typical of Middle Eastern, African, and (to some extent) southern European women. It is produced with a high-pitched, loud voice, accompanied by rapid movement of the tongue and the uvula. (The right hand is usually extended horizontally over the upper lip.) It may simply be an expression of joy, but it is also an act of power. It would be most unfortunate for any significant event to pass without *zaghrīṭ.* Clearly women's monopoly of this device enhances their status. Most regions have conventions specifying greater length, more iterations, or more volume for the *zaghrīṭ* of a male birth. The *tarḥība* (welcoming) is a rhythmic fanfare (Example 13.3) produced by one or more women on a *bandīr* (round, snared frame-drum) or *darbūka.* It likewise has ritual value and may not be omitted on this and other important occasions. Men are certainly capable of producing the *tarḥība,* and I know of no prohibitions or penalties, but it counts, like the *zaghrīṭ,* as the exclusive province of women.

EXAMPLE 13.3. *Tarḥība,* a welcoming drum fanfare (Tunisia)

The women also sing. The specific repertoire for birth celebrations is quite small, but many songs of well-wishing, religious praise, and thanksgiving, also used at weddings and circumcisions, are appropriate here. Most important is the *taᶜlīla* for the occasion. This is a traditional song, considered to be of old and venerable vintage, whose melody summons nostalgia and whose text may contain obsolete or even "forgotten" words. Every important ritual occasion has a *taᶜlīla* or (in the case of weddings) several *tᶜallal* that are to be sung at appropriate moments.

Weddings are genuine community events and involve much more than the joining of a couple. They are the most elaborate, prolonged, and expensive ritual celebrations in Tunisian society. A full-scale, traditional Tunisian wedding may last up to seven days, each packed with events that require special food, special acts, and special music. The sexes are segregated for many of these events. Women's activities generally center on the bride's house, men's on the groom's. Often there is a kind of neutral ground as well.

The musical repertoire for Tunisian weddings is vast, rivaled perhaps only by that of Sufi religious groups, which may also play a prominent role at weddings. Music is ubiquitous, but there is very little "performance." Music making is a communal undertaking, inseparable from the other acts of celebration. *Zaghrīṭ* and *tarḥība* are *de rigueur* at specified moments. The *ᶜashshāqa* is there, as are other wedding professionals, who may sometimes have selections to sing or play on instruments while others listen; but the tone throughout is that of collective music making, certainly never the performer/listener "concert" setting that pervades much of Western music.

Principal women-only events are *līlt al-ḥannā* (night of henna, when an herbal dye is applied to the hands and feet of the bride and, optionally, of members of the wedding party) and *līlt al-jilwa* (night of glory, when the bride is displayed in all her finery). Each event has a set of ritual acts to be performed in prescribed sequence and a set of *tᶜālil* to be sung at specified points of the celebration. Women usually sing together, but occasionally there is antiphony between groups, such as the bride's attendants and the wedding guests. *Darbūka* or *bandīr* drums are always on hand and usually get passed around in the course of the evening. Example 13.4 (*taᶜlīlat al-ᶜarūsa*) is sung in the bride's house by the women of both families, just before the bride takes leave of her parents and is borne in solemn procession

EXAMPLE 13.4. *Taʿlīlat al-ʿarūsa,* a wedding song (Tunisia)

by the groom's family to the house of her future husband. This song is ostensibly in 6/8 rhythm, but it has measures of hemiola within the verses. The melodic range is narrow, and small motivic patterns repeat.

Besides the *tʿālil* there are many other wedding songs, and the praise repertoire of Sufi groups enjoys great favor. Well-liked folk songs and popular mass-media songs come up as well. The women may also dance, usually as a group, with rhythmic body movements, as in Sufi events. Occasionally individuals come forward impromptu and dance before the others to display their finery and skill. Without the restrictive presence of men, these dances can become very sexually explicit, but this is hardly the rule.

Sometimes all-women ensembles are hired for their (particularly rhythmic) skills, their instruments, and their intimate knowledge of the wedding repertoire. They are paid (or at least fed) and may be genuine professionals, but it is difficult to consider them performers in the Western sense. Their role is rather to enhance the music making of the group and to reinforce the good feelings and propitious tone of the occasion, perhaps also to display the wealth of the family or to encourage the flow of small contributions from the guests.

Women also have a leading role at times of death, particularly as mourners. Mourners may be hired professionals, family members, or the entire community, but they are usually only women. Mourning, like religious ceremony, involves what Western observers would readily label "music," although the participants may fail to see what it has in common with music making at festive events and may be offended by the implied comparison.

Elizabeth Mathias describes wake ceremonies in rural Sardinia, where women sing extemporaneous dirges.[6] Men may not be present, nor are they allowed to show signs of mourning. The information that comes out at a wake is equally important to them, but they are allowed to learn of it only secondhand. Women from the family predominate, telling in their song of the deceased's life and virtues, but also expressing their own problems and complaints. Wakes are very long, and all the women in the community have an opportunity to be heard. The wake thus fills an important social function, and it is a major source of power for women, since they control the flow of information in the community. Men have no similar opportunity to vent their feelings and needs, and must depend on women for this.

Control of official religion is often in the hands of men, who allow women only a helpmate role. Men have codified into religion curious notions about women, associating them with sin and evil and labeling them as distractions from men's higher spiritual aspirations. Religion is a source of many prohibitions against women's musical activities. Sīdī ᶜAbd as-Salām, a venerable North African saint of the fifteenth century, called women's religious ceremony the "ceremony of the devil" and forbade them to touch the sacred drums of his brotherhood.[7] Muslim tradition anathematizes the female voice to the extent of commanding women to clap their hands when answering the door, so that a caller will not be troubled by hearing their voices.[8] Jewish groups are not far behind, some forbidding women to sing, even religious songs, in front of men.[9]

Nevertheless, religion is a major context for women's music making, even within systems where orthodoxy is severe. There are many examples of women providing spiritual exercise, including music, for other women, and not infrequently their influence extends to male devotees. Tunisia has female groups within the Tijānī Sufi order. They operate loosely under a male grand *shaykh* but are largely independent in both the content and the conduct of their ceremonies. Each group is led by a *mqaddma,* who fills the function of *shaykh*. She is normally an older woman of piety and experience whom circumstances (such as widowhood) have rendered relatively independent of male control. She shares her home with a circle of devotees, usually needy women who live from the contributions she collects. They are her assistants in ceremony and constitute a vocal/instrumental ensemble for the music.

Typically there are weekly ceremonies (Thursday or Friday) at a *zāwīya* (shrine) and many additional appearances at weddings or in the homes of women who have special (spiritual or health) needs. Their standard instrument is a large bowl-shaped drum with a single laced head (*ṭabla,* or *ṭablat sīdī ḥmād*). They may use other instruments as well. The repertoire consists chiefly of songs in praise of the Prophet or of Sīdī Aḥmad, the founder of the order. The women share some repertoire with male brotherhoods, but most of it is their own. *Tijānīya* songs are much appreciated by women and are sung with or without occasion. An important function of the female *Tijānīya* ceremony is therapeutic. Through the blessings (*baraka*) of Sīdī Aḥmad, the personal powers of the *mqaddma,* and the beneficent effect of music and motion, many women seek relief from their physical and emotional afflictions. There are secular spin-offs of the *tijānīya*, called *ḥadḥriya,* who work weddings and celebrations, providing similar music but with little claim to spiritual powers.

There are also women's religious ceremonies in Tunisia involving spirit possession and oracular demonstrations (such as glossolalia), but this sort of musical/spiritual activity has been studied more elsewhere. In Korea, a *kut* (shamanic ceremony) is frequently led by a woman who can take on hundreds of different spirits. It is possible, but rare, for men to have this role. The style of ceremony may vary with the occasion, but there is always music. The female shaman (*mansin*) is accompanied by two double-head laced drums (*chango*) and a double-reed aerophone (*piri*). A woman may become a shaman by inheritance or by divine inspiration.

In the rich cultural heritage of Bali, spirits enter virtually every aspect of life. They function through both men and women mediums (*sadeg*) in a variety of ceremonies involving music. Young girls may also enter trance and become *sanghyang* vehicles of the spirits' musical utterances. Though not exclusive to women, practices of possession with song and dance constitute a significant context for women to make music and to assert their importance in society. The ceremonies are necessary to the community and important in the official, sanctified realm of the temple.

Performing Music

Performance is the realm of the star, the diva, the virtuoso, the rock group; also of the sequestered composer and of the silent, appreciative audience. It is the stratified structure for music making perhaps most familiar to people in the West; and it is threatening to become a norm for the rest of the world, with the irresistible thrust of mass media. Lofty though its spiritual summits may be, it breeds atrophy in the musical laity, who risk losing a cherished boon companion for the delights and pains of their lives. I find the transformation palpable in my Tunisian friends. People who brought out their pipes and drums for my evenings with them fifteen years ago now offer me a cushion in front of the television.

The story of professional women performers outside the West is an old and curious one, with many turns we may not expect from the standpoint of our occidental bias. Yet it is similar in many respects to stories we know very well: women struggling to achieve a balance between their private and public lives; attempting to maintain respectability in the face of their obvious deviation from expected female behavior; revered for their artistic prowess and reviled for their violation of cultural norms; envied and admired for their freedom and allure and decried for their refusal to be normal. It is a story of women's lives that bears telling and retelling with each set of individual details in order to achieve its full impact on our consciousness, and for which bland generalizations appear a violation, a betrayal.

Other societies than ours have had their Maria Callas, their Billie Holiday, their Edith Piaf, and their fortunate ones. There are tales of ecstasy and of tragedy. But the stories are often told in tones of masculine mentality, with male fantasies and judgments. Women need to get behind the myths and retell these stories in terms of real life. Two recent essays have undertaken this in a general way,[10] but more specific focus on individuals is needed.

Transmitting Music

Paco de Lucía is one of today's leading flamenco guitarists. Lucía is his mother. There may be many reasons why he chose this stage name, but we might surmise that one of them is an acknowledgment of his musical debt to a woman. Music, as we have stressed, is a basic human activity that all people may enjoy. Nevertheless, it must be learned. No one is born with the songs and tunes of her or his culture. Our society provides music education in schools and conservatories. In the world at large, however, throughout human history, very few people have received formal music training; yet music belongs to everyone. Many who gain much from music and who are able to give much are unschooled, but they have learned well.

A great many vectors combine in transmitting musical traditions; no one of them is sufficient by itself. It is obvious, however, that women have an immense share in this process. One might, indeed, assert that women are the principal transmitters of music. It would be difficult to dispute this claim, yet it has an odd ring to our ears, for it is still not common among us to attribute such strong roles to the "weaker" sex. Women's music receives relatively less public exposure, certainly less attention, than men's, and the scarcity of women among music's leading figures is proverbial. Yet it is largely women who give us music—our first melodies and much that we acquire thereafter. This is tacitly confessed even in our word "music," for the Muses were females. The great Orpheus learned his art from these divine women, a pattern that has been repeated countless times since then.

If Orpheus owed his music to the Muses, and Paco to Lucía, the same is true of many other men who have become prominent in music and for whom music has become a prominent part of life. It is also true, of course, for many women. In reminiscences of the great Tunisian *mālūf* composer Aḥmad al-Wāfī, ᶜUthmān al-Kaᶜᶜāk mentions that al-Wāfī's mother and sisters were skilled in *mālūf*. The boy Aḥmad first learned from his mother the instruments and repertoire for which he was to become famous, a music that she and her daughters would never have been able to perform in public. Al-Kaccāk further notes that al-Wāfī's older sister knew and loved Ṭayyibīya Sufi music, a male repertoire. It was from her that al-Wāfī first acquired this music. The same woman was also al-Kaccāk's grandmother. It is thus not surprising to read that when al-Kaccāk participated in his first Ṭayyibīya session, he already knew the repertoire.[11] Several Maltese men have told me that they learned *spirtu pront* from their mothers. *Spirtu pront* is a difficult improvisational art, demanding both musical and poetic virtuosity. Women do not engage in it publicly, but they are capable of teaching it to their sons. Such examples could be multiplied. One might say that the voice that sings at the cradle sets the tone for the world's music.

It is not only as mothers that women enrich the musical heritage of their own and future generations. They also perform an important service in cross-cultural fertilization. In Arab-Islamic civilization of the Middle Ages it was customary for wealthy men to purchase "singing slave girls" from foreign climes, not infrequently from Christian lands, East and West. (The practice continued until the end of the nineteenth century in Tunisia and may still persist in some places.) These women were consummate virtuosi in their own music and fetched a high price. They often became the teachers of musicians in their involuntarily adopted country. We know few of their names, but their legacy is with us. Much of the musical wealth of the Arab world was brought and bequeathed by these anonymous women slaves.[12] Examples of this process may be drawn from other cultures as well, including our own.

Conclusion

This time is not ripe for conclusions. Serious gender studies in music are just beginning to emerge. Many old prejudices about women and music have yet to be unmasked. Much of the world's music still remains beyond our ken. If concluding words are to be spoken, they must come from a future generation of ethnomusicologists.

NOTES

In the years between the first and second editions of this book, L. JaFran Jones passed away. Out of respect for her scholarship, this chapter is being reprinted unchanged.

1. William Marçais and Abderrahman Guiga, *Textes Arabes de Takrouna,* vol. 1 (Paris: Imprimerie National Ernst Leroux, 1925), pp. 330–32.
2. Marcia Herndon and Norma McLeod, "The Bormliża: Maltese Folk Song Style and Women," *Journal of American Folklore* 88 (1975): 81–100.
3. cAbd as-Salām Ibrāhīm Qādridūh, *Ughnīyāt min bilādī* (Beirut: Maṭbaca Samaya, 1974), pp. 81ff.

4. Marius Schneider, "A propósito del influjo de la música árabe. Ensayo de etnografía musical de la España medieval," *Annuario Musical* 1 (1946): 31ff.

5. Aṣ-Ṣādiq ar-Rizqī, *Al-Aghānī at-Tūnisīya* (Tunis: ad-Dār at-Tūnisīya lin-Nashr, 1967), pp. 284–90.

6. Elizabeth Mathias, "Funeral Laments and Female Power in Sardinian Peasant Society," in *Contributions to Mediterranean Studies* (Malta: Malta University Press, 1977), pp. 153–64.

7. Muhammad ᶜUmar Salīm Makhlūf, *Mawāhib ar-raḥīm fī manāqib mawlānā ash-shaykh Sīdī ᶜAbd as-Salām Ibn Salīm* (Beirut: al-Maktaba ath-Thaqāfīya, 1966), pp. 197–99.

8. Abdelwahab Bouhdiba, *La Sexualité en Islam* (Paris: Presses Universitaires de France, 1975), p. 53.

9. Ellen Koskoff, "The Sound of a Woman's Voice: Gender and Music in a New York Hasidic Community," in *Women and Music in Cross-Cultural Perspective,* ed. Ellen Koskoff (Westport, CT: Greenwood Press, 1987), pp. 213–23.

10. L. JaFran Jones, "A Sociohistorical Perspective on Tunisian Women as Professional Musicians," and Jennifer Post, "Professional Women in Indian Music: The Death of the Courtesan Tradition," in Koskoff, *Women and Music*, pp. 69–83 and 97–109.

11. *at-Turāth al-Mūsīqī at-Tūnisī* (Tunis: al-Maᶜhad al-Watanī lil-Mūsīqā wa-r-Raqṣ, n.d.), vol. 5, pp. 5, 9, 18.

12. Ḥ. Ḥ. ᶜAbd al-Wahhāb, "Taqaddum al-mūsīqā fi-sh-sharq wa-l-andalus wa-tūnis," in *Waraqāt* (Tunis: Maktabat al-Manār, 1966), vol. 2, pp. 196–205. Al-Kaᶜᶜāk (note 11) also alludes to this on pp. 5, 11–12.

SUGGESTIONS FOR FURTHER READING

In addition to sources cited in the text or in the footnotes, the following offer additional information.

Belo, Jane. *Trance in Bali.* New York: Columbia University Press, 1960.

Bergman, Billy. *Goodtime Kings: Emerging African Pop.* New York: Quill (William Morrow and Co.), 1985.

Covell, Alan Carter. *Ecstasy: Shamanism in Korea.* Elizabeth, NJ: Hollym International Corp., 1983.

Henry, Edward. *Chant the Name of God.* San Diego: San Diego State University Press, 1988.

Huhm, Halla Pai. *Kut: Korean Shamanist Rituals.* Elizabeth, NJ: Hollym International Corp., 1980.

Jackson, Irene V., ed. *More Than Drumming: Essays on African and Afro-Latin American Music and Musicians.* Westport, CT: Greenwood Press, 1985.

Keil, Charles. *Tiv Song.* Chicago: University of Chicago Press, 1979.

Kendall, Laurel. *Shamans, Housewives, and Other Restless Spirits: Women in Korean Ritual Life.* Honolulu: University of Hawaii Press, 1985.

Koskoff, Ellen. "When Women Play: Musical Instruments and Gender Style." In *Violet Archer Festschrift,* ed. Regula Qureshi and Christopher Lewis. Edmonton: University of Alberta Press, forthcoming.

Merriam, Alan P. *The Anthropology of Music.* Evanston: Northwestern University Press, 1964.

Nettl, Bruno. *The Study of Ethnomusicology: Twenty-Nine Issues and Concepts.* Urbana: University of Illinois Press, 1983.

Nketia, J. H. Kwabena. *The Music of Africa.* New York: W. W. Norton and Co., 1974.

XIV. Women in the World of Music: Latin America, Native America, and the African Diaspora

Robert Whitney Templeman

Introduction

The Andes Mountains run north to south along the western edge of South America through parts of Colombia, Ecuador, Peru, Bolivia, and Chile. Ethnomusicologists often group these countries together because of their shared history and, related to this, musical forms, styles, and aesthetics that Andean people hold in common. In my research in Bolivia, I have focused on the music of Quechua-speaking Indians, who in some social contexts, self-identify as *campesinos* (people of rural agricultural lands); black Bolivians who mainly self-identify as *negros* (black people); and *mestizos,* a social category that some people use when referring to themselves or to others who are of mixed European and indigenous cultural heritages. As labels, we must recognize that these terms are relative to the social and historical contexts in which people use them. This results in fluid terms that are difficult to define. Because of this fluidity, I find it more useful to discuss the social and musical practices of individuals and small communities rather than generalizing about indigenous, *mestizo,* or black people of the Americas.[1] Thus, in doing ethnographic research, I concentrate my efforts on interviewing, observing, and participating with people to learn about their musical interests, involvement, and values. I also learn about the terms people use in self- and other identifications and the associations that they make between these social identifiers and music. When Bolivians, for example, refer to *el rítmo negro,* or "the black rhythm," they are binding the color of a people's skin with an essentialized notion of rhythmic competency, thus reproducing a stereotype. Understanding these social identifiers and the associations that people make enables me to avoid the problems inherent in generalizing about people as a "culture" (e.g., "that culture has rhythm"). What I find most interesting are the creative contributions and leadership styles and skills of individuals, and how these affect social dynamics and musical productivity within their communities. In recognizing the musical work and contributions of individual women, we begin to understand how some work to maintain, revitalize, and reinvent historically gendered aspects of their musical heritage, while other women cultivate more radical change and redefine ascribed musical roles. Not surprisingly, I observed that the women who succeed in effecting change are recognized leaders within their own communities. To be effective they must win the support of their peers and communities. Ethnomusicologists have found that leadership styles are radically different among indigenous Andeans, black Bolivians, and *mestizos*.[2]

Whether describing the musical practices of individuals from a specific community or surveying the music of indigenous, *mestizo*, and black people of South America, it is helpful to recognize that composers, performers, and dancers have historically drawn upon resources of three musical heritages: Native American, European, and African. The music of rural Quechua-speaking Bolivian farmers, for example, often reveals both Native American and European influence, but to understand how they use music as a means of resistance to European cultural and economic domination, we must view this within the historical context of five hundred years of European imperialism in the Andes. Similarly, while the music of black Bolivians reveals African and European musical heritages, to account for musical revitalization and an Africanization of their music during the last two decades of the twentieth century, one must understand the issues of racial discrimination and inter-ethnic group competition in Bolivia. Ethnomusicologists identify both the tri-ethnic musical heritage and people's social and class struggles in relation to their musical productivity and consumption throughout Latin America. Recognizing this tri-ethnic heritage alone does not account for the enormous variety of musical creativity and expression found throughout the Americas; we must also take a critical look at issues of nationalism, racism, and class stratification, and processes of gender and identity constitution.[3]

Like leadership styles, the roles, participation, and visibility of women in music are not equal across indigenous, black, and *mestizo* people. As I draw upon case studies from the Andean region, I dedicate a larger portion of this chapter to the black women of Bolivia because of their relatively higher level of involvement and visibility in community-based musical ensembles. I begin by looking at colonial documents from the central Andes to establish a baseline from which to measure both continuity and change in women's music in the region and the ways in which their musical and leadership roles are historically engendered. From there, I present examples of contemporary rural Bolivian women in indigenous, black, and *mestizo* communities. I introduce two parallel case studies of women in music for comparison with those that I have researched myself. The first of these features Native-American Shoshone women of Wyoming, as reported by ethnomusicologist Judith Vander. For the second, I draw upon the research of anthropologist Sally Price as she reports on a song tradition of another people of African musical heritage, the Saramaka of Suriname.

WOMEN AND MUSIC IN THE INCA EMPIRE

In the late fifteenth century, when the Spanish conquistadors arrived in South America, the Inca Empire governed the Andean region. From chronicles written by Spanish and first-generation, native Andean authors, we know that as the empire expanded and conquered new territories and people, the Inca rulers imposed linguistic and other cultural changes onto what had been a plurality of indigenous ethnic groups.[4] They forced people of hundreds of unique languages (e.g., Puquina and Mochica) to speak Quechua, itself a Native-American language and the imperial language of the Inca. Because of this common history of domination, a large proportion of Andean people still speaks Quechua. One Native American language that survived with some predominance in the central Andes is Aymara. Beginning in the late fifteenth century, the historical time of transition from Inca to Spanish rule in the Andes, we can learn about the women's musical roles, and more specifically, their musical participation, education, and visibility. Besides chronicles, we can look to colonial Quechua and Aymara language dictionaries, and to archeological findings such as musical instruments and iconographic depictions of people playing them.[5]

One author, a Quechua Indian who claimed descent from Inca nobility, wrote a chronicle in the form of a letter to King Phillip III of Spain that exceeded one thousand pages. His name was Felipe Guaman Poma de Ayala, and he wrote his *Primer nueva corónica y buen gobierno* in the late sixteenth and early seventeenth centuries. His hope in addressing his chronicle to Phillip III was that the king would honor his hard work by publishing it.[6] In his chronicle Guaman Poma describes the history of the Inca Empire and the first decades of Spanish colonization, informing the king about abuses of the indigenous people by the Spanish conquistadors. Through hundreds of drawings and their accompanying descriptions, he also documents aspects of social, religious, economic, and political life, beginning with the first Inca ruler. In his drawings he features Inca and colonial festivals, some of which picture women playing drums, singing, and dancing, and he provides dozens of pages of text describing musical instruments and the contexts for performance. He depicts, for example, women from three of the Inca Empire's four geographical quadrants (Chinchaysuyo, Collasuyu, and Condesuyo) playing hand drums that he labels with the Quechua term *tinya* during their respective fiestas.[7] In his descriptions of these festivals, Guaman Poma mentions several flutes, such as the *quena-quena* (vertical, end-notched flute) and *pingollo* (vertical duct flute), but in these contexts the flutes were played by men, never women.[8] He shows us that women accompanied the men on their drums, and they played the larger *guayyaya* drum for solemn dances attended only by Inca royalty and blood relatives (see Figure 14.1).

FIGURE 14.1. For the Fiesta of the Chinchaysuyos, Guaman Poma illustrates women playing a hand drum called *tinya*. The men in this drawing are playing flutes made from deer skulls.

In the mid-fourteenth century the Incas established schools in Cuzco, the seat of the empire, where *amautas* (wise elders) taught science, art, poetry, and music to the royal family and to selected girls from the four quadrants of the empire. They called these girls *acllas* or "chosen ones." The Inca selected them based on their physical beauty and the quality of their voices. There were six houses set aside for their education, and of those, the fourth house, called *taquiaclla* (*taqui* means "song") was for the musically gifted. It housed girls between the ages of nine and fifteen who were excellent singers. Women, especially young women we learn, were the preferred singers. Besides singing and drumming, the *amautas* may have taught women to play flutes.[9] It is likely that indigenous Andeans from this period had an aesthetic preference not only for women singers but also for high range. There are no musical scores or transcriptions to indicate this, but archaeologists have uncovered a variety of ceramic, animal-bone, and cane flutes. Ethnomusicologists have measured and documented the pitch sets of these instruments and found that they consistently reveal a high range.[10]

Today, in some parts of the Andes, indigenous women play drums called *tinyas,* and they are often considered the preferred singers. Ethnomusicologists report an aesthetic preference among Andean Indians for high range.[11] While I am not suggesting that indigenous Andeans continue pre-Hispanic styles or aesthetics as if they were a timeless and unchanging people, such historical continuity is significant to considerations of people's active resistance to centuries of cultural domination. As I will show, there have also been and continue to be substantial changes, such as in women's public musical participation and visibility.

Indigenous Andeans Today

The most common form of musical participation for Quechua women of rural agricultural villages is dancing and singing. During my research among Quechua communities of Bolivia's Charazani Valley (1990, 1992, and 1995), people referred to a variety of forms of musical participation with the Quechua word *tusuy*; they use *tusuy* to refer to a complex of dancing, music making, and general fiesta participation. In Charazani *tusuy* involved men singing, playing in village-based flute ensembles (e.g., panpipes), or dancing, while women sang and danced. For the individuals among whom I researched, and as reported for other Quechua- and Aymara-speaking people of the Bolivian and Peruvian *altiplano* (high plateau), music making is a group activity that happens only on special occasions. People do not dance or practice instruments by themselves, but they do participate in community-based ensembles at fiestas.[12]

In the rural Andes, the occasions for dancing are Catholic holidays, such as Corpus Christi (movable date), Carnival (movable date), and *Navidad* (25 December). Every village and town has a patron saint whom locals celebrate on a specific day of the year (e.g., San Juan's Day is 24 June).[13] The musical instruments and genres to which rural farmers dance vary with the agricultural seasons. During the highland dry season (May to October), for example, Quechua people of the Charazani Valley, such as the village of Niñokorín, celebrate their patron saint holidays with large ensembles of panpipes, a style they call *kantus*. During the period of my research, women of rural *altiplano* villages did not play panpipes or other flutes. In the *kantus* tradition of the Charazani Valley, women sing and dance. *Kantus* ensembles are made up of pairs of men; each individual plays one half of a double-row panpipe, and pairs create melodies by playing in hocket. Playing in this way, each musician "answers" the notes played by his partner. A community *kantus* ensemble consists of at least six pairs of musicians playing panpipes of six different sizes or voices, tuned in fourths, fifths, and octaves. Pairs of *kantus* musicians strive to "equalize" or balance with other pairs in the ensemble so that no player or pair is heard above any other.[14]

The ensemble voicing, instrumentation, tuning, tempo, rhythmic patterns, and the manner of articulating notes differentiate the *kantus* style from other styles of the Bolivian and Peruvian *altiplano*. In smaller villages of the Charazani Valley, communities celebrate the same holidays of the dry season with ensembles of *pífanos* (transverse bamboo flutes). During the rainy season, women and men dance with their village-based ensembles to the music of *pinkullus* (vertical duct flutes), *chatres* (vertical, end-notched flutes), and *tarkas* (vertical duct flutes).[15]

The town of Charazani hosts annual regional fiestas such as Corpus Christi and Bolivian Independence Day. All fiestas have designated sponsors who have the obligation of contracting at least one musical ensemble. This can be a brass band or popular group from a nearby city, or it can be one of the larger rural village ensembles. As part of this contract, the sponsors typically provide meals, refreshments, a place to sleep, and a new consort of instruments, such as panpipes. Quechua-speaking people from villages throughout the valley walk to Charazani. Some, especially those who have been contracted by a fiesta sponsor, bring instruments and arrive in organized village ensembles, while others come to dance and observe the festivities. Young, unmarried women prepare for fiestas like these by weaving colorful *llikllas* (shawls) that they pin around their necks and drape over their backs (see Figure 14.2). These fiestas present the best opportunities for people of different villages to meet, and dancing at fiestas is a first step in courtship.

Village music ensembles organize themselves into two dance formations.They first enter the plaza performing on the vespers of the fiesta in a

FIGURE 14.2. Wearing their finest woven fabrics, Quechua women dance to Kantus panpipes during the highland dry season. Photo by the author.

processional or parade formation. Once in the plaza the musicians form a large circle, about twenty to thirty feet in diameter. When in the processional formation, musicians and dancers parade through the streets and plazas of the town, sometimes visiting the homes of sponsors who invite them to food and drinks before they continue back to the central plaza. In this formation couples precede the music ensemble by dancing in a long line that weaves through the streets and plazas. The fiesta sponsors lead these processions, and by making sharp turns and doubling back, they inscribe the streets and plazas with long serpentine designs. Women sometimes dance together as couples, but more often they pair up with men, in which case they dance on the left side, offering their right hands to their partners. In mixed couples the men usually lead, guiding the women through turns by raising their left arms high; the women first turn counterclockwise and then back. The dance itself involves an uncomplicated forward shuffle of feet as dancers rotate their upper torsos in toward their partners, then out to face forward while swinging, and sometimes pulling their partners' arms as the entire procession speeds up and slows down. In the stationary circular dance formation, couples dance inside of the circle of musicians. While the shuffling steps and turns are similar to those of the processional choreography, dance partners face each other, often holding and swinging both hands.

When not dancing, women sit together on the ground conversing. They form a circle around one or more woven shawls, on which they place a communal pile of coca leaves that they chew. Some bring plastic bottles containing a prepared alcoholic drink, and they share this by passing around shots from a single cup. This is recognized as active fiesta participation, an integral component of the *tusuy* concept; not to participate would mean to stay at home as some people do to avoid the social obligations of dancing and consuming alcohol.

Some men choose not to play instruments; instead they dance or support their communities by serving alcoholic beverages to the musicians. Men sit together with other men in straight lines, sometimes on benches or chairs against a wall. While they might serve drinks to the women, men never join a circle of women to sit together with them on the ground. The participation of women and men at fiestas, whether by singing, dancing, or socializing, is vital to the multifaceted complex of music, dance, and interaction referred to as *tusuy* by the Quechua people of Charazani. Without community members participating in these ways, there would be no music.[16]

Aymara-speaking people represent another linguistic group of the Andes mountains. They are predominant in the state or "department" of La Paz, Bolivia, especially on the *altiplano* around the shores of Lake Titicaca. Aymara-speaking people play many of the same instruments as the Quechua, but they do not sing as much, at least not in public fiestas. The ways in which Aymara women participate are otherwise similar to those of the Quechua women.[17] In the Aymara village of Compi on the Bolivian shore of Lake Titicaca, anthropologist Hans Buechler illustrates how the involvement of women is changing in fiestas. One woman from that village named Lucía took it upon herself to organize and sponsor a new *comparsa* (costumed dance genre) for the fiesta of San Pedro. This involved making dance uniforms, finding other sponsors to help her finance and organize the dance, and hiring a brass band from the city of La Paz. Together with a girlfriend, she decided to name the dance group *Hijos de Tupac Yupanqui* (Children of Tupac Yupanqui). Until then, sponsorship roles like this in Compi were primarily the domain of men. Because of the obstacles this presented, Lucía secured the support of some men to help her complete the endeavor.[18]

Some migrant women living in major Andean cities now learn to play the panpipe, *tarka*, guitar, and *charango* (a small lute with five double courses) at local folkloric schools. Others choose to dance in any of the many costumed dance genres that are a regular feature of Andean festivals. In doing so, women are broadening and redefining their roles in music. With the adoption of these new musical practices, together with changes in dress, hairstyle, language, and the consumption of recorded music, people begin to identify them not as *campesinas* (rural peasants) or *indias* (Indians; this often carries pejorative connotations), but as *mestizas.*

ANDEAN MESTIZO WOMEN

Mestizo, a term found throughout Latin America, refers to people of mixed Spanish and indigenous cultural heritages. In Bolivia the term is not limited to racially mixed persons, but rather has significant cultural connotations expressed in part by peoples' cultural productivity and habits of consumption. The process of becoming *mestizo* is a strong ideological current throughout Latin America.[19] There are musical genres and dances that people associate with *mestizo* culture in Bolivia. In the 1990s the most popular dance *comparsa* was *Los Caporales* (The Foremen). As with most *mestizo* dances, brass bands accompany *Los Caporales.* The participants of a *caporal* dance troupe often number in the hundreds, and they are divided into *bloques* (blocks or sections). Some dance groups are large enough that they may have two or more brass bands interspersed between the enormous sections of dancers. *Caporal* dancers divide themselves into blocks along gender lines; men and women dance as separate blocks. Within each section are characters distinguished by their costumes and *pasos* (dance steps). The typical dance costume for women is a bowler hat, a colorfully sequined blouse, a short skirt held out by thick petticoats, pantyhose, and high-heeled shoes (see Figure 14.3). The men wear cowboy hats, shirts similar to those worn by the women, long slacks, and tall boots adorned with large jingle bells (Figure 14.4). The individuals whom I interviewed in 1995 enjoyed dancing as *Caporales* because the dozens of complicated, and sometimes acrobatic, dance moves were challenging to perform.

I interviewed one unusually talented *caporal* dancer from La Paz named Claudia. Like others whom I met, Claudia knew a great deal about *Los Caporales,* including the dance's history, symbolism, choreography, costumes, and music. As she and several other *caporal* dancers explained to me, the *Caporal* himself was a black foreman who controlled African slaves during Bolivia's colonial period. Claudia had participated as a *caporal* dancer for three consecutive years, becoming a *guía* (guide or leader) among the women. In 1995, the year that I saw her dance, Claudia decided to dance in the men's costume so that she could learn and dance the more difficult *pasos* that the men do. She told me that "[I] wanted [to dance] something different, more difficult." She wore the costume and boots of the men (see Figure 14.4).

The musical roles, participation, and visibility of Native American women from North America in some ways parallel those of Quechua,

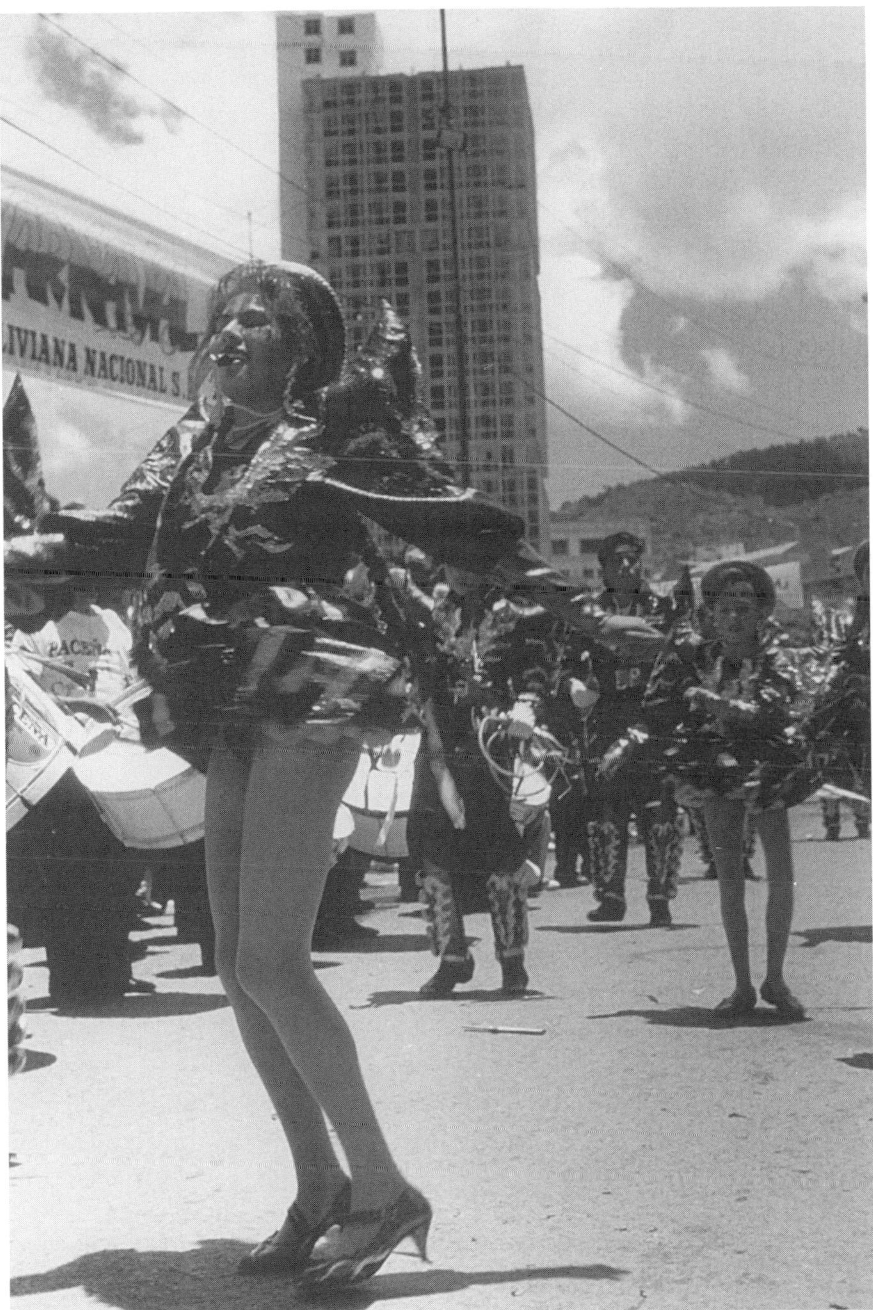

FIGURE 14.3. Woman *guía* (leader) of *Los Caporales*. Note that her costume includes high-heeled shoes. Photo by the author.

FIGURE 14.4. Claudia's *bloque* in *Los Caporales*. Note how the costume differs from those of the women (Figure 14.3) and enables acrobatic dance choreography. Photo by the author.

Aymara, and *mestizo* women in the Andes. Ethnomusicologist Judith Vander carried out ethnographic research among the Shoshone, a Native American tribe that lives in Wyoming's Wind River Reservation. Vander interviewed women of different generations who ranged in age from twenty to seventy, and she contrasted their musical lives in *Songprints: The Musical Lives of Five Shoshone Women*. In her book Vander presents examples of highly gendered, yet constantly changing, musical roles in social, religious, and ceremonial life.[20] In comparing the song repertoires of young and old women, she found that the song genres that women perform and prefer have changed considerably throughout the twentieth century. The Shoshone songs of *Naraya huvia*, which pertain to the pan-tribal Ghost Dance religious movement that spread across the Great Basin and the Plains in the late nineteenth century, are a clear example of such a genre. Another is the War Dance song, now sung during powwow ceremonies. Emily, the eldest Shoshone woman whom Vander interviewed, maintains a repertoire of 147 *Naraya* songs, but she sings no War Dance songs. By contrast, the youngest woman, Lenore, sings fifty-nine War Dance songs but no Ghost Dance songs. Emily laments the disappearance of *Naraya* and Women's Dance songs, and she views the War Dance as foreign to Shoshone culture.[21] Lenore, on the other hand, is a powwow singer, part of a new generation of women who have increased the participation and visibility of women in powwow ceremonies. Lenore, like the Aymara woman Lucía, has expanded women's roles in music by starting a women's family drum group as a counterpart to the traditional Shoshone men's drum groups.[22]

Vander found that the support of male community members is important not just in making changes in practices associated with music and dance but also in gaining community support for these changes.[23] The musical participation and visibility of women like Lenore parallels the self-determination of Lucía, the Aymara woman who took the initiative to form a new dance *comparsa,* and Claudia, who shed the constraining dance costume of women *caporal* dancers so that she could redefine the participation of women in *Los Caporales.*

WOMEN OF THE AFRICAN DIASPORA

The character of the *Caporal,* or slave foreman, alludes to Bolivia's colonial history and the importation and enslavement of African people. Today, most of the descendants of Bolivia's African slaves live in the state or "department" of La Paz, and thus coexist with indigenous and *mestizo* people. Not surprisingly, these people, who self-identify as *negros,* sometimes take offense at *Los Caporales* and other *mestizo* dance genres that in some way mock their African ancestors. In *tundiki,* another *mestizo comparsa*, dancers paint their faces black and parody *saya,* a traditional song, drumming, and dance genre of black Bolivians. Since the mid-1980s, black Bolivians have organized a social movement through which they work to reclaim *saya* and raise the levels of consciousness among Bolivians and tourists regarding these offensive dance parodies. Black Bolivians accomplish this, in part, by performing what they call the "original *saya*" of their ancestors. Through *saya* songs like "*Todo es de fruta*" ("Everything Comes from Fruit"), they tell people about their history and cultural heritage and seek recognition as a *grupo legitimo*, a legitimate ethnic group among their country's citizenry. Women play a central leadership role in this movement and in organizing *saya* music performances.[24]

Todo es de fruta, café y coca,
el lugar donde vivimos se llama Tocaña.
De nuestra cultura,
hemos traido la saya, pueblo Boliviano.

Everything comes from fruit, coffee, and coca;
The place where we live is called Tocaña.
From our culture,
We have brought *saya,* Bolivian people.

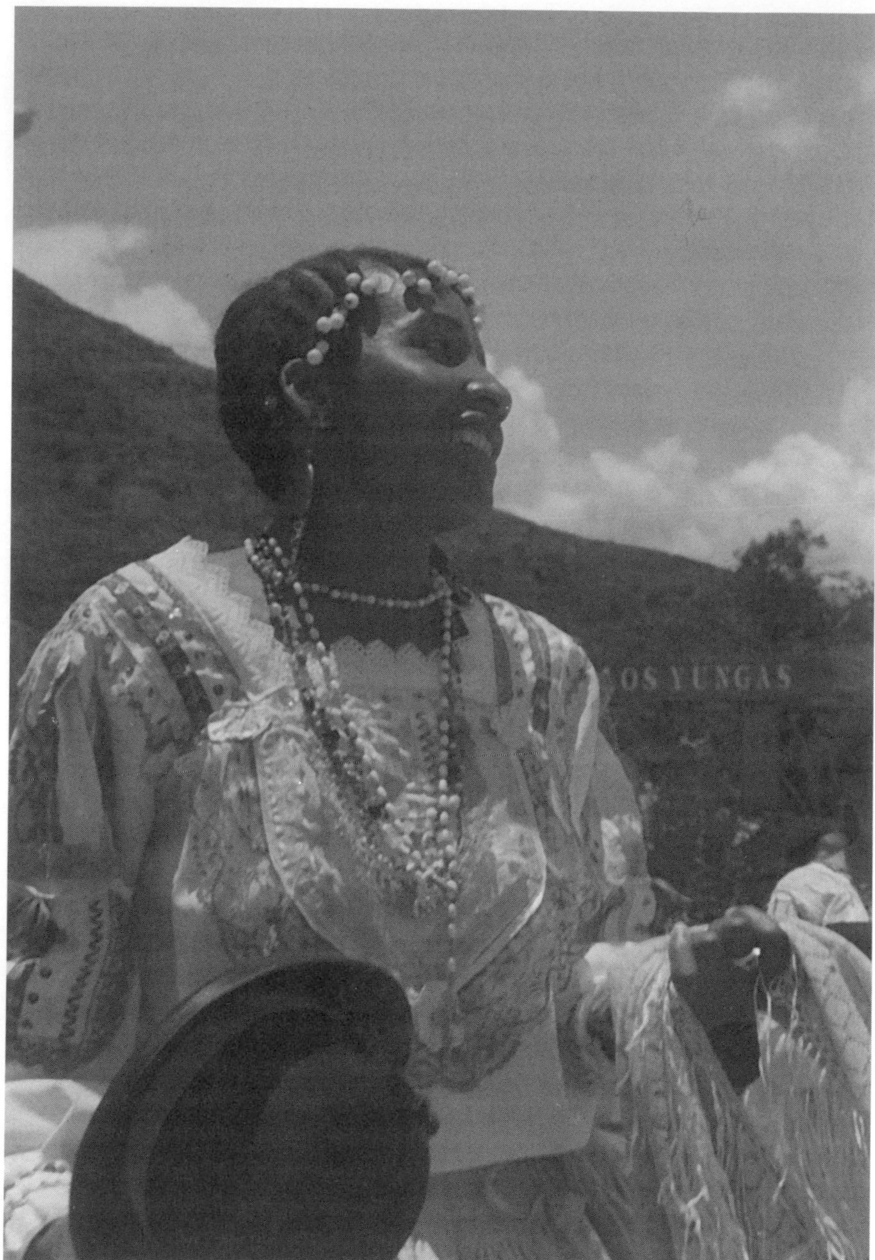

FIGURE 14.5. Fortunata, President of the Afro-Bolivian Cultural Movement, in her *saya* dance costume. Photo by the author.

Women in the Black Movement in Bolivia

The state of La Paz is divided into provinces, such as Bautista Saveedra, where the Charazani Valley is located, and the provinces of Nor Yungas and Sud Yungas, where the largest populations of black Bolivians live. The *yungas* is a semitropical valley region on the eastern slopes of the Andes Mountains. It is different from other parts of Bolivia in climate, landscape, ecology, and agriculture—as well as people's cultural practices. In Bolivia people associate dress, dialect, music, dance, and other forms of cultural expression with specific regions. The *yungas* is one such region that has its own cultural charm. Bolivians call people from there *yungueños* (people of the *yungas*). Because of the relatively large proportion of black people in the *yungas,* Bolivians associate them with this region.

Tocaña is a village of the Nor Yungas province, known by people of the region for its unique cultural practices, especially its music. A farming community, Tocaña consists of some thirty-five families (about 130 people). Each family has a home made from adobe and one or more agricultural fields on the terraced sides of the steep mountain on which they live. To generate income Tocañans harvest coca leaf, coffee, oranges, mangos, and bananas. They sell these products at markets in a nearby town named Coroico or in the city of La Paz, some four hours away by bus or truck. The village has no plaza per se, but people gather and children play in a level area between a community-run cooperative store and a small adobe Catholic church. As of this writing, the village has had no electricity, and the water system is not sanitary.[25]

In 1982 young women from Tocaña attending high school in Coroico led the revitalization of *saya* so that they would have something unique to their black heritage to which they could dance. Other students—*mestizos,* Aymara Indians, and *blancos* (white people)—danced to brass-band music, such as *Los Caporales,* or to panpipe music, such as *ayarichis* (a style danced by Aymara people of this region), but the black students never participated in these dance traditions. As one woman told me, they wanted "something they could call their own and take pride in." Until then, black cultural practices like *saya* had all but disappeared.

Fortunata, one of the young women who led this revitalization, recalled for me how her teen-aged friends felt so ashamed of *saya* and their black heritage that many chose not to participate in its revitalization. She told me that parodies of *saya,* like *Los Caporales* and *Tundiki,* caused feelings of humiliation and fear among black people of her generation. When confronted with the prospect of singing and dancing *saya* publicly, some individuals felt that this would worsen matters by fueling racist and disparaging acts.[26] Others, like Fortunata, were not willing to give in and forsake their heritage and traditional forms of cultural expression. She, together with her classmates, sought instead to reclaim *saya* and to redefine it as something of which they could feel proud. The students returned to Tocaña, where they set out to reconstruct *saya* music and its associated costumes and dance choreography. To accomplish this they visited village elders, women like Doña Angelica, to learn how to embroider colorful *saya* blouses and skirts and how to sing and dance *saya* (see Figure 14.5). Led by these young women, the high school students reconstructed the traditional *saya* of their parents and ancestors and danced it publicly on October 20, 1982, in Coroico (the town of their high school) for its patron saint festival.

Upon graduation from high school, some students returned to Tocaña to be farmers, while others migrated out of the *yungas* to the city of La Paz. In La Paz, Fortunata and her colleagues from the *yungas* organized a *saya* ensemble for black migrants. They began by calling themselves *El Movimiento Cultural Grupo Afro-Boliviano* (The Afro-Bolivian Cultural Movement), a social movement that had as its main activity the performance of *saya*. In 1994 in an effort to unify other black movements that had emerged around Bolivia, the leaders of this movement invited black activists from La Paz, Cochabamba, and Santa Cruz to an assembly in Tocaña. There they elected new leaders for the combined pan-regional social movement and named their joint effort *El Movimiento Negro* (The Black Movement). Besides leading the Black Movement, women constitute the majority of musicians in the *saya* ensemble.

In rural Tocaña people define musical roles more strictly along gender lines than do the black migrants in La Paz. Women sing and dance; men sing, dance, and drum. There are levels of expertise among the women (e.g., *guías* or leaders), and while some sing *coplas* (paired couplets or verses), others shy away from this individualistic behavior. Men compose most *saya* songs, but nothing prohibits women from doing so. Women change lyrics and compose verses to existing *sayas*. Only a few talented men take on the responsibility of composing *saya*, and they are continually encouraged through positive feedback by other *saya* musicians. *Saya* texts are often about black women—and more specifically *sayeras* (women *saya* musicians). Like *copla* texts, some are love songs, while others have profound messages of encouragement to their people to take pride in their color and to join the *saya* movement. "*La Vueltita*" is one such *saya* that compliments black women as it challenges them to "take a turn" and invites them to join the movement:

Cantaremos, bailaremos,
todos de la saya, nuestra cultura.
Alegría chicas,
dense una vueltita, se ve bonita.

We will sing, we will dance,
everyone of the *saya,* our culture.
Be happy girls,
take a turn, you look beautiful.[27]

Traditionally, *saya* served black people of the *yungas* as a vehicle for their oral history and as a way of educating children. *Saya* melodies are usually diatonic and in the major mode. The form of *saya* is strophic, comprised of verses and a refrain sung in call-and-response fashion between soloists and the chorus of musicians. Afro-Bolivians accompany *saya* songs with bells and scrapers, and they interlock three differently voiced drums to create a dense polyrhythmic texture. They begin every *saya* with a single couplet that is a dedication to Manuel Isidoro Belzu, the Bolivian president they revere for freeing their ancestors from slavery. The captain of the drummers begins this dedication, and the *guía* (leader) of the women then joins him in a repetition. The entire chorus of singers responds to this dedication with the *saya* refrain. Individual musicians, women and men, then call out *coplas,* to which the group responds with the *saya.* Although *copleros* (couplet singers) sometimes improvise verses, commenting on a situation or topic, more often they make social commentary by drawing *coplas* from a repertoire. The topics they address seem limitless, especially considering the element of improvisation, but most popular topics include unrequited love, self-affirmation, history, and the advances and goals of the Black Movement.

La lucha de este grupo
es integrarlos a todos.
Queremos que participan;
vengan chicas a la saya.

The struggle of this group
is to integrate with everyone.
We want you to participate;
young women, come join the *saya.*

Participating in a social movement, the Afro-Bolivian musicians travel to music festivals that take place in cities throughout Bolivia. The most common performance context at these festivals is the street parade. During parade performances it is critical that spectators hear and understand the *saya* texts, and to accomplish this the black musicians must compete with brass bands, crowd noise, and fireworks. In their parade choreography, women organize themselves into two blocks, one in front of and one behind the all-male *batería* (drum group). The women of each block dance in parallel lines along the edges of the street. As they progress through the streets, each line faces out toward the spectators to whom they direct their singing. Several men, rather than one, sing the *coplas,* to which all of the other musicians respond with the *saya* chorus. The group draws considerable media attention at their performances, and the women leaders are cooperative about granting interviews (see Figure 14.6).

The highly visible leadership and participatory roles that these women assume are common among black Bolivians, especially among urban migrant women. I found that women maintained a far more integrated and active role in musical performance than the Quechua women from Charazani. Black migrant women not only control the leadership of the Black Movement; they also manage their households and are at the center of domestic and public social activities.

Matrifocality is an anthropological term that refers to kinship and social patterns in which women are the focus of domestic and public social life. Ethnographers have reported other cases of matrifocal kinship patterns in the African diaspora, and some researchers trace this and other black cultural practices to an African heritage.[28] There is a classic debate in the fields of black studies and anthropology that concerns whether such cultural patterns are Africanisms brought by slaves to the New World or whether they emerged as vital and creative responses, under European or American social, economic, and cultural domination, to the destruction that slavery

FIGURE 14.6. Wearing their *saya* dance costumes, the women leaders of the Black Movement answer questions about their social movement at a conference on racism in Bolivia. Photo by the author.

wrought on their kinship, cultural practices, and social organization. The scholarship into these issues is known as the Herskovits/Frazier debate. Melville Herskovits, a cultural anthropologist who conducted research in Africa and among black people of South America and the Caribbean, advocated a theory of "retentions" or Africanisms in the New World.[29] Ethnomusicologists following Herskovits might interpret not just the apparent matrifocal social organization of black Bolivians but also the interlocking drums, call-and-response singing, open vocal timbres, and other stylistic and aesthetic criteria of their music as African carryovers. E. Franklin Frazier, a pioneer in African-American sociological studies, found virtually no Africanisms among African Americans of the United States. He and his followers argued that both kinship and music were, and continue to be, creative responses to the New World predicament of slavery and the destruction of kinship and cultural patterns.[30] The followers of Frazier's approach credit slaves and their descendants for their resourcefulness in surviving and proliferating despite the inhuman conditions of slavery and for their abilities to assimilate themselves into American culture. Herskovitz's approach favored parentage, historical memory, and enduring cultural traditions, whereas Frazier's credited resourcefulness, inventiveness, and adaptation.

When considering the Afro-Bolivian case, there is value in both sides of this classic debate. Rather than interpreting their cultural practices from one perspective or the other, I find it useful to combine them. Although the call-and-response practice and interlocking drum parts resonate with sub-Saharan African style and aesthetics, the diatonic melodies, triadic harmonies, and eight-syllable couplets exemplify the influence of Western European music. Some researchers have argued, as black Bolivians do, that *saya* music is *netamente Africano* (purely African), but I do not feel this gives the musicians and their ancestors proper credit for the ingenuity that *saya* reveals. As they did with the revitalization of *saya* in 1982, black Bolivians continually reinvent the tradition. With every performance they are capable of altering it and of keeping these changes when they become useful or meaningful.

Some Afro-Bolivian women showed an interest in changing their prescribed gender roles for participating in music. They told me, for example, that they were learning to play *saya* drums. They felt that *saya* was such an essential aspect of their social movement that they needed to be able to play the drums, should a performance opportunity arise when the *sayeros* (male *saya* musicians) were unavailable. In 1994 I attended Fortunata's marriage to Felix, an Afro-Bolivian musician. At this wedding men drummed popular dance rhythms (e.g., *huaynos, cuecas*) and a dance genre called *baile de tierra*, which is part of traditional Afro-Bolivian weddings. Susana, a migrant woman who participates in the Black Movement as leader and musician, sat down, pulled a drum in front of her, and played together with the men as they accompanied the wedding party. It was clear that she was learning to drum, for she paid careful attention to the hand strokes of Roberto, her brother. No one challenged her as black men typically do when a drummer is not capable. This was significant to me since it represented the fluidity and continuity of change in musical roles among black Bolivians.

Saramaka Seketi Songs

Saramakas are another New World people of African heritage, but with a history quite different from that of black Bolivians. The Dutch imported Africans as slave laborers to work on plantations in Suriname, a Dutch colony on the northeast corner of South America. Between the mid-seventeenth and late eighteenth centuries, scores of slaves escaped and fled to the inland rainforests of Suriname, where they established villages. Armies of Dutch plantation owners pursued them and engaged them in battle, but the escaped slaves, often called *maroon*s, were able to defend themselves and eventually won their freedom. Today Saramakas, descendants of those escaped slaves, number approximately twenty thousand. They maintain a sophisticated knowledge system of oral history about the time of slavery and the battles waged by their ancestors. They call this historical knowledge *fesi-ten* (First-Time, in Saramaccan). They guard this knowledge, knowing that it is a powerful resource. Should they ever forget or misuse it, history might repeat itself, and they could lose the liberty won by their ancestors.[31]

Saramaka social organization consists of *lô* (matrilineal clans), which, by definition, trace their ancestry through women. These clans are at the center of social activities among Saramakas, and women comprise the center and foundations of the clans. Saramaka men and women pray to their gods for female babies, knowing that without them their lineages cannot continue. This matrilineal ideology permeates all aspects of daily life, affecting inheritance, fosterage, spiritual beliefs, and art.[32] Matrilineality, however, is not the same as matrifocality. Although Saramakas trace descent and lineage through women, men go unchallenged in managing the clans as well as administrating other social and cultural activities.[33] Saramaka men are *polygynous* (they have two or more wives), and one way that women air their frustrations with their husbands and co-wives is through song.

In addition to singing, Saramaka artistic creativity includes drumming, dancing, woodcarving, storytelling, and weaving. Women and men share a musical tradition of composing and singing popular songs they call *sêkêti kandá*. The ways women and men use their *sêkêti* songs, however, are quite different. Women compose them more often than do men, and women's songs are more often motivated by emotions of despair and loneliness.[34] Women compose songs spontaneously, often as an explicit response to or commentary on a social predicament. Through *sêkêti* songs they express personal frustration, inner conflict, and interpersonal tensions. One woman noted that *sêkêti* songs articulate one of three emotions: *lóbi* (love), *kósi* (cursing), or *fuká* (hardship).[35] *Sêkêti* songs are also about the everyday happenings of village life. Price reports on a *sêkêti* song in which a Saramaka woman accused her husband of favoritism toward her co-wife:

> You've neglected me for her,
> But don't neglect me anymore.
> We're *both* your wives.[36]

As women continually compose new songs, older ones that gained popularity within their villages fall into disuse. Saramaka women have begun taping these songs so that they can listen to and remember them for years to come.

Conclusion

One conclusion I draw from these examples of indigenous and *mestizo* women and women of the African diaspora is that change in their musical roles and participation is the rule, not the exception. By focusing on individuals, like Lucía, Claudia, Emily, Lenore, Fortunata, and Susana, we see that meaningful change occurs when individuals discover the need for it or find the motivation to effect it either for themselves or for their communities. By focusing on the practices of individuals in specific historical and social contexts, rather than generalizing about entire "cultures" or ethnic groups, we can discover the importance and meaning of music as well as the creative and resourceful ways Latin American women use it.

NOTES

1. Some people identified themselves to me as such, "*Yo soy mestizo*" (I am a *mestizo*), while others avoid being thus classified. *Mestizo* has become a fluid social category that is difficult to define. Such terms as *vecino* (residents of a rural town) and *misti,* a shortened form of *mestizo* that indigenous people of some regions use synonymously with *mestizo*, add difficulty.

2. See Robert Whitney Templeman, "Afro-Bolivians," *Encyclopedia of World Cultures,* vol. 7, *South America,* ed. Johannes Wilbert (Boston: G. K. Hall/Macmillan, 1994); and "We Are People of the *Yungas,* We Are the *Saya* Race," *Blackness in Latin America and the Caribbean: Social Dynamics and Cultural Transformations,* vol. 1, ed. Norman E. Whitten Jr. and Arlene Torres (Bloomington: Indiana University Press, 1998).

3. See Gerard Béhague, "Folk and Traditional Music of Latin America: General Prospect and Research Problems," *The World of Music* 25/2 (1982): 3–18.

4. For examples of chronicles, see Felipe Guaman Poma de Ayala, *Nueva Corónica y Buen Gobierno,* ed. Franklin Pease (Caracas: Biblioteca Ayacucho, 1980) and Garcilaso de la Vega, *Royal Commentaries of the Incas* (1609), trans. Harold V. Livermore (Austin: University of Texas Press, 1966).

5. For colonial Quechua and Aymara dictionaries, see Diego González Holguín, *Vocabulario de la lengua general de todo Peru llamada Qquichua, o del Inca.* Edición del Instituto de Historia (Lima: Imprenta Santa Maria, 1952) and Ludovico Bertonio *Vocabulario de la lengua Aymara* (1612; La Paz, 1956). For archaeological findings, see Robert Stevenson, *Music in Aztec & Inca Territory* (Berkeley: University of California Press, 1968) and Marguerite and Raoul d'Harcourt, *La musique des Aymara sur les hauts plateaux boliviens.* Société des américanistes (Paris: Palais de Chaillat—Place du Trocadéro, 1959).

6. Rolena Adorno, *Guaman Poma: Writing and Resistance in Colonial Peru* (Austin: University of Texas Press, 1986).

7. Poma de Ayala, pp. 225–35 (fol. 316–30). From Diego Gonzales Holguin's dictionary of the Quechua language, we learn that the *tinya* was in fact a drum played by women.

8. Poma de Ayala, p. 226 (fol. 317). See also Stevenson, p. 263.

9. Stevenson, p. 275.

10. Ibid., pp. 243–58.

11. Thomas Turino, *Moving Away from Silence: Aymara Music of the Peruvian Altiplano and the Experience of Urban Migration* (Chicago: University of Chicago Press, 1993). Examples of this can be heard on Thomas Turino, *Mountain Music of Peru,* vol. 2 (Washington, DC: Smithsonian/Folkways Recordings, 1994).

12. Robert Whitney Templeman, "We Answer Each Other: Musical Practice and Competition among *Kantus* Panpipe Ensembles in Bolivia's Charazani Valley" (M.M. thesis, University of Illinois, 1994). See also Hans C. Buechler, *The Masked Media: Aymara Fiestas and Social Interaction in the Bolivian Highlands* (The Hague: Mouton Publishers, 1980); Raul Romero, "Musical Change and Cultural Resistance in the Central Andes of Peru," *Latin American Music Review* 11/1 (1990): 1–35; Turino, *Moving Away from Silence.*

13. See Templeman, "We Answer Each Other"; Turino, *Moving Away from Silence.*

14. For more on the *kantus* panpipe style, see Templeman, "We Answer Each Other."

15. Ibid.

16. From what I observed, women did not challenge their musical roles or work toward altering or expanding them. However, it is possible that I was not privileged to private forms of contestation or dissent that may have existed. Women ethnographers working in central highland Andes have reported similar participatory roles for women. See, for example, Catherine J. Allen, *The Hold Life Has: Coca and Cultural Identity in an Andean Community* (Washington, D.C.: Smithsonian Institution Press, 1988); Billie Jean Isbell, *To Defend Ourselves: Ecology and Ritual in an Andean Village* (Prospect Heights, IL: Waveland Press, 1978).

17. See Buechler and Turino, *Moving Away from Silence.*

18. See Buechler, p. 337.

19. See Whitten and Torres.

20. Judith Vander, *Songprints: The Musical Experience of Five Shoshone Women* (Urbana: University of Illinois Press, 1988), pp. xi and xvi.

21. Ibid., p. 48.

22. Ibid., pp. 283–84.

23. Ibid., p. xvi.

24. Templeman, "We Are People of the Yungas."

25. Templeman, "Afro-Bolivians."

26. Templeman, "We Are People of the Yungas."

27. For translation, ibid., p. 438.

28. For examples, see Hortense Powdermaker, *Stranger and Friend: The Way of an Anthropologist* (New York: W. W. Norton, 1966); Raymond T. Smith, *The Negro Family in British Guiana: Family Structure and Social Status in the Villages* (New York: Humanities Press, 1971); Roger Bastide, *African Civilization in the New World* (New York: Torchbook Library, 1971).

29. Melville J. Herskovits, *The Myth of the Negro Past* (Boston: Beacon Press, 1990, first published in 1941).

30. E. Franklin Frazier, *The Negro Family in the United States* (Chicago: University of Chicago Press, 1939).

31. Richard Price, *First-Time: The Historical Vision of an Afro-American People* (Baltimore: Johns Hopkins University Press, 1983).

32. Sally Price, *Co-wives and Calabashes* (Ann Arbor: University of Michigan Press, 1984).

33. Ibid., p. 11.

34. Ibid., p. 168.

35. Ibid., p. 167.

36. Ibid., p. 181; emphasis original.

I am grateful to the people of Charazani, Tocaña, and La Paz for their participation in my ethnographic research. I am equally thankful to the Wenner-Gren Foundation for Anthropological Research, the Inter-American Foundation, the Fulbright Foundation (IIE), and the Tinker Foundation. Finally, I want to thank Karin Pendle, bruce d. mcclung, Debra Templeman, Stephanie Schlagel, Christy Holland, and Amy Dix for their feedback and editorial suggestions.

SUGGESTIONS FOR FURTHER READING

In addition to the items mentioned in the text or cited in the footnotes, the following sources provide information on women in world music.

Guillermoprieto, Alma. *Samba.* New York: Vintage Books, 1991.

Kisliuk, Michelle. "Musical Life in the Central African Republic." *The Garland Encyclopedia of World Music.* Vol. 1, *Africa,* ed. Ruth M. Stone, pp. 681–97. New York: Garland Publishing, 1998.

Koskoff, Ellen, ed. *Women and Music in Cross-Cultural Perspective.* Urbana: University of Illinois Press, 1989.

Rose, Tricia. *Black Noise: Rap Music and Black Culture in Contemporary America.* Hanover: Wesleyan University Press, 1994.

XV. American Women in Blues and Jazz

Michael J. Budds

Introduction

Beginning in 1619, Africans were brought to the American colonies to endure the humiliation of slavery. In most instances slaves were stripped of all traces of their native cultures, indoctrinated in European ways, and expected to worship in the European manner. Yet these adverse circumstances produced one of the most powerful musical developments in history. Since the time when African slaves began to render European hymns according to the music-making practices of their homelands, a dynamic tradition of African-American music has evolved. Because this music developed as an oral tradition, much of its history has been lost. Yet even if the music had been written down, European notation cannot communicate its essence.

Although much African-American music, especially jazz, is often described as the combination of a European "what" and an African "how," such an explanation oversimplifies the complex process of acculturation. Among the most distinctive features of making music in African-American culture are an emphasis on improvisation and the use of preexisting musical patterns as the basis for elaboration; an acceptance of the performer as a creative partner with the composer; the presence of "hot" rhythm and the cultivation of swing; an acceptance of a heterogeneous sound ideal permitting a great variety of colors; and a range of emotional expression that dismisses mainstream society's notions of decorum and propriety. Texts in vocal music often mirror the lives of black Americans quite realistically.

The participation of women in the African-American music tradition has always been of vital importance. As wives, mothers, and caretakers of family souls, African-American women found many opportunities to sing. Secular music, such as lullabies and play songs, and sacred pieces, such as spirituals, were passed from one generation to another, as was the distinctive style of performance. For worship services, talented women developed keyboard skills. Indeed, as a haven for honest expression and as the focus of community life, the church must be recognized as the primary institution responsible for nurturing and preserving the black tradition in music. In addition, women assumed leading roles in religious practices in which African spirit beliefs and customs survived: "While men served 'aboveground' as preachers in the Afro-American churches, women held sway as 'underground' priestesses."[1] In the rites of vodun, commonly known as voodoo, for example, the central figures were the so-called voodoo queens, and many songs celebrate the dynamic personalities and powers of these women. Such portrayals recur during the 1920s in the theatrical posing of "blueswomen."

Yet the opportunities for women to pursue careers as musicians and entertainers were exceedingly few. Participation in the minstrel tradition after the Civil War affected only a small number of performers. During the twentieth century, however, as various streams of black music occupied prominent places in the world of commercialized entertainment, black women became supremely successful as singers and rather well accepted as pianists, both functions enjoying the sanctions of tradition.

THE BLUES

The blues, the primary stream of black folk music, arose in rural areas during the eighteenth and nineteenth centuries, its antecedents both secular (work songs and field hollers) and sacred (spirituals and singing sermons). Its practice was probably codified near the end of the nineteenth century, although regional and local dialects have been cultivated throughout its recorded history. In the twentieth century, a process of urbanization has taken the blues into the realm of popular music as well. The modern history of the blues is a distinctive one, but its influence on other strains of African-American music, such as jazz and gospel, has been fundamental. The blues has also influenced the white rural tradition (country) and, since the advent of rock 'n' roll in the 1950s, the popular music of mainstream America.

Several features give the blues its special identity. The first relates to a state of mind. The term, which usually designates a highly personal condition of melancholy or depression, did not enter American usage until after the Civil War, and its application to music expressing the emotional state of American blacks may not have occurred until after 1900. The act of performing the blues is believed to be cathartic, an emotional release. Some also contend that, because of social conditions in the United States, only African Americans can meaningfully perform the blues.

The blues is a form of improvised song. At the heart of the music is a flexible series of elemental chords, related to the harmony of hymns, popular songs, and the "amen cadence." A twelve-measure pattern has been widely adopted and has served as the basis for great elaboration; the distinctive melodic and harmonic language uses pitches outside the European-tempered system. A characteristic aspect of performance is a procedure from Africa known as call-and-response: the alternation of phrases or verses of text by the singer with purely instrumental fill. An extraordinarily compelling tradition has also arisen in the treatment of the improvised text in blues performances, and a vernacular language rich in imagery and double entendre has emerged. The blues deals with human existence at its most realistic; its point of view ranges from anguished to angered and from playful to defiant.

The blues tradition may be divided into two practices: rural and urban. Country (or rural) blues, the older form, is less regular because of the idiosyncrasies of its self-taught, independent-thinking practitioners. The country blues typically takes the form of solo performance: a male vocalist singing to his own instrumental accompaniment. Whereas male performers have dominated this part of the tradition, women have been ever-present as the subjects of their songs. Remarkable among the few women who sang the country blues was "Memphis Minnie" McCoy (1896–1973), who also earned considerable respect for her forceful guitar playing.

When African Americans migrated to cities in the early twentieth century, they took their music with them. In the process, the blues was transformed into a popular music and subjected to commercial influences. The so-called classic urban blues of the 1920s became a mainstay of black public entertainment. Charismatic women soloists who combined physical glamour, a bold social stance, and emotionally powerful singing created a memorable repertoire that admitted a wide variety of instrumental accompaniments. Some of the most celebrated performances of the period featured Mamie Smith (1883–1946), Gertrude "Ma" Rainey (1886–1939), Bessie Smith (1894–1937), Clara Smith (1894–1935), Ida Cox (1896–1967), Beulah "Sippie" Wallace (1898–1986), Bertha "Chippie" Hill (1905–1950), and Victoria Spivey (1906–1976). These artists achieved celebrity status as captivating entertainers, both in personal appearances and on records. As they sang of lost love and broken dreams, of sexual politics and moments of glory, they were providing important models of independence for other black women.

Rhythm and blues, an umbrella term for a varied body of black popular music created since the late 1940s, is thought to reflect the growing confidence among African Americans following World War II. Although the melancholy of early blues was not dismissed, the rhythmic vitality, upbeat tempos, and emphasis on the good-time lyrics of rhythm and blues added new dimensions. The participation of women in rhythm and blues at this time may be symbolized by Willie Mae "Big Mama" Thornton (1926–1984), whose career is described in an earlier chapter. Other significant women blues singers, such as Dinah Washington [Ruth Jones] (1924–1963), Mabel Louise "Big Maybelle" Smith (1924–1972), Etta James (b. 1938), and Cora "Koko" Taylor (b. 1938) have carried on this tradition. Whereas men dominated the rural blues and women reigned as the significant interpreters of the classic urban blues of the 1920s, both sexes have participated fully in the rhythm and blues tradition since the 1940s, although women have remained in the minority. The absence of women instrumentalists in the blues tradition is closely related to the social and professional prohibitions described below in the discussion of jazz.

"Ma" Rainey

Mamie Smith may have been the first woman to record the blues, but it was Gertrude "Ma" Rainey who popularized the genre for mass audiences. She was Paramount Records' biggest-selling star of the 1920s, performing with some of the greatest instrumentalists of the era—Coleman Hawkins, Fletcher Henderson, Blind Blake, "Georgia" Tom Dorsey, and Louis Armstrong.

The woman now known as the "Queen of the Blues" was born Gertrude Pridgett in Columbus, Georgia, in 1886. Her parents were troupers in minstrel shows, and she followed in their footsteps from the age of fourteen. In 1904 she married Will "Pa" Rainey; they toured as the song-and-dance team of Ma and Pa Rainey, then as Rainey and Rainey, Assassinators of the Blues. Their repertoire consisted of minstrel and novelty songs, dancing, humor, and a little blues singing. For a while young Bessie Smith was a member of the ensemble and learned about the blues from the Queen Mother herself. By 1917 "Ma," now billed as "Madame," had formed her own Georgia Jazz Band, and "Pa" was no longer her partner. From 1920 until 1935, when she retired from the stage, she performed chiefly in vaudeville, her repertoire including an ever-larger proportion of the blues.

Rainey's recording career with Paramount began in 1923 and ended in 1928, when the company refused to renew her contract because her style of down-home singing and the blues had gone out of fashion. On her more than one hundred discs the accompaniments ranged from simple guitar and piano (in blues such as "Sweet Rough Man") to jazz ensembles of cornet, trombone, clarinet, bass saxophone, piano, and banjo (in "Chain Gang

Blues"). Although recordings are an important legacy of Rainey's long career, it was her live performances that moved her mainly poor, rural black audiences. These people understood they were hearing a woman who knew firsthand about their troubles. The usually frank lyrics dealt with loneliness, violence, men who do women wrong, prostitution, trouble with the law, drinking, and even sexual brutality. A stanza from Rainey's own "Bo-weavil Blues" illustrates the use of double meanings:

> I don't want no man to put sugar in my tea.
> I don't want no man to put sugar in my tea,
> Some of 'em is so evil, I'm 'fraid he might poisin [*sic*] me.

The earthy sound of Rainey's full-voiced contralto comes through even on the rather primitive recordings of the 1920s. Her voice could sound harsh, sometimes guttural, and it was often tinged with melancholy. The influence of rural African-American folk music is evident in her moaning style, which is sometimes echoed in the wailing instrumental accompaniments of her recordings. Rainey varied the melody and rhythm to suit her interpretive purposes and often held back a bit in the middle of a line or at the beginning of a repeated line for emphasis. Although she never learned to read music, "Ma" Rainey composed at least twenty-four of the songs she performed. One of her showstoppers was "See See Rider," which, like "Bo-weavil Blues," exemplifies the classic AAB form of blues lyrics, where B serves as a kind of stinger or punch line. Among the other well-known songs she wrote are "Don't Fish in My Sea," "Weepin' Woman Blues," and "Moonshine Blues."

"Ma" Rainey was a total performer who wanted to please audiences with her appearance as well as with her music. Her smile shone with gold-capped teeth, and she dressed flamboyantly in sequin and rhinestone gowns, often also wearing diamond jewelry and carrying an ostrich feather fan. One of her monikers, "The Golden Necklace of the Blues," derived from her trademark necklace made of twenty-dollar gold pieces. A sound businesswoman both on the road and, after her retirement, as the owner-manager of two theatres, she went home to Georgia in 1935, kept house for her brother, and joined the Friendship Baptist Church. It is no small irony that after such a long and successful career as a performer, her death certificate lists her occupation as "housekeeper." "Ma" Rainey died in December 1939 and was buried in the family plot in the town of her birth.

Bessie Smith

The life of the woman known as the "Empress of the Blues" was itself a blues litany. The place of Bessie Smith's birth, Chattanooga, Tennessee, is not disputed, but the date is. Most recent sources say 1894; 1895 is on her

FIGURE 15.1. Bessie Smith in 1923. The Frank Driggs Collection. Used by permission.

gravestone. An orphan by the age of eight, Bessie sang in the streets of Chattanooga for spare change before joining a minstrel troupe as a child performer. In 1912 she met and worked with "Ma" Rainey in Moses Stokes's Show. Her 1923 marriage to a Philadelphia policeman ended when he deserted her for another woman, although his leaving may have been caused in part by Bessie's drinking problem. Her career reached its apex in the 1920s, when she performed for large audiences in both the North and South and frequently appeared at New York City's Apollo Theatre. Smith may have earned as much as $2,500 a week, making her one of the highest-paid black performers of this era. Yet she found herself earning half her usual salary following the stock market crash of 1929 and learned the hard lesson of being out of fashion and without the resources to adapt to new trends. Bessie Smith's life ended in a car crash in Clarksville, Mississippi, in 1937. She was buried in an unmarked grave on the outskirts of Philadelphia.

Smith's recording career, like Rainey's, began in 1923. Although Smith recorded some two hundred discs over the next decade, her prime recording years were 1923–1928. Her first recording was a new version of "Down-Hearted Blues," a song popularized by another famous blues singer, Alberta Hunter, and Lovie Austin, the equally famous female jazz pianist. Smith's rendition sold 780,000 copies in less than six months. Other recordings sold as many as ten million copies. Smith collaborated with various members of Fletcher Henderson's band, including Louis Armstrong, with whom she made a justly famous duet of W. C. Handy's "St. Louis Blues." Although she is best known for her slow blues, Smith also recorded Irving Berlin's "Alexander's Ragtime Band" and other up-tempo standards.

A blues singer who never betrayed her rural Southern roots, Bessie Smith preferred to play to live audiences, even in the North. Unfortunately, her refusal to "whiten" her act for urban, middle-class audiences probably hastened her loss of popularity in the 1930s. Possessor of a warm, powerful, resonant voice, Smith could shout or moan, sound plaintive or languorous. Because she normally worked within an interval of a sixth, her range of an octave proved no limitation. She tended to concentrate on focal tones within the key, then embellish them with microtonal slides. The result was an expressive, personal shaping of the original tune. She further shaped songs by modifying the lyrics to enhance their meanings. Working contextually, she would eliminate words and interpolate "hmms" and "ahs," alter vowels, drop or add syllables, repeat or interject words. Her clear diction makes all this lyrical alteration extremely effective. In addition, Smith had a sure understanding of how and when to use rubato. She bent the rhythm by leaning into it, and preferred to sing without a drummer so that she could control the rhythmic flow of a performance.

The liberties Smith took served the same expressive end. A recorded example demonstrating her style is the popular song "Nobody Knows You When You're Down and Out." Cast in the typical Tin Pan Alley structure of verse and chorus, the song approximates the blues because of her particular interpretation. Her treatment of the verse is conversational, as if she is confessing her own sad story. At the beginning of the chorus Smith reshapes the well-known tune by sliding into, then stretching, its opening "nobody" and later by dropping syllables and phrases and inserting heartfelt "hmms" to enhance the absent lyrics. She also adds text, most noticeably at the end of the chorus, when she slides into "when you're down and out" as a tag line.

Smith had a regal presence on stage. She was good-looking, with a pleasant round face and dimples, and her shapely body swayed to the rhythm as she sang. "Empress" is a fitting title for her, as she dominated her own era. Among her most important legacies is the tremendous influence she had on contemporary and later generations of blues singers and jazz performers, such as Louis Armstrong, Billie Holiday, Mahalia Jackson, Willie Mae "Big

Mama" Thornton, Dinah Washington, Odetta, and Janis Joplin. Her artistry survives through her recordings, which Columbia reissued in full in the early 1970s, now available on CDs. For more than three decades after Smith's death, her grave at Mount Lawn Cemetery in Sharon, Pennsylvania, remained unmarked. When this became widely known, Janis Joplin and Juanita Green, a nurse who then headed the North Philadelphia chapter of the NAACP (and who had scrubbed Bessie Smith's floors as a child), bought a gravestone. The inscription reads: "The greatest blues singer in the world will never stop singing."

Jazz

Jazz is another significant stream of music created primarily by African Americans since the early twentieth century. Although improvisation by individual performers is central to jazz, a variety of performance contexts have been embraced in a series of rapidly changing substyles. Throughout its history jazz musicians have drawn on the resources of folk music, popular music, and fine-art music and have, in turn, exerted an immeasurable influence on music outside the nebulous borders of jazz. Although black musicians must be identified as the major figures in the evolution of jazz, white musicians have also worked successfully in this tradition almost from its beginning.

More than other musical traditions, jazz has been viewed by the musicians who produce it and by the society it serves as a male reserve. As late as 1973 an anonymous male pianist declared: "Jazz is a male language. It's a matter of speaking that language and women just can't do it."[2] More recently, in his discussion of "the gender problem" in jazz, the historian Neil Leonard observed: "Women function in secondary roles as pianists, singers, dancers, den mothers, homemakers, breadwinners, and sex objects, but seldom are first-line musicians."[3] The truth of these statements must be qualified, although women have been most successful and best accepted in the world of jazz as singers and pianists. Because jazz is primarily an instrumental music and because its history has been largely shaped by wind players, women have been at a considerable disadvantage. The direct precursors of jazz were the blues, ragtime,[4] and the marching band traditions, each of which is strongly associated with men and their fraternal pleasures. Although in mainstream society young women were encouraged to become proficient as singers and pianists, in part with the hope of making successful marriages, rarely were they encouraged to pursue careers. Playing wind instruments was not considered decorous, and the thought of women marching down the street as band members was inconceivable. Among the lower classes there were economic obstacles as well: instruments and lessons were luxuries, and money was rarely to be wasted on the education of girls.

In a sense, the very venues for jazz performance served as discriminatory social filters. Ragtime and early jazz found homes in the rough-and-tumble night spots of turn-of-the-century American cities, where a host of unsavory behaviors flourished by night. Because of its association with early jazz, Storyville, the pleasure district of New Orleans, has become legendary, but similar areas existed in other cities. If a woman, musician or not, valued her reputation, she would not be seen in such precincts. Indeed, the initial objections of the establishment to ragtime and jazz were based on their African-American origins and their whorehouse associations.

In subsequent decades the factors that contributed to the jazz musician's precarious lifestyle continued to inhibit the participation of women. The scarcity of musical opportunities, the instability of employment, the resulting financial insecurity, the loose code of morality that flourished in night spots, and the temptations of liquor and drugs were obstacles confronting all jazz artists. For women, additional challenges relating to sexist notions prevailed in society. Men typically refused to take women seriously as gifted musicians and did not welcome them as competitors for jobs. At the same time, almost no role models existed for women as jazz artists, and their families seldom supported their career aspirations. One final circumstance made the barriers to a career almost insurmountable for women: jazz is fundamentally an oral tradition, which the young typically learn by playing with established figures. Systematically excluded from entry-level opportunities and denied the essential period of apprenticeship, women players were rarely able to develop their talents to a professional level, let alone establish themselves as viable jazz artists.[5]

One response to this dilemma was the formation of ensembles made up exclusively of women. In general, such an artificial solution contributed as much to the double standard as it strengthened the rights of women performers. Two ensembles, however, made important strides in improving the position of women jazz musicians, although both were forced to make concessions to sexism. The Melodears, formed in 1934 and led by singer Ina Ray Hutton (Odessa Cowan, 1916–1984), became one of the popular swing bands of the decade. Although Hutton was billed as "the blonde bombshell" and was obliged to parade around in extravagant costumes, the members of her all-white ensemble were highly competent and played arrangements comparable to those of male bands. Perhaps the most highly respected all-women big band was the International Sweethearts of Rhythm, formed in 1939 in Piney Woods, Mississippi. From the time of its debut at the Howard Theatre in Washington, D.C., in 1940 until it was disbanded late in the decade, the International Sweethearts of Rhythm was accepted not only as the premier female band but also as a first-rate ensemble. Through tours of the United States and Europe, and through such recordings as "Don't Get It Twisted," this band, which took pride in the ethnic diversity of its membership, reached a broad audience and enjoyed real success.[6]

Yet today's jazz legacy would not be as substantial as it is without the enduring contributions of women singers and pianists. Many indeed stand as artists of the highest calibre. In addition to Billie Holiday, Ella Fitzgerald, and Mary Lou Williams, notable African-American women jazz performers include the singers Ethel Waters (1896–1977), Helen Humes (1913–1981), Carmen McRae (1922–1994), Sarah Vaughan (1924–1990), Betty Carter (b. 1930), and Nancy Wilson (b. 1937); the pianists Lovie Austin (Cora Calhoun, 1887–1972), Sweet Emma Barrett (1897–1983), Lillian "Lil" Hardin Armstong (1898–1971), Hazel Scott (1920–1981), Dorothy Donegan (1926–1998), and Alice Coltrane (b. 1937); and the organist Shirley Scott (b. 1934). Women of comparable stature as jazz makers from beyond the African-American community include the singers Mildred Bailey (1907–1951), Anita O'Day (Anita Belle Colton, b. 1919), and Peggy Lee (Norma Delores Engstrom, b. 1920), and the pianists Marian McPartland (b. 1920), Toshiko Akiyoshi (b. 1929), and Carla Bley (b. 1938).

Lil Hardin Armstong

Born in Memphis, Tennessee, Lil Hardin Armstrong was something of a child prodigy on piano and organ, abilities that led the Chicago music store where she worked as a demonstrator of sheet music to bill her as "the Jazz Wonder Child." Well trained in her craft, Hardin was soon working in Chicago nightclubs. In 1921 she joined King Oliver's Creole Jazz Band, where she met and married Louis Armstrong. In the 1920s she branched out from performance and into composition and arranging for Armstrong and for her own group, the Harlem Foot-Warmers. In the 1930s she worked in a number of big bands, including two composed entirely of women, and served as house pianist for Decca records. Testimonies to her long and successful career are her recordings and more than 150 jazz compositions.

Billie Holiday

Struggle and misery mark the lives of many artists. Few, however, contain the elements of tragedy and pathos to the same degree as the life of Billie Holiday, the woman considered by many to be the most important singer in the history of jazz on the basis of her originality, artistry, and influence. The poverty of her childhood in the slums of Baltimore, the institutionalized racism and sexism of her time, the unforgiving nature of the entertainment business all exacted powerful tolls on her outwardly tough but inwardly fragile sensibility. Highly temperamental in both personal and professional dealings, she suffered from what has been called "a staggering lack of self-esteem."[7] Her private search for the love she sang about so eloquently yielded failed relationships that left her victimized and exploited. She did not possess the personal resources to sustain her own existence, and so retreated into the private hell of alcohol and drug addiction. Her autobiography, *Lady Sings the Blues* (1956), and the film biography of the same name (1972), though marred by inaccuracies and sensationalism, succeed in communicating the sordid details of her life.

Born in 1915 to a teen-aged unwed mother and soon abandoned by her father, Eleanora Fagan was given little education. Reportedly raped at the age of ten and arrested for prostitution after following her mother to Harlem, she embarked on a career as a singer in the 1930s. Her only musical education took the form of listening to recordings of Bessie Smith and Louis Armstrong loaned to her by a madam for whom, as a child, she worked as a messenger. In 1933 Holiday was discovered by producer John Hammond and, with his assistance, began recording and performing in prominent New York clubs. Her collaborations with pianist Teddy Wilson, Lester Young, and others brought her greatest recognition, though her public appeal never equaled the respect accorded her by musicians and musical connoisseurs. In 1937 she toured with Count Basie's band, and in 1938 she became one of the first black female soloists to cross the racial barrier by performing publicly as a member of Artie Shaw's band. In spite of her success, both affiliations were sources of great personal humiliation: for appearances with Basie, Holiday was forced to darken her face with makeup; traveling with the all-white Shaw band presented a regular series of confrontations in restaurants, hotels, and nightclubs.

One must assume that the plaintive, almost wounded quality so characteristic of Holiday's singing and so much a part of her attraction to listeners was a musical mirror of her own personal anguish. Her assumed name—a combination of the names of her movie idol Billie Dove and guitarist Clarence Holiday, the father who abandoned her—represents an apt symbol of her suffering. Her nickname, "Lady Day," coined by saxophonist Lester Young, paid tribute to her dignified bearing. Her trademarks were a white dress and a white gardenia, worn in her hair.

The last years of her life were tainted by arrests for narcotics possession, a public trial, a prison term, and revocation of the cabaret card that permitted her to work in New York City. Her recordings in the 1950s bear witness to the ravages of liquor, drugs, and a deteriorating personal life on her voice. She died alone in 1959, her fortune dissipated by her own mismanagement and the expenses of her addictions.

Holiday, a singer of uncommon expressive power, lacked a naturally beautiful voice. Yet she created a dynamic, individual world of expression. By exploring the continuum between heightened speech and singing, by recasting well-known tunes to reach their essential musical qualities, by applying the jazz instrumentalist's manner of phrasing to her singing, and by interpreting sad songs with disarming personal emotion, she almost single-handedly raised the singer's role in jazz to the level of creativity expected of instrumental soloists. At the same time her singing was colored by the tonal inflections, urgency, and realism associated with the blues. Her primary vehicle was the torch song, which she transformed into some of the most immediate jazz of her time. Among many memorable performances, Holiday's renditions of "Them There Eyes," "All of Me," "I Can't Get Started," and "Georgia on My Mind" demonstrate her talents magnificently.

Ella Fitzgerald

Perhaps no one symbolizes the very concept of a jazz singer as much as Ella Fitzgerald. For more than fifty years she reigned as a superlative interpreter of the American popular song and participated in the jazz tradition as one of its most versatile artists. In so doing, she commanded the highest

FIGURE 15.2. Ella Fitzgerald in 1966. Photo by Joe Alper. The Frank Driggs Collection. Used by permission.

respect of musicians and the adoration of an international public. Her knowledge of musical style and her awareness of her own capabilities resulted in stunning musical creations. She demonstrated repeatedly the uncanny capacity to transform the most conventional melody and the most banal lyrics into memorable music.

Born in Newport News, Virginia, in 1918, Fitzgerald was reared as an orphan in Yonkers, New York. Youthful aspirations to become a dancer enticed her to enter an amateur contest at Harlem's famous Apollo Theatre in 1934. Too "stagestruck" to dance, she won by singing. This surprising turn of events brought her to the attention of drummer Chick Webb, who engaged her to sing with his ensemble. After his death in 1939, Fitzgerald led the band until 1942. Early success as a big-band singer not only brought her national celebrity but also provided invaluable on-the-job training during her teen years, as she heard instrumentalists improvise and explore the rhythmic and melodic subtleties of jazz.

Her solo career, which dated from 1942, acquired an important dimension in 1946, when Fitzgerald became associated with the impresario Norman Granz and his Jazz at the Philharmonic tours. In 1955, on Granz's new record label Verve, Fitzgerald embarked on a milestone venture—a series of albums devoted to the great composers of American popular song. This twelve-year project yielded a treasury of performances of some of the finest works of Arlen, Berlin, Ellington, Gershwin, Kern, Mercer, Porter, and Rodgers. Fitzgerald's discography ranks among the most impressive in the history of jazz.

Fitzgerald's universal and long-standing success as a singer can be attributed to a number of factors: a genuine and endearing personality; an appealing voice with true intonation and an extraordinary range; an intuitive knowledge of her own considerable vocal technique that allowed her to emphasize her strengths; an impeccable sense of rhythm and harmony; and a seemingly inexhaustible gift for melodic invention. Whether Fitzgerald was embellishing a classic love ballad, as in Gershwin's "I've Got a Crush on You" or "Someone to Watch over Me," or astonishing her listeners with her justly famous virtuoso scat improvisations, as in "How High the Moon," her performances presented a quality of musical rightness and inevitability that defied explanation. Loved, honored, and revered, Fitzgerald died on June 15, 1996, at the age of 78.

Mary Lou Williams

Pianist, composer, and arranger Mary Lou Williams must be remembered as a true pioneer. For much of her career she was regarded as the only female instrumentalist to demonstrate the highest level of achievement in

FIGURE 15.3. Mary Lou Williams in 1944. Photo by Charles B. Nadell. The Frank Driggs Collection. Used by permission.

jazz circles. Her full measure of success was often explained with the dubious justification that she "played like a man." In fact, although Williams was fully aware of the playing styles of many male pianists, she modeled herself after pianist and composer Lovie Austin. Williams was also exceptional for her important contributions to jazz arranging and composition. By the end of her long and multifaceted career, she had revealed not only a remarkable talent, unending resourcefulness, and a high sense of purpose, but an equally rare ability to move on with the times without losing touch with the historical foundations of jazz, especially the blues.

Born in Atlanta, Georgia, on May 8, 1910, Mary Elfrieda Scruggs learned about spirituals and ragtime literally on her mother's knee. From the age of four she astonished her family and her neighbors with her piano playing. Claiming never to have received a formal lesson, she taught herself by listening closely to other musicians, then working out at the keyboard what she had heard. By the age of ten she had performed publicly in Pittsburgh, where she was reared, and sat in with visiting bands whenever possible. At the age of fifteen, Mary joined a band led by saxophonist John "Bearcat" Williams, whom she married in 1926. In 1929, with him, she began her professionally rewarding association with Andy Kirk and his Clouds of Joy, a Kansas City–based band that featured both "hot" and "sweet" music. Many attribute a substantial part of the high reputation of Kirk's band to Williams's arrangements, compositions, and solos, which included "Froggy Bottom" (1936) and "Mary's Idea" (1938). Benny Goodman, Jimmie Lunceford, Earl Hines, Bob Crosby, Louis Armstong, Tommy Dorsey, Duke Ellington, and Dizzy Gillespie also performed her polished arrangements.

With the ascendancy of the bop style, Williams formed a combo in 1942 with trumpet player Shorty Baker, her second husband, and became prominent on the New York scene. In 1945 she led a short-lived all-women ensemble, which included the talented guitarist Mary Osborne (b. 1921). After a brief stint as the staff arranger for Duke Ellington, Williams established herself as a soloist and trio player and toured at home and abroad. Except for a three-year hiatus (1954–1957), she worked continuously as a performer and composer and ultimately as a teacher, notably at Duke University, until her death on May 28, 1981. Toward the end of her life, critics, scholars, and jazz lovers recognized her stature as a musician and her authority as a participant in much of the history of jazz. In addition, Williams served as president of her own recording company and established and guided the Bel Canto Foundation, a charitable organization dedicated to helping needy musicians.

The piano style of Mary Lou Williams is marked by experimentation and eclecticism. She established herself as a swing-era pianist with elements of the stride style and boogie-woogie. Her transition to the bop idiom, with its irregular and sometimes relentless "noodling," was accomplished with such convincing ease that it seemed natural. By the 1960s, moreover, she had enriched her vocabulary with gestures of rhythmic and harmonic intricacy not unlike those found in the creations of many of the so-called radicals of the day. Nevertheless, she never turned her back on "the beat."

Just as in her playing, Mary Lou Williams exhibited an unusually broad scope as a jazz composer in more than 350 works. Firmly grounded in spirituals, ragtime, the blues, and the swing-era style, she nevertheless embraced new ideas. Her first extended work, *Zodiac Suite* (1945), in twelve movements, was premiered by her trio on her New York radio show; in 1946 a part of this work was performed by members of the New York Philharmonic and the composer at Carnegie Hall. She collaborated with Milton Orent in creating a fairy tale in the bop style, *In the Land of Oo Bla Dee,* recorded by Dizzy Gillespie's big band. After her conversion to Catholicism in the mid-1950s, Williams often used her gifts for composition as a form of religious expression. Her most celebrated work in this sphere is *Mary Lou's Mass* (1969; excerpt in CAWM) for jazz combo and solo vocalists, which was commissioned by the Vatican, written in Rome, and choreographed by Alvin Ailey. This score has been praised as an encyclopedia of black music and has received many performances in both liturgical and concert settings.

Mary Lou Williams was willing to embrace new developments and was able to explore new idioms without sacrificing tradition. Through the force of her musicianship and the strength of her character, she was able to weather the storms of an inhospitable system and to flourish admirably in spite of it. For these reasons, during the later years of her life, she was often justifiably acknowledged as the "First Lady of Jazz."

The Younger Generation

Among the current generation of jazz women, Toshiko Akiyoshi and Carla Bley have made their marks as composers and pianists and are especially noteworthy as leaders of successful mixed-gender jazz ensembles. Akiyoshi often creates distinctive sounds by fusing traditional elements of jazz with sounds that draw on her Japanese musical heritage. Bley first gained wide notice in 1964 as leader of the avant-garde Jazz Composers Orchestra, for whom she created her pseudo-opera *Escalator over the Hill.* Bley's awareness of a broad range of musical genres and idioms comes through in her varied productions in the course of the last twenty years. Saxophonist and composer Jane Ira Bloom has "made a successful career as a woman in a male-dominated profession" and has done so "playing the soprano saxophone, an uncommon instrument on which to specialize."[8] With bachelor's and master's degrees in composition from Yale University, Bloom has established a solid reputation as performer and composer. This route eventually took her, in 1994, to the American Composers Orchestra and her largest work to date, *Einstein's Red-Blue Universe,* which mixes jazz idioms with conventions of Western art music.

Developments of the Recent Past

Just as it would be irresponsible to suggest that racism and sexism have disappeared from American musical circles at the end of the twentieth century, it would be equally unthinkable not to take stock of important changes in terms of opportunities for women participating in the jazz tradition during the past three decades. The contributions of women to jazz history and to contemporary musical life have been highlighted in numerous ways, most notably through well-publicized performances at prestigious festivals and venues and, because of their enduring testimony, through recordings featuring the artistry of women performers. Events devoted specifically to women professionals, such as Women's Jazz Festival in Kansas City and New York City, and recorded anthologies, such as *Forty Years of Women in Jazz: A Double Disc Feminist Retrospective* (Jazz Records, 1989), have helped to raise awareness to an unprecedented level. The enthusiastic advocacy of veteran Marian McPartland on her popular National Public Radio broadcast *Piano Jazz* has introduced the work of her jazz sisters to countless new listeners. Positive assessments by leading male critics, such as Leonard Feather, John S. Wilson, Whitney Balliett, and Nat Hentoff, as well as recognition by jazz historians,[9] have provided additional "legitimizing" support and encouragement. Most important, of course, are the individual women who have stubbornly followed their talents and dreams and sought out audiences. The long-held myth that only men can play jazz has suffered a terminal, if not quite lethal, blow.

During this recent period the number of women jazz musicians in the United States has grown. The number of jazz ensembles of various kinds comprised exclusively of women has likewise grown dramatically. Large ensembles such as the Los Angeles–based Maiden Voyage (formed in 1980) and New York–based Diva (formed in 1993) have garnered well-deserved attention and critical appreciation. Although the reality of men and women sharing the jazz bandstand is still not the norm, it is certainly no longer uncommon or controversial. The 1995 publication of *Madame Jazz: Contemporary Women Instrumentalists* by Leslie Gourse serves as a provocative status report on this phenomenon.[10] In the appendix to that text the author documents the careers of more than 300 musicians active during the 1980s and early 1990s. What is especially noteworthy and, in fact, of historical notice is the number of non-keyboard instrumentalists. The gamut of jazz instrumentation is fully represented: women horn players, bassists, and drummers have taken their places beside singers and pianists. Women have also joined the ranks of composers, arrangers, and business figures.

In spite of these undeniable successes, the career of the contemporary jazz musician—whether African American or white, female or male—remains a precarious one. Since the heyday of the swing era in the 1930s and 1940s, jazz has become increasingly a connoisseur's art: the majority of jazz musicians have cast aside the entertainer's pose and have chosen to concentrate on creating music that challenges and edifies; the majority of consumers have found musical satisfaction elsewhere. The fragmentation of the jazz style since the 1960s has further weakened the interest of the general public. Today very few jazz musicians—female or male—command a sizable cadre of concert-going, record-buying fans. With such limited patronage, competition for existing opportunities has become even keener. Although what must be understood as full sexual integration has yet to occur, women have more than made their presence known and have struggled alongside their male colleagues for recognition with as much talent, imagination, and dedication. Together they will determine the evolving nature of jazz to come.

NOTES

1. Linda Dahl, *Stormy Weather: The Music and Lives of a Century of Jazzwomen* (New York: Pantheon Books, 1984), p. 6.

2. Ibid., p. 3.

3. Neil Leonard, *Jazz: Myth and Religion* (New York: Oxford University Press, 1978), p. 24.

4. In spite of its origins, ragtime was quickly embraced in the parlors of middle-class American homes, and among its most devoted consumers and champions in the first decades of the twentieth century were white women pianists. A number of women, most notably May Aufderheide (1890–1972), were active as ragtime composers. See Max Morath, "May Aufderheide and the Ragtime Women," in *Ragtime: Its History, Composers, and Music,* ed. John E. Hasse (New York: Schirmer Books, 1985), pp. 154–65.

5. In her important study *Stormy Weather,* Linda Dahl discusses a number of women pioneers—instrumentalists and singers—who struggled to achieve recognition as jazz musicians. She also includes profiles of ten women who were enjoying successful careers in jazz at the beginning of the 1980s as well as a selective discography (pp. 307–54) devoted to women jazz musicians as vocalists, instrumentalists, and composers.

6. For a detailed account of this ensemble, see D. Antoinette Handy, *The International Sweethearts of Rhythm* (Metuchen, NJ: Scarecrow Press, 1983).

7. James Lincoln Collier, *The Making of Jazz: A Comprehensive History* (Boston: Houghton Mifflin, 1978), p. 310.

8. Patrick Lewis Harbison and Gregory Kehl Moore, "Jazzwomen Compose," *Contemporary Music Review* 16 (1997): 119.

9. Especially significant is Jan Leder, *Women in Jazz: A Discography of Instrumentalists, 1913–1968* (Westport, CT: Greenwood, 1985).

10. Leslie Gourse, *Madam Jazz: Contemporary Women Instrumentalists* (New York: Oxford University Press, 1995). This volume consists of a series of profiles of significant musicians, based on interviews and organized primarily by instrument.

SUGGESTIONS FOR FURTHER READING

In addition to the items mentioned in the text or cited in the notes, the following sources provide information on women involved in blues and jazz.

Bourgeois, Anna Stong. *Blueswomen: Profiles of Thirty-Seven Early Performers, with an Anthology of Lyrics, 1920–1945.* Jefferson, NC: McFarland, 1996.

Bowers, Jane. "'I Can Stand More Trouble than Any Little Woman My Size': Observations on the Meanings of the Blues of Estelle 'Mama' Yancey." *American Music* 11 (Spring 1993): 28–53.

Dahl, Linda. "Equal Time: A Historical Overview of Women in Jazz." In *America's Musical Pulse: Popular Music in Twentieth-Century Society.* Westport, CT: Greenwood Press, 1992, pp. 205–12.

Dje Dje, Jacqueline, and Eddie S. Meadows, eds. *California Soul: Music of African Americans in the West.* Berkeley: University of California Press, 1998.

Floyd, Samuel, Jr. *The Power of Black Music.* New York: Oxford University Press, 1995.

Gourse, Leslie, ed. *The Billie Holiday Companion: Seven Decades of Commentary.* New York: Schirmer Books, 1997.

Harrison, Daphne Duval. *Black Pearls: Blues Queens of the 1920s.* New Brunswick: Rutgers University Press, 1988.

James, Etta, and David Ritz. *Rage to Survive: The Etta James Story.* New York: Da Capo, 1998.

Kay, Jackie. *Bessie Smith.* Bath, UK: Absolute, 1997.

Kernodle, Tammy. "'Anything You Are Shows Up in Your Music': Mary Lou Williams and the Sanctification of Jazz." Ph.D. diss., Ohio State University, 1997.

Lieb, Sandra. *Mother of the Blues: A Study of Ma Rainey.* N.p.: University of Massachusetts Press, 1981.

Monson, Ingrid. "The Problem with White Hipness: Race, Gender, and Cultural Conceptions in Jazz Historical Discourse." *Journal of the American Musicological Society* 48 (1995): 396–422.

Placksin, Sally. *American Women in Jazz: 1900 to the Present.* New York: Wideview Books, 1982.

Southern, Eileen. *The Music of Black Americans,* 3rd ed. New York: W. W. Norton, 1997.

Tucker, Sherrie. "Female Big Bands, Male Mass Audiences: Gendered Performances in a Theater of War." *Women and Music: A Journal of Gender and Culture* 2 (1998): 64–89.

———. "Telling Performances: Jazz History Remembered and Remade by the Women in the Band." *Women and Music: A Journal of Gender and Culture* 1 (1997): 13–23.

Unterbrink, Mary. *Jazz Women at the Piano.* Jefferson, NC: McFarland, 1983.

The Special Roles of Women

XVI. Women's Support and Encouragement of Music and Musicians

Linda Whitesitt

Introduction

"Culture, like automobiles, lighting fixtures, and bread, is produced by the integrated actions of people filling a variety of roles."[1] Far from the Romantic ideal of art as the product of individual and isolated genius, musical culture is the outcome of actors in socially defined roles playing parts in socially constructed institutions. It is the result of performers, listeners, teachers, instrument makers, publishers, critics, ticket purchasers, managers, helpmates, fundraisers, administrators, and volunteers interacting in private and public institutions—family, church, court, salon, concerts, symphony orchestras, festivals, and conservatories. By transcending the myth of the great artist and looking at systems rather than individuals as the architects of art, women become visible as starring actors in the institutional creation of musical culture.

Limited by familial and societal conventions from entering the public professions of composition and performance, women have turned to other ways of participating in musical culture. In the private sphere of home, court, and salon, they have encouraged the musical education of their children, engaged the services of composers and performers, and promoted the careers of virtuosi. In the public sphere of symphony orchestras, music festivals, community recital series, and educational institutions, women have founded performing ensembles, coordinated fund-raising efforts, managed appearances of touring artists in their communities, started music libraries, donated land for music parks, established instrument collections, and joined together to solicit financial backing for large musical institutions.

Although women have viewed their support of music from a variety of vantage points, most have sought the role of friend to music for similar reasons: a deep love of music, a belief in the value of musical experiences in the life of a community, and an appreciation of the rewards of musical training in the education of the young. Many have come from musical backgrounds to their commitment of nurturing the lives of musical individuals and institutions, and many see their work as an opportunity to give back to the community and to music the enrichment they experienced as music students. Discouraged from entering the labor market, educated and displayed as status symbols for their husbands, wealthy women with leisure time looked to involvement in cultural activities to escape the isolation of the home. Only in the twentieth century, with the necessity of coordinated group support for ever-larger musical institutions, have women of lesser means pooled their resources to support musical organizations.

Although much of women's work has been in the form of financial subsidy, their support of musical activities calls for a broader definition of

FIGURE 16.1. Isabella d'Este. Leonardo da Vinci's cartoon (in bistre) for a portrait. Musée du Louvre, Paris. Photo courtesy of Alinari/Art Resource.

patronage: one that includes the encouragement of child by mother and husband by wife; the donation of hours, energy, and organizational skill; and the fashioning of nurturing environments for musical culture. In view of how many women have been active supporters of music and how little scholarly attention has been paid to the area of patronage in general, the scarcity of primary sources, the dearth of reliable secondary studies, and the invisibility of women's activities in historical documents, this chapter is but a brief exploration of what has been an unknown terrain. What follows is only a beginning—a brief chronological sketch of women's part in helping to create musical culture.

SUPPORT IN PRIVATE INSTITUTIONS OF MUSIC MAKING

Until the development of public institutions of music making in the late eighteenth century, classical music was cultivated in the private institutions of church and court by persons holding positions of power. On occasion and under certain circumstances, these might include women. During the Middle Ages the most significant was Eleanor of Aquitaine (1122–1204), who, along with her family and her descendants, influenced the course of medieval music.[2] By the thirteenth century, Europe's feudalism began to be replaced by a hegemony based on royal dynasties. Numerous noblewomen of Europe's castles and manors directed musical courts where composers and performers flourished: Mary of Burgundy (1457–1482) retained the services of chanson composer Antoine Busnois as her *prêtre chapelain;* Margaret of Austria (1480–1530) reestablished the musical brilliance of the Burgundian court with her special protégé Pierre de la Rue; Mary of Hungary (1505–1558) succeeded Margaret as Regent of the Netherlands and followed her lead as patron by nurturing an active musical chapel in Brussels.

The power enjoyed by some women under the feudal and monarchical system of Western Europe was far less common in the sovereign states in Renaissance Italy. Nevertheless, two women exerted an enormous influence on the course of native Italian music in the sixteenth century: Lucrezia Borgia (1480–1519) in Ferrara and Isabella d'Este (1474–1539) in Mantua. Both women paid exclusive attention to secular music for voice and strings, but Isabella focused her patronage on a single type of music, the frottola, while Lucrezia concentrated on music for banquets and dances for court celebrations. In addition, both women employed one of the greatest frottolists of the period, the composer Bartolomeo Tromboncino, who served Isabella from 1489 to 1505, when he left for Lucrezia's court. Both Isabella and Lucrezia encouraged Tromboncino to create musical settings of the poems of Petrarch and his most talented successors, thus raising the literary standards of the frottola. Because of Isabella's greater commitment to high-quality poetry, "and because her determined patronage stretches over a longer period than Lucrezia's, it may be that Isabella is the more important patron. Nevertheless, both women contributed profoundly to the rise of native Italian music and to its development."[3]

Women of noble rank continued to hold sway over the course of musical styles and composers' careers through the nineteenth century. In England, Elizabeth I (1533–1603) encouraged the flowering of keyboard music during her reign not so much by direct patronage as by her example as an amateur singer, dancer, and virginalist. In Rome, Queen Christina of Sweden (1626–1689) gathered around her an incredible entourage of poets, musicians, artists, and intellectuals; they became the nucleus of the Arcadia, one of the most famous academies in Rome. As her *maestro di cappella* Christina employed Alessandro Scarlatti, who remained in her retinue from ca. 1680 to 1684. Scarlatti probably also provided music for Christina's successor as patron of the arts in Rome, Maria Casimira of Poland (1641–1715), who in 1696 settled into voluntary exile in that city. Her fifteen years of distinguished and far-reaching patronage in Rome included support of Alessandro's son, Domenico Scarlatti. Today the latter Scarlatti's renown as a composer of keyboard sonatas is due to the woman he served first as teacher and then as music master, the woman who commissioned for her own use most of the composer's 550 harpsichord sonatas: Princess Maria Barbara of Bragança (1711–1758).

The revolutions at the end of the eighteenth century shook the social foundation of music making, dependent as it was on the wealth of the aristocracy. Now the growth of independent concerts, opera, and musical societies caused the structure of musical life to develop different institutions and social organizations. By the middle of the nineteenth century, the growing economic power and stability of the middle class supported a public world of commercial concert establishments, and "by 1870 there was little in the new concert world which would seem anachronistic today."[4]

The nineteenth century also witnessed the emergence of two different musical worlds: high art—that is, the music of the German classical school—and music that was more popular—that is, opera and music of the virtuosi. Each had its own public, institutions, and activities. Benefit concerts and salons provided a setting for the dazzling displays of the virtuosi and offered musicians the opportunity to build followings for themselves. Orchestral and chamber music concerts furnished an arena for classical music. Until the middle of the nineteenth century, concerts of popular music overshadowed concerts of classical music in London, Paris, and Vienna. Not until the 1860s did "serious" music encompass both the virtuosic and the German schools.

Given the close link between the popular-music world and the world of the family (benefit concerts grew out of salons in the home), women played critical roles in the foundations: they took charge of their children's musical education, continued their own musical training, and directed the salons. In the public world of classical concerts, however, "Males imposed . . . a lofty intellectual definition through which—thanks to the traditional conception that men were more serious than women—they excluded the other sex from leadership, even though women attended classical-music concerts just as much as men."[5] Women would not be awarded formal public authority over such concerts until the twentieth century.

With the soaring popularity of the piano at the turn of the nineteenth century and its importance as a woman's instrument, many composers made their livings by teaching and composing for women as well as by performing in women's salons. Beethoven honored many women with dedications: Eleonore von Breuning, Christiane Lichnowsky (1765–1841), Anna Luise Barbara Keglevich, Antonie Brentano, and Dorothea Ertmann, among others. His participation in the musical gatherings of Nanette Streicher and her husband, Johann Andreas Streicher, led to a close "motherly" relationship with Frau Streicher, a type of nurturing association characteristic of many of Beethoven's alliances with other women. Other sponsors in the nineteenth century include Countess Maria Wilhelmine of Thun-Hoherstein (mother of Christiane Lichnowsky), who was a patron of Haydn, Beethoven, and Mozart; Countess Delphine Potocka (1807–1877) the dedicatee of many of Chopin's works; and Pauline Viardot-Garcia (1821–1910), who helped foster the careers of Gounod and Saint-Saëns.

In addition to arranging salons, women of wealth continued their private subsidy of composers. For Grand Duchess Elena Pavlovna (1807–1873), sister-in-law of the tsar, Anton Rubinstein served as accompanist to palace singers (he jestingly referred to his position as "Janitor of Music"), lived as a guest at the Kàmennoiòstrov Palace, wrote a series of short operas to illustrate the different nationalities of Russia, accompanied his patron to Nice, and helped the duchess plan the establishment of the Russian Musical Society and the Russian Conservatory. Another Russian composer, Tchaikovsky, was awarded a number of commissions followed by an annual allowance for fourteen years by the wealthy widow Nadezhda von Meck (1831–1894), who later employed Debussy as her pianist. She and Tchaikovsky had a unique association in that they never met; both needed the illusion of close emotional support without the obstructions an actual meeting might incur.

Women have long served as sources of support for their partners, dedication generally inspired by deep commitment and admiration for the artistic ability of their lovers or husbands both during their lives and after their deaths. Clara Schumann (1819–1896) gave sustained emotional, financial, and artistic sustenance to Robert at the same time as she managed their household, bore eight children, and pursued her own successful composing and performing career. Other helpmates in the nineteenth century included George Sand (1804–1876), pseudonym of the writer Amantine Lucile Aurore Dudevant (helpmate to Chopin), Countess Marie d'Agoult (1805–1876) and Princess Carolyne Sayn-Wittgenstein (1819–1887; Liszt), Cosima Wagner (1837–1930), Giuseppina Verdi (1815–1897), and Alma Mahler (1879–1964). A women's negation of self on behalf of her partner's art is epitomized in Alma Mahler's acquiescence to her husband's wish that she abandon her own composing career:

> I buried my dream and perhaps it was for the best. It has been my privilege to give my creative gifts another life in minds greater than my own. And yet the iron had entered my soul and the wound has never healed.[6]
>
> I lived his life. I had none of my own. He never noticed this surrender of my existence. He was so self-engrossed that any disturbance, however slight, was unendurable. Work, exaltation, self-denial and the never-ending quest were his whole life on and on and forever.[7]

With the consolidation of modern concert institutions in the second half of the nineteenth century, salons declined in importance. However, the practice of inviting musicians to perform for guests in one's home continues to this day. Composers and performers of the early twentieth century won unwavering support from the woman whose salon became the crossroads in new musical developments in Paris: Princesse Edmond de Polignac (1865–1943), who for more than half a century promoted the talents of young performers, commissioned new works, and ensured the performance of new music. The list of those she supported reads like a register of the primary actors on the musical and artistic scene from 1880 to 1940: Gabriel Fauré, Ernest Chausson, Vincent d'Indy, Emmanuel Chabrier, Maurice Ravel, Ethel Smyth, Claude Debussy, Manuel de Falla, Jean Cocteau, Serge Diaghilev, Darius Milhaud, Igor Stravinsky, Erik Satie, Germaine Tailleferre, Karol Szymanowski, Nadia Boulanger, Paul Hindemith, Francis Poulenc, Kurt Weill, and Jean Françaix.

Support of Public Institutions

Although individual women have continued to support composers in the twentieth century, much of women's gift giving to music has been directed toward public institutions in their communities: concert and opera series, symphony orchestras, educational institutions, music festivals, and the like. Combining a view of music as necessary for the cultural life of their communities with a commitment to social services for the masses and education for the young, women have joined together to provide rich musical environments. Nowhere has this support been so vital as in the United States.

The role of cultural supporter was first championed among American women by Fanny Raymond Ritter (1830–1890) at the 1876 meeting of the Association for the Advancement of Women:

> Every American lady who possesses the indispensable kindness of heart, refinement, generosity and culture, as well as influence—the wives of men with intellectual power, inherited wealth, or great commercial prominence, more especially—can accomplish a great deal in her own small circle. . . .
>
> With lady amateurs, then, will chiefly rest the happy task of preparing, by a beneficent use of such abilities as they may possess, the soil which must foster the young germs of future American art. . . .[8]

In the United States there was a common notion that men guarded the precincts of business and politics while women oversaw the domains of home and culture. Many women triumphed in the socially sanctioned separate sphere of musical patronage without questioning the construct of separate spheres itself, and they did it, as Ritter suggests, "in [their] own small circle."

Women began their group patronage of music in women's music clubs and music departments of women's clubs, part of a long line of nineteenth-century women's organizations that included charitable and missionary societies, moral reform and welfare groups, and women's study clubs. Organized initially to provide forums for women trained as musicians but unable to practice music professionally, women's music clubs soon turned to stimulating the musical culture of their communities by sponsoring concerts of touring artists. They were so successful that by 1927 it was reported that, outside of large cities, individual clubs handled three-fourths of the concert engagements in the United States, spending approximately one million dollars to engage concert artists.[9] Club efforts were a major force in the growth and education of concert audiences at the turn of the century, and they played a significant role in molding the musical values of their communities and shaping the nature of concert life in America.[10]

One outstanding music club leader was Ella May Smith (1860–1934), president of the Music Club of Columbus (Ohio). Coming to the presidency of her club in 1903 from a career as a piano teacher, vocal coach, instructor of music, lecturer on music history, music journalist, composer, and author, Smith increased the membership of the once-disbanded club to 850 by the end of her first year and 3,500 by the end of her fourth year. During thirteen years as president (1903–1916), this talented leader established a yearly series of six artists' and six members' concerts, free public organ recitals, a choir, the Altruistic Department, an exchange program with other clubs, extension lectures and recitals, a student organization, community music schools in settlement houses, and a music library and a trust for its continuation at the Columbus Public Library. The club also donated an organ to the city. Many women, using the experience gained in directing club activities, entered the world of music management and became role models for a growing number of women professional managers in a variety of arts organizations. In Washington, D.C., Mamie Hilyer founded the Treble Clef Club, whose nationally recognized aim was to bring the "best music" of African-American composers and musicians to the city. In addition, it was Hilyer's idea to found the successful Coleridge-Taylor Choral Society.[11]

Women have been indispensable in championing the symphony orchestras in their communities, shaping their development, organizing financial support, and developing educational programs. They have also been influential in the founding of orchestras. In Cleveland, Adella Prentiss Hughes (1869–1950) enlisted the aid of wealthy businessmen to bring conductor Nikolai Sokoloff to that city in 1918. She persuaded them to pay his salary, thus founding the Cleveland Orchestra, which she managed for fifteen years. Hughes helped raise money for operating expenses; encouraged the securing of Cleveland's first adequate concert auditorium, Severance Hall; arranged tours for the orchestra; and developed a comprehensive educational program. Likewise, Ima Hogg (1882–1975) engineered the founding of the Houston Symphony in 1913, served twelve terms as president of its board of directors, initiated the Women's Committee, and directed fund-raising campaigns.

Women were essential in the establishment and growth of symphony orchestras in other cities as well. In Cincinnati in 1894, members of the Ladies' Musical Club led the way in founding and supervising the Cincinnati Symphony Orchestra. Prominent in these efforts were Helen H. Taft (1861–1943), first president of the Orchestra Association Board; Bettie Fleischmann Holmes, a later president; and Annie Sinton Taft, who with her husband, Charles Taft, provided major financial support for the orchestra. In Washington, D.C., the Friday Morning Music Club was one of the founding members and a major financial supporter of the National Symphony Orchestra. Composer Mary Howe (1882–1964) was important in this early relationship, and later in the century Marjorie Merriweather Post (1887–1973) donated more than one million dollars to the orchestra. Women exerted tremendous influence on the course of the New York Philharmonic:

> To anyone who examines without prejudice the history of the Philharmonic it is a perpetual source of wonder that, ever since that fateful moment in 1909

> when Mrs. George Sheldon helped to marshal the forces that reorganized the old Philharmonic, the Society has been blessed with an unfailing supply of rich, hard-working, intelligent, loyal, and public-spirited women who have been willing to give their time and money for the good of the city's musical life. Some of them may have had nobler motives than others, but whether they did what they did out of generosity, or vanity, or love of music, or just to keep busy, the results for the Philharmonic have been always salutary and sometimes salvatory.[12]

In Philadelphia the early work of informal committees of women and the efforts after 1904 of the formal Women's Committees were integral to the success of the Philadelphia Orchestra. Such achievement has been echoed in women's work in symphony auxiliaries and on symphony boards throughout the United States.

Similar activities on behalf of opera companies may be found in numerous cities. Perhaps the most outstanding examples have been the efforts spearheaded by Eleanor Robson (Mrs. August) Belmont in support of the Metropolitan Opera Guild, the founding work by Helen Huntington Hull of what would later become the New York City Opera, and the initial efforts by Mary Cardwell Dawson (1894–1962) to establish the National Negro Opera Company (1941).

Women have also been active in founding educational institutions. One of the first of them was Clara Baur (d. 1912), who in 1867 founded and directed the Cincinnati Conservatory of Music. Twenty years later, Jeannette Thurber (1850–1946) organized the ill-fated National Conservatory of Music in 1885 and persuaded Antonín Dvořák to assume its directorship in 1892; he remained for three seasons. In 1894 May Garrettson Evans (1866–1947) founded the Peabody Graduates' Preparatory and High School of Music, which was incorporated into the Peabody Conservatory as the Preparatory Department two years later. Close by, pianist Harriet Gibbs Marshall (1869–1941) founded the Washington (D.C.) Conservatory of Music in 1903. As the first black pianist to graduate from Oberlin Conservatory, Marshall's goal was to provide black students with a rigorous musical education. In Philadelphia the Curtis Institute of Music was founded in 1924 by Mary Louise Curtis Bok (later Zimbalist; 1876–1970), who served as president until 1969.

Women have been fervent advocates of music festivals. The first woman in the United States to found a music festival was Maria Longworth Nichols Storer (1849–1932). In 1871 she established the Cincinnati May Festival and convinced Theodore Thomas to conduct it. After two years of diligent planning and fund-raising, the first festival took place in May 1873. America's first summer music festival, the Norfolk Music Festival, located in the Litchfield Hills of northwestern Connecticut, was founded by Ellen Battell

Stoeckel (1851–1939) and her husband, Carl, in 1900; it was a direct outgrowth of the Litchfield County Choral Union, which they had begun in 1899. A significant part of this festival was the commissioning of new works by such composers as George Chadwick, Victor Herbert, Horatio Parker, Samuel Coleridge-Taylor, Percy Grainger, and Jean Sibelius. Although the festival ceased in 1922, Ellen Stoeckel continued her generous gifts to music and her community. She willed much of her property for the use of Yale University, a bequest that led to the establishment of the Yale Summer School of Music and Art.

The Berkshires of western Massachusetts are the scene of two of America's best-known summer music festivals—South Mountain and Tanglewood. The first of these grew out of the efforts of Elizabeth Sprague Coolidge (1864–1953), whom many view as the most important patron of music in the twentieth century. Coolidge began her career as "Lady Bountiful of Chamber Music" with the founding of the Berkshire Quartet in 1916. Two years later, she established the annual Berkshire Festival of Chamber Music at South Mountain, near Pittsfield. The Berkshire Quartet and the new Coolidge-supported Elshuco Trio presented newly commissioned works alongside classical repertoire. The success of these festivals led her to sponsor similar festivals in cities throughout Europe.

Composer-conductor Henry Hadley's idea for an orchestral music festival, the Berkshire Symphonic Festival, was carried forward by three women: Gertrude Robinson Smith (1881–1963), Mrs. Owen Johnson, and Mrs. William Fulton Barrett. It opened its doors in August 1934, and in 1936 the Boston Symphony Orchestra was engaged as its permanent orchestra. In the same years, Rosamund Dixey Brooks Hepburn (Mrs. Andrew H., 1887–1948) and Mary Aspinwall Tappan (1851–1941) donated a permanent home for the festival, the Tanglewood estate, which has since served as the site of an annual international festival of music.

Wolf Trap, the only national park in the United States dedicated to the performing arts, is the result of the creative imagination and financial backing of Catherine Filene Shouse (1896–1994). Donor of the land and the funds for both the outdoor and indoor theatres, Shouse is dedicated to the educational and performing opportunities offered at the park. Other communities across the country have been blessed with women who have given or raised the funds for new arts centers. In San Francisco, Louise M. Davies (b.1900) gave $5 million toward the erection of the concert hall that bears her name and an additional $3 million to the orchestra's endowment fund. Los Angeles's Dorothy Buffum Chandler (1901–1997) almost single-handedly raised $18.5 million for the building of the Music Center, then organized a company to float $13.7 million in bonds to finish the work.

The love of music has also been behind the generous patronage of Alice Tully (1902–1993), from her support of major cultural institutions and the careers of promising singers to her contributions to the chamber music hall at Lincoln Center that bears her name. On the occasion of her eighty-fifth birthday, Will Crutchfield addressed the nature of a patron's involvement in the outcome of her patronage:

> Some people adhere to the view that patrons ought simply to write their checks and never dream of influencing ("interfering in") artistic results. Miss Tully, bestowing her philanthropies from a highly discriminating point of view, has represented the opposite tradition. I prefer it.[13]

Many women have given financial backing and energetic support to composers through stipends, commissions, and moral encouragement. Elizabeth Sprague Coolidge shaped the course of chamber music in the twentieth century, first by founding the Berkshire Chamber Music Festival, then, in 1925, by establishing the Elizabeth Sprague Coolidge Foundation at the Library of Congress, along with the auditorium that bears her name. Other women who have supported the creative efforts of composers and performers include Mary Louise Curtis Bok (George Antheil, Samuel Barber, Gian-Carlo Menotti), Isabella Stewart Gardner (1840–1924; Charles Martin Loeffler, Clayton Johns), Gertrude Vanderbilt Whitney (1875–1942; Edgard Varèse), Alma Morgenthau Wertheim (Aaron Copland, Roy Harris), Blanche Walton (1871–1963; Henry Cowell), and Clair Raphael Reis (1888–1978; numerous modernist musicians; Reis was the executive director of the International Composers' Guild and the League of Composers).

This brief survey of women's patronage has merely begun to suggest the richness of women's contributions to musical culture. Each woman's gift to music making is a story in itself, and the areas not discussed call for additional volumes of study. Women have built and supported retreats and working communities for musicians and artists (Katrina Trask, 1853–1922, Yaddo; Marian MacDowell, 1857–1956, the MacDowell Colony); donated scholarships for young composers and performers (the National Federation of Music Clubs); established grants for music making and scholarship (Martha Baird Rockefeller, 1895–1971); contributed to music libraries (Lila Acheson Wallace, 1889–1984, the Juilliard School Library); offered commissions in memory of loved ones; and donated instruments to performers and collections (Gertrude Whittall, 1867–1965, the Gertrude Whittall Foundation and Pavilion at the Library of Congress). They have furthered music making through writing and editorial efforts (Minna Lederman, b. 1898, the journal *Modern Music*); founded publishing firms (Alma Wertheim, d. 1953, Cos Cob Press; Sylvia Smith, b. 1948, Smith Publications and Sonic

Art Editions); founded organizations to further the careers of both musicians and composers (Nora Douglas Holt, 1885–1974, journalist and founder of the National Association of Negro Musicians in 1919); contributed far-reaching scholarship aid (Emma Azalia Hackley, 1867–1922, an important supporter and encourager of African-American musicians and composers); and worked to support new music (Betty Freeman, b. 1921, patron of composers John Cage, Steve Reich, Philip Glass, Daniel Lentz, Ingram Marshall, and Paul Dresher).

CONCLUSION

Other aspects of women's support remain to be examined. How have women of other cultures and other colors worked to facilitate the making of music? What has been the relationship between giver and recipient? And what have been the effects of the gifts on the artists and the art? How have women's efforts been viewed by other contributors to musical culture—press, critics, teachers? How has patronage changed the lives of the patrons? Why have women seemingly failed to support women composers and performers? Conversely, how have they fostered the activities of other women? Many questions remain to be answered before we can begin to understand how women's supportive efforts have altered the fabric of our musical culture. By changing our perspective of music culture from one focused on individuals of genius to one centered on institutions of creative interactions, we have at least begun to ask the right questions.

NOTES

1. Gaye Tuchman, "Women and the Creation of Culture," *Sociological Inquiry* 45 (1975): 192.

2. Rebecca A. Baltzer, "Music in the Life and Times of Eleanor of Aquitaine," in *Eleanor of Aquitaine: Patron and Politician,* ed. William W. Kibler (Austin: University of Texas Press, 1976), p. 61.

3. For a detailed study of the patronage of these two Renaissance noblewomen, see William F. Prizer, "Isabella d'Este and Lucrezia Borgia as Patrons of Music: The Frottola at Mantua and Ferrara," *Journal of the American Musicological Society* 38 (Spring 1985): 1–33.

4. William Weber, *Music and the Middle Class: The Social Structure of Concert Life in London, Paris, and Vienna* (New York: Holmes & Meier Publishers, Inc., 1975), p. 7.

5. Ibid., p. 126.

6. Alma Mahler, *Gustav Mahler: Memories and Letters,* trans. Basil Creighton (New York: The Viking Press, 1946), p. 21.

7. Ibid., p. 104.

8. Paper written by Fanny Raymond Ritter and read by Mrs. Churchill at the Centennial Congress in Philadelphia of the Association for the Advancement of

Woman (1876) and published in *Woman's Journal.* It is quoted here as it was published (with additions) as *Woman as a Musician: An Art-Historical Study* (New York: Edward Schuberth & Co., 1876), pp. 15–17.

9. *Past Presidents Assembly (A Fraternity of Presidents) of the National Federation of Music Clubs. Blue Book* (N.p.: National Federation of Music Clubs, 1927), p. 1.

10. For more detail concerning women's concert management efforts, see Linda Whitesitt, "The Role of Women Impresarios in American Concert Life, 1871–1933," *American Music* 7/2 (Summer 1989): 159–80.

11. For more information, see Doris Evans McGinty, "The Black Presence in the Music of Washington, D.C.," in *More Than Dancing: Essays on Afro-American Music and Musicians,* ed. Irene V. Jackson (Westport, CT: Greenwood Press, 1985), pp. 81–106.

12. Howard Shanet, *Philharmonic: A History of New York's Orchestra* (Garden City, NY: Doubleday & Company, 1975), p. 294.

13. As quoted in Dorle J. Soria, "A Wonderful Woman," *Opera News* 52/14 (March 26, 1988): 44.

SUGGESTIONS FOR FURTHER READING

In addition to the items mentioned in the text or cited in the footnotes, the following sources provide information on women's encouragement and support in the music world.

Barr, Cyrilla. *Elizabeth Sprague Coolidge: Portrait of a Patron.* New York: Schirmer Books, 1998.

———."The Faerie Queene and the Archangel: The Correspondence of Elizabeth Sprague Coolidge and Carl Engel." *American Music* 2 (1997): 159–82.

———. "The Musicological Legacy of Elizabeth Sprague Coolidge." *Journal of Musicology* 2 (1993): 250–68.

Bernhard, Virginia. *Ima Hogg: The Governor's Daughter.* Austin: Texas Monthly Press, 1984.

Blair, Karen. *The Clubwoman as Feminist: True Womanhood Redefined, 1868–1914.* New York: Holmes & Meier, 1980.

———. *The History of American Women's Voluntary Organizations, 1810–1960: A Guide to Sources.* Boston: G. K. Hall, 1988.

———. *The Torchbearers: Women and Their Amateur Arts Associations in America, 1890–1930.* Bloomington: Indiana University Press, 1994.

Cossart, Michael de. *The Food of Love: Princess Edmond de Polignac (1865–1943).* London: Hamish Hamilton, 1978.

Feldman, Ann E. "Being Heard: Women Composers and Patrons and the Development of Modernism in America." M.A. thesis, American University, 1992.

Keefer, Lubov. *Music Angels: A Thousand Years of Patronage.* Baltimore: Sutherland Press, Inc., 1976.

Lesinski, Carolyn Homan. "Unsung Heroines: Women Patrons at the 1893 World's Columbian Exposition." *Notes* 47/1 (September 1990): 7–20.

Leung-Wolf, Elaine. "Women, Music, and the Salon Tradition: Its Cultural and Historical Significance in Parisian Musical Society." D.M.A. thesis, University of Cincinnati, 1996.

Locke, Ralph. "Music Lovers, Patrons, and the 'Sacralization' of Culture in America." *Nineteenth-Century Music* 17 (1993–1994): 149–73; and 18 (1994–1995): 83–84.

———. "Paradoxes of the Woman Music Patron in America." *Musical Quarterly* 78 (1994): 798–825.

———. "Women in American Musical Life: Facts and Questions about Patronage." *repercussions* 3, no. 2 (Fall 1994): 81–95; and 4, no. 1 (Spring 1995): 102.

——— and Cyrilla Barr, eds. *Cultivating Music in America: Women Patrons and Activists since 1860.* Berkeley: University of California Press, 1997.

Marshall, Kimberly, ed. *Rediscovering the Muses: Women's Musical Traditions.* Boston: Northeastern University, 1993.

Martin, Theodora Penny. *The Sound of Our Own Voices: Women's Study Clubs 1860–1910.* Boston: Beacon Press, 1987.

McCarthy, Kathleen D., ed. *Lady Bountiful Revisited: Women, Philanthropy, and Power.* New Brunswick, NJ: Rutgers University Press, 1990.

Perry, Pamela J. "The Role of Women as Patrons of Music in Connecticut during the Nineteenth and Twentieth Centuries." D.M.A. thesis, Hartt School of Music, University of Hartford, 1986.

Rosaldo, Michelle Zimbalist, and Louise Lamphere, eds. *Woman, Culture, and Society.* Stanford: Stanford University Press, 1974.

Viles, Elza Ann. "Mary Louise Curtis Bok Zimbalist: Founder of the Curtis Institute of Music and Patron of American Arts." Ph.D. diss., Bryn Mawr College, 1983.

Whitesitt, Linda. "'The Most Potent Force' in American Music: The Role of Women's Music Clubs in American Concert Life." In *The Musical Woman.* Vol. III*: An International Perspective,* ed. Judith Lang Zaimont. Westport, CT: Greenwood Press, 1991.

General Bibliography

SUGGESTIONS FOR FURTHER READING

The following resources are more general than the items listed at the end of each chapter or cover more than one period, country, or topic.

The New Grove series of dictionaries includes much information about women in all areas of music. Check for general articles on "Women in Music" as well as articles on particular women in *The New Grove Dictionary of Music and Musicians, The New Grove Dictionary of American Music, The New Grove Dictionary of Jazz,* and *The New Grove Dictionary of Opera.* Of particular value is the *Norton/Grove Dictionary of Women Composers,* ed. Julie Anne Sadie and Rhian Samuel (New York and London: W. W. Norton, 1995). Publishers are now working on second editions of these helpful reference books.

The second edition of *Die Musik in Geschichte und Gegenwart* contains many articles on women. Short but informative articles can also be found in Riemann's *Musiklexikon, Baker's Biographical Dictionary2,* and Oscar Thompson's *International Cyclopedia of Music and Musicians* (11th edition, 1985). For information on women singers or singing actresses, try *Enciclopedia dello spettacolo.*

Indiana University Press publishes two anthologies of music by women, both ed. James Briscoe. The first, *Historical Anthology of Music by Women* (Bloomington, 1987), contains music from the twelfth through the twentieth centuries. The second, *Contemporary Anthology of Music by Women* (Bloomington, 1997), contains twentieth-century music in a variety of genres.

Barbara Garvey Jackson's ClarNan Editions publishes music by women from the seventeenth and eighteenth centuries, along with a few items from the nineteenth and twentieth centuries. Her approach combines scholarly standards with practical issues of performance. Contact her at ClarNan Editions, 235 Baxter Lane, Fayetteville, AR 72701.

Sylvia Glickman and Martha Furman Schleifer are editors of a thirteen-volume anthology of music by women, *Women Composers: Music through the Ages* (New York: G. K. Hall, 1996–). Volumes are in chronological order and contain music by women from medieval times to the present, along with helpful essays about each composer and the music in the anthology. Performing editions of all works in these volumes, along with many other works by women, are available from Hildegard Publishing Company in Bryn Mawr, Pennsylvania. Hildegard is also the American distributor for many scores of women's music from European publishers. Check their Web site at http: //www.hildegard.com.

Da Capo Press has published much worthwhile music of women of the past in its Women Composers Series. Three recently initiated journals deal exclusively with women's music. *The International Alliance of Women in Music Journal,* a cross between journal and newsletter, is sent to IAWM members three times a year. The organization also publishes *Women & Music: A Journal of Gender and Culture,* which began in 1997. Copies are sent to members of IAWM free of charge in the fall of each year. Editor Barbara Harbach brings out a journal that, though small in size, contains valuable information on women composers and musicians; *Women of Note Quarterly.* Harbach's Vivace Press publishes music by women and men; for more information, consult the Web site: http: //www.vivacepress.com.

The Leonarda record label issues works almost exclusively by women; their Web site is: http: //music.acu.edu/www/iawm/leonarda/

BOOKS

Ammer, Christine. *Unsung: A History of Women in American Music.* Westport, CT: Greenwood Press, 1980; 2d ed., 2000.

Anderson, Bonnie S., and Judith P. Zinsser. *A History of Their Own.* 2 vols. New York: Harper and Row, 1988.

Barkin, Elaine, and Lydia Hamessley, eds. *Audible Traces: Gender, Identity, and Music.* Zurich and Los Angeles: Carciofoli, 1999.

Battersby, Christine. *Gender and Genius: Towards a Feminist Aesthetics.* London: Women's Press, 1989; Bloomington: Indiana University Press, 1989.

Bergeron, Katherine, and Philip Bohlman, eds. *Disciplining Music: Musicology and its Canons.* Chicago: University of Chicago Press, 1992.

Blackmer, Corinne, and Patricia Julianna Smith. *En travesti: Women, Gender Subversion, Opera.* New York: Columbia University Press, 1995.

Block, Adrienne Fried, and Carol Neuls-Bates. *Women in American Music, a Bibliography of Music and Literature.* Westport, CT: Greenwood Press, 1979.

Boenke, Heidi M. *Flute Music by Women Composers: An Annotated Catalogue.* New York: Greenwood Press, 1988.

Bowers, Jane, and Judith Tick, eds. *Women Making Music.* Urbana: University of Illinois Press, 1986.

Brett, Philip, Elizabeth Wood, and Gary Thomas, eds. *Queering the Pitch.* New York: Routledge, 1994.

Bridenthal, Renate, Claudia Koonz, and Susan Stuard, eds. *Becoming Visible: Women in European History.* 2d ed. Boston: Houghton Mifflin, 1987.

Carroll, Berenice A., ed. *Liberating Women's History.* Urbana: University of Illinois Press, 1976.

Chiti, Patricia Adkins. *Donne in musica.* Rome: Bulzoni, 1982. Also available in Spanish as *Mujeres en la musica.* Madrid: Alianza Editorial, 1994.

Christiansen, Rupert. *Prima Donna: A History.* New York: Viking, 1985.

Citron, Marcia. *Gender and the Musical Canon.* Cambridge: Cambridge University Press, 1994.

Claghorn, Charles. *Women Composers and Songwriters: A Concise Dictionary.* Lanham, MD: Scarecrow, 1996.

Clément, Catherine. *Opera, or the Undoing of Women.* Trans. Betsy Wing. Minneapolis: University of Minnesota Press, 1988.

Cohen, Aaron. *International Discography of Women Composers.* Westport, CT: Greenwood Press, 1984.

———. *International Encyclopedia of Women Composers.* 2d ed. New York: Books and Music, 1987.

Cook, Susan, and Judy Tsou, eds. *Cecilia Reclaimed: Feminist Perspectives on Gender and Music.* Urbana: University of Illinois Press, 1994.

Cooper, Sarah, ed. *Girls! Girls! Girls! Essays on Women and Music.* New York: University Press, 1996.

Drinker, Sophie. *Music and Women.* New York: Coward-McCann, 1948; reprint, Boston: Northeastern University Press, 1995.

Dunn, L. C., and N. A. Jones, eds. *Embodied Voices. Representing Female Vocality in Western Culture.* Cambridge: Cambridge University Press, 1994.

Edwards, H. Sutherland. *The Prima Donna.* New York: Da Capo Press, 1978.

Erickson, Mary. *Women and Music: A Selective Bibliography on Women and Gender Issues in Music, 1987–1992.* New York: G. K. Hall, 1995.

Farkas, Andrew. *Opera and Concert Singers: An Annotated International Bibliography of Books and Pamphlets*. New York: Garland, 1985.

Fuller, Sophie. *The Pandora Guide to Women Composers*. London: Pandora, 1994.

Gill, John. *Queer Noises: Male and Female Homosexuality in Twentieth-Century Music*. Minneapolis: University of Minnesota Press, 1995.

Goss, Madeleine. *Modern Music Makers*. Westport, CT: Greenwood Press, 1952.

Gourret, Jean, Jean Giraudeau, and François Lesure. *Dictionnaire des cantatrices de l'Opéra de Paris*. Paris: Albatros, 1982.

Grattan, Virginia. *American Women Songwriters: A Biographical Dictionary*. Westport, CT: Greenwood Press, 1993.

Green, Lucy. *Music, Gender, Education*. Cambridge: Cambridge University Press, 1997.

Green, Miriam Stewart. *Women Composers: A Checklist of Works for the Solo Voice*. Boston: G. K. Hall, 1980.

Halstead, Jill. *The Woman Composer: Creativity and the Gendered Politics of Musical Composition*. Aldershot, England: Ashgate, 1997.

Herndon, Marcia, and Susanne Ziegler, eds. *Music, Gender, and Culture*. Wilhelmshaven: F. Noetzel; New York: Peters, 1990.

Hipsher, Edward Ellsworth. *American Opera and Its Composers*. Philadelphia: Theodore Presser, 1934; reprint New York: Da Capo Press, 1978.

Hixon, Donald L., and Don Hennessee. *Women in Music: A Bio-Bibliography*. Metuchen, NJ: Scarecrow Press, 1975; 2d ed., 2 vols., 1995.

Hoffman, Freia. *Instrument und Körper: Die musizierende Frau in der bürgerlichen Kultur*. Frankfurt: Insel, 1991.

International Dictionary of Black Composers, ed. Samuel A. Floyd, Jr. Chicago: Fitzroy Dearborn Publishers, 1999.

International Who's Who in Music. 15th edition, 1996/97. Cambridge, England: International Who's Who in Music, 1996.

Jackson, Barbara Garvey. *Say Can You Deny Me: A Guide to Surviving Music by Women from the Sixteenth through the Eighteenth Centuries*. Fayetteville: University of Arkansas Press, 1994.

James, E. T., J. W. James, and P. S. Boyer, eds. *Notable American Women*. 3 vols. Cambridge: Harvard University Press, 1980.

Jewish Women in America: An Historical Encyclopedia. Ed. Paula Hymna and Deborah Dash Moore. New York: Routledge, 1997.

Jezic, Diane Peacock. *Women Composers: The Lost Tradition Found*. New York: Feminist Press, 1988; 2d ed., ed. Elizabeth Wood, 1994. Cassettes illustrating points or composers discussed in the book are available from Leonarda Records.

Koskoff, Ellen, ed. *Women and Music in Cross-Cultural Perspective*. Urbana: University of Illinois Press, 1989.

Kutsch, K. J., and Leo Riemens. *Grosses Sängerlexikon*. 2 vols. Bern: Francke Verlag, 1987.

Le Page, Jane Weiner. *Women Composers, Conductors, and Musicians of the Twentieth Century*. 3 vols. Metuchen, NJ: Scarecrow Press, 1980–88.

LeFanu, Nicola, and Sophie Fuller, eds. *Reclaiming the Muse*. Full issue of *Contemporary Music Review* 11 (1994).

Lerner, Gerda. "Placing Women in History: Definitions and Challenges." *Feminist Studies* 3/2 (Fall 1975): 5–14.

Loesser, Arthur. *Men, Women, and Pianos: A Social History*. New York: Simon and Schuster, 1954.

Lyle, Wilson. *A Dictionary of Pianists*. New York: Schirmer, 1985.

MacAuslen, Janna. *A Catalogue of Compositions for Guitar by Women Composers*. Portland, OR: Dear Horse Publications, 1984.

Manning, Jane. *New Vocal Repertory*. Vol. 1, Basingstoke: MacMillan, 1986; vol. 2, Oxford: Clarendon Press, 1998.

Marcus, Adele. *Great Pianists Speak with Adele Marcus*. Neptune, NJ: Paganiniana, 1979.

Marshall, Kimberly, ed. *Rediscovering the Muses: Women's Musical Traditions*. Boston: Northeastern University Press, 1993.

Matheopoulos, Helena. *Diva. Great Sopranos and Mezzos Discuss Their Art*. Boston: Northeastern University Press, 1992.

Migel, Parmenia. *The Ballerinas, from the Court of Louis XIV to Pavlova*. New York: Da Capo Press, 1980.

McClary, Susan. *Feminine Endings: Music, Gender, and Sexuality*. Minneapolis: University of Minnesota Press, 1991.

Neuls-Bates, Carol. *The Status of Women in College Music: Preliminary Studies*. Binghamton, NY: College Music Society, 1976. Rev. ed., Boston: Northeastern University Press, 1996.

———, ed. *Women in Music: An Anthology of Source Readings from the Middle Ages to the Present*. New York: Harper and Row, 1982. Rev. ed., Boston: Northeastern University Press, 1996.

Nies, Christel. *Komponistinnen und ihr Werk: Eine Dokumentation*. Cologne: Heinrich Boll, 1992.

Nishimura, Mari. *The Twentieth-Century Composer Speaks: An Index of Interviews*. Berkeley: University of California Press, 1993.

Olivier, Antje, and Karin Weingartz, eds. *Frauen als Komponistinnen*. 2d ed. Düsseldorf: International Arbeitskreis Frau und Musik, 1987.

Olivier, Antje, and Karin Weingartz-Perschel, eds. *Komponistinnen von A–Z*. Düsseldorf: Tokkata Verlag, 1988.

Pendle, Karin, ed. *American Women Composers*. Full issue of *Contemporary Music Review* 16 (1997).

Pleasants, Henry. *Great Singers from Jenny Lind to Callas and Pavarotti*. Rev. ed. New York: Simon and Schuster, 1981.

Rasponi, Lanfranco. *The Last Prima Donnas*. New York: Knopf, 1982.

Reich, Nancy, ed. *Women's Studies, Women's Status*. CMS Report No. 5. Boulder: College Music Society, 1988.

Rieger, Eva. *Frau, Musik und Männerherrschaft*. 2d ed. Kassel: Furore, 1988.

———. *Frau und Musik*. Frankfurt: Fischer Taschenbücher, 1980.

Rosen, Judith, and Grace Rubin-Rabson. "Why Haven't Women Become Great Composers?" *High Fidelity/Musical America* 23/2 (February 1973): 46, 51–52; 47–50.

Schlegel, Ellen Grolman. *Catalogue of Published Works for String Orchestra and Piano Trio by Twentieth-Century American Women Composers*. Bessemer, AL: Colonial Press, 1993.

Schonberg, Harold. *The Great Pianists*. New York: Simon & Schuster, 1963.

Shepherd, John. "Music and Male Hegemony." in *Music and Society: The Politics of Composition, Performance and Reception*, ed. Richard Leppert and Susan McClary. Cambridge: Cambridge University Press, 1987.

Showalter, Elaine, ed. *The New Feminist Criticism: Essays on Women, Literature, and Theory*. New York: Pantheon, 1985.

Silverman, Kaja. *The Acoustic Mirror: The Female Voice in Psychoanalysis and Cinema*. Bloomington: Indiana University Press, 1988.

Solie, Ruth, ed. *Musicology and Difference: Gender and Sexuality in Music Scholarship*. Berkeley: University of California Press, 1993.

Sonntag, Brünhilde, and Renate Mathei, eds. *Annäherung an sieben Komponistinnen*. 4 vols. Kassel: Furore, 1986.

Story, Rosalyn M. *And So I Sing: African-American Divas of Opera and Concert*. New York: Warner Books, 1990.

Straus, Joseph. *Music by Women for Study and Analysis*. Englewood Cliffs, NJ: Prentice-Hall, 1990.

Walker-Hill, Helen. *Music by Black Women Composers: A Bibliography of Available Scores.* Chicago: Center for Black Music Research, 1995.
———. *Piano Music by Black Women Composers.* New York: Greenwood Press, 1992.
Weissweiler, Eva. *Komponistinnen aus 500 Jahren.* Frankfurt: Fischer, 1981.
Zaimont, Judith Lang, et al., eds. *The Musical Woman.* 3 vols. Westport, CT: Greenwood, 1984, 1987, 1991.
Zaimont, Judith Lang, and Karen Famera. *Contemporary Concert Music by Women.* Westport, CT: Greenwood Press, 1981.

RECORDINGS

A companion set of three audio cassettes or CDs contains most of the music given in score in *Historical Anthology of Music by Women,* ed. James R. Briscoe (Bloomington: Indiana University Press, book 1987). It includes the following works:

Kassia: "The Fallen Woman."
Hildegard von Bingen: "In Evangelium."
———: "Kyrie."
Anne Boleyn (?): "O Deathe, Rock Me Asleepe."
Maddalena Casulana: "Morte—Che vôi—Te chiamo" (Madrigal VI).
Francesca Caccini: "Maria, dolce Maria."
———: "Aria of the Shepherd," from *La Liberazione di Ruggiero.*
Isabella Leonarda: Kyrie, from *Messa Prima.*
Elizabeth-Claude Jacquet de la Guerre: *Semelé.*
Maria Margherita Grimani: Sinfonia, from *Pallade e Marte.*
Anna Amalie: Adagio, from Sonata in F for Flute and Basso Continuo.
Marianne von Martinez: Allegro, from Sonata in A for Piano.
Maria Theresia von Paradis: "Morgenlied eines armen Mannes."
Maria Agata Szymanowska: "Nocturne" for Piano.
Josephine Lang: "Frühzeitiger Frühling."
Fanny Mendelssohn Hensel: "Schwanenlied."
Clara Schumann: "Liebst du um Schönheit."
———: Allegro moderato, from Piano Trio in G Minor.
Louise Farrenc: Allegro deciso, from Trio in E Minor for Flute, Cello, and Piano.
Pauline Viardot-Garcia: "Die Beschwörung."
Amy Marcy Beach: "Elle et moi."
———: "A Hermit Thrush at Morn" for Piano.
Dame Ethel Smyth: Scene from *The Wreckers.*
Lili Boulanger "Je garde une médaille d'elle" and "Demain fera un an," from *Clairières dans le ciel.*
Alma Mahler: "Der Erkennende." Laurel Goetzinger, soprano; Anna Briscoe, piano.
Rebecca Clarke: Allegro from Piano Trio.
Germaine Tailleferre: Modéré sans lenteur from Sonata in C# Minor for Violin and Piano.
Ruth Crawford Seeger: Prelude No. 2 for Piano.
———: "Rat Riddles."
Miriam Gideon: *The Hound of Heaven.*
Grazyna Bacewicz: Sonata No. 2.
Louise Talma: "La Corona," from *Holy Sonnets of John Donne.*
Julia Perry: *Homunculus C. F.*
Vivian Fine: "The Triumph of Alcestis," from *Alcestis.*
Violet Archer: "Preamble," from Sonata for Saxophone.
Thea Musgrave: "Monologue for Mary," from *Mary, Queen of Scots.*
Ellen Taaffe Zwillich: Symphony No. 1, first movement

The companion set of CDs for James R. Briscoe's *Contemporary Anthology of Music by Women* (Bloomington: Indiana University Press, 1997) contains the following:

Emma Lou Diemer, *Fantasy on "O Sacred Head."*
Elena Firsova, "What has caused my heart to feel songful" from *Three Poems by Osip Mandelstam.*
Jennifer Fowler, *Blow Flute: Answer Echoes in Antique Lands Dying.*
Sofia Gubaidulina, *Garten von Freuden und Traurigkeiten.*
Barbara Heller, *Tagebuch für Violine und Klavier, Teil II: Die Linien,* movements 1 and 2.
Adriana Hölszky, *Hängebrücken: Streichquartett an Schubert,* excerpt.
Betsy Jolas, *Plupart du temps II.*
Barbara Kolb, *Millefoglie,* beginning.
Joan La Barbara, "to hear the wind roar," excerpt.
Libby Larsen, *How It Thrills Us.*
Hope Lee, *Tangram.*
Nicola LeFanu, *Old Woman of Beare,* conclusion.
Tania León, *Momentum.*
Alexina Louie, "Ritual on a Moonlit Plain" from *Music from Night's Edge,* electronic.
Babbie Mason, "Standing in the Gap for You."
Joni Mitchell, "Hejira" from the album *Hejira.*
Meredith Monk, "Airport," from *Atlas.*
Undine Smith Moore, *Mother to Son.*
Alice Parker, "Lethe," from *Songstream.*
Dolly Parton, "Coat of Many Colors."
Marta Ptaszyńska, Movement III ("Thorn Trees"), "Tema con 7 variazione," from Concerto for Marimba and Orchestra.
Jean Ritchie, "The L and N Don't Stop Here Anymore."
Lucy Simon and Marsha Norman, "Come to My Garden" from *The Secret Garden.*
Natalie Sleeth, "Hymn of Promise."
Grace Wiley Smith, *A Distant Dream.*
Joan Tower, *Night Fields* for string quartet.
Nancy Van de Vate, *Chernobyl.*
Judith Weir, *The Consolations of Scholarship,* excerpt.
Gillian Whitehead, *The Journey of Matuku Moana,* beginning.
Mary Lou Williams, "Our Father," from *Mary Lou's Mass.*
Judith Lang Zaimont, *Parable: A Tale of Abraham and Isaac,* excerpt.

Discographies are notorious for being out of date the minute they are published. However, discographies in journals can be more up-to-date because they get into print faster than most books. One good starting place is Barbara Harbach, "A Compact Discography: Women Composers on CD," *Women of Note Quarterly* 4 #4 (November 1996), complete issue. Some ongoing discographies are also very helpful. They include the following:

Elizabeth Hinkle-Turner, "Currently Available Women's Classical/Experimental Music on Compact Disc," *IAWM Journal* 1 #2 (October 1995): 15–23.
———, "Update—Compact Discs of Classical and Experimental Music by Women," *IAWM Journal* 2 #2 (June 1996): 20–22.
"Broadcast News" series (play lists from radio programs of women's music) appear in most issues of the *IAWM Journal* starting with vol. 2 #3 (October 1996): 40–45.

In this book, recent recordings are often listed among the footnotes for any given chapter.

Index

Note: Italicized page numbers refer to illustrations.

Contributors

Adrienne Fried Block is a musicologist who has long specialized in music by American women. Her book *Amy Beach, Passionate Victorian: The Life and Work of an American Composer* has won several awards.

Michael J. Budds is a musicologist on the faculty of the University of Missouri, Columbia. He is author of *Jazz in the Sixties: The Expansion of Musical Resources and Techniques.*

Marcia Citron, professor of musicology at Rice University, is author of the award-winning study *Gender and the Musical Canon* and two other books on women in music, *Letters of Fanny Hensel to Felix Mendelssohn* and *Cécile Chaminade: A Bio-Bibliography.* Her most recent book, *Opera on Screen*, deals with the aesthetics of opera when transferred to the medium of film or video.

J. Michele Edwards, conductor and musicologist, is professor of music and teaches in the Women's and Gender Studies Program at Macalester College, St. Paul, Minnesota. Recent projects include a recording of Marta Ptaszyńska's *Holocaust Memorial Cantata,* essays about Julia Perry and Frédérique Petrides, articles for the *Revised New Grove Dictionary of Music and Musicians,* and presentations about Japanese women composers. She is currently preparing a book about Ruth Crawford Seeger's String Quartet (1931).

S. Kay Hoke chairs the Division of Fine Arts at Brevard College in the mountains of North Carolina. Currently she serves as a national workshop leader for the *Music! World! Opera!* program sponsored by Opera America and is writing a book on Douglas Moore's opera *The Ballad of Baby Doe.*

Barbara Garvey Jackson is a professional violinist and professor emerita of music at the University of Arkansas. She is founder and publisher of ClarNan Editions, a firm specializing in music by women of the seventeenth and eighteenth centuries.

The late L. JaFran Jones, an ethnomusicologist, was head of the music department at the University of Toledo, Ohio. She died of cancer on March 1, 1997.

Leslie Lassetter has published articles on Philip Glass and Meredith Monk. Her current research concerns the rise of English country dance in America, with a focus on the work of Pat Shaw. She has graduate degrees from the University of Cincinnati and the Graduate Center of the City University of New York.

Renée Cox Lorraine teaches at the University of Tennessee in Chattanooga. Her articles on music aesthetics have been published in several journals.

Ann N. Michelini is professor of classics in the College of Arts and Sciences, University of Cincinnati.

Karin Pendle is professor of musicology at the College-Conservatory of Music, University of Cincinnati. Her publications include several studies on eighteenth- and nineteenth-century opera and on women in music.

Nancy B. Reich is working on nineteenth-century topics and has prepared a new edition of her book *Clara Schumann: The Artist and the Woman*, slated for publication in 2000.

Catherine Roma is associate professor of music at Wilmington (Ohio) College and the founding director of MUSE, Cincinnati's Women's Choir, and Ujima, a male chorus at Lebanon (Ohio) State Prison. Her D.M.A. thesis for the University of Cincinnati concerned choral music by British women.

Robert Whitney Templeman is assistant professor of ethnomusicology at the University of Cincinnati. His specializations include the Andean music of Latin America and the African diaspora. He has conducted extensive research among people of African ancestry in Bolivia and among Quechua and *mestizo* people of the highland Bolivian Andes.

Linda Whitesitt, music education specialist, coordinates string programs for Miami–Dade County Public Schools. Her writings on women's support of music and the arts have appeared in several journals and in Ralph Locke and Cyrilla Barr's *Cultivating Music in America* (1997).

Robert Zierolf is professor of music theory at the University of Cincinnati and heads the Division of Music Theory, History, and Composition there.